THE NOVEL 100

REVISED EDITION

THE NOVEL 100

REVISED EDITION

A Ranking of the Greatest Novels of All Time

Daniel S. Burt

The Novel 100, Revised Edition

Checkmark Books
An imprint of Infobase Publishing
132 West 31st Street
New York NY 10001

Library of Congress Cataloging-in-Publication Data
Burt, Daniel S.
The novel 100, revised edition : a ranking of the greatest novels of all time / Daniel S. Burt.
p. cm.
Includes bibliographical references and index.
ISBN 978-0-8160-7859-2 (hc : alk. paper) ISBN 978-0-8160-7860-8 (pb: alk. paper)
1. Fiction—History and criticism. 2. Fiction—Stories, plots, etc. 3. Fiction—Themes, motives. I. Title. II. Title: Novel one hundred, revised edition.
PN3491.B87 2010
809.3—dc22 2009034906

Checkmark Books are available at special discounts when purchased in bulk quantities for businesses, associations, institutions, or sales promotions. Please call our Special Sales Department in New York at (212) 967-8800 or (800) 322-8755.

You can find Facts On File on the World Wide Web at http://www.factsonfile.com

Text design by Annie O'Donnell
Composition by Hermitage Publishing Services
Cover printed by Art Print, Taylor, Pa.
Book printed and bound by Maple Press, York, Pa.
Date printed: July 2010
Printed in the United States of America

10 9 8 7 6 5 4 3 2 1

This book is printed on acid-free paper.

CONTENTS

PREFACE TO REVISED EDITION

Afforded the opportunity to add an additional 25 books to my ranking of the greatest novels of all times, I have undertaken a full-scale review of *The Novel 100* rather than simply promote the most deserving candidates from the honorable mentions list. Rarely is an author given a "do-over," and more than five years after the initial conception of *The Novel 100*, I have been allowed to test my first choices from my current perspective, while adding another 25 titles to the mix.

In making my choice and arranging the ranking, I have been guided, as with the original edition of *The Novel 100*, by a self-imposed selection criteria to try to identify the novels that have exerted the strongest impact, that have changed or altered the form in significant ways, and, based on critical consensus and the test of time, that continue to deliver importance, relevance, and enjoyment years, decades, or centuries after publication.

Among the new entries selected, nine are additional works by novelists already represented—Austen, Defoe, Dickens, Eliot, Faulkner, Lawrence, Nabokov, Stendhal, and Woolf—that have allowed me to increase consideration of the range and achievement of these superb writers. The remaining 16 novels represent works published between 1731 (*Manon Lescaut* by Abbé Prévost) and 1997 (*American Pastoral* by Philip Roth) and originate from 12 different countries—Austria, Brazil, Britain, Canada, China, Czechoslovakia, France, India, Japan, Russia, Trinidad, and the United States. All of the novels selected are more than able to withstand a comparison with the greatest of the form, and I hope, by including them in the ranking, I have given readers a chance to reencounter old favorites and possibly make some new acquaintances as well.

As to the ranking, I will let the changes I have made stand on their own without specific comment, only to say that any such ranking is of course subjective and unstable over time. To the great chagrin of my students, I often comment that you need to reread the greatest works of literature perhaps every five years, not because they change but because you do. Since first making my choices and rankings for *The Novel 100* six years ago, I have become, if not a better reader, at least a different one, and my decisions reflect that (for better or worse). The ranking of greatest novels of all time may appear to some as misguided and foolish in the extreme—too much subjectivity masquerading as objective truth—but it has been done primarily to provoke consideration and comparison of literary greatness to further appreciate the achievement that is on display in these 125 novels.

INTRODUCTION

As the author of *The Literary 100: A Ranking of the Most Influential Novelists, Playwrights, and Poets of All Time* I am no stranger to the challenges and perils connected with devising a listing and ranking of literary greatness. By choosing what I believe to be the most significant novels of all time, I have embarked on an enterprise that some may claim is doomed from the start. One can argue that to attempt to quantify the qualitative is simply capricious and arbitrary. The field of choice is too varied: there are too many apples to be compared with too many oranges. Ultimately the whole enterprise, some may say, is personal preference masquerading as objective truth. Let me plead at the outset guilty as charged. I claim neither a scientific method nor indisputable logic for my choices. *The Novel 100* is one reader's attempt to identify and compare the novels that have had the greatest impact in defining or modifying the genre. Disagreement with my listing is not only inevitable, it is encouraged. As novelist and critic Anthony Burgess declared in introducing his own selections of the best modern novels, "If you disagree violently with some of my choices, I shall be pleased. We arrive at values only through dialectic." Like Burgess, I believe provocation is a good thing when it stimulates debates about literary values. Inevitably, to answer the question "Which novels are best?" you must read the works and yourself more deeply. By weighing novels on a scale of importance and significance, you test your own values and perspectives in a way that makes you a better and more thoughtful reader.

What makes a listing of the greatest novels even more problematic is the lack of any consensus about which works rightfully constitute the genre. The exact point of origin of the novel is disputed, and because the novel is such a hybrid and adaptive genre, assimilating other prose and verse forms, it is difficult to establish with any precision one's selection criterion of the works making up the genre. A standard definition of the novel—an extended prose narrative—is so broad that it fails to limit the field usefully, while begging an essential question: what exactly does "extended" mean? As in choosing what is best, deciding which novels to consider requires some risky judgment calls. I have been influenced in this regard, like many, by literary critic Ian

Watt's groundbreaking 1957 study, *The Rise of the Novel,* which contends that the novel as a distinctive genre emerged in 18th-century England through the shifting of the emphasis of previous prose romances and their generalized and idealized characters, settings, and situations to a particularity of individual experience. In other words, the novel replaced the romance's interest in the general and the ideal with a concern for the particular. The here and now substituted for the romance's interest in the long ago and far away. As 18th-century novelist Clara Reeve observed, "The Novel is a picture of real life and manners, and of the times in which it was written. The Romance, in lofty and elevated language, describes what has never happened nor is likely to." Novelists began to represent the actual world accurately, governed by the laws of probability.

Such a radical change in storytelling to a more faithful representation of actuality can be more broadly explained by the overall mimetic trends in Western art beginning with the Renaissance, and, as in the case of Lady Murasaki's 11th-century masterpiece, *The Tale of Genji,* even earlier in Asian narrative traditions. It would be far too reductive and misleading, however, to define the novel only by its realism or accurate representation of ordinary life. Rather, in 18th-century England and earlier throughout Europe and Asia, a realistic alternative to the make-believe of the romance established an alternative direction for prose narratives. It would be far more accurate to say that the novel as a distinct genre attempts a synthesis between romance and realism, between a poetic, imaginative alternative to actuality and a more authentic representation. For purposes of my listing, I have narrowed the field by categorizing as novels works that engage in that synthesis. Some narrative works judged too far in the direction of fantasy—Rabelais's *Gargantua and Pantagruel,* Bunyan's *The Pilgrim's Progress,* Swift's *Gulliver's Travels,* Carroll's *Alice in Wonderland*—have been excluded. I have also made judgment calls on the question of the required length of a novel and have ruled out of contention such important fictional works as Joseph Conrad's *Heart of Darkness* and Franz Kafka's *The Metamorphosis* as falling short of the amplitude expected when confronting a novel.

Having been forced in certain ways to be reductive in coming up with a workable list of novels, I nonetheless derived a major part of the intellectual thrill in producing this book from looking at the novel as a literary form as broadly as possible, across cultural and historical divisions, to ponder the key question of what makes a novel great and how that greatness can be measured and compared. Although I have taught many of these novels for more than 20 years, I make no special claim to universal expertise or authority. I have gratefully sought out the judgments of others, including my students, colleagues, and literary specialists in print to broaden and refine my views and inform my selections. Ultimately, however, these are my choices alone, arrived at by balancing competing standards derived from the literary canon, contemporary literary values, and personal preferences. The first standard is the "test of time" measure that ranks as best those novels that have maintained their importance over the long haul. The second is the prevailing conventions of a particular time that esteem certain works and devalue others based on current ideology; the third asserts the inevitable power of age, culture, gender, and personal experience that form each person's idiosyncratic tastes. Each standard has its merits as well as its limitations. The "test of time" measure asserts that literary greatness is inherent and absolute. Because *Tom Jones* continues to be read and esteemed, it must be great. It is certainly useful to consider what literary history has deemed important, providing you also recognize its sliding scale. Each age ranks based on what it values. We read and appreciate a different *Tom Jones* today than the one read by Fielding's contemporaries or the Victorians. In this way, the "test of time" is as much a relative standard as current fashions or personal bias. Literary greatness, therefore, has less to do with intrinsic worth than adaptability, in a masterwork's capacity to engage very different readers with varying assumptions, experiences, and techniques of interpretation. In making my selections for *The Novel 100*, I have tried to make choices that were neither unduly influenced by the weight of critical consensus, nor overly trendy in disregarding established views in favor of contemporary fashion, nor have I allowed my personal preference undue sway.

I ultimately constructed my listing and ranking by considering which novels dominated their eras; in other words, what novels are indispensable for the fullest understanding of the novel as a unique artistic form. The next step was to evaluate each novel's impact comparatively. I have tried in my analysis of the novels to give you a sense of why each work is important as well as what each is about, along with some biographical and literary historical context to aid your own evaluation. The intention has been to stimulate greater appreciation of the literary achievement so clearly on display.

1

DON QUIXOTE

(1605, 1615)

by Miguel de Cervantes

What is prodigious about Don Quixote *is the absence of art, and that perpetual infusion of illusion and reality which makes the book so comic and so poetic. All others are such dwarfs beside it! How small one feels, oh Lord, how small one feels!*

—Gustave Flaubert, *Letters*, November 22, 1852

For more than 400 years *Don Quixote* has served, in the words of the 19th-century French literary historian Sainte-Beuve, as the "Bible of Humanity" and as *the* indispensable novel. The second best-selling book in history, *Don Quixote* has become so much a part of our culture that, as Miguel de Unamuno has observed, "There scarcely exists a person of even average education who does not have some idea of Don Quixote and Sancho." Among subsequent novelists, it is virtually impossible to identify any who are not in Cervantes's debt or who do not consciously or unconsciously participate in the exploration of the irony of human existence that *Don Quixote* pioneered. Cervantes fashioned in his rich masterpiece a central, enduring human myth and exploited essential fictional implications and possibilities in his dramatization of the conflict between the real and the ideal, what can be sensed and what can be imagined, between appearance and actuality. No other novel has proven to be as influential or as crucial for an understanding of the form in its blending of literary elements from the epic, drama, and poetry as well as for its complex synthesis of social satire and psychological insights.

Ortega y Gasset asserted that "every novel bears the *Quixote* within it like an inner filigree, just as every epic poem contains the *Iliad*, like the fruit its core," a testimony echoed by Lionel Trilling, who observed that "All prose fiction is a variation of the theme of *Don Quixote*." The novel's impact extends through the entire subsequent history of Hispanic literature. In England during the 18th century, when the novel was formulated by such writers as Fielding, Smollett, and Sterne, the influence of Cervantes is unmistakable. Cervantes's influences are detectable in Dickens (beginning with his own Quixote-Panza-like pairing of Mr. Pickwick and the Cockney Sam Weller through his mature novelistic intention to portray the "romantic side of familiar things") and in James Joyce's collision of myth and reality. In America, Melville regarded Cervantes as a personal hero on the same level as John Bunyan and Andrew Jackson; Twain not only echoes *Don Quixote* in his own fiction (teaming the questing Huck, for example, with the Sancho-like Jim) but took on the Cervantine role himself as the opponent of pretense and romantic excess; while Faulkner reread *Don Quixote* yearly to sustain himself as a writer. Among the French, Stendhal regarded his first encounter with the novel as "perhaps the greatest epoch of my life," while Flaubert, who traced his imaginative origins from the novel, incorporated its central themes into the tragedy of his "female Quixote" in *Madame Bovary. Don Quixote* echoes are equally evident in Balzac and Proust. Finally, the great Russian novelists Turgenev, Tolstoy, and Dostoevsky all reveal residual debts to Cervantes. Few writers and readers have been able to avoid, directly or indirectly, the novel's spell. As critic Harold Bloom observes, *Don Quixote* "remains the best as well as the first of all novels, just as Shakespeare remains the best of all dramatists."

Don Quixote is the work of an artist whose life combined to a remarkable degree the conjunction of high adventure and intractable, disappointing reality that his novel reflects. After having being severely wounded at the sea battle of Lepanto in 1571, permanently losing full use of his shattered left hand, Cervantes was captured by pirates and sold into slavery in Algiers (experiences reflected in the Captive's Tale in *Don Quixote*, Part I, Chapters 39–41). Ransomed after five years in 1580, Cervantes returned to Spain at the age of 33, partially crippled and with scant prospects. He spent the next 25 years desperately struggling to earn a living. As a writer Cervantes took up the popular genres of the time, pastoral romance and drama, but found little success with either. He secured positions as a commissary, buying supplies for the Armada that was preparing for its invasion of England, and as a tax collector. He was imprisoned several times for shortcomings in his accounts, and tradition asserts that while Cervantes was in prison in Seville he began work on *The Ingenious Gentleman Don Quixote de la Mancha*, the first part of which appeared in 1605. It became an immediate, though not financially rewarding, success in Spain and abroad. The novel's second part appeared in 1615, shortly before Cervantes's death in 1616, written at least partially in response to an unauthorized continuation of the novel. Cervantes was uniquely fitted for his role as the progenitor of the novel by his varied experiences as well as by the detached, critical, outsider status gained from his lack of success and frequent disappointments. It is not surprising, therefore, that Cervantes found the popular prose romance form inadequate and discovered a new prose form in the conjunction between chivalric idealism and the commonplace.

Each successive era has seen its own features and preoccupations reflected in *Don Quixote.* The novel has been read as both comic and tragic, as burlesque and serious moral and psychological exploration. It has been interpreted as a cautionary tale on how not to live by misidentifying appearance and reality, as well as a positive heroic example of how to redeem a diminished, tawdry world. Despite the book's expansive mythmaking and profundity about the nature of human identity and of art's grappling with the problematic nature of experience, real and imagined, Cervantes makes clear that his principal motivation in writing the book was the comic puncturing of the popular indulgence in tales of chivalry and readers' preference for make-believe over the actual and the probable. Urged by a friend, as he reports in the Prologue, to "keep your aim fixed on the destruction of that ill-founded edifice of the books of chivalry, hated by so many yet praised by many more; for if you succeed in this you will have achieved no small success," Cervantes returns to this theme in the novel's final chapter, stating that "my desire has been no other than to cause mankind to abhor the false and foolish tales of the books of chivalry, which, thanks to that of my true Don Quixote, are even now tottering and doubtless to fall for ever."

Cervantes mounts his attack on the falsity and idealization of the escapist chivalric romances by dramatizing the adventures of a country gentleman who is an addictive reader of chivalric romances and so convinced by their truth that he remakes himself a knight errant, seeking in everyday life the marvels he has encountered in his reading. Don Quixote, in an outdated suit of armor and a homemade helmet, mounted on a skinny nag, and inspired by a humble farm girl, Dulcinea, as his lady fair, struggles to sustain his illusions, while the reader revels in the irony and comedy of the self-styled knight's confusion between an actual country inn and imagined castle, between giants and windmills, a barber's basin and an enchanted helmet, and a flock of sleep and contending armies. Don Quixote's attempt to repossess his ordinary world as a stage for his inflated dreams of chivalry is tested by the real that refuses to conform easily. By teaming Quixote with his squire, the practical Sancho Panza, Cervantes embodies the novel's dialectic between common sense and dreams, the real and the ideal, and body and spirit in his questing pair.

With his central motive and comic types in place, Cervantes manages a remarkable chronicle of his age, connecting Quixote and Sancho to an ever-growing cast of representative figures in some of the most amusing situations in literature. However, the novel resists confinement to a single dimension of the comic picaresque, and Quixote resists a simple role as a target of mockery. His misidentification between the real and the ideal is not so easily diagnosed as insanity. As the novel proceeds, the nature of Quixote's misperceptions is given a convincing psychological basis, and the reader can watch for one of the first times in fiction as characters change and develop under the pressure of circumstances and personality. The interpenetration of opposites begun

2

WAR AND PEACE

(1869)

by Leo Tolstoy

Reading War and Peace *for the first time is one of the greatest literary experiences; reading it again and again is to realize the immeasurable gulf that is fixed between a merely good book and a great one. . . . Here is a novel that is worth whatever time one gives to it. There is more of life between its cover than in any other existent fictional narrative. All the normal human emotions find play in this novel; practically every facet of human experience is there. Its characters become as real to us as people whom we have known all our lives. . . . It is a novel of which one cannot accurately state the theme. One can say that it is a broadly inclusive picture of Russian life during the Napoleonic period, but that is merely the accident of its setting and time. In its universal value it is simply human life, greatly grasped and extraordinarily presented over a period of something less than a generation. No intelligent person can read it without a deep enrichment of experience. And having once read it, he is certain to turn to it again, to be amazed once more by its veracity, its tremendous vitality, its epic scope.*

—J. Donald Adams, quoted in the Inner Sanctum edition of *War and Peace*, 1942

It has been said that every traveler has two favorite cities: Paris and some other. Adapting this observation to the novel, *War and Peace* is fiction's Paris, the novel that has gained possibly more consensus than any other as the form's supreme achievement. *War and Peace* has been called "a dictionary of life, where one may look up any passion, any ambition, and find its meaning" (William Lyon Phelps), in which there is "hardly any subject of human experience that is left out" (Virginia Woolf), and a book that "helps to restore the balance and to recall our vision of humanity" (E. M. Forster). A synonym for massiveness, *War and Peace* more than justifies a designation as a narrative epic, combining an enormous cast of real and imagined characters with actual and invented events, and subsuming history, fiction, and philosophy into an immense construct that is simultaneously intimate, private, abstract, and universal. It is ironic, however, that this candidate for the greatest novel ever written, was, according to its author, not a novel at all. For Tolstoy, *War and Peace* was "not a novel, even less is it a poem, and still less an historical chronicle." Instead Tolstoy considered it a new species entirely: fictionalized history and historicized fiction, family saga, and philosophical treatise combined into what Tolstoy would categorize only as "what the author wished and was able to express in the form in which it is expressed." There is, therefore, at the core of *War and Peace* a radical reconception of the conventional ends and means of the novel, as well as a testing of the accepted fictional boundary lines. As Tolstoy commented, *War and Peace* "is not a novel because I cannot and do not know how to confine the characters I have created within given limits." No other single novel stretches the form so grandly or dares so much by excluding so little.

Tolstoy was 35 when, in 1863, he began work on the novel that he would complete six years later. He originally conceived of a near-contemporary story to be set in 1856 concerning an aging participant in the Decembrist uprising of 1825 who returns with his wife from Siberian exile (the initial conception of Pierre and Natasha). To understand his central figure and how historical events shaped his ideas and motives, Tolstoy was forced further back in time. "Without intending to do so," Tolstoy recounted,

> I moved from the present time to the year 1825, a period of error and unhappiness for my hero, and I abandoned what I had begun. But even in the year 1825 my hero was already a grown-up family man. In order to understand him, I had to move once again back to his youth, and his youth coincided with the period of 1812, so glorious for Russia. I abandoned for a second time what I had started and began to write about the year 1812. The odors and sounds of that time are still dear to us but also so remote from us that now we can think about them calmly. But for a third time I abandoned what I had started, not because it was necessary for me to describe the earliest days of my hero's youth but, on the contrary, because among the half-historical, half-social, half-invented great characters of the great era, the personality of my hero was being pushed into the background, and the foreground was being occupied with an equal interest for me, by old and young people and by men and women of that time. For the third time I turned back to an earlier period.

Tolstoy eventually traced the source of his novel to the events of 1805 in which Russia's initial defeat at the hands of Napoleon at Austerlitz becomes the appropriate starting point to measure Russia's eventual victory in 1812, as well as the conditions that would shape his hero from youth to maturity. The task that Tolstoy ultimately set himself was the imaginative reconstruction of the defining events of Russia's national history, a past that explains the present in the coming of age of the generation that endured the French invasion of 1812.

Begun in monthly installments under the title *1805*, the novel was eventually published in volume form in 1868–69. Reflected by its eventual all-encompassing title, *War and Peace*, Tolstoy's conception grew into a massive panoramic summary of a historical era that also comprehended much of the human condition as one generation is succeeded by the next and characters evolve through time and circumstances from youth to experience in the complicated interplay between private and public life. The novel's centrifugal movement, extending an almost encyclopedic range outward, is organized on its fictional level by the interlocking relationships of three principal families—the Rostóvs, the Kurágins, and the Bolkónskis. Five primary characters eventually emerge to claim predominance: the awkward, bearlike, illegitimate Pierre Bezúkhov, who inherits his father's title and immense wealth; his friend Prince Andrei Bolkónski, the scion of a wealthy landowning family who, dissatisfied with his wife and his societal life, seeks glory on the battlefield. Both men's contrasted search for life's meaning ultimately leads them to Natasha Rostóv, the novel's vital life principle, who will be loved by each man. Her brother, Nicholas, and Andrei's sister Mary (modeled on Tolstoy's parents) complete the cast of primary characters. Each is shown in the process of development that tests their conception of the world against maturing experience and the forces of history. Interlinked with an expansive fictional cast is an equally extensive gallery of historical figures, including Napoleon, Alexander I, and the Russian general Kutúzov. The fate of the novel's fictional cast is displayed against the backdrop of such historical events as the battles of Austerlitz and Borodino, Napoleon's meeting with Alexander at Tilsit, the French invasion of Russia in 1812, the destruction of Moscow, and the disastrous winter retreat of the French invaders.

By the novel's conclusion, a generation has come of age and a way of life has been replaced by a new set of national and personal realities enforced by the passage of time and history. Supporting the sense of change that Tolstoy stresses is continual are the fixed conditions of life that give life meaning: family and feeling. By connecting the grand movement of history with the personal experiences of his characters, Tolstoy makes his central point that life is both determined and redeemed not by the great but by the ordinary, that "there is no greatness where simplicity, goodness, and truth are absent." Tolstoy's scorn is reserved for those, like Napoleon, who think they can control their own and others' fate, while they are actual in the grip of forces beyond themselves that they are too egotistically blind to see or understand. That is the central insight that makes Kutúzov, whose motto is "patience and time," superior to all the strategists on the battlefield and insures Napoleon's defeat and Russia's victory. It is also the crucial lesson that both Pierre and Andrei struggle to incorporate into their view of the world, as each is pushed close to death to discover life's essentials. To dramatize his sense of life's limits and possibilities, Tolstoy constructs some of the most memorable scenes in literature: Andrei's view of the sky high above the Austerlitz battlefield that makes insignificant the individual's will and reduces the words of the great Napoleon to the buzzing of a fly; Natasha's gypsy dance at "Uncle's," her first grand ball, and her heartbreaking seduction by Anatole; Pierre's experiences at Borodino, his near-execution, and rebirth through the nurturing peasant Platon Karataev; Andrei's terrifying death scene; and the climactic joyful affirmation that closes the novel, as the two characters that Tolstoy originally conceived as his protagonists—Pierre and Natasha—finally, appropriately, come together.

The challenge that Tolstoy set himself with such a massive historical and fictional canvas is how to sustain his extended vision, wide enough to connect the fates of several protagonists with a sense of life that contains both the grandest historical moment and the quietest private insight. For several critics, *War and Peace* is a magnificent failure that is simply too vast, too disparate in intention between Tolstoy's role as artist and didact, too diffuse between private and public life that it ultimately fails to coalesce. For Henry James, *War and Peace* is a "the loose baggy monster," filled with impressive touches but structurally bad art. "Tolstoy is a reflector as vast as a natural lake;" James declares, "a monster harnessed to his great subject—all human life—as an elephant might be harnessed, for purposes of traction, not to a carriage, but to a coach-house. His own case is prodigious, but his example for others dire: disciples not elephantine he can only mislead and betray." James and like-minded critics who deplore the panoramic novel of the social group as written by Tolstoy and Dickens, as shapeless, the art of accumulation rather than selection, have judged *War and Peace* as disjointed, really two novels (or multiple novels) that fail to cohere. As Percy Lubbock commented, "*War and Peace* is like an *Iliad*, the story of certain men, and an *Aeneid*, the story of a nation, compressed into one book by a man who never so much as noticed that he was Homer and Virgil by turns." Such complaints seem more the dissatisfaction over an embarrassment of riches that Tolstoy provides (How many novelists could, for example, invite simultaneous comparisons to Homer and Virgil?), a lament for the novel Tolstoy did not write rather than the one he did, and a preference for fiction on a narrower gauge: the art of the microscope versus Tolstoy's telescope. While it is certainly true that the novel's search for the widest possible totality threatens to unravel into its constituent parts—battlefield and domestic life, historical chronicle/exegesis on the meaning of history and bildungsroman—with Tolstoy the supreme animator of life competing with Tolstoy the moralist and pedagogue, ultimately the novel's unities predominate, with its unmatched triumphs of psychological and sensual portraiture largely making irrelevant the questions of methods.

Ultimately, what sustains Tolstoy's masterpiece is an unprecedented ability to shock the reader with both the familiar and the unexpected. Scenes and characters are visualized to such an extent that all seems foreground, all equally demanding the reader's attention. As one of the triumphs of psychological realism, *War and Peace* refuses to idealize its characters. Even such a potential villain as Dólokhov, a contributing agent of so much of the novel's suffering, is granted a devoted mother. Characters we eventually admire—Pierre, Andrei, and Natasha—are shown as complex mixtures of strengths and weaknesses. This sense of the widest conception of humanity is echoed by Tolstoy's expansive exploration of experience itself that again resists simplified formulation. Beginning in Anna Schérer's fashionable Petersburg drawing room, allegedly far from the battlefields to come, Tolstoy initiates the connection between war and peace by describing the social maneuvering in military terms of strategy and conquest. He will similarly emphasize images of domestic life on the battlefield, where, for example, Pierre experiences in the midst of Borodino's carnage a concept of family that he had long struggled to realize. Again, at Borodino, as the wounded Andrei is brought to a dressing station amid massive human suffering, Tolstoy directs the reader's attention to a nearby birch wood where "The horses were eating oats from their movable troughs and sparrows flew down and pecked the grains that fell." This close-up image of the life cycle juxtaposed with that of the wounded filling five acres around the operating tent presses home Tolstoy's point that his novel will force his readers to widen their perspective, with life always an accompaniment to death (and vice versa), with the individual always placed in context of a larger process beyond self, beyond the narrow reach of reason alone, ultimately discovered by instinct and feeling.

The supreme test for the greatest novels is whether a conception of life is deepened in the drama provided. Simply put, life has rarely been captured in language better than what Tolstoy manages in *War and Peace.* If Cervantes establishes the novel's potential as a medium to reflect a massive criticism of life, Tolstoy delineates the novel's epic border, elastic enough to contain more of life than it seemed possible to circumscribe before. In a sense, like Shakespeare's plays, Tolstoy's novel defines a conception of greatness that future novelists may imitate, modify, or challenge but cannot avoid.

3

ULYSSES

(1922)

by James Joyce

I hold this book to be the most important expression which the modern age has found; it is a book to which we are all indebted, and from which none of us can escape.

—T. S. Eliot, "*Ulysses*, Order and Myth"

Only a handful of books alter the very concept of what a novel is and how it can be read and understood. *Don Quixote*, *War and Peace*, *In Search of Lost Time* all do so, and *Ulysses* must be grouped alongside these works. *Ulysses* could be described as an imaginative explosion whose aftershocks continue to be felt. Nearly 90 years after *Ulysses* was published, we are, in the words of the Joyce scholar Richard Ellmann, "still learning to be Joyce's contemporaries, to understand our interpreter." Those who have not read what is surely the most famous novel of the 20th century have grown used to seeing *Ulysses* selected as one of the novel's greatest achievements and are often puzzled by the praise lavished on a book that seems to overwhelm and intimidate the uninitiated or uncommitted. Resisters of *Ulysses* have some distinguished company. D. H. Lawrence found in the book "Nothing but old fags and cabbage-stumps of quotations from the Bible and the rest, stewed in the juice of deliberate, journalistic dirty-mindedness." H. G. Wells called *Ulysses* a "dead end," and Virginia Woolf labeled it "an illiterate, underbred book . . . the book of a self-taught working man." Wyndham Lewis could detect only a vacuum at its core, "An absence of meaning, an emptiness of philosophic content, a poverty of new and disturbing observation," while the Soviet literary critic Karl Radek castigated the novel as an outrage: "A heap of dung, crawling with worms." Joyce has been excoriated as a pornographer, an anarchist, and a self-indulgent aesthete who subverted the novel tradition and left only wreckage in his wake. After violating all of the novel's assumptions and expectations, Joyce replaced what was lost with a brilliant technical virtuosity pursued so relentlessly that even a supporter like Ford Madox Ford complained that "I am inclined to think that Mr Joyce is riding his method to death." Joyce himself contributed to the notion that the established compact between novelist and his audience has been altered and that his reader must rise to his demanding level, identifying his ideal reader as someone suffering "from an ideal insomnia," and gleefully proclaiming that he put into *Ulysses* "so many enigmas and puzzles that it will keep the professors busy for centuries arguing over what I meant." Many have been willing to let the scholars tuck in, while looking for their novelistic sustenance elsewhere in books more seemingly designed to be enjoyed rather than studied, to be read rather than reread.

It is understandable, therefore, that those whose rest is not jeopardized or whose passion for literary conundrums is insufficient to the occasion of tackling *Ulysses* to ask for some assurance of compensation for their labors. My placing *Ulysses* so high in this ranking rests on a contention that its greatness is due not to its daring, its arcane allusions, or its stylistic pyrotechnics but to its status as one of the supreme human documents in all of literature. No other single day has been as fully or as brilliantly captured than June 16, 1904, nor has any novelist created a greater protagonist than Leopold Bloom, whom critic Harold Bloom called "the most *complete* figure in modern fiction, if not indeed in all Western fiction." At the novel's core is an unprecedented apprehension of the multiplicity of life itself. As one of the novel's consummate realists, Joyce ventured further than anyone previously into the complex labyrinth of modern experience, while as one of the novel's supreme symbolists he set out to irradiate the myriad mundane data of existence with universal significance. The greatest novels—*Don Quixote, War and Peace, In Search of Lost Time, Bleak House*—are all special cases that synthesize everything that has come before and create utterly new fictional constructs. *Ulysses* is such an achievement, a paradoxical, bewildering, and glorious celebration of the novelist's ability to distill meaning from chaos, while radically redefining the ways and means of the novel.

The last words of *Ulysses*, following Molly Bloom's life-affirming "Yes," form the byline: *Trieste-Zürich-Paris, 1914–1921*, testifying to a literary odyssey no less circuitous or tortuous as that of Joyce's modern epic hero. Joyce had been fascinated by Homer's *Odyssey* since childhood and regarded the theme of Ulysses's homeward journey as "the most beautiful, all-embracing . . . greater, more human, than that of *Hamlet*, *Don Quixote*, Dante, *Faust* . . . the most human in world literature." Having experimented in the short story "Grace" with echoing Dante's *Divine Comedy* in using a structural and mock-heroic allusive method, Joyce began to transpose the lineaments of Homer's epic to Dublin on a single June day in 1904, casting as his Ulysses a middle-aged, middle-class Jewish canvasser for newspaper advertisements. Writing to a friend in 1920 as he neared completion of his novel that had grown in scope and deepened with an evolving experimental method, Joyce commented that "The character of Ulysses always fascinated me—even when a boy. Imagine, fifteen years ago I started writing it as a short story for *Dubliners!* For seven years I have been working at this book—blast it! It is also a sort of encyclopaedia. My intention is to transpose the myth *sub specie temporis nostri.* Each adventure (that is, every hour, every organ, every art interconnected and interrelated in the structural scheme of the whole) should not only condition but even create its own technique." Through an intricate patterning of correspondences, parallels, and contrasts Joyce arranges the undramatic activities and experiences of three principal characters—his Ulysses, Leopold Bloom, his Telemachus, Stephen Dedalus, and his Penelope, Molly Bloom—into a modern equivalent of Homer's epic, an all-embracing documentary and symbolic summary of a time, place, and culture. Finally published in Paris on the author's 40th birthday, in 1922, *Ulysses* was a notorious succès de scandale. Banned from publication and importation into Britain and the United States as obscene, *Ulysses* would through a decade exert its revolutionary influence through smuggled copies until the 1933 landmark ruling by U.S. District Court judge John W. Woolsey, who, declaring that "whilst in many places the effects of *Ulysses* on the reader undoubtedly is somewhat emetic, nowhere does it tend to be an aphrodisiac," lifted the ban on the novel and cleared the way for U.S. and subsequent British publication.

Initial readers were shocked by the novel's massive realism, as *Ulysses* invades territory previously regarded as off limits for the novelist. We meet the novel's hero, for example, in his morning routine, which includes a trip to the privy, the first representation of this basic human activity in a novel. Later Bloom will masturbate while watching a young woman from afar, and the novel concludes with Molly Bloom's long soliloquy as she reviews her sexual history, which includes her affair with Blazes Boylan, whom she welcomed into her bed earlier in the day. More shocking, however, than any outré incident or sexual or physical candor is Joyce's presentation of his characters' thoughts, associations, and feelings, which appear unedited and unexpurgated in the famous stream-of-consciousness technique with which he experimented in *A Portrait of the Artist as a Young Man.* In *Ulysses* entire chapters register the complex, often baffling associational logic of his characters, as the data of urban life are mixed with memory and emotion. By eliminating the cushioning barrier of the omniscient narrator, Joyce treats his characters in a radically original fashion in which their very human ordinariness and the intricate web of consciousness itself stand out in refreshing, challenging relief. Bloom is, therefore, a radical stand-in for the heroic Ulysses, whose claims on the reader's sympathies occur despite his average talents, evident failings, his status as a cuckold, and the unremarkable accomplishments of this day's ordinary routine.

It is this very ordinariness that perplexes but ultimately sustains the novel's reader. In such a massive book, almost nothing of note happens, and Joyce sets himself the challenge of involving his reader in the mostly undramatic activities of his characters and the specific data of Dublin city life. Joyce would proudly claim that should Dublin be destroyed, one could use his books in the reconstruction efforts. Arranged into 18 unnumbered chapters, the novel proceeds chronologically through the long June day from morning to night. Each segment is a discrete unit with transitions eliminated and connections to be worked out by the attentive reader, who must play an active role in joining the novel's parts. The novel's first three chapters follow the morning progress of young Stephen Dedalus, whose story from *A Portrait of the Artist as a Young Man* is resumed after his aborted Parisian exile. Stephen is shown increasingly alienated from his friends, from the older and younger generation at the school where he works, and finally from the world itself. Intensely introspective, Stephen is adrift in his Irish homeland, lacking the means to break out of a torturous isolation. In the Homeric schema that patterns the novel, he is the son in search of a father to assure his birthright and inheritance, Telemachus searching for Ulysses. It is Leopold Bloom, Stephen's opposite, who in essential ways fills in the sensual gaps in Stephen's mercilessly abstract perception of the world and serves as his surrogate father. Bloom's day will send him on a circuitous odyssey from his home on various errands across the city, including attendance at the funeral of a friend, a confrontation with a belligerent Irish nationalist in a pub, the visit to a maternity hospital, and finally the rescuing of Stephen from an evening's debauch. Although the stream of consciousness is the centerpiece of Joyce's narrative strategy, the novel offers additional demanding stylistic experiments, filtering the characters' experiences through verbal patterns that approximate newspaper reportage, a fugue-like musical composition, montage, a parody on the development of English prose, expressionistic drama, and pseudo-scientific questions and answers. Each section is designed to expand the events of June 16, 1904, into a wider comprehension. Like T. S. Eliot's modern poetic epic, *The Waste Land* (1922), which *Ulysses* resembles, Joyce offers a new definition of narrative in which coherence and meaning are generated not linearly through dramatic action but through complex, fragmented verbal structures, allusions, and associations.

Throughout the day, Stephen's path crosses Bloom's, and the novel's dramatic curve builds to a climax at Bella Cohen's brothel, where Stephen's guilt over the death of his mother and Bloom's over the death of his son will establish the pair's kinship. Stephen accompanies Bloom home to 7 Eccles Street but resists Bloom's offer to stay. The novel concludes with Bloom back in bed beside his wife, with Molly's concluding affirming thoughts on her husband, the muted triumphant return and victory of the formerly displaced, wandering hero. Bloom can claim his heroic status not because of any notable achievement, in fact despite circumstances that are determined to cast him in the role of outsider and fool, but because of his humanity, his persistent striving curiosity and engagement in the multiple complexity of experience that Joyce arranges through the course of his day. It is finally the richness of

4

IN SEARCH OF LOST TIME

(1913–27)

by Marcel Proust

But just as the reader is sinking delectably into the feather-bed of the small town, Proust snatches him up in eagle's talons and swings him over the darkest abysses of passion and intrigue—showing him, in the slow tortures of Swann's love for Odette, and of Saint-Loup's for Rachel, the last depths and involutions of moral anguish, or setting the frivolous careers of the two great Guermantes ladies, the Duchess and the Princess, on stage vaster than any since Balzac's, and packed with human comedy as multifarious. . . . Every reader enamoured of the art must brood in amazement over the way in which Proust maintains the balance between these two manners—the broad and the minute. His endowment as a novelist—his range of presentation combined with mastery of his instruments—has probably never been surpassed.

—Edith Wharton, *The Writing of Fiction*

Like other inevitable pairings of the dominant novelists of their era—Richardson and Fielding, Dickens and Thackeray, Tolstoy and Dostoevsky—Proust and Joyce are forever linked as the towering twin peaks of fictional modernism. More than any other novelists in the 20th century, Proust and Joyce altered the very conception of the novel's capacity and method. Joyce in *Ulysses* showed how a single day in all its myriad triviality could be patterned into an equivalent of a modern epic; Proust builds his epic, *À la recherche du temps perdu* (first translated into English by C. K. Scott Moncrieff as *Remembrance of Things Past* but increasingly referred to by the more literal title, *In Search of Lost Time*), out of an individual's memories. Proust's innovations fundamentally redefined fiction's operating principles of both causality and chronology, in which conventional plot and stable characterization are bypassed for a complex and intimate unlocking of the essential, buried, multivariable texture of experience itself. As José Ortega y Gasset asserted, Proust "stands as the inventor of a new distance between things and ourselves. . . . The whole of the novel that preceded him suddenly appears like a bird's eye literature, crudely panoramic, when compared to that delightfully near-sighted genius."

Proust and Joyce met only once, in 1922, a few months after the publication of *Ulysses*, at a party in Paris celebrating the premiere of Stravinsky's new ballet *Renard*. In attendance were Diaghilev and Picasso, and the moment seems perfectly designed for a fateful encounter in the history of modernism. Each novelist was aware of the other's reputation; neither, however, was familiar with the other's work, and they discussed, according to poet William Carlos Williams, mainly their respective physical complaints. Joyce would later embroider on the encounter, recalling that "Proust would only talk about duchesses, while I was more concerned with their chambermaids." Proust's reaction to the Irishman is unrecorded. Given the egos involved, it is perhaps inevitable that so little came of this fateful meeting, one of literary history's great anticlimaxes, a scene that could easily have been incorporated into Proust's masterpiece as each author made little headway in understanding the other. Had they managed the sophisticated assessment Proust arranges in his masterpiece, they could have detected key resemblances.

Each writer became a kind of secular priest of the imagination, obsessively devoted to the transformative power of their art. Joyce's artistic vocation was announced early and confidently; for Proust the process that turned him into a great novelist was far more intermittent and gradual. Like Joyce, however, he would eventually become a novelist by writing about the process of becoming a novelist. Debilitated by an asthmatic condition from childhood, supported by his family's fortune, Proust indulged in a lifestyle of the neurotic invalid, artistic dilettante, and social raconteur until the death of his mother in 1905. At that time, he initiated a long period of self-assessment that would eventually lead him to the discovery of his lifework, the massive project of self-projection and imaginative recovery of his multivolume masterpiece, which he labored to complete until his death in 1922. The trigger that would unlock his theme and method occurred in 1909 when a sensory illumination from drinking a cup of tea and a bit of toast suddenly restored his past, opening up a previously unexplored region of experience. The interstices between the past and the present would become his central subject, and Proust replicated his epiphany in the best-known scene of his novel's first volume. His protagonist, taking tea and madeleine cake, suddenly perceives the long-forgotten world of his childhood:

> And as in the game wherein the Japanese amuse themselves by filling a porcelaine bowl with water and steeping in it little pieces of paper which until then are without character or form, but, the moment they become wet, stretch and twist and take on color and distinctive shape, become flowers or houses or people, solid and recognizable, so in that moment all the flowers in our garden in M. Swann's park, and the water-lilies on the Vivonne and the good folk of the village and their little dwellings and the parish church and the whole of Combray and its surrounding,

taking shape and solidity, sprang into being, towns and gardens alike, from my cup of tea.

Proust's immense novel would become an exploration in the recovery and the redemption of the past, an infinitely rich and shifting domain of subjective and sensual associations in which the empirical could be made to release its emotional and intellectual essence. Patterned from Proust's own experiences, his novel was conceived as Proust's version of *A Portrait of the Artist as a Young Man*, a first-person narrative of his protagonist's eventual emergence as the novelist of the book we read. Proust wrote the novel's opening volume—the childhood and early experiences of the speaker occasionally identified as Marcel—as well as the novel's conclusion—Marcel's final acceptance of his artistic vocation—simultaneously, intending a much more compact two-volume work. The first volume, *Du côté de chez Swann (Swann's Way)* was published at the author's expense after being turned down by four publishers in 1913. During the war years, the project eventually expanded into five volumes—*À l'ombre des jeunes filles en fleurs* (1919; *Within a Budding Grove*). *Le Côté de Guermantes* (1920–21; *The Guermantes Way*), *Sodome et Gomorrhe* (1921–22; *Sodom and Gomorrah*), *La Prisonnière* (1923; *The Captive*), and *Albertine disparue* (1925; *The Fugitive*)—before reaching the concluding volume, *Le temps retrouvé* (1927; *Time Regained*). At more than 4,000 pages, *In Search of Lost Time* is one of the most ambitious novels ever attempted, in which the years between about 1840 and the opening decades of the 20th century, with a cast of some 200 characters, are depicted with an incomparable poetic intimacy and subtlety that the novel had never previously managed.

Readers attuned to the more direct, logical progression of conventional novels must readjust their expectations under the pressure of Proust's dislocations and digressions. Action is intermittent, and narrative progression circles backward and forward in time. Moments are extended through multiple pages; while years can shift within a single paragraph. Motive as well as cause and effect are made problematic with multiple, often contradictory explanations for behavior asserted. Often settings and events are overlaid on each other so the reader faces not so much a forward progress as a deepening. Time for Proust is not linear but simultaneous, with multiple pasts interacting. Time and space, generally reliable coordinates in most novels, are in Proust's handling destabilized. Central as well to Proust's innovations in the novel is the way in which characters are not fixed entities but are contradictory and fluid, to be revealed only gradually and tentatively, shaped by context and the perceiver's bias. In this sense, the character of Charles Swann is typical. A neighbor of Marcel's family at Combray, the small village the narrator and his parents visit, Swann is condescendingly tolerated. Few suspect that he is on intimate terms with the aristocratic and cultural elite, nor the depth and anguish of his passion for Odette, the former prostitute whom he marries. The contradictory depths of Swann and literally dozens of other characters, misperceived or overlooked through conventional eyes, are what Proust's novel tries to penetrate. In the infinitely refracted vision of Proust's minute observations and analysis, delivered in his highly allusive, metaphorical style of seemingly countless comparisons and qualifications, forming what the Proust critic Roger Shattuck has labeled his "transcontinental sentences," nuance is everything. To see clearly, Proust suggests, depends on multiple vantage points and various contexts with the novelist providing a radical redefinition of experience itself that seems to add an additional dimension to our view of the world. The result is an enriched intimacy that makes previous attempts to capture experience seem shallow and superficial in comparison. As the critic Raymond Mortimer has observed, "No novelist has made his characters more real to us than Proust, and we know much more about them than about any other figure in fiction. For this reason alone, I believe him to be incomparably the greatest writer who has flourished in my lifetime." Proust is no less adept at extending his view from the individual to society itself, and the novel moves from Marcel's family and friends to a growing awareness of complex interrelationships and social patterns as easily misperceived and ignored as Swann himself.

The complex art of seeing the world in all its dimensions is the theme of Proust's novel. As the novel opens, all that Marcel recalls about his past is a night in which his mother was prevented from giving him his customary kiss. Frustrated desire sets the tone of the novel's grand symphony as the child's longing is felt again by the narrator but without the capacity to objectify its reality fully. It is the association of sense and memory stimulated by a madeleine cake dipped in tea that manages to unlock the world of the narrator's past, and the novel's initiation rite of comprehension begins. The narrator's understanding of himself and his world is continually tested in a landscape in which appearance clashes with reality, people are rarely who they seem, and conventional methods to categorize individuals and behavior prove inadequate. Combray is mapped in the narrator's mind by the two routes the family takes on its walks: one to Swann's house, the other to the distant estate of the aristocratic Guermantes family. The novel's enormous cast will all derive from associations with one or the other of these paths. Marcel will become the playmate of Swann's daughter. Later, through a trip to the fashionable resort of Balbec, he will meet the Baron de Charlus and Robert de Saint-Loup, who will provide his entry into the Guermantes's Parisian salon. In Balbec he will also meet and fall in love with the enigmatic Albertine, whose ambiguous sexuality Marcel will attempt to decipher, while his jealous obsessions will resemble the tortuous love between Swann and Odette. Alternately dazzled by the brilliance of the salon world and disappointed by the mediocrity and corruption of its denizens, Marcel at a final reception hosted by the Prince and Princess de Guermantes experiences a series of shocking revelations, resembling the initial madeleine incident, that restores his memory and perception about the passage of time and his own life and finally convinces him that the only sure way to redeem the past is through art itself.

In a kind of infinite loop, Marcel reaches the point of becoming the novelist of the book that the reader has just completed, with beginning and ending, past and present, merged. For the reader who persists in the journey that Proust arranges, the cumulative effect is surely one of discovery. As Proust has orchestrated a redemption for his narrative consciousness in accepting his vocation as an artist, he supplies one for his reader as well in breaking down the intractable barriers of time and space into a rich artistic whole.

5

THE BROTHERS KARAMAZOV

(1880)

by Feodor Dostoevsky

The Brothers Karamazov *is the most magnificent novel ever written: the episode of the Grand Inquisitor, one of the peaks in the literature of the world, can hardly be valued too highly. Before the problem of the creative artist, analysis must, alas, lay down its arms.*
—Sigmund Freud, "Dostoevsky and Parricide"

Ever since it first appeared serially in Russia in 1879, *The Brothers Karamazov* has been recognized as exceptional in its profundity, ambition, and achievement as a social, psychological, and spiritual exploration. Sigmund Freud's comments on Dostoevsky's final and greatest novel are perhaps the most extravagant in a chorus of famous advocates, including Virginia Woolf and André Gide. Albert Einstein, for example, found in it "the emotional, psychological and aesthetic equivalent" of his own theories. The novel has been offered as a factor in cultural developments as diverse as existentialism and Latin American magic realism. Even well-known resisters of Dostoevsky's spell, including Henry James, Joseph Conrad, D. H. Lawrence, and Vladimir Nabokov, have been hard pressed to avoid its influence. As critic W. J. Leatherbarrow has observed, "It is arguable that *The Brothers Karamazov* has contributed more to the content and shape of modern fiction than any other single novel. . . . The central themes of the novel—its concern with human alienation and exposure of the inadequacy of reason, its depiction of a fragmented, unstable world, and its attempts to rediscover a core of permanent values—have all become the common currency of twentieth-century fiction." Its polyphonic structure, "fantastic realism," and reliance on dreams and fables all give the novel a modernist texture that anticipates the works of Franz Kafka, William Faulkner, Thomas Pynchon, and others. Whether through its method or its message, *The Brothers Karamazov* remains one of the key fictional texts that establishes a significant outer boundary for the novel in the exploration in breadth and depth of the fullest dimensions of human experience. Few other novels have dared to ask so many essential questions, including whether God exists, the origins of evil, and how faith is possible in a world full of suffering and injustice. Fewer still manage to combine metaphysical speculation with the visceral power of human tragedy.

At the center of Dostoevsky's monumental conception is the fate of the Russian family, whose breakdown and disintegration represent in the writer's mind symptoms of a general cultural collapse. Dostoevsky writes in *The Diary of a Writer*, the seedbed of many of the ideas he would treat in *The Brothers Karamazov:*

> Never has the Russian family been more shaken loose, more degraded, more unsorted and unformed than now. Where will you now find such "Childhoods and boyhoods" as have been depicted so harmoniously and graphically by Count Leo Tolstoy as representative of *his* epoch and his family, or those shown in *War and Peace?* . . . In my view the accidental quality of the modern Russian family consists in the loss by the present-day fathers of a general idea with regard to their families, an idea common to all fathers, which would bind them together, in which they could themselves believe, and which they could teach their children to believe, passing on to them this faith in life. . . . The very presence of such a general idea binding together society and the family is already the beginning of order, i.e., moral order . . . In our age there is no such order, since there is nothing general or binding.

The Brothers Karamazov illustrates the principles of this disintegration and fragmentation while exploring the means by which healing and redemption might be possible through love, self-sacrifice, and faith. The basic plot situation of a man mistakenly sentenced for the murder of his father was suggested by a fellow convict during Dostoevsky's Siberian exile. Equally important sources came from Dostoevsky's autobiography, including his ambivalent feelings toward his own father, who met a violent death, and the death of his three-year-old son, Alyosha, from an apparent epileptic seizure just as Dostoevsky was beginning the book. The injustice of an innocent child's death would become one of the central issues to be treated in his novel that would turn on the relationship between a father and his sons. As in most of Dostoevsky's novels, a crime dramatically centers the book, and parricide serves as the extreme circumstance with which he would push his characters to a display of their essential natures and values.

Set in the middle of the 19th century in the Russian provincial town of Skotoprigonyvski, the novel depicts an archetypal dysfunctional Russian family. At its head is Fyodor Karamazov, a successful but corrupt provincial landowner, a crude, self-destructive hedonist, given to miserliness and debauchery, willing to violate every moral law to gratify his desires. Karamazov is the progenitor of "the spirit of the Karamazovs," sensualism that he passes on to his children, affecting each in different ways. He has fathered three sons: Dmitri by his first wife, and Ivan and Alyosha by his second. After the death of both of his wives, whom he mistreated, Karamazov hands the care of his sons over to his servants, Grigory and his wife, Marfa, the adoptive parents of an epileptic orphan, Smerdyakov, who is said to be Karamazov's illegitimate son, the product of his rape of a local idiot girl. As the novel opens, the now grown sons are reunited in the town of their birth for a fatal confrontation with their father. The eldest, Dmitri, who has served in the army and become a wastrel, the most obvious inheritor of "the spirit of the Karamazovs," has returned for the legacy he believes he is owed from his mother's estate. Ivan, educated in Moscow and—having achieved a modest reputation as an intellectual—humiliated by his boorish father, has returned to pursue Katerina Ivanovna, Dmitri's betrothed. Aloysha, the youngest, has secured his father's scornful permission to enter the local monastery and become the pupil of the famous elder of the Orthodox church, Father Zosima. On a psychological level, Dostoevsky has subdivided the integrated, whole individual into component parts of body (represented by the passionate Dmitri), mind (by the intellectual, rationalistic Ivan), and soul (in the spiritual Aloysha), and the novel explores the means of integration as well as reformulating a redeemed family through the crime of parricide that tests each of the brothers' capacities and moral, philosophical, and spiritual values.

The ensuing domestic tragedy becomes the means for Dostoevsky's widest possible meditation on crime and punishment in the context of spiritual belief. At the center of the debate is the rationalistic skepticism of Ivan, who has transferred his hatred of his father into his rejection of God the father. In a challenge to Aloysha's orthodox faith, Ivan narrates to Aloysha his "Legend of the Grand Inquisitor," one of the most powerful indictments against God ever written. Set in 15th-century Seville, Ivan's fable imagines Christ's return in the worst days of the Spanish Inquisition. After raising a dead child to life, Christ is immediately seized by order of the Grand Inquisitor and imprisoned, condemned to burn as an enemy of the church. In conversation with Christ, the Inquisitor indicts him for bestowing on mankind free will, the cause of suffering and disharmony because "Man is weaker and baser by nature than Thou hast believed him." In the Inquisitor's views Christ has given a gift to man beyond his means and thereby "burdened the spiritual kingdom of mankind with its suffering for ever." The church, according to the Inquisitor, has corrected Christ's error by coercive control: "We shall give them the quiet humble happiness of weak creatures such as they are by nature. . . . We shall show them that they are weak, that they are only pitiful children, but that childlike happiness is the sweetest of all. They will become timid and will look to us and huddle close to us in fear, as chicks to the hen. They will marvel at us and will be awestricken before us, and will be proud of our being so powerful and clever, that we have been able to subdue such a turbulent flock of thousands of millions." Instead of freedom, the church offers oblivion in obedience, alleviation of suffering on earth at the cost of individuality. The full meaning of Dostoevsky's fable, with its anticipation of the psychology of the modern totalitarian state, has been continually and inconclusively debated since its first publication. Of primary importance is the connection between the issues it raises about the nature of belief, will, and moral law with the larger fable surrounding it, namely the murder of Karamazov and its impact on the rationalistic view that Ivan advocates. When "The Grand Inquisitor" chapter first appeared, the patriarch of the Russian Church became so upset by the force of the Inquisitor's arguments that he wrote Dostoevsky asking how they would be refuted. Dostoevsky remarked that "the whole book serves as an answer."

The enmity, suspicion, and jealousy among the family members explode into a violent confrontation as father and his eldest sons visit Aloysha and Father Zosima at the monastery. There Karamazov accuses Dmitri of wanting money to support his mistress, Grushenka (whom Karamazov also desires). It is revealed that Dmitri is actually desperate for his money to repay 3,000 rubles he has misappropriated from Katerina and squandered in an orgy with Grushenka. Aloysha, who is asked by Dmitri to mediate with their father, learns that Karamazov is afraid of both Dmitri and Ivan, and that both brothers distrust each other and share a deep aversion for their father. At this stage in the novel we are about as far from the sunny, domestic family world of Tolstoy as can be. Here the Russian family is a veritable hell on earth of disharmony and rivalry, and the novel proceeds with an almost unbearably escalating intensity toward its climax. Karamazov is killed under circumstances that implicate each of the brothers. Dmitri's violent outbursts against his father and motive in feeling he has been cheated out of his inheritance mark him as the prime suspect. However, Ivan's religious doubts and rationalistic philosophy suggesting that if there is no God "all is permitted" play a part in the crime, as does Aloysha's religious despair after the death of Father Zosima, which leads him to ignore Zosima's warning that a family catastrophe is coming and to his disobeying his father's final order to attend to him that might have prevented his murder. Each, therefore, is complicit in the murder, and each will be forced to deal with the implication on their various ideologies for understanding the world and their nature.

The law responds shallowly to circumstantial evidence, and Dmitri is charged with the murder. At his trial Ivan comes to his brother's defense, telling how Smerdyakov confessed to the crime before his suicide, but Ivan's testimony is undermined by his guilt over his having hinted to Smerdyakov that it would be best for everyone if Karamazov were dead. Ivan's intellectual rebellion that has denied God's existence and the claims of moral law leads to the perversion of his ideology by Smerdykov as justification for his crime. The realization undermines Ivan's view of the world and results in his breakdown, haunted by a devil who exposes the dead end of a rationalistic explanation of existence used to insulate Ivan from a full understanding of himself. Also damning is the letter Katerina reveals in which Dmitri threatens to kill his father to gain the money he owed her. The jury returns a guilty verdict, and Dmitri, an innocent man, is condemned to Siberian exile. Despite the injustice, Dmitri accepts the verdict willingly as a sign of a more fundamental guilt. By doing so, Dostoevsky suggests, Dmitri's moral and spiritual rebirth has begun. As the novel closes, reconstituted family groupings take shape, along the principles of love, suffering, and Christian faith, as Aloysha and Grushenka plan to accompany Dmitri in his exile, and Katerina ministers to Ivan. By the end of the novel each of the brothers' characteristic initial responses to life has been exposed as inadequate. Dmitri's emotional sensuality has led to enmity and despair; Ivan's cold rationalism is incapable of contending with mixed human nature which is Dmitri's important lesson drawn from his experience: "I was a scoundrel, yet I loved the good . . . Good and evil are monstrously mixed up in man." Even Aloysha, who lacks the more obvious sins of his brothers, must reassess his simple assumptions about faith to accommodate a wider conception of the world's disorder as well as the existence of evil in the world and humanity's susceptibility to it. Neither logic, nor passion, nor simple faith alone provides the answer, but each must play a role in reformulating the integrated self that the novel seeks to define. Unlike the suffering that Ivan cites as grounds for rejecting God, the novel suggests that suffering is actually the means for man's rebirth based on the novel's central ethical point that "all are responsible." In this sense, Dostoevsky has answered the Grand Inquisitor, suggesting that freedom of choice is both a blessing and a burden, and until each accepts the notion that we are all guilty, all conjoined, all a mixture of animal and angel, humanity will remain unreformed and damned.

Dostoevsky intended to say more about the fate of the Karamazovs but died before he could accomplish the task. However, it is finally Dostoevsky the novelist, the powerful visualizer of man's dilemmas, who ultimately predominates over the philosopher and the solver of metaphysical and existential enigmas. What marks *The Brothers Karamazov* as one of the towering narratives is its sheer daring in coming to terms with the knottiest problems of the human heart, mind, and soul.

6

MOBY-DICK

(1851)

by Herman Melville

Moby-Dick *is fiction, not history—beside James or Dickens, how thin and few its characters, how heroic and barbarous its adventure. As a librettist once said to me, "Not the faintest whisper of a female voice." Often magnificent rhythms and a larger vocabulary make it equal to the great metrical poems. Parts, of course, are not even prose, but collages of encyclopedic clippings on cetology. It is our best book. It tells us not to break our necks on a brick wall. Yet what sticks in mind is the Homeric prowess of the extinct whaleman, gone before his prey.*

—Robert Lowell, "Epics," *New York Review of Books*, February 21, 1980

When *Moby-Dick* first appeared in 1851, its mixed reception was far from its eventual appreciation as an American epic and arguably the greatest novel America has yet produced. Bafflement about its meaning and methods is the dominant strain in the initial reviews in which *Moby-Dick* is described as an "odd book, professing to be a novel" and a "rhapsody run mad." Melville's unconventional medley of narrative forms—documentary, metaphysical, and dramatic—prompted the novel's first readers to scramble for a term to contain its variety, including "an intellectual chowder of romance, philosophy, natural history, fine writing, good feeling, bad sayings," and a "salmagundi of fact, fiction and philosophy." Even a sympathetic reader such as George Henry Lewes, George Eliot's common-law husband, who was fascinated by the book's daring, found it "a strange, wild, weird book." Revival of interest in Melville and his masterpiece began in earnest in the 1920s, long after the writer's death in 1891 and too late to rescue Melville from the obscurity of his final years or to redeem a career that the author regarded as a failure. Despite being long out of print at the time of Melville's death, with fewer than 3,000 copies sold during his lifetime, *Moby-Dick* has subsequently achieved canonical status, along with *The Scarlet Letter* and *Adventures of Huckleberry Finn*, as the essential 19th-century American novels. It is certainly the most written-about American novel, the interpretation and investigation of which, in the words of the critic Harry Levin, "might be said to have taken the place of whaling among the industries of New England." Levin's remark, made in the 1950s, is no less true today, although the *Moby-Dick* "industry" has now gone global, in pursuit of some of the grandest themes ever attempted in the novel and a delineation of a narrative strategy that challenged prior fictional assumptions and anticipated the experimental blending of forms that the literary modernists in the 20th century used to transform the novel's methods.

When Melville began *Moby-Dick* in early 1850, he was a 30-year-old author of five previous novels, all of which had drawn on his brief sea voyage in 1839 and his extended time at sea from 1841 to 1844, spent on several ships and various locales ashore in the Pacific. His 18-month voyage aboard the American whaling ship *Acushnet* remained the one episode of his sea experience that he had not yet chronicled, and he proposed it as the subject to his English publisher, Richard Bentley, as "a romance of adventure, founded upon certain wild legends in the Southern Sperm Whale Fisheries, and illustrated by the author's own personal experience, of two years & more, as a harpooner." Although Melville misrepresented his whaling experience by promoting himself from seaman to harpooner, there is truth in his subsequent statement to Bentley that "I do not know that the subject treated of has ever been worked up by a romancer; or, indeed, by any writer, in any adequate manner." Melville, at least initially, set out to document the American whaling industry based on his personal experience. After achieving some notoriety and financial success with his first two novels, *Typee* (1846) and *Omoo* (1847), gaining him a reputation that he derided in 1851 as "the man who lived among the cannibals," Melville ventured beyond a straightforward "narrative of facts" for romantic fancy and metaphysical speculation in *Mardi* (1849). The result baffled his dwindling audience, and Melville reluctantly returned to documentary narratives based on his first voyage to Liverpool in *Redburn* (1849) and his few weeks' service in the U.S. Navy in *White-Jacket* (1850), dismissed by the writer as "two *jobs,* which I have done for money—being forced to it, as other men are to sawing wood." Feeling constrained by the personal adventure-travel narrative from the self-expression and intellectual speculation that interested him, Melville took up his whaling story aware that "What I feel most moved to write, that is banned,—it will not pay. Yet, altogether, write the *other* way I cannot."

The factors influencing the personal departure, expansion, and deepening philosophical and psychological complexity of Melville's whaling tale include the author's extensive reading of Shakespeare, which contributed notably to the novel's poetic style and tragic resonance, and Thomas Carlyle's *Sartor Resartus,* a possible model for *Moby-Dick's* combined philosophical and autobiographical narrative strategy. The greatest influence, however, on Melville's evolving masterpiece, based on the author's own estimation, was his friendship with Nathaniel Hawthorne, to whom *Moby-Dick* is dedicated. Having relocated to the Berkshires for the summer of 1850, Melville met Hawthorne for the first time in August at a picnic near Pittsfield, Massachusetts. Melville's nearly simultaneous first acquaintance with Hawthorne's writing was a revelation and an encouragement to undertake his own original and ambitious creation. As Melville acknowledged in his essay, "Hawthorne and His Mosses," written during this period, it was the "blackness in Hawthorne . . . that so fixes and fascinates me" in which the older writer "has dropped germinous seeds into my soul." Sustained by letters and meetings in which the two men engaged in sessions of "ontological heroics," in Melville's phrase, *Moby-Dick* grew in scale—as Ishmael reports, "To produce a mighty book, you must choose a mighty theme"—and darkened in tone as Ahab's pursuit of the white whale began to reflect a tragic human and philosophical quest after the "ungraspable phantom of life."

The reader's guide and interpreter of the symbolically expansive world of *Moby-Dick* is the novel's narrator, whose ambiguous introduction—"Call me Ishmael"—is arguably the most famous opening sentence in fiction. Ishmael, a former schoolmaster and a wanderer of philosophical temperament, has returned to the sea to relieve the "damp, drizzly November in my soul" and to restore his sense of the world and his place in it. There are actually two Ishmaels between whom the novel modulates: the innocent seaman uninitiated to the ways of whaling whose education and development are traced and the lone survivor of the *Pequod*'s destruction, in which Ishmael recollects the events that in retrospect seem inevitably leading him and the crew to the "one grand hooded phantom, like a snow hill in the air." Ishmael's attempt to make sense of his experiences and the speculative testing of everything he encounters give the novel its peculiarly modern tone of indeterminacy as open-ended questions of free will and determinism, the source of human identity, purpose, and destiny, and what with any certainty can be known are debated. W. H. Auden remarked, that "the whole book is an elaborate synecdoche," in which the crew of the *Pequod*, their activities, and the anatomy of the whale from its head to tail are plumbed for their symbolic significance as the quest for Moby Dick takes on the expansive coloration of the epic heroic and intellectual quest.

Providing the tragic shape and momentum for Ishmael's attempt to understand and interpret his world is the "grand, ungodly, god-like man, Captain Ahab." With his massive, destructive ego, "a crucifixion in his face," and a tendency toward iambic pentameter, Ahab is one of fiction's most oversized, suggestive characters, derived from Attic and Shakespearean tragedy and the brooding, romantic questers of Byron and Shelley. Like Ishmael, Ahab is driven to confront the significance of things, and, since his maiming by the white whale, "all the subtle demonisms of life and thought; all evil" is embodied in Moby Dick, "the monomaniac incarnation of all those malicious agencies which some deep men feel eating in them." Ahab's "wild vindictiveness against the whale" infects the crew through the magnetism of his will to join him in the hunt. Like Hawthorne and his scarlet letter, Melville thereby places at the center of his novel an endlessly suggestive central symbol in his albino rogue whale. For Ahab, Moby Dick personifies cosmic evil, a mask of the inscrutable "unknown but still reasoning thing"; for Ishmael the white whale points to an existential blankness, suggesting "the heartless voids and immensities of the universe . . . a colorless, all-color of atheism from which we shrink." Moby Dick becomes the measure by which all of the other crew members—Starbuck, Stubb, Flask, Pip, Fedallah, Queequeg, and others—reveal their characters, mirroring their (and mankind's) fears and desires.

To prepare for the novel's climactic confrontation with Moby Dick, Melville alternates philosophical speculation with dramatic tableaux. Ishmael's introspective questioning of the nature of the whale and whaling is joined with theatrical set pieces, such as "The Quarter-Deck," presented as if for the stage. Ishmael's limited first-person perspective gives way to soliloquies and psychological omniscience, in violation of narrative decorum as the novel incorporates the methods of the epic and the tragic. The voyage of the *Pequod* is marked by nine encounters with other ships to offer various views on the white whale and the increasing desperation of Ahab's pursuit. Eventually Melville reaches a symbolic crescendo in anticipation of the fateful sighting of the white whale in which all of human destiny, human nature, and the meaning of existence itself is bound up with Ahab's quest.

Rejecting a final appeal by chief mate Starbuck to "fly these deadly waters! let us home," Ahab condemns himself to his dark cause even against "all natural lovings and longings." The white whale is finally sighted, and in the apocalyptic confrontation, Ahab, ship, and all the crew except Ishmael are destroyed with the frenzy of violence replaced by the tragic catharsis of pity and terror:

> Now small fowls flew screaming over the yet yawning gulf; a sullen white surf beat against its steep sides; then all collapsed, and the great shroud of the sea rolled on as it rolled five thousand years ago.

Ishmael, kept afloat by his friend Queequeg's coffin, is rescued, fated, like Coleridge's Ancient Mariner, to repeat his dark sea exploration of the inscrutable. Melville's "wicked book" that he claimed was "broiled in hell-fire" comes to rest on the final word "orphan," suggestive of Ishmael's and mankind's separation from ultimate answers to questions of origins, identity, and destiny. The novel, finally, is not about resolving the issues raised but framing essential questions for the reader to ponder. It is a facing down of the unfathomable and giving form to the ineffable. In summarizing his feeling to Hawthorne after completing his masterpiece, Melville stated that "I have written a wicked book, and feel spotless as the lamb. . . . It is a strange feeling—no hopelessness is in it, no despair. Content—that is it; and irresponsibility; but without licentious inclination. I speak now of my profoundest sense of being, not of an incidental feeling." For the first and only time on such a scale in his career Melville had ventured as deeply as any novelist would ever go to probe existential questions, satisfied that he had unlocked significance in a creation, to borrow a phrase of F. Scott Fitzgerald from another great American myth, *The Great Gatsby*, "commensurate to his capacity for wonder."

7

MADAME BOVARY

(1857)

by Gustave Flaubert

Madame Bovary *has a perfection that not only stamps it, but that makes it stand almost alone; it holds itself with such a supreme unapproachable assurance as both excites and defies judgment. . . . The work is a classic because the thing, such as it is, is ideally done, and because it shows that in such doing eternal beauty may dwell.*

—Henry James, "Style and Morality in *Madame Bovary*," *Notes on Novelists with Some Other Notes*

In several crucial ways, the modern novel begins with *Madame Bovary*. Prior to Flaubert, the novel was chiefly regarded as a popular entertainment, lacking in intellectual seriousness or aesthetic accomplishment; he would help to turn it into an art form so patterned that every detail contributed to the intended effect and as capable of rendering beauty and truth as poetry, drama, or the epic. Flaubert's 56-month, nightly seven-hour struggle to complete his masterpiece—the descent of his title character, deluded by romantic illusion, into tawdry affairs and finally destroyed by the conjunction of her nature and an inhospitable provincial environment—represents the birthing pains of a new kind of fictional narrative. Flaubert devoted weeks to individual scenes and days to a single page, sustained by the originality of his groundbreaking efforts. "The goal I have set for myself will be achieved by others," he wrote in a remarkable series of letters that charts his progress during the composition of *Madame Bovary*, "thanks to me, someone more talented, more instinctive, will be set on the right path. It is perhaps absurd to want to give prose the rhythm of verse (keeping it distinctly prose, however), and to write of ordinary life as one writes history or epic (but without falsifying the subject). I often wonder about this. But on the other hand it is perhaps a great experiment, and very original."

Flaubert accomplished a revolution in the novel's subject matter and style by presenting such an unrelenting objective depiction of ordinary life, making the trivial and the mediocre the source for the deepest moral and poetic exploration. He replaced fictional idealization and falsification of character and scene with an accurate portrait of the mundane and the ignoble. No previous novel had been so carefully designed with each part fitted into an elaborate whole. To decipher the novel's significance, the reader needs to employ the same skills usually reserved for poetry, discerning the implications of diction, image, repetition, contrast, and comparison. According to Flaubert, "The artist in his work must be like God in his creation—invisible and all-powerful: he must be everywhere felt, but never seen." Flaubert denied the reader direct, subjective narrative guidance and in doing so established an important modernist principle of composition, raising the bar in the art of the novel by insisting that the reader play an active role in uncovering the patterns beneath the surface of things, subverting the expected fictional delights, and substituting a coherent fictional universe held together by the force and clarity of the novel's vision.

Contributing to the nature and originality of *Madame Bovary* are the character of Flaubert's temperament and his redefinition of the role of the novelist and his place in society. Rescued from a law career by a seizure in 1844, Flaubert "retired" at the age of 23 to his family's estate at Croisset, near Rouen, where he devoted himself to his writing, surrounded by a solicitous mother and an adored orphaned niece. Freed from the financial need to publish or the desire to court fame through gratifying conventional literary tastes, Flaubert, with a priestlike devotion, began to evolve his narrative aesthetic, attempting to reconcile what he perceived was the duality of his nature: "There are in me, literally speaking, two distinct persons: one who is infatuated with bombast, lyricism, eagle flights, sonorities of phrase and lofty ideas; and another who digs and burrows into the truth as deeply as he can, who likes to treat the humble fact as respectfully as a big one, who would like to make you feel almost *physically* the things he reproduces." Flaubert's early writing is marked by the romantic and exotic excesses of his nature; *Madame Bovary* was conceived as a needed corrective to discipline his imagination and reveal his other side.

Having finished an early version of what would eventually become *La Tentation de Saint Antoine* in 1849, which his friends Maxine du Camp and Louis Brouilhet criticized mercilessly as formless and vague, Flaubert was encouraged to take up a story of ordinary life, borrowed from the actual circumstances of the wife of one of his father's former medical students, whose love affairs and debts lead her to suicide. With a mixture of abhorrence and fascination for this somewhat tawdry story of provincial life, Flaubert began on St. Gustave's Day, September 9, 1851, the nearly five-year effort to penetrate imaginatively his characters and their environment. With a combination of sympathy and satire, Flaubert mounted a withering indictment of his society's most cherished illusions: material satisfaction, faith in science and progress, religious consolation, and the enobling power of love and passion.

He aspired to write "a book about nothing," in which the trivial details of stultifying bourgeois life would replace the expected dramatic stimulus of other novels, held together not by action but by ideas and sustained by his pursuit of *le mot juste*, in which every word, image, and scene contributed to an underlying pattern of meaning with denotation and connotation joined to elaborate both surface and symbol, the particular and the universal. Compared to his previous efforts, Flaubert observed that "I am trying to be as buttoned up in this one as I was slovenly in the others and to follow a geometrically straight line. No lyricism, no commentaries, author's personality absent. It will make depressing reading. There will be atrocious things in it—wretched, sordid things."

The "geometrically straight line" Flaubert pursued is the undermining of romance by the vulgar. His central character, Emma Bovary, is a convent-educated beauty with peasant roots. She has been described as a "female Don Quixote," who, like Cervantes's hero, is similarly infected by the dreams from her reading of romances. Emotional rather than affectionate, sentimental rather than genuine, Emma is incapable of reconciling her desires and responsibilities. Like Quixote, she becomes a martyr to her illusions, crushed when she attempts to embody her fantasies of passion and spirituality in a provincial world that values only the material, not the spiritual or the passionate that Emma craves. Wed to a doctor of plodding mediocrity, Charles Bovary, Emma is disappointed in her marriage and unfulfilled in her expected role as wife and mother. Fueled by the stimulants of passion and the accoutrements of refinement that her limited means cannot sustain, she compensates with affairs with two men who fail her. Her first lover, Rodolphe, is a caddish libertine, a chivalric parody who exploits romantic clichés to gain Emma as his mistress but refuses to assist Emma's desired escape from her hateful life. Léon is Emma's pallid, timorous second lover, who seduces her not on horseback like Rodolphe, but during a cab ride through the streets of Rouen. Inevitably, the prosaic, limiting reality of provincial life triumphs over her illusions and desires. Emma's life in the narrow confines of Yonville is governed by the pedantic hypocrite Homais, Yonville's pharmacist, and the ineffectual parish priest, Bournisien, so lacking in his spiritual mission that he is incapable of recognizing even the proverbial cliché that men and women do not live by bread alone. Her dream world collapses from deceit and debt and climaxes in suicide. Emma is finally given the ultimate opportunity of sacrificial martyrdom to become the romantic heroine that she had always aspired to be, but her death, like her life, is undermined by reality. Her death throes are described by Flaubert with an unflinching, clinical scrupulousness that subverts the sentimental. Emma's last vision is of the blind beggar, the novel's death's-head figure, who mirrors her own blindness and corruption. Her final dignity is undercut by the opposed representatives of bourgeois life, Homais and Bournisien, who guard her corpse. By the end, Flaubert has taken the reader simultaneously outward for a satirical portrait of provincial life and inward to the formation of a mental landscape, tracing the way in which thoughts, feelings, memories, and needs conspire to produce consciousness.

To reveal the significance of Emma's history, Flaubert orchestrates his presentation through repetition, contrast, and juxtaposition. Each of Emma's three loves (Charles, Rodolphe, and Léon) follows the same pattern of illusion, disappointment, reintensification, and final disillusionment. Episodes such as Emma's wedding, the ball at La Vaubyessard, Emma's seduction on horseback by Rodolphe, and the cab seduction with Léon are linked through contrast. In one of the novel's greatest innovations, Flaubert arranges a series of simultaneous actions, such as the famous Agricultural Fair at Yonville, in which the public event takes place concurrently with the private affair of Rodolphe and Emma. The elevated political rhetoric at the fair counterpoints and parallels Rodolphe's language of love. Flaubert presents both without authorial commentary. Finally, Flaubert's focus on details, such as the Viscount's cigar case, Emma's wedding bouquet, the plaster priest, and Binet's lathe, establishes an elaborate figurative pattern of symbols that causes a vividly realized scene to resonate with wider meaning and thematic coherence.

After completing *Madame Bovary* in 1856, Flaubert first brought out his novel serially in the *Revue de Paris*, reluctantly allowing some cuts in an attempt to ward off the storm of controversy that followed but resisting others, arguing to his editor that "You are objecting to details, whereas actually you should object to the whole. The brutal element is basic, not superficial. Negroes cannot be made white, and you cannot change the *blood* of a book. All you can do is weaken it." Charged with "outrage of public morals and religion," Flaubert faced a trial in which he bitterly predicted a guilty verdict, ironically finding in the legal affair "sweet recognition for my labors, noble encouragement to literature." Instead he was acquitted, and the novel became a notorious succès de scandale.

Madame Bovary has served ever since it first appeared as one of the landmarks in the history of the novel. Besides opening up fiction by its frank realism and uncompromising honesty and authenticity, Flaubert established the notion of the novelist as craftsman and social critic, offering the permanence and order of his art as an alternative for the sordid chaos of experience. In Flaubert's revolutionary achievement in subject matter and method it is possible to view the novel prior to *Madame Bovary* as distinctly different from the novels that followed his masterpiece. As Vladimir Nabokov argued, "Without Flaubert there would have been no Marcel Proust in France, no James Joyce in Ireland. Chekhov in Russia would not have been quite Chekhov. So much for Flaubert's literary influence."

8

MIDDLEMARCH

(1871–72)

by George Eliot

What do I think of Middlemarch? *What do I think of glory? . . . The mysteries of human nature surpass the "mysteries of redemption."*

—Emily Dickinson, *Letters*, 1874

Few would dispute the placement of *Middlemarch* among the very greatest novels; it is generally regarded as a landmark achievement that established the standard by which realism in the novel can be measured and expanded the boundaries of what a novel could be in its comprehensiveness, truthfulness, and artistic, moral, and intellectual ambitions. It has been called "the summa of Victorian realism" (George Levine); "one of the supreme classics of European fiction" (David Daiches); and "the only truly representative, truly great Victorian novel—all other candidates, including the rest of George Eliot's fiction, being either too idiosyncratic or too flawed" (David Lodge). Straining the limits of the novel's expandability, pushing the form's capacity to accommodate multiple plotlines and an extensive cast of characters into a massive, panoramic whole, George Eliot certainly produced one of the most ambitious English novels. "No other Victorian novel approaches *Middlemarch*," V. S. Pritchett has argued, "in its width of reference, its intellectual power, or the imperturbable spaciousness of its narrative." Despite such high praise, dissenting views are also part of the novel's critical heritage. Contemporary readers acknowledged the novel's genius but greatly preferred the human warmth of George Eliot's earlier novels, such as *Adam Bede* and *The Mill on the Floss*, to the perceived chilly behaviorism and analytical dissection of *Middlemarch*. Henry James found the novel's amplitude structurally problematic, calling *Middlemarch* "at once one of the strongest and one of the weakest of English novels," and a "treasure-house of details" but "an indifferent whole" that set "a limit . . . to the development of the old-fashioned English novel." There is something of the same note of qualification in Virginia Woolf's well-known appreciation that held that "with all its imperfections," *Middlemarch* remains "one of the few English novels written for grown-up people." If subsequent novelists turned away from Eliot's panoramic method for depth rather than her unsurpassed breadth, *Middlemarch* remains, like Tolstoy's *War and Peace*, an exemplary novel because it both risked and achieved so much in pursuit of a comprehensive vision of human nature and experience.

The novel's core aesthetic strategy is the realistic and moral aims that defined Eliot's purposes as a novelist from her start. Coming to fiction late, at the age of 38, following a career a reviewer and critic, Eliot set out to widen the intellectual range of the novel by making fiction a medium for serious social, psychological, and moral inquiry. She also was determined to alter the basic Victorian fictional formula by replacing the appeal of idealization and the melodramatic with a careful analysis of commonplace experience and mixed characters. Her first book of stories, *Scenes from Clerical Life* (1858), set the pattern for her subsequent novels with its insistence that ordinary life is the proper realm for fiction, that flawed characters should be viewed with tolerance and sympathy, and that dramatizations of human behavior should be accomplished through what she called "aesthetic teaching." She declared, "Art must be either real and concrete or ideal and eclectic. Both are good and true in their way, but my stories are of the former kind. I undertake to exhibit nothing as it should be; I only try to exhibit some things as they have been or are." The three novels that followed—*Adam Bede* (1859), *The Mill on the Floss* (1860), and *Silas Marner* (1861)—owe much of their power and appeal to the author's childhood memories of provincial Warwickshire. When these sources began to run dry, Eliot attempted a departure in *Romola* (1863), a historical novel of 15th-century Florence. Eliot traveled to Italy and researched the customs and values of a different time and culture with the eye of the social scientist. With *Romola,* Eliot learned to go beyond her own memories to see an entire society as a complex, interconnected whole. This deepened and widened her scope as a novelist when she returned to more familiar English scenes for her last three novels—*Felix Holt* (1866), *Middlemarch* (1871–72), and *Daniel Deronda* (1874–76). All three are massive novels of the social group in which Eliot attempted to display what she called the "invariability of sequence": the laws of social order and principles of moral conduct, including both the complex forces underlying characters' actions and the social, historical, and political climate in which her characters move.

Middlemarch began to form in the writer's mind as early as 1869 in a journal entry listing a "Novel called Middlemarch" as one of her proposed tasks for the year. Originally, her scheme concerned the single figure, Tertius Lydgate, the doctor whose altruistic and scientific aspirations would be tested against the limitation of English provincial life. Eliot set his story during the period 1829–31, the crucial years of Catholic Emancipation, the death of George IV, the general election of 1831, and the passage of the first Reform Bill of 1832 in which traditional English authority and values were tested and out of which Eliot's contemporary world emerged. It is estimated that between 1868 and 1871, Eliot read more than 290 works of history, philosophy, and science to help her reconstruct the past and gain a critical perspective on it. Yet the story languished, and Eliot turned in 1870 to the story of another idealist, Dorothea Brooke, whose aspirations for a wider life would, like Lydgate's, be similarly hampered by actual life. At some point in 1871, Eliot decided to join her manuscript of "Miss Brooke" with the early "Middlemarch" material. The challenge the novelist then faced was the "fear that I have too much matter, too many 'momenti.'" Eliot needed to solve the dramatic problems of joining an expanded novel reconstructing an entire social scene with four major plot centers: the story of Dorothea Brooke's marriage to the pedant Casaubon and her subsequent attraction to his nephew, the artistic Will Ladislaw; Lydgate's marriage to the conventionally materialistic Rosamond Vincy and his professional life in Middlemarch; a third individual in search of a vocation, Fred Vincy, and his relationship with the sensible, practical Mary Garth; and the circumstances surrounding the self-righteous businessman Bulstrode, whose secret and fall from grace in the Middlemarch community Eliot used to join the novel's many parts.

To complete her ambitious plan, Eliot realized that she required four volumes, not the standard three, and, as her common-law husband, George Henry Lewes, proposed to her publisher, the scheme, borrowed from Victor Hugo's plan for *Les Misérables,* was to bring the book out in half-volume bimonthly parts at a total cost double the usual one pound for an installment novel, like those of Dickens and Thackeray. The arrangement was a significant departure from Victorian publishing practices. Eliot's novel would be carefully crafted and composed before it began to appear in parts and at a cost that restricted a wide popular readership. *Middlemarch* was thereby aimed at a highbrow audience that reflected the heightened intellectual ambitions and assumptions of its author. For good or ill, the English novel after *Middlemarch* would begin to challenge the old three-volume format that had dominated the form since Walter Scott's Waverley novels, while unraveling the synthesis between popular and serious literature that Victorian novelists such as Dickens and Thackeray had fashioned since the 1830s. The battle to secure the novel's respectability as more than popular entertainment, to claim equal footing with poetry and drama as an instrument of truth and moral seriousness, was finally won with Eliot's challenge both to the novel's accepted methods and aims.

Middlemarch, with its subtitle, "Study of Provincial Life," shares Balzac's intention in his *Human Comedy* to relate individual lives to the wider historical scene as well as Thackeray's interest in observing society in depth. Challenging novel readers' conventional expectations, Eliot insisted that ordinary life and unexceptional, often flawed characters are the novel's proper subject matter. Dorothea Brooke is a "latter-born" St. Theresa, "helped by no coherent social faith and order which could perform the function of knowledge for the ardently willing soul." She is a zealous neophyte and idealist in search of a great cause and opportunity for self-expression who is shown in conflict with her own nature and the narrowness of her circumstances. Rejecting the standard notion that marriage should be the novel's climax, Eliot substitutes a detailed study of the aftermath of Dorothea's choice as she accepts a man whom she perceives to be a kindred spirit, the scholarly Casaubon, who fails to provide her with the expansion into the noble life of mind and spirit she seeks. Lydgate's desire to advance medical science and to remain independent to do good works is similarly compromised by the petty and practical world of Middlemarch and what Eliot calls his "spots of commonness," his conceit and ambitions for social advancement that cause him to succumb to the superficial charms of the materialistic Rosamond. Dorothea and Lydgate, as well as a wide cast of characters, are all examined against a fully elaborated social hierarchy, from Middlemarch's gentry and farm families through the professional and laboring classes. All are related to a particular historical moment in which traditional values face the pressure of change in the reforming spirit of the age.

The major action in the novel is brought on mainly by such natural circumstances as marriage and death. Resisting exceptional dramatic situations, the novel's integrative narrative perspective concentrates on what Eliot calls "the suppressed transitions which unite all contrasts," the buried threads of personality and circumstance that explain and cause the novel's relationships, conflicts, and resolutions. *Middlemarch* presents an elaborate social web needing mainly ordinary pressure to set the whole in motion. The novel's major plot stimulant is Bulstrode's secret that leads to the novel's major crisis, which brings about Lydgate's diminished prospects and produces Dorothea's final self-assertion in accepting her affection for Will Ladislaw in defiance of propriety. In the end, idealism is tested in an arena of conventionality with mixed outcomes. Fred Vincy finds his way through practical, earned labor; Lydgate manages a respectable, successful career but regards his life as ultimately a failure; and Dorothea's triumph of spirit and ultimate satisfaction are muted and misunderstood by the world. Eliot concludes, "Certainly those determining acts of her life were not ideally beautiful. They were the mixed result of young and noble impulse struggling amidst the conditions of an imperfect social state, in which great feelings will often take the aspect of error, and great faith the aspect of illusion." To see the world and individuals correctly, Eliot asserts, readers must extend their sympathy and widen their understanding to the causes and effects of human behavior from a comprehensive vantage point that the novel provides.

The greatness of *Middlemarch* derives ultimately from Eliot's taking the novel simultaneously to the inwardmost recesses of private consciousness and outwardly to the weblike complexity of social life in which each individual is a

9

THE MAGIC MOUNTAIN

(1924)

by Thomas Mann

Der Zauberberg [The Magic Mountain] *is Thomas Mann's most complex creation. It is the summa of his life, thought, and technical achievement to the age of fifty. It is spiritual autobiography, confession and apologia, an intricate allegory, a kind of historical novel, an analysis of Man and a declaration of principle for practical humanism.*

—T. J. Reed, *Thomas Mann: The Uses of Tradition*

The Magic Mountain is *the* great philosophical novel of the 20th century. In it Thomas Mann undertakes a radical reformulation and renewal of the bildungsroman, the German term for the novel of growth and development, as well as a massive extension of Voltaire's *conte philosophique.* In Mann's novel the clash of ideas moves to the foreground of an intellectual drama that manages to be emotionally gripping at the same time it queries the meaning of Western culture. Along with the other great novelistic achievements of European modernism—*In Search of Lost Time*, *The Man without Qualities*, *The Sleepwalkers*, and *Ulysses*—*The Magic Mountain* helped redefine what the novel could be. All in their different ways expanded the epic tradition and charted an experiential search for significance. The cultural impact of Mann's novel, in particular, has been immense. As the German critic Arthur Eloesser observed in 1925, "With this novel the German people learned to read again," and in a sense we are continuing to learn how and why *The Magic Mountain* should be read: as a challenge to our widest and fullest consideration of the mystery of existence.

The genesis of *The Magic Mountain* can be traced to the summer of 1912, when Mann visited his wife in Davos, where she was being treated for a touch of tuberculosis at a sanatorium. Like his novel's central character, Hans Castorp, Mann became a potential patient: after 10 days, Mann caught a cold and consulted the sanatorium's specialist, who discovered a moist spot in his lung and urged him to remain for treatment. He refused. As he later recalled, "If I had been Hans Castorp, the discovery might have changed the whole course of my life. The physician assured me that I should be acting wisely to remain there for six months and take the cure. If I had followed his advice, who knows, I might still be there! I wrote *The Magic Mountain* instead." Nearing completion of the novella *Death in Venice* when he went to Davos, Mann conceived the notion of converting his experiences there into a "humorous companion piece," like a "satyr-play after the tragedy." It would be a satirical complement to his portrayal of the writer Aschenbach's fatal destruction, which was due, in Mann's diagnosis, to "the fascination of the death idea, the triumph of drunken disorder over the forces of life consecrated to rule and discipline." Like his views of Venice, Mann saw his Swiss sanatorium as symbolic and symptomatic, a "charmed circle of isolation and invalidism." Ironically, in Mann's view, while offering a cure from tuberculosis, the sanatorium could "wholly wean a young person from actual and active life," to the point that "after the first six months the young person has not a single idea left save flirtation and the thermometer under his tongue. After the second six months in many cases he has even lost the capacity for any other ideas. He will become completely incapable of life in the flatland." Mann's original conception called for a "simple-minded hero, in conflict between bourgeois decorum and macabre adventure." Work on the story, which grew in the writer's mind into a "dangerously rich complex of ideas," was halted by World War I. Mann felt compelled to defend Germany's plunge into war with the polemical *Reflections of a Non-Political Man.* In Mann's view, both the war itself and his wrestling with the ideas and values underlying the conflict prepared him for a greatly expanded artistic project and "incalculably enriched its content." Published in 1924, *The Magic Mountain* solidified Mann's international reputation as the greatest German writer since Goethe. As a novelist, Mann had in his first novel, *Buddenbrooks* (1901) produced what some see as Germany's greatest realistic novel; with his third, he revitalized the classical bildungsroman as a symbolic novel that radically redefined time, characterization, and dramatic action in an unprecedented intellectual and aesthetic construct. "The work, as a work of art," Theodore Ziolkowski has argued, "approaches perfection to a degree rarely achieved on such a monumental scale."

Patterned on the conventional novel of initiation and development, transmuted into a spiritualized quest-adventure, *The Magic Mountain* introduces Hans Castorp, a recently certified naval engineer from Hamburg, to the "strange mixture of death and lightheadedness" in the remote, rarefied mountain setting of the fashionable International Sanatorium Berghof. His three-week visit to his cousin Joachim, intended as a holiday for Hans before he begins his career, turns into a seven-year residence that takes him from 1907 to the beginning of World War I. Reflecting Mann's notion of "disease and death as a necessary route to knowledge, health, and life," the novel enacts "therapy" that proceeds parallel to the sanatorium's medical cure for

Castorp; "in the hermetic, feverish atmosphere of the enchanted mountain, the ordinary stuff of which he is made undergoes a heightening process that makes him capable of adventures in sensual, moral, intellectual spheres he would never have dreamed of in the 'flatland.'" Castorp slips into the unvarying routine of the sanatorium and the companionship of its international collection of patients. Like Robert Musil's protagonist Ulrich in *The Man without Qualities* who takes a "leave from life" to reassess the most effective ways to live, Hans Castorp leaves the flatland and its numbing routine for the freedom and recreation afforded by this mountain retreat, where temporality gives way to the timeless, and action is replaced by the clash of opposing ways of understanding human experience and nature in the face of the omnipresent threat of disease and death. In Mann's portrayal, Castorp is a "typical curious neophyte . . . who voluntarily, all too voluntarily, embraces disease and death, because his very first contact with them gives promise of extraordinary enlightenment and adventurous advancement, bound up, of course, with corresponding great risks." Like other bildungsroman heroes, Castorp is as yet unformed, a malleable quester, who, in the words of Hermann J. Weigland, "develops from a simple young man to a genius in the realm of experience." His is an internal initiation, an adventure in the formation of personality and a worldview with the assistance of an assortment of mentors. Virtually eliminating external action, populating his setting with characters who are "something more than themselves—in effect they are nothing but exponents, representatives, emissaries from worlds, principalities, domains of the spirit," Mann skillfully draws the reader into the novel's dialectical clashes. As Henry Hatfield has observed, "It is a tribute to the book that one rarely hears criticism against it like 'Nothing happens,' 'There is no real hero,' or even 'There are no credible characters.'"

One of Castorp's first acquaintances is the Italian humanist Settembrini, whose advocacy of Western rationalism comes into conflict with the younger man's attraction to the sensual Clavdia Chauchat. Later Settembrini is paired with his intellectual opposite in a series of dazzling verbal duels with the Jewish Jesuit Communist Naphta. The opposed positions of both men—reason versus faith, discipline versus destruction, nationalism versus anarchy—effectively cancel each other out, and in the end Castorp resists either would-be mentor's domination. A fourth influence is the Dutch hedonist Mynheer Peeperkorn, who, like Madame Chauchat, offers emotion as an alternative to the intellectualism of Settembrini and Naphta, whom Peeperkorn contemptuously dismisses as "chatterers," characterizing their talk as "cerebrum cerebral." No ideology remains untested or unopposed in Mann's ironic symphony of clashing views, and each representative proves ultimately disappointing. Naphta, challenged to duel Settembrini, turns the gun on himself in a frustrated rage; Settembrini, the advocate of committed engagement, retreats to his bed; Peeperkorn, the representative of the vital, sensual life force, commits suicide when his physical strength fails, and Clavdia Chaucat, the emblem of passive receptivity, simply drifts away. Ultimately, no single ideology or attitude to life rules Castorp's development; rather, all contribute to an evolving philosophy based on intense exposure to the many contradictory positions that the novel embodies in engaging characters. This philosophy, a view of human possibilities that does not privilege any single system of belief, enables Hans Castorp finally to break the spell of the magic mountain and to reemerge into life below.

Castorp's crucial epiphany occurs in the chapter titled "Snow," when he sets out alone on skis, leaving behind the protection of the sanatorium, is caught in a blinding snowstorm, becomes disoriented, and risks death by exposure in the "white, whirling nothingness." Castorp is vouchsafed a dream vision of an earthly paradise conjoined with images of destructive horror and human sacrifice, in Nietzsche's terms, the Apollonian offset by the Dionysian, in an imaginative synthesis that neither Settembrini nor Naphta could attain. "The recklessness of death is in life," Castorp recognizes, "it would not be life without it." Recognizing that "Man is the lord of counter-positions," Castorp resolves to oppose the intractable antimonies of life and death:

> Love stands opposed to death. It is love, not reason, that is stronger than death. Only love, not reason, gives sweet thoughts. And from love and sweetness alone can form come: form and civilization, friendly, enlightened, beautiful human intercourse—always in silent recognition of the blood sacrifice. Ah, yes, it is well and truly dreamed. I have taken stock. I will remember. I will keep faith with death in my heart, yet well remember that faith with death and the dead is evil, is hostile to humankind, so soon as we give it power over thought and action. *For the sake of goodness and love, man shall let death have no sovereignty over his thoughts.*

Although his dream realization begins immediately to fade as Castorp regains the safety of the sanatorium, it is his and the book's essential awareness that death cannot be ignored but can be opposed. To do so, Castorp must come down from the magic mountain, gaining the final insight that the freedom and relief his hermetic world offers is a kind of death by stagnation. The impetus to break its spell is ironically the war that engulfs the flatland, which Castorp willingly joins. The reader receives a final glimpse of Hans Castorp in the midst of the actual blood sacrifice on the western front, and Mann ends the novel with an unanswered question regarding Castorp's and the human race's fate: "Moments there were, when out of death, and the rebellion of the flesh, there came to thee, as thou tookest stock of thyself, a dream of love. Out of this universal feast of death, out of this extremity of fever, kindling the rain-washed evening sky to a fiery glow, may it be that Love one day shall mount?"

The novel has led Hans Castorp and the reader to "an understanding of a humanity that does not, indeed, rationalistically ignore death, nor scorn the dark, mysterious side of life, but takes account of it, without letting it get control over his mind." The larger question of what will be done with such an insight is left unanswered. To a group of American high school students who inquired of the novelist what became of Hans Castorp, Mann replied that if he survived the war, "surely he would have remained the learner, the listener, testing, rejecting, choosing, no one's servant . . . his own self and the friend of all good men." Mann's prediction is actually a fitting analysis of the method and intention of *The Magic Mountain:* not a philosophy of life but an imaginative projection how a philosophy might be gained, by the fullest appreciation of how human life can be understood.

THE TALE OF GENJI 10

(11th Century) *by Murasaki Shikibu*

The Tale of Genji . . . *is the highest pinnacle of Japanese literature. Even down to our day there has not been a piece of fiction to compare with it. That such a modern work should have been written in the eleventh century is a miracle, and as a miracle the work is widely known abroad. . . . It is the* Genji, *I think, that has meant the most to me. For centuries after it was written, fascination with the* Genji *persisted, and imitations and reworkings did homage to it. The* Genji *was a wide and deep source of nourishment for poetry, of course, and for the fine arts and handicrafts as well, and even for landscape gardening.*

—Yasunari Kawabata, 1968 Nobel Prize acceptance speech

Western literary tradition traces the origin and development of the novel from Cervantes in the 16th century and European writers of the 17th and 18th centuries such as Madame de Lafayette, Defoe, Richardson, and Fielding. A less ethnocentric view needs to acknowledge the remarkable fictional accomplishment of Murasaki Shikibu, who formulated the novel's primary ingredients out of a previous romance tradition 500 years before Cervantes attempted a similar revolution of fiction's ways and means. *The Tale of Genji* (or the *Genji monagatari*) is as central as a national epic and treasure in Japan as *Don Quixote* is in the Hispanic world, a foundation text in the cultural literacy for all educated Japanese. Largely unknown in the West until Arthur Waley's English translation (1925–33), *The Tale of Genji* has rightfully been recognized as one of the landmarks of world literature. With its realistic social setting, individualized characters, and psychological richness, the *Genji* is deservedly considered unprecedented and the first great novel.

We lack essential information about the woman who wrote *The Tale of Genji*, beginning with her name. Identified by a combination of a nickname from the main female character in the *Genji* and a position, Shikibu ("Bureau of Ceremonial"), once held by her father, the author was the daughter of a scholar/poet of the middle rank of the Japanese aristocracy. Widowed in 1001,

Murasaki began in 1002 or 1003 the fictional narrative that brought her notoriety and, it is thought, helped secure for her a position as a lady-in-waiting to the Empress Shōshi, with access to the court world that Murasaki would exploit in her evolving masterpiece. *The Tale of Genji* gradually emerged from chapter installments enjoyed by a small aristocratic audience into a narrative twice the length of *War and Peace*, ranging over a period of 75 years and three generations with more than 500 characters, combining, like all great literature, the literary traditions of its times and the innovations of genius.

That a woman should stand as the fountainhead of the Japanese vernacular fiction tradition is logical, given the customs of Heian Japan. Following Chinese tradition, only poetry, history, and philosophy in Japan during this period were regarded as distinguished literary genres, with vernacular poetry alone taken seriously as a worthy indigenous artistic form. Japanese men devoted themselves primarily to writing in Chinese, the official language of religion and government; women were relegated to the vernacular, and in prose had two genres to choose from. One is the literary diary, a record of activities, observations, and feelings, in which Murasaki's own diary of her experiences at court is one of the leading examples. The other available prose form is the vernacular tale, or *monogatari*, fanciful, often supernatural storytelling derived from the folk tradition, a debased literary form intended mainly for women and children that carried a strong Buddhist opprobrium for its fabrication and encouragement of immoral behavior. Murasaki's innovation in *The Tale of Genji* is her creative fusion of both forms, replacing the fantasy and idealization of the *monogatari* tradition with the specificity and psychological insight derived from the literary diary form. *The Tale of Genji* presented for the first time in Japanese and world literature a prose narrative infused by the power of the actual that opened up new realistic and truth-telling resources for fiction. Reflecting the shift from romantic invention to the treatment of recognizable experience, Murasaki writes, "Anything whatsoever may become the subject of a tale provided only that it happens in mundane life and not in some fairyland beyond our human ken."

The Tale of Genji begins with an accepted convention of the *monogatari* tradition: the complication of an illustrious noble's love for a heroine of unsuitable rank. Murasaki dramatizes this theme, usually treated as a pleasing fantasy by storytellers, from the perspective of its social, political, and psychological consequences as it is played out, repeated, and compared over three generations. The emperor's violation of the established rules of conduct by loving a woman of considerable lower rank, of letting his passion overrule his duty, produces the novel's hero, "The Shining Prince," Genji. It also leads to the loss of his mother when she is hounded to an early death in consequence of the emperor's indiscretion and a lifelong search for compensation in love through surrogate females and in rank when he is dispossessed of his birthright by his father, who makes him a commoner. Genji's search to find the perfect woman and redemption through love causes him, like his father, to pursue affairs that challenge social standards and complicate fulfillment. Genji's early idealism is tested in his disastrous affair with his father's consort, which causes his exile, and his repetition of his father's passion for a woman of unsuitable rank in his relationship with Murasaki. Through its first 41 chapters, the novel chronicles the life story of Genji, a Prince Charming and paragon of manly virtues, possessing wit, sophistication, and great physical attraction, who is humanized by his shortcomings and redeemed not by conventional heroic strengths but by his vulnerability and emotional needs. Genji's growth and development through disappointment and suffering are presented in realistic, recognizable situations from the historical past, not with the expected marvelous events, generic settings, and typical behavior of the *monogatari* tradition.

Of equal interest to the maturation of her male hero is Murasaki's psychological penetration into the psyches of the various women whom Genji encounters, whose stories represent not the expected fulfillment of love and social redemption through contact with the highborn, captivating Genji, but love's costs in dependence on man's unsteady devotion, threat to desired independence, and fear of abandonment and betrayal. There is simply no better window on the relationship of the sexes and the customs and values during the writer's time than what Murasaki provides in her intense and nuanced individualized portraits in which political pressure, custom, and individual needs and identity conspire to shape the novel's personalities and drama.

After chronicling Genji's development up to his death, Murasaki devotes her final 13 chapters to the succeeding generation, focusing on the relationship among Kaoru, Genji's putative son (actually the illegitimate child of Genji's wife and the son of his best friend), Genji's grandson, Niou, and the three daughters of Prince Hachi. Patterns established in the earlier generations by the emperor and Genji regarding passion and betrayal are repeated but ultimately unresolved, reflecting the indeterminate, open-ended form of Murasaki's massive novel that proceeds by a successive deepening of understanding of human nature and experience in an expansive accumulation of episodes over time. Murasaki's method echoes both the picaresque tradition of the early novel in the West and modernist strategies by writers such as Faulkner and García Márquez. At the novel's deepest level, however, is an intensity of awareness and comprehensive imaginative vision that secures Murasaki's place as a consummate artist and establishes *The Tale of Genji* as one of the novel's supreme achievements. Widening fiction's reach into the actual world and private consciousness, Murasaki legitimizes the truth-telling possibility of the novel by its reflection of the world while uncovering underlying universal patterns of thought and feeling.

In the midst of Murasaki's own narrative, which transformed the function and focus of the prose narrative tradition, the writer offers a defense of fiction. Genji, who is at first skeptical about the utility and seriousness of the vernacular tale, eventually accepts that its aims are different from historical narrative but valuable nevertheless, stating that a "storyteller certainly does not write about specific people, recording all the actual circumstances of their lives. Rather it is a matter of his being so moved by things, both good and bad, which he has heard and seen happening to men and women that he cannot keep it all to himself but wants to commit it to writing and make it known to other people—even to those of later generations. This, I feel sure, is the origin of fiction." Murasaki Shikibu, speaking through her hero, pronounces an essential defense of her artistic form: derived from the actual but transformed by the shaping power of the artist into both beauty and truth.

11

EMMA

(1816)

by Jane Austen

At every turn we are kept so dancing up and down with alternate rage and delight at Emma that finally, when we see her self-esteem hammered bit by bit into collapse, the nemesis would be too severe, were she to be left in the depths. By the merciful intention of the book, however, she is saved in the very nick of time, by what seems like a happy accident, but is really the outcome of her own unsuspected good qualities, just as much of her disasters had been the outcome of her own most cherished follies.

—Reginald Farrer, *Jane Austen*

If *Pride and Prejudice* remains Jane Austen's most popular and endearing novel, the exuberant achievement of her youth, *Emma* is her mature masterwork, the apex of Austen's skills as a social satirist, psychologist, and dramatist—the ultimate justification of her assertion that "3 or 4 Families in a Country Village is the very thing to work on." *Emma* combines both the comic social drama of Henry Fielding and the inner exploration of character derived from Samuel Richardson in such a masterful, culminating synthesis that a case can be made that it is the first great display in English of the novel's fullest potential and mastery. Such recognition certainly was not immediate. The novel's first edition, 1,500 copies published in 1816, sold quickly, but a second edition did not appear until after Austen's death in 1833. Jane Austen herself had misgivings about her novel, fearing that "to those readers who have preferred 'Pride and Prejudice' it will appear inferior in wit, and to those who have preferred 'Mansfield Park' very inferior in good sense." Even more troublesome was her fear that she had created a heroine "whom no one but myself will much like." *Emma* is the longest of Austen's novels and the most psychologically rich, with the closest focus on her heroine's inner development, signaled by its being the only one of her novels named for its central protagonist. It is also most fully exploits Austen's reliance on the commonplace details of ordinary life with which to construct her social dramas. *Emma* depicts a year in the life of the Surrey village of Highbury in which nothing unusual happens beyond the natural cycle of births, deaths, and marriages, and the various unexceptional comings and goings in a self-enclosed, provincial community.

Like all of Austen's novels, *Emma* treats the progress of its heroine to the altar; a romantic drama, it fundamentally delineates a process of growth and education into the ways of the world and human nature. Unlike her other novels, *Emma*'s protagonist is hampered neither by a lack of fortune nor status, having only the disadvantage of her own immaturity to complicate her destiny: "Emma Woodhouse, handsome, clever, and rich, with a comfortable home and happy disposition seemed to unite some of the blessings of existence; and had lived nearly twenty-one years in the world with very little to distress or vex her." With her mother dead, her older sister married and living in London, and her father a hypocondriacal "valetudinarian," Emma is the uncontested mistress of Hartfield, the most prominent household in Highbury, which she dominates. With only her sister's brother-in-law, Mr. Knightley, willing to criticize her, Emma is afflicted with the "power of having rather too much her own way, and a disposition to think a little too well of herself."

The novel opens significantly with the departure from Hartfield of Emma's former governess and companion, Miss Taylor, who has married the Woodhouses' neighbor, Mr. Weston, leaving Emma on her own for the first time. Emma flatters herself that she has succeeded in arranging the match, and she looks about for another opportunity for matchmaking. She befriends Harriet Smith, "the natural daughter of somebody," and recklessly decides that Harriet is the perfect match for the local vicar, Mr. Elton. To clear the way, Emma must convince Harriet that her attachment to the local farmer Robert Martin is beneath her and intimidates Harriet into rejecting his proposal when it comes. Indulging in a romantic fantasy, Emma is guilty of a series of social errors that underscore her blindness, vanity, and snobbery. Her encouragement of Mr. Elton on behalf of Harriet is ultimately misperceived by the clergyman as Emma's own interest in him, and she is comically blindsided by Mr. Elton's proposal following a Christmas party at the Westons' that concludes the novel's first volume. Mr. Elton's drunken impertinence exposes Emma's errors of judgment in which her exaggerated sense of her own importance, of her infallibility and snobbish prejudices, prevent her from seeing correctly the social reality or the natures of those around her. She ends this first stage of her development swearing off future matchmaking (while violating her prohibition almost instantaneously). Emma has played with love and romance by proxy through Harriet; however, the stakes will subsequently increase as she allows her own affections to be engaged and when she finds herself the victim of another's scheming and manipulation.

Part of Emma's problem is that life in Highbury has grown too stale and complacent, and Emma's superiority has been assumed rather than earned.

Three newcomers will help Highbury to awake from its moribund routine, revive its social obligations, and reaffirm its principles. They will also help Emma complete her education. One is the estimable Jane Fairfax, the talented young niece of Miss Bates, the garrulous Highbury spinster. Brought up and educated by Colonel and Mrs. Campbell as a companion to their daughter, Jane has returned to Highbury to visit her aunt and grandmother after her friend's marriage to Mr. Dixon. Jane is Emma's equal (or superior) in everything but fortune and is consequently not one of Emma's favorites. The other is Mr. Weston's son by his first marriage, Frank Churchill, who lives with his aunt and uncle and has finally come to Highbury to pay his respects to his father's new bride. The agreeably sociable Frank flirts with Emma, and the pair enjoys a secret joke at Jane's expense alleging that she has had an unhappy love affair with her friend's husband, Mr. Dixon, who seems to be the only possible source for the gift of a piano that Jane receives. The third newcomer is the former Augusta Hawkins, now married to Mr. Elton. An ill-bred parvenu, Mrs. Elton challenges Emma for social dominance in Highbury and offers her a pointed comparison to her own tendency toward vanity and snobbery: "Mrs. Elton was a vain woman, extremely well satisfied with herself, and thinking much of own importance. . . . She meant to shine and be very superior, but with manners which had been formed in a bad school, pert and familiar." The bad breeding of both husband and wife is in evidence at the long-awaited ball at the Crown Inn. Their snub of Harriet is answered by Mr. Knightley, who, forgoing his previous reluctance to dance, saves the embarrassed Harriet by becoming her partner. It is a fateful act that causes Emma to acknowledge his superiority and to see Knightley as a potential partner as well. The following day, Harriet is beset by a band of gypsies (the novel's one extraordinary circumstance) and is rescued by Frank Churchill. Harriet's later confession to Emma that she is now over Mr. Elton and prefers someone more superior leads Emma to think that Harriet must mean Frank and willingly accedes to her friend's preference, matchmaking yet again.

As summer arrives, the complicated tangle of relationships reaches a crisis point. Jane prepares to accept a governess position arranged through Mrs. Elton; Frank is unexplainably out of humor at the news; and Mr. Knightley has finally reasserted his social responsibilities as one of the principal landowners by reviving the social life of his estate, Donwell Abbey. The excursion to his home stimulates a more ambitious journey to Box Hill, where Frank caters to the worst of Emma's imperious tendencies with a game in which each of the party is commanded to entertain Miss Woodhouse by saying one clever thing, "or two things moderately clever—or three things very dull indeed." Miss Bates chooses the later, prompting Emma's unpardonably rude remark: "Ah! ma'am, but there may be a difficulty. Pardon me—but you will be limited as to number—only three at once." The entire novel will turn on this witty remark at Miss Bates's expense, which crystallizes all of Emma's shortcomings. These are made painfully (and tearfully) clear to Emma in Mr. Knightley's later rebuke. She is mortified for the hurt she has caused an old family friend deserving her respect and compassion and in eliciting Mr. Knightley's poor opinion of her behavior. Repentant, Emma visits Miss Bates the next day, an act of reformation and an acknowledgment of her error that paves the way for the comic conclusion of the novel, which depends on Emma's maturation.

In rapid succession, complications give way to three weddings. Frank's aunt dies suddenly, and it is revealed that he has been secretly engaged to Jane all along. His duplicity and manipulation are the final telling comparison with Emma's own behavior, which at times also has been far from open and honest. Emma's first thought, however, is for "poor Harriet," who is assumed to be in despair over the news. Instead, in the great comic revelation in the novel, Harriet admits that she has set her sight not on Frank but on Mr. Knightley. It was Knightley's chivalric treatment of Harriet at the ball, not Frank's rescue of Harriet from the gypsies, that has gained Harriet's affections, encouraged by Emma to aim higher than her station might otherwise have allowed. Emma is shocked into a recognition of her own blindness and folly: "With insufferable vanity had she believed herself in the secret of everybody's feelings; with unpardonable arrogance proposed everybody's destiny. She was proved to have been universally mistaken. She had brought evil on Harriet, on herself, and she too much feared, on Mr. Knightley." Equally powerful is her realization "that darted through her with the speed of an arrow that Mr. Knightley must not marry anyone but herself."

After two previous proposals—Mr. Elton's and Frank's confession that is misperceived as a proposal by Emma—the way is now clear for the culminating and appropriate third. Misperceiving initially the other's feelings—Knightley, that Emma is in despair over Frank's engagement and Emma over the presumed affection between Knightley and Harriet—the couple comes to a satisfactory understanding in the end. To the exact words of Knightley's proposal and Emma's acceptance, the author retreats to a discreet, generalizing distance: "What did she say?—Just what she ought, of course. A lady always does.—She said enough to show there need not be despair—and to invite him to say more himself." To add to the happy conclusion of reconciliation and unity, Harriet is granted a second proposal from Robert Martin to make up the third match that ends the novel. Emma has learned crucial lessons about her own nature and her responsibilities in an adult world. The final view is provided by Mrs. Elton, who laments the absence of white satin and lace that makes Emma's nuptial a "most pitiful business." However, Emma's maturation in her nature and her social responsibility makes it one of the most satisfying comic culminations in which someone who, in her own words, seems "to have been doomed to blindness" finally sees clearly, the essential step in Austen's mind for a heroine to assume her proper station as an adult and a wife.

As in all her novels, marriage is not a simple, sentimental climax, but the result of a complex moral and social negotiation that reveals much about human nature and experience. To reach the altar triumphantly, Emma must first learn painful lessons about self-deception and the ego's often dangerous drive for mastery and control. Emma, like the reader, is schooled in the complicated matter of living, in which common sense and clarity replace self-deception and delusion.

12

BLEAK HOUSE

(1852–53)

by Charles Dickens

The movement of Bleak House *becomes a centripetal one like a whirlpool, at first slow and almost imperceptible, but fatefully drawing in successive groups of characters, circling faster and faster, and ultimately sucking them into the dark funnel whence none will escape uninjured and where many will be crushed and destroyed. In pure emotional power* Bleak House *ranks among Dickens's greatest books.*

—Edgar Johnson, *Charles Dickens: His Tragedy and Triumph*

In deciding which of the many worthy Dickens novels to include in this ranking, I was tempted to employ the distinction made by G. K. Chesterton that there is in fact no single Dickens novel; they are "simply lengths cut from the flowing and mixed substance called Dickens." Taken all of a piece, I could, therefore, have found room for all, or at least more than the limitations on the works of a single author I forced myself to abide by in this ranking, balancing a competing desire for inclusiveness and wide representation. In the end, my Dickens choices—*The Pickwick Papers*, *David Copperfield*, *Bleak House*, and *Great Expectations*—still retain something of a representative quality, characterizing particular aspects of Dickens's genius and method. *Pickwick* heralded Dickens's arrival and his unsurpassed inventive animation of character and scene. His first novel also revolutionized Victorian publishing practices while setting the early, improvised, picaresque method that would define his novels through *David Copperfield*. *Pickwick*, therefore, initiates and characterizes a distinctive grouping of Dickens's novels that culminates in *David Copperfield*. *Bleak House* is the first of Dickens's massive social panoramas, setting the structure and concerns of the darker, socially obsessed novels of Dickens's maturity. It is the greatest of Dickens's monthly installment novels, as *Great Expectations* is the finest of his weekly serials. Readers interested in marking Dickens's remarkable progression as a novelist cannot do better than to compare the joyful, seemingly spontaneous generation of *Pickwick*, in which Dickens claimed that, given his desultory mode of installment publication, no artful plot could even be attempted, with the intricate, brooding design of *Bleak House*, published in the same monthly installment form, but organized by the most demanding narrative method of all: that of the mystery. *Bleak House* is Dickens's most ambitious work, the book that set the terms for all the novels that would follow, and very nearly justifies Geoffrey Tillotson's impossibly grand claim that it is "the finest literary work the nineteenth century produced in England."

In 1852, when *Bleak House* began its serialization, Dickens was 40 years old and at the peak of his artistic powers and popularity. After eight novels in 14 years, Dickens had mastered the challenge of installment construction, learning how to connect all the elements of characters, action, and atmosphere by a central purpose. With *Martin Chuzzlewit*, Dickens had widened his exploration of human nature and society into a general indictment of human selfishness and greed. In *Dombey and Son*, he had for the first time employed a contemporary setting and traced its impact on characters who display a growing psychological depth and who become not merely the victims of the novel's plot but its cause. Finally, with *David Copperfield*, Dickens reopened the trauma of his own early life, taking account of both the social and psychological factors that formed him in a first-person narrative that is simultaneously a private confession and public analysis. With *Bleak House*, Dickens attempted nothing less than a comprehensive anatomy of Victorian society. None of his novels are designed with such a purpose to show how society operated from the highest class to the lowest, along with its important institutions of law, government, and religion. Eighteen fifty-one was the year of the Great Exhibition in London, a self-satisfied celebration of Victorian progress and ingenuity. *Bleak House* is a dissenting vision in which Dickens portrayed not an age of progress but a stagnated society ruled by a crippling selfishness that refused to acknowledge social obligations or the inextricable link between the haves and the have-nots. With *Bleak House*, Dickens set out to make that connection and the cost of doing nothing about it clear.

At the center of *Bleak House* is a sensational mystery around which several lesser secrets, surprises, and a large cast revolve. Dickens had employed mystery before in his novels, most notably in *Oliver Twist*, but in *Bleak House* the mysteries are truly labyrinthian. Esther Summerson, who shares half of the book's narration, is, like Oliver, illegitimate, and her identity remains in doubt for the first half of the novel. Also, as in *Oliver Twist*, there is a disputed inheritance, and the secret of Esther's identity is joined to the interminable and destructive Chancery case of Jarndyce versus Jarndyce. However, in *Bleak House* Dickens greatly expands his range from *Oliver Twist*, connecting two plots rather than combining them in one character's history like Oliver's. Sylvère Monod has observed that the Jarndyce plot resembles the more typical Dickensian plot of the earlier books in which John Jarndyce, Esther, Ada Clare, and Richard Carstone can be seen as members of a kind of Pickwickian

Club who "go from city to city and keep meeting eccentrics. . . . By adhering to that line, Dickens might have turned *Bleak House* into a work resembling *Nickleby*. He needed only to add to the number of Jarndyce's picturesque friends and to the careers attempted by Richard." To this more characteristic plot of an inheritance that hangs in the balance until the novel's climax, Dickens adds the more extraordinary and sensational plot of Lady Dedlock's secret. The two plots are united in a network of coincidences, mysteries, and detection.

It is ultimately the plot of *Bleak House*, not its social criticism or its symbols, such as the fog in its famous opening, that unifies the novel's massive social panorama. The process of the narrative is the uncovering of the buried past and the interconnection of the novel's many parts. Lady Dedlock is linked to an anonymous and dissipated legal writer; Mrs. Chadband is the former maid of Esther's aunt; Smallweed is Krook's brother-in-law; George turns out to be both the friend of Captain Hawdon and the long-lost son of the housekeeper of Chesney Wold. Dickens has reversed the centrifugal pressure of his earlier novels in which the parts threaten to break away from the whole into glorious irrelevance. As Dickens's friend and first biographer, John Forster, observed, in *Bleak House* "nothing is introduced at random; everything tends to the catastrophe."

The center of the novel's dramatic action is the sensational mystery surrounding Lady Dedlock. As Inspector Bucket points out, "She is the pivot it all turns on." The novel is organized by the unraveling of her secrets, her relationship to Nemo, to Esther, whether she killed Tulkinghorn, and where she has gone after her past has been uncovered. It is her surprise at the handwriting of the copyist in the book's second chapter and her resemblance to Esther that Guppy notices that start the machinery of her detection. The fitting together of the past with the present and the many chance encounters, resemblances, and relationships join the narrative puzzle into a significant dramatic as well as social design. The consequences of Lady Dedlock's secret result in Tulkinghorn's murder, Lady Dedlock's flight, and her pursuit, which ends with her death at Nemo's grave. The sensational mystery, therefore, gives *Bleak House* its method of narration—information withheld and gradually revealed—and a series of startling revelations and incidents that builds up to a dramatic climax.

If the method of the novel is the discovery of connections among its many parts, coincidences make many of these possible. The novel is in fact a compendium of the accidental and the fortuitous. Characters' paths and histories are forever crossing, as if to illustrate Tim Linkinwater's remark in *Nicholas Nickleby* that "There's no such place in all the world for coincidence as London is!" Dickens's many coincidences show the operation of fate in the novel and, more important, Dickens's social theme of the linkage of the social classes. The destiny of the aristocracy is by chance entangled with the humblest characters. The disreputable rag-and-bones man Krook is made to resemble the Lord Chancellor, and lowly characters like the Necketts and the brickmaker's family become tied up in the affairs of the respectable Jarndyces and the fashionable Dedlocks. In this regard, the lowest character of them all, the crossing sweeper Jo, serves as a kind of linchpin joining the entire social world of *Bleak House.* "What connexion can there be," Dickens writes, "between the place in Lincolnshire, the house in town, the Mercury in powder, and the whereabouts of Jo the outlaw with the broom, who had the distant ray of light upon him when he swept the churchyard-step? What connexion can there have been between many people in the innumerable histories of the world, who, from opposite sides of great gulfs, have, nevertheless, been curiously brought together!" *Bleak House* works toward unraveling these questions while making Dickens's central social point of the linkage of classes.

When Jo infects both Charley and Esther with typhoid, Dickens underscores the connection between the squalid Tom-All-Alone's and the regal Chesney Wold. The physical contagion that Jo spreads from the lowest rung of the society is matched by the moral corruption spread from the top. Jo's downfall comes from befriending Nemo and becoming involved in Lady Dedlock's past. Jo is actually "infected" by Lady Dedlock and is kept "moving on" by Bucket because he knows too much. The coincidental connection of the humblest characters with the highest makes Dickens's point that society is bound tightly together. Lady Dedlock is brought down from her aristocratic, haughty isolation to her end in the clothes of a brickmaker's wife atop a pauper's grave.

Bleak House unquestionably has one of Dickens's most elaborate and intricate melodramatic plots, consisting of multiple secrets, suspended outcomes, and often violent, extraordinary turns of events, such as Tulkinghorn's murder and Krook's spontaneous combustion. *Bleak House* set the pattern of the so-called Sensation Novel of the 1860s, novels such as Wilkie Collins's *The Woman in White*, Mary Elizabeth Braddon's *Lady Audley's Secret*, and Mrs. Henry Wood's *East Lynne*, that used extraordinary events such as crimes, violence, bigamy, disputed fortunes, hidden and multiple identities, presented by surprising turns of plot, startling revelations, and suspense. The Sensation Novel, far different in emphasis from the novels of domestic realism, updated the gothic romance, giving it a contemporary setting and realistic background. Dickens's intention in *Bleak House* to portray "the romantic side of familiar things" typifies the sensation novelist's merging of surface realism and sensational incident. Dickens, moreover, anticipated not just the entire mystery genre (employing, in Inspector Bucket, the novel's first professional detective) but the key ingredient of secret and suspense that other literary novelists—Hardy, Dostoevsky, and Faulkner most notably—would use to structure their own social and psychological explorations.

The advantages and disadvantages of Dickens's sensational, mystery construction have been contentious from the novel's first appearance. Dickens's first reviewers complained that the lively, comic exuberance of the earlier novels was stifled in the unrelieved dreariness of his design. Others could not detect any design at all. As one reviewer observed, "*Bleak House* is, even more than any of its predecessors, chargeable with not simply faults, but absolute want of construction." Modern critics have been far kinder to the novel's symbolic, antirealistic method and more sympathetic to its darkened social vision. As Edmund Wilson argued, in *Bleak House* Dickens

> discovers a new use for plot, which makes possible a tighter organization. . . . Dickens creates the detective story which is also a moral fable. . . . It is one of Dickens' victories in his rapid development as an artist that he should succeed in transforming his melodramatic intrigues of stolen inheritances, lost heirs and ruined maidens—with their denunciatory confrontations that always evoke the sounds of fiddling in the orchestra—into devices of artistic dignity. Henceforth the solution of the mystery is to be also the moral of the story and the last word of Dickens' social "message."

No other Victorian novel and few other novels at any time dared so much or delivered so much, and *Bleak House* is deservedly placed in the select company of novels by Balzac, Tolstoy, and Joyce that aspire to the epic. Dickens's subsequent novels would consolidate and amplify the social vision and narrative methods that *Bleak House* pioneered. Dickens shows in *Bleak House* his willingness to press his storytelling into the service of a massive criticism of life, expanding the descriptor "Dickensian" to include more than the comforts of hearth and home but the darkest recesses of self and society.

ANNA KARENINA 13

(1877)

by Leo Tolstoy

There are many characters in Anna Karénine*—too many if we look in it for a work of art in which the action shall be vigorously one, and to that one action everything shall converge. There are even two main actions extending throughout the book, and we keep passing from one of them to the other—from the affairs of Anna and Wronsky to the affairs of Kitty. People appear in connection with these two main actions whose appearance and proceedings do not in the least contribute to develop them; incidents are multiplied which we expect are to lead to something important, but which do not. . . . But the truth is we are not to take* Anna Karénine *as a work of art; we are to take it as a piece of life.*

—Matthew Arnold, "Count Leo Tolstoi," in *Essays in Criticism: Second Series*

The Tolstoy scholar John Bayley has written that the "best books, the most full of infectious feeling, are those in which the author's intention is lost sight of, or even contradicted by, the close attention or 'love' which he devotes to his characters." Bayley's comment is particularly appropriate in regard to *Anna Karenina*, one of the supreme novels of the 19th century, a contender, in the view of many, as the world's greatest novel. It is certainly a triumph of psychological realism and incomparable in its distillation of observation and analysis into powerful essence. However, *Anna Karenina* is also one of the most fascinating novels in revealing the inner struggle of its creator for control of his work. In *Anna Karenina,* Tolstoy the matchless artist battled with Tolstoy the implacable moralist for predominance. In the end, he wrestled himself to a draw with his characters' humanity and their creator's vitalism triumphing over any lesson that Tolstoy felt compelled to pursue. At the beginning of his labors to produce *War and Peace,* in 1865 Tolstoy asserted that "The aim of an artist is not to solve a problem irrefutably, but to make people love life in all its countless, inexhaustible manifestations." *Anna Karenina* would be the last instance in Tolstoy's career in which this credo would still apply. Tolstoy the holy man, sermonizer, and sage would emerge after the battle to produce *Anna Karenina,* and the novelist would give way to the preacher who would eventually forsake his greatest imaginative achievements as worthless. *Anna Karenina* is, therefore, a culmination of Tolstoy's art, a book that he regarded as his "first real novel," and in essence the last one he managed in which his mighty gifts of animation and analysis were so magnificently joined.

The long gestation and compositional struggle to complete *Anna Karenina* reflect Tolstoy's inner conflict following the completion of *War and Peace.* Fitfully at work on another historical novel set during the era of Peter the Great, Tolstoy offers the first glimmer of *Anna Karenina* in 1870, when he told his wife that he was intrigued by "a type of married woman from the highest society, but who had lost herself" and whom he intended to show as "pitiful and not guilty." This core idea of a fallen woman was given shape and direction by the death in 1872 of a neighbor's mistress, Anna Pirogova, who in despair over her lover's abandonment committed suicide by throwing herself under a freight train. Tolstoy, who inspected the woman's mangled corpse, now had his protagonist's first name and her violent end. The spark that would finally ignite Tolstoy to begin writing, however, occurred a year later. Leafing through Pushkin's *Tales by Belkin,* Tolstoy was struck by the opening sentence of the story "Loose Leaves": "The guests were arriving at the country house." Tolstoy's reaction was "That is the way to begin. Pushkin plunges his readers right into the middle of the action. Others would describe the guests, the rooms, but Pushkin at once gets down to business." Here was the way to get under way by thrusting himself directly into an active fictional world. Tolstoy picked up his pen and began a sentence that would begin Chapter 6 or Part II of *Anna Karenina:* "After the opera, the guests reassembled at the home of the young Countess Vraski," and he was launched. "Yesterday Leo suddenly started to write a novel on contemporary life. The subject is the unfaithful wife and the ensuing tragedy," Tolstoy's wife wrote to her sister. "Involuntarily, unexpectedly, without knowing myself why or what would come of it," Tolstoy observed to a friend, "I thought up characters and events, began to continue it, then, of course, altered it, and suddenly it came together so neatly and nicely that there emerged a novel, which I have today finished in rough, a very lively, ardent and finished novel, with which I am very pleased and which will be ready, if God grants me health, in two weeks." Instead of the impossibly unrealistic two weeks, it would take Tolstoy five years, until 1878, to reach book publication.

Early drafts featured only the adulterous triangle of Anna, Vronsky, and Karenin, who, rather than his wife, was marked for the tragic role with his virtue besmirched by his wife's lecherous and irresponsible passion. Anna initially lacked her attractiveness in the final version, with Tolstoy casting her originally in the role of a fleshy she-devil whose lust Tolstoy viewed as "terribly repulsive and disgusting." However, Anna's hold on Tolstoy gradually forced a change. By incorporating the parallel story of Levin and Kitty to his tale of adultery, Tolstoy altered his initial scheme. As John Bayley argues, "It is Levin who liberates the novel from itself." Absorbing the moral focus that Tolstoy derived from his own married life and spiritual struggles, Levin deflected Tolstoy's moral attention and allowed Anna to become more than an archetype and warning about the destruction of passion but a truly complex, sympathetic figure and one of fiction's greatest heroines. Richard Pevear, one of the novel's recent translators, contends that Tolstoy "gradually enlarged the figure of Anna morally and diminished the figure of the husband; the sinner grew in beauty and spontaneity, while the saint turned more and more hypocritical."

By spring 1874 Tolstoy sent the first 31 chapters to the printers but then changed his mind about publishing them. In November, however, he agreed to have the novel serialized in the *Russian Messenger*, and after four monthly installments appeared in 1875 work broke off. He would eventually resume his labor but not without duress, declaring, "My God, if only someone would finish *Anna Karenina* for me!" Additional installments appeared in 1876 and, after another long interruption, more in 1877. Part VIII, the final part of the novel, was refused by his editor because of Tolstoy's unpatriotic ridicule of the Volunteers' movement to help the Balkan Slavs in Russia's war with Turkey, and was eventually printed as a separate pamphlet. Each installment was avidly read and greeted enthusiastically by the public with Tolstoy receiving word from friends that "There is a roar of satisfaction as if you were throwing food to starving men" and that "Only Gogol and Pushkin have ever been read like this." Reviewers, however, were not as supportive. Many were disappointed in this follow-up to the epic *War and Peace* in which Tolstoy was accused of wasting his talent "on absolutely insignificant subject-matter, such as the depiction of empty lives, foolish concepts, and petty interests." The novelist was also roundly censured as a reactionary enemy of progress with his conservative moral vision celebrating married and country life and derided for his novel's "idyllic aroma of babies' nappies." Others could not decipher the novel's plan, seeing only a teeming sprawl or a ungainly collection of tedious or memorable parts. "I don't care for *Anna Karenina*," Turgenev commented, "although one comes across truly magnificent pages (the horse race, mowing, hunting). But it is all sour, with an odor of Moscow, incense, spinsterhood, the Slavophil thing and the gentry thing, etc." Dostoevsky, however, was appreciative and generous in his praise: "*Anna Karenina*, as an artistic product, is perfection. . . . Nothing in the literature of Europe at the present time compares with it."

Following the expansiveness of *War and Peace*, there is certainly a narrowing of scope in *Anna Karenina* but a compensating increase in depth and intensity. The novel is a triumph of psychological penetration as Anna's doomed passion moves toward its tragic culmination, balanced by the contrapuntal design of Levin's comic history in love and marriage that Tolstoy animates with autobiographical details and a merciless self-analysis. Although both protagonists meet only once in the novel, Tolstoy was confident that their connections were closely fitted and thematically appropriate. Writing to a reviewer who had complained about the lack of architectural unity in his novel, Tolstoy is emphatic:

> Your judgment about *Anna Karenina* seems to me wrong. I am, on the contrary, proud of the architecture—the arches are brought together in such a way that it is impossible to notice even where the keystone is. And that is what I was trying for most of all. The connection of the structure is made not on the level of the story and not on the relationships (acquaintances) of the characters, but on the inner connection.

For Tolstoy the "inner connection" is announced by the novel's first sentence: "All happy families are alike but an unhappy family is unhappy after its own fashion." His novel would explore the various social, psychological, and moral factors that destroy Anna's married life and the essential condition that will insure Levin's happiness as a husband and father. As Tolstoy observed, "For a work to be good one must love the main, basic idea in it. So in *Anna Karenina* I love the *family* idea, in *War and Peace* I loved the *national* idea as a result of the war of 1812." From his basic idea of family Tolstoy alternates the contrasting though linked histories of love and marriage between Anna and Vronsky and Levin and Kitty. The novel opens with the disruption in the Oblonsky household with Dolly's discovery of her husband and Anna's brother Stiva's affair. Anna arrives in Moscow to restore domestic peace while her own married life is threatened by her fateful encounter with Vronsky. Both Anna and Vronsky are impediments to Kitty's and Levin's marriage plans, with Anna a rival to Kitty for Vronsky and he the reason that Kitty rejects Levin's initial proposal. Through the rest of the novel the theme of love and marriage plays out through comparison between the two couples. As Anna struggles to reconcile with Karenin and give up Vronsky, Kitty and Levin come together, and as Anna and her lover begin their version of married life in restless travel and social ostracism, Kitty and Levin marry. With Anna's return to claim her son and resolve the hopeless situation that has cut her off from society and, without any object beyond her obsessive desire that has trapped her in an increasingly mutually destructive dependency on Vronsky, Kitty gives birth, and Levin glimpses a wider and richer basis for his relationship with his wife. Finally, Anna's passion, which unlike Levin's is not a means to a wider spiritual growth but an end in itself, becomes the poison that destroys her. Suicide is the only relief, as Levin's own spiritual crisis in the face of the reality of death is resolved by the sustenance of family and country life, freed from the social and personal torments that punish Anna mercilessly.

Through his contrasted stories of the workings of the human heart and soul, Tolstoy erects a remarkable social panorama that links city and country life and a wide cast in which each character is simultaneously unique and universal. All is sustained by Tolstoy's inimitable power of animation, which he shares with Dickens, showing us the world and its inhabitants newly minted but eerily familiar and recognizable. "Every twig, every feather sticks to his magnet," Virginia Woolf wrote in an appreciation of Tolstoy's skills, "and what his infallible eye reports of a cough or a trick of the hands his infallible brain refers to something hidden in the character so that we know his people, not only by the way they love and their views on politics and the immortality of the soul, but also by the way they sneeze and choke. Even in a translation we feel we have been on a mountain-top and had a telescope put into our hands. Everything is astonishingly clear and absolutely sharp." *Anna Karenina* ultimately compels its readers as few other novels have done as well that life itself hangs in the balance of Tolstoy's representation and that the fate of his characters touches at critical points who we are and how we understand our world.

14

ADVENTURES OF HUCKLEBERRY FINN

(1884)

by Mark Twain

But more truly with Huckleberry Finn *than with any other book, inquiry may satisfy itself: here is America. . . . The book has the fecundity, the multiplicity of genius. . . . It is a passage through the structure of a nation. . . . It is an exploration of the human race.*
—Bernard De Voto, *Mark Twain's America*

It is fair to say that *Adventures of Huckleberry Finn* exerts a hold on the American consciousness and conscience like no other American novel. It is a story about liberation and limitations: what Americans would like to believe about themselves and their nation as well as fear to acknowledge. The Mississippi River of Huck's self-reliant journey is an ever-flowing American highway of boundless possibilities, where the darker, sinister consequences of American democracy may also lurk along the shore. By liberating Huck from the confinements of civilization and sending him down the Mississippi to confront the various expressions of American culture and identity, by linking him with the escaped slave Jim and his own pursuit down America's racial divide of freedom and humanity, Twain transforms a boy's adventure tale into what Lionel Trilling asserted is "One of the world's great books and one of the central documents of American culture." In tapping the poetic resources of the American vernacular and the dramatic and thematic possibilities of the American landscape, Twain can also withstand the high praise of William Dean Howells, who called the writer "the Lincoln of our literature," and justify Hemingway's oft-quoted overgeneralization that "All modern American literature comes from one book by Mark Twain called *Huckleberry Finn*. . . . All American writing comes from that."

Initially condemned and banned by the Public Library Committee of Concord, Massachusetts, in 1885 as "rough, course, and inelegant . . . more suited to the slums than to intelligent, respectable people," *Huckleberry Finn* continues to elicit contentious reaction and remains the only 19th-century American classic under threat of censorship and removal from school required reading lists. School board debates on inclusion of the novel in the curriculum prompted a 1985 ABC *Nightline* feature called "*Huckleberry Finn:* Literature or Racist Trash." Like *Don Quixote*, Twain's masterpiece serves a multiple function in our literature and culture: as a literary fountainhead, as a work of powerful mythic expression, and as a disturbing challenge to how Americans see themselves and their history.

Despite Twain's achievement, there is something of the accidental and the spontaneous combustion of significance in the making of the masterpiece. *Huck's Autobiography*, as it was first titled, was begun in the summer of 1876 after the publication of *The Adventures of Tom Sawyer*. It was conceived as "another boys' book," undertaken, according to its initially dismissive author, "more to be at work than anything else." Twain partially completed the first 16 chapters but grew discouraged and lost interest, writing that "I like it only tolerably well as far as I got and may possibly pigeonhole or burn the MS when it is done." Instead he set his manuscript aside, fitfully returning to it in 1879–80, and again when his imagination finally caught fire as a result of an 1882 trip on the Mississippi to refresh his recollections. Twain's return to the West and the sites of his boyhood and early days as a riverboatman inspired him to complete *Life on the Mississippi* (1883) and the remaining 22 chapters of *Huckleberry Finn*. Published first in England in December 1884, the novel appeared in America in February 1885, after 40,000 copies had been ordered by subscription. Both praised and condemned by early and later critics, *Huckleberry Finn* attracted the support of such writers as Robert Louis Stevenson, who considered the book one of the greatest American novels, H. L. Mencken, who judged it "one of the great masterpieces of the world," and T. S. Eliot, who argued that Twain "wrote a much greater book than he could have known he was writing." Others, such as Van Wyck Brooks, have granted the book's episodic brilliance but overall inferiority as a work of art, citing particularly the return of Tom Sawyer at the novel's disappointing climax as evidence of the novel's ultimate failure. Some critics, such as William Van O'Connor and Leo Marx, have also accused others of overvaluing Huck as a mythic hero and the implication of his adventures, as well as charging Twain with mishandling the book's central moral conflict regarding Jim's slave status and humanity. Despite its shortcomings, the novel continues to hold its contested place, along with *The Scarlet Letter* and *Moby-Dick*, as one of the trio of essential and defining 19th-century American novels.

Adventures of Huckleberry Finn generates its comedy, satire, pathos, and dramatic irony by having the adolescent Huck tell his own story, keeping his misspellings, solecisms, and naiveté intact. His story begins in the aftermath of the climax of *Tom Sawyer* with Huck chafing under the "sivilizing" of the Widow Douglas and her sister Miss Watson and under the sway of Tom Sawyer's Quixote-like chivalric playacting. Tom recruits Huck to join his robbers' band, whose adventures confuse hogs with "ingots," turnips with "julery," and a Sunday school picnic with Spanish and Arab merchants and their elephants and camels loaded with diamonds. Huck finds little profit in either the unnatural hypocrisy of respectability or the romantic fantasy that distorts actuality, establishing the theme of lying, pretense, and gamesmanship that will define Huck's maturation. With the appearance of his brutal father, Huck is reclaimed as the son of a violent drunk, prompting his escape by staging his own death and beginning his downriver "rebirth" in which to survive he assumes a succession of identities—"Sarah Williams," "George Peters," "son of a family who knows Miss Hooker," "son of a father with smallpox," an orphan slaveowner, "George Jackson," "the servant Adolphus," an English valet, and finally "Tom Sawyer"—while dealing with threats on the river and along the shore. Accompanying Huck is Miss Watson's runaway slave, Jim, fleeing to avoid being sold down the river and permanent separation from his wife and children.

Huck's relationship with Jim and his role in the slave's escape form the novel's core moral conflict that tests Huck's sense of the world and his identity. Although Jim proves to be an invaluable companion as well as a more reliable guide than Huck's schooling and prior experience, Huck alternates between respect for Jim's practical and oracular insights and demeaning ridicule of his friend. Huck ignores Jim's injunction against handling snakeskin and places a dead snake under Jim's blanket as a joke, with painful results when the joke on Jim misfires. When the pair are finally reunited after being separated in a fog, Huck reverts to the earlier Tom-inspired foolery, dismissing Jim's relief at his friend's safety by trying to convince Jim that he had only dreamed the danger. Finally realizing the truth, Jim comments that "When . . . my heart wuz mos' broke bekase you wuz los' . . . all you wuz thinkin' 'bout wuz how you could make a fool uv ole Jim wid a lie. Dat truck dah is *trash;* en trash is what people is dat puts dirt on de head er dey fren's en makes em ashamed." Jim's words hit their target, and Huck is forced to reassess his shabby behavior: "It was fifteen minutes before I could work myself up to go and humble myself to a nigger; but I done it, and I warn't ever sorry for it afterward, neither. I didn't do him no more mean tricks, and I wouldn't done that one if I'd 'a' knowed it would make him feel that way." The biggest challenge to Huck's growing respect for Jim as a man and a friend is his realization that his assistance in Jim's escape goes against established authority and his previously accepted moral code in which Jim is property that should be returned to its owner. Although his conscience, schooled by custom and civilization, tells him that "people that acts as I'd been acting about that nigger goes to everlasting fire," Huck resolves "All right, then I'll *go* to hell," committing to protect Jim's freedom, a decision that marks Huck's independence, maturation, and rejection of hypocrisy and injustice.

On the river, the pair experiences its liberation from socially imposed constraints, mutual respect, and a sustaining relationship with nature, uncontaminated by the threat that will arrive from the shore:

> Sometimes we'd have that whole river all to ourselves for the longest time. Yonder was the banks and the islands, across the water; and maybe a spark—which was a candle in a cabin window—and sometimes on the water you could see a spark or two—on a raft or a scow, you know; and maybe you could hear a fiddle or a song coming over from one of them crafts. It's lovely to live on a raft.

These lyrical moments are interrupted by episodes and characters that allow Twain to explore the discrepancy between American ideals and reality exemplified by violence, knavery, and delusions. The chivalric pretenses of Tom's playacting are embodied in disturbing actuality. On board the ironically named steamboat *Walter Scott*, Huck and Jim encounter a real-life robber band and the grisly truth of their "brotherhood." The Grangerford-Shepherdson feud translates notions of inviolate family honor and heroic glory into a cold-blooded murder that shakes Huck to his core:

> The boys jumped for the river—both of them hurt—and as they swum down the current the men run along the bank shooting at them and singing out, 'Kill them, kill them!' It made me so sick I most fell out of the tree. I ain't a-going to tell *all* that happened—it would make me sick again if I was to do that. I wished I hadn't ever come ashore that night to see such things. I ain't ever going to get shut of them—lots of times I dream about them.

Further downstream, violence is unredeemed by anything honorable among a citizenry that is a brutal, idle mob in which "There couldn't anything wake them up all over, and make them happy all over, like a dog-fight—unless it might be putting turpentine on a stray dog and setting fire to him, or tying a tin pan to his tail and see him run himself to death." Playacting as performed, not by Tom, but by the professional rogues and aristocratic pretenders, the Duke and the Dauphin, lacks any end but greed and victimization, with their targets escalating in human cost from the suckers tricked by the Royal Nonesuch, who deal with their deception by deceiving their neighbors, to the Wilks orphans to be stripped of their sustenance, and finally to Jim himself, sold back into captivity.

Jim's final "liberation" from the Phelps farm and the novel's climax mark the return of Tom Sawyer and the boyish, romantic playacting of the novel's opening. Although Twain punctures through ridicule the romantic excesses derived from Tom's reading, he eliminates the crucial moral conflict of what should be done with the now humanized Jim by having Miss Watson repent her decision to sell him down the river, a fact that Tom knows but conceals to act out Jim's elaborate, unnecessary escape. Tom's "trash," in the word of Jim's accusation of Huck's earlier behavior, is counterbalanced by the life-and-death reality of the situation that emerges, by Huck's genuine concern for Jim, and by Jim's own sacrificial decision to risk his freedom to help the wounded Tom. Many readers have resisted the shift of focus from Huck to Tom, from the novel's realism and moral seriousness to the boyish escapade and the author's belabored contrivance. In defense of Twain's ending, T. S. Eliot rationalizes the author's diminished focus on Huck and his development, stating that "For Huckleberry Finn, neither a tragic nor a happy ending would be suitable . . . He has no beginning and no end. Hence, he can only disappear; and his disappearance can only be accomplished by bringing forward another performer to obscure the disappearance in a cloud of whimsicalities." Before passing into silence and joining the pantheon of American literary heroes that includes Natty Bumppo, Ishmael, Nick Adams, and Jay Gatsby, Huck is given the final word on behalf of mythic American freedom: "But I reckon I got to light out for the territory ahead of the rest, because Aunt Sally she's going to adopt me and sivilize me, and I can't stand it. I been there before."

TOM JONES 15

(1749)

by Henry Fielding

Character, Painting, Reflection, Humour, excellent each in its Kind, in short I found every thing there. . . . If my design had been to propagate virtue by appearing publickly in its defence, I should rather have been ye Author of Tom Jones than of five Folio Volumes of sermons.

—Captain Lewis Thomas in a letter, 1749

With Fielding's *Tom Jones*, the English novel had its first colossal masterpiece. Called "the greatest single literary work of the eighteenth century" (Leopold Damrosch, Jr.) and "at once the last and the consummate literary achievement of England's Augustan Age" (Martin C. Battestin), *Tom Jones* was an immediate, notorious popular success, selling out its entire first edition of 2,000 copies before the official publication date, February 10, 1749; by the end of the year three additional editions had appeared. Fielding's first readers were both entranced and appalled by the novel's rough-and-tumble exuberance, wide social canvas, and frank urbanity, dubbing it both "the most lively book ever published," as well as "low" and "vicious." The novel's precise title, *The History of Tom Jones, a Foundling*, clearly announced its assault on conventional decency and artistic propriety by putting at the center of the fiction a young man of dubious birth and questionable morality. One contemporary even suspected that the earthquakes that shook London in 1750 were divine retribution for the book's popular success.

The book's seismic jolts have been felt ever since. Among critics and literary historians, Fielding and *Tom Jones* have commonly been paired with Samuel Richardson and his contrary, nearly contemporaneous masterwork, *Clarissa* (1747–48), marking out the two different paths the English novel would take: inward, in Richardson's treatment, to explore the wellsprings of human personality and consciousness, or in Fielding's outward movement toward the rich panorama of English society, customs, and human affairs. In Dr. Johnson's famous denigration of Fielding's achievement, Richardson's "characters of nature" were judged superior to Fielding's "characters of manners," with as great a difference between the two novelists "as between a man who knew how a watch was made, and a man who could tell the hour by looking on the dial-plate." Coleridge counters, asserting that *Tom Jones*, along with *Oedipus Tyrannus* and *The Alchemist*, were "the three most perfect plots ever planned," and that reading Fielding after Richardson "is like emerging from a sick-room heated by stoves into an open lawn on a breezy day in May." Fated to be continually linked in the literary mind, like Tolstoy and Dostoevsky, Keats and Shelley, Hemingway and Fitzgerald, Fielding and Richardson have long served as the rivals they were in life, representing central opposed tendencies in the novel between plot and character, comedy and tragedy, manners and consciousness, the telescope versus the microscope.

Fielding's background, compared to Defoe's and Richardson's, was not middle class but distinguished, and his classical education, legal training, and wide exposure to high and low life, as well as his experience as a dramatist who came to the novel late, provided the ideal conjunction of personal qualities and the cultural moment to establish the novel in England as a rival form to poetry and drama. The novel's eventual emergence as a dominant artistic medium owes much to Fielding's genius in blending his comic and dramatic vision to the flexible and expansive narrative form of the novel that he helped devise. Fielding's career as a dramatist ended in 1737 with the passing of legislation restricting the number of authorized theaters, prompted by Fielding's attack of the Walpole government in his plays. The same year, Fielding entered the Middle Temple to study law, and the legal career that took him throughout the country increased his wide knowledge of English life. After 1748 Fielding became one of the most famous of the Bow Street magistrates, closely associated with human suffering and the moral issues that absorbed him and are reflected in his writing.

Fielding took up fiction prompted in part by the publication in 1740 of Samuel Richardson's first novel, *Pamela, or Virtue Rewarded*, arguably, after *Don Quixote*, the second international best-selling novel. It is the story of a virtuous maidservant who rebuffs the unwanted attentions of the rakish Mr. B. before winning his genuine affection and marriage. Fielding set out to puncture Richardson's genteel sentiment and what he perceived to be his false idealization, first in the pastiche *Shamela* (1741), in which a heroine's virtue is only a pretense to inflame her lover and to manipulate an advantageous marriage. A similar attack on Richardson's sentimentality provides at least the initial ironic focus of Fielding's other masterwork, *Joseph Andrews* (1742). In Fielding's comic parody, Richardson's Pamela is now married to Squire Booby, and her brother, Joseph Andrews, has his virtue assaulted by Booby's sister in a delightful reversal of Richardson's plot. However, what began as a satire on Richardson's perceived narrow and hypocritical sentimental virtue in *Pamela* grows in *Joseph Andrews* to one of the English novel's first great social satires, in which Fielding's good humor and sympathy embrace a wider comic conception of human nature as a blend of frailty and goodness, corruption and virtue. *Joseph Andrews* is also significant for announcing and previewing in its preface Fielding's radical narrative departure, "hitherto unattempted in our language." Fielding's version of the novel—his "comic romance" or "comic epic poem in prose"—draws on the conventions of the earlier prose romance, epic, and drama, but differs from them by

> its action being more extended and comprehensive, containing a much larger circle of incidents, and introducing a greater variety of characters. It differs from the serious romance in its fable and action in this, that as in the one these are grave and solemn, so in the other they are light and ridiculous; it differs in its characters by introducing persons of inferior rank, and consequently of inferior manners, whereas the grave romance sets the highest before us; lastly, in its sentiments and diction, by preserving the ludicrous instead of the sublime.

Fielding offers a new definition for the fledgling novel as a hybrid form incorporating the epic's wide vision of central cultural values, comedy's admission for attention of ordinary characters and scenes, and drama's artful arrangement of incident into a skillful plot.

Fielding's claim of creating a comic epic is most masterfully fulfilled in *Tom Jones*. In his story of the adventures of the low-born protagonist, whose generic name suggests an English Everyman, Fielding brings to the center of the novel a character whose disreputable birth and blend of virtues and flaws extend the novel's realism. By rejecting previously idealized character types Fielding paves the way for a frank consideration of the actual ways of the world and a clear-headed conception of human nature. Tom is no paragon; he has all the excesses of youth, perfectly suitable for his entry into a wider world of dupes and knaves, whose outstanding characteristics are their imperfections. The novel begins in the Somersetshire of Fielding's youth, where Tom, whose indiscretions include his daring to love his neighbor's daughter, Sophia Western, loses the support of Squire Allworthy and is cast out of the rustic, Edenic Paradise Hall to embark upon a revealing journey through English society. Fielding's account of Tom's education in the ways of the world combines the episodic looseness of the picaresque road narrative—in which the novelist presents an ever-widening cast of characters, scenes, and incidents—with the tight control of the mystery and suspense novel, putting at the center of Tom's story the sensational secret of his birth. Supporting Fielding's social panorama is a formal structure of breathtaking symmetry. The novel is divided into 18 books and subdivided into three equal portions corresponding to the story's principal settings—Somerset, the road to London, and London itself. Each setting features a female—Molly Seagrim, Mrs. Waters, and Lady Bellaston—to tempt Tom and complicate his true love for Sophia. At the inn at Upton, the novel's exact midpoint, Fielding reverses the novel's narrative pressure from Sophia's pursuit of Tom to his pursuit of her, which will be resolved only when the questions of Tom's identity are revealed and his own recognition of his moral failings is accepted at the novel's breathless and triumphant conclusion. All is controlled by the shaping presence of the book's narrator, whose ironic, though compassionate, sympathy insists on a moral standard that embraces man's weaknesses as well as his vitality and accepts the world as it is, even as it is shown very much in need of the good sense the narrator supplies.

There had simply never been anything quite like Fielding's performance in English fiction before. The author of the play *Don Quixote in England* succeeded in a Cervantine equivalent in the English novel, sharing with *Don Quixote* an epiclike depiction of his age's customs and values, and offering the amplitude that had previously been achieved in English narrative only by Chaucer, England's first great literary artist. Like Chaucer, Fielding numbered the classes of men, while providing both delight and instruction in human nature and action. If breadth dominates over depth in Fielding's bravura performance, if a convincing inwardness of character is missing in the often emblematic Hogarth-like quality of Fielding's portraiture in pursuit of the universals of human nature, *Tom Jones* compensates in unparalleled enjoyment. It also reflects the crucial innovations the author brings to the novel form: the harnessing of wide learning and classical tradition to fashion an imaginative structure that rivals poetry and drama as a medium for truth-telling and a massive criticism of life. In the wake of *Tom Jones,* the commonplace realism of Jane Austen, the picaresque and suspenseful marvels of Dickens, Sterne's self-reflective novel as artifice, and the prose epic of Joyce become conceivable.

16

GREAT EXPECTATIONS

(1860–61)

by Charles Dickens

The book will be written in the first person throughout and during these first three weekly numbers you will find the hero to be a boy-child, like David. Then he will be an apprentice. You will not have to complain of the want of humour as in The Tale of Two Cities. *I have made the opening, I hope, in its general effect exceedingly droll. I have put a child and a good-natured foolish man in relations that seem to me very funny. Of course I have got in the pivot on which the story will turn too—and which indeed, as you will remember, was the grotesque tragi-comic conception that first encouraged me. To be quite sure I had fallen into no unconscious repetitions, I read* David Copperfield *again the other day, and was affected by it to a degree you would hardly believe.*

—Charles Dickens, letter to John Forster, 1860

George Bernard Shaw called *Great Expectations* Dickens's "most compactly perfect book." It is certainly mature Dickens at the height of his powers as a novelist. All of the characteristic Dickensian strengths are evident: humor, pathos, and satire, but here supported by a tightly constructed mystery plot, employed not only to captivate and hold an audience but pressed into service as a means of illuminating character and a social theme. Dickens followed his friend Wilkie Collins's *The Woman in White* with his own version of the sensation novel, the thriller with a secret at its center. There is perhaps no better illustration of the remarkable development of Dickens as a novelist than by a comparison between the exuberant, picaresque improvisation of *The Pickwick Papers* and the taut control of *Great Expectations*, produced under the even more challenging conditions of weekly serialization. *Great Expectations* belies Henry James's contention that Dickens produced undisciplined fictional extravaganzas, what James's scornfully classed as loose, baggy monsters. *Great Expectations* is one of the greatest bildungsroman ever crafted, one of the central 19th-century social fables, and one of the supreme mystery novels that does not exhaust its appeal once the reader knows whodunit.

In working out *Great Expectations*, Dickens decided again to use a first-person narrator and to reexamine the same autobiographical territory previously explored in *David Copperfield* (1849–50), Dickens's "favorite child." Both books deal with the taint of commonness, the central trauma of Dickens's own life. David Copperfield, like the young Charles Dickens, is a sensitive youth sent off to labor in a factory, abandoned and neglected. What follows in Dickens's reworking of aspects of his own past is a fictional compensation for those early humiliations. *David Copperfield* becomes a powerful and compelling fairy tale of success, a make-believe equivalent of the hard-fought, realistic struggle for achievement and respectability that Dickens's own career represented. Young David is rescued from his descent into the lower depths by a fairy godmother, Aunt Betsey, and the novel shows David's ascent into gentility. As Cinderella rises above drudgery and gets her prince and a title, David gets his pot of gold, a respectable position in society, and a wife. *David Copperfield* is, therefore, a Victorian Horatio Alger story, a social fable from rags to riches, but more important from rags to respectability.

By the time Dickens wrote *Great Expectations*, a decade had passed, and much had changed in Dickens that would alter the societal wish fulfillment of *David Copperfield.* The novels that followed it—*Bleak House*, *Hard Times*, and *Little Dorrit* (a novel Shaw called "a more seditious book than *Das Kapital*")—show Dickens's societal view darkening. The genteel society that he previously showed David so unquestioningly joining is found sinister and corrupt. Pip's autobiography, compared to David's, shows Dickens returning to the same personal material but with radically altered conclusions. We have the same sensitive boy from a humble background that he resents. Pip's secret desire to escape his commonness is miraculously granted. Yet *Great Expectations* is a perverse fairy tale of success in which the presumed fairy godmother, Miss Havisham, is a life-hating old witch, Pip's true benefactor is a common criminal, and Pip's aspirations are shown to be all pretensions and snobbery. Eventually, Pip's fortune is lost rather than gained, and in terms of the view of society Dickens presents, it is a fortune that is well lost. Pip's success, as opposed to David's, is in self-understanding rather than in material satisfaction, and Pip's history is an inward, self-critical psychological journey rather than David's fall and rise of fortune and adventure. In *Great Expectations*, therefore, Dickens rewrites a version of his own history from an altered viewpoint. By 1860, Dickens was able to objectify and criticize his past and his former attitudes that go considerably further than self-pity and self-fulfillment. Shaw observed that by the time Dickens wrote *Great Expectations* Dickens had learned that "making a living by sticking labels on blacking bottles and rubbing shoulders with boys who were not gentlemen, was as little shameful as being the genteel apprentice in the office of Mr. Spenlow. . . . The reappearance of Mr. Dickens in the character of a blacksmith's boy may be regarded as an apology to Mealy Potatoes [one of David's fellow laborers]."

The success fable that is offered in compensation to David and Dickens's feelings of victimization and neglect is reworked in *Great Expectations.* It is the humbler life of Joe Gargery's smith shop, which Pip is so desperate to escape, that is the moral corrective to the false assumptions and distortions of gentility and privilege in Pip's desire to be a gentleman. David's dream world of success becomes Pip's nightmare. The novel turns on the recognition of Pip's self-deception and ingratitude, on the awakening of Pip from his false dream of gentility and privilege. Pip is made to learn the bitter lesson through the agency of Dickens's remarkable plot, which eventually reveals that Pip's real fairy godmother is a an outcast and a criminal, his love is a heartless victimizer, and his fortune has made him an ungrateful snob.

The novel begins on the fateful day of, in Pip's words, "my first most vivid and broad impression of things." Standing before the graves of his mother, father, and five siblings, Pip for the first time in his recollection reflects on his position alone in the midst of a harsh, hostile, and threatening world, a "small bundle of shivers." Actual threat arrives by the novel's fourth paragraph: "'Hold your noise!' cried a terrible voice, as a man started up from among the graves at the side of the church porch. 'Keep still, you little devil, or I'll cut your throat!'" Magwitch, who is to become "my convict," compels Pip's assistance in bringing him food and a file to assist his escape from a nearby prison ship. Pip's generosity on behalf of the convict forces his own first criminal act and establishes the connection, the "pivot" of Dickens's "tragi-comic conception" that will shape Pip's career and produce both the novel's plot surprises and Pip's self-awareness. Magwitch is eventually recaptured, and this vivid opening incident is allowed to subside in Pip's memory, replaced by another turning point: his summons to Satis House by Miss Havisham.

The conception of a woman jilted at the altar who stops time to perpetuate her humiliation by remaining attired in her decaying wedding gown, surrounded by the now moldering, untouched wedding breakfast, is one of Dickens's most outlandish inventions. However, Miss Havisham and Satis House combine elements of the gothic and fairy tale with plausible psychological and social elements. Miss Havisham is the ultimate victim of a social system that values form and appearance over reality. She psychologically paralyzes herself, a self-sacrifice to a set of false social values. To extract vengeance, she raises Estella to become her proxy, to break others' hearts as Miss Havisham's heart has been broken. Pip is summoned as a companion to Estella to test her growing skills as a heartbreaker, and it is in loveless, stagnant, prisonlike Satis House, under the perverse influence of Miss Havisham and her creation Estella, that Pip becomes "infected" by class consciousness for the first time. Playing cards with Estella, he becomes aware that jacks should be knaves and that he is a coarse and common boy. His experience at Satis House begins his dream to become a gentleman that will cause him to forget the tender comradeship and humane council he has received from

Joe Gargery and to feel ashamed of Joe's ignorance and clumsiness and his own background.

Miss Havisham's lawyer, Mr. Jaggers, brings Pip word that he has a secret benefactor who intends Pip to become a gentleman. Pip (and the first-time reader) naturally assumes that Miss Havisham is the benefactor, part of her plan to make him a worthy suitor for Estella. Pip leaves the world of the marsh and forge for London, which is characterized by its artificiality and repression of everything natural. Perhaps the greatest embodiment of the distortion of modern city life is Jaggers's clerk, Wemmick, a thoroughly self-divided man, forced to behave coldly and calculatingly at work, reserving his humanity for his home, which is constructed literally as a castle with drawbridge. In this world of self-interest and self-protection, of appearance over reality, Pip begins his education in becoming an idle, extravagant, ungrateful gentleman who is mortified by his common origin and terrified that he might be exposed for what he was.

The exposure comes in one of the greatest surprise scenes in all of Dickens—Magwitch's return and his revelation that he is Pip's benefactor: "Yes, Pip, dear boy, I've made a gentleman on you! It's me wot has done it! I swore that time, sure as ever I earned a guinea, that guinea should go to you. I swore arterwards, sure as ever I spec'lated and got rich, you should get rich. I lived rough, that you should live smooth; I worked hard, that you should be above work. What odds, dear boy? Do I tell it, fur you to feel a obligation? Not a bit. I tell it, fur you to know as that there hunted dunghill dog wot you kep life in, got his head so high that he could make a gentleman—and, Pip, you're him!" Magwitch shows himself in his scheme to be as much a victim of the tyranny of gentility as Miss Havisham. Treated by society as a "hunted dunghill dog," Magwitch's revenge is to enter that same society by creating his own proxy, like Miss Havisham's Estella. Pip's first reaction to the truth of his circumstances is horror and dread that Magwitch's identity will be found out. Magwitch is a ticking time bomb. If he is discovered, he is a condemned man, but more, Pip's great expectations would be exposed as a fraud perpetrated by a common criminal.

The novel accelerates from this point into a breathless rush of exciting scenes and revelations (including the symmetrical news that Estella is Magwitch's daughter). Orlick, Pip's old nemesis from the forge, threatens Pip's life and pushes him at the brink of death to his key realizations: "Softened as my thoughts of all the rest of men were in that dire extremity; humbly beseeching pardon, as I did, of Heaven; melted at heart, as I was, by the thought that I had taken no farewell, and never could take farewell, of those who were dear to me, or could explain myself to them or ask their compassion on my miserable errors. . . ." Rescued, Pip now treats Magwitch with sympathy and compassion, standing by him as he is once more taken by the law. Pip finally recognizes the superiority of Joe Gargery's commonness to all his former notions of gentility. But Pip is prevented from returning to that world, and he is forced to make his way by his own labors, sobered and matured in an ambiguous world in which a criminal can still claim sympathy as, in Joe's words, "a poor miserable fellow-creatur," and the genteel are little more than respectable criminals.

Central to Dickens's original conception was a conclusion in which Pip's only profit from his great expectation should have been in self-knowledge. He was, however, persuaded by his friend the writer Edward Bulwer-Lytton to "unwind the thread that I thought I had wound for ever," to rewrite his original conclusion, which ended with a reunion with Estella that only implies her suffering and her sharing with Pip a similar life of bleak loneliness. "I was very glad afterwards to have had the interview;" Pip observes in the original ending, "for in her face and in her voice, and in her touch, she gave me the assurance that suffering had been stronger than Miss Havisham's teaching, and had given her a heart to understand what my heart used to be." Instead, Dickens softens the blow to imply a romantic consolation for both sufferers: "I took her hand in mine, and we went out of the ruined place; and, as the morning mists had risen long ago when I first left the forge, so the evening mists were rising now, and in all the broad expanse of tranquil light they showed to me, I saw the shadow of no parting from her." Most critics have preferred Dickens's original intention as more psychologically believable and artistically consistent, and virtually every modern edition of the novel now offers both endings for the reader to decide. It is a debatable flaw in what is otherwise, in the words of Dickens's biographer Edgar Johnson, "the most perfectly constructed and perfectly written of all Dickens's works."

17

ABSALOM, ABSALOM!

(1936)

by William Faulkner

Absalom, Absalom! *is a unique fictional experiment—unique in relation to Faulkner's other novels and to modern fiction generally. Indeed, it is not too much to claim that in point of technique it constitutes the last radical innovation in fictional method since Joyce. . . . Broadly stated, the intention of* Absalom, Absalom! *is to create through the utilization of all the resources of fiction, a grand tragic vision of historical dimension. As in the tragedies of the ancients and in the great myths of the Old Testament, the action represents issues of timeless moral significance. That Faulkner here links the decline of a social order to an infraction of fundamental morality cannot be doubted. Sutpen falls through innate deficiency of moral insight, but the error which he commits is also socially derived and thus illustrates the flaw which dooms with equal finality the aspirations of a whole culture. Events of modern history, here viewed as classic tragedy, are elevated through conscious artistry to the status of a new myth.*

—Ilse Dusoir Lind, "The Design and Meaning of *Absalom, Absalom!*"

In the euphoria William Faulkner experienced when in 1936 after a nearly five-year struggle he finished the final draft of *Absalom, Absalom!* he declared that "I think it's the best novel yet written by an American." It has certainly proven to be one of a very few candidates for that distinction as America's great modernist classic, appropriate to be discussed alongside the other towering achievements in the novel during the first half of the 20th century—Proust's *In Search of Lost Time*, Joyce's *Ulysses*, and Mann's *Magic Mountain*. *Absalom, Absalom!* is the most ambitious of Faulkner's novels, the culmination of a remarkable sequence of technical and thematic explorations beginning with *Sartoris* (1929) through *The Sound and the Fury* (1929), *As I Lay Dying* (1930), *Sanctuary* (1931), and *Light in August* (1932). Collectively, in imitation of Balzac's *Human Comedy*, each forms a chapter of Faulkner's expansive saga of Yoknapatawpha County, his recreated version of his native region of Mississippi. With repeated characters and a cumulatively revealed pattern that reflects the rise and fall of the South—from the displacement of the Indians to the rise of a plantation society and its attendant code of chivalry and honor, to its destruction through the tragedy of slavery—Faulkner dramatizes a mythic cycle of paradise lost through human limitations and the inexorable process of history. The archetypes that define a people, a region, and an era are most expressively represented in the haunted story of Thomas Sutpen and his family in *Absalom, Absalom!*

Chronicling almost 100 years of American history, from the early 1800s to the early 1900s, *Absalom, Absalom!* is in a sense the American version of Emily Brontë's *Wuthering Heights.* Like Brontë's masterwork, Faulkner similarly adapts an existential drama out of a tangled and portentous family history, derived in unequal mixture from Attic and Shakespearean tragedy, gothic traditions, and biblical cadences. Also like *Wuthering Heights,* a complicated chain of events, genealogy, and chronology must be reconstructed from witnesses and interpreters. At the center of Faulkner's drama, like Brontë's Heathcliff, is the grandiose and puzzling figure of Thomas Sutpen, part dreamer, like Fitzgerald's Jay Gatsby, part monomaniacal overreacher, like Melville's Ahab. Faulkner's novel is patterned by the central enigmas—the who and why of Thomas Sutpen—and a crucial mystery—why Sutpen's son kills his close friend Charles Bon, the suitor of Sutpen's daughter, the act that brings down the House of Sutpen. Answering these questions and assessing significance are a number of narrative guides—Rosa Coldfield, Sutpen's sister-in-law; Jason Compson, who has heard Sutpen's story from his father; and Compson's son Quentin who attempts to arrive at the full story along with his Harvard roommate Shreve McCannon. Each perspective is subjectively clouded and ultimately unreliable, forcing the reader into an active role of weighing the available evidence, resolving contradictions, and evaluating multiple versions of what happened to the Sutpen family and why. Employing the multilayered narrative technique of Joseph Conrad that creates a complex double focus on narrator and story, Faulkner fractures chronology and causality into a remarkable experiment in literary perspectivism that blurs distinctions between actuality, history, legend, and myth.

Eventually, a chronology and a sequence of cause and effect emerge. Born in the first decade of the 19th century, the son of a poor mountain family of western Virginia, Thomas Sutpen moves with his family to Tidewater Virginia. Sent by his father with a message to a plantation owner, Sutpen is turned away from the front door of the plantation house by a house slave, and the affront is the catalyst for his launching his great design of acquisition and power: "to combat them you have got to have what they have that made them do what the man did. You got to have land and a fine house to combat them with." Leaving Virginia for Haiti, Sutpen works as an overseer on a sugar plantation and marries the rich planter's daughter, who bears him a son. Putting wife and child aside as contrary to "the design I had in mind," Sutpen arrives in the frontier town of Jefferson, Mississippi, where he manages to obtain 100 square miles of land from the Indians. He erects a mansion in his wilderness and becomes the biggest cotton planter in Yoknapatawpha County. His second wife, Ellen Coldfield, bears him a son, Henry, and a daughter, Judith, and Sutpen's ruling passion to revenge himself on the rich and the powerful by outdoing them and founding a dynasty seems assured. Nemesis, however, arrives in the person of Henry's college friend Charles Bon, who falls in love with and wishes to marry Judith. Sutpen, who learns that Bon is his first son by his Haitian wife, orders him from the house without acknowledgment or explanation. Henry and Bon serve together during the Civil War, and, in the spring of 1865, when Bon returns to marry Judith, Henry kills him and disappears. Henry's act of killing his best friend and stepbrother, along with the attendant act of Sutpen's refusal to acknowledge Bon's birthright, precipitate the collapse of Sutpen's grand design and the ruin of his family, as well as the key puzzle that each of the novel's narrators attempts to solve.

In the aftermath of the Civil War, with his wife now dead, his son a fugitive, his slaves dispersed, and his land seized for debt, Sutpen doggedly makes a final attempt to realize his design. He proposes to his wife's sister, Rosa Coldfield, but is rejected when he offers marriage only after she provides him with a son and heir. Sutpen restores neither his land nor his power and provokes his own death by seducing his business partner's granddaughter and dismissing her when she gives birth to a daughter instead of the male heir he craves. After his death, his great house falls into ruin, haunted by Clytie, Sutpen's daughter by one of his slaves, and by the fugitive Henry Sutpen, who has come home to die. Both will be consumed in a fire that destroys the house and completes the destruction of Sutpen's family and dream.

Such a plot summary does little to capture the essence of *Absalom, Absalom!*, or the reading experience in which the various pieces of the puzzle occur out of sequence and must be reassembled. The even greater question of motive and significance must be deciphered with the assistance of the various narrative guides whose own stories, obsessions, and sensibilities shape and distort the Sutpen saga. The three Southerners who interpret the Sutpen story—Rosa Coldfield, Mr. Compson, and Quentin—create a legend that serves to mirror their private selves and collective identities as Southerners. For Rosa, the frustrated spinster, Sutpen can only be understood as a demon, a violator of the aristocratic code that defines her sense of the South as a gothic battleground of nobility versus villainy, unable to penetrate her own complicity through pride and prejudice that links her to Sutpen's rise and fall. The key issue of Sutpen's motivation to forbid the marriage between Bon and Judith remains a mystery for Rosa, "without rhyme or reason or shadow of excuse." Mr. Compson, less subjectively blinded than Rosa, grants Sutpen considerably more heroism in the grandeur of his design. However, his version of Sutpen's story is a romanticized portrait of a larger-than-life, defeated South, haunted by fallen heroes, suited to Compson's own romantic fatalism. Although more informed and comprehensive than Rosa in his judgment of Sutpen, Mr. Compson still is unable to uncover adequately the reason for his fall and ultimately its larger significance. For Mr. Compson, it is Bon's mulatto mistress that is offered in explanation of Sutpen's opposition and Henry's subsequent murder of his best friend, but even he realizes the inadequacy of this explanation: "It just doesn't explain. . . . They are there, yet something is missing."

It is finally Quentin Compson's imaginative engagement with Sutpen's story, fueled by his own personal demons, that penetrates most deeply into the core mystery. Quentin has learned from his grandfather that Bon was Sutpen's son, and incest offers one plausible explanation for the family's tragedy. Quentin, whose own incestuous fears are explored in *The Sound and the Fury*, eventually decides that incest alone is insufficient to cause Bon's murder and reaches an alternative conclusion to explain Sutpen's refusal to acknowledge his first son's birthright and Henry's act: Bon's mother "was part negro." This shattering revelation is the key that finally clarifies the undermining of Sutpen's design as a moral transgression, deeply rooted in the miscegenation that ultimately cripples and destroys the South. Faulkner would later summarize that Sutpen "violated all the rules of decency and honor and pity and compassion, and the fates took revenge on him." Ultimately, Sutpen's design, like that of the South and its social order based on the denial of human dignity and values, is a reckless, self-destructive passion for order and control with its violations of humanity and kinship the inner rot that brings down the entire social structure. Sutpen has embarked on a plan to revenge himself on a world that had denied his own humanity and has become that world.

Faulkner turned his operatic family history, fashioned out of the stuff of Horatio Alger, gothic romance, biblical archetypes, folklore, and classical tragedy, into an expansive, expressive psychological and social allegory, an investigation into the causes of a tragic history of a man, a family, a region, and a nation.

18

THE AMBASSADORS

(1903)

by Henry James

Seen in the light of its inventions, its original style, its psychology, [The Ambassadors] *can be recognized in literary history as a Stendhalian mirror in the roadway, past which Marcel Proust, James Joyce, Virginia Woolf, William Faulkner and so many others have since travelled. It might be called the first authentic masterpiece of the "modern movement." Its pattern-structure prefigures* Ulysses; *its long river-like sentences anticipated the reflective novel of Proust. Its quest of "auras" of feeling foreshadowed the experiments of Virginia Woolf.*

—Leon Edel, *The Life of Henry James: The Master*

Support for the selection and placement of Henry James's novels in this ranking comes in part from the novelist himself. James regarded *The Ambassadors* as "frankly, quite the best, 'all round,' of my productions," with *The Portrait of a Lady* next in his ranking of his works. James's own valuation has been echoed by a host of subsequent critics. *The Portrait of a Lady,* the culmination of James's initial achievement in realistic social comedy, may be a more accessible and emotionally satisfying book for many readers, but *The Ambassadors* is the more important novel in terms of literary history. It initiated the novelist's final phase of creative fulfillment in a trilogy that included *The Wings of the Dove* (1902) and *The Golden Bowl* (1904) that would define the Jamesian novel and the ways and means of modern fiction. As a crucial text in the development of the modern poetic novel of consciousness, *The Ambassadors* sets a standard that shaped writers as diverse as Joseph Conrad, D. H. Lawrence, Ford Madox Ford, Edith Wharton, Marcel Proust, James Joyce, F. Scott Fitzgerald, Virginia Woolf, William Faulkner, and others. Critics and scholars have been no less affected by the book's implication about how the novel should be read and understood. As Philip Fisher has argued, *The Ambassadors* is "perhaps from an academic point of view the most perfect text written by an American," in which "an entire academic generation saw its own love of criticism, observation, nuance, disappointment, myth and defeat."

Written between 1900 and 1901 but not published until 1903, when James was 60 years old, *The Ambassadors* was a restatement and synthesis of the writer's preoccupations developed from his first successes in the 1870s. The novel revisits the international theme of such works as *The American*, *Daisy Miller*, and *The Portrait of a Lady*. It is the story of an American in Paris who is forced to reassess his previous conception of the world and himself when confronted by a European alternative to his rigidly myopic New England views. The germ of James's novel was an anecdote related to him in 1895 by his friend Jonathan Sturges concerning their mutual friend, American novelist and editor William Dean Howells. Sitting in the Parisian garden of painter James McNeill Whistler, Howells, regretting his age and lost opportunities, had expostulated to Sturges in James's reconstruction: "Oh, you are young, you are young—be glad of it and *live*—Live all you can: it's a mistake not to. It doesn't so much matter what you do—but live. This place makes it all come over me. I see it now. I haven't done so—and now I'm old. It's too late. It has gone past me—I've lost it. You have time. You are young. Live!" From Howells's words, mood, and exhortation, James began to conceive "the little idea of the figure of an elderly man who hasn't 'lived,' hasn't at all, in the sense of sensations, passions, impulses, pleasures—and to whom, in the presence of some great human spectacle, some great organization for the Immediate, the Agreeable, for curiosity, and experiment and perception, for Enjoyment, in a word, becomes, *sur la fin*, or toward it, sorrowfully aware." To dramatize the midlife crisis of awareness he wanted to explore, James returned to the familiar imaginative territory of an American's transforming encounter with Europe, but with a heightened and more fundamental moral and psychological dimension added to the social one. American innocence would not be simply tested by European experience but the paradoxes of both would be explored directly in the evolving consciousness of his central protagonist, Lambert Strether.

Completed in about eight months in a rush of inspiration in which, as James recalled, "Nothing resisted, nothing betrayed; it shed from any side I could turn it to the same golden glow," *The Ambassadors*, despite its nuanced, complex tangle of half-concealed relationships and problems of perceptions, has one of James's simplest story lines. Lambert Strether, a 55-year old native of Woollett, Massachusetts, is dispatched to Paris by his rich patron and purported fiancée, Mrs. Abel Newsome, to retrieve her son and heir Chad, whom it is feared has fallen under the influence of an unsavory Frenchwoman. Gradually succumbing to the delights of Paris that open up new possibilities in his life, Strether observes what he perceives to be Chad's improvement from the ill-formed and shallow American youth he had been through exposure to Europe and the influence of Marie de Vionnet, a married French noblewoman. Strether concludes that Chad should not return home. Having reversed his initial motive for his journey, defied Mrs. Newsome's wishes, and contradicted his previous Woollett standards, Strether changes diplomatic sides from advocacy on behalf of the mother to the son, supporting Chad's desire to remain in Europe. Mrs. Newsome responds by sending to Paris a second ambassadorial delegation made up of her daughter, the daughter's husband, and her husband's younger sister, intended as Chad's future wife. Sustained in his opposition to their wishes by the belief that Chad's and the Contesse de Vionnet's is a beneficial, "virtuous attachment," Strether next must contend with a series of jolting realizations. Chad proves to be only too willing to return to Woollett and resume the life his mother has planned for him and is equally ready to forgo his liaison with Marie. Even more seriously, Strether finally discovers that Chad and the Contesse have been lovers all along, and Strether's mission shifts yet again from Mrs. Newsome to Chad to Marie in her attempt to prevent the loss of her lover. In the end, Strether has lost everything: his fiancée, his occupation as an editor of a journal that Mrs. Newsome supports, and his idealized romantic notions of Madame de Vionnet, with whom he is half in love. Strether finally renounces even Europe, which has expanded his view of the world, others, and himself, including the sympathetic offer of his confidante, Maria Gostrey, resolving to return home to face the responsibilities for his actions. He concludes, "But all the same I must go. . . . To be right. . . . That, you see, is my only logic. Not, out of the whole affair, to have got anything for myself." In the endlessly refracted irony of James's artistry, what on the surface is Strether's ostensible failure as an ambassador and the loss of everything he had previously held valuable, masks a far more crucial victory. Through the process of his experiences and development Strether sheds his innocent provincialism and narrow intolerance and adopts an expanded awareness of human nature and experience that takes on the depth, ambiguity, and challenge that James's novel so remarkably replicates.

Interestingly, *The Ambassadors* is such a constructive marvel largely because James initially prepared his novel to reach a wide popular audience as a magazine serial. Divided into 12 books to conform to monthly installments, the novel is a model of balanced, symmetrical design. Each book presents a series of dramatized climaxes reflecting Strether's developing consciousness. During the first six books the movement of the novel is a progression toward Strether's completing his mission to retrieve Chad. At the end of the sixth book, Strether is "recalled," and the narrative movement is reversed with its central irony established: Strether, sent to bring Chad home, has been converted to the opposing view, arguing that he should stay, setting in motion the implication of Strether's decision. In the second half of the book, roles are reversed as previous attitudes shift. Chad is now ready to go home, having been only superficially changed by Europe; while it is Strether who will be unalterably transformed by his European encounter. The climax of each half of the novel is reached neatly in the penultimate books of each section.

In Book 5, Strether has the Howells's inspired moment that causes him to reassess all his previous values. In Book 11, Strether by chance meets Chad and Marie in the countryside where the true nature of their relationship is finally, inescapably realized.

Other design features include parallel and contrasting situations and characters. There are a series of balcony scenes, like Hawthorne's scaffold scenes in *The Scarlet Letter*, each serving to reflect Strether's psychological and emotional development and change. Characters and settings are similarly balanced and contrasted: the artist Gloriani and the lawyer Waymarsh, Mrs. Newsome and Marie de Vionnet, rigid and parochial Woollett versus flexible and cosmopolitan Paris. The novel's greatest achievement other than the elegance of its form, however, is James's masterful handling of point of view. By restricting the view to Strether's perceptions, by, in James's words, keeping "it all within my hero's compass," James achieves an intensity and compression that turns ostensibly ordinary events into a compelling inner drama. Forgoing omniscience, which had been the stock-in-trade for novelists from the beginning, James limits and restricts the reader's view, turning perception itself into an experiential process of shifting angles of vision that has held sway over the novel ever since. By becoming, in Joseph Conrad's phrase, a "historian of fine consciences," James located the novel's power to penetrate the recesses of consciousness itself while investing relatively simple circumstances with an unprecedented complexity and subtlety.

Lambert Strether is in a sense a model for the reader. Both are subjected to a reeducation process, tutored by James in the complex art of seeing life fully. Narrow assumptions about the world, human relationships, and human nature are broadened through the testing ground of James's drama. To catch significance, Strether must learn to decipher what has been hidden from him both in others and in himself, and James turns the novel into a drama of self-awareness that readers ignore at their peril. It may be true that James in his final phase beginning with *The Ambassadors* began to write "more and more about less and less," permanently solidifying the gap between the highbrow and lowbrow, popular fiction and literary fiction, but the reader interested in the challenges and compensations of the modern novel can find no better blueprint for the resources or techniques of the modern novel than in James's masterly *The Ambassadors*.

19

ONE HUNDRED YEARS OF SOLITUDE

(1967)

by Gabriel García Márquez

One Hundred Years of Solitude *is the first piece of literature since the Book of Genesis that should be required reading for the entire human race. It takes up not long after Genesis left off and carries through to the air age, reporting on everything that happened in between with more lucidity, wit, wisdom, and poetry than is expected from 100 years of novelists, let alone one man. . . . Mr. García Márquez has done nothing less than to create in the reader a sense of all that is profound, meaningful, and meaningless in life.*

—William Kennedy, *New York Times Book Review*

Only a handful of novels written in the second half of the 20th century seem certain to endure, and *One Hundred Years of Solitude* must surely be one of these. First published in 1967 in South America, *Cien años de soledad* caused, in the words of Mario Vargas Llosa, "a literary earthquake in Latin America," the reverberation of which stunned the world. It is that rarest of fictional achievement: a critical and popular success that is challenging and complex, yet accessible and enthralling. Pablo Neruda called the novel "the greatest revelation in the Spanish language since *Don Quixote* of Cervantes," and it remains the most acclaimed product of *el Boom*, the remarkable explosion of Latin American fiction that many believe defines the shape and achievement of the postmodern novel. As critics in Europe and North America began to lament the death of the novel in the face of the declining energy of modernism, García Márquez offered an invigorating renewal, synthesizing elements from Kafka, Joyce, Hemingway, and Faulkner, and others from Hispanic oral and literary traditions, with the novel's most basic resource of storytelling to fashion a narrative that is simultaneously a family saga, historical chronicle, and universal myth.

So dominating and influential has *One Hundred Years of Solitude* become that its composition has, like the novel itself, assumed the qualities of legend. Colombian-born García Márquez's first three novels, despite evident merit, were largely ignored by readers and reviewers. Having settled in Mexico

City after journalistic stints in Colombia, Cuba, New York, and Paris, García Márquez lacked the key to unlock the novel he wished to write about his childhood home with his maternal grandparents in Aracataca, where he lived until his grandfather's death when García Márquez was eight. According to the novelist, "Nothing interesting has happened to me since," and he has asserted that all his writing "has been about the experiences of the time I spent with my grandparents." In January 1965, while on a drive along the Mexico City–Acapulco highway with his family, the shape and the words of the long-dormant novel struck him with visionary force. "It was so ripe in me," he would later recall, "that I could have dictated the first chapter, word by word to a typist." García Márquez spent the next 18 months in his apartment composing his manuscript as his wife pawned their valuables to meet living expenses. He finally emerged to exchange his manuscript for $10,000 of unpaid bills.

The revelation García Márquez had in his car that offered him the means and the method for his long-contemplated novel was that his story should replicate the oral storytelling style of his grandmother:

> She told things that sounded supernatural and fantastic, but she told them with complete naturalness. . . . What was most important was the expression she had on her face. She did not change her expression at all when telling her stories. . . . In previous attempts to write, I tried to tell the story without believing in it. I discovered that what I had to do was believe in them myself and write them with the same expression with which my grandmother told them: with a brick face.

It was his grandmother's ability to create believable fantasy that would make *One Hundred Years of Solitude* so distinctive in its dual presentation of the marvelous as plausible and matter-of-fact and the infusion of the commonplace with wonderment. "I wanted only to give a poetic permanence to the world of my childhood," García Márquez observed, "which as you know took place in a large, very sad house, with a sister who ate dirt and a grandmother who predicted the future, and numerous relatives with the same name who never made much distinction between happiness and madness." García Márquez has always regarded himself as a realist but with a concept of realism wide enough to include the grotesque and the impossible.

To capture his own, his family's, and his country's history, García Márquez constructs a multigenerational family saga around the creation, growth, and eventual destruction of the town of Macondo, a fictional equivalent of his native Aracataca. Like Trollope's Barchester, Hardy's Wessex, Joyce's Dublin, and Faulkner's Yoknapatawpha County, García Márquez's locale and history have simultaneous real and fabled coordinates, anchored both in actuality and in the archetypes of innocence and experience, paradise gained and lost. From the novel's memorable first sentence—"Many years later, as he faced the firing squad, Colonel Aureliano Buendía was to remember that distant afternoon when his father took him to discover ice"—the reader enters a fictive world with its own unique operating principles, in which past and future conjoin to form a continual present, in which the extraordinary (the firing squad) meets the commonplace (ice) to defamiliarize and release an aura of strangeness and wonder. In García Márquez's handling, the real and the fantastic coexist and reinforce the novel's texture of captivating specificity and universality. Elements of traditional Hispanic literature and modernist technical disruptions support one another with traditional oppositions—realism and fantasy, fact and illusion, history and myth, reason and irrationality—coming together in an astonishing complex of significance.

Designed to replace causality and chronological time with mythic recurrence, the novel proceeds indirectly through interruptions and flashbacks, tracing a history of a place and a time through the rise and fall of successive generations of the Buendía family. Patriarch José Arcadio Buendía has married his cousin Ürsula, an incestuous act that carries a curse of bearing a child with a pig's tail. This "original sin" leads to violence and a pattern of sin, guilt, madness, and retribution that will haunt the family through succeeding generations. García Márquez asserted, "I merely wanted to tell the story of a family who for a hundred years did everything they could to prevent having a son with a pig's tail, and just because of this very effort to avoid having one they ended by doing so." The inevitable destiny of the Buendías is related to their founding the community of Macondo in the wilderness. It is initially a remote, primitive Edenic world, "built on the bank of a river of clear water that ran along a bed of polished stones, which were white and enormous, like prehistoric eggs. The world was so recent that many things lacked names, and in order to indicate them it was necessary to point." However, Macondo falls into time and historical progression as outsiders arrive with the wonders of civilization—magnets, telescopes, magnifying glasses—knowledge that produces technological change and disruptions. Knowledge, a philosophical variant of the incest theme, threatens a reversion into solitude, an internal migration into obsession and madness that will afflict the Buendías. As the nurturing matriarch, Ürsula attempts to hold the family together, and her husband, fatally infected by the knowledge brought in from the outside world, obsessively tries to comprehend that world and goes mad, tied to a chestnut tree where he eventually dies, establishing a pattern that successive Buendías will follow.

García Márquez's first-generation version of Adam and Eve gives way to the second-generation Cain and Abel—Colonel Aureliano Buendía and his brother José Arcadio. It is among this generation that the novel begins to reflect more explicitly a version of Colombia's and Latin America's past.

García Márquez has stated that *One Hundred Years of Solitude* is not a history of Latin America but a metaphor for Latin America, and the second generation of Buendías embodies the personality traits and temperament that will plunge the region into an endless cycle of civil war and susceptibility to foreign intervention. José Arcadio aggressively expropriates his neighbors' lands and jealously protects his property interests, setting in motion the reformist reaction that his brother will lead through 32 failed military campaigns. Eventually, Colonel Aureliano Buendía's power corrupts him completely as generous and humane idealistic principles are forgotten, and both brothers become tyrants on opposite ends of the political spectrum. Their crippling isolation is made clear when the colonel has a chalk circle drawn around him that he forbids anyone from penetrating, and ends his career creating golden fish that he sells for gold coins to make into more fish.

In succeeding generations, among other Aurelianos and Arcadios, technological change and historical forces continue to affect Macondo's fate, while repeated traits among the Buendías, particularly an incapacity to love or to break out of their obsessive isolation, push the family to extinction. Following the civil wars, there are brief boom times with the arrival of a North American company that creates a banana plantation. Labor unrest explodes into a massacre of 3,000 strikers. José Arcadio Segundo is the sole survivor of the massacre, but he goes mad when the townspeople refuse to believe that the killings took place. Heavy rains that continue for four years, 11 months, and two days destroy the plantation, and Maconda begins a steady decline. The novel finally concludes with the end of the Buendía line. A son with a pig's tail is born from the incestuous relationship of a nephew and his aunt, finally bearing out the curse that has taken seven generations to realize. The last of the Buendías is abandoned after his mother's death in childbirth, a corpse consumed by ants, which provides a key for his father, Aureliano Babilonia, to decipher the ancient manuscript of the gypsy Melquíades with the epitaph: "The first of the line is tied to a tree, and the last is being eaten by ants." Melquíades's text is revealed as the complete history of the Buendías family in which Aureliano is able to read his own and the town's final destruction in a hurricane. Family, town, and book come to a simultaneous end, like a conjuror's trick in which fact and illusion intermingle, as the reader reads about a character reading his own demise in a history of his family that is brought to a climactic halt as the novel itself ends.

Excluded by necessity in this brief synopsis are dozens of other characters and incidents that give *One Hundred Years of Solitude* its remarkable appeal. García Márquez's "magic realism," which would help define Latin American modernism—deadpan, objective reporting of the marvelous—is a variant of Kafka's haunting dislocations of reality, made chilling by treating the extraordinary as commonplace. Like Kafka, García Márquez composes a verbal texture that is simultaneously real and symbolic, specific and universal. Unlike Kafka's dark, often suffocating nightmares, however, García Márquez's transformations suggest an astonishing, ultimately liberating vitality, a world alight with marvels in which a priest can levitate 12 centimeters above the ground after drinking hot chocolate, in which a beautiful girl can ascend into heaven while hanging up sheets, and a dead man's blood can drain across distance to his home. Each impossibility helps to restore a lifeless, routinized world and offers new possibilities and insights, tapping into a vast storehouse of liberating dreams that García Márquez regards as the writer's principal resource in the face of internal and external destructive forces that afflicted his Buendías and their Macondo. As he stated in his Nobel Prize acceptance speech in 1982, "We, the inventors of tales, who will believe anything, feel entitled to believe that it is not yet too late to engage in the creation of the opposite utopia. A new and sweeping utopia of life, where no one will be able to decide for others how they die, where love will prove true and happiness be possible, and where the races condemned to one hundred years of solitude, will have, at last and forever, a second opportunity on earth."

20

THE GREAT GATSBY

(1925)

by F. Scott Fitzgerald

I want to write something new, something extraordinary and beautiful and simple and intricately patterned.

—F. Scott Fitzgerald, letter to Maxwell Perkins, July 1922, as he began to formulate his third novel, which became *The Great Gatsby*

That Fitzgerald fulfilled his literary desire, announced above, by writing the defining novel of the lost American dream is only one of the many ironies surrounding *The Great Gatsby.* Another, given the novel's eventual recognition as one of America's greatest, is the initial lack of critical and popular recognition for what Fitzgerald called his "consciously artistic achievement." After *The Great Gatsby* appeared in 1925, sales never approached the totals of the best-selling *This Side of Paradise* (1920) and *The Beautiful and Damned* (1922). Despite appreciative recognition by T. S. Eliot, who called *Gatsby* the "first step that American fiction has taken since Henry James," reviewers labeled the novel a "dud," "an absurd story," and a "trifle . . . neither profound nor durable." H. L. Mencken considered the novel's plot as "no more than a glorified anecdote" and judged *Gatsby* not deserving "to be put on the same shelf with, say, 'This Side of Paradise.'" When Fitzgerald died in 1940, his *Time* magazine obituary did not even mention *The Great Gatsby,* and its creator was remembered not as an enduring novelist but as the celebrated Jazz Age chronicler whose early promise was sadly squandered. *The Great Gatsby* has subsequently been added to an exclusive group of fictional masterworks forming the American literary canon, as well as an even more select handful of novels, including *The Scarlet Letter, Moby-Dick,* and *Adventures of Huckleberry Finn,* that significantly define a peculiarly American myth of identity and experience.

The complexity of character, language, and theme that earns *Gatsby* such high praise can be traced to several influences. One is T. S. Eliot's *The Waste Land,* published in 1922, the year in which *Gatsby* is set. Fitzgerald similarly explores a rootless and sterile, unredeemed modern landscape, with its equivalent of Eliot's "unreal city," and, at its approach, a "solemn dumping ground," where "ashes grow like wheat," under the mockingly unseeing eyes of Doctor T. J. Eckleburg, a symbol of the moral and spiritual blindness of the novel's fallen world. Incorporating the modernist techniques of Eliot's poem, one of the earliest American novelists to do so, Fitzgerald, through sharply focused dramatic scenes, telling dialogue, heroic allusion, and an intricate image pattern, achieves a similar symbolic expansion that universalizes the story of Gatsby's quest for transcendence into an American-located, prose version of *The Waste Land.*

If T. S. Eliot helped Fitzgerald clarify the wider theme and poetic method of *Gatsby*, the novel's aesthetic theory can be traced to Joseph Conrad, whose critical preface to *The Nigger of the Narcissus* (1898) Fitzgerald reread and considered crucial during the composition of his novel. "A work of art," Conrad writes in his preface, "that aspires, however humbly, to the condition of art should carry its justification in every line." This sense of intricate patterning, of loading every sentence with significance, marks the difference between *Gatsby* and Fitzgerald's previous novels, and is reflected in his contention during composition that "I feel I have an enormous power in me now. . . . In my new novel I'm thrown directly on purely creative work—not trashy imaginings, as in my stories but the sustained imagination of a sincere and radiant world." *Gatsby* thereby also aims at what Conrad identified as the writer's primary goal: to stimulate "our capacity for delight and wonder . . . the sense of mystery surrounding our lives." To reach it, Fitzgerald tells Gatsby's story, in imitation of Conrad's method in *Lord Jim* and *Heart of Darkness*, at a remove, through the perspective of Conrad's Marlow-like narrator, Nick Carraway. Like Gatsby, Nick is a westerner who has come east to seek his fortune and who gains sympathy for Gatsby the dreamer while remaining detached enough to assess the impact and wider significance of his dream. Echoing Keats's concept of negative capability, Fitzgerald would later observe in the posthumous collection, *The Crack-Up* (1945), that "the test of a first-rate intelligence is the ability to hold two opposing ideas in the mind at the same time, and still retain the ability to function." *Gatsby* achieves this dual focus with his twin protagonists, conveying the delight, wonder, and mystery of his title character's sustaining illusions and their inevitable destruction, both ineffable desire and its betrayal by intractable reality.

At the novel's center is the enigmatic contradiction of Gatsby himself, who grows in Nick's view from a representative of "everything for which I have an unaffected scorn" to one who, despite his preposterous aspirations and sordid death, wrongly murdered by a jealous husband, "turned out all right at the end," who was "worth the whole damn bunch put together." Eventually Nick and the reader learn Gatsby's secret and sustaining core—the grounds that justify the term of greatness confirmed by the novel's title. The awkward figure in the white suit, "whose elaborate formality of speech just missed being absurd," lost in the shuffle of partygoers in his faux-Norman castle in West Egg, Long Island, is actually the western roughneck James Gatz of North Dakota. Self-made and self-generating, Gatsby "sprang from his Platonic conception of himself," remade as an embodiment of his heroic vision of himself in pursuit of a "vast, vulgar, and meretricious beauty." Fitzgerald presents Gatsby's identity as an American archetype, part Horatio Alger rags-to-riches figure, part western frontiersman, with his Benjamin Franklin-like program of self-improvement to equip him for his great destiny written on the fly-leaf of his copy of *Hopalong Cassidy*. Nick eventually realizes that "this has been a story of the West, after all," in which Gatsby, Tom and Daisy Buchanan, and Nick himself, westerners all, have reversed Horace Greeley's direction to seek their fates in the East. It is in the settled, corrupt East, not on the now closed western frontier of unlimited possibilities, where Gatsby's dream will be corrupted and his destiny decided.

"The whole idea of Gatsby," Fitzgerald observed, "is the unfairness of a poor young man not being able to marry a girl with money. This theme comes up again and again because I lived it." If war was Hemingway's continual subject, Fitzgerald's was the betrayal of the American dream, a subject that linked his personal life, his writing career, and the subjects of his books into a thematic whole. In this sense, Gatsby is another in a long line of Fitzgerald's failed romantics, driven to realize their ideals of fulfillment, but destined to fail, held back by a world that refuses to conform to their transcendent dreams. It is Gatsby's ultimate embodiment of all his desires in the form of his "Golden Girl," Daisy Buchanan, Fitzgerald's version of Keats's "La Belle Dame sans Merci," that will be his undoing. For Gatsby, Daisy is the "king's daughter" in his fairy-tale illusion. With a voice "full of money," Daisy is the incarnation of Gatsby's deepest aspiration, the ultimate prize and the fulfillment of his heroic vision of himself, "a promise that the rock of the world was founded securely on a fairy's wing." However, Daisy requires wealth to win her, which Gatsby lacked five years before when he lost her to the brutal materialist Tom Buchanan. Through his underworld connection with Meyer Wolfsheim, Gatsby has acquired the means that he hopes will allow him to realize his desire. Set up in his West Egg mansion, across from Daisy's East Egg home, Gatsby constructs a stage upon which his romantic fantasy can be acted out with Daisy his fairy-tale heroine. To Nick's cautionary warning that "I wouldn't ask too much of her. . . . You can't repeat the past," Gatsby counters, "Can't repeat the past? he cried. Why of course you can!" The novel traces not only the falsity of Gatsby's assertion, but the truth that Fitzgerald summarized in *The Crack-Up:* "It is sadder to find the past again and find it inadequate to the present than it is to have it elude you and remain forever a harmonious conception of memory."

As the novel makes clear, both Gatsby's past and the present are built on a series of lies, not only that he is the fanciful construct of his own romantic imagination, that his veneer of wealth and respectability has a criminally unsavory source, that the material allure to capture Daisy is hollow and tawdry, but that Daisy herself is a cheat, unworthy of his consummate desire. Like her husband Tom (and virtually all who inhabit Gatsby's world), Daisy is a rapacious consumer of things and people, a base betrayer, lacking Gatsby's idealism that gives his world value and the moral sense that Nick ultimately finds wanting in their self-indulgence and self-protection: "They were careless people, Tom and Daisy—they smashed things and creatures and then retreated back into their money or their vast carelessness, or whatever it was that kept them together, and let other people clean up the mess they had made. . . ." The novel records one of their messes, as Tom's mistress, Myrtle Wilson, is killed by Daisy at the wheel of Gatsby's car, and Tom arranges the death of his rival for the possession of Daisy by allowing Myrtle's husband, George, to think that Gatsby was responsible for Myrtle's death. Left to clean up, Nick Carraway takes the responsibility to provide some kind of eulogy for Gatsby to explain the significance and meaning of his rather banal end. One of three attendants at Gatsby's funeral is his father, Henry C. Gatz, who supplies a glimpse of how far Gatsby has come and his potential greatness: "If he'd of lived, he'd of been a great man. A man like James J. Hill. He'd of helped build up the country." Another attendee is the anonymous owl-eyed man whose epitaph is franker: "The poor son-of-a-bitch." But the book's ultimate summary of Gatsby's tragedy and his entitlement to greatness takes the form of Nick's closing reverie, one of the most lyrically resonant passages in American literature. What separates Gatsby from everyone else in the novel's diminished world is his defiance of limits by his capacity for wonder, which Nick connects to what the first European must have felt standing "face to face for the last time in history with something commensurate to his capacity for wonder." Gatsby, therefore, becomes the prototypical American for whom anything is possible. The "green breast of the new world" is further linked to the green light at the end of Daisy's dock across from Gatsby's mansion, and Nick typifies Gatsby's fate shared with all Americans, tantalizingly close to grasping our greatest desires but forever frustrated by the current of reality:

> He had come a long way to this blue lawn, and his dream must have seemed so close that he could hardly fail to grasp it. He did not know that it was already behind him, somewhere back in that vast obscurity beyond the city, where the dark fields of the republic rolled on under the night.
>
> Gatsby believed in the green light, the orgiastic future that year by year recedes before us. It eluded us then, but that's no matter—

TO THE LIGHTHOUSE

21

(1927)

by Virginia Woolf

Never have I written so easily, imagined so profusely.
—Virginia Woolf, *Diary*, February 8, 1926, during the composition of *To the Lighthouse*

The fifth of Virginia Woolf's eight novels, *To the Lighthouse*, is unquestionably her greatest, one of the seminal works of modernist fiction and the ultimate justification for her experimental method in her ability to give form to the flux of human experience and consciousness. Like D. H. Lawrence's *Sons and Lovers* and James Joyce's *A Portrait of the Artist as a Young Man*, *To the Lighthouse* derives its power from the novelist's exploration of her own past and her grappling with the artist's mission. Having proclaimed that "On or about December 1910, human character changed," Virginia Woolf set out to reflect that change in a radically redefined novel. In her important essay written in 1924, "Mr Bennett and Mrs Brown," Woolf laid down the challenge for the modern novelist: how best to capture ordinary life personified by the unremarkable, obscure Mrs. Brown. Rejecting the surface materialism and moralism of the Edwardian novelists Arnold Bennett, John Galsworthy, and H. G. Wells as insufficient to the task, Woolf predicts that eventually Mrs. Brown will be caught, and that "The capture of Mrs Brown is the title of the next chapter in the history of literature." Making her own contribution to this effort, Woolf announced, in her essay "Modern Fiction," an aesthetic principle that would govern her fictional approach:

> Examine for a moment an ordinary mind on an ordinary day. The mind receives a myriad of impressions—trivial, fantastic, evanescent, or engraved with the sharpness of steel. . . . Life is not a series of gig lamps symmetrically arranged; but a luminous halo, a semi-transparent envelope surrounding us from the beginning of consciousness to the end. Is it not the task of the novelist to convey this varying, this unknown

> and uncircumscribed spirit, whatever aberrations or complexity it may display, with as little mixture of the alien and external as possible?

For Woolf's purposes, fictional realism, conventional characterization, and plot were inadequate, missing the drama of consciousness and existence itself. The artistic problem she faced in *To the Lighthouse* was how to give shape and form to the "luminous halo."

The incident at the core of *To the Lighthouse* occurred in 1892 at her family's vacation home at St. Ives in Cornwall, recorded by the 10-year old Virginia Stephen in her chronicle of her family's activities, the *Hyde Park Gate News:*

> On Saturday morning Master Hilary Hunt and Master Basil Smith came up to Talland House and asked Master Thoby and Miss Virginia Stephen to accompany them to the light-house as Freeman the boatman said that there was a perfect tide and wind for going there. Master Adrian Stephen was much disappointed at not being allowed to go.

The frustrated trip to the lighthouse would recur to Woolf's imagination 34 years later, in 1925, as she finished *Mrs. Dalloway* and began to conceive her next novel, a book that would reach back to the novelist's past and would be inspired by her attempt to deal with her feelings about her dead parents, the domineering, brilliant Leslie Stephen and her mother, Julia. In a 1925 diary entry, Woolf summarized her intention for her proposed novel: "This is going to be fairly short: to have father's character done completely in it; & mother's; St. Ives; & childhood; & all the usual things I try to put in—life, death, etc. But the centre is father's character, sitting in a boat, reciting We perished, each alone, while he crushes a dying mackerel." Woolf would later recall in her essay "Sketch of the Past" that the memory of her mother dominated her plan: "It is perfectly true that she obsessed me, in spite of the fact that she died when I was thirteen, until I was forty-four. Then one day walking round Tavistock Square I made up, as I sometimes made up my books, *To the Lighthouse;* in a great, apparently involuntary rush . . . I wrote the book very quickly; and when it was written, I ceased to be obsessed by my mother. I no longer heard her voice; I do not see her. I suppose that I did for myself what psycho-analysts do for their patients. I expressed some very long felt and deeply felt emotions. And in expressing it I explained it and then laid it to rest." Both Leslie and Julia Stephen are refracted in the novel as Mr. and Mrs. Ramsay, and Woolf managed her greatest fictional achievement in her attempt to capture both clearly, her version of Mr. and Mrs. Brown, while making sense of her own past and its impact on her career as an artist.

The novel, which is patterned by the painter Lily Briscoe's attempt to complete her portrait of Mrs. Ramsay—the symbolic equivalent of Woolf's own struggle to embody her sense of the past in the permanence of her narrative art—is divided into three sections, like a medieval triptych, or as Woolf described it, "two blocks joined by a corridor." The record of two days before and after World War I is bridged by a brief impressionistic passage reflecting the passage of 10 years. The first section, "The Window," deals with the activities of the large Ramsay family and their house guests in late September before the war at their island vacation home in the Hebrides. Shifting in and out of multiple perspectives, Woolf plunges the reader into the life of the Ramsay family that is marked by an initial conflict. Mrs. Ramsay has agreed that her young son James may undertake an expedition to the offshore lighthouse the next day, a plan that the sensible, rational Mr. Ramsay spoils by pointing out that the weather will make the trip an impossibility. *To the Lighthouse* has been described as a novel constructed around an interruption, and the completion of this family outing and the revelation of its deeper significance will pattern the entire novel. The two conflicting views of Mr. and Mrs. Ramsay, the former dominated by negation and fact, the latter by imaginative sympathy and affirmation, represent the two poles that the novel attempts to resolve, connected in Woolf's imagination in the image of her father and mother. At the still center of the family's movement and underlying conflict is Mrs. Ramsay, knitting before the window, whom Lily Briscoe chooses as the subject for her painting. Lily's struggle to isolate Mrs. Ramsay's essential qualities and significance in her art is the other major interruption of the novel, to be achieved only with the passage of time in the novel's final section. "One wanted most some secret sense," Lily observes, "fine as air, with which to steal through keyholes and surround her where she sat knitting, talking, sitting silent in the window alone, which took to itself and treasured up like air which held the smoke of the steamer, her thoughts, her imaginations, her desires." Lily is initially unable to solve the compositional and imaginative "problem" of capturing her subject on canvas, but Woolf's narrative method provides the required "secret sense." In the subtle interpenetration of thought, dialogue, and action, Mrs. Ramsay is illumined as an artist in her own right: a domestic mediator and shaper who through her sympathy and affection unites her family and friends into a greater whole, like the lighthouse that momentarily fixes the flux and chaos of experience and gives it shape and significance. The climax of the first section of the novel is Mrs. Ramsay's dinner party, which like its main course, the wondrous *boeuf en daube*, joins disparate elements into a harmonious unity. The section closes with the resolution of the opening conflict between the married couple: Mrs. Ramsay concedes the point that her husband was right about the impossibility of the trip to the lighthouse, while Mr. Ramsay craves more than the satisfaction of his victory in the completion of wife's love. Husband and wife are conjoined symbolically to represent two alternative views of the world, united in a stability that at least momentarily resolves all difference and redeems the moment.

22

CRIME AND PUNISHMENT

(1866)

by Feodor Dostoevsky

[Crime and Punishment] *is easily the greatest book I have read in ten years. I am glad you took to it. Many find it dull; Henry James could not finish it: all I can say is, it nearly finished me. It was like having an illness.*

—Robert Lewis Stevenson, letter to J. A. Symonds, 1886

Subscribers to the periodical *The Russian Messenger* in 1866 were beneficiaries of what must be one of the greatest values for money spent in literary history, as the serialized *Crime and Punishment* alternated with the opening books of what would eventually become Tolstoy's *War and Peace.* Dostoevsky and Tolstoy began their public and critical linkage as their respective novels marked out in significant ways the opposing boundaries of the novel—between Tolstoy's expansive inclusiveness and Dostoevsky's intensive narrowing, between Tolstoy's Olympian clarity and Dostoevsky's dark tunneling into the wellsprings of the human psyche and core existential truths. What Dostoevsky's first readers were forced to confront and subsequent readers have continued to acknowledge is the extraordinary intensity of the novelist's dramatic method. What is so striking about Dostoevsky's masterpiece is its tapping into the power source of human consciousness, itself in the grip of overpowering fixations and emotional stress. As Harold Bloom asserts, "No other narrative fiction drives itself onwards with the remorseless strength of *Crime and Punishment,* truly a shot out of hell and into hell again. To have written a naturalistic novel that reads like a continuous nightmare is Dostoevsky's unique achievement." Poe had earlier shown how crime and detection could serve a psychological purpose. Dickens preceded Dostoevsky in the use of adversity to illuminate character, in employing crime as a means of revealing a character's inner state of mind. Think of Sikes's expressionistic circular journey after he kills Nancy in *Oliver Twist* or Jonas Chuzzlewit psychically leaving his respectable double safely in his room while he stalks his prey in *Martin Chuzzlewit.* Dickens also pioneered the use of crime and detection as structural principles in such novels as *Bleak House*, *Little Dorrit*, *Great Expectations*, and *Our Mutual Friend*, in which secrets and sensation link an expansive cast and make a social point. It is Dostoevsky, however, who brought the plot devices of mystery and suspense to a masterly fulfillment, who transformed the crime novel into one of the most searching moral and psychological explorations ever attempted in fiction.

In 1859 Dostoevsky returned to St. Petersburg after a decade in exile when his promising literary career had been abruptly interrupted by his arrest as a member of the Petrashevsky Circle of socialist utopians. An execution order was commuted to four years of hard labor and four years in the army in Siberia. He published a graphic account of his experiences in *Memoirs from the House of the Dead* (1861–62), followed by the watershed *Notes from the Underground* (1864), in which he explored the psychological terrain of an ideological rebel and deeply divided obsessive. Both works anticipate the preoccupations of his subsequent major novels, but it would be *Crime and Punishment*, the first of his masterpieces and arguably the most powerful and best constructed of his books, that finally secured Dostoevsky's reputation. Writing from Wiesbaden in September 1865, unable to pay his hotel bills after a bout of gambling, Dostoevsky proposed to the editor M. N. Katkov his plan for a new work. It would be "the psychological account of a crime" in which "A young man, expelled from the student body of the university, of lower-class origins and living in utter poverty through thoughtlessness, through an infirmity of notions, having come under the influence of some of those strange 'incomplete' ideas which go floating about in the air, has decided to break out of his loathsome situation in one stroke. He has decided to kill a certain old woman, the widow of a titular councilor, who lends out money at interest." Central to Dostoevsky's scheme was the impact of the murder on his protagonist, with his motive and the significance of his act forming the core questions that Dostoevsky struggled to answer from the beginning:

> Insoluble questions confront the murderer; unsuspected and unanticipated feelings torment his heart. Divine truth and justice, the earthly law, claim their rights, and he ends by being *compelled* to give himself up. Compelled so that even if he perish in penal servitude, nonetheless he might once again be united to men. The feeling that he is separated and cut off from mankind, which he experienced immediately upon the completion of the crime, has tortured him. The law of justice and human nature have taken hold. . . . The criminal himself decides to accept suffering in order to atone for his deed. But, then I find it difficult to elucidate my thought fully.

Dostoevsky would go back and forth trying to account for the murderer Raskolnikov's motivation and the appropriate solution to what would become the novel's central mystery, not a whodunit, since the identity of the murderer is clear from the beginning, but a "whydunit," with Raskolnikov himself one of the novel's primary detectives in untangling his own complex motives and identity. Dostoevsky at first experimented with a first-person narrative with his murderer in prison, reflecting on his crime. The author's choice of a third-person point of view that could move from subjective confinement to Raskolnikov's perspective to other angles of view resulted in the novel taking on its final coloration, linking the intensity of Raskolnikov's inner anguish with the wider story of his mother and sister, the Marmeladovs and their daughter Sonia, his fellow student Razumihin, his sister's two suitors, Luzhin and Svidrigailov, and the investigating detective Porfirii Petrovich.

By placing Raskolnikov's murder of the pawnbroker and her stepsister in the first of the novel's six parts, Dostoevsky shifts the emphasis from the crime to its aftermath and impact on Raskolnikov. In Dostoevsky's handling, why Raskolnikov kills is connected to the complex psychological question of his identity. An impoverished student forced to withdraw from the university for a lack of funds, supported by his mother and his sister, who is contracting a undesirable marriage to aid him, Raskolnikov hatches a plan to kill the moneylender Alyona Ivanovna, whom he regards as a worthless parasite, living off others' misery. Initially, the novel poses an ethical dilemma: whether an evil act can be justified by a positive outcome if the moneylender's stolen money serves to relieve Raskolnikov's and his family's misery as well as to contribute to the greater good in helping to make Raskolnikov the benefactor to humanity that he aspires to be. Raskolnikov eventually acts out his plan in one of the most gripping and horrifying scenes in fiction, killing with an ax Alyona Ivanovna as well as the hapless Lizaveta, who witnesses the crime:

> He flung himself forward with the axe; her lips writhed pitifully, like those of a young child when it is just beginning to be frightened and stands ready to scream, with its eyes fixed on the object of its fear. The wretched Lizaveta was so simple, brow-beaten, and utterly terrified that she did not even put up her arms to protect her face, natural and almost inevitable as the gesture would have been at this moment when the axe was brandished immediately above it. She only raised her free left hand a little and slowly stretched it out towards him as though she were trying to push him away. The blow fell on her skull, splitting it open from the top of the forehead almost to the crown of the head, and felling her instantly. Raskolnikov, completely beside himself, snatched up her bundle, threw it down again, and ran to the entrance.

After the crime, the cat-and-mouse suspense of detection is joined to the larger issues of Raskolnikov's guilt as he tries to rationalize his action based on his conception of himself and the world. In the pivotal confession scene to the prostitute Sonia, Raskolnikov provides multiple explanations for his crime. The simplest solution, that he killed to profit from the robbery, is quickly dismissed. As Raskolnikov observes, "If I'd killed because I was hungry . . . then I should be happy now." He then offers another alternative, connected with his theory that a superior man is not bound by conventional moral sanctions: "I wanted to make myself a Napoleon, and that is why I killed her." However, the alienating guilt that torments Raskolnikov suggests another, more fundamental explanation. Raskolnikov finally narrows his self-analysis to the terrifying revelation that he killed simply as an assertion of self:

> I wanted to murder without casuistry, to murder for my own sake, for myself alone! I didn't want to lie about it even to myself. It wasn't to help my mother I did the murder—that's nonsense—I didn't do the murder to gain wealth and power and to become a benefactor of mankind. Nonsense! I simply did it . . . It was not so much the money I wanted, but something else. . . . I wanted to find out then and quickly whether I was a louse like everybody else or a man. Whether I can step over barriers or not, whether I dare stoop to pick up or not, whether I am a trembling creature or whether I have the *right* . . .

Stripped of all former rationalization, Raskolnikov faces the horror of his act: that by violating the barrier of restraint in self-assertion he has annihilated himself. As he ironically discovers and Dostoevsky's drama reveals: "I murdered myself, not her!" Throughout the novel, Raskolnikov is beset by an irresolvable duality in which his rational mind battles with deeper emotional needs, which Dostoevsky brilliantly exploits in the delirium of his illness following the murders and the series of dreams that embody the contours of Raskolnikov's conflicted psyche. Generous and sympathizing, morose and vain, a split Raskolnikov corresponds to his friend Razumihin's analysis that "it is exactly as though he were alternating between two opposing characters." His complex contradictions are what set *Crime and Punishment* apart from other novels in its depiction of the multifariousness of motivation and the fundamental irresolvability of the character's complex inner needs.

Dostoevsky contemplated suicide for Raskolnikov as the final solution to the enigma of the character's nature, but eventually opted for redemption through confession and suffering. Recognizing his transgression for what it is—a violation of conditions that make him human—Raskolnikov eventually takes responsibility for his act; the possibility of redemption follows. It is Svidrigailov who goes beyond the barrier dividing self from others and is left in a void with only suicide as an answer. For Raskolnikov, confession implies a recognition of limits and participation in the human community he has previously despised and from which he has withdrawn. As Dostoevsky indicates in his notebook, the "idea of the novel" is that "There is no happiness in comfort; happiness is purchased at the price of suffering. . . . Man is not born for happiness. Man earns happiness, and this always through suffering." While critics continue to debate the effectiveness of Dostoevsky's conclusion in *Crime and Punishment*, suggesting Raskolnikov's torment is far more convincing than his consolation, the more significant point is clearly how the novelist has managed through the genius of his imagination to make the predictable elements of crime and detection into a profound exploration of the human heart and soul.

23

THE SOUND AND THE FURY

(1929)

by William Faulkner

[The Sound and the Fury] *was the one that I anguished the most over, that I worked the hardest at, that even when I knew I couldn't bring it off, I still worked at it. It's like the parents feel toward the unfortunate child, maybe. The others that have been easier to write than that, and in ways are better books than that, but I don't have the feeling toward any of them that I do toward that one, because that was the most gallant, the most magnificent failure.*

—William Faulkner, *Faulkner in the University: Class Conferences at the University of Virginia, 1957–1958*

Faulkner's fourth published novel is his first undisputed masterpiece, the beginning of his artistic mastery, the book that has become synonymous with his ruling preoccupations and technical experiments. Like Dickens's *David Copperfield*, it was Faulkner's "favorite child," the novel that continued to haunt his imagination, as expressed by the multiple versions he offered about its genesis, his reuse of the Compson family in *Absalom, Absalom!*, as well as the fully worked out fate of his characters he would later provide. Prior to *The Sound and the Fury* there is little to predict Faulkner's quantum leap of accomplishment. His three previous novels are conventionally structured, chronological, and omnisciently narrated. The third, *Sartoris*, a curtailed version of *Flags in the Dust*, which no publisher wanted, is the first use of his fictional Yoknapatawpha County, a version of his native region of Mississippi, and his initial, tentative attempt to deal with the complex social, historical, and psychological legacy of the South. *The Sound and the Fury* marks the discovery of both Faulkner's dominant themes and the experimental means to display their richness, grafting onto a believable social and historical background deep symbolic, mythic, and psychological resonances. *The Sound and the Fury* is the first great modernist American novel, a book that reflects the native tradition of Poe, Hawthorne, and Melville and the European innovations of Conrad, Joyce, and others.

Faulkner traced the genesis of this novel to the image of a young girl's muddy drawers glimpsed as she climbed a pear tree. "It started out as a short story about two children being sent out to play in the yard during their grandmother's funeral," he later recounted. "It was going to be a story of blood gone bad." The girl who climbs the tree became the headstrong and fallen Caddy Compson, whose story is extended to typify the decay and dissolution of the entire Compson family and with it the tragedy of southern history. Caddy's three brothers—Benjy, Quentin, and Jason—elaborate her story and their family history, with a fourth objective section added for a concluding context. In the process, Faulkner forgoes a linear narrative for a multivocal approach beginning in the limited and confused perspective of the severely retarded Benjy, "since I felt that it would be more effective as told by someone capable only of knowing what happened, but not why." After completing Benjy's version of the Compson story, Faulkner explained, "I saw that I had not told the story that time. I tried to tell it again, the same story through the eyes of another brother. That was still not it. I told it for the third time through the eyes of the third brother. That was still not it. I tried to gather the pieces together and fill in the gaps by making myself the spokesman." The novel, therefore, provides four different perspectives on the same circumstances, proceeding by a progressive deepening of the view as additional perspectives and contexts are added. The first, third, and final sections cover three consecutive days in April 1928, symbolically echoing the Christian liturgical calendar of Good Friday, Holy Saturday, and Easter Sunday, and the second section depicts a single day in June, 18 years earlier.

The first section, from the perspective of Benjy, is the most daring, and perhaps Faulkner's most famous technical experiment. It establishes the significance of the novel's title from Macbeth's description of life as "a tale/Told by an idiot, full of sound and fury,/Signifying nothing." Benjy, in the words of one character, has "been three years old thirty years." He is incapable of reasoning; his mind works through associations of sight, sound, and smell. Without a concept of linear time, Benjy's perspective continually shuffles between an undifferentiated present and past. By deciphering Benjy's shifting responses, however, the reader begins to piece together the main circumstances of the Compson family history. They are a once-prominent Mississippi family in decline, headed by Jason senior, a retired lawyer given to drink and cynical self-pity, and his hypochondriacally narcissistic wife, Caroline, a self-described "burden" to all. To finance a Harvard education for their eldest son, Quentin, Benjy's birthright, his pasture, is sold to developers who turn it into a golf course where a golfer's call for his caddie prompts Benjy's recollection of his lost sister. Benjy is considered either a family embarrassment or an annoyance by all except Caddy, who provided Benjy with the only love and understanding he received from his family. His practical caretakers are the relations of the family's black cook, Dilsey, who becomes Benjy's primary nurturer when Caddy leaves home. Comforted only by Caddy's presence, Benjy is haunted by her loss, and in fragmented images and flashbacks he recalls the circumstances that led to her departure and the steady decline of the Compson family, including his grandmother's and father's death; his brother Quentin's suicide; his own castration after he confuses a passing schoolgirl for his absent sister, the arrival of Caddy's daughter, also named Quentin, who comes to live with the family, and her final departure after stealing the child support money her mother has sent that has been secretly hoarded by her uncle Jason. At this stage in the narrative, most of these details are out of sequence and out of focus in Benjy's fuguelike account and will be clarified only by juxtaposing and comparing the subsequent versions.

The second section, "June Second, 1910," is set at Harvard on the day of Quentin Compson's suicide. Although far more sophisticated intellectually than Benjy, Quentin is no less haunted by Caddy and no less a prisoner of his past. Like Benjy's narrative, Quentin's is a stream-of-consciousness interior monologue in which present details prompt flashbacks that add to the previous section's account. Quentin spends his final day organizing his affairs and meditating on his past, particularly his sister's loss of virginity and the hastily arranged marriage that conceals her pregnancy. Although Quentin is convinced that his feelings for Caddy are incestuous, his actual trauma seems to stem more from his desire to regress to their previous childhood state of innocence and his inability to protect his sister from sexual corruption, captured in the image of Caddy's muddy drawers. Quentin is obsessed by the loss of his sister's and his own purity. Unable to halt the process of time and change that seem to herald only decline and corruption, unable to face the overturning of the heroic southern chivalric code that equates chastity with honor, Quentin ultimately responds to the tyranny of time and his own and his family's defeat by suicide.

The third section, "April Sixth, 1928," is narrated by the bitter, grasping, bigoted Jason Compson, in whom the complete moral collapse of the family is made manifest. Now the head of the family after the death of Quentin and his father, Jason exacts his frustrations on Caddy's daughter Quentin, who has come to live with the family after Caddy's husband, realizing the child is not his, has abandoned his wife. Lacking the emotional or intellectual sensitivities of his brothers, Jason's more matter-of-fact recollections serve to clarify the details and the sequence of Caddy's seduction by Dalton Ames, followed by her marriage, abandonment by her husband, and her parting from her daughter. Jason has secretly kept the money Caddy has sent for child support, letting his mother self-righteously burn phony checks in place of the real ones that Jason cashes and keeps. Denied the opportunity afforded his brother of a college education, Jason is further disappointed by the failed promise of a banking career with the assistance of Caddy's husband. Instead he is the limited partner in a hardware store. Contemptuous of the townspeople and driven by his insistence that the Compsons are still a family of importance, Jason rages at the Jews and Yankees who take his money in his cotton speculation, the blacks whose emancipation implies only his own servitude, and the entire community for not recognizing his worth. His niece's rebellion and sexual indiscretions with one of the traveling performers serve as an echo of his sister's promiscuousness that toppled his expectations, the latest assault on Jason's misguided sense of his importance and his futile attempt to maintain his family's diminished honor. Jason is a portrait in frustration, a petty tyrant whose venom and paltry materialist fantasies make him one of the most fascinating, forsaken figures in American literature.

The fourth part, "April Eighth, 1928," set on Easter Sunday, is narrated in the third person and describes what happens when it is discovered that Quentin has run away after having stolen Jason's secret cache of money intended for her. The perspective alternates among Jason's futile attempt to get his money back and the experiences of Dilsey, who emerges as the calm eye at the center of Jason's storm, Mrs. Compson's crippling narcissism, and Benjy's helpless madness. Dilsey's selflessness, sacrifice, and protection of both Benjy and Quentin mark her as the only figure in the Compson household whose love and nurturing contrasts with its absence and the evasion of parental responsibility that hastens the Compsons' decline. As Jason pointlessly pursues his vanished niece for the money he has stolen from her, Dilsey, her family, and Benjy attend Easter services, where the preacher's stirring sermon on sin and redemption stimulates Dilsey's tears. Dilsey simply accepts what the Compsons rail against in their fate and fortune. Unlike the Compsons' obsession with the past, Dilsey firmly inhabits the present. In the mythical and spiritual cycle of sin, sacrifice, and redemption that the preacher celebrates, Dilsey glimpses an alternative vision to the tyranny of time and collapse that has beset the Compsons. If the novel has been a series of sound and fury signifying nothing, Dilsey's vision of a mutuality of suffering and endurance offers coherence and meaning.

The novel ends with Dilsey's grandson Luster driving Mrs. Compson and Benjy to the cemetery, when a wrong turn, a violation of the routine, prompts Benjy to hysterics, and Jason, suffering a final public humiliation, returns to restore control over his diminished family. As the novel concludes, the reader realizes that the story of the Compsons has been unified by an absence, by the departed presence of Caddy, who is never allowed to give her version of the story, based on Faulkner's contention that she was "too beautiful and too moving to reduce her to telling what was going on, that it would be more passionate to see her through somebody else's eyes." Seen from the perspective of her three brothers, Caddy (and her daughter

24

VANITY FAIR

(1847–48) *by William Makepeace Thackeray*

He dissects his victims with a smile; and performs the cruellest of operations on their self-love with a pleasantry which looks provokingly very like good-nature.

—Robert Bell, review of *Vanity Fair* in *Fraser's Magazine*, 1848

Anthony Trollope's ranking of his English novelist contemporaries placed Charles Dickens third, George Eliot second, and William Thackeray first. "His knowledge of human nature was supreme," Trollope asserted, "and his characters stand out as human beings, with a force and a truth, which has not, I think, been within the reach of any other English novelist in any period." Even Thackeray's temperamental opposite, Charlotte Brontë, who dedicated the second edition of *Jane Eyre* to him, regarded Thackeray as a "Titan" and "unique," unrivaled in his capacity "to distinguish so exquisitively as he does dross from ore, the real from the counterfeit." Before she began her own novelist career, George Eliot corroborated the views of both writers, judging Thackeray "the most powerful of living novelists." Such high praise may strike the modern reader as inexplicably overgenerous. Many would reverse the order of Trollope's ranking, and, while granting inclusion of *Vanity Fair* as an undisputed classic, many may fail to appreciate what his contemporaries saw so clearly: how unique and groundbreaking was Thackeray's achievement. Flaubert, Eliot, James, Conrad, Joyce, and others have taught us to prefer a different kind of novel. We value elaborately structured works rather than the improvised vehicle Thackeray provides in which his characters seem to be given their freedom, and the narrator and reader follow along after them. We regard a tighter dramatic focus as ideal, a centripetal rather than the centrifugal motion of Thackeray's expansive social panorama with its intrusive, garrulous, and guiding narrator that the modern novel prohibits. However, in essential ways, the modern novel is inconceivable without Thackeray's clearing the ground for its construction. *Vanity Fair* is as revolutionary a fictional departure as any modernist masterpiece. It initiated one of the greatest periods in the novel's history, while it established a realistic standard with which all subsequent novelists have had to contend and shifted the emphasis of the novel from entertainment toward an extensive criticism of life.

Vanity Fair is both a great personal and artistic achievement, comparable to the impact of Dickens's *Pickwick Papers* 10 years before. As a young man Thackeray lost through gambling and financial setbacks the inherited means to enjoy the life of the idle, genteel clubman of his snob satires. He spent a decade, from 1837 to 1847, "writing for his life," turning out reviews, sketches, and parodies under such aliases and personae as Charles Yellowplush, Ikey Solomon, Fitz-Boodle, Our Fat Contributor, and Michael Angelo Titmarsh. *Vanity Fair* was his first book with his own name on its title page. Its eventual popular and critical success allowed Thackeray to gloat that he had suddenly "became a sort of great man . . . all but at the top of the tree . . . indeed there if truth were known and having a great fight up there with Dickens." After *Vanity Fair* there would be two undisputed masters of the Victorian novel, and an alternative fictional direction initiated by Thackeray that would influence Dickens himself and the major novelists, such as Trollope and Eliot, that followed.

Prior to *Vanity Fair*, Thackeray had found a journalistic niche as a social and literary satirist, a cynical puncturer of his era's pretensions and foibles in such works as *The Yellowplush Papers* (1837–38), *The Luck of Barry Lyndon* (1844), *Jeames's Diary* (1845), and *The Snobs of England* (1847). He also targeted the ways in which contemporary fiction falsified and distorted experience and human nature, through sentimentality and idealization in the popular Newgate Novels that exalted criminality and the Silver-Fork Novels that glamorized upper-class life, in such burlesques as *Catherine* (1839–40) and the series of *Punch* parodies collected in *Novels by Eminent Hands* (1847).

Both social satire and the fictional means by which life might best be measured and treated informed Thackeray's mission as he began *Vanity Fair*. What prevented the novel from being simply another of his detached and noncommittal portraits of the world inhabited by either knaves or dupes was a growing moral seriousness derived from his personal setbacks and family disappointments. Thackeray's second daughter had died, and his wife, despondent after the birth of their third child, succumbed to depression, suicide attempts, and ultimately madness. The experience caused Thackeray to reevaluate his life, informed by his sense of the world made up of fellow sufferers and sinners, and to reassess his responsibility as a writer. The change of attitude that deepened and extended the moral purpose of *Vanity Fair* is evident from this letter extract, written as the novel got under way:

> What I mean applies to my own case & that of all of us—who set up as Satirical-Moralists—and having such a vast multitude of readers whom we not only amuse but teach. And indeed, a solemn prayer to God

> Almighty was in my thoughts that we may never forget truth and justice and kindness as the great ends of our profession. There's something of the same strain in *Vanity Fair.* A few years ago I should have sneered at the idea of setting up as a teacher at all, and perhaps at this pompous & pious way of talking about a few papers of jokes in *Punch*—but I have got to believe in the business, and in many other things since then. And our profession seems to me as serious as the Parson's own.

His readers were meant to profit from the sobering lesson of seeing themselves and their world clearly, treated not with the scornful bitterness of his earlier fiction but with tolerance and sympathy, narrated by a worldly fellow sufferer.

Published in monthly installments beginning in 1847 with the author's own illustrations, *Vanity Fair* was unlike any previous Victorian novel. Not since Fielding's *Tom Jones* had an English novelist ranged so widely in a depiction of social customs, and no writer since Jane Austen had based so much on the appeal of the actual. As Thackeray's biographer Gordon Ray has asserted, "Thackeray's novel achieves for the first time in English the effects of massive realism: among the novelists of the world, indeed, only Stendhal and Balzac had earlier shown how to establish character in society by deluging the reader with information concerning the daily routine, the employments, the pleasures, and the manners of their figures." Furthermore, almost everything about *Vanity Fair* seemed aimed to confound standard fictional expectations. As Thackeray announces in his preface, "Before the Curtain," readers should expect a genre-defying variety:

> There are scenes of all sorts: some of dreadful combats, some grand and lofty horse-riding, some scenes of high life, some of very middling indeed: some love-making for the sentimental and some light comic business; the whole accompanied by appropriate scenery, and brilliantly illuminated by the Author's own candles.

Vanity Fair expanded the novel's usual focus on a few central characters to chronicle the full range of society itself. The book's most radical innovation, however, is announced in its subtitle: "A Novel Without a Hero." Thackeray suggests a new realistic standard for the novel in which not paragons but unexceptional, flawed individuals and their far-from-idealized daily routine should take center stage in his drama, initiating the psychological realism of characterization and the drama of ordinary life that would be adapted and modified by many subsequent novelists.

The unifying principle for the exploration of the novel's world came from the book's title, derived from Bunyan's *Pilgrim's Progress,* which occurred to Thackeray in the middle of the night. He remembered, "I jumped out of bed and ran 3 times round my room, uttering as I went Vanity Fair, Vanity Fair, Vanity Fair." Thackeray had discovered his moral focus, allegorized in the conception of the world as a glittering carnival of often tawdry attractions and gimcracks that rarely satisfy. Thackeray summarizes the novel's essential lesson in its final paragraph, "Ah! Vanitas Vanitatum! Which of us is happy in this world? Which of us has his desire? or, having it, is satisfied?"

The means for mounting Thackeray's massive critique on human nature and social life are the contrasting careers of his two female characters, Amelia Sedley and Becky Sharp. Their story begins, "While the present century was in its teens," with their departure from Miss Pinkerton's academy for young ladies. Amelia is the well-to-do daughter of an affluent London merchant and stockbroker, pretty and petted, who "had twelve intimate and bosom friends out of the twenty-four young ladies" and whose empty head can manage only two responses: laughing and crying. Becky is a socially valueless orphan ticketed for servitude as a governess and forced to make her way in the world by her wiles and physical allure that she will wield like a weapon. Becky is a social upstart and a toppler of order and tradition like the infamous Napoleon, to whom she vows allegiance when she throws away her presentation copy of Dr. Johnson's dictionary and blasphemously proclaims: "*Vive la France! Vive l'Empereur! Vive Bonaparte!*" Her campaign in the adult world into which both girls are graduating is thereby joined, and the novel follows their rise and fall over the course of nearly 20 years as England's Regency period gives way to the Victorian era of Thackeray's contemporaries.

Having learned to survive by playing on the vanities and hypocrisies of those around her, Becky seems made for success in the world of *Vanity Fair;* while Amelia's affectionate, sentimental nature, unschooled by judgment, will guarantee her heartbreak and victimhood. Exploiting others' weaknesses and desires, Becky soon has a succession of men at her feet, including Amelia's gluttonous and vainglorious brother, Jos, the brutish baronet Sir Pitt Crawley, his feckless son, the Regency buck, Rawdon, and even Amelia's childhood intended, George Osborne. That both Becky and Amelia secure husbands so early in the novel alerts the reader that Thackeray's plan will not be cut to the romantic pattern of a wedding climax but will deal realistically with the aftermath of the choice of partners. Becky becomes Mrs. Rawdon Crawley, shedding "genuine" tears at the fortune she has lost when she is forced to tell Rawdon's proposing father in one of the novel's triumphant surprises, "Oh, sir—I—I'm *married already!*" Meanwhile, despite the financial collapse of the Sedleys, George's devoted friend William Dobbin, equally devoted to Amelia, convinces the caddish, superficial George to marry Amelia. The reader is left with few illusions in this battle of self-interest for supremacy. Neither family devotion, friendship, nor the honor of the nobility, military, or clergy are spared Thackeray's sober moral assessment. Perhaps the most devastating assault on romantic and fictional conventions is the shocking intelligence from the Waterloo battlefield that George Osborne, the novel's one potential hero, is denied the opportunity to reform, "lying on his face, dead with a bullet through his heart" at the novel's midpoint.

The second half of the novel continues Becky's conquests in the postwar world while "living well on nothing a year," as Amelia slips into grinding poverty, blindly worshipping the memory of her dead husband, who has been false to her. Becky's greatest triumph is her presentation at court in a stolen dress and borrowed diamonds, followed by a precipitous fall through a scandalous affair with a noble roué, Lord Steyne. Becky's descent into the demimonde on the Continent is paralleled by Amelia's gradual ascent. Forced to bargain away her son to her still unforgiving father-in-law, Amelia is reclaimed when Jos returns from India with the always hopeful Dobbin, and the Sedleys' fortunes are restored. For the last time, Becky ingratiates herself with her old schoolmate, and Dobbin finally takes a stand. Rebuked for reminding Amelia of George's flirtation with Becky, he finally realizes what the reader had known about Amelia from the start, "You are not worthy of the love which I have devoted to you. I knew all along that the prize I had set my life on was not worth the winning. . . . I will bargain no more: I withdraw." Amelia is left to contemplate the loss of Dobbin and the truth of his words before eventually calling him back to marriage and the novel's long-delayed, still barbed and muted, romantic fulfillment:

> Here it is—the summit, the end—the last page of the third volume. Goodbye, colonel—God bless you, honest William!—Farewell, dear Amelia—Grow green again, tender little parasite, round the rugged old oak to which you cling!

But it is not the last page of the third volume. There are still final glimpses of Becky, first as the suspected murderer of Jos for his life insurance and finally in the novel's final illustration, titled "Virtue Rewarded: A Booth in Vanity Fair," demurely and piously selling her wares.

As Thackeray's irony makes clear, there is precious little poetic justice in the world of *Vanity Fair*. More often than not, virtue is not rewarded. Even Amelia's faithfulness and Dobbin's long-suffering nature are flaws, though clearly less reprehensible than others' heartlessness. The novel achieves an alternative way of viewing life and human nature, replacing pleasing illusion with a bracing, often unforgiving, reflection of not who we would like to be but who we are. Novel readers had never had such a massive dose of truth, and fiction would follow Thackeray's lead, outward to decipher the complex web of human relationships and inward to the contradictory core of human nature.

25

DEAD SOULS

(1842)

by Nikolai Gogol

I have begun to write Dead Souls. *The subject has stretched itself into a most lengthy novel and, it seems, will be tremendously funny. . . . In this novel I want to show all Russia, at least from one side.*

—Gogol to Pushkin, October 7, 1835

Like English literature's most eccentric novel, Laurence Sterne's *Tristram Shandy*, Gogol's *Dead Souls* continues both to impress and perplex. *Dead Souls*, like *Tristram Shandy*, comes early in its country's novel tradition, in Gogol's case, taking pride of place as Russia's first great novel. Both are regarded as comic masterworks that achieve their dazzling effects by challenging and extending novelistic boundaries. Both books, viewed by contemporaries with dismay, have proven to be far from outlandish exceptions to the rules, however, but have found themselves more and more regarded from the perspective of literary modernism on fiction's main track in their astonishing verbal display and radical redefinition of plot and character. *Dead Souls* in particular is an attempt to extend to the Russian tradition a conception of the novel wide enough to encompass the innovations of Cervantes in *Don Quixote* by making the novel serve as a massive, imaginative criticism of life.

Like so much in Russian literary history, Pushkin provided the initial genesis for Gogol's masterpiece. Having achieved notoriety with his collections of sharply depicted scenes of Ukrainian life (*Village Evenings Near Dikanka*, 1831–32) and as a dramatist, Gogol met Pushkin in 1835. Pushkin encouraged the younger writer to test his talents against the more extended challenge of the novel. As Gogol recalled in "An Author's Confession," Pushkin urged him to undertake a longer work: "He gave me a plot of his own, which he himself had wanted to make into something of a long poem, and which, as he put it, he would not have given to anyone else. This was the plot of *Dead Souls*." Pushkin had suggested the means for Gogol to supply a panoramic portrait of Russian life and behavior through his characteristic grotesque comic lens. The suggested plot is based on a curious loophole in the Russian tax law under serfdom. Every 10 years landowners were required to supply a census of their "souls," or male serfs, and pay a poll tax on the numbers provided. If serfs died before the next census, the landowner still was financially liable for the valuation based on the original number. If a swindler purchased these "dead souls" (at a discount to relieve a landowner's tax burden), he could then use these "holdings" as collateral to secure a mortgage on property, becoming in effect a person of landed wealth based on his title to no longer existent but still precious "souls." Such an ironic situation gave Gogol a ready means with which to sardonically survey and criticize Russian customs and behavior. The grotesque trading in dead souls commented on an institution that treated living humans as chattel, and even more devilishly called into question who were in fact the deader souls, the departed serfs or the living gentry, enclosed by a stifling conventionality. By dramatizing the swindlers's trafficking in dead serfs, Gogol had a narrative means with which to portray a virtually inexhaustible supply of characters and potentially grotesque situations. "I began to write with no definite plan in mind," Gogol recalled, "without knowing exactly what my hero was to represent. I only thought that this odd project . . . would lead to the creation of diverse personalities and my own inclination toward the comic would bring on amusing situations that I could alternate with pathos." Pushkin's narrative anecdote, however, grew in Gogol's handling from an extended satirical attack on Russian mores and traits to a national and comic prose epic that outgrew the strictures of the conventional novel.

What Gogol had begun to envision as the first installment of a multivolume work was published in 1842. He struggled for the next nine years to complete a sequel, burning what he had accomplished 10 days before his death in 1852. (What survived is included in most modern reprints of *Dead Souls*.) Although a fragment of the grander scheme that Gogol intended, there is something thematically appropriate in the unresolved nature of *Dead Souls*, a novel in which confusion, contradiction, and frustrated expectations play such vital roles. The first of these assaults on expectations confronts the reader on the title page. What is initially most striking about *Dead Souls* is its unusual subtitle: "A Poem." By refusing to label his work a novel, Gogol seems to be announcing his break with previous fictional conventions and demanding a different set of associations with which to view his creation. Clearly the poetical form Gogol had in mind is the epic, a poetic narrative form that better suited his overall intentions. According to Gogol, the conventional novel, closer to drama, "does not take in all of life, but a remarkable event in life." In contrast, the epic "embraces not just certain features, but an entire epoch of time in which there acts a hero with the type of thoughts, beliefs, and even confessions that mankind made at that time." It is the encyclopedic nature of the epic in which character and events become representative of a people and a time that Gogol was after in *Dead Souls.* Wide enough to contain all of Russia, *Dead Souls* conforms to a different shape and principle than other novels, closer to the intentions of the epic, but a particularly diminished form of epic. In what Gogol calls "a sort of middle ground between the novel and the epic," the hero is "a private and insignificant figure, but one who is nonetheless significant in many respects for the observer of the human soul." The diminished hero is presented against what the author detects as the traits and mores of the time: "that earthy, almost statistically grasped picture of shortcomings, abuses, faults, and all he has noticed in the chosen epoch and time. . . . It is not the whole world that is portrayed, but there is often a full epic range of remarkable individual phenomena." Gogol suggests here his interest in a wider range than conventional novels provided, as well as an epic subject marked more by its insignificance and typicality. His novel would be, therefore, an epic of ordinary life in which banality is the norm, and heroism and adventures, usually associated with the novel, are unsettlingly absent. It is, in a sense, the same formula that James Joyce would use 80 years later with *Ulysses* and equally revolutionary.

From the beginning of *Dead Souls,* the reader's expectations are undermined and subverted. Pavel Ivanovich Chichikov, the novel's putative hero, arrives in an unnamed provincial Russian town on an unidentified mission. A traveler, Chichikov seems a figure from the picaresque tradition, a quester, ready for a series of road adventures. However, until the very end of the novel the reader learns almost nothing about Chichikov's background or history, and, until the novel is well under way, no clear understanding about what he is up to as he begins to ingratiate himself with the town's powerful elite. Far from the expected idealized hero, Chichikov is denied an expected love interest and is closer to a nonentity than to a conventional hero. He is intentionally malleable and faceless, offering little more than a pleasing veneer meant to impress but not too memorably, more a mirror than an individual. His scheme to acquire dead souls to advance himself is actually more prosaic than daring or diabolical, with Chichikov anxious to join the ranks of the landed gentry whom he exploits. Furthermore, dramatically, nothing really comes of the intended swindle. Although Chichikov does in fact acquire 400 dead souls, he is exposed before he can complete the transaction, and the novel ends with his hasty departure, presumably to another promising venue. As a cheat Chichikov is a failure; as a symbolic instigator or provocateur, he is equally ineffectual, leaving the town completely intact, its banalities and hypocrisies exposed but still fully functioning. In Gogol's version of the picaresque adventure it is not the novel's hero or the outcome of his actions that finally matter but the milieu, the rich texture of observed life, that claims the reader's attention. Ultimately, *Dead Souls* sustains interest not from the usual novelistic drama or idealization of characters into assigned roles as heroes, villains, and support but as an unsurpassed gallery of comic characterization, grotesque episodes, and imaginative sleights of hand. Here is Gogol's justifiably famous description of a party at the governor's house that Chichikov attends:

> The black tailcoats flickered and fluttered, separately and in clusters, this way and that, just as flies flutter over dazzling white chunks of sugar on a hot July day when the old housekeeper hacks and divides it into sparkling lumps in front of the open window; all the children look on as they gather about her, watching with curiosity the movements of her rough hands while the airy squadrons of flies that the light air has raised, fly boldly in, complete mistresses of the premises and, taking advantage of the old woman's purblindness and of the sun troubling her eyes, spread all over the dainty morsels, here separately, there in dense clusters.

Gogol's version of the epic simile conjoins two worlds in a dazzling verbal display. Gogol identifies in the novel his intention to "evoke all such things that are constantly before one's eyes but which idle eyes do not see—the shocking morass of trifles that has tied up our lives, and the essence of cold, crumbling, humdrum character with whom our earthly way, now bitter, now dull, fairly swarms."

Chichikov's main strength is his skill in sizing up those around him and identifying the means to flatter his way into their good graces. The petty vanities of the provincial town offer him plenty of opportunities (and Gogol a chance to anatomize and ridicule Russian society). Gaining access to and acceptance by the most important officials, Chichikov is now ready to set out on his mission to acquire dead souls. The novel's long central section describes Chichikov's visits with neighboring gentry in a series of memorable character portraits that have been described as the most famous grotesque comic types in Russian literature: Manilov, the vacuous sentimental dreamer; the widow Korobochka, whose domesticity drives her to demand the best possible price for her formerly worthless departed serfs; the braggart and hyperbolic Nozdev; the bearlike, boorish Sobokevich; and the frighteningly avaricious Plyushkin. Each has entered the Russian consciousness as an identifiable character type, and collectively they serve as a devastating attack on the gentry with Chichikov's unusual (and illegal) scheme the means to expose their true natures.

Back in town, Chichikov is in turn inflated by rumors as a purported man of means and deflated by equally outlandish rumors of his nefarious intentions. In a swirl of what Gogol called "extreme vacuousness, empty chatter. Uncontrolled gossip stemming from a lack of anything to do," the novel collapses in a Kafkaesque world of threat, confusion, and stupidity: a withering exposé of contemporary Russian society. Exposed as a fraud, Chichikov departs hastily, allowing Gogol a final, famous grotesque generalization in the comparison between Russia and a careening carriage:

> Rus, are you not similar in your headlong motion to one of those nimble troikas that none can overtake? The flying road turns into smoke under you, bridges thunder and pass, all falls back and is left behind! The witness of your course stops as if struck by some divine miracle: is this not lightning that dropped from the sky? And what does this awesome motion mean? . . . Rus, whither are you speeding so?

Gogol labored in vain to answer the question of whither in subsequent attempts to resolve the implication of the marvelous comic world that he created. Critics have joined in the attempt to reduce the novel to a conventional interpretation. Is it, as has been suggested, a marvel of social realism, an elaborate symbolic allegory, or a novel about the art of writing or imagining the world? All seem plausible but ultimately inadequate to capture Gogol's animation of the world lit by his peculiar genius.

26

LE PÈRE GORIOT

(1835)

by Honoré de Balzac

Anyone interested in the novel must eventually come to Balzac; anyone who comes to Balzac must eventually encounter Le Père Goriot. *In fact, to have read a nineteenth-century novel is to have felt, knowingly or not, the influence of this extraordinary work, for* Le Père Goriot *is the keystone of the* Comédie humaine, *itself a vast monument of Western prose fiction.*

—Martin Kanes, *Père Goriot: Anatomy of a Troubled World*

For Henry James in his essay "The Lesson of Balzac," the French writer is the master of the "conditions" of his characters, showing the reader "*how* we all are, and how we are placed and built-in for being so. What befalls us is but another name for the way our circumstances press upon us—so that an account of what befalls us is an account of our circumstances." Balzac is one of the first novelists to anatomize the effects of environment on the individual, while directing the novel outward to an unprecedented expansion and reflection of those conditions, achieving for the first time in the novel a massive criticism of life. Among Balzac's novels, for James *Le Père Goriot* (Old Goriot) is his "supreme case of composition, a model of that high virtue that we know as economy of effect, economy of line and touch."

Le Père Goriot is the foundation work in Balzac's monumental fictional edifice that he conceived in the 1830s. "I am about to become a genius," he wrote to his sister in 1833, explaining that he envisioned a sequence of novels in which he would create "the history of a whole society," in which "not a single situation of life, not a face, not the characters of any man or woman, not a way of life, not a profession, not a social group, will be missing. Not an aspect of childhood, maturity, old age, politics, justice, war, will be left out. On this foundation, I shall examine every thread of the human heart, every social factor and it will be real." Virtually all the fiction Balzac wrote after he began publishing under his own name in 1829, a series of nearly 100 novels, contributed to the project that Balzac titled in 1840, *La Comédie humaine* (The

Human Comedy), in a secular contrast to Dante's *Divine Comedy*. Nothing so expansive or in depth, nothing so telescopic or microscopic—the attempt to render an entire society in all its complexity—had ever been attempted in fiction before. With *Le Père Goriot*, the 41st of the 94 novels he would publish under his name, Balzac substantially transformed his plan from a loose succession of thematically linked works into an elaborate web of connections and interrelationships. In his manuscript, the young law student to be introduced to the ways of the world in the novel was originally named "Massiac," but Balzac changed it to "Rastignac," the name of one of his minor characters in a previous novel, *The Wild Ass's Skin* (1831). The alteration signals Balzac's decision in effect to turn his novels into chapters of one great comprehensive narrative in an ever-expanding fictional universe connected through his diagnoses of human experience and society and by recurring characters. Individuals would be studied at various stages of their careers (the mature Rastignac from *The Wild Ass's Skin* would be given a background and a history); secondary characters or those merely passing through one book would dominate the action in another. The effect is a social panorama that is both broad and deep. *Le Père Goriot* functions, therefore, as the single most important work of the *Comédie humaine* in its refinement of Balzac's grand scheme. It also serves as a kind of microcosm of the entire plan, showing Balzac's intentions to unlock underlying universal principles from the seeming chaos of experience.

Set in Paris in 1819, *Le Père Goriot* opens with an elaborate, room-by-room description of Madame Vauquer's shabby boardinghouse in an impoverished corner of the Latin Quarter. With the eye of a scientist minutely recording data, Balzac first establishes his characters' milieu that will help condition their actions, becoming the first novelist to establish in depth the link between the social environment and human behavior. As the critic M. A. Crawford has observed, "No novel ever had its setting more exactly visualized." It is this concreteness of detail that would establish Balzac as the master of fictional mimesis and the realistic predecessor of his countrymen Flaubert and Zola. The boardinghouse's ostensibly respectable façade is shown to conceal a shabby, dirty interior, establishing the discrepancy between appearance and reality that the novel will dissect in Paris society as a whole. Also apparent is the money ethic that dominates every relationship as the boarders form a microhierarchy based on their means. No one, however, is who he seems, particularly the resident enigma, Jean-Joachim Goriot, an impoverished gentleman of previous means who is sometimes visited by two beautiful and apparently wealthy women. It is the secret of Goriot's relationship to these women, his daughters, that helps drive the narrative while establishing the connection between the disreputable Rue Nueve-Sainte-Geneviève of Madame Vauquer's boardinghouse and the fashionable salons of the Faubourg Saint-Germain.

The bridge between these worlds will be made by another boarder, the impoverished law student, Eugène de Rastignac. Family connections gain him access to a prominent social lady, Madame de Beauséant, who facilitates Rastignac's meeting one of Goriot's female visitors, Countess Anastasie de Restaud. However, when Rastignac mentions to her that they have the acquaintance of Goriot in common, he is snubbed. It is from Madame de Beauséant that Rastignac learns the truth, that Goriot's visitors are his daughters for whom he has sacrificed his entire fortune from the flour trade to provide them with sufficient dowries to make fashionable marriages. Spoiled and indulged by their doting father, who lives vicariously through his children, the daughters have repaid his devotion by concealing their connections with their now shabbily genteel and less-than-respectable parent.

At the center of the novel, therefore, is the perversion of the family unit, the disintegration of the affection, loyalty, and respect due a parent by a money ethic and selfishness that begin to typify all relations in the Parisian world that Rastignac is slowly made to understand. It is from Madame de Beauséant that Rastignac gains his first lesson in the ways of getting on: "You are determined to succeed? I will help you. You shall sound the depths of corruption in woman; you shall measure the extent of man's wretched vanity. . . . The more cold-blooded your calculations, the further you will go. Strike ruthlessly; you will be feared. Men and women for you must be nothing more than post-horses; take a fresh relay, and leave the last to drop by the roadside; in this way you will reach the goal of your ambition." Rastignac's mentor urges him to court Goriot's other daughter, Madame Delphine de Nucingen, as his initial relay to his Paris success, a cynical scheme for advancement that is contrasted by only a slightly more immoral proposal by another of Madame Vauquer's boarders, the equally cynical Vautrin. Sensing Rastignac's ambition, Vauquer proposes that the younger man secure the affections of another boarder, a disinherited daughter of a banker, Victorine Taillefer. In exchange for a percentage of their take, Vautrin will arrange to have her brother disposed of in a duel, assuring that Victorine will inherit her father's fortune. The similarity between Madame de Beauséant's and Vautrin's plan in its manipulation of others for personal gain is not missed by either Rastignac or the reader, and Balzac makes clear that what is criminal in the seedy world of the strivers at Madame Vauquer's is only given a more respectable veneer in the fashionable salons. Both Madame de Beauséant and Vautrin provide the same lesson in self-interest in which all human relationships are measured by a cash return on investment.

Despite Rastignac's hesitancy over Vautrin's scheme, Vautrin proceeds with the plan, misconstruing Rastignac's flirtation with Victorine as compliance, and kills her brother in a duel. Vautrin, however, is exposed as the infamous criminal Jacques Collin by two of his fellow boarders who turn out to be police informers. Vautrin will be seen again in subsequent novels, the embodiment of the corruption and criminality that exist beneath the respectable surface of things and the extreme version of the individual who rejects the limitations of law and morality to further his drive for mastery. Like Dickens, Balzac makes his melodrama serve a larger social vision, suggesting the connection among classes, between the fashionable and the criminal. If Rastignac fails to accept a partnership with Vautrin, he does pursue Madame de Beauséant's advice by becoming Delphine's lover, to the pleasure of Goriot, who hopes their relation will allow him at least a vicarious involvement in his daughter's life. Described as the "Christ of paternity," Goriot is a victim of his daughters' heartlessness, but he is also the agent of their and his own ruin by his indulgence and selfish, obsessive aspirations. Translating love into cash, giving them everything he has, Goriot eventually has nothing left to gratify their continual demands, and he is finally drained and broken under the strain and the growing realization of his daughters' monstrous ingratitude. He dies alternating in his mind between self-pity and self-justification, between the vain hope that his daughters will return the love he has lavished on them and his understanding that "It is all my own fault, I taught them to trample upon me. I loved to have it so." Neither of his daughters is with him at his deathbed, and Goriot is buried in a pauper's grave at Rastignac's expense. Goriot's daughters send only empty carriages for the funeral procession.

In a novel that has punctured virtually every noble ideal of humanity, the conclusion is the most devastating blow of all. Presumably Rastignac has learned a lesson in the shallowness and venality of the world he was anxious to master. Money and status have eroded the most fundamental bonds between a father and his children, and no crime is seemingly beyond the realm of the possible among those determined to get on at all cost. However, instead of deciding that this world is not worth the price, Rastignac finds himself committed to a redoubled effort to force the world to yield to his will:

> His eyes turned almost eagerly to the space between the column of the Place Vendôme and the cupola of the Invalides; there lay the great world that he had longed to penetrate. He glanced over that humming hive, seeming to draw a foretaste of its honey, and said magniloquently:
>
> "We'll fight this out, you and I."
>
> Then, as a first challenge to Society, Rastignac went to dine with Mme. De Nucingen.

Rastignac's career has been launched as he stifles the novel's moral lesson and pursues his conquest of Delphine. It is a devastating climax in a novel that has penetrated beneath the glittering social surface to reveal the economic and selfish principles linking the highest to the lowest, master to victim. *Le Père Goriot* is both a triumph of narrative construction that weaves its multiple strands into a convincing social panorama, and a lens to show a world free of the illusions that flatter but obscure. In summarizing the novel's significance, the critic David Bellos has stated that "Balzac's novel abandons the love intrigue as the central plot element of its analysis of feelings; it incorporates a properly tragic element in the principal narrative of the death of Goriot; and it brings an entirely new seriousness to the description of the physical setting in which its characters live. In these ways, *Old Goriot* makes a major development of the novel as a form, and contributes significantly to its emergence from the limbo of popular entertainment as the dominant form of serious cultural expression in the nineteenth century." Like Rastignac, Balzac announces the novelist's ongoing battle with the way things are: "We'll fight this out, you and I."

27

THE PORTRAIT OF A LADY

(1881)

by Henry James

Over and above its substance The Portrait of a Lady *established itself, by degrees, as one of the best-written novels of its age. In a prose of high style, with a narrative unsurpassed for its rhythmic development, with a mastery of character and of all the threads of his complicated story, Henry had created a novel that could be placed among the supreme works of the century. It introduced into a Europe that was reading Turgenev and Flaubert, and would soon be reading Tolstoy, a distinctly American heroine.*

—Leon Edel, *Henry James: The Conquest of London, 1870–1881*

The critic R. P. Blackmur has called *The Portrait of a Lady* "the first of Henry James's books to sound with the ring of greatness." The culminating work of James's early period that included *Roderick Hudson* (1875), *The American* (1877), and *Daisy Miller* (1879), *Portrait* is one of the novel's greatest achievements in the 19th century, the first American novel to absorb and expand upon the lessons of social and psychological realism by such European practitioners as Stendhal, Balzac, Flaubert, Turgenev, and George Eliot. According to Richard Chase, it was the "first novel by an American that made, within the limits of its subject, full use of the novel form." Replacing the American storyteller's previous reliance on romantic adventure for the internal drama of consciousness in a solidly rendered social setting, James pointed the way the novel would increasingly follow in the modern period, while adding to an impressive roster of fictional heroines that includes Elizabeth Bennet, Emma Bovary, Becky Sharp, Jane Eyre, Dorothea Brooke, Gwendolen Harleth, and Anna Karenina, an American, Isabel Archer, whose psychological and moral development is one of the singular achievements by any novelist. James himself ranked *The Portrait of a Lady* behind only his great achievement of his final period, *The Ambassadors*. *Portrait* marked James's arrival in the first rank of novelists, and he would triumphantly claim about his novel on publication, "It is from that I myself shall pretend to date, on that I shall take my stand."

The germ of James's novel was his conception of his central character, an idealistic, vital young American woman whose freedom and sense of self and possibility are tested in the social drama James arranges for her. As the novelist recorded in his *Notebooks*, "The idea of the whole thing is that the poor girl, who has dreamed of freedom and nobleness, who has done, as she believes, a generous, natural, clear-sighted thing, finds herself in reality ground in the very mill of the conventional." Isabel's process of character formation takes place in her contact with Europe, James's characteristic laboratory to study the operation of innocence giving way to experience. In America, she is a naive, headstrong, and deluded young woman, isolated from the world in her grandmother's Albany home. As her aunt, Mrs. Touchett, explains to her son Ralph about her motive for bringing Isabel back with her to England: "I found her in an old house in Albany, sitting in a dreary room on a rainy day, reading a heavy book, and boring herself to death. . . . I thought she was meant for something better. It occurred to me that it would be a kindness to take her about and introduce her to the world. She thinks she knows a great deal of it—like most American girls; but like most American girls she's ridiculously mistaken." The novel will test Isabel's notion of the world, presenting her with a series of suitors as well as a fortune that will aid her independence and allow her choices to be hers alone. What Isabel makes of her freedom and the consequences of her actions form the novel's internal drama, patterned by what James called his "primary question, 'Well, what will she do?'" Despite his fear that his novel was "too exclusively psychological—that it depends too little on incident," James persisted in structuring his novel by the inner dynamics of Isabel's predicament and perception: "'Place the centre of the subject in the young woman's consciousness,' I said to myself, 'and you get as interesting and as beautiful a difficulty as you would wish.'"

At the outset of Isabel's encounter with the world beyond her Albany home, she prides herself on her independence and autonomy and blithely announces that she is "not a candidate for adopting" while she rejects two marriage proposals—one from her American suitor, Caspar Goodwood, and the other from the English Lord Warburton—as premature given her desire to see the world for herself and as too restrictive to her desired self-definition. "I don't want to begin life by marrying," Isabel asserts to Ralph. "There are other things a woman can do." However, Isabel lacks the means to avoid dependency until Ralph convinces his father to divert a substantial portion of his inheritance to her, to "put a little wind in her sails." As Philip Rahv has pointed out, "the stage is set for the essential Jamesian drama of free choice." Ralph gives Isabel the means to decide for herself how to invest her freedom.

Isabel eventually succumbs to the manipulation of Madame Merle and the American expatriate and dilettante Gilbert Osmond to exchange her freedom for incarceration. Osmond, the man she finally chooses to marry, is someone with "No career, no name, no position, no fortune, no past, no future, no anything," nothing except a highly cultivated taste and a few "good things." A connoisseur, "a critic, a student of the exquisite," Osmond has managed "to renounce everything but Corregio." He is the cicerone of his own museum, closed up in his house as in a display case. Isabel sees Osmond as having succeeded in refining life down to its essential values, purifying reality into a work of art. In marrying Osmond, Isabel decides to bring her tour of the world to a close, to sacrifice her freedom by becoming the possession of Gilbert Osmond. Telling Ralph that "the desire for unlimited expansion had been succeeded in her soul by the sense that life was vacant without some private duty that might gather one's energies to a point. . . . she had 'seen life' in a year or two and . . . she was already tired, not of the act of living, but of that of observing," Isabel chooses instead to be observed, as one of Osmond's precious objects.

Isabel's marriage proves to be a tragic failure. Ralph's confidence that "she'll please herself, of course; but she'll do so by studying human nature at close quarters and yet retain her liberty" is shattered as Isabel finds herself, like Osmond's daughter Pansy, "immured in a kind of domestic fortress." The reader's view of Isabel recedes at this point from her consciousness to seeing her from the vantage point of those around her. Ralph, Warburton, Goodwood, her American friend Henrietta Stackpole, and Rosier, Pansy's suitor, all examine and evaluate her. All measure their picture of the "real" Isabel with the one found in Osmond's Roman palazzo: "framed in the gilded doorway, she struck our young man as the picture of a gracious lady." To Ralph such a picture is a counterfeit of the actual Isabel, submerged under her function as a decoration in Osmond's house: "The free, keen girl had become quite another person; what he saw was the fine lady who was supposed to represent something. What did Isabel represent? Ralph asked himself; and he could answer only by saying that she represented Gilbert Osmond."

It is the recognition of Osmond's immorality—his use of people as means rather than as ends—that completes Isabel's education and prepares the way for the novel's climactic moral decision. The climax of *Portrait* occurs in Chapter 42, when Isabel sees her life with Osmond elucidated for the first time. Suspecting that she has been used by Madame Merle and Osmond, her mistrust of her husband isolates her enough so that she begins to see her circumstances clearly: "She had taken all the first steps in the purest confidence, and then she had suddenly found the infinite vista of a multiple life to be a dark, narrow alley, with a dead wall at the end. Instead of leading to the high places of happiness, from which the world would seem to lie below one, so that one could look down with a sense of exaltation and advantage and judge and choose and pity, it led rather downward and earthward, into realms of restriction and depression where the sound of other lives, easier and freer, was heard as from above, and where it served to deepen the feeling of failure."

Isabel's perception takes her out of the world of romance and the quest for freedom and into a painfully real world of suffering and responsibility. The final refinement of Isabel's moral education comes with her decision to leave Rome to be with Ralph on his deathbed. It is compassion for another that compels Isabel out of her confinement and to break with her husband. Yet why must Isabel return to Osmond at the novel's conclusion? Every critic who examines *Portrait* has been forced to weigh in on the implication of James's ending, and readers must come to terms with what William Gass has called the "high brutality of Isabel's good intention." The ambiguity implied in Isabel's final rejection of the release offered by Goodwood for the sake of her duty in Rome has been variously explained as Isabel's sexual timidity, her masochism, and her self-deception. An explanation of James's ending that is consistent with the novel as a whole is possible if one examines the alternative that Goodwood offers Isabel. In stating that "the world's all before us—and the world's very large," Goodwood offers Isabel her freedom in the same Miltonic language at the beginning of her European career. Again, Isabel must choose how to invest her freedom. In answering the question, "Why should you go back—why should you go through that ghastly form?" Isabel asserts that the form—her commitment to the world of conventions, customs, and traditions—cannot be avoided. Goodwood's proposal is a retreat to Isabel's earlier state of idealistic isolation. In this sense, Isabel's decision to return to Rome can be viewed not as a denial of life but as an affirmation of the actual world of boundaries, responsibilities, and suffering. Isabel's decision is a reversal of the archetypal American direction, into the frontier, away from the restraints and responsibilities of society. Huckleberry Finn's plan to "light out for the territory" to avoid civilization, is in James's view a child's wish to void inevitable constraint. Isabel rejects such an independent and ideal existence as finally impossible. The adult must be expected to reside in the actual world, and James ends his novel with Isabel standing on the threshold of maturity, exchanging her freedom for self-understanding. The process of Isabel's education, and vicariously the reader's, has shifted from solipsism to society, from abstraction to a reality shaped by a deepened sense of self and the world.

James fashioned in *The Portrait of a Lady* a remarkable social drama, expanding the archetype of American innocence and European experience into a rich moral and psychological exploration of the nature of freedom and destiny, choice and consequence, dependent not on plot but on the contingencies of character. As Leon Edel has observed, *The Portrait of a Lady* "established once and for all Henry James's 'international theme' on a truly large scale. . . . Isabel Archer brought to the Old World a pair of eyes that would look upon it with all the freshness of vision of the New World. . . . This was the 'Americano-European legend' of Henry James, the myth that he was to explore definitively for us: the ambivalence of a nation that was turning its back upon the past, yet could not wholly ignore it, while forging its new life with energy and self-reliance. In observing this, James was foreshadowing, in the nineteenth century, America's role in the twentieth." In James's masterly handling, the American novel is Europeanized; the European novel is Americanized, and the complex, realistic drama of an individual in society becomes part of American fiction.

28

WOMEN IN LOVE

(1920)

by D. H. Lawrence

There is another novel, sequel to The Rainbow, *called* Women in Love. . . . *I don't think anybody will publish this, either. This actually does contain the results in one's soul of the war: it is purely destructive, not like* The Rainbow, *destructive-consummating. It is very wonderful and terrifying, even to me who have written it. I have hardly read it again. I suppose, however, it will be a long time without being printed—if ever it is printed.*

—D. H. Lawrence, letter to Waldo Frank, July 27, 1917

D. H. Lawrence's *Women in Love* is unquestionably one of the groundbreaking masterpieces of the 20th century. Nothing remotely like its treatment of sexual relationships and personal identity had previously been written, and few other novels have ever attempted such an ambitious interweaving of its psychological-moral-cultural-historical themes. Lawrence considered it the best of his books, and most subsequent critics have concurred. For F. R. Leavis, perhaps the novel's most passionate advocate, *Women in Love* is "one of the most striking works of creative originality that fiction has to show." It is the third and the most accomplished of Lawrence's remarkable sequence of novels that redefined conventional fictional forms and practices. *Sons and Lovers* (1913) provided a radical repossession of the bildungsroman that, like Joyce's *A Portrait of the Artist as a Young Man*, makes other attempts to depict growth and development seem shallow and uninspired by comparison. In *The Rainbow* (1915) Lawrence turned the family saga into a social and psychological critique, while denying at virtually every point the novel's expected idealized romance pattern, ending not in his heroine's marriage but with a hard-won, yet ambiguous independence. *Women in Love* depicts, in Lawrence's words, "*the* problem of today, the establishment of a new relationship, or the readjustment of the old one, between man and woman." Lawrence looks searchingly at relations between the sexes to reflect the fate of modern civilization. The novel offers a double courtship, echoing the pattern employed by Jane

Austen in *Pride and Prejudice* in which two sisters are wooed by two friends, but in Lawrence's version one couple is destroyed; while the other achieves only the most fragile, tentative equilibrium. After Lawrence, any attempt to render this "new relationship" that does not similarly come to terms with sexuality and the power of the unconscious seems slight and inadequate. *Women in Love* also established an influential, poetically inspired logic for the novel, proceeding not forward but deeper, in a series of fragmentary scenes in which contrasting forces, feelings, and ideas face off. It is a novel that begins and ends in mid-conversation, suggesting an open-ended form that defies virtually every previous narrative convention. As in a modern poem that is organized by image and by a sequence of symbolic scenes, what actually happens and what is said is of less importance than what is implied in the realm of the unconscious and instinctual that is shown as the truer guide to the novel's characters and the novel's meaning. It is finally one of the greatest novels of ideas in which battling ideologies are visualized in a series of unforgettably powerful scenes.

The origin of *Women in Love* is traceable to 1913 when Lawrence conceived a "pot boiler" for "jeune filles" to be called "The Sisters." The evolving story of Ursula and Gudrun Brangwen seized Lawrence's imagination, and expanded so that he eventually divided his tale into two novels—*The Rainbow*, providing the Brangwen family background and the stages of Ursula's maturation, and *Women in Love*, the story of the sisters' contrasting courtships. *The Rainbow* was suppressed as obscene upon publication in 1915, and copies were seized and burned. As Lawrence began work on its sequel, he was convinced that there was little possibility of its publication. Completed in 1916 at the end of what Lawrence would call a "nightmare year," *Women in Love* reflects, though never mentions, the Great War, which Lawrence regarded as the greatest of calamities. "The War finished me," he wrote. "It was the spear through the side of all sorrows and hopes." Enduring a kind of internal exile in England, married to a distant cousin of Manfred von Richthofen, Germany's greatest war hero, Lawrence was a target for abuse by his neighbors and surveillance by the police. The Cornish cottage where he composed the novel was repeatedly searched, and Lawrence was evicted in 1917 and ordered to report his whereabouts regularly to the police. The experience of a world gone mad, of technology producing refined instruments of mass slaughter, ended Lawrence's hope for progress and the redemption of art, and *Women in Love* attempts at the level of personality and private relationships to come to terms with how it all came about and what, if anything, could be done. The novel was published first privately in the United States in 1920, and appeared amid libel threats in England in 1921.

The novel is constructed as a prolonged mating dance among its four principal characters—Ursula Brangwen, a teacher, and Rupert Birkin, an idealistic, fatalistic school inspector, Gudrun Brangwen, an artist, and Gerald Crich, a coal mine owner. As the novel opens, Ursula and Gudrun, while watching the wedding of Gerald's sister, have resolved that marriage is "intolerable." The novel works out the emotional and psychological logic of how this is true, and the degree to which male-female relations can both destroy and nurture the individual.

Ursula and Birkin are attracted to each other, but their relationship stalls due to Birkin's cynicism and his wish to avoid the struggle for dominance implied by sexual relationships. Having endured a mutually destructive affair with the wealthy intellectual Hermione Roddice, Birkin tries to articulate the way in which separateness can be reconciled with union while each mate can thrive. Compared to the conventional romantic notion of love based on self-sacrifice and mutuality, Birkin, who becomes easily identifiable throughout the novel as Lawrence's principal spokesman, attempts to outline a new kind of love relationship, what he calls a "strange conjunction . . . an equilibrium, a pure balance of two single beings: as the stars balance each other." Eventually, Ursula understands and accepts Birkin's abstractions and they are reconciled into a tenuous alliance.

Meanwhile, the very process of mutual destruction that Birkin hopes to avoid is being acted out in the relationship between Gudrun and Gerald, who seek not a balance but the absorption of the other's being. Theirs is a dance of death, a sadomasochistic pairing that reveals the hollowness and inadequacies of both partners. Gerald takes over the operation of his family's mine, committed to the principles of machinelike efficiency, and he becomes the main representative of the repressed, mechanized civilization that Lawrence holds responsible for the war. Gerald's drive for mastery and dominance is best glimpsed in the scene in which he brutally reins in his Arab mare as she shies at an oncoming train. Ursula observes Gerald's actions with horror, but Gudrun is fascinated. The two come together when Gerald, lacking any inner resources to deal with his father's death, seeks a kind of oblivion in Gudrun's arms, and their relation is consummated, significantly in the chapter titled "Death and Love," as a kind of war of machines: "It was wonderful, marvelous, it was a miracle. This was the ever-recurrent miracle of his life, at the knowledge of which he was lost in an ecstasy of relief and wonder. And she, subject, received him as a vessel filled with his bitter poison of death. She had no power at this crisis to resist. The terrible frictional violence of death filled her, and she received it in an ecstasy of subjection, in throes of acute, violent sensation."

The novel's climax occurs as the two couples decide to vacation together in the Austrian Alps. There Gudrun and Gerald's relationship deteriorates when she meets Loerke, a German sculptor who offers her an alternative to the role she is expected to assume with Gerald. Meanwhile, Ursula and Birkin have decided to go south to Italy. Gerald tries to kill Gudrun when he finds her walking in the snow with Loerke. When he fails, he wanders through the mountains and valleys, where he dies in a symbolic setting reflecting the frigidity, sterility, and barrenness of his soul. As critic Julian Moynahan has rightly asserted, "The scenes in the snow valley constitute the most brilliant writing that Lawrence ever did, and some of the finest writing in the history of the English novel as well." Gerald's suicide by exposure as a form of spiritual death is matched by Gudrun's drift to aestheticism and the sensual offered by the cynically self-enclosed Loerke to end as a cheap artist's model.

Only Ursula and Birkin have managed to find a way out of the destructive process that destroys sex partners as it destroys civilizations in the rush to mastery and dominance. Yet theirs is more a process of becoming rather than an achieved end, represented by their disagreement that closes the novel as Birkin wonders whether his love for Gerald could have saved him and whether his achieved equilibrium could manage an even more radical expansion. As he confesses to Ursula,

> "Having you, I can live all my life without anybody else, any other sheer intimacy. But to make it complete, really happy, I wanted eternal union with a man too: another kind of love," he said.
>
> "I don't believe it," she said. "It's an obstinacy, a theory, a perversity."
>
> "Well—" he said.
>
> "You can't have two kinds of love. Why should you!"
>
> "It seems as if I can't," he said. "Yet I wanted it."
>
> "You can't have it, because it's wrong, impossible," she said.
>
> "I don't believe that," he answered.

It is ultimately Birkin's daring theorizing and Lawrence's that makes *Women in Love* such a monumental achievement. Both who we are and what we can become undergo one of the most extreme experiments in Lawrence's daring laboratory of heart and head.

29

THE RED AND THE BLACK

(1830)

by Stendhal

In so far as the serious realism of modern times cannot represent man otherwise as embedded in a total reality, political, social, and economic, which is concrete and constantly evolving . . . Stendhal is the founder.

—Erich Auerbach, *Mimesis*

If it is true, as the German critic Walter Benjamin has asserted, that "all great works of literature found a genre or dissolve one . . . they are, in other words, special cases," then there is perhaps no more special case than Stendhal's masterpiece, *The Red and the Black*. It is a novel that does both: undermines previous fictional assumptions and sets in motion elements that will define a new kind of novel. Called by Robert Alter "one of the most boldly original masterworks of European fiction" and by Emile J. Talbot "the first great post-Revolutionary novel in France," *The Red and the Black* exemplifies a crucial turning point in the history of the novel. There had simply never been anything like Stendhal's approach to fiction: an attempt to extend the range of the novel in two different directions simultaneously—outwardly to capture in depth a particular historical moment and inwardly to reveal the concealed recesses of the human heart and psyche. Stendhal transformed unalterably the capabilities of the novel, making the fictional methods that preceded *The Red and the Black* seem increasingly insufficient for the task at hand, while predicting in central ways the course the novel would take.

Stendhal's originality stems from a lifetime in opposition. Born Marie-Henri Beyle in provincial Grenoble, whose conservative, materialistic values he despised, Stendhal, like Julien Sorel in *The Red and the Black*, tried to reinvent himself, as a Parisian, a Bonapartist, and finally as an Italian. Each new identity proved either inadequate or poorly timed, given the political and cultural shifts from the Revolution through Napoleon's rise and fall and the Restoration. Notions of alienation and displacement are at the core of Stendhal's life and provide his central themes in his fiction. Few other writers have examined themselves so continuously or as rigorously as Stendhal, and the same unblinking honesty of presentation informed his novels and helped to redefine fictional realism. Stendhal's discovery of his vocation as a novelist came after years as a critic and historian. The inspiration for *The Red and the Black* originated in two court cases that Stendhal had read in the *Gazette des Tribunaux* concerning two murderers. One was the son of a blacksmith who spent four years in a seminary before becoming the tutor of a well-to-do couple. Dismissed from his position, he blamed the wife of the family for his setback, shooting her and himself during a Mass. The other was a cabinet-maker who killed his lover and was sentenced to 25 years in prison. Stendhal conjoined both stories into his narrative, reworking the sordid circumstances of these two case histories into the epitome of an era.

It is perhaps hard from a modern vantage point to comprehend fully just how shocking Stendhal's novel must have seemed when *The Red and the Black* appeared in 1830. Readers had never before seen their world reflected so immediately. Stendhal dedicated his story of how a provincial nobody manipulates his way to a distinguished position in society before shooting his ex-mistress during Mass to the "Happy Few," presumably those who could cope with the precept contained in the novel's initial epigram from Danton: "The truth, the truth in all its harshness." Central to the novel's strategy is an unsparing honesty that subjects cherished illusions about the clergy, nobility, love, and honor to a test that exposes the gap between appearance and reality. In the process, Stendhal provides one of the groundbreaking statements of the novel's realistic intentions and a defense of the novelist's truth-telling responsibility: "A novel is a mirror going along a main road. Sometimes it reflects into your eyes the azure of the sky, sometimes the mud of the quagmires on the road. And the man carrying the mirror in the basket on his back gets accused by you of being immoral! His mirror shows the mire, and you accuse the mirror! You'd do better to accuse the road where the quagmire is, and better still the inspector of roads who allows the water to stagnate and the quagmire to form."

Stendhal mounts his assessment of the quagmire—the hypocrisy, deviousness, and crass self-interest of the contemporary scene—through the career of his protagonist, Julien Sorel, the archetypal young man from the provinces who sets out to make his way in the wider world. The son of a sawmill owner, Julien is an intelligent, sensitive, and ambitious young man who despises his hometown of Verrières, his common background, and the pettiness that surrounds him. One of the novel's first great antiheroes, Julien is determined to rise in the world by exploiting the illusions and weaknesses of others. The title of Stendhal's novel alludes to the two courses available at the time for a man on the make: the red of the military or the black of the church. Julien's dilemma is that he is a Napoleon-like figure in the black world of the Restoration, in which the egoist is expected to conform and the revolutionary must abide by the rules of rank and hierarchy. To rise in such a society, Julien decides to subvert the system by trading on its hypocrisies, mounting an assault on prestige and power, setting out to bend the world to his will, and in the process becoming a new kind of fictional hero. "The modern hero," critic Irving Howe observes, "the man who forces society to accept him as its agent—the hero by will rather than birth—now appears for the first time. . . . Before the revolution men had been concerned with privileges, not expectations; now they dream of success, that is, of a self-willed effort to lift oneself, through industry or chicanery, to a higher social level. Life becomes an experiment in strategy, an adventure in plan, ruse, and combat; the hero is not merely ambitious but sensitive to the point of paranoia, discovering and imagining a constant assault upon his dignity; and Stendhal carries this outlook to its extreme limit, perhaps even to caricature, by applying it to the affairs of love." What sets Julien Sorel apart from other ambitious young men setting out to make their fortunes is not just his calculation but Stendhal's attempt to understand him more fully than any other previous character in fiction. Innovative in its realism, *The Red and the Black* is also one of the first novels to turn its focus inward toward an unprecedented intimate presentation of private consciousness and the absorbing mystery of human desires.

Appointed tutor in the household of Verrières' mayor, Julien begins an affair with the mayor's wife, Madame de Rênal. Julien's initial romantic experiment to test his mastery over another turns unexpectedly into a sincere passion, the exposure of which causes Julien to be sent away to a seminary. There Julien finds a repetition of the petty meanness and hypocrisies of his provincial hometown. Alienated from his fellow seminarians, former peasants who preferred "to earn their living by reciting a few Latin words than by digging dirt," Julien finds his only friend in the Abbé Pirard, whose moral honesty has in turn alienated him from the seminary officials. Eventually dismissed from the seminary, Pirard secures a position in Paris from the Marquis de La Mole and hires Julien as his secretary. Julien's route to advancement in the marquis's service lies ultimately through the marquis's daughter Mathilde, who yields to Julien's sexual advances and becomes pregnant. The marquis deals with the crisis by making Julien a respectable husband for his daughter by agreeing to give him a fortune, a title, and a commission in the army.

At this point, Julien has achieved all he had dreamed of, but nemesis strikes in the form of a letter from Madame de Rênal that reveals her relationship with Julien to the marquis, prompting him to withdraw his support and permission to let Julien marry his daughter. Enraged, Julien returns to Verrières and shoots Madame de Rênal while she is kneeling at church. She does not die, yet Julien is condemned to death for the attack. In fact, Madame de Rênal is contrite and reaffirms her passion for Julien. As Mathilde attempts to bribe the jury, and his friends urge Julien to appeal his conviction, he accepts his sentence with serenity, in fact taunting his jurors to condemn him. Executed and buried in a cave in the mountains where he had daydreamed his heroic ascent as a boy, Julien is mourned by Madame de Rênal, who dies shortly afterward, and memorialized by Mathilde, who turns his tragedy into a romantic echo of a past increasingly distant from the tawdry and prosaic present.

No other aspect of Stendhal's radically unsettling novel has been so controversial as its conclusion. Exploding the convention that a novel should end with a wedding or at least the morally reassuring rewarding of virtue and punishment of vice, Stendhal leaves his reader perplexed at the implications of Julien's career. The trajectory of Julien's ambitious pursuit of self-fulfillment reaches a terminus in a prison cell. Yet in the logic of the novel, it is clear that his cell is a superior destination to the life of privilege Julien ultimately rejects. The madness of Julien's act, which costs him his dreamed-of fortune, is actually the fulfillment of his heroic destiny and a form of redemption. In an escalation of irony, Julien allows passion and instinct to overrule his carefully laid plan of advancement, achieving a genuine heroism in defiance of the societal values he spurns. The result is the discovery of an authentic self. As Victor Brombert has asserted, "Tired of heroic poses, freed from the compulsions of his own ambitious temperament, Julien can finally devote himself to the *present* situation; he is delivered from time. The stripping of false values allows him to relive the past and to make a new present." Julien, in his prison cell, passionately embracing Madame de Rênal, accepting the dictates of the heart over the head, achieves a status of existential hero.

Stendhal forces the reader to abandon unexamined or reassuring moral categories and to consider the full implication of Julien's case, while raising important questions, such as, how can a truly authentic self be formed? and how can human desire be understood and expressed? The novel's honesty, its clear-eyed assessment of cherished illusions, its morally suspect protagonist, and its unornamented, functional prose style gives the novel the feel of a new departure, justifying André Gide's contention that "*The Red and the Black* had been written for the pleasure of the 20th century." Stendhal himself believed that it would be 50 years before the audience for his kind of novel would be ready for his art, a prediction that came true. Zola and the naturalists at the end of the 19th century claimed Stendhal as their realistic forebear; Tolstoy would insist that he learned more from Stendhal than from any other writer, and the influence of Stendhal on such modern novels as Camus's *The Stranger* is unmistakable. *The Red and the Black* is one of the paradigm-shifting books in literary history that helps introduce its readers to the modern world and to themselves.

TRISTRAM SHANDY 30

(1760–67)

by Laurence Sterne

Recently I took another glance at Sterne's Tristram *which, at the time that I was a miserable student, had caused much sensation in Germany. With the years my admiration has increased and is still increasing; for who in 1759 recognized pedantry and Philistinism so well and described it with such good humor. I still have not met his equal in the broad field of literature.*

—Johann Wolfgang von Goethe, letter to C. F. Zelter, October 5, 1830

In charting the progress of the English novel in the 18th century from the perspective of the ascendancy of realism, Sterne's *Tristram Shandy* is the glaring, subversive exception. It is a work that undermined novelistic conventions, substituted for the first time the associational logic of consciousness for narrative chronology, and established an alternative, antirealistic course for the novel to follow. Despite Samuel Johnson's premature obituary for the novel—"Nothing odd will do long; *Tristram Shandy* did not last"—and F. R. Leavis's inability to find room for the novel in his Great Tradition, dismissing it as "irresponsible (and nasty) trifling," the influences of Sterne's masterpiece are unmistakable and persistent. Echoes of Sterne can be found in Dickens's characterization, in his reconception of Sterne's hobbyhorse theory of personality into the Dickensian obsessive. Tolstoy, who named Sterne his favorite author, found in Sterne's novel a model for his own expansive narrative hybrid of history, fiction, and essay in *War and Peace*, so much so that Russian formalist critics have described Tolstoy's masterwork as a Russian version of *Tristram Shandy*. However, the full implication of Sterne's method would not be fully realized until modernist novelists exploited *Tristram Shandy* as a prototype for their own fictional forms and preoccupations. As Benjamin H. Lehman wrote in an important 1941 study of Sterne's novel, "If *Tristram Shandy* as we have it did not exist, we should have to say that that achievement also, twenty years after *Pamela*, was not to be imagined. . . . To see what Sterne's achievement really was, is I believe only in these last years possible, in a mind made aware by *The Magic Mountain*, *Ulysses*, and *Remembrance of Things Past*." Dorothy Van Ghent, one of many critics who has identified the kinship between Sterne and Proust, has observed that "We think of *Tristram Shandy*, as we do of Proust's *Remembrance of Things Past*, as a mind in which the local world has been steeped and dissolved and fantastically re-formed, so that it issues brand new." Joyce, in trying to explain his experimental intentions in *Finnegans Wake*, offered the following: "Time and the river and the mountain are the real heroes of my book. Yet the elements are exactly what every novelist might use: man and woman, birth, childhood, night, sleep, marriage, prayer, death. There is nothing paradoxical about this. Only I am trying to build as many planes of narrative with a single esthetic purpose. . . . Did you ever read Laurence Sterne?"

That Sterne's ribald, iconoclastic, and idiosyncratic novel should emerge in the 20th century as an influential mainstream source for groundbreaking modernist masterpieces is the ultimate irony in a writer's career that defied prediction. Forty-six years old when he began *Tristram Shandy* in 1759, Sterne had since 1738 served quietly and unremarkably as an Anglican vicar of a rural parish eight miles north of York. He was the author of some political writings and sermons published locally and a satire on diocesan squabbles, *A Political Romance*, that had been suppressed. A dilettante and dabbler with an interest in painting and music, Sterne reveals little in his background to forecast the imaginative resources or the eccentric genius that would produce one of the most extraordinary novels in English literature. The first two volumes of *Tristram Shandy*, completed in May 1759, were rejected by a London publisher. Brought out at his own expense in York, the novel was an immediate success, selling 200 copies in two days. By March 1760, Sterne had sold the copyright in London for the first four volumes for a sum three times his annual income as a clergyman and had agreed to write new volumes annually. Eventually, nine volumes appeared, from 1760 until 1767 when the consumption that afflicted him most of his life prevented continuation. Sterne died in London in 1768 at the age of 54.

The full title of the novel, *The Life and Opinions of Tristram Shandy, Gentleman*, gives the reader the first indication of the gap between the expected fictional conventions and what Sterne provides in his work. "I have undertaken, you see," Tristram announces to his readers at the outset, "to write not only my life, but my opinions also . . . if you should think me somewhat sparing of my narrative on my first setting out,—bear with me,—and let me go on, and tell my story my own way:—or, if I should seem now and then to trifle upon the road,—or should sometimes put on a fool's cap with a bell to it, for a moment or two as we pass along,—don't fly off,—but rather courteously give me credit for a little more wisdom than appears upon my outside:—and as we jog on, either laugh with me, or at me, or in short, do any thing,—only keep your temper." Testing the reader's patience, Tristram narrates the story of his life in a manner that frustrates expected forward progress and demolishes chronological sequence. He does not arrives at his birth until the book is one-third complete, reaches the age of five at the midway point, and gains his first breeches two-thirds of the way to the end. Indeed, a summary of the novel's dramatic action surrounding the title character is wholly inadequate to encompass what this novel is about. Tristram is conceived, a victim of coitus interruptus (serving as an appropriate metaphor for the novel's narrative act itself), and is finally born after his nose is crushed by a doctor's forceps. He is baptized and given the wrong name. His father, Walter, sets to work on an educational treatise for his upbringing, while his Uncle Toby deals with his own wounding at the Siege of Namur by reconstructing model fortifications on the bowling green behind Shandy Hall. At the age of five, Tristram is accidentally circumcised by a faulty window sash, the weights of which have been removed to make miniature cannons for Toby's ruling passion, his hobbyhorse. The novel concludes with the adult Tristram visiting France, while the story of Uncle Toby's courtship of the Widow Wadman is described as she tries unsuccessfully to ascertain the exact nature of his groin injury.

In place of the expected narrative adventures of the protagonist are Tristram's reflections and observations that follow an associational logic, cycling backward and forward in time, blocking any desired chronological progression. Digressions become the book's major operating principle. "Digressions, incontestably," Tristram declares, "are the sunshine;—they are the life, the soul of reading;—take them out of this book for instance,—you might as well take the book along with them;—one cold eternal winter would reign in every page of it; restore them to the writer;—he steps forth like a bridegroom,—bids All hail; brings in variety, and forbids appetite to fail." Following the train of his thought rather than the progress of action, Tristram struggles to tell his story in full, seemingly opposed at every turn by context, clarification, and the equally important claims of others in the expanding world of his novel. Calling attention to the narrative act itself, undermining it to reveal the novel's component parts of character, plot, and theme, Sterne tests the reader's assumptions about the novel's means and methods, substituting the lineaments of consciousness itself as the novel's appropriate domain. Described by various critics as the first truly psychological novel and the first to put the method of the stream of consciousness into practice, *Tristram Shandy* has also been regarded as the first antinovel or metafiction, a novel about itself, whose self-reflexivity dismantles narrative and rearranges it with an enhanced awareness of the illusions of character, plot, and sequence.

As Tristam points out, "Every thing in this world, said my father, is big with jest,—and has wit in it, and instruction too,—if we can but find it out." To do so, Sterne turns his lens on the trivial and the absurd, importing into the novel the oversized appetite for experience found in Rabelais and the comic inversions derived from Cervantes. Sterne declared that "I am perswaded that the happiness of the Cervanic humour arises from . . . describing silly and trifling events, with the circumstantial pomp of great ones." The corollary of great events, such as birth, marriage, and death, described by their silly and trifling aspects is also in play in his novel. Fundamental to Sterne's vision is the notion that life is far too complex to be contained by the standard novelistic treatment, by a linear sequence of dramatic incidents, consistent characters, or by a simplistic moral interpretation. Experience instead is fragmentary and shifting, a rich tangle of associations pointing backward and forward in time. If the mind is infinite, so too should be the novel, and Sterne liberates fictional form to encapsulate the rich and contradictory contours of life and consciousness itself while achieving some of the most entertaining and cherished portraits of individuals in fiction. Characters such as Walter Shandy, the theorizing master of pseudo-nonsense, and his unforgettable brother Toby, who has been described as the highest compliment ever paid to human nature, are revealed simultaneously as great eccentrics and representatives of universal human traits. For writer Katherine Anne Porter, *Tristram Shandy* "contains more living, breathing people you can see and hear, whose garments have texture between your finger and thumb, whose flesh is knit firmly to their bones, who walk about their affairs with audible footsteps, than any other one novel in the world, I believe." Virginia Woolf contends that Sterne brings us "as close to life as we can be." By eliminating the "usual ceremonies and conventions which keep reader and writer at arm's length" Sterne manages "to speak to the reader as directly as by word of mouth . . . No writing seems to flow more exactly into the very folds and creases of the individual mind to express its changing moods, to answer its lightest whim and impulse, and yet the result is perfectly precise and composed." The novel after *Tristram Shandy* had a new set of possibilities as well as a new set of challenges to contain the infinite prospects of the human mind and experience that Sterne displays in all their rich variety.

31

FINNEGANS WAKE

(1939)

by James Joyce

The last book of James Joyce is a very great poem, one of the top works of literature of our time. It is in some ways, in fact, a more extraordinary production than Ulysses*—digging deeper into human psychology, breaking new intellectual ground and exhibiting Joyce's musical genius as perhaps none of his other books does. Yet* Finnegans Wake *has acquired the reputation of being inordinately difficult to read, and Joyce has even been accused in some quarters of having perpetuated an insolent hoax or executed an insane mess of gibberish . . . it is time that these doubts and inhibitions were dispelled. . . .* Finnegans Wake *is one of the few great intellectual and aesthetic treats that these last bad years have yielded.*

—Edmund Wilson, "A Guide to *Finnegans Wake*," 1944

Finnegans Wake absorbed the last 17 years of James Joyce's creative life. He regarded it as his masterpiece, and it is by any measure one of the most challenging works of the imagination ever produced. Its legendary impenetrability has stopped many readers in their tracks after its initial incomplete sentence: "riverrun, past Eve and Adam's, from swerve of shore to bend of bay, brings us by a commodius vicus of recirculation back to Howth Castle and Environs." It is scant reassurance to learn that the sentence begins nearly 700 pages later, forming an immense, infinite loop. Having exploded most of the accepted novel conventions in *Ulysses,* Joyce proceeds in *Finnegans Wake* with an even more radical narrative and linguistic experiment, designing with infinite care a kind of perpetual story and interpretation generator, a "funferal" and a "colliderorscape" that is in turn maddening, profound, exhilarating, tedious, astonishingly funny, lyrically moving, impenetrable, and ultimately irreducible. It is perhaps the most famous "untranslated" great book in modern literature. For sheer verbal daring it is also unavoidable in a listing of the greatest novels of all time. Advocates have called it "perhaps the single most intentionally crafted literary artifact that our culture has produced" (John Bishop) and "the most revolutionary book" of the 20th century and "what may prove to have been the most influential and liberating" (David Hayman). Others have viewed the novel as a massive exercise in self-indulgence and impossibly arcane erudition—the ultimate expression of the forsaking of the reader's needs for the author's amusement. Joyce's brother Stanislaus called it "drivelling rigmarole" and "the witless wandering of literature before its final extinction." Max Eastman in a famous dismissal equated reading *Finnegans Wake* with chewing gum: "It has some flavor at the start but you soon taste only the motion of your jaws." Perhaps the most encouraging comment for readers contemplating an assault on Mount Finnegan is the reassuring suggestion of Joyce critic Harry Levin, who declares that the prerequisite for the attempt "is not omniscience. It is no more than a curiosity about Joyce's unique methods and some awareness of his particular preoccupations." And the rewards? Levin states that *Finnegans Wake* "is enriched by such large resources of invention and allusion that its total effect is infinite variety." To enter and sustain a visit to Joyce's dream world, the reader must accept a radical reorientation of language and narrative that makes *Finnegans Wake* one of the most challenging and experimental novels ever attempted.

Joyce began *Finnegans Wake* in March 1923, a little more than a year after the publication of *Ulysses.* It began with a series of pastiches and burlesques ("King Roderick O'Conor," "Tristan and Isolde," and "St. Patrick and Druid") that would be incorporated in the novel's long-evolving thematic and structural pattern that was determined only when the novel was published in 1939. Joyce likened the process of finding his way through his dense narrative and linguistic construct to "an engineer boring through a mountain from two sides. If my calculations are correct we shall meet in the middle. If not . . ." Throughout the long composition Joyce was alternately confident and despairing, as he recorded in a letter: "Complications to right of me, complications to left of me, complex on the page before me, perplex in the pen beside me, duplex in the meandering eyes of me, stuplex on the face that reads me. And from time to time I lie back and listen to my hair growing white."

Sections of his novel appeared serially under the title *Work in Progress,* with Joyce keeping the book's eventual title a secret until publication, revealing it only to his wife, Nora. Like *Ulysses,* set on the day of Joyce's first date with his future life companion, *Finnegans Wake* similarly contains an echo of tribute to Nora Barnacle with the Finn in its title a verbal reminder of Finn's Hotel, where Nora was working when Joyce met her. The title's source is a comic Irish-American ballad about Tim Finnegan, a hod carrier who falls off a ladder and is presumed dead. At his wake, the rowdy mourners spill whiskey on him, and he revives. The title, therefore, announces the overall thematic pattern of the novel with its concern with life and death and the cycle of the fall and resurrection. By eliminating the apostrophe, Joyce suggests that Tim

Finnegan is the comic prototype for all mankind's cyclical fall and rise. The word *wake* serves both as a noun denoting a period of mourning for the dead and a verb suggesting rebirth and resurrection. The fusion of opposites is also expressed in the proper name that combines Fin (or end) with Again. Joyce's dense verbal mix has only just begun with its title.

Finnegans Wake commences at the point where *Ulysses* leaves off. Having exhaustively chronicled one of the longest days in literature, Joyce brings *Ulysses* to rest in Molly Bloom's monologue as she drifts toward sleep. With *Finnegans Wake* Joyce enters that dream world. "Having written *Ulysses* about the day," Joyce explained, "I wanted to write this book about the night." To do so, Joyce attempts to replicate, in the words of his confidant Frank Budgen, "the night mind of man, his timeless existence in sleep, his incommunicable experience in dreams." If *Ulysses* records the mind and adventures of man awake, *Finnegans Wake* will deal with the timeless, illogical, nonlinear domain of his subconscious and unconscious nocturnal existence. To do so, he abandons narrative sequence—as Joyce states, "the book has no beginning or end"—or conventional characters. "There are," Joyce explains, "so to say, no individual people in the book—it is as a dream, the style gliding and unreal as is the way in dreams. If one were to speak of a person in the book, it would have to be of an old man, but even his relationship to reality is doubtful." The old man is *Finnegans Wake*'s dreamer, whose identity has been a major source of critical speculation. Suffice to say that in *Finnegans Wake* we enter the psyche of a dreamer whose mental gyrations spin out a world embodying all human history and myth into a "nonday diary" and an "allnights newseryreel." Having perfected in *Ulysses* the stream-of-consciousness technique to replicate human thought, *Finnegans Wake* employs a "stream-of-unconsciousness" technique in which character, time, and space morph, and English itself is reformulated into a fusion of words and phrases from as many as 70 of the world's languages. As in a dream, characters and language have both a literal and a figurative meaning, and Joyce proceeds "two thinks at a time," in a language of "punns and reedles" to form an immense verbal "crossmess parzel" of etymological, associative, and acoustic wordplay. Justifying his dislocations and linguistic inventions, Joyce argues that "They say it's *obscure* . . . It's natural things should not be so clear at night, isn't it now?" and that "One great part of every human existence is passed in a state which cannot be rendered sensible by the use of wideawake language, cutanddry grammar and goahead plot."

If Joyce threads the daylong wanderings of Stephen Dedalus and Leopold Bloom onto the mythical structure of Homer's *Odyssey*, his "trellis" for supporting *Finnegans Wake* is Giambattista Vico's theory of the cyclical pattern of history in which mankind continuously cycles through three ages—the age of gods, the age of heroes, and the age of men—with a *recorso*, a brief period of renewal and regeneration before the cycle is repeated. The Viconian pattern is evident in the novel's four books and its reflections of the stages of history, beginning with the archetypal fall of the everyman and father HCE (Here Comes Everybody/Haveth Childers Everywhere), who takes local shape as the Dublin pubkeeper Humphrey Chimpden Earwicker. This prototypical male figure is paired with an everywoman, Anna Livia Plurabelle, the universal female, identified with Dublin's River Liffey and her initials, ALP. HCE's fall is due to some unnamed obscure crime committed in Dublin's Phoenix Park that reverberates through the entire novel, while the male principle that he embodies appears in many other forms through the course of the night, including Jarl van Hoother, Festy King, Persse O'Reilly, and Mr. Porter. The children of HCE and ALP are male twins and a daughter. Shem the Penman is Joyce's self-parody of the artist and rebel, a "fraid born fraud" who is mocked as the author of "inartistic portraits of himself," "his usylessly unreadable Blue Book of Eccles," and "one continuous present tense integument slowly unfolded all marryvoising moodmoulded cyclewheeling history." His opposite is the industrious, pragmatic, pompous Shaun the Postman (reflecting Joyce's long-suffering dutifully subservient brother Stanislaus), fated to carry messages without grasping their meaning. The twins, in their various manifestations, embody multiple opposite character types—artist and bureaucrat, introvert and extrovert, relativist and dogmatist. Their sister, Issy, is the provocative, divisive female, in contrast to her peacemaking, nurturing mother. Joyce, therefore, cycles through myth and history, as he did in *Ulysses*, through the relationships and conflicts in the life of an archetypal Irish family. In Joyce's version of the collective unconscious, the Earwickers are an aspect of a grand human allegory of archetypes that rings the changes on the themes of death and resurrection, family dynamics, generational conflict, sexual identity, human desire, and the manifold challenge of embodying human experience in language.

Dawn finally arrives after "a long, very long, a dark, very dark, an allburt unend, scarce endurable, and we could add mostly quite various and somewhat stumbletumbling night," and as in *Ulysses*, the final words are given to the novel's female principle, Anna Livia, who wakes her husband, telling him, "You came safe through," and resignedly comments on the "bitter ending" of the human condition, which she captures simply and forcefully: "It's something fails us. First we feel. Then we fall." She then completes her journey seaward and reaches the point that cycles back to the novel's beginning: "We pass through grass behush the bush to. Whish! A gull. Gulls. Far calls. Coming, far! End here. Us then. Finn, again! Take Bussofthlhee, mememormee! Till thousendsthee. Lps. The keys to. Given! A way a lone a last a loved a long the."

Joyce predicted that *Finnegans Wake* would keep the professors busy for centuries, and thus far a seemingly endless flow of interpretive studies has failed to exhaust its riches or find its bottom. In a way, *Finnegans Wake* is so complex that it is the simplest of all novels. It allows us entry at any point, permitting us to read ourselves in its funhouse mirrors. Ultimately it derives its power and importance in dealing so directly, so elementally, with origins and essentials: of language, of storytelling, of dreams, of consciousness itself. It may in fact be an elaborate game, but it is one that we revisit each night when all is possible in the dark.

32

TESS OF THE D'URBERVILLES

(1891)

by Thomas Hardy

The book stands at the center of Hardy's achievement, if not as his greatest then certainly his most characteristic. . . . For in Tess he stakes everything on his sensuous apprehension of a young woman's life, a girl who is at once a simple milkmaid and an archetype of feminine strength. Nothing finally matters in the novel nearly so much as Tess herself: not the other characters, not the philosophic underlay, not the social setting. In her violation, neglect and endurance, Tess comes to seem Hardy's most radical claim for the redemptive power of suffering; she stands, both in the economy of the book and as a figure rising beyond its pages and into common memory, for the unconditional authority of feeling.

—Irving Howe, *Thomas Hardy*

For sheer grandiosity of vision alone, Hardy's *Tess of the D'Urbervilles* is one of the supreme fictions of the 19th century. Hardy is the pivotal link between the methods and concerns of such great Victorians as Dickens, Thackeray, Eliot, and Trollope and modern writers as diverse as Conrad, Kafka, Lawrence, Faulkner, and Gárcia Márquez, the writer who adapted Dickens's theatrical, melodramatic method to embody what is identified in *Tess* as the "ache of modernism." Although both the novels that preceded and followed *Tess*—*The Mayor of Casterbridge* and *Jude the Obscure*—deserve consideration in any ranking of the greatest novels, I have selected *Tess of the D'Urbervilles* as the most powerful and enduring example of Hardy's idiosyncratic and challenging genius as a novelist.

To understand Hardy's fictional approach, one must begin with his avowed role as a storyteller. Through his father and his rural background, Hardy absorbed the rustic, oral storytelling traditions, and his novels resemble ballads, with their emphasis on tragic events arranged in a highly contrived, symmetrical narrative that Hardy, a former church architect, loved. In a Hardy novel dramatic events are not only numerous but exceptional enough to merit the telling. As Hardy observed, "We tale-tellers are all Ancient Mariners, and none of us is warranted in stopping the Wedding Guests (in other words, the hurrying public) unless he has something more unusual to relate than ordinary experiences of every average man and woman." For Hardy, unlike Jane Austen or George Eliot, the value of the novel was not its faithful representation of actuality but its penetration of surface reality to reveal a deeper significance of universal truth. Hardy's fictional formula, therefore, depended upon a blend of surface realism derived from the partly observed, partly imagined Wessex countryside—his equivalent of southwest England—and a series of extraordinary events, relying on coincidence, melodramatic or theatrical staging, and symbolic underscoring to attain a deeper realism. Hardy believed that the aim of art was "to be more truthful than truth. . . . Art is the secret of how to produce by a false thing the effect of a true." The false things in Hardy's fictions—the improbable and melodramatic deviations from the real—provided him with the means to reach certain truths closed by a more restrictive realistic means. For Hardy, "Art is disproportioning—(ie, distorting, throwing out of proportion)—of realities, which if merely copied or reported inventorily, might possibly be overlooked. Hence realism is not Art." The measure to judge Hardy's novels, therefore, is consequently different from that used to evaluate Austen or Eliot. In Hardy's fiction veracity of vision or feeling is more important than fidelity to normative fact. He is more concerned with the violent dislocations of his dramatic contrasts than an eye-deceiving realism of proportion and perspective. The challenge in Hardy's approach to the novel is to extend the sensational, nonrealistic conventions to express not simply thrilling and unusual adventure but emblematic actions: to elevate ordinary experience and to raise the theatrical to the level of the genuine tragic, mythic, and universal.

There is no better expression of Hardy's fictional method than the dramatic collisions and epic magnification of *Tess*, a work of such radical "disproportioning," of such uncomfortable truths, that it effectively ended Hardy's career as a novelist. Begun in 1888, *Tess* was conceived as a full-frontal assault on Victorian hypocrisy regarding sexual matters. Hardy's subject was the fate of a ruined maiden, a popular theme of the English novel from Richardson's *Clarissa* through Scott's *Heart of Midlothian*, Dickens's *David Copperfield*, and Eliot's *Adam Bede*, as well as countless lesser works, which mainly supported the conventional view that once a seduction occurred, death or exile was the end of the matter, a climax to be avoided at all cost. Hardy took an opposite view, arguing for the interest in his heroine *after* her fall, shifting the focus from the heroine's moral corruption to the circumstances that caused her fall and their wider implications. Of humble birth and background but with an innate goodness and a fateful vulnerability, Tess Durbeyfield is compelled by the economic collapse that threatens her family to claim connection with the well-to-do, parvenu D'Urberville family, whose son, Alec, seduces her. Occurring in the first third of the novel, Tess's fall is actually the beginning of her career as a heroine and her interest as a character. Tess is blighted by heredity and environment, betrayed by her lovers, and finally ground down by social laws and conventions through rape, an illegitimate birth, bigamy, and finally murder. Yet, as Hardy asserts in his provocative subtitle, she is a "Pure Woman Faithfully Presented," and the reader is challenged to suspend conventional moral judgments in favor of the greater claims of Tess's suffering, integrity, and humanity. Hardy's defense of Tess is based on the contention that it is not circumstances but an individual's will that determines innocence or purity. Events are loaded against Tess from the start, and fate, as it is suggested through Hardy's theatrical plot, seems to conspire to ruin her. In her struggle against society's unnatural code that condemns her and the human condition that governs her, Tess is raised to the level of the heroic, the mythic, and the universal.

Hardy faced the challenge of gaining an audience for his radical reinterpretation of the ruined-maiden theme, and his novel's censorship would contribute to his abandoning the novel completely, after firing off a final vitriolic attack on Victorian complacency and hypocrisy in *Jude the Obscure*. Unwilling to forgo the lucrative market of serial publication, Hardy submitted his manuscript to two different magazine editors who contended that the book's "improper explicitness" made it unfit for family reading. Hardy eventually provided a bowdlerized, sanitized version to a weekly newspaper, ironically called *The Graphic*, which accepted his story after Hardy had eliminated objectionable material and had rewritten sections in different colored ink so that the original version could be later easily restored. In the serial form, Tess's seduction follows a mock marriage ceremony, and no illegitimate child or its baptism are mentioned. Angel Clare is given a wheelbarrow to transport Tess and her three dairymaid companions across a flooded lane rather than carrying them in his arms. Hardy approached the drudgery of these changes with, in the words of the veiled autobiography nominally written by his wife, "cynical amusement, knowing the novel was moral enough and to spare" despite the required changes. Although complaints continued about the book's indecency, and a bishop consigned the book to the flames, *Tess* was a popular and critical success. The reviewer for the London *Times* declared, "Mr. Hardy's latest novel is his greatest. . . . he has found a story, daring in its treatment of conventional ideas, pathetic in its sadness, and profoundly stirring in its tragic power." Despite such praise, Hardy would eventually seek relief from censorship by abandoning the novel for poetry, bitterly and ironically contending that "If Galileo had said in verse that the world moved, the Inquisition might have let him alone."

In the restored original version published in volume form in 1891, Tess's doom is chronicled with a daring frankness and with her suffering unalloyed. After her baby dies, Tess enjoys a brief respite at a dairy farm where she meets a minister's son, Angel Clare. Tess eventually marries him after her confession of her past by letter slipped under his door before their marriage goes under the carpet unseen. After listening to Angel's confession of the debauchery in his own past, thinking she is likewise forgiven Tess speaks freely of Alec and her dead baby. Angel reacts with horror and abandons his wife. Despite Angel's freethinking opposition to orthodoxy, he is revealed as morally rigid, one who cannot accept the human, fallible Tess over the ideal figure he has created to love. Angel, therefore, harms Tess as much as Alec through his lack of human sympathy. Again on her own, dispossessed from the bower of bliss of the dairy, Tess finds herself in Hardy's version of the rural wasteland, condemned to grinding labor in a countryside devoid of comfort or community. Tess will be again beset by Alec, and in despair of Angel's return to her, finally agrees to live with Alec as his wife. Eventually a contrite Angel does return, and Tess responds by murdering Alec, rejoining Angel for a few days of happiness before the authorities inevitably close in on the couple.

The novel's climactic scene at Stonehenge has been called Hardy's "most ambitious attempt at rendering the world of the action in metaphoric and symbolic terms" (Bert G. Hornback) and as a "grandiose conception . . . somehow blurred" (Walter Allen). That the scene is enacted on a grand scale is unquestionable. In terms of Hardy's use of heightened effects to underscore and intensify his drama, Stonehenge is a suggestive triumph. Beyond the question of probability that these two fugitives should accidentally come upon Stonehenge on their final night together, Hardy's use of this setting seems symbolically appropriate. In a novel obsessed with the past—of past generations and actions—and natural or primitive instincts struggling against social morality, Tess's resting on a pagan altar prior to her societal sacrifice is fitting for the emblematic nature to which her drama has been raised. Yet Tess is not reduced merely to symbolic importance. Her resignation—"It is as it should be. . . . I am ready"—transcends the melodramatic extremes of sentiment and the overly expansive symbolic setting. Her humanity dominates the heavier strains of her implied martyrdom. It is in such a scene as at Stonehenge that Hardy's fiction overpowers suspension of disbelief by the full weight of his conception. At Stonehenge Tess's character is not dwarfed by the monolithic stones or the cosmic symbolism or reduced by the machinations of plot. She has instead found a fit stage for her tragedy to be completed.

Tess is in one sense a victim, ground up by social conventions and economic forces, but the novel is not so easily reducible to a social thesis or a narrow pathetic response. Tess's tragedy goes far beyond a societal explanation or an identifiable moral or legislative cure. She is as much a victim of fate as social conventions. Dorothy Van Ghent has argued that the novel's principal subject is "mythological, for it places the human protagonist in dramatic relationship with the nonhuman and orients his destiny among preternatural powers." This is the effect of the novel's close in which the "President of the Immortals" ends his sport with Tess. In this manner, Hardy attempts a kind of epic magnification of Tess's history, placing her, and by implication the novel, on a much larger, grander stage of mythic and tragic proportions. *Tess* shows Hardy working out a definition of the novel that would become an important legacy for modern fiction with its poetic method of argument through imagery, its symbolic rather than realistic plot, its artful arrangement of significant, vivid action to bring to the surface deep-seated emotional and psychological realities.

Hardy, who had come of age during the High Victorian period dominated by Dickens, Thackeray, and Eliot, lived long enough to watch the production of a film version of *Tess*, his most popular novel. Content as a poet, Hardy observed that "I seldom read novels now, but I understand that today they no longer have plots." He speculated that storytelling might now belong to the filmmakers and that "Perhaps the cinematograph will take the place of fiction, and novels will die out, leaving only poetry." In one sense Hardy was correct, though the marginalization of poetry in our era and, one would suspect, the routinized stories of many of our films would have shocked him. In another sense the synthesis between poetry and story that Hardy found missing in the modern era defines the modern novelist's challenge: how to recapture, like the Ancient Mariner, the hurrying Wedding Guests and grip them with a story that is both profound and captivating, precisely the kind of novels that Hardy crafted.

33

BUDDENBROOKS

(1901)

by Thomas Mann

In his middle years Thomas Mann once likened Buddenbrooks *to a musical instrument he had constructed "in the vigour of youth freely to play on it in his later life." When he said this, he could hardly have known how true it was to become. . . .* Buddenbrooks . . . *contains almost all the elements of vision and thought of which the later works are made. If his play becomes ever more assured, if the pieces are ever more complex and ambitious, the performance is yet rendered on the strings strung across the body of his first novel.*

—Erich Heller, *The Ironic German: A Study of Thomas Mann*

Mann's first novel, one of the masterworks of European realism, published when he was only 26, brought the German novel into the 20th century and established Mann's reputation as a major international literary figure. Mann would later call *Buddenbrooks* the only great naturalist novel in German, and it is certainly true that in it Mann extends the realistic tradition in the German novel, widening the range from the individual to an extended family and community, while exploring the means by which actuality could be blended with the symbolic to force the particular to yield universal significance. In *Buddenbrooks* Mann draws upon the model of the realistic Scandinavian family novel, infusing his narrative with the spirit of European fin de siècle decadence as he chronicles the decline of a North German family. The story of the Buddenbrooks, inspired by Mann's own family history, covers four generations, in which decline manifests itself through a progressive diminution of physical robustness and business acumen, accompanied by increased inwardness and emotional sensitivity. Mann's first novel would set many of the dominant themes for the rest of his career in his preoccupation with decadence, illness, death, and the isolation of the artist in modern culture. It would also feature his characteristic literary technique of the verbal leitmotifs, the device consciously borrowed from Richard Wagner, to establish pervasive themes and characters' salient traits. In emphasizing decline in a work completed at the threshold of a new century, Mann suggests a crisis in the values of the European bourgeoisie, a crisis he treats with delicate irony and a love of telling detail.

Mann was born in the Baltic seaport town of Lübeck into a prosperous merchant family and broke with his background to declare his vocation as a writer. In 1897, Mann, who had previously written only a few stories, was encouraged by his publisher to attempt a more extended work. His original plan was to draw on his own conflict with his family over his ambition as a writer as well as his fascination with the tension between art and ordinary middle-class life. His novel would, therefore, fall into the established German fictional pattern of the bildungsroman, the novel of education and growth, or more specifically the *Künstlerroman*, which deals with the development of the artist. It initially was to treat only the relationship between the artist Hanno Buddenbrooks and his businessman father, Thomas, the third and last of his eventual novel's four generations. However, to tell the story of both fully, Mann widened his focus, placing his own story in an extended context of a family saga whose members are both the product and expression of social and historical forces. Mann also ironically reverses the expected progress of the bildungsroman to document a family's decline. *Buddenbrooks*, therefore, became both an analysis of the writer's own origins and a wider cultural meditation. As the novelist later observed: "I am a town dweller, a citizen, a child and great-grandchild of German bourgeois culture. . . . Were my forefathers not artisans from Nuremburg of that type which Germany exported throughout the world and even to the Far East, as a proof that it was the country of towns? They sat as town councilors in Mecklenburg, they came to Lübeck, they were merchants of the Holy Roman Empire—and by writing the story of their house a *civic* chronicle modulated into a naturalistic novel . . . I proved to be much less removed from their way of life than I allowed myself to imagine."

The essential conflict between bourgeois and artistic values that fascinated Mann remains, but it was shaped into an elaborate multicharacter narrative to comprehend not just personal and local story but a complex, symbolic, universal history. Mann indicated his thematic intention by the novel's subtitle: "*Verfall einer Familie*" ("Decline of a Family"), and in *Buddenbrooks* attempted to identify the social, cultural, and psychological forces that dissolve a representative German family. Their decline is set against the background of Mann's native Lübeck, the novel's unnamed but unmistakable locale, and the evolution of German unity, prosperity, and power from the 1830s to the 1870s.

The novel opens in 1835 with three generations of the Buddenbrook family at a celebratory dinner party in the family's grand new house, symbolic of the prosperity and achievement of patriarch Johann Buddenbrooks, head of a thriving grain firm founded in 1768. Although in his 70s, the patrician Johann is still a robust, uncomplicated, single-minded businessman, sustained by the integrated ideals and tastes of the Enlightenment. He becomes the standard of stability and the measure of decline in the succeeding generations. His son, also named Johann, but called Jean, is described as the first Buddenbrook to possess "other than the normal, every-day sentiments proper to good citizens." For Jean, who is far more sensitive and religious than his father, the family business is a moral burden and a responsibility. His doubts and business scruples are balanced by a greater capacity for artistic enjoyment and a more spiritual introspection. The difference between father and son, between the first and second generation, establishes the novel's core dilemma and cause of the family's decline. Johann, possessing solid German burgher values, through ambition and drive, has produced prosperity and comfort for his descendants, but with greater luxuries and refinements comes a problematic sensitivity and a split between the inner and outer world that results in a slackening of the life force. An artistic sensibility then emerges that is estranged from the bourgeois world and its sustaining values and is instead drawn toward disease and death. Jean is the first indication of this process that accelerates inexorably in the career of Jean's son Thomas and culminates with Thomas's son Hanno.

After the death of his father in 1855, Thomas becomes the head of the firm. As critic Henry Hatfield observes, "Thomas is the most appealing and impressive of the line. Cultivated, able, and enormously conscientious, he guides the family to its greatest successes, but he has no real belief in the value of his enterprises; his energies are eaten away. Despite all his efforts, he cannot overcome the somehow innate tendency to dissolution which has overtaken the family like a sort of fate." This dissolution is represented by the idleness, self-indulgence, and hypochondria of Thomas's brother Christian, and the succession of failed marriages of his sister Tony. As his siblings lose focus and control, Thomas struggles to keep in balance two sides of his temperament, that of the practical businessman and the dreamer, having inherited from his father an introspection from which he derives few benefits other than a painful self-consciousness. "What is success?" Thomas ruefully reflects. "The awareness that alone by virtue of my presence I can exert pressure on the movements of life all around me. . . . luck and success are in us. We must hold on to them, firmly, profoundly. As soon as here inside us something begins to weaken, to grow slack and tired, then everything comes loose all around us, rebels, withdraws from our influence." Thomas is depicted as trapped between his will and his intellect with the conflict manifested in an increasing hatred of life and signs of premature aging and disease. Ultimately, Thomas succumbs to the forces of death and decay that have progressively infected the family, and his end is heralded by a collapse in the street that Mann records with unsentimental accuracy: "He had fallen on his face, from under which a pool of blood at once began to spread out. His hat rolled down a way on the road. His fur coat was spattered with filth and melting snow. His hands, in their white kid gloves, lay outstretched in a puddle."

The final stage of the family's disintegration is chronicled in the experiences of Thomas's son Hanno, a talented musician with a full-blown artistic temperament of painful hypersensitivity that ill-equips him for involvement in the world. Hanno is described as "afraid of life" and never "disturbed by breakings-up, closings, endings, disintegration." Shown as a student in a rigid school devoted exclusively to the scientific and practical, Hanno is stifled and retreats inwardly, unable to break through into any active engagement with life. Instead he succumbs to a death wish that seems as responsible for his demise as the typhoid fever that kills him at age 15. With Thomas's death the family business is sold; with Hanno's end the family itself is extinguished, and Mann records a decadent process with far-reaching implications on European culture. *Buddenbrooks* traces the fatal dynamic of a mercantile, materialistic ethos lacking in self-knowledge or any sense of deeper values beyond the practical. It is pitted against a problematic spirituality and aestheticism cut off from the vital resources to sustain an inward-directed life. The Buddenbrooks, therefore, represent a fatal split in European society in which the practical and the artistic are inimical with each tendency lacking needed elements from the other.

Mann's remarkable achievement in *Buddenbrooks* is his ability to turn a family history into an exploration of a profound cultural and psychological crisis. Sustained by a minute fidelity to the surface details of commonplace life that makes it one of the high points of the realistic novel, *Buddenbrooks* simultaneously reaches a depth that refashions a family saga into a sustained criticism of life and the human condition. As critic Martin Swales argues, "*Buddenbrooks* is a supreme example of how novelistic strategies of inwardness, thoughtfulness, and reflectiveness can coexist with a realistic allegiance to the social and institutional substantiality of a specific historical world. It is a novel that fuses inwardness and outwardness; it makes the inner expressive of realistic concerns, and it makes realistic concerns not just outwardly accurate but also inwardly truthful insofar as they are shown to be inseparable from the abundantly portrayed psychological and mental life of the characters." Writing in Italy of his northern German hometown and background and the bourgeois cultural values he rejected for an artistic career, Mann held both the practical and the introspective in a creative balance that neither Thomas nor Hanno Buddenbrooks are able to achieve. Mann's first extensive diagnosis of this European cultural dilemma established his essential themes for the remainder of his distinguished career in the opposing tendencies that hurtle his protagonists between intellect and passion, engagement and detachment, citizenship and art. *Buddenbrooks* is the first expression of Mann's mastery in capturing with exquisite irony and fidelity the conflicting forces in human behavior and thought that give life its fullest meaning and at the same time constitute its greatest peril.

34

INVISIBLE MAN

(1952)

by Ralph Ellison

Invisible Man *has as much claim to being that mythical, unattainable dream of American literature, the "great American novel," as any book in our literature.*

—Jonathan Yardley, "30 Years on the 'Raft of Hope,'"
Washington Post, April 1982

Ralph Ellison's only completed novel, *Invisible Man*, is one of the landmark texts by an American writer in the 20th century. The literary critic Frederick Karl has called it an achievement that "needs no second act" and "a touchstone of the 1950s," while a *Book Week* poll of prominent authors, critics, and editors conducted in 1965 ranked *Invisible Man* "the most distinguished single work" published in the previous two decades. Judged by F. W. Dupee "the veritable *Moby-Dick* of the racial crisis," *Invisible Man* has entered the canon of American and world literature, as Saul Bellow observed in 1995, as a book that "holds its own among the best novels of the century."

Critics continue to debate the degree to which *Invisible Man* is a universal or racial expression and the implications of the novel's lessons in democracy, identity, and history. What is unquestionable is that for the first time in literature Ellison illuminated the African-American experience with the sophistication, density, and daring of the modernist masters, such as T. S. Eliot, William Faulkner, and James Joyce, whom he admired. By suffusing his narrative with the American vernacular, Ellison also created something uniquely his own, refracting African-American experience into a groundbreaking and influential prose equivalent in his themes and structure of two of America's greatest cultural contributions: the blues and jazz. As his friend the novelist Albert Murray explained, *Invisible Man* represents "par excellence the literary extension of the blues. It was as if Ellison had taken an everyday twelve bar blues tune (by a man from down South sitting in a manhole up North in New York signifying about how he got there) and scored it for full orchestra." In this sense Ellison should be compared with the American musical geniuses Louis Armstrong and Duke Ellington, whose works and methods echo throughout his novel, as a similar artistic originator, synthesizer, and liberator. *Invisible Man* is equally one of the most profound meditations on what it means to be an American and one of the great artistic battles to contain identity, consciousness, and the complexity of the American experience in a radical new form consistent with the novelist's mission that Ellison embraced. As the writer remarked in a 1955 interview:

> I feel that with my decision to devote myself to the novel I took on one of the responsibilities inherited by those who practice the craft in the United States: that of describing for all that fragment of the huge diverse American experience which I know best, and which offers me the possibility of contributing not only to the growth of literature but to the shaping of the culture as I should like it to be. The American novel is in this sense a conquest of the frontier; as it describes our experience, it creates it.

According to Ellison, the conception for his novel came to him in the summer of 1945 while on sick leave from the merchant marine, recovering from a kidney infection at a friend's Vermont farm, while "reading *The Hero* by Lord Raglan and speculating on the nature of Negro leadership in the United States." Ellison recalled that "creatures from Afro-American fables—Jack-the-Rabbit and Jack-the-Bear—blended in my mind with figures of myth and history," and "images of incest and murder, dissolution and rebirth whirled in my head," when he suddenly typed "I am an invisible man," the novel's opening line, "and I gasped at the range of implication." The novel, finally published in 1952, would take him the next five years to complete. As Ellison summarized his challenge and intention in his introduction to the novel's 30th anniversary edition, "I knew that I was composing a work of fiction, a work of literary art and one that would allow me to take advantage of the novel's capacity for telling the truth while actually telling a 'lie,' which is the Afro-American folk term for an improvised story. . . . I knew that I could draw upon the rich culture of the folk tale as well as that of the novel, and that being uncertain of my skill I would have to improvise upon my material in the manner of a jazz musician putting a musical theme through a wild star-burst of metamorphosis. By the time I realized that the words of the Prologue contained the germ of the ending as well as that of the beginning, I was free to enjoy the surprises of incident and character as they popped into view."

Framed by its prologue and epilogue of Ellison's nameless protagonist who has retreated to his basement room illuminated by 1,369 lightbulbs, *Invisible Man* traces the theme of selfhood and invisibility through his central character's recollections from boyhood, through college, exile to New York City, infatuation and ultimately betrayal by the manipulative Brotherhood, to eventual insights into the meaning of his racial, national, and personal identity. The stages of *Invisible Man*'s development proceed through a series of reversals dramatized by surrealistic dislocations and symbolically haunting imagery. There is simply no greater dramatic scene in modern fiction than the "Battle Royal" that initiates the protagonist's career. He is asked to deliver his high school valedictory address on racial deference at a smoker attended by white community leaders but must first participate with nine other young black men, all blindfolded, in combat with one another. They are rewarded in a scramble for coins on an electrified rug. This chilling, expressionistic scene forecasts much of the novel and crystallizes black experience into rich symbolism while initiating Invisible Man's discovery of his invisibility. Armed with a college scholarship in his presentation briefcase that will bear the totems of his encounters with the wider world that refuses to see him beyond its own projections and manipulative needs, Invisible Man will be tested into self-knowledge and awareness. "It's a novel about innocence and human error," Ellison remarked, "a struggle through illusion to reality." Invisible Man is initially disturbed and puzzled by his grandfather's deathbed advice, so different from the humility and deference his grandson initially accepts as the means for success: "Live with your head in the lion's mouth. I want you to overcome 'em with yeses, undermine 'em with grins, agree 'em to death and destruction, let 'em swoller you till they vomit or bust wide open." This riddle—how *yes* can become *no* and vice versa—will not be finally solved until the novel's conclusion in which the novel's protagonist has learned the lesson of his invisibility, its consequences and responsibilities.

At college, modeled on Ellison's own alma mater, Tuskegee Institute, the naively earnest Invisible Man is initially eager to succeed by endorsing the school's mission of racial accommodation. However, he is expelled after he accidentally exposes a white trustee, Mr. Norton, to a lowly sharecropper, Trueblood, who captivates the white man with the heartrending story of his incestuous relations with his daughter, and takes Norton to recover at the Golden Day, a saloon-brothel frequented by black veterans on an outing from their asylum. Allowing an unflattering view of black experience, Invisible Man has committed an unpardonable error, according to the school's manipulative president, Dr. Bledsoe, who declares that "the only way to please a white man is to tell him a lie!" Black power and success are reached, according to Bledsoe, by subterfuge and illusion: by wearing a mask and letting whites see only what they think they want to see. Dispatched to New York to expiate his crime, Invisible Man is given a stack of introductory letters to help him find work that eventually are discovered to be the equivalent of his grandfather's interpretation of the testimonial he carries in his briefcase: "To Whom It May Concern . . . Keep This Nigger-Boy Running."

Invisible Man's experiences in New York include work for the Liberty Paint factory, mixing in black drops to make its white paint whiter ("If It's

Optic White, It's the Right White"), confinement at the factory's hospital, and identity reprogramming until finally discharged back to Harlem. Through his oracular skills Invisible Man comes to the attention of the white-controlled Brotherhood who provide him with a new identity and occupation as "chief spokesman of the Harlem District" for their radical cause. Eventually Invisible Man learns that despite the Brotherhood's rhetoric of equality and social justice, the group is as manipulative and unwilling to grant the autonomy of blacks as the community leaders at the smoker. Neither radical politics, black nationalism as represented by the rabble-rouser Ras the Exhorter, nor the shapeshifting hipster Rinehart and his "vast seething, hot world of fluidity" provide Invisible Man with a workable solution for his dilemma to define himself and his responsibilities, though all help to define his challenge. Others he encounters—Trueblood, Wheatstraw, Mary Rambo, Brother Tarp, and Tod Clifton—offer alternatives in transcendence and survival that echo the insight of the veteran he meets on the bus north: "Play the game, but don't believe in it . . . Learn how it operates, learn how *you* operate. . . . The world is possibility if only you'll discover it." As Harlem explodes into riot in one of the novel's most impressive expressionistic scenes, Invisible Man is betrayed yet again. The betrayal forces him underground where the act of recalling his experiences leads to the novel's final illumination.

Ultimately, by accepting his invisibility, Invisible Man asserts control of his destiny. Invisibility offers possibilities, a liberating nullity upon which identity can be creatively fashioned. As Invisible Man gradually understands, "When I discover who I am, I'll be free." Through confronting the challenge of his invisibility, he can penetrate to the core of the American experience in which the delineation of identity is the central cultural imperative. He also approaches the full implication of his grandfather's deathbed advice "to overcome 'em with yeses": Take America at its word. By affirming the principles of American democracy, despite all the evidence to the contrary, the individual can validate and vindicate his humanity and begin to give shape and purpose to his identity.

Few novels have more powerfully exposed the essential American problem of identity and democracy as *Invisible Man.* Richard Wright asserted that the Negro is "America's metaphor," and Ellison, his former protégé, has applied it expertly. As Ellison conceived it, his novel framed the essential questions: "Who am I, what am I, how did I come to be? What should I make of the life around me? . . . What does American society mean when regarded out of my *own* eyes, when informed by my *own* sense of the past and viewed by my *own* complex sense of the present?" Ellison's answers in *Invisible Man* reach far beyond protest, victimhood, and sociology through its aspirations and achievement to the universals implied in the novel's concluding sentence: "Who knows but that, on the lower frequencies, I speak for you?"

35

THE MAN WITHOUT QUALITIES

(1930–43)

by Robert Musil

No other work of literature goes farther in laying bare for its readers the moral dilemmas of life in western civilization of the twentieth century. No other novel makes its readers aware to the same extent of these moral conflicts within themselves.

—Burton Pike, *Robert Musil: An Introduction to His Work*

Robert Musil's *The Man without Qualities*, unfinished at nearly 1,800 pages, has been called "the supreme example in Western literature of the novel of ideas" and a "compendium of contemporary uncertainty." Formidable as it is in length and complexity, uncertain as it remains regarding its author's ultimate intentions, *The Man without Qualities* is as much of a landmark in modern thought and artistic conception as *Ulysses*, *In Search of Lost Time*, and *The Magic Mountain*, entitling Musil to comparison with the very greatest of literary artists. Like Joyce, Musil attempted a massive reconstruction of experience with a mythic substructure; like Proust, Musil offered a colossal repossession not of the past but the present. Finally, like Mann, Musil arranged his novel against the backdrop of the breakdown of contemporary values into a dialectical clash of ideas to reach a new synthesis and understanding. *The Man without Qualities*, like all of these modernist masterworks and such predecessors as Tolstoy's *War and Peace*, tests the limits of the novel to contain the widest possible perception of experience and the moral, philosophical, and psychological currents underlying human action. Like Tolstoy, Musil blurred the distinction between fiction and essay, novel and philosophy, creating a new narrative hybrid. There are few novels better at diagnosing the breakdown of beliefs and values in the modern world or as intriguing in their search for a way out of the morass of doubt and despair.

Monumental is by far the best descriptor of Musil's remarkable fictional exploration of the modern landscape. The Austrian author struggled for nearly two decades to control his ever-expanding fictional universe, completing only about half of what he intended his novel to become. In 1920, the project had the title *Der Spion (The Spy)*, later changed to *Der Erlöser* (The Redeemer) and *Die Zwillinsschwester (The Twin Sister)*. Each title reflected themes, character, and plot developments eventually fused in a proliferating, all-encompassing structure in pursuit of an elusive unity. By 1927 Musil arrived at the final title, *Der Mann ohne Eigenschaften (The Man without Qualities)* and a multi-part plan for the novel. The first two sections were published in 1930 and a second volume appeared in 1933. A perfectionist and continual reviser, Musil wrestled with his ungainly manuscript through the rise of the Nazis, which cost him financial support in the demise of his German-Jewish publisher. Musil was exiled from Vienna to Switzerland when Hitler annexed Austria, and he died in Switzerland in near destitution in 1942, having finished only a couple dozen more chapters since 1933. Although it is impossible to ascertain how Musil would have resolved and concluded the many strands of his enormous project, he left tantalizing clues, as the recent English translation of the novel by Sophie Wilkins and Burton Pike with its 600 pages of drafts and fragments shows. Destined to retain its fractured, open-ended form, *The Man without Qualities* still commands attention for what Musil managed to accomplish: one of the novel's most ambitious experiments in fully capturing not only an era but the multifarious complexity of modern life and thought in which such crucial concepts as self, beauty, and love are deconstructed and reformulated in ways never before attempted by a novelist.

An encyclopedic panorama of fin-de-siècle Vienna, *The Man without Qualities* is set during the 12 months leading up to August 1914. As in Thomas Mann's *The Magic Mountain*, the cataclysm of war is the inevitable, ironic conclusion for Musil's contemplation of a society on the brink. Again, like Mann, Musil diagnoses the ailments of European life via an observer protagonist pulled out of his routine to allow a consideration of essentials. The reader is initially thrust into the maelstrom of city life, Musil's metaphor for the fragmentation and disunity the novel will expose and attempt to answer: "Like all big cities it was made of irregularity, change, forward spurts, failures to keep step, collisions of objects and interests, punctuated by unfathomable silences; made up of pathways and untrodden ways, of one great rhythmic beat as well as the chronic discord and mutual displacement of all its contending rhythms. All in all, it was like a boiling bubble inside a pot made of durable stuff of buildings, laws, regulations, and historical traditions." Observing the traffic and pedestrians outside his window, stopwatch in hand, "gauging their speeds, their angles, all the living forces of mass hurtling past," is Ulrich, the man without qualities and the novel's central consciousness. Ulrich is an intensely introspective veteran of three careers—army, engineering, and mathematics—who at the age of 32 has found no sustaining belief and cannot commit to any clear course of action. Instead he takes a "leave from life" to choose how he may most effectively live. Ulrich represents Musil's prototypical modern man: disengaged, adrift, paralyzed by doubt, unable to bridge the gap between thought and action or to make the disparate parts of experience fit into a sustaining unity. His dilemma is symptomatic of what Ulrich later diagnoses as the modern malaise: "There is no longer a whole man confronting a whole world but a human something floating about in a universal culture-medium." Ulrich's existence has been defined for him externally, by the social role he is given, by his environment, by others' expectations and demands, leaving his core a blank and a void. Ulrich is, therefore, a man not without talent or characteristics but without a primary, self-defining essence. "Nothing is stable for him. Everything is fluctuating," his friend Walter, who names him a man without qualities, observes, "a part of a whole, among innumerable wholes that are presumably part of a super-whole, which, however, he doesn't know the slightest thing about. So every one of his answers is a part-answer, every one of his feelings only a point of view, and whatever a thing is, it doesn't matter to him what it is, it's only some accompanying 'way in which it is,' some addition or other, that matters to him." However, it is Ulrich's very impersonality, his lack of a fixed character and certainties, that equips him well in Musil's view as the skeptical tester of essential values that can form the basis for a redeemed private and public life. Ulrich's ensuing search for answers becomes a journey of social satire and self-awareness, revealing the inadequacy of tradition and conventions, as well as the social and psychological causes of the debacle to come. The novel largely replaces dramatic action with the states of mind and emotions of characters forced to make sense of their world. Fragmented and limited, all of Musil's characters fall short of the integration and unity that the book strives to provide in its massive criticism of life.

Ulrich's internal quest for redefinition and renewal is initially sidetracked by his being recruited to participate in the "Parallelaktion," or Parallel Campaign, in which a group of prominent citizens meet to determine how best to celebrate the 70th anniversary of the Austrian emperor's rule in 1918, an occasion calling for consensus on a society's achievement and values. This becomes the opportunity for Musil's ironic critique of contemporary political and social life, as well as an expansion of his theme of the breakdown of private life and the loss of national and social identities. The group's endless contradictory wrangling, given the futility that history will deal it, inspires some of Musil's most brilliant satire as well as his creation of a vivid gallery of contemporary character types and animating scenes, variations linked by analogy and contrast to display Musil's multiple themes of the chaotic and corrupting nature of modern life and inadequate personal responses. Characters include revolutionary socialists as well as aristocrats trumpeting a return to "true" feudalism, the complacent and sinister industrialist Arnheim, the altruist Feurermaul, the mentally unstable Nietzschean Clarisse, and the sex murderer Moosbrugger, whose irrational violence becomes one of the novel's central tests of the characters' responses to questions of human nature and social responsibility.

Eventually, Ulrich realizes that the Parallel Campaign has failed, that there can be no way to resolve its cacophony of contradictory ideas, and the novel turns inward for solutions to Ulrich's disengagement and dissatisfaction. Feeling his loneliness "ever thicker or ever larger," Ulrich experiences a crisis that is heightened by the sudden news of his father's death. Reunited with his younger sister, Agathe, after five years at his father's funeral, Ulrich is shocked into a sympathetic identification with her: "He felt that it was he himself who had come in through the door and was he walking up to him. . . . For the first time the thought seized him that his sister was a dream-like repetition and alternation of himself." Both view each other as two halves of a fractured whole, and Ulrich accepts his sister's proposal that they form a "utopia of the Siamese twins." Ulrich's passion for his sister, expressed as a variation of the myth of Isis and Osiris, becomes the impetus to compel him into taking action, breaking down his isolation, and opening up a previously untapped emotional life. As rich as *The Man without Qualities* has been up to this point in psychological exploration and social satire, the novel here shifts gear to become one of the great modern explorations of passion. It is interesting that like another great 20th-century novel of passion, Nabokov's *Lolita*, *The Man without Qualities* follows desire from a taboo source: pedophilia and incest. Ulrich's search for solutions to his and his society's dilemma turns increasingly toward mysticism and the completion possible through love to bind the disjunction between the self and the world.

The novel breaks off with the outcome of Ulrich's utopian plan in doubt but with the clear suggestion that historical events will eventually triumph, destroying any possibility for a separate, private solution. Ulrich's fate is fundamentally beyond his control, and Musil has identified in his novel as powerfully as any novelist has ever done the testing ground of modern identity. If the narrative impetus finally is slowed by thinly disguised essays or is stalled in a tangle of alternate directions that frustrates a desire for closure, *The Man without Qualities* still exerts considerable power to evoke at the highest level a view of modern experience that resists simplification. It offers instead a novelistic structure and meditation consonant with Musil's diagnosis of a fractured modern world. Like the efforts of the romantic visionary William Blake in his epic and prophetic works, Musil's novel offers a program for revitalization and rebirth based on a challenge of the reader's perception of the world and an imaginative transcendence of the most intractable of limitations, including thought and action, reason and emotion, subject and object, past and present. If ultimately Musil's questions are more compelling than any answers he reached, *The Man without Qualities* remains one of the most ambitious and intriguing attempts to locate key truths about human nature and existence ever undertaken by a novelist.

36

A PORTRAIT OF THE ARTIST AS A YOUNG MAN

(1916)

by James Joyce

There once was a lounger named Stephen
Whose youth was odd and uneven
He throve on the smell
Of a horrible hell
That a Hottentot wouldn't believe in.

—James Joyce in a letter to Ezra Pound, April 9, 1917

"At the age of twenty-one," Joyce's biographer Richard Ellmann astutely observed about the origins and impact of *A Portrait of the Artist as a Young Man*, "Joyce had found he could become an artist by writing about the process of becoming an artist." The shape and texture of the modern novel and the literary revolution that Joyce would help to initiate are clearly glimpsed in his interpretation of one of the novel's most traditional subjects—the story of a youth's education and development. Literary critic Harry Levin has argued that "The history of the realistic novel shows that fiction tends toward autobiography," that "the increasing demands for social and psychological detail that are made upon the novelist can only be satisfied out of his own experience." Joyce responded by transforming the bildungsroman (or more precisely the *Künstlerroman*, the story of the formation of an artist), previously attempted by such novelists as Goethe in *Wilhelm Meister*, Dickens in *David Copperfield*, Flaubert in *The Sentimental Education*, and Samuel Butler in *The Way of All Flesh*, with an experimental daring, concentration, and symbolic density that make other versions seem shallow and stale by comparison. In its focus on the formation of consciousness and identity, in its fusion of the realistic and the symbolic, and in its grafting of the subjective expressiveness of the lyric and the compressed economy of the short story onto the longer narrative form, *Portrait* is in many ways the prototypical modern novel.

Joyce's decadelong labor on a fictional version of the development of an Irish renegade artist in *Portrait* reflects the critical stages of his evolution as a novelist. The first version of his self-portrait, written on a single day in January 1904, was the narrative essay, "A Portrait of the Artist," which anticipated both Joyce's eventual intention—to capture the stages of an artist's development from infancy—and his method of recreating the past as a "fluid succession of presents." Joyce incorporated several of the epiphanies or fragmentary revelatory incidents he had collected to dramatize his version of the artist's evolving sensibility from religious zeal, through sexual awareness, to secular celebration, as well as the artist's necessary liberation from the constraints of homeland, church, and family. The essay was rejected by the Dublin magazine editor who had first commissioned it with the justification that "I can't print what I can't understand." Responding to this rejection, Joyce on his birthday (February 2, 1904), in the words of his brother Stanislaus, "decided to turn his paper into a novel. . . . It is to be almost autobiographical, and naturally as it comes from Jim, satirical. He is putting a large number of his acquaintances into it, and those Jesuits he has known." Joyce set out to record in naturalistic detail his life up to his accepting his artistic vocation and exile from Ireland. Portions shared with the Irish writer and editor George Russell led to an invitation to write a short story for the *Irish Homestead.* This resulted in Joyce's beginning the groundbreaking sequence of stories that became *Dubliners* and the refinement of Joyce's epiphanic and symbolic methods, the essential components of his future novels. Called *Stephen Hero,* the manuscript grew by 1906 to 914 pages, about half its proposed length. The 383 pages that survive, rescued by Joyce's sister Eileen after the author had thrown the manuscript into a fire, are longer than the final published version and cover what would be eventually reduced to the final 80 pages of *Portrait.* The cuts and the radical contraction of his autobiographical material are a result of Joyce's decision in 1907, after finishing "The Dead," the final story of *Dubliners,* to rewrite *Stephen Hero* completely "in five chapters—long chapters." Serialized in *The Egoist* from 1914 to 1915, *Portrait* was finally published in America in 1916 and in England in 1917, after it had been rejected by every London publisher to whom it was submitted and printers refused to take the job when *The Egoist* attempted to publish it in book form.

With an emphasis on selection, compression, and intensity, in its final version Joyce pared the episodic, naturalistic *Stephen Hero* down to the essential, intimate stages of his surrogate Stephen Dedalus's developing consciousness. Transitions and authorial comment were eliminated. Fully elaborated supporting characters recede from the stage, and clarifying dramatic incidents serve only as a shadowy backdrop or sounding board for Stephen's internalized drama. Compared to the characterized members of the Dedalus family in *Stephen Hero,* for example, in the reshaped *Portrait* Stephen is not even clear on the exact number of his siblings, and his love, Emma Clery, has been reduced to initials only and the occasion for a poem and a later resentment over a perceived slight. Joyce filters all through Stephen's consciousness, which processes events past and present into a network of significance through association. As Harry Levin has observed, in the revised *Portrait* "Drama has retired before soliloquy." Although Joyce sacrificed a richness of background, he gained a closeness of focus that directly reproduces the internal dynamic of Stephen's identity and the pressures that shape his consciousness in ways that had never previously been attempted in a novel. In place of a conventional narrative unity, Joyce establishes a poetic, cinematic logic in which the reader must be alert to recurrent images, parallels, and juxtapositions that elucidate the stages of Stephen's emotional, intellectual, and artistic evolution.

Stephen's development from infancy through childhood, adolescence, and maturity is organized into five chapters, made up of a series of episodes, each an epiphany illuminating a significant step in Stephen's education and gestation as an artist. The novel begins with a brilliant, fuguelike overture recording Stephen's earliest recollections and infant capacities. Differentiating reality only very broadly through his senses, Stephen can distinguish between his mother and father by touch and smell. As an incipient artist he responds to his father's stories, to the power of language, and expresses his first creativity in song and dance. However, when he declares that he will become a father himself by marrying the girl next door, Stephen is ordered to apologize under threat of eagles who will pull out his eyes. The scene closes with Stephen's first poem and a symbolic summary of much of the novel in miniature: Stephen in defensive hiding against vengeful authority, representative of the various father figures—his own father, the Jesuit fathers, and his fatherland—that he must eventually overcome.

Each of the subsequent stages of Stephen's education is characterized by a different school. In the first chapter, Stephen is a boarder at the prestigious Clongowes Wood, in which the sensitive boy endures bullying and the school routine while attempting to make sense of the baffling larger world. The novel's first great dramatic scene—the Christmas dinner dispute that splits his family over whether the church was right or wrong in deserting the Irish nationalist leader Parnell—becomes a crucial lesson for Stephen in his own testing of authority that culminates in his first rebellion, in which he stands up to the undeserved "pandying" by Father Dolan.

In Chapter 2, Stephen's short-lived triumph of self-assertion is undercut by a financial decline that takes the Dedaluses from the respectable suburbs to grim Dublin and Stephen's next school at Belvedere. Stephen struggles to maintain his independence and to achieve his dreams of beauty and fulfillment against increasingly squalid family conditions and pressures to submit to the conventional beliefs of his schoolmates and the Jesuit fathers, culminating in his second major rebellion: his carnal sin with a prostitute that ends the chapter. Representing the final assault on Stephen by the forces of authority, Chapter 3 takes the form of a hellfire-and-brimstone sermon that produces in Stephen a temporary repentance and mortification of the senses. Chapter 4 leads to the novel's climax, Stephen's epiphany on Dollymount Strand, in which he accepts his vocation as an artist: "He would create proudly out of the freedom and power of his soul, as the great artificer whose name he bore, a living thing, new and soaring and beautiful, impalpable, imperishable." Stephen embraces not the cold certainty of religious faith or conformity before an intractable Irish reality but the call to create permanent beauty out of the sensual world that surrounds him: "To live, to err, to fall, to triumph, to recreate life out of life!"

Chapter 5, Stephen's undergraduate education, the longest section of the book, shows his preparation for his artistic life and exile by formulating the aesthetic theories that will sustain him and the nets of family, friends, church, and homeland that continue to exert their pull on his independence. In this section, the reader's sympathy toward Stephen is most severely tested. Unwilling to make any concessions that might humanize him, priggish and pedantic, Stephen gathers strength for his flight into exile, but the novel offers little confirmation of Stephen's gifts beyond his assertions of artistic integrity and a collection of aesthetic declarations.

To assess Stephen's final progress, it is essential to remember Joyce's qualifying phrase in his title: "as a Young Man," which suggests that Stephen has still a long way to go to become a mature artist. The degree to which Joyce meant Stephen to be viewed ironically is one of the central critical debates over the novel. Clearly the reader is meant to sympathize with Stephen's facing down the obstacles that stand in his way, but throughout the book his triumphs are quickly deflated, with Stephen's rhapsodic assertions the only evidence of his artistry. Joyce himself confessed to being "extremely hard on that young man. . . . I haven't let this young man off very lightly, have I? Many writers have written about themselves. I wonder if any of them has been as candid as I have." As the novel concludes in Stephen's diary fragments on the verge of his departure from Ireland, he is given a final, famous, lyrical exultation: "Welcome, O life! I go to encounter for the millionth time the reality of experience and to forge in the smithy of my soul the uncreated conscience of my race." However, Joyce was not yet done with his young artist. Stephen is next seen back in Ireland from his short-lived Parisian exile to refight his previous struggles and to encounter a new surrogate father: the cuckolded Irish Jew, Leopold Bloom, in *Ulysses*. Joyce had shifted, as Stephen's aesthetic theory forecast, from the lyrical mode of *Portrait* to the epical and dramatic mode of *Ulysses* and the ultimate confirmation of the artistic process that he began in *Portrait*.

MOLLOY, MALONE DIES, THE UNNAMABLE

37

(1951–53)

by Samuel Beckett

We may say that the discovery that freed Beckett to write his major fiction was the discovery, about 1945, of the first person; as simple as that, but no first-person novels before had so fully exploited the uncertainties of someone remembering, distorting, narrating.

—Hugh Kenner, *A Reader's Guide to Samuel Beckett*

Beckett's artistic turning point came in 1946 while on a visit to see his mother in the Dublin suburb of Foxrock. Following the war and his experience with the French Resistance that involved his escape from imminent arrest by the Nazis into the French countryside where he subsisted as a farm laborer, Beckett was struggling to restart his interrupted and stalled literary career. He would later transfer the epiphany that gave him a new subject and method to the more dramatic setting of the pier in Dún Laoghaire on a stormy night in *Krapp's Last Tape:*

> Spiritually a year of profound gloom and indigence until that memorable night in March, at the end of the jetty, in the howling wind, never to be forgotten, when suddenly I saw the whole thing. The vision at last. . . . What I suddenly saw then was this . . . that the dark I have always struggled to keep under is in reality my most. . . .

Krapp's revelation breaks off, but Beckett completed his sentence, saying that the "dark I have always struggled to keep under" was "my most precious ally." To mine those inner recesses, Beckett reversed the centrifugal direction of most novelists to bring the world under control for the centripetal, of reduction down to essentials, completing the process begun by Knut Hamsun in *Hunger* and by Kafka to make consciousness itself the novel's center. Beckett, who had assisted fellow Dubliner James Joyce in the proliferating *Finnegans Wake*, would reverse the method of his mentor. "I realized that Joyce had gone as far as one could in the direction of knowing more, in control of one's material,"

Beckett would observe. "He was always adding to it; you only have to look at his proofs to see that. I realized that my own way was in impoverishment, in lack of knowledge and in taking away, in subtracting rather than in adding."

This realization required a means of presentation that Beckett found in the dramatic monologue and composition in French, which he found "easier to write without style." Restricted to a voice and its consciousness, Beckett eliminated the conventional requirements of the novel, such as specificity of time and place, elaborate background for characters, and a complex sequence of causes and effects to form a plot. As the Beckett biographer James Knowlson summarizes, Beckett's insight meant that he would "draw henceforward on his own inner world for his subjects; outside reality would be refracted through the filter of his own imagination; inner desires and needs would be allowed a much greater freedom of expression; rational contradictions would be allowed in; and the imagination would be allowed to create alternative worlds to those of conventional reality." Beckett would find the way to bypass the particular to deal directly with the universal. His fiction would not be social or psychological but ontological, treating, as no writer had done before, existence in terms of essence.

Beckett's epiphany resulted in "a frenzy of writing" that produced between 1946 and 1950 four *nouvelles*, or stories, two plays (including *Waiting for Godot*), and four novels that would establish Beckett as one of the leading forces in modern drama *and* fiction. "I wrote all my work very fast—between 1946 and 1950," he later recalled. "Since then I haven't written anything. Or at least nothing that has seemed to me valid." Beckett's greatest achievement as a novelist is the trilogy that began with *Molloy*, which Beckett began to write in 1947 and finished in 1948. *Malone Dies* followed, and *The Unnamable* concludes the sequence, written in 1949 after Beckett completed *Waiting for Godot*. "Malone came from Molloy and the Unnamable from Malone," Beckett observed, and the trilogy can be viewed as variations on the prototypical Beckett preoccupations of exile, alienation, and the impossibility of language, thought, and action ever to arrive at meaning.

Molloy divides into two sections that reflect each other. Molloy narrates his futile quest to find his mother, first by bicycle, then on crutches, and finally crawling through a series of bizarre encounters. He eventually finds himself in his mother's bed, rescued by unknown forces. The second monologue is that of Moran, who has been dispatched to locate Molloy. Moran eventually shares so many of the same experiences as Molloy that he may in fact be an aspect of the other, ending up similarly motionless, his mission a failure. In *Malone Dies* the terminus for both Molloy and Moran, their beds, is the locus for Malone's final reflections as he awaits his death: "It is in the tranquility of decomposition that I remember the long confused emotion that was my life." Malone writes to relieve his misery and boredom, inventing stories of a boy named Saposcat, of a Jew who tries to teach a parrot

Latin, of the itinerant Macmann, frustrated efforts in self-understanding that are Malone's only option as he is compelled to compose his stories and his life. Moving progressively inward, from story to storyteller, from *Molloy* to *Malone Dies*, *The Unnamable* features a disembodied persona, a voice, morphing into such characters as Mahood, Basil, and Worm but ultimately reflecting the boundaries and dictates of human consciousness itself. The pattern in the trilogy reveals itself as soliloquies in which Beckett explores language, existence, and consciousness itself.

In *Molloy* both Molloy and Moran recite their present states and their present possibilities. Both describe the ambivalence and the angst resulting from what one can and cannot know, see, and do with the mind's obsession for analysis, reduction, and classification. In describing his mind, Molloy remarks, "In forever reminding me thus of my duty was its purpose to show me the folly of it?" To the mind the world presents itself in a limited number of ways. "It is midnight," Moran observes. "The rain is beating on the windows. It was not midnight. It was not raining." The mind's ability to finalize these possibilities leaves little else to occupy it once the job is completed. In *Molloy* there is also no satisfaction in making sense of the senseless. Molloy's joy is "to speak of the things that are left . . . to fill in the holes of words till all is blank and flat and the whole ghastly business looks like what it is, senseless, speechless, issueless, misery." Man's thought is a rehearsal of fixed principles of sense about boundless nonsense.

In *Malone Dies* the narrator is the creator of Molloy and Moran. After having reached the end of the existential ropes of these two, *Malone Dies* mentally jumps further back into a mind concerned with making imaginary sense, or at least interpretation. There is a self-conscious author interrupting his story with present history. The world fatally deciphered in *Molloy* is in *Malone Dies* material for mental games. The novel's drama is in the workings of the imagination, an imagination that is coming apart: "That the noises of the world, so various in themselves and which I used to be so clever at distinguishing from one another, had been dinning at me for so long, always, always the same old noises, as gradually to have merged into a single noise, so that all I heard was one vast buzzing." The inventiveness that the mind performs to distinguish and satisfy is found by Malone to be a mental diversion of the issues: "If this continues it is myself I shall lose and the thousand ways that lead there. And on the threshold of being no more I succeed in being another." In *Malone Dies* the narrator reflects on his own reflections, incapable of breaking free from the fictions his mind devises. Malone is unable to find a means to talk about himself that does not become characters and situations—constructs of his imagination—that do not express him adequately or at all. Molloy worries about the subjective buzzing of man about the silent object, the self. The imagined self must always exclude its conjurer and must forever be incomplete.

The Unnamable draws again one step further back. The narrator here is the source of Malone, who is in turn the creator of Molloy and Moran. In *Malone Dies* the speaker reflects on his imaginings. Here the speaker—thought, imagination, mind, voice—reflects on itself. Malone makes his thoughts objects of study; here thought objectifies itself, a mind freed from a body thinking about its thinking. The mind in *Molloy* and *Malone Dies* dead-ends or loses itself in the real and the imagined (for the mind, both are the same). It devises answers to questions; it manufactures stories that fail to explain it. In *The Unnamable* thought attempts to free itself of the real and the imagined to answer its own questions about itself: "Ah yes, all lies, God and man, nature and the light of day, the heart's outpourings and the means of understanding, all invented basely by me alone, with the help of no one, to put off the hour when I must speak of me."

Thought is caught between itself as fabrication, as fiction, and as the unidentified speaker who produces the voice, the thought. The voice is up against its own subjective core. Who is the subject of its own object? Thought is without the language or the ability to express its own subjectivity. The mind is in the curious position of being its own best object. The words of the voice, thought, can never say themselves. Beckett has unraveled and reduced the process of the mind to an initial tautology: One cannot explain something one is explaining; an object cannot become a subject to apprehend its own objectivity. The voice in *The Unnamable* is forced to play a circular game. The object that the mind makes itself presumes a subject from which to start. Thought as object peeks over that final binary wall and sees itself thinking itself seeing itself thinking itself. The ultimate question of the self's effort to know itself awaits the perfect silence of the answer that can never apprehend the question. Molloy makes an object of the world and dreams of his own silence, his own objectivity. Malone objectifies his imagination and wants to forget his own fiction. In *The Unnamable* thought makes an object of itself, and the coil of subject and object disappears like a slipknot. The entire procedure is a bit like the bullfighter turning the bull in smaller and smaller circles around itself until the bull is fixed in one place, allowing the bullfighter to walk away. The trilogy is a spiraling down to a point that contains the entire spiral. Reducing the mind to its final or initial object, itself, completes the circle of the mind spinning on. You cannot go any further. You have not gone anywhere at all. Beckett has described the mind down to an infinite loop of subject and object. The mind continues, though exasperated, to make objects, even objects that try to make it. The mind, however, cannot think itself the means to shut itself off. Its only silence is a noisy fraud. The Unnamable is caught in the prototypical Beckett existential moment: unable to stop but also unable to go on:

> If only I knew if I've lived, if I live, if I'll live, that would be simply everything . . . what's a door doing here? . . . perhaps they have carried

> me to the threshold of my story, before the door that opens on my own story. . . . I don't know, I'll never know, in the silence you don't know, you must go on, I can't go on, I'll go on.

For all its dislocations and frustrations, Beckett's trilogy is one of the most exhilarating of modern novels, treating the dilemma of existence in a radically new manner that forces the reader to reevaluate virtually every assumption about life, language, thought, and expression.

THE TIN DRUM 38

(1959)

by Günter Grass

In the 20 years since its publication, Die Blechtrommel*—as it is called in German—has not been surpassed; it is the greatest novel by a living author. More than 14 books later, Grass himself has not surpassed* The Tin Drum, *but—more importantly—he hasn't limited himself by trying.*

—John Irving, "Günter Grass: King of the Toy Merchants," 1982

"Whoever fights monsters should see to it that in the process he does not become a monster," Friedrich Nietzsche observed in *Beyond Good and Evil.* "And when you look into an abyss, the abyss also looks into you." Nietzsche's caution captures the spirit and the technique of the distorting lens and mirror of Günter Grass's *The Tin Drum.* Grass's first novel remains his finest, one of fiction's most unflinching and disturbing reflections of the first half of the 20th century, a work that succeeds by making the monstrous ordinary and the ordinary monstrous. Grass blends matter-of-fact realism with caricature, playful fantasy with the grotesque as part of his strategy to make believable and real the horrors of Nazism but also to provoke a postwar society suffering from cultural amnesia into remembrance and responsibility. Although accepted internationally as an outstanding modern novel, *The Tin Drum* has also been condemned as obscene, banned, and burned—evidence that Grass's iconoclastic, scatological, and witheringly satirical novel has found its targets. As Grass's early supporter Walter Höllerer observed about the controversy the novel generated when it was published in 1959, "Why is it that Grass's novel gets people wound up? Just because of his motifs? Hardly. It is rather that he has probed a hidden, neuralgic web of nerve-fibres that lies entangled in the deepest recesses of our society, and to which all of us, whether we like it or not, are connected."

Two English writers pioneered some of the narrative methods Grass uses in *The Tin Drum:* Jonathan Swift and Laurence Sterne. Grass borrows Swift's technique of dislocating perspective through magnification and diminution, the technique central to *Gulliver's Travels*, by deploying as the narrator of *The Tin Drum* Oskar Matzerath, who at the age of three, decides to halt his growth into an adult world that has repeatedly disappointed him. Twentieth-century German history is, therefore, viewed from Oskar's peculiarly sinister perspective, that of an adult in a child's guise. Oscar looks up from below and behind the scenes at the towering, menacing, corrupt grownup world that surrounds him; his perspective subverts normality, subjecting it to the unrestrained demands of the preternatural child. From 1952 to 1954, Oskar tells his life story, up to the age of 30, from his cell in a mental hospital for the criminally insane, where he is incarcerated for a murder he may or may not have committed. Oskar's unreliability is one of the novel's operating principles, forcing the reader to question repeatedly what can be believed. Like Sterne's narrator in *Tristram Shandy*, Oskar also reaches back in time to before his birth in 1924, tracing his biological origin to the chance meeting in 1899 of his grandparents in a potato field, where Oskar's Polish grandfather, being pursued by authorities for committing arson on behalf of Polish independence, takes refuge under the skirts of Oskar's grandmother. Oskar's mother is thereby conceived, while the police interrogate his grandmother. Again, like *Tristram Shandy*, *The Tin Drum* presents an endlessly tangled narrative reconstruction of the past that frustrates the reader's desire for clear motives, straightforward linear progression, and certainty. Beginning at the end of his adventures, Oskar works backward to trace the multiple causes that have landed him in a mental hospital. Grass forces his reader to confront the question of who Oskar Matzerath is: alienated victim, artist rebel, Hitler manqué, or delusionary psychopath? And what of his story? Is it a perverse exercise in shock therapy or one of the great monitory fables for our times? No other living novelist has penetrated so deeply into the psyche and psychoses of the 20th century, and *The Tin Drum* has become, in critic John Reddick's phrase, "one of the monumental reference points of post-war writing": the defining fictional rendition of the Nazi experience and all that it more broadly implies about human nature.

In the distorted, expressionistic mirror of *The Tin Drum* autobiographical correspondences can be glimpsed, and the novel derives a good measure of its power from the author's probing of his own and his country's past. Like Oskar, Grass was a native of the Free City of Danzig (now the Polish city of Gdansk), a mixed community of Poles, Germans, Slavs, and Jews. Hitler's "liberation" of Danzig's German population became the pretext for the invasion of Poland that touched off the war in 1939. Partitioned at the end of World War I, Danzig was effectively dissolved at the end of World War II as the entity Grass had known, and *The Tin Drum* represents the imaginative reclamation of the lost world of Grass's childhood, as well as a diagnosis of how and why Danzig was lost. Like one of Oskar's two purported fathers, Alfred Matzerath, Grass's father was a German grocer, and his grandmother and mother, like Oskar's, were Kashubian, members of a Slavic people indigenous to the rural areas around Danzig with their own language and culture. Grass was five years old when the Nazis gained political control of the city, and he became a willing recruit to the Nazi's youth organizations. As Grass recalled, "At the age of ten, I was a member of the Hitler Cubs; when I was 14, I was enrolled in the Hitler Youth. At 15, I called myself an Air Force auxiliary. At 17, I was in the armored infantry." In Grass's view, one of the greatest of the Nazi perversions was its appropriation of childhood. Grass's retaliation can be seen in his conception of the perversely persistent child Oskar, who forces the adults to serve his will in a world turned topsy-turvy. Leaving Danzig as a soldier in 1944, Grass was wounded and captured by U.S. troops; he became one of the first Germans to be marched through Dachau to confront the enormity of the Nazi holocaust. A patriotic and a self-styled "dutiful youth," Grass confessed that although he was too young to have been a Nazi, he was "old enough to have been moulded by a system, that, from 1933 to 1945, at first surprised, then horrified the world." Grass's reassessment of his own and Germany's past has been a constant in his writing, and may be seen as elaboration, expansion, and variation on themes that he introduced in *The Tin Drum.* "A writer," Grass observed in *From the Diary of a Snail* (1973), "is someone who writes against the passage of time," and *The Tin Drum* and his subsequent works all return to the notion of how the past can be reclaimed, its continuity restored, and the reader's complicity in its creation revealed.

After the war, Grass worked on farms, in a potash mine, and as a stonemason's apprentice before enrolling in 1948 at the Düsseldorf Academy of Art as a student of painting and sculpture, supporting himself as a drummer in a jazz band. In 1952 he moved to Berlin to work as a sculptor and graphic designer. Grass's initial literary efforts took the form of poetry and plays. In 1955 his wife submitted a selection of Grass's poems to a radio contest for which he won third prize. This brought him to the attention of Group 47, a gathering of young German writers dedicated to restoring German literature after the Nazis. In 1956 Grass moved his family to Paris where he began work on *The Tin Drum.* In 1958, nearly penniless, Grass attended the annual Group 47 meeting, where on the basis of his reading from the first two chapters of his unfinished novel he won the group's literary prize. The funds allowed him to revisit his hometown and complete his manuscript, which appeared to great acclaim and condemnation in 1959. Grass has subsequently grouped *The Tin Drum* with the novella *Cat and Mouse* (1961) and *Dog Years* (1963) to form a "Danzig Trilogy," unified by shared characters and a common setting, a fictional landscape like Hardy's Wessex, Faulkner's Yoknapatawpha County, and García Márquez's Macondo.

Divided into three parts that correspond to prewar, wartime, and postwar German history, *The Tin Drum* invites the reader to compare the rise and fall of the Nazis with Oskar's family chronicle. Like Danzig itself, Oskar has a mixed heritage, and through his part-Kashubian mother's affair with her cousin, Jan Bronski, claims both Polish and German paternity, as well as an even more extraordinary legacy. "I may as well come right out with it," Oskar confesses. "I was one of those clair-audient infants whose mental development is completed at birth and after that merely needs a certain amount of filling in." Blessed or cursed with an adult consciousness from infancy, Oskar is, in the words of the critic Robert Maurer, "the youngest of the world's angry young men." His defiance of conventional values and alienation from his community and family are crystallized on his fateful third birthday, when he receives a tin drum that will become his indispensable means to express "the necessary distance between grownups and myself." Responding to his father's vow that he should inherit the family's grocery shop, Oskar hurls himself down the cellar steps to stop his growth, an act that works just as intended, and for the next 18 years Oskar views the world from the safe haven of his three-year-old body, forcing the world to accede to his demands by his drumming and glass-shattering scream.

From Oskar's unique perspective, Grass reconstructs his Danzig world and the historical events that intersect with his family history. The rise of the Nazis is shown not as a fatal capitulation to an overpowering, irresistible force imposed from above but as the result of the latent petty frustrations, aggressions, and boredom of ordinary Germans. Hitler is shown to be not the cause but the effect of the circumstances that condition the Mazeraths and their community. Oskar's ability to see through the hypocrisies and the fixations of the child-adults around him serves the interest of Grass's satire, but the novel resists any self-righteous moralizing. Hiding beneath the stands and staring up at the fat backsides of the local Nazis, Oskar subverts the rhythms of a Nazi rally with his drumming, but he is far from an active or consistent Nazi resister; rather, complicity and guilt are central to Grass's projection. Oskar, in fact, shares some features with Hitler himself. A failed artist, Hitler saw himself as a savior of his people, and even had the nickname "Der Trommler" (The Drummer). There is, therefore, in Oskar a complex dual role: He provides an angle from which to view the forces that destroyed Germany, while he shares complicity in its destruction.

Oskar's biography, particularly his ambiguous role in the deaths of his three parents, further elaborates the question of guilt and complicity. Oskar's mother dies from a surfeit of fish, having first been physically repelled, in one of the novel's most infamous scenes, by the severed horse's head that a fisherman is using to catch eels. Oskar's complicity in his mother's death is alternately denied and accepted, and her death is one of a series of grotesque scenes that underscore Oskar's dislocation and intimacy with existential terror. He is more directly responsible for the death of Jan Bronski, whom Oskar cajoles into entering the Polish Post Office during the German siege in 1939. During the war, Oskar plays a more active role not as observer but as participant, entertaining German troops with his glass shattering skills. Finally, in 1945, as his family cowers before their Russian conquerors, Oskar forces his father to take back the Nazi badge he was trying to make disappear, the act that leads directly to Alfred Matzerath's death. At his father's funeral, Oskar tumbles into his father's open grave and reemerges determined to resume his growth and enter as an adult the postwar world. The one death for which Oskar is accused, that of a young nurse, he may or may not be responsible for, and the novel ends with the news that his case is about to be reopened, allowing Oskar to be released into an uncertain future.

Oskar's memoirs evoke a nightmarish yet strangely familiar petty bourgeois milieu, in which a horrendous chapter in history reveals itself as the cumulative effect of many "little" people's bad faith, evasion, and cowardice, rather than as the work of a few incomprehensibly evil leaders. The vividness of Grass's language and the baroque imagination that informs his imagery compel Germans and non-Germans alike to recognize the presence of the monstrous in the midst of everyday life.

39

WUTHERING HEIGHTS

(1847)

by Emily Brontë

I've been greatly interested in Wuthering Heights, *the first novel I've read for an age, and the best (as regards power and sound style) for two ages. . . . But it is a fiend of a book, an incredible monster. . . . The action is laid in Hell,—only it seems places and people have English names there.*

—Dante Gabriel Rossetti in a letter to William Allingham, 1854

There are simply no satisfying fictional precedents to explain the elemental intensity, structural sophistication, and unique vision of Emily Brontë's *Wuthering Heights.* The book's lineage and influences are traceable more from the Greek tragedians, Shakespeare, and the Romantic poets than from any novel that preceded her masterpiece. *Wuthering Heights* is easily the strangest and most disturbing novel published in the 19th century, a work of supreme contrariness to the reader's expectations of what should be found in the novel. Popularly regarded as a classic love story, as writer and critic V. S. Pritchett observed, "Never, in a novel, did so many people hate each other with such zest." No other Victorian novel penetrated so deeply the depth of passion or existence in which ordinary, average experience—the central defining convention of the novel—is not only avoided but violated and defied. The novel dramatizes not the expected conflict between the individual and society but the combat with the ultimate conditions of existence itself: time, space, and the very notion of selfhood. *Wuthering Heights* shifts the novel into a different poetic universe where the tragic and the cosmic intersect and where the resources and boundaries of fiction are profoundly extended.

The uniqueness and unorthodoxy of *Wuthering Heights* are attributable to the author's imaginative development in the isolated world of Yorkshire and her reclusive family circle. Born in 1818 in the Yorkshire town of Haworth, Emily was the fourth daughter in a family of five girls and a boy. After their mother's death in 1821 and the deaths of their two eldest sisters from tuberculosis contracted at school, Charlotte, Emily, Anne, and Branwell were raised by their stern clergyman father, Patrick, and an aunt. The major imaginative event of their young lives took place in 1826, when Patrick Brontë brought home a box of wooden soldiers for his son. Each child claimed one, and the toy figures became the dramatis personae in an ever-lengthening series of fantasy stories eventually involving imaginary kingdoms, populated with historical, literary, and invented characters whose exploits were developed in endless nightly walks around their drawing room and celebrated in minuscule handmade books. Emily's first poems and stories chronicled the history of Gondal, a large Pacific island with a climate and topography that resembled Yorkshire, made up of a hardy, elemental race, whose intense, heroic conflicts animated her imagination. Emily's fantasy world persisted well beyond childhood and coexisted equally with her actual domestic circumstances, as suggested in this 1841 journal entry:

> It is Friday evening, near 9 o'clock in wild rainy weather. I am seated in the dining room, having just concluded tidying our desk boxes, writing this document. . . . Keeper is in the kitchen—Hero in his cage. We are all stout and hearty. . . . The Gondaland are at present in a threatening state, but there is no open rupture as yet.

Emily's Gondal writings shed light on the values and perspective in *Wuthering Heights* by expressing her admiration of intensity, strength, and willpower in which nature is often savage but essential, and humanity is seen in stark, existential, and amoral terms.

Ultimately forced to earn their livings, the three Brontë daughters pursued schemes that would allow their tight family circle to remain together, collaborating on a volume of poetry before turning to the commercial potential of fiction. Emily adapted her Gondal characters and themes to a Yorkshire setting for *Wuthering Heights*, which was accepted by a publisher to be brought out with Anne's *Agnes Grey*, while Charlotte's second effort, *Jane Eyre*, became a phenomenal best seller in 1847. When *Wuthering Heights* finally appeared, it was falsely advertised as the work of the author of *Jane Eyre* and ignored. Regarded, in Charlotte's words, as "an earlier and cruder attempt of the same pen," it became the only major Victorian novel that was not also a popular success. Those who noticed the book at all were baffled by the novel's complex, intricate structure—its nonchronological arrangement, filtered by at least two major removes by unreliable narrators, Lockwood and Nelly Dean—and detected little structure at all in a book that is now considered a formal marvel. The novel's first readers also responded to the relationship between Catherine Earnshaw and Heathcliff conventionally, viewing it as a story of reckless passion and the harm done by the unchecked ego. Even Charlotte Brontë judged it, in her preface to the novel's 1850 edition, a tale of "perverted passion, and passionate perversity" with Heathcliff "unredeemed," views that have been challenged by later readings that have done more justice to the challenging unconventionality of the novel's method and themes.

Turning the liabilities of her limited experience into the novel's chief strength, Emily Brontë consciously restricts the world of *Wuthering Heights* to three local yet universalized, symbolic settings, ideal for the larger-than-life, starkly heroic drama she enacts: the Heights itself, a utilitarian fortresslike structure occupied by the Earnshaw family that is characterized by its stormy exposure; Thrushcross Grange, the cultivated and sheltered property of the Linton family that provides a calming, civilized alternative to the Heights; and the moors in between, a beautiful, dangerous landscape that represents for the novel's protagonists, Cathy and Heathcliff, ultimate liberation and self-fulfillment, a metaphor for the heightened, unfettered existence that the pair aspire to but are tragically denied.

The chronological story of their relationship and its consequences for two generations, which must be reassembled by the reader through an intricate retrospective filtered through unreliable witnesses, begins with the uneasy absorption of the young Heathcliff, a dark, gypsylike foundling rescued from the Liverpool streets, into the Earnshaw family. He becomes the indispensable soul mate of the headstrong Cathy, and the novel's tragedy begins when they are separated as Cathy is drawn to the civilized world of Thrushcross and the respectable Edgar Linton. Cathy struggles to reconcile the conventional life Linton offers while attempting to maintain her essential identification with Heathcliff. Overhearing only Cathy's contention that it would degrade her to marry him, not her assertion, meant to be taken literally, that "I am Heathcliff," Heathcliff departs. Returning some years later after Cathy's marriage to Linton, Heathcliff is now rich and powerful, with his life plan firmly established: to bring both the Earnshaw and Linton families under his domination. Revenge, pursued with unmitigated cruelty and violence, becomes the central motive for his existence, but his plan breaks down when to best his rival, Linton, he must destroy Cathy as well. Unable to keep both Linton and Heathcliff and the separate worlds of Thrushcross and the Heights with all they represent—acquiescence and rebellion, responsibility and freedom, civilization and eros—from colliding, Cathy starves herself in one of the harshest, unrelieved deathbed scenes in literature. Heathcliff offers her no forgiveness and can find no consolation, cursing, "May she wake in torment! . . . You said I killed you—haunt me then! The murdered *do* haunt their murderers, I believe—I know that ghosts *have* wandered on earth. Be with me always—take any form—drive me mad! only *do* not leave me in this abyss, where I cannot find you!"

Heathcliff's revenge scheme is then played out on a second generation, with Cathy's daughter (also named Catherine) and another young primitive (Hareton) repeating the cycle of the first generation. The two are a paler, more diluted version of Cathy and Heathcliff, who are finally able to resolve the polarities that the novel has so vividly dramatized, between love and hate, liberation and confinement, the rational and the irrational, the elemental and the civilized. Heathcliff, having ultimately failed in his mission of destruction, like the first Cathy, wills his own death as the only available means of reuniting with his love.

Emily Brontë provided the reader with an intricate web of human relationships that extends our notions of both passion and human existence. In a novel that resists conventional moral judgment, the reader is asked to consider a love that often resembles hatred and a curse, as well as to balance the paradoxical image of Heathcliff, as faithful, tormented lover and as brutal, sadistic monster. In *Wuthering Heights* the conventional barriers of time, place, and identity itself are not absolutes but relative, allusive concepts in a world of destructive but fundamentally heroic intensity. Emily Brontë's greatness as a novelist rests in her ability to reach the profundity of tragic drama in which the cathartic expression of pity and terror is the reader's final appropriate response.

40

PRIDE AND PREJUDICE

(1813)

by Jane Austen

Read again, and for the third time at least, Miss Austen's very finely written novel of Pride and Prejudice. . . . *The Big Bow-wow strain I can do myself like any now going; but the exquisite touch which renders ordinary commonplace things and characters interesting, from the truth of the description and the sentiment, is denied to me.*

—Sir Walter Scott, *Journal*, March 14, 1826

Few readers have been able to resist Jane Austen's remarkable second published novel. *Pride and Prejudice* brings together an utterly charming, headstrong heroine, Elizabeth Bennet, and a hero, Fitzwilliam Darcy, who is undervalued and misunderstood until the novel's romantic climax, when reader and heroine alike change their estimation of his true worth. The novel also claims one of the most memorable supporting casts in fiction, including the ultimate parental embarrassment, the marriage-hungry Mrs. Bennet, the oily, toadying Mr. Collins, and the fire-breathing social dragon Lady Catherine de Bourgh, whom Elizabeth slays in one of the funniest, most satisfying confrontations in literature, as well as an ingenious courtship plot that combines psychological, social, and moral drama. Jane Austen herself referred to the novel as "my own darling child" and thought Elizabeth "as delightful a creature as ever appeared in print, and how I shall be able to tolerate those who do not like *her* at least I do not know." The novelist need not have worried, since most readers have shared the author's pleasure in her heroine, shortlisting her as one of fiction's strongest female presences, while valuing *Pride and Prejudice* as Austen's masterpiece and as one of the wittiest romantic comedies of manners ever written.

Pride and Prejudice: A Novel. In three volumes. By the Author of 'Sense and Sensibility' was published in 1813, anonymously like all of Austen's books during her lifetime, in a first edition of 1,500 copies. The reviewer for *The British Critic* ranked it as "very far superior to almost all the publications of the kind which have lately come before us." *Pride and Prejudice* became the fashionable novel of the season, with its first edition selling out in six months, a second edition appearing in November 1813, and a third in 1817. Despite the book's popularity, because Austen had sold her copyright for £110 with no royalty arrangement, she earned less for *Pride and Prejudice* than any of her other novels.

The novel's first readers were struck by its originality. As one contemporary recorded, "It depends not on any of the common resources of novel-writers, no drownings, no conflagrations, nor runaway horses, nor lap-dogs and parrots, nor chambermaids and milliners, nor rencontres and disguises. I really think it is the *most probable* I have ever read. It is not a crying book, but the interest is very strong." What Austen had accomplished was to shift reader interest from the extraordinary to the ordinary, from what might or should be to what was, eliminating idealization and exaggeration and substituting the surprising appeal of the recognizable, the realistic, and the truthful. As Somerset Maugham observed about all of Austen's novels, "Nothing very much happens in her books, and yet, when you come to the bottom of the page, you eagerly turn it to learn what will happen next. The novelist who has the power to achieve this has the most precious gift a novelist can possess." *Pride and Prejudice* is not just an admirably crafted, satisfying story, but one of the crucial books in the history of the novel. In it Jane Austen helped reclaim the novel as an instrument for truth and for a serious criticism of life. The future of the novel as written by William Thackeray, Gustave Flaubert, George Eliot, and Anthony Trollope can be glimpsed in Jane Austen's masterpiece, derived from her conscious restriction to what she knew best. As she indicated, "three or four families in a country village is the very thing to work on."

Born into the English gentry, whose customs and values would become her exclusive fictional concern, Jane Austen was the youngest daughter of the eight children of George Austen, the rector of Steventon in Hampshire. Although all her books concern the crucial domestic drama of matrimony, Jane Austen never reached the goal of her novels, though several affairs of the heart are suspected and at least one rejected marriage proposal is known. Austen knew intimately the challenge that courtship represented and used the difficult, complex private, moral, and social issues contained in the marriage decision as the central subject of all her books.

Pride and Prejudice delivers a mastery only fitfully glimpsed in Austen's first published novel, *Sense and Sensibility* (1811) and combines to a greater degree than any other of her novels a freshness and youthful exuberance with a mature perspective. The reason stems from the novel's long evolution from its first appearance as a playful literary entertainment written when she was 21 to her revision 15 years later. Her first version of the novel, called *First Impressions*, was the Austen family's favorite among the literary fragments, satires, parodies, and burlesques that she produced throughout her girlhood to entertain her family and friends (juvenilia that included the first version of *Sense and Sensibility* and the novel that would become *Northanger Abbey*). Written between 1796 and 1797 and rejected for publication, *First Impressions* (the manuscript of which has been lost) is thought to have been an epistolary novel that Austen recast and substantially revised beginning in 1809, returning to writing after a long and unhappy period following her father's retirement and the relocation of the family to Bath in 1801. Returning to the Hampshire countryside at Chawton Cottage, aged 34 with no further hope of marriage, Jane Austen concentrated on succeeding as a novelist, and she again picked up her youthful story, this time with the advantage of experience gained during the intervening years. The novel retains both the exuberance of the young writer joyfully animating her world with a mature assessment of the wider meaning and significance of the courtship drama that she had unsuccessfully negotiated in life.

From its opening sentence—"It is a truth universally acknowledged, that a single man in possession of a good fortune, must be in want of a wife" (along with Tolstoy's initial sentence in *Anna Karenina*, one of the most famous epigrammatic openings in fiction)—Austen explores the conflict between appearance and reality, a central theme of the novel dating from Cervantes's *Don Quixote*. Four strangers, all to a greater or lesser degree eligible bachelors (Bingley, Darcy, Collins, and Wickham), arrive in the provincial Hertfordshire community to test the novel's opening statement. All four will be married by the novel's conclusion with the question of pursuer and pursued delightfully scrambled and their marriage choices shown as a far more complex matter than the opening truism suggests. Elizabeth Bennet, the second of five marriageable sisters, finds herself in conflict with the aristocratic Mr. Darcy, and both misperceive the other due to their pride and its resulting prejudice. As much as the novel is about the challenges of the heart, it also concerns the ways in which judgment is confounded and can be schooled. Darcy initially cannot imagine that there is anyone deserving of his attention in the narrow, provincial world in which he finds himself; Elizabeth can see only his vanity and snobbery and is wounded by his superior airs. In a series of verbal skirmishes that compare favorably with those waged between Beatrice and Benedick in Shakespeare's *Much Ado About Nothing*, Elizabeth and Darcy battle through their senses of themselves and their society until Darcy's surprising marriage proposal. Elizabeth's rejection of Darcy's offer at the novel's midpoint is followed by an artfully arranged sequence of events, including a chance meeting between Elizabeth and Darcy at his ancestral home at Pemberley, in which a very different genteel host is glimpsed, and the sensational elopement of the caddish Wickham with Elizabeth's coquettish and irresponsible younger sister, Lydia. These events contribute to Elizabeth's ultimate recognition that she has been "blind, partial, prejudiced, and absurd" regarding Darcy and much more, a realization that prepares the way for the reconciliations and unions that the comedy demands.

By the novel's end, both Elizabeth and Darcy see each other and their world more clearly, as a complex network of interconnections and interdependencies in which the mature individual must reach a delicate balance between social and personal claims. In a novel that is as much a story of education and development as it is a romantic comedy, the match between Elizabeth and Darcy is a social as well as personal fulfillment. Elizabeth brings to the marriage an "ease and liveliness" to soften the stiff and austere Darcy, while his knowledge of the world and his wider, less mediocre field of opportunities made possible by his wealth and position are the ideal completions for his intended's character. By following the complications that eventually lead to Elizabeth and Darcy's marriage, Austen's readers also come to understand and appreciate that *how* we see often determines *what* we see, that to live both rightly and fully much more than the primacy of the individual is at stake, and that love and marriage are moral as well as an emotional states.

In Austen's masterly handling, *Pride and Prejudice* becomes one of the rarest of fictional achievements: a romantic comedy that entertains and enlightens. Combining elements of the Cinderella fable, sentimental romance, and serious reflections on the nature of society and morality, the novel's characters are both unique and familiar, and their fates both grounded in the accurate details of its era and universal. Although convincing arguments can be made for the superiority of Austen's later novels—*Mansfield Park*, *Emma*, and *Persuasion*—*Pride and Prejudice* retains for many readers pride of place in the Austen canon, announcing the arrival of a great novelist and her most endearing achievement.

41

THE SCARLET LETTER

(1850)

by Nathaniel Hawthorne

Hawthorne finished The Scarlet Letter *on February 3, 1850. On the evening of that day he read the latter part of the book to his wife who—as always—had religiously refrained from any inquiry or intermeddling during the process of composition. "It broke her heart," Hawthorne wrote . . . "and sent her to bed with a grievous headache, which I look upon as a triumphant success."*

—Randall Stewart, *Nathaniel Hawthorne*

With *The Scarlet Letter* the American novel achieved its first undisputed masterpiece, a book of such remarkable and unique moral and psychological exploration and artistic design that it far surpassed any previous American novel and rivaled the greatest European works. Hawthorne's focus on the hidden recesses of human nature, the consequences of moral transgressions, the conflicts between authority and personal freedom and responsibility, as well as his distinctive use of romance elements to explore his themes established the primary characteristics of the American novel that have dominated ever since. Hawthorne also anticipated the direction toward the elusive "great American novel" that would be followed by Melville, Faulkner, Fitzgerald, Ellison, Pynchon, and others in his wake, not toward the central realistic tradition of the European novel but toward the mythic and symbolic.

Hawthorne's early artistic development together with his family and financial circumstances were crucial in shaping his masterpiece. His first published work was the novel *Fanshawe*, based on his experiences at Bowdoin College, which appeared anonymously in 1828. The novel was ignored and so dissatisfied its author that he would later seek out available copies to destroy. Hawthorne devoted the next 20 years to the shorter form of the prose tale and sketch. In the absence of an international copyright agreement, native novelists struggled in the marketplace since American publishers had no financial incentive to cultivate homegrown talent because they were able to pirate the best English writers, like Scott and Dickens, for free with impunity.

Hawthorne did find a market of sorts for his short fiction in New England magazines and newspapers and in *The Token*, a Boston gift book annual where most of the works collected in *Twice-Told Tales* (1837) first appeared. Between his graduation from college in 1825 and 1837, Hawthorne lived mainly in seclusion in his mother's house in Salem, Massachusetts, reading histories of early New England and perfecting his craft, learning to project the moral and existential themes that fascinated him in fictional characters and situations. "Had he been born without the poetic imagination," poet and critic James Russell Lowell observed, "he would have written treatises on the Origin of Evil." Hawthorne's early tales, such as "The Gentle Boy," "Young Goodman Brown," "The Minister's Black Veil," "Rappaccini's Daughter," "The Birthmark," "Ethan Brand," and "Endicott and the Red Cross," all anticipate such preoccupations—the Puritan past, the ambiguity of sin, the conflict between heart and head, and the corrosive power of guilt—as well as character types and settings that he would return to in *The Scarlet Letter*. His tales and sketches also helped Hawthorne work out and refine his fictional methods, including the symbolic, "atmospheric medium" that permeates his work, as well as the compression and intensity of the short form in which each element of plot, characterization, setting, and surface detail contributes to an overall unity of focus and impact. If the epic and drama were the key literary genres that helped shape the English novel, it was the short story and its artistic effects, devised and formalized by Washington Irving, Hawthorne, and Edgar Allan Poe, that would provide the greatest impact on the American novel. Hawthorne's long apprenticeship as a writer of tales and sketches is, therefore, crucial to the evolution of the American novel, and *The Scarlet Letter* is the first great expression of the wider reach of the novel supported by the artistic techniques of the short story.

The Scarlet Letter became a novel almost by accident. Hawthorne had married Sophia Peabody in 1842, and, unable to earn a sufficient income to support his growing family from his writing, he gained employment from 1846 to 1849 as an official at the Salem Custom-House. Hawthorne's was a Democratic political appointment that he lost with the Whig election victory of Zachary Taylor. Hawthorne's dismissal, prompted by false charges by Salem Whigs of "corruption, iniquity, and fraud," received national attention, and the notoriety contributed to the success Hawthorne would achieve with *The Scarlet Letter*. Returning to writing in earnest to make up for his lost income after his dismissal, Hawthorne began *The Scarlet Letter* in September 1849, as a tale for a projected new volume to be called *Old-Time Legends: Together with Sketches, Experimental and Ideal*. The novel's themes and situations reflect ideas earlier recorded in his notebook. Hester Prynne, his heroine, is anticipated in the entry: "The life of a woman, who, by the old colony law, was condemned always to wear the letter A, sewed on her garment, in token of her having committed adultery." Hester's lover, Dimmesdale, and his secret, are suggested by the interesting idea "To symbolize moral or spiritual disease by disease of the body;—thus, when a person committed a sin, it might cause a sore to appear on the body; this to be wrought out." Chillingworth is forecast in the notation: "A story of the effects of revenge, in diabolizing him who indulges in it."

James T. Fields of Ticknor and Fields, the proposed book's publisher, read the uncompleted manuscript and encouraged Hawthorne to expand the story and publish it as a separate work. Finished in February 1850, the novel became an immediate popular success, with the first edition of 2,500 copies selling out in three days. Two more editions appeared before the end of the year, and, although only 7,500 copies would be sold in Hawthorne's lifetime, earning him a total of $1,500, *The Scarlet Letter* has never gone out of print since it first appeared, becoming, along with *Moby-Dick* and *Adventures of Huckleberry Finn*, the most popular and most written-about 19th-century American novels.

To understand his methods and intentions in *The Scarlet Letter*, it is important to emphasize that, according to Hawthorne, the book was not a novel at all. It was instead a romance, with the distinction clarified in the long introductory chapter titled "The Custom-House" that precedes the story. If the novel shows the world in sunlight, aiming, as Hawthorne later explained in the preface to *The House of the Seven Gables*, "at a very minute fidelity, not merely to the possible, but to the probable and ordinary course of man's experience," the romance is moonlit:

> Moonlight, in a familiar room, falling so white upon the carpet, and showing all its figures so distinctly—making every object so minutely visible, yet so unlike a morning or noontide visibility—is a medium the most suitable for a romance-writer to get acquainted with his illusive guests. . . . Thus, therefore, the floor of our familiar room has become a neutral territory, somewhere between the real world and fairy-land, where the Actual and the Imaginary may meet, and each imbue itself with the nature of the other.

Central to Hawthorne's fictional strategy is this conjunction of the actual and imaginary in which the familiar is "spiritualized by the unusual light" of the romance writer's art. In *The Scarlet Letter* Hawthorne borrows elements of romance and the gothic novel, such as archetypal settings, the aura of the uncanny, secrets, and suspense, to aid the exploration of psychological and moral themes that would be prohibited by a more restrictive realistic method. His novel is concerned with the consequence of sin on the individual and the community, projected against the background of Puritan New England, illuminated by the implication of Hester Prynne's adultery. Hawthorne explores the effects of human sin and guilt particularized by an actual time and place—colonial Boston in the 1640s—populated by historical as well as invented characters, but with an imaginative pressure that suffuses the specific with symbolic associations and universal implications.

The power of *The Scarlet Letter* stems from Hawthorne's tight concentration on his four major characters—Hester, her lover, Arthur Dimmesdale, her husband, Roger Chillingworth, and her daughter, Pearl—in a series of striking tableaux that animate the novel's action and the characters' moral and psychological natures. We learn little about the causes of Hester's sin; instead, Hawthorne focuses on its consequences, beginning the novel after Hester's fall with the first of three scenes on the scaffold in the public square. There, Hester's repentance is extracted by the Puritan authorities with the ambiguous nature of her sin underscored by the multiple associations of the scarlet letter she is forced to wear as a public acknowledgment of her fallen nature. Like Melville's white whale, the scarlet letter becomes the novel's magnetic central symbol, attracting all the characters' reactions and inviting diverse interpretation. For Hester, the letter is a sign of her fallible human nature which she acknowledges; for Dimmesdale it is a symbol of his sinful nature and complicity which he denies until the novel's climax when he finally reveals his own "red stigma"; for Chillingworth the letter forces him to hide his connection with his wife and causes him to embark on a self-destroying pursuit of revenge and retribution; finally, for Pearl, brilliantly dressed in scarlet as the living symbol of Hester's sin, the letter denies her membership in the human family as an uncanny outsider until Dimmesdale's dying recognition of his paternity.

Chapters of character analysis alternate with dramatic scenes of character conflict underscored by symbolic associations: Hester and Pearl's visit to the governor's mansion; Dimmesdale's night vigil on the scaffold during which he glimpses a meteor in the shape of the letter A; Hester and Dimmesdale's forest meeting with its interplay of light, shadow, and reflecting surfaces; and the novel's climax, paralleling the opening, when Dimmesdale publicly acknowledges Hester and Pearl on the scaffold before the community who had previously viewed him as an untainted saint. The result is a richly textured inquiry into human nature fueled by Hawthorne's daring inversions. Hester, the fallen woman, by acknowledging her nature and accepting her fate, is shown far more worthy of sympathy than the narrow, intolerant Puritan community of the righteous. Chillingworth, the man of intellect and science, is condemned as more corrupt than the two lovers, and Dimmesdale, the community standard for moral authority, is presented as a case study in repression, whose public identity isolates him from himself and sentences him to a crippling guilt.

There had never been anything quite like Hawthorne's symbolic drama in American fiction before, with its rich evocation of internal states cast in a historical setting that is both sharply imagined and symbolically suggestive. There had never before been a comparable American attempt to reach so profound an understanding of humanity's moral nature and the impact of sin and guilt on the human psyche. As a work of art, Hawthorne's novel points both toward the economy and intensity of fictional means that Flaubert would elaborate in another story of adultery, *Madame Bovary*, and the expansive reverberations of the symbolic form that Hawthorne's future protégé, Herman Melville, recognized and imitated to transform his whaling tale into an equivalent existential drama. Hemingway, in an often quoted comment, traced the origin of American literature to Twain's *Adventures of Huckleberry Finn*. An alternative compelling case can be made that it was really Hawthorne who was the American novel's progenitor, with Melville and Twain the tragic and comic inheritors of the romance tradition that Hawthorne pioneered.

42

GRAVITY'S RAINBOW

(1973)

by Thomas Pynchon

Pynchon's work takes its place in that line of dazzlingly daring, even idiosyncratic American writing which leads back through writers like Faulkner to Mark Twain and Hawthorne, and above all to Melville and Moby-Dick. *And, taking yet another view, we might want to cite* Tristram Shandy *as an earlier experimental novel that lies behind him; but then Sterne points us in turn back to Rabelais, and both bear the mark of* Don Quixote *(as does Pynchon)—which is, in a manner of speaking, where the novel as we know it in the West began. Few major modern novels have not in some fashion returned to these origins, and thus we can see Pynchon continuing that series of radical shifts and innovations in fictional technique which was started by Conrad and James, and continued by Joyce—all of whom are more or less audible in his work. Which is all to say that he is both creatively eclectic and unmistakably original. From one point of view, the novel from its inception has always been a mixed genre with no certain limits or prescribed formal constraints; Pynchon, then, is in no way an "eccentric" novelist, for the novel has no determined centre. Rather he is a key contemporary figure in the great tradition of those who extend the possibilities of fiction-making in arresting and enriching ways—not in this or that "Great Tradition," but in the great tradition of the novel itself.*

—Tony Tanner, *Thomas Pynchon*

No other American novel written after 1950 approaches *Gravity's Rainbow* for sheer invention, cultural synthesis, and imaginative reach. For the critic Edward Mendelson, *Gravity's Rainbow* is not a novel at all but should be included in "the most important single genre in Western literature of the Renaissance and after" that he describes as the "encyclopedic narrative," along with "Dante's *Commedia*, Rabelais's five books of Gargantua and Pantagruel, Cervantes' *Don Quixote*, Goethe's *Faust*, Melville's *Moby-Dick*, and Joyce's *Ulysses*." For Khachig Tololyan, *Gravity's Rainbow* is best described as "a cosmography, that is, a fictional alternative to available historical versions of the real world, made up of fragments of reality wielded together by an extraordinary imagination." Having found a wide-enough and distinguished-enough category to contain Pynchon's work, however, does little to mitigate the difficulty and challenge of coping with a text that includes more than 400 characters and their intersecting (and dissolving) plots, as well as a range of historical, literary, scientific, and popular-culture allusions that makes mastery the equivalent of a liberal education in itself. David Leverenz summarizes the initial reaction of many by describing the novel as "an act of calculated hostility against my own need to find out what it was about." Many readers have become disoriented in Pynchon's labyrinth, consigning the novel, along with Joyce's *Finnegans Wake*, Beckett's trilogy, and other notoriously difficult modernist texts, to the category of respected but unread. *Gravity's Rainbow*, however, deserves the effort for its mind-stretching pleasures, dizzying thrills, and the brilliance of its exploration that seemingly attempts to contain all modern experience between its covers. Not since Melville's white whale has an American writer seized upon a more complex or resonant symbol than the V-2 rocket that centers the action of *Gravity's Rainbow* and, like Ishmael's and Ahab's confrontation, forces a similar consideration of mankind's ultimate questions.

Gravity's Rainbow placed Pynchon in the forefront of postwar American novelists and led to a critical scramble to decipher its significance and measure its considerable impact. Attaining a short stay on the best-seller list, an unheard-of accomplishment for such a demanding, unwieldy novel, *Gravity's Rainbow* is perhaps the only novel that was reviewed in general interest periodicals, literary journals, *and Scientific American*. In 1974, it was unanimously selected by the judges for the Pulitzer Prize in literature, but their decision was overruled by their advisory board, whose members called it "unreadable," "turgid," "overwritten," and "obscene." When Pynchon was named corecipient with Isaac Bashevis Singer of the 1973 National Book Award, the double-talking comic "Professor" Irwin Corey accepted the award for the notoriously reclusive Pynchon. In 1975, *Gravity's Rainbow* was awarded the Howells Medal as the best novel of the first half of the decade, an honor that Pynchon politely but firmly declined. In the years that followed, Pynchon has mostly succeeded in eluding his public, forcing his critics to guess about his intentions and influences without the usual reliance on biographical coordinates or authorial assistance to aid interpretation. As in all of Pynchon's fiction, the reader is forced into the role of detective, sorting through all available evidence for the key to unlock the mystery of meaning and significance. *Gravity's Rainbow*, however, is simultaneously the ultimate paranoid's fantasy that truly everything is connected and the supreme nihilistic nightmare that connections are delusions and meaning an impossibility. As in all postmodernist texts, the search for meaning and the art of reading itself become fundamental issues in a narrative that seems both to move forward and dissolve, frustrating the reader's inquiry while insisting that all will be revealed. Like *Moby-Dick* and *Ulysses*, *Gravity's Rainbow* pursues a strategy of multiple narrative styles blending serious metaphysical inquiry with slapstick, lyrical moments with outrageous puns and eschatological high jinks, and a dense verbal pattern of scientific arcana with fantasy.

"A screaming comes across the sky. It has happened before, but there is nothing to compare it to now." The novel's first section, "Beyond the Zero," is set in London in September 1944 under V-2 bombardment. In three more sections, the novel continues through the final months of the war and the first months of the peace until September 1945, during the decisive period that would reshape the map of Europe, transform modern warfare and technology, and usher in the cold war and the forces that would define postwar history. The V-2 is the first guided ballistic missile, which (along with the nearly simultaneous American development of the atomic bomb) represents the perfection of the technology of death that Pynchon suggests is the modern world's primary legacy. Produced by the same German scientists who would design the prototypes of the space-traveling rockets whose triumphs were manifest during Pynchon's writing of the novel, the V-2 combines in its parabola of flight (represented by the novel's title) the contradictions of mankind's ultimate transcendence and destruction, of escape from the constraints of nature and confirmation that our technological mastery resides in affirming our basest natures as killing animals.

What also makes the V-2 so special (and sinister) is that the sound of its coming *follows* its impact, suggesting a technology that undermines causality and the tyranny of time. The disjunction caused by the rocket is mirrored by *Gravity's Rainbow* itself, in which the reader faces a series of narrative shifts and explosions whose full significance only begins to make sense after the pieces of the novel's immense sociopolitical panorama drop into place. A similar disjunction defines the novel's initial narrative situation, an anomaly whereby the hapless American lieutenant Tyrone Slothrop's erections and sexual conquests predict the V-2's targets. Slothrop's uncanny response to the V-2 attracts the scrutiny of researchers at the White Visitation (a group doing psychic research on behalf of the war effort), notably the Pavlovian Ned Pointsman and the statistician Roger Mexico. Their contrasting views set up the novel's opposing existential philosophies. The Pavlovian necessarily believes that everything has a cause and effect, while the statistician sees a universe governed by the principle of randomness. The statistician's job is to measure these random movements, but he knows that these measurements can only be approximate. Pointsman's universe is ordered and controlled, while Mexico's is not. Slothrop's reaction and the correlation between his lovemaking and the explosions defy both the statistician's concept of randomness and reverses the Pavlovian concept that a stimulus should precede a response, that an effect should follow a cause. Pointsman's conviction that there must be a connection between Slothrop and the rocket, confirming a deterministic order to the universe, sets the novel in motion and Slothrop on a surrealistic quest into his own background, modern history, and the world that the war has wrought.

In the second section, "*Un Perm' au Casino Hermann Goering*," Slothrop is assigned to a tour of duty on the French Riviera as part of an elaborate experiment to expose him to rocket data while monitoring his sexual activity with the triple Dutch agent Katje Borgesius. As various political and corporate interests begin to converge over Slothrop, whose ultimate significance is by no means clear, he initiates a search for his identity, integrating his past with present developments, including the existence of the plastic imipolex-G, a mysterious rocket called the 00000, and his relationship to the inventor of imipolex, Laszlo Jamf. Becoming increasingly aware that he is being used by a sinister military-industrial complex, Slothrop decides to escape and pursue his own search for the rocket technology that may hold the answers.

In the third and longest section of the novel, "In the Zone," Slothrop enters the phantasmagoric domain of occupied Europe hovering between the Nazi collapse and Allied partition. Assuming various identities, including the cartoonish superhero Rocketman and Plechazunga, the pig hero in a German village's fertility festival, Slothrop gradually morphs out of the novel, his interest in locating the rocket and in returning home fading, as the reader's attention is focused on a variety of characters who reflect aspects of his story and represent thematic multipliers of the novel's diagnosis of the paranoid's dilemma. They include Oberst Enzian, the leader of the Schwartzkommando, a displaced band of militant Africans brought to Germany after the slaughter of the Herero tribe in South-West Africa in 1904, who pursues the rocket as a means of tribal rebirth. He is in turn pursued by Vaslav Tchitcherine, a Russian intelligence officer, who is actually Enzian's half brother. As they seek the rocket components, Pynchon makes clear that despite the armistice the real war for global control by the world's corporations never ends: "Don't forget that the real business of the War is buying and selling. The murder and violence are self-policing, and can be entrusted to non-professionals. The mass nature of wartime death is useful in many ways. It serves as spectacle, as diversion from the real movements of the War. It provides raw material to be recorded into History . . . as sequences of violence, battle after battle . . . The true war is celebration of markets."

In the fourth part of *Gravity's Rainbow*, "The Counterforce," Mexico, Katje, and others attempt to rescue the lost Slothrop, but their efforts are unresolved, as are many of the novel's plotlines that simply fade from view. All that matters is their intention to oppose the System that determines behavior and dictates control. The counterforce that Pynchon offers as an alternative to the powerful is identified as "creative paranoia," in which "For every They there ought to be a We." Chance and chaos are the alternatives to the inevitability of modern conditioning. The novel's many dualities—They/We, Preterite/Elect, White/Black, Life/Death—are ultimately focused in the rocket itself, described as "a good rocket to take us to the stars, an evil rocket for the World's suicide, the two perpetually in struggle." The story of the launch of Rocket 00000 by German scientist Major Weissmann/Captain Blicero with his lover Gottfried as the payload closes the novel, described in a style that suggests the reader is viewing Gottfried's last moments on film. We are finally in contemporary Los Angeles's Orpheus Theatre as *Gravity's Rainbow*, the "film" we had been "reading" all along, concludes and the descending rocket is about to find its target "above the roof of the old theatre."

Part slapstick, part film, cartoon, technical manual, and revisionist history, *Gravity's Rainbow* maps the landscape of our worst fears. In the process, war and peace, love and death, They and We are redefined with a striking potency that does not evade the complexity of modern experience but mines it.

43

BELOVED

(1987)

by Toni Morrison

Beloved *is Toni Morrison's fifth novel, and another triumph. Indeed, Ms. Morrison's versatility and technical and emotional range appear to know no bounds. If there were any doubts about her stature as a preeminent American novelist, of her own or any other generation,* Beloved *will put them to rest. In three words or less, it's a hair-raiser.*

—Margaret Atwood, "Haunted by Their Nightmares," *New York Times Book Review*, 1987

There is perhaps no better justification for the challenging modernist methods of chronological dislocation, fragmentation, and blending of fantasy and realism than Toni Morrison's remarkable attempt to come to imaginative terms with the enormity of slavery and the American past in *Beloved.* How better to emphasize a repressed, traumatizing past than to bury it and allow it only gradually to emerge in disjointed, lethal images? How appropriate in a present haunted by the past that a spirit from the host of the anonymous dead should magically appear and compel an exorcism? *Beloved* is thus far Morrison's most ambitious and most fully realized novel, a masterpiece of almost unbearable power and seemingly inexhaustible cultural, psychological, and human relevance. In a work of shattering emotional intensity and historical synthesis Morrison has crafted one of the essential fictional works of the second half of the 20th century.

Having come to novel writing late in a career occupied by teaching and editorial work, Morrison published her first novel, *The Bluest Eye,* in 1970, when she was 39. This lyrical exploration of racial and gender identity was followed by *Sula* in 1974. Both books were critically praised for their poetic prose, emotional intensity, and unique interpretation of African-American experience from the largely neglected woman's perspective. Neither book was a popular success, and both novels were out of print when Morrison published her breakthrough novel, *Song of Solomon,* in 1977. *Song of Solomon* established her reputation as a dominating voice in contemporary fiction worldwide. The novel shows Morrison extending her range, employing a male protagonist for the first time, Milkman Dead, whom critic Margaret Wade-Lewis has called "undoubtedly one of the most effective renderings of a male character by a woman writer in American literature." His quest to find a family legacy and to decipher his racial identity is a complex and resonant interweaving of myth and history that draws on black folklore, oral tradition, and classical archetypes. This expansiveness is continued in her next novel, *Tar Baby* (1981), in which Morrison pursues the imaginative search for identity in the confrontation between blacks and whites, along with her characteristic fusion of fantasy derived from the black American folktale and realism, but here placed in a global setting that encompasses the entire African diaspora.

Tar Baby was a best seller and prompted *Newsweek* to do a cover story on the writer. Ironically, Morrison felt at the time that her writing days were over. "I would not write another novel to either make a living or because I was able to," she later recalled. "If it was not an overwhelming compulsion or I didn't feel absolutely driven by the ideas I wanted to explore, I wouldn't do it. And I was content not to ever be driven that way again." The compulsion came reluctantly as Morrison began to confront the legacy of slavery, a subject obscured, in Morrison's words, by a "national amnesia." *Beloved* would become an effort of "re-memory," the deliberate act of reconstructing what has been forgotten, which the author defined as "a journey to a site to see what remains have been left behind and to reconstruct the world that these remains imply." In an act of bearing witness, of giving voice to the unspeakable, Morrison set out "to fill in the blanks that the slave narrative left," to "part the veil that was frequently drawn" in which the full ramifications of the slave experience could be probed, and its costs embodied in psychological, emotional, social, and cultural terms.

The inspiration for her story came from Morrison's editorial work on Middleton Harris's documentary collection of black life in America, *The Black Book* (1974). Morrison became fascinated by a historical incident from a newspaper clipping contained in Harris's volume entitled "A Visit to the Slave Mother Who Killed Her Child." It is a journalist's report on a runaway slave from Kentucky, Margaret Garner, who in 1855 tried to kill her children rather than allow them to be returned to slavery. Successful in killing one, Margaret Garner would provide the historical access point for *Beloved* as Morrison explored imaginatively the conditions that could have led to such a horrific act and its consequences on the survivors.

Narrated in a series of flashbacks, assembled gradually from the limited perspective of its characters, *Beloved* opens in 1873, 18 years after the defining trauma in the life of Sethe, a former slave on a Kentucky farm called Sweet Home. Sethe lives in an isolated house outside Cincinnati with her 18-year-old daughter, Denver, and the ghost of Sethe's dead baby girl, named by the inscription on her tombstone, Beloved. The novel's setting during Reconstruction is symbolically appropriate for its search for wholeness, the effort to rebuild an identity, a family, and a community shattered by the enormous human waste and dehumanization of slavery. A clear chronology of events in Sethe's life emerges only eventually as numerous characters—Sethe's mother-in-law, Baby Suggs; the black river man, Stamp Paid; Sethe's fellow slave, the last of the Sweet Home Men, Paul D; and others—allow their experiences to emerge painfully through a protective repression.

In 1848 the teenage Sethe had been sold to Mr. Garner at Sweet Home as the replacement for Baby Suggs, whose freedom had been purchased by her son Halle, whom Sethe marries. When Mr. Garner dies in 1853, the farm is run by an overseer called Schoolteacher, who replaces Mr. Garner's more benign regime with a brutal and calculated indifference to the humanity of the Sweet Home slaves. When one is sold, the rest plot their escape in 1855. On the eve of departure, the pregnant Sethe is attacked by Schoolteacher's two nephews. As one holds her down, the other submits her to "mammary rape," sucking the milk from her breasts. Unknown to Sethe, this violation is witnessed by Halle, who is incapable of assisting his wife. The event leads to his derangement and disappearance. Sethe sends her three children to join the emancipated Baby Suggs in Ohio and eventually reaches freedom there herself after giving birth to her daughter, Denver. The four other Sweet Home men are either brutally killed or imprisoned. Sethe enjoys only 28 days of freedom before Schoolteacher arrives to take her back. Rather than allowing her children to be returned to slavery, Sethe tries to kill them. Three survive, but Beloved's throat is cut. Arrested and sentenced to hang, Sethe is pardoned due to the intervention of abolitionists and allowed to return to Baby Suggs's home at 124 Bluestone Road, where she is shunned by the black community. The vengeful spirit of her murdered child also takes up residence, drives away Sethe's two sons, contributes to Baby Suggs's retreat to her bed and death, and holds Sethe and Denver in her spell until the arrival in 1873 of Paul D.

Paul D is able to expel the ghost, temporarily breaking the hold of grief, seclusion, and despair that has locked Sethe and Denver in a continual, debilitating past. Paul D offers the possibility of family and future, but neither Paul D nor Sethe are truly ready to put their past behind them. As if to insist that both must confront that past, the ghost returns in bodily form as a young woman the age Beloved would have been had she survived and claims sanctuary. A sinister presence, Beloved's voracious obsession for food and Sethe's love splits the incipient family apart. Beloved prompts the revelation that Sethe has killed her daughter, driving Paul D away, and Beloved claims complete dominance over Sethe as the physical embodiment of her crippling conscience. Increasingly obsessed with righting the uncorrectable wrong to Beloved, Sethe loses her job and all contact with the outside world. Neglected and starving, Denver is forced to reach out to the larger community for assistance, an act that finally breaks the hold Beloved has over Sethe. As the black women of the community who had previously ostracized Sethe for her murder now come to her assistance, an echoing of Schoolteacher's arrival at the house at 124 Bluestone is reenacted as the elderly Mr. Bodwin, who had gained Sethe's pardon in 1855, is mistaken by the deranged Sethe as a slave catcher. She is prevented from stabbing him with an ice pick, but her climactic gesture of striking out, not at the victims of slavery in her former assault on her children but at its presumed agent, causes Beloved to vanish and prepares the way for the novel's concluding reconciliations and affirmations. Sethe at first despairs at losing her child yet again, but her complete breakdown and retreat from life, following the previous example of Baby Suggs, is halted by the return of Paul D, whose acceptance of Sethe and the past asserts his willingness and Sethe's ability to face the future. Contrary to Sethe's belief that her children were her "best things," that her all-encompassing love was the essential justification for her to kill them rather than allow them to be returned to slavery, Paul D insists that "You your best thing, Sethe. You are." The revelation he offers Sethe suggests that the past need not tyrannize but must be fully confronted, with wholeness the result of self-respect *and* selflessness, of individual autonomy and participation in a sustaining wider human community.

From a perspective that has previously been ignored, Morrison has supplied a unique lesson in the ramifications of the legacy of slavery as an institution with devastating consequences on the family, sexuality, and psychological and emotional wholeness. In her handling, racial, personal, and national history comes together in an essential myth that probes a collective scar and suggests where healing can be found.

44

NOSTROMO

(1904)

by Joseph Conrad

I'd rather have written Conrad's Nostromo *than any other novel. First, because I think it is the greatest novel since* Vanity Fair *(possibly excluding* Madame Bovary*), but chiefly because Nostromo, the man, intrigues me so much. . . . [Conrad] took this man of the people and imagined him with such a completeness that there is no use of any one else pondering over him for some time. He is one of the most important types in our civilization. In particular he's one that always made a haunting and irresistible appeal to me. So I would rather have dragged his soul from behind his astounding and inarticulate presence than written any other novel in the world.*

—F. Scott Fitzgerald, letter, *Chicago Tribune*, May 19, 1923

When Joseph Conrad began the two-and-a-half-year labor that would produce his most ambitious and profound novel—what he would later describe as his "largest canvas" and what critic F. R. Leavis called "Conrad's supreme triumph"—he was convinced that "there was nothing more in the world to write about." Conrad felt that he had exhausted the storehouse of experiences derived from his nautical career, but a chance discovery of "a vagrant anecdote completely destitute of valuable details" provided the stimulus for the creation of the writer's richest fictional world. In a memoir of an American seaman that Conrad happened to read, there was a fleeting mention of an encounter with a man who in the midst of the turmoil of a Central American revolution single-handedly stole a boat laden with silver, sank it in shallow water, and enriched himself by drawing on his hoard gradually. It reminded Conrad of a story that he remembered hearing on his only voyage into the Gulf of Mexico in the 1870s. The anecdote began to germinate in his mind as the possibility for a new fictional subject. As Conrad recalled in his Author's Note for *Nostromo:*

> Perhaps, perhaps, there still was in the world something to write about. Yet I did not see anything at first in the mere story. A rascal steals a

> large parcel of a valuable commodity—so people say. It's either true or untrue; and in any case it has no value in itself. To invent a circumstantial account of the robbery did not appeal to me, because my talents not running that way I did not think that the game was worth the candle. It was only when it dawned upon me that the purloiner of the treasure need not necessarily be a confirmed rogue, that he could be even a man of character, an actor, and possibly a victim in the changing scenes of a revolution, it was only then that I had the first vision of a twilight country which was to become the province of Sulaco, with its high shadowy Sierra and its misty Campo for mute witness of events flowing from the passions of men short-sighted in good and evil.

Like the ivory in *Heart of Darkness*—the catalyst for Conrad's earlier study of greed and human corruptibility—the silver in *Nostromo* infects an entire country and animates the novelist's most extensive anatomy of human nature and behavior. "Silver is the pivot of the moral and material events," Conrad later summarized about his conception, "affecting the laws of everybody in the tale." In working out its impact on several individuals, a community, and a nation, Conrad achieved, in the words of Robert Penn Warren, "his total vision of the world, his sense of human destiny, his sense of man's place in nature, his sense of history and society."

The personal, political, and social forces Conrad examined are set in motion by the return of idealistic Englishman Charles Gould to the country of his birth, the imaginary South American republic of Costaguana, to take up his inherited ownership of the San Tomé silver mine that has already claimed the obsessions and lives of two generations of his family. He arrives at Sulaco, the regional capital, with a new wife, Emilia, and the financial backing of an American industrialist determined to make the mine pay. As Gould succeeds, the mine begins to figure prominently in the political destiny of Costaguana. The enlightened dictator Don Vincente Ribiera, propped up by Gould's silver, is overthrown by the demagogic head of the armed forces, General Montero, and Monterist troops try to seize the mine. Desperate to protect his treasure, Gould entrusts the annual supply of silver to a small boat and the presumed incorruptible Giovanni Battista Fidanza, a former Italian seaman, nicknamed Nostromo, or "our man," a trusted factotum of the powerful and an admired figure of the Sulaco populace. Accompanying Nostromo is the cynical journalist Martin Decoud, who is fleeing as a marked man due to his newspaper attacks on the Monterists. The pair tries to deliver the treasure to an offshore European vessel to be transported to safety, but their boat collides with the rebel troopship. They manage to run their damaged boat ashore and to hide the silver on a deserted island. There Decoud remains in hiding while Nostromo returns to Sulaco to play a crucial part in the defeat of the Monterists and the secession of Sulaco from Costaguana.

Decoud, unable to cope with his isolation on the island, drowns himself using four silver bars as ballast. Nostromo eventually returns to the island to find Decoud vanished and some of the treasure missing. Valuing his unblemished reputation above all, Nostromo finds it now impossible to confess what has truly happened to the silver since he cannot account for the four missing ingots and fears he will be suspected of stealing them. Instead he allows the notion to stand that the treasure was lost at sea, while succumbing to its lure, secretly dipping into his cache "to grow rich slowly."

As progress grows in the now politically stable, flourishing Occidental Republic, a lighthouse is built on the deserted island where the treasure is concealed. Nostromo, considered a state hero, uses his influence to have his friend Giorgio Viola made lighthouse keeper to justify his secret withdrawals from the hidden treasure under cover of social visits to Viola and his two daughters. Courting the eldest, Linda, Nostromo is increasingly attracted to the youngest, Giselle, but he is unable to avoid being betrothed to Linda. Eventually, his duplicity and his enslavement by the treasure result in his death as he is accidentally shot by Viola. On his deathbed, Nostromo tries to confess to Emilia Gould, but she does not allow him to reveal the location of the remaining treasure, preferring the less complicated illusion that the silver should be "lost for ever." The novel concludes with the betrayed Linda mourning the dead Nostromo, whose genius "dominated the dark gulf containing his conquests of treasure and love."

Such a chronological summary considerably simplifies the actual progress of Conrad's narrative that scrambles cause and effect into a nonlinear sequence of events so that the reader often feels trapped within unfolding circumstances, the full significance of which is only gradually revealed. Flowing backward and forward in time, with seemingly insignificant details elaborately described and crucial facts mentioned in passing and possibly overlooked on a first reading, *Nostromo* is one of the first great experimental narratives of literary modernism in which conventional novelistic structure is redefined. The novel works by juxtaposition in which the reader must play an active role, reassembling the various parts of the story into coherence. Adding to the complication is Conrad's abandonment of a single narrative viewpoint. In works such as *Heart of Darkness* and *Lord Jim* the reader's guide and interpreter of events is the seaman Marlow. Described in *Heart of Darkness*, Marlow's storytelling avoids the simplicity of typical seaman's yarns in which meaning "lies within the shell of a cracked nut" for a more impressionistic approach in which "the meaning of an episode was not inside like a kernel but outside, enveloping the tale which brought it out only as a glow brings out a haze." Marlow's impressionism gives way in *Nostromo* to a kind of literary cubism, in which viewpoints shift from character to character with what one critic has described as a "bewildering mobility." The effect is to immerse the reader in experience sustained by the writer's incomparable ability to visualize scenes and anatomize complex behavior in which gesture and dialogue always have extensive contexts and often contradictory explanations.

On one level, *Nostromo* is a brilliant social drama that shows the evolution of civilization, as a wilderness is brought under control and a dynamic of confrontation and compromise is set in motion, reflecting the ways in which history emerges out of chaotic experience. On a deeper, psychological level, the novel, in the phrase of critic Albert Guerard, is a "critique of idealization," in which moral, social, and political principles are all tested by the corrupting influences of the San Tomé silver. In dealing with the implications of the silver the characters reveal themselves and what they stand for. For Charles Gould, the mine represents a principle of good intended to bring progress and order. Charles could not "act or exist without idealizing every simple feeling, desire, or achievement. He could not believe his own motives if he did not make them first a part of some fairy tale." To sustain his beliefs, Charles must blind himself to their full impact, making him, in the clearer vision of his wife, little more than a child. At the other end of the idealization spectrum is the nihilist Decoud, who is destroyed by "disillusioned weariness," lacking any sustaining ideals in the face of his existential isolation. Between the two is Nostromo, who is revealed not so much as a man but an image of one, a prisoner of his reputation and his own conception of his greatness that is finally transferred to the silver he has stolen: "He could never shake off the treasure. His audacity, greater than that of other men, had wielded that vein of silver into his life." Like the protagonist in *Lord Jim*, Nostromo is "one of us," knocked from his heroic pedestal and revealed as human, but unlike Jim, Nostromo is destroyed rather than redeemed, a self-divided man whose heroism and cupidity pull him apart.

Ideals in Conrad's diagnosis both kill and sustain. They drive a country into revolution and civil war, exploit the labor of others under the guise of progress; they imprison the individual in an illusion, yet they allow greatness of action, grand gestures, and a way to fill a meaningless void of existence. In the end, there are no true winners in Conrad's exploration of human nature and history. Only the silver retains its power, captured in the vision of Emilia Gould as she contemplates her diminished world: "She saw the San Tomé hanging over . . . the whole land, feared, hated, wealthy; more soulless than any tyrant, more pitiless and autocratic than the worst Government, ready to crush innumerable lives in the expansion of its greatness." No other novel that Conrad produced achieves so vast and so comprehensive an assessment of human motives and relationships. By turning from the sea to the land, Conrad showed he could create a world and one of the novel's great achievements in the 20th century.

45

FATHERS AND SONS

(1862)

by Ivan Turgenev

No author in Russia or the West was able to assemble such burning ideological and personal issues and to show their interconnections and universality quite in the way Turgenev has with Fathers and Sons.

—Edward Wasiolek, *Fathers and Sons: Russia at the Cross-roads*

According to Henry James, Turgenev was "the only real beautiful genius," and a writer he called "the novelist's novelist, an artistic influence extraordinarily valuable, and ineradicably established." Central to the artistic refinement of the novel in the 19th century, Turgenev had a crucial influence on modern fiction both as a short story writer and novelist and as a mentor to such writers as Flaubert, James, Conrad, and Hemingway. His greatest achievement is the novel *Fathers and Sons,* a work that scholar David Lowe has described as the "quintessential Russian novel," which absorbed the influences of the first great wave of Russian writers—Pushkin, Lermontov, and Gogol—and anticipated the direction of the next led by Tolstoy and Dostoevsky. Additionally, *Fathers and Sons* is the indispensable text for an understanding of the intellectual and social climate at the crucial moment in Russian history leading up to and immediately following the emancipation of the serfs in 1861. As Sir Isaiah Berlin has argued: "If the inner life, the ideas, the moral predicament of men matter at all in explaining the course of human history, then Turgenev's novels, especially *Fathers and Sons,* quite apart from their literary qualities, are as basic a document for the understanding of the Russian past and of our present as the plays of Aristophanes for the understanding of classical Athens, or Cicero's letters, or novels by Dickens or George Eliot, for an understanding of Rome and Victorian England." Invaluable as a window into the Russian mind and the ideological issues that shaped it, *Fathers and Sons* is equally remarkable for introducing a new type of fictional hero, the nihilist Bazarov, who in many ways set the pattern for the modern alienated outsider and antihero, an incendiary figure whose meaning and importance continue to be critically debated.

Having established his reputation as one of Russia's leading writers in the 1850s with the brilliantly observed depictions of Russian village life collected in *A Sportsman's Sketches* (1852), Turgenev in his fourth novel took up the subject of the ideological clash between reformers and revolutionaries, between his own generation of liberals who came of age in the 1840s and the next generation impatient with the pace of social change and scornful of those it held responsible. Called the first Russian ideological novel, *Fathers and Sons*, as its title indicates, embodies the ideological conflict of Turgenev's era in a generational battle in which two opposed value systems are tested dramatically in the return home of the recent university graduate Arkady Kirsanov to his widowed father's country estate, accompanied by his friend, medical student Evgeny Bazarov. With his gruff manners and self-styled nihilistic philosophy that refuses to accept any ideals or principles untested by practicality and elevates science and reason over art and emotion, Bazarov becomes the provocateur to challenge the conventional wisdom and verities of the gentry, typified by the kind-hearted but ineffectual father of Arkady, Nikolay Petrovich, and his brother, the pompous and self-righteous dandy Pavel. Fastidious in his dress and manners, a self-styled custodian of established views, Pavel quickly becomes Bazarov's antagonist in a series of verbal sparring matches that eventually escalates into a duel. Through the conflict that Bazarov supplies by his unconventional views, each of the novel's characters reveals his values and beliefs as a multidimensional portrait of a time and place begins to emerge.

Supporting Turgenev's didactic purpose is his observational skill in carefully rendering customs and milieu as well as his characteristic stance of sympathetic detachment, which allows him to reveal his characters by fully recording gesture, reaction, and context. Responding to the charge that his fiction was dominated by the general rather than the specific, Turgenev declared that "I have heard it said . . . not once but many times that in my works I always 'started with an idea or developed an idea'. . . . I never attempted 'to create character' unless I had as my starting point not an idea but a living person to whom the appropriate elements were later added. Not possessing a great amount of free inventive power, I always felt the need of some firm ground on which I could plant my feet." The starting point for Turgenev's conception of the age's new man, Bazarov, was a young provincial doctor the writer had met on a train in England, through whom, Turgenev later reported, he "could watch the embodiment of the principle which had scarcely come to life but was just beginning to stir at the time which later received the name of 'nihilism.'"

At the center of the vituperative storm that followed publication of *Fathers and Sons* in 1862, which Russian scholar A. V. Knowles asserts was "possibly the greatest controversy that has ever greeted a Russian novel," was what to make of Turgenev's central character and Turgenev's intentions concerning his story in which the nihilist, who succeeds in exposing the shallowness of those around him, is eventually himself bested by a combination of uncontrolled emotion and mortality. Turgenev would later call Bazarov his "favorite offspring" and declare his agreement with all of Bazarov's views except on the worthlessness of art. "I wanted to create a character who was shadowy," Turgenev asserted, "strange, life-size, only half-developed, yet strong, fearless, and honest, but nonetheless doomed to failure because he still stands only on the threshold of the future." Although the reader is clearly invited to admire Bazarov's uncompromising testing stance, particularly against the comically ineffectual Nickolay and the pompously reactionary Pavel, and his devotion to his philosophy compared to those like Arkady who merely copy the nihilist style while missing its substance, Bazarov is also shown to be severely limited in self-understanding. His nothing-sacred attitude is shown to be inadequate, particularly when his philosophy proves to be no match for the claims of love when he cannot resist the attractions of Anna Odintsova or as a prescription against mortality and human frailty when he is fatally infected with typhoid. Having dismissed love as sentimental nonsense, Bazarov is himself a victim of an uncontrolled passion for the cold-hearted Anna. Having broken with Arkady over the latter's conventionality, Bazarov returns home to his adoring parents where, performing an autopsy on a peasant, he is mortally stricken with a disease whose cure is unavailable at his parents' rural home. He dies, therefore, needlessly but resignedly, in a deathbed scene the writer V. S. Pritchett has called "one of the most moving and beautifully observed things that the great observer ever wrote."

Is Bazarov, therefore, meant to be seen as a tragic hero, a victim, or a fool? Evidence for each can be readily found in the novel, and the contradictions formed the basis for the argument surrounding *Fathers and Sons* when it first appeared. Radicals on the Left saw Bazarov as an insulting caricature, a parody of their generation's attitudes and leading figures, showing that Turgenev had joined forces with the reactionaries in opposition to the new ideas of the younger generation. Those on the Right accused Turgenev of currying favor with the younger radicals by memorializing one of their number and glorifying the destruction of essential values in Bazarov's easy victories over establishment representatives like the Kirsanovs. In retrospect, the offending of both sides in the ideological divide of the 1860s is proof of Turgenev's superior artistry and nonpartisan, nondidactic aspirations in the novel. It is also why *Fathers and Sons* continues to be read with interest long after the ideological issues and contemporary relevance have faded into the background. The novel's drama seems to work out a far more complicated and universal assessment of the human condition than the narrower didactic purpose that Turgenev's first readers suspected. As Henry James observed about Turgenev's great gifts as a novelist, "If his manner is that of a searching realist, his temper is that of a devoutly attentive observer, and the result

THE TRIAL

46

(1925)

by Franz Kafka

In chronicling Joseph K.'s struggle to discover the nature of his guilt, the identity of his judges, the letter of the law, and his stubborn efforts to pit reason and common sense against the flawless logic of a sentence based on a verdict beyond rational comprehension, Kafka quietly, without fanfare, without stylistic extravagance or verbal excesses, demolished the solid, taken-for-granted certitudes of nineteenth-century realism with its black-and-white contrasts and sharply defined outlines, not unlike the way in which post-Newtonian physics had begun to dismantle the commonsense notions of matter and dissolved the familiar world of solid objects in a space-time continuum governed by forces of terrifying potential.

—Ernst Pawel, *The Nightmare of Reason: A Life of Franz Kafka*

There is something eerily prophetic in the fact that Franz Kafka composed the opening sentence of his masterpiece—"Someone must have maligned Josef K., for without having done anything wrong, he was arrested one morning"—around August 1914, at the outset of World War I as the modern world began to assume its characteristic shape, and Kafka's unsettling conception of irrational persecution and victimization was on the verge of being converted into global fact. Kafka introduces his readers to the contemporary world and their deepest fears in a prescient novel that from the perspective of history since 1914 seems far more realistic than surrealistic. As Erich Heller has observed, "There can be no other novel so thoroughly pervaded by the sense of nightmare and paranoia as *The Trial*." It could indeed be argued that Kafka's *The Trial* is in fact the archetypal modern novel: fragmentary, bewildering, disturbing, and inexhaustibly challenging in its symbolic and interpretive possibilities. It is certainly the defining fable of the modern bureaucratic victim, of contemporary alienation and the ultimate persecution complex, as Josef K., a respectable bank officer, awakes to find himself charged with an unspecified crime by a shadowy legal system that frustrates any defense. In one sense, Josef K. is the representative victim of a Gestapo-like arrest and a show trial in which there is no defense possible in a modern justice system that has been perverted into an instrument for irrational persecution. At a deeper level, however, *The Trial* is an even more demanding and revealing exploration of universal, existential guilt in which Josef K.'s complicity becomes the novel's inescapable central lesson.

Like Kafka's other two novels, *The Castle* and *Amerika*, *The Trial* was left unfinished and consigned along with the nearly four-fifths of the author's oeuvre that Kafka instructed his friend and literary executor, Max Brod, to destroy after the writer's death. Brod disobeyed Kafka's wishes and began the process of reconstructing the writer's intentions in *The Trial* from an unsorted collection of unnumbered chapters, fragments, and notes. Unlike his other novels, however, *The Trial* does have a definite conclusion since Kafka composed the novel out of linear sequence, writing the end chapter immediately after the opening. Scholars have subsequently worked out a plausible sequence for the intervening chapters. While most agree that *The Trial* is Kafka's greatest extended narrative, there is little consensus on the definitive meaning of Kafka's text, which in many ways frustrates the reader in the same way that Josef K. is impeded from learning what crime he is guilty of or how he can demonstrate his innocence. At the center of Kafka's conception is the radical repossession of the novel of crime and punishment, a novel of detection transformed from the expected "who did it?" to "what was done?" Unlike a detective writer, however, Kafka never solves this mystery, and the reader, kept within the limited and unreliable perspective of Josef K., experiences directly his claustrophobic frustrations and ambiguities.

The Trial opens, like Kafka's other masterpiece, the novella *The Metamorphosis*, in which Gregor Samsa awakes one morning to find himself transformed into an insect, with its central protagonist, Josef K., waking up on his 30th birthday to find his normal respectable world utterly and irrevocably transformed. Two warders have come to arrest him, and neither they nor the inspector who questions K. are willing or able to inform him of his crime. No evidence is provided of K.'s guilt; neither is the identity of his accuser (if any) revealed. Moreover, Josef K. is not taken into custody but merely informed that he has been charged and allowed to resume his normal daily activities. His initial reaction is righteous indignation, assertion of his innocence, and blame of others, be they the unknown figure who has denounced him or the justice system itself that seems to operate outside the expected rules. Josef K. demands to know the law he is supposed to have broken, and one of his guards remarks to his partner: "He admits that he doesn't know the Law and yet he claims he's innocent." The inspector who questions him advises K. to "think less about us and of what is going to happen to you, think more about yourself instead. And don't make such an outcry about your feeling innocent." Both guard and inspector suggest that K.'s crime and the secret court that will judge him are *extra*ordinary, a more fundamental tribunal to consider an interior and existential crime, a lesson that eludes K. even as the evidence proves unavoidable.

Ordered to appear before the court on the following Sunday, Josef K. is surprised to discover that the court is located in a huge, factorylike, shabby apartment building. Directed by a washerwoman to the fifth-floor attic room filled with drying laundry and old men with long beards, K. contemptuously addresses those assembled and mounts an indignant defense:

> There can be no doubt that . . . behind my arrest and today's interrogation, there is a great organization at work. An organization which not only employs corrupt warders, oafish Inspectors, and Examining Magistrates . . . but which also has at its disposal a judicial hierarchy of high, indeed of the highest rank, with an indispensable and numerous retinue of servants, clerks, police, and other assistants, perhaps even hangmen, I do not shrink from that word.

He is interrupted in his consoling conception of a vast judicial conspiracy by the shrieks of a young man lustily holding onto the washerwoman, and K. storms indignantly out of the room. The absurd details of K.'s court appearance, like those of his arrest, should point him to the revelation that this court is unlike any other, not a civil authority but a far more elemental one. By setting himself in opposition to an imagined system that seems bent on his destruction, Josef K. misses the point of a universalized guilt that he refuses to acknowledge. In his demand for a judgment, he misses the larger point that guilt in his world is a steady state, not an exception but the rule.

Throughout the rest of the novel there is a growing disjunction between Josef K.'s actions and his increasing fixation on his guilt. On the one hand, he seeks whatever assistance he can manage in order to approach the court and resolve his case; on the other hand, nothing he does makes any difference, and Josef K. must adjust to a new sense of circumstances in which it is no longer a matter of guilt or innocence but guilt *and* innocence. On the advice of his uncle, Josef K. hires a lawyer, but the lawyer is ineffectual. Frustrated by the lack of progress, Josef K. seeks other assistance. Visiting Tintorelli, the court painter, who presumably has some influence, Josef K. learns that no one charged is ever acquitted and that the best one can expect is an indefinite postponement of a judgment. Finally, in the next-to-last chapter, "In the Cathedral," Josef K. meets with a priest who repeats the inspector's earlier advice to give over his efforts to shift the guilt to others and to acknowledge his culpability. To Josef K.'s assertion of his innocence, the priest replies, "That's how all guilty men talk." To illustrate his lesson, the priest tells Josef K. a parable of a man who seeks entrance to the law but is blocked by a doorkeeper. After a lifetime of waiting and futile efforts to convince the doorkeeper to relent, the man learns that, although he could never enter the door, nevertheless it was meant for him alone. Although the relevance of the parable to Josef K.'s dilemma continues to be debated, it seems clear that the man in the parable has wasted his life confusing a prohibition (the doorkeeper's refusal to let him pass) with a greater truth: that the entrance is intended only for him, an irrevocable absolute. By shifting the blame for his circumstances to the doorkeeper who forbids entry but cannot prevent it, the man has mistaken who ultimately is responsible for his wasted life—himself. It is a lesson that Josef K. also misses by apprehending the lesson of the parable as the deception of the doorkeeper. The priest offers alternative interpretations, altering the emphasis from the doorkeeper to the man himself, suggesting by the connection with Josef K.'s own circumstances that he has missed the true point of the court. "The Court wants nothing from you," the priest concludes. "It receives you when you come and it dismisses you when you go." As elliptical as Kafka's allegory may appear, the end effect of the priest's lesson and the details of Josef K.'s circumstances transfer the focus from the external to the internal, from persecution to conscience.

Equally challenging as the interpretation of the priest's parable is the novel's conclusion, in which on the eve of his 31st birthday Josef K. awaits his executioners—two men in frock coats and top hats—who lead him to a quarry. Rejecting their implied suggestion that he should carry out the sentence himself by suicide, Josef K. dies in shame "like a dog," with one of his executioners holding his throat and the other stabbing him in the heart, turning the knife around twice.

The attempt to wrestle final meaning from the implications of Josef K.'s experiences, like the experiences themselves, frustrates resolution. More symbolic than allegorical, multiple interpretations are not only possible but inescapable. As the ultimate victim, Josef K. is trapped in a modern version of Dickens's Circumlocution Office from his own novel that displays society as a prison, *Little Dorrit.* Frustrated at every turn by a system that seems to require victims, Josef K. can only look forward to his execution, which reduces him to the level of ignoble brute. In this reading the law is a fantasy, justice a sham, and every effort of social structure—church, state, family—a conspiracy to impede essential self-knowledge. On the psychological level, however, Josef K. can be viewed not as a blameless victim but as guilty as charged. In the same way that Gregor Samsa living an insect-like life becomes an insect, Josef K. under an open-ended charge is awakened to the inescapability of his own crimes and guilt. On the point of execution, Josef K. manages for the first time a self-judgment that helps to redeem, if for only an instant, the irrational persecution. "I always wanted to snatch at the world with twenty hands," he acknowledges, "and not for a very laudable motive, either. That was wrong, and am I to show now that not even a year's trial has taught me anything? Am I to leave this world as a man who has no common sense? Are people to say of me after I am gone that at the beginning of my case I wanted to finish it, and at the end of it I wanted to begin it again? I don't want that to be said. I am grateful for the fact that these half-dumb, senseless creatures have been sent to accompany me on this journey, and that I have been left to say to myself all that is needed." In Kafka's remarkable narrative, the trial is the unavoidable state of existence, not an exceptional or terminal circumstance. Josef K. is left suspended in the anxiety of conscience that defines the modern dilemma.

47

LOLITA

(1955)

by Vladimir Nabokov

What is the evil I have committed?
Seducer, criminal—is this the word
for me who set the entire world a-dreaming of my poor little girl?
—Vladimir Nabokov, from "What Is the Evil Deed," in *Poems and Problems*

Lolita, decried by one of the many American publishers who turned the novel down in 1954 as "sheer pornography," has also been praised by writer Edmund White as "the supreme novel of love in the twentieth century," as well as by Garry Wills as "an even rarer thing than an honest love story. It is our best modern hate story." The chronicle of Humbert Humbert's doomed and damning passion for adolescent Dolores Haze, Humbert's Lolita, proved to be both an irresistible, unsettling best seller and the text that secured Nabokov's reputation as an erudite and demanding modernist master, a rare combination indeed. Even nonreaders understand a reference to a "Lolita," a name that has entered the English sexual lexicon conjuring the allure of the prepubescent nymphet (a term Nabokov also coined) and a sexual attraction that flirts dangerously with pedophilia. Eventually accepted in the literary canon as, in the words of Alfred Appel Jr., "one of the few supremely original novels of the century," *Lolita* still shocks and is still censored, even in a society in which sex is marketed by high-fashion models who may be over the hill and used up at age 17. *Lolita* remains one of the great controversial enigmas in fiction. Is Humbert Humbert, its poetic pedophile, a monster, magician, or eventual moralist? Are his desires and his aesthetic transformations to be abhorred or admired, and is his story merely the playful trickery of the puzzle-loving Nabokov or something far more complex, disturbing, and enduring? Nabokov's novel assaults the reader's moral assumptions and sympathies while it destabilizes the familiar and constructs a shimmering verbal playground that is both seductive and dangerous.

Nabokov traced the origin of *Lolita* to his chance reading in a French newspaper in 1939 of an ape "who, after months of coaxing by a scientist, produced the first drawing ever charcoaled by an animal; this sketch showed the bars of the poor creature's cage." The incident, suggestive of a captive whose only artistic transcendence is a reflection of his captivity, inspired an aborted initial short story of a man enthralled by nympholepsy. "The Magician," set in France, was abandoned because, as Nabokov recalled, "the little girl wasn't alive. She hardly spoke. Little by little I managed to give her some semblance of reality." By the 1940s Nabokov had immigrated to the United States, begun composing in English, and returned to his story, now with an American setting and verisimilitude provided by Nabokov's cross-country summer butterfly hunts and motel stays as well as research forays on school buses to learn how American teenagers talked. "The book developed slowly," Nabokov recalled, "with many interruptions and asides. It had taken me some forty years to invent Russia and Western Europe, and now I was faced by the task of inventing America."

After a five-year labor *Lolita* was delivered to American publishers who balked, fearing prosecution over the book's incendiary, taboo subject. Turning to European publishers, Nabokov agreed to publication in France by the Olympia Press, headed by Maurice Girodias. Although Olympia did publish such literary authors as Henry Miller and Jean Genet, it was known primarily for the sexual content of its offerings with such titles as *White Thighs* and *The Sexual Life of Robinson Crusoe.* According to Girodias, "I sensed that *Lolita* would become the one great modern work of art to demonstrate once and for all the futility of moral censorship, and the indispensable role of passion in literature." Nabokov, unaware that *Lolita* would be joining a pornographic catalog, was a reluctant First Amendment crusader who asserted to Girodias that "*Lolita* is a serious book with a serious purpose. I hope the public will accept it as such. A succès de scandale would distress me." The novel sold poorly in its first year and was not reviewed. However, when Graham Greene named *Lolita* one of the best books of the year in the London *Times*, it became an underground sensation. The novel finally appeared in the United States in 1958 after the U.S. Customs Bureau released confiscated copies of the Olympia edition, thus opening the way for American publication. Nabokov described what followed the book's American release as "Hurricane Lolita." An immediate best seller, *Lolita* became the first book since *Gone with the Wind* to sell 100,000 copies in its first three weeks. The novel's success allowed Nabokov to retire from university teaching to devote himself full time to his writing. Nabokov later observed, "I never imagined that I should be able to live by my writing, but now I am kept by a little girl named Lolita."

The novel takes the form of the European émigré scholar Humbert Humbert's prison confession, written while awaiting trial for the murder of playwright Clare Quilty, his rival for the possession of Lolita. The narrator's pseudonymous matching names are the perfect signs of the ultimate narcissist. Humbert's defense chronicles his life and obsessive passion, including an unrequited boyhood love that he offers as the cause for his nymph fixation, his disastrous first marriage before his relocation to America, and a chance encounter with the 12-year-old Dolores Haze, the daughter of his landlady, Charlotte Haze, whom Humbert marries to secure his access to the young girl he renames Lolita. Humbert resists murdering Charlotte, only to find that she is conveniently eliminated after discovering Humbert's incriminating diary of his obsession with Lolita ("hurrying housewife, slippery pavement, a pest of a dog, steep grade, big car, baboon at the wheel"). Humbert retrieves Lolita from summer camp, and as her nominal stepfather takes her to the aptly named hotel, "The Enchanted Hunters," where they become "technically lovers," although Humbert insists that "it was she who seduced me." Dad and daughter begin a year-long driving tour of the United States. Here Nabokov offers some of his most mordant satire as Humbert's guilty possession of his prize is played out across an American landscape of majestic vistas desecrated by Humbert's violation and littered with vulgar roadside kitsch, a perfect emblem for Humbert's doomed affair with his dream child. As Humbert recalls, "We had been everywhere. We had really seen nothing. And I catch myself thinking today that our long journey had only defiled with a sinuous trail of slime the lovely, trustful, dreamy, enormous country that by then, in retrospect, was no more to us than a collection of dog-eared maps, ruined tour books, old tires, and her sobs in the night—every night, every night—the moment I feigned sleep." Returning east, Humbert enrolls Lolita in a girls' prep school where Humbert enforces Lolita's sexual compliance with threats and bribes while she plots with Quilty her escape on a reprise of the earlier cross-country trip.

Humbert searches in vain for the couple for three years before hearing from Lolita, now Mrs. Richard F. Schiller, pregnant, and in need of money. Her nymphet charms have vanished, but Humbert still begs her to rejoin him and makes a claim for his moral redemption: "You may jeer at me, and threaten to clear the court, but until I am gagged and half-throttled, I will shout my poor truth. I insist the world know how much I loved my Lolita, *this* Lolita, pale and polluted, and big with another's child." To bolster his contrition, Humbert recalls during his search hearing the sounds of children at play and realizing that "the hopelessly poignant thing was not Lolita's absence from my side, but the absence of her voice from that concord." Humbert finally confesses to having stolen Lolita's childhood from her, to have remade her to serve his will, a violation and sacrifice to his unappeasable desires. Yet even as Humbert claims regret, he embarks on an equally monstrous appropriation of his rival's life. Quilty proves difficult to kill ("I rolled over him. We rolled over me. They rolled over him. We rolled over us.") and equally resistant in conforming to Humbert's righteous indignation over the callousness of Quilty's manipulation of Lolita, to contrast with the purity of Humbert's passion ("My memory and my eloquence are not at their best today but really, my dear Mr. Humbert, you were not an ideal stepfather, and I did not force your little protégée to join me. It was she made me remove her to a happier home."). Eventually, Quilty is silenced after one of the funniest murders in literature. Ultimately, Humbert offers his own verdict on his crimes: "Had I come before myself, I would have given Humbert at least thirty-five years for rape, and dismissed the rest of the charges."

Many readers, seduced by the narrator's verbal wizardry and the poetic intensity of his passion, have been inclined to concur, going so far as to mitigate the rape conviction as well. Even such a sophisticated and moral reader as Lionel Trilling has confessed that "I was plainly not able to muster up the note of moral outrage. . . . Humbert is perfectly willing to say that he is a monster; we find ourselves less and less eager to agree with him." Nabokov, however, disagrees, calling Humbert "a vain and cruel wretch who manages to appear 'touching.'" The uncritical reader should never forget that Humbert Humbert is one of fiction's most insidious, unreliable narrators, that to take him at his word is a trap as difficult to resist and as dangerous as any of the other violations that the novel arranges. Humbert *is* a monster, one of fiction's cruelest, but also one of the most compelling, whose verbal spell, withering scorn, and poetic rapture help to make the reader complicit in his crimes.

Nabokov, however, is equally adept in providing the clues to resist Humbert's version of events and their full significance. As the Nabokov biographer Brian Boyd points out, "The whole of *Lolita* inverts the detective story pattern: we begin with a murderer, identified on the first page of the novel and have to guess at the victim: we face not a whodunit but a 'whocoppedit.'" Reaching the identity of Humbert's victim, the reader can relish the clues that were missed all along as well as the more compelling inquiry into the nature of the novel's criminal and the fate of the book's principal victim. Buried in the editor's foreword and meaningless on first reading is the crucial nugget that "Mrs. 'Richard F. Schiller' died in childbed, giving birth to a stillborn girl, on Christmas Day 1952, in Gray Star, a settlement in the remotest Northwest." Like Humbert, who has died of coronary thrombosis before going on trial, Lolita has died shortly after Humbert's last visit, a victim of what Humbert terms "McFate," which haunts the book. Death as much as desire is a determining motive of Humbert's redeeming, diabolic, and ultimately destructive wish to halt time, recapture the departed past, and construct and inhabit an imagined paradise. The greatness of *Lolita* is Nabokov's skill in capturing such a world and its underlying human cost. Like many of the great modernist masterpieces, *Lolita* is fundamentally about

48

MRS DALLOWAY

(1925)

by Virginia Woolf

Mrs Dalloway *was the first novel to split the atom. If the novel before* Mrs Dalloway *aspired to immensities of scope and scale, to heroic journeys across vast landscapes, with* Mrs Dalloway *Virginia Woolf insisted that it could also locate the enormous within the everyday; that a life of errands and party-giving was every bit as viable a subject as any life lived anywhere; and that should any human act in any novel seem unimportant, it has merely been inadequately observed. The novel as an art form has not been the same since.* Mrs Dalloway *also contains some of the most beautiful, complex, incisive and idiosyncratic sentences ever written in English, and that alone would be reason enough to read it. It is one of the most moving, revolutionary artworks of the twentieth century.*

—Michael Cunningham, quoted in *Mrs Dalloway,* Harcourt edition

Virginia Woolf's fourth novel, *Mrs Dalloway,* shows the full emergence of her distinctive literary voice and the experimental method she would employ in her subsequent fiction. Written in the shadow of Joyce's towering achievement in *Ulysses, Mrs Dalloway* similarly records the events of a single day in June in a single place—London—linking, as in *Ulysses,* the separate progress of two central protagonists, while turning the novel's drama inward for a direct apprehension of human consciousness itself that probes the elusive contours of memory and identity. If, however, *Ulysses* aspires to the status of modern epic, *Mrs Dalloway* is far more lyrical in its aims, more personal and centripetal, less encyclopedic and centrifugal, in attempting to render human experience, though no less profound in its representation of the mysteries and wonderment of a morning walk to buy flowers, a suicide, or a successful dinner party. With *Mrs Dalloway,* Woolf pioneered a new subspecies of fiction—the poetic novel—a narrative manifesting the lyric poem's preoccupation with private thoughts and emotions and structured by tone and imagery rather than by plot. In rewriting the rules of narrative fiction, *Mrs Dalloway* is the most impressive, earliest British example of modernism's assault on literature's ends and means.

The modernist revolution of the first two decades of the 20th century passed through Bloomsbury for Virginia Woolf's approval and assistance. Joyce's patron, Harriet Shaw Weaver, arrived in 1918 with Joyce's manuscript, hoping that the Woolfs might publish it through their Hogarth Press. Woolf had read the serialized excerpts, and, at least publicly, she ridiculed Joyce's novel as "underbred" and tortuous: "Never did I read such tosh," she famously complained to her friend Lytton Strachey. "As for the first chapters we will let them pass, but the 3rd 4th 5th 6th—merely the scratching of pimples on the body of the bootboy at Claridges." On finishing the manuscript, Woolf declared, "my martyrdom is over." Privately, however, her diary records a deeper appreciation of Joyce's accomplishment: "It is an attempt to get thinking into literature—hence the jumble . . . Here is thought made phonetic—taken to bits . . . The inner thought, & then the little scatter of life on top to keep you in touch with reality . . . the repetition of words like wormwood and ashes." Woolf would revisit *Ulysses* in 1922 when it was published, urged on by T. S. Eliot, whose own modernist masterwork, *The Waste Land*, Woolf accepted for the Hogarth Press and set into type. Eliot had declared Joyce "a great genius" and *Ulysses* "the greatest work of the age." Rankled by such praise for a novel she claimed she despised, Woolf took up the novel again just as she was at work on a short story, "Mrs Dalloway in Bond Street," and finished it several months later as she was writing a sequel to the Dalloway story called "The Prime Minister," about an assassination attempt by a deranged man. Joyce's novel would play a part in both confirming the interior direction she intended to pursue in her fiction and showing Woolf how to connect her two stories into the novels that began to take shape in Woolf's mind.

Other factors in the evolving shape of *Mrs Dalloway* can be traced from Woolf's writing that preceded the novel, marking the growing break in her thinking away from established fictional conventions. As early as 1919 in her essay "Modern Novels" (revised as "Modern Fiction" and published in *The Common Reader*, 1925), Woolf rejected the external preoccupations of contemporary realistic fiction that she labeled "materialistic." Content at rendering only the surface of things, such novelists missed the point in Woolf's view. "Is life like this?" she asked. "Must novels be like this?" Her answer, exhorting readers to "Examine for a moment an ordinary mind on an ordinary day" with all its myriad impressions—"trivial, fantastic, evanescent, or engraved with the sharpness of steel"—describes the operating principles that would characterize *Mrs Dalloway*'s depiction of: "an ordinary mind on an ordinary day." Her first attempt to embody these principles was her third novel, *Jacob's Room* (1922), a significant break from her more conventionally structured preceding novels, *The Voyage Out* (1915) and *Night and Day* (1919). In it, the story of Jacob Flanders's life is assembled from brief, disconnected scenes and indirectly from the possessions that remain following his death in the

Great War. With its emphasis on the fragmentary nature of experience and the difficulty of authentically capturing identity, *Jacob's Room* constituted a new form for her fiction in which she saw "immense possibilities" and caused her to declare just after its completion, "There's no doubt in my mind that I have found out how to begin (at 40) to say something in my own voice." She would later report that *Jacob's Room* had been "a necessary step" on the way to *Mrs Dalloway*. Another was the seminal essay "Mr. Bennett and Mrs Brown," published in 1923 as she was working on *Mrs Dalloway*. It was a response to the novelist Arnold Bennett's review of *Jacob's Room* (one of the "materialists" Woolf had earlier criticized) titled "Is the Novel Decaying?" which held Woolf culpable for the decay as one whose "characters do not vitally survive in the mind, because the author has been obsessed by details of originality and cleverness." Woolf's rebuttal on behalf of her new generation of writers like Joyce and Eliot takes the form of her conjuring as a stand-in for human nature an ordinary woman named Mrs Brown traveling in a railway carriage and imagining how the novelists of the preceding generation—H. G. Wells, John Galsworthy, and Arnold Bennett—would have attempted to depict her by attending to her class, manners, and particulars of dress and gesture and thereby failing to capture her essence:

> There she sits and not one of the Edwardian writers has so much as looked at her. They have looked very powerfully, searchingly, and sympathetically out of the window; at factories, at Utopia, even at the decoration and upholstery of the carriage; but never at her, never at life, never at human nature. And so they have developed a technique of novel-writing which suits their purpose; they have made tools and established conventions which do their business. But those tools are not our tools, and that business is not our business. For us those conventions are ruin, those tools are death.

By employing different tools and conventions to capture life and the elusive Mrs Brown, Woolf urges readers to "Tolerate the spasmodic, the obscure, the fragmentary, the failure" because "we are trembling on the verge of one of the great ages of English literature. But it can only be reached if we are determined never, never to desert Mrs Brown. . . . The capture of Mrs Brown is the title of the next chapter in the history of literature . . . the most important, the most epoch-making of them all."

Mrs Dalloway, therefore, is Woolf's effort to capture Mrs Brown. Her first attempt at rendering "an ordinary mind on an ordinary day" was a short story, "Mrs Dalloway in Bond Street," in which the well-to-do, middle-aged Clarissa Dalloway ventures from her Westminster home to buy gloves. Clarissa's background and temperament are glimpsed from fragments of her perceptions and memories. Additional sketches concerning Mrs Dalloway eventually "branched into a book" that was first tentatively titled "At Home: or The Party." Woolf increasingly struggled to connect scenes involving her society matron with those concerning a madman plotting to kill the prime minister who became Septimus Warren Smith, the damaged war veteran. Here, the example of Joyce's *Ulysses* would be applied in which the separate progress of Stephen Dedalus and Leopold Bloom are connected through the unities of time and place, image and theme. "Suppose," Woolf pondered in her diary, "it be connected this way: Sanity & insanity. Mrs D. seeing the truth, S. S. seeing the insane truth . . . the contrast must be arranged," and in another entry, "All inner feelings to be lit up. The two minds Mrs D. & Septimus." In this expanded concept of a network of associated sympathies, emotions, and experiences, now titled *The Hours*, Woolf labored to find the necessary balance between "design and substance" as a diary entry shows: "Am I writing *The Hours* from deep emotion? . . . Have I the power of conveying the true reality? Or do I write essays about myself? . . . This is going to be the devil of a struggle. The design is so queer and so masterful. I'm always having to wrench my substance to fit it." Woolf's solution for her internalized narrative came to her suddenly: "My discovery: how I dig out beautiful caves behind my characters: I think that gives exactly what I want; humanity, humour, depth. The idea is that the caves shall connect and each comes to daylight at the present moment." Woolf's "tunneling process" allowed her to forgo a linear narrative, replacing the impressionism of *Jacob's Room* with a stream of consciousness method in which external events are filtered almost entirely through the feelings, perceptions, and memories of her characters. Moving without transition from various centers of consciousness and through interweaving of image and preoccupations, Woolf arrived at a form which could "use up everything I've ever thought." "In this book," Woolf realized, "I have almost too many ideas. I want to give life and death, sanity and insanity; I want to criticize the social system, and to show it at work, at its most intense."

The novel opens with Clarissa Dalloway, aged 52, the wife of a Conservative M.P. leaving her house in Dean's Yard, Westminster, for Bond Street to buy flowers for the party she is giving that evening. Present and past collide in Clarissa's perception and memory as details about her girlhood and her relationship with her cherished friends Sally Seton, Peter Walsh, and the man she would eventually marry, Richard Dalloway, gradually take shape amid Clarissa's present anxieties about her age and health: "What a lark! What a plunge! For so it had always seemed to her, when, with a little squeak of the hinges, which she could hear now, she had burst open the French windows and plunged at Bourton into the open air. How fresh, how calm, stiller than this of course, the air was in the early morning; like the flap of a wave; the kiss of a wave; chill and sharp, and yet (for a girl of eighteen as she then was) solemn, feeling as she did, standing there at the open window, that something awful was about to happen. . . ." While Clarissa buys the flowers, an automobile carrying some important person passes; it also goes past a young married couple, Septimus and Lucrezia Warren Smith. He is an estate agent's clerk and shell-shocked veteran of the war haunted by the death of his friend Evans and voices that have necessitated his seeking medical help, first from a G.P., Dr. Holmes, and later at noon with the noted nerve specialist Sir William Bradshaw. As the Smiths pass the time in Regent's Park before the appointment, Clarissa returns home where she learns that her husband is having lunch with Lady Bruton. Disappointed not to be included, Clarissa begins to mend her party dress, but she is surprised by the unexpected visit from Peter Walsh, her former suitor whom she rejected to marry Richard. Peter has returned after years in India, a widower, now in love with a young married woman with two children. After Peter departs with the narrative entering his consciousness, he passes the Smiths on their way to see Sir William. After a brief assessment, the doctor insists that Septimus be committed to a country sanitarium under his direction. Meanwhile, Richard Dalloway helps Lady Bruton write a letter to the *Times* before returning home to find Clarissa annoyed that she must invite an unwanted relative to her party and that her 17-year-old daughter, Elizabeth, is under the sway of her possessive history tutor, Miss Kilman. The Warren Smiths also return home, and Septimus's brief respite of lucidity and calm is interrupted by the arrival of Dr. Holmes to take him to the sanitarium, and Septimus jumps out of the window to his death. Peter, who is passed by the ambulance carrying Septimus's body, arrives at Clarissa's party and is surprised to find Sally Seton, about whom both Peter and Clarissa had been thinking throughout the day, an uninvited surprise guest. The party in fact brings together many of the various characters who have been seen or mentioned throughout the day, including Sir William Bradshaw who explains his late arrival because of the suicide of one of his patients. Clarissa's intense sympathy for Septimus in which his death seems more a liberation from the social constraints and life-denying imperatives that have haunted Clarissa throughout the day ultimately liberates Clarissa from confinement to her defined roles as wife, mother, and perfect hostess and provokes a concluding appreciative wonderment from Peter:

> What is this terror? What is this ecstasy? He thought to himself.
> What is it that fills me with extraordinary excitement?
> It is Clarissa, he said.
> For there she was.

Peter models the wonderment, the catharsis of pity and terror, that the attentive reader feels at the novel's conclusion and in our appreciation for Woolf's achievement in *Mrs Dalloway*. Recounting the trivial details of an ordinary June day bombarding the consciousness of several characters, Woolf manages

49

DREAM OF THE RED CHAMBER

(1791)

by Cao Xueqin

With one book, the genius of Cao Xueqin proves to have the universality of Shakespeare. Its combination of intellectual scope and immediate human drama has no counterpart in Western fiction. To appreciate its position in Chinese culture, we must imagine a work with the critical cachet of James Joyce's Ulysses *and the popular appeal of Margaret Mitchell's* Gone with the Wind*—and twice as long as the two combined.*

—Dore J. Levy, *Ideal and Actual in the Story of the Stone*

As national and cultural epics only Cervantes's *Don Quixote* and Lady Murasaki's *Tale of Genji* rival Cao Xueqin's 18th-century novel, *Hong Lou Meng*, known in the West as *Dream of the Red Chamber* (alternatively, *Dream of Red Mansions* or *The Story of the Stone*). The greatest of all Chinese novels, Cao Xueqin's masterpiece is the standard by which previous and subsequent fiction in China is measured. "To show his scorn for contemporary Chinese writing," literary historian C. T. Hsia has observed, "a scholar versed in traditional literature would often ask, 'What has been produced in the last fifty years that could equal *Dream of the Red Chamber?*' But one could also turn the tables on him and ask with equal expectation of a negative answer: 'What work previous to *Dream* could equal it?' . . . *Dream* which embodies the supreme tragic experience in Chinese literature is also its supreme work of psychological realism." *Dream of the Red Chamber* revolutionized the novel in China, turning it away from a previous reliance on well-known myths and legends and stereotypical, idealized characters that earned fiction a reputation for moral irrelevance and a lack of artistic and intellectual seriousness. Cao Xueqin substituted the worldly and spiritual strivings of believable characters in a realistically conceived network of recognizable social and psychological relationships. Like such progenitors of the novel in the West as Cervantes, Fielding, Stendhal, and Thackeray, Cao Xueqin deepened the resources of the novel in China by opening up actuality while achieving a comparable effect of massive realism, documenting virtually every aspect of his era's life and culture. Like most Chinese novels, *Dream of the Red Chamber* is massive: an episodic 120-chapter narrative of about 1 million words with 421 named and described characters. No other Chinese novel, however, approaches it in depth and scope. Simultaneously a deeply personal exploration of love and passion, a family saga, and a philosophical, moral, and spiritual critique of an entire culture's values, *Dream of the Red Chamber* in its range, seriousness of purpose, and comprehensive vision is one of the touchstones of literary history, one of a handful of novels that radically redefined the resources and capabilities of the form.

No less daunting than the novel's great length are the scholarly controversies surrounding its author, composition, and publishing history. Cao Xueqin (1715–63) was a member of a prominent and prosperous Chinese family whose dramatic collapse provides one of the central themes of *Dream of the Red Chamber*. Cao Xueqin's family had for three generations been important bondservants to the Manchu emperors, holding the lucrative and powerful post of commissioner of the Imperial Textile Mills in Nanjing. Managing a staff of as many as 3,000, Cao Xueqin's grandfather, a patron of letters and a poet, lived lavishly and entertained the emperor in his home at least four times, a sign both of great distinction and means. In 1728 the new emperor dismissed Cao Xueqin's father from his post, ordered his house raided, and confiscated most of his property. The family moved to Beijing, where Cao Xueqin endured extreme poverty. An accomplished painter, Cao Xueqin supported himself by selling his works and possibly as a private tutor or schoolmaster. Cao Xueqin was described by friends as short, plump, and dark, in marked contrast to the striking beauty of his central protagonist, Jia Bao-yu, in *Dream*, the author's surrogate. Cao Xueqin was also called a charming and witty conversationalist who "wherever he was, he made it spring." One intimate recorded a description of Cao Xueqin "discoursing of high, noble things while one hand hunts for lice." Encouraged by his friends to complete his masterpiece, Cao Xueqin's efforts—writing without a patron and uncertain how the finished novel would be received by the state—are prodigious and heroic, particularly by breaking with established traditional conventions on which the Chinese novel depended for success. His manuscript circulated among Cao Xueqin's friends during his lifetime, and the version that has come down to us includes the commentary and corrections of another person with the pseudonym "Red Inkstone," thought to be a close friend or relative of Cao Xueqin, that help to establish the novel's autobiographical correspondences. After the novelist's death, the unfinished manuscript came into the hands of the writer Gao E, who, claiming to work from original manuscript sources, completed the story by adding its final 40 chapters, with the degree of Gao E's invention and direct reliance on Cao Xueqin the basis for ongoing scholarly debate. It was published in 1791.

Whether the work of a single author or a collaboration, *Dream of the Red Chamber* is conspicuous by its originality and break with previous Chinese fictional traditions. Chinese novels prior to *Dream* impersonally reworked familiar stories of the exploits of mythological heroes. Cao Xueqin expanded the novel's resources with private material based on his own family history, producing the first Chinese novel to utilize autobiographical experience on such a grand scale to become simultaneously a deeply felt personal statement, a massive social panorama, and a serious criticism of everyday life. To justify the novel's seriousness and claims on the reader's attention, Cao Xueqin established an allegorical frame for his tale that serves both to universalize his story and to establish the superiority of his novel based on its faithful representation of actuality. According to the novel's opening conceit, the ensuing story is actually a transcription on a magical, conscious stone, recording the stone's passage to enlightenment, incarnated as the human being Bao-yu. Its first reader, a Taoist called Vanitas, finds it wanting in historical accuracy and moral grandeur. "All I can find in it," he declares, "in fact, are a number of females, conspicuous, if at all, only for their passion or folly or for some trifling talent or insignificant virtue." The stone defends its story by contrasting it with other historical or romantic narratives whose artificiality, falsification, and idealization undermine truthfulness:

> Surely my "number of females," whom I spent half a lifetime studying with my own eyes and ears, are preferable to this kind of stuff? I do not claim that they are better people than the ones who appear in books written before my time; I am only saying that the contemplation of their actions and motives may prove a more effective antidote to boredom and melancholy. . . . All that my story narrates, the meetings and partings, the joys and sorrows, the ups and downs of fortune, are recorded exactly as they happened. I have not dared to add the tiniest bit of touching-up, for fear of losing the true picture.

Vanitas reads the inscription again in the light of the stone's defense and concludes that as a "true record of real events" the story deserves publication, and its readers are thereby alerted that Cao Xueqin's novel with its recognizable, flawed human characters and its seemingly inconsequential accumulation of day-to-day events and details would offer a new kind of fictional experience.

The novel presents the intimate and complex family relationships of the Jai clan, a prosperous family in decline. Bao-yu, the family's heir and great hope, is the central figure, whose intellectual, emotional, and spiritual development provides the narrative unity in a story that can be read on multiple levels: as autobiographical commentary on Cao Xueqin's family history, as social critique of the external forces that challenge the individual's quest for fulfillment, and as an allegorical drama on the nature of love and its relationship with the soul's striving for enlightenment. Bao-yu's triangular relationship with his female cousins, the neurotically self-centered Dai-yu and the more robust, practical Xue Bao-chai, forms the dramatic core of the novel that extends outward to an ever-widening circle of relationships and masterful character portraits. At liberty in the spacious garden of his family's residence to enjoy the company of his female cousins and devoted servants, Bao-yu is gradually faced with the external pressures of family expectations in his choice of career and a wife as well as the internal pressure in selecting a suitable mate and discovering a satisfying life. Both Dai-yu and Bao-chai correspond to certain aspects of Bao-yu's temperament, but neither individually typifies the ideal he wishes to embody. Dai-yu, with whom he has the greatest sympathy, grows increasingly mentally and emotionally unstable, causing the family to prefer Bao-chai for his wife. In the novel's climax, Bao-yu is tricked into marrying Bao-chai, while Dai-yu is dying of consumption, but he renounces the world and his family obligation by becoming a monk.

The novel charts with mastery a search for the proper course between self-realization and self-sacrifice, while dramatizing the central cultural and spiritual conflict between the age's defining beliefs, between the Buddhist-Taoist imperatives to renounce the world and the Confucian obligation to recognize family and personal responsibility. If the resolution of Bao-yu's story tilts toward the Buddhist-Taoist solution, the novel is no less adept in countering Bao-yu's withdrawal with a sense of its human cost in human sympathy and fellowship. Ultimately, it is Bao-yu's inability to bring the various aspects of his sensibility, the various factions of his family, and the embodiments of his desire into balance that gives *Dream* its tragic depth. Suffused with profound allegorical and philosophical significance, the novel is finally sustained by its masterly realism that roots the novel's many characters and episodes to the actual with psychological precision and skill. The culminating effect of the novel is a comprehensive view of the entire civilization and culture of Imperial China seen through the detailed exploration of everyday life. Like Chaucer in *Canterbury Tales*, Cao Xueqin numbered the class of men, achieving both a profundity of theme and subtlety of presentation that secure the status of *Dream of the Red Chamber* as one of the masterworks of world literature.

CLARISSA

50

(1747–48)

by Samuel Richardson

I spoke to him once about Clarissa—"*Not read* Clarissa*!" he cried out: "If you have once thoroughly entered on* Clarissa, *and are infected by it, you can't leave it. When I was in India I passed one hot season at the hills, and there were the governor-general, and the secretary of government, and the Commander-in-Chief, and their wives. I had* Clarissa *with me; and, as soon as they began to read, the whole station was in a passion of excitement about Miss Harlowe and her misfortunes and her scoundrelly Lovelace. The governor's wife seized the book, and the secretary waited for it, and the chief justice could not read it for tears."*

—W. M. Thackeray in conversation with Lord Macaulay, 1860

It is certainly possible to agree with Angus Ross that to read Samuel Richardson's masterpiece, *Clarissa*, "is not only to meet an indispensable document in the history of English (and indeed European) fiction in the eighteenth century, but also to become engaged with one of the greatest European novels, the haunting life of which has been acknowledged by many and diverse successors of Richardson himself and which in surprising places in the text still has the force to startle, and the spirit to enmesh, its modern audience." However, F. R. Leavis's qualification is no less valid: "It's no use pretending that Richardson can ever be made a current classic again." At a daunting length of nearly 1 million words—one of the longest novels ever written—*Clarissa* presents a formidable challenge for the modern reader. Even its creator's great contemporary champion, Samuel Johnson, contended that "if you were to read Richardson for the story, your impatience would be so much fretted, that you would hang yourself." Johnson's advice to read the novel "for the sentiment, and consider the story as only giving occasion to the sentiment" is no less a problem for a modern reader who will have a harder time empathizing with an exemplary heroine's moral certainty threatened through seven long volumes.

The justification to include *Clarissa* in this ranking of the greatest novels, however, is overwhelming. Richardson can claim a major share in the title of progenitor of the English novel. If Defoe is widely credited with first tapping into the novel's primary resource of ordinary life, and Fielding is mainly responsible for establishing the affinity between the novel and the epic and drama, then Richardson played two equally crucial roles in establishing the novel in the Western literary tradition: He made the novel respectable as a vehicle for serious moral and social exploration, and he began the process of turning the novel inward to delineate the private realm of consciousness itself, showing how an individual perceives the world and the complex psychological and emotional issues underlying motivation. Technically, Richardson's epistolary method—his surrender of omniscience for a direct view of his characters and the relativity of viewpoints—is an unmistakable influence on modern fiction with echoes of Richardson detectable in writers as different as Goethe, Jane Austen, Stendhal, Charlotte Brontë, Henry James, Joseph Conrad, William Faulkner, and many others. *Clarissa* deserves its place in this ranking ultimately not just for its importance in literary history, but for the daring of Richardson's conception and the power of its execution. Richardson changed immeasurably what the novel could do and how it could do it, and to overlook Richardson's achievement in *Clarissa* is to miss a remarkable performance as well as the discovery of some of the novel's most enduring capabilities.

Compared to the extravagant praise of Diderot, who eulogized the novelist's achievement after his death in 1761 by ranking Richardson with Homer, Euripides, and Sophocles as one who "carries the torch to the depths of the cave" of human nature, subsequent critical appreciation have been considerably more qualified and more patronizing. For many the middle-aged London printer who stumbled onto fiction by accident with trade as much as inspiration on his mind was, in the harsh words of R. F. Brissenden in the 1950s, "an affront to every conception of what an artist should be." Richardson was a self-educated businessman who had risen from apprentice and journeyman to respected tradesman and official printer for the House of Commons. His skill as a letter writer resulted in a publisher's offer to write a book of sample letters, models of style and behavior for an increasingly literate but unpolished public. Richardson's efforts in imagining various responses to different experiences led him in 1740, at the age of 51, to interrupt his work on *Familiar Letters* and expand a story he was told of a beautiful young serving girl who resisted her master's seduction attempts until, won over by her virtue, he married her. "Little did I think," Richardson remarked concerning the origin of *Pamela*, "of making one, much less two volumes of it. But when I began to recollect what had, so many years before, been told me by my friend, I thought the story, if written in an easy and natural manner, suitable to the simplicity of it, might possibly introduce a new species of writing." Nothing quite like the immediacy and intensity had ever been achieved in the novel before in the series of letters Pamela wrote to her parents concerning Mr.

B.'s assault on her virtue. *Pamela* became an international sensation. Scenes from the novel decorated ladies' fans, and the book's popularity spawned sequels as well as attacks, most notably Fielding's *Shamela* and *Joseph Andrews*, which comically ridiculed the moral seriousness of Richardson's contention, announced in the novel's subtitle, of "Virtue Rewarded."

Compared to his first novel, Richardson's second, *Clarissa*, is an improved, symphonic orchestration of the plan for *Pamela*, which occupied Richardson for nearly five years, from 1743 to 1748, when the last of the novel's seven volumes appeared. Its full title is *Clarissa, or, The History of a Young Lady: Comprehending the Most Important Concerns of Private Life and Particularly Showing the Distresses that May Attend the Misconduct Both of Parents and Children in Relation to Marriage.* Instead of *Pamela*'s reassuring notion of "Virtue Rewarded," *Clarissa* aims at a darker, tragic outcome and a more sophisticated and challenging portrait of human behavior and virtue's costs. Clarissa Harlowe is the youngest daughter of a merchant family who wish her to marry their rich, elderly neighbor, Mr. Solmes, to advance their interests. She is also pursued by the aristocratic rake Robert Lovelace, whom her family opposes as a libertine. Desperate to avoid a forced marriage to Solmes, Clarissa reluctantly accepts Lovelace's assistance to escape her family's campaign to compel her submission but is tricked by him into virtual imprisonment in a brothel. There Lovelace duels with Clarissa in a long series of stratagems to gain her sexual compliance, finally drugging and raping her. Convinced that "once subdued, always subdued," Lovelace is, however, surprised by Clarissa's continued resistance, and his marriage proposal, guiltily offered in compensation for his act, is firmly rejected. Clarissa eventually manages to escape from him and under the strain of her experiences, she dies, with her family's and Lovelace's repentance coming too late to save her. Lovelace is finally killed in a duel by Clarissa's cousin.

Compared to the Cinderella-like wish fulfillment of *Pamela*, in which the heroine's virtue rehabilitates her rakish pursuer, *Clarissa* offers a far more realistic challenge to the concept of "Virtue Rewarded" that must accommodate Clarissa's elopement with a libertine, her rape, and eventual demise unalloyed by poetic justice beyond a spiritual consolation that virtue is its own reward. Compared to *Pamela*, Richardson's social observation is more acute and his psychological exploration far more complex. His heroine, like Pamela, is still a moral paragon, but Clarissa's self-awareness is brought to the forefront of the drama as she is pressed to hold onto her idealistic principles in a complex practical world of mixed and disguised motives. As in *Pamela*, Richardson's epistolary method achieves a closeness of view and immediacy through his strategy of writing "to the moment," with the correspondent dealing directly with experiences as they occur, as Richardson declares in his Preface, "while the hearts of the writers must be supposed to be wholly engaged in their subjects." However, *Pamela* is close to a monologue in which almost all of the letters are written by the heroine to her parents, with Pamela's naiveté crucial for the unfolding action. In *Clarissa*, Richardson widens his focus and drama by including multiple correspondents. Through contrasting viewpoints, the reader, therefore, gains access to both Clarissa's and Lovelace's thoughts as well as a multidimensional perspective on their circumstances. Both central protagonists write to trusted confidants—Anna Howe and John Belford—with whom they share their intimate thoughts and who in turn offer alternative interpretations for them and the reader to consider. By strategically cutting from one correspondent to another, Richardson aids verisimilitude by advancing the story more plausibly from several angles of view. Richardson also can fully exploit dramatic irony by contrasting one character's knowledge with another's while orchestrating a fuller social context to the ongoing crises. The overall effect is an enhancement of both breadth and depth over Richardson's achievement in *Pamela*, while involving the reader actively in the complex issues of right behavior and self-awareness that the novel raises.

While it is possible to judge Clarissa and Lovelace as impossibly idealistic projections of virtue in the grips of equally unmitigated villainy, they actually emerge through the pressure Richardson extracts from their situation and what adversity causes them to show about themselves as believable and interesting characters. Clarissa is immediately assaulted by conflicting aims: How can she love whom she wishes and still retain the support of her family? Faced with the far more attractive option of Lovelace versus the vulgarian Solmes, Clarissa is emotionally tempted to give in to her desires while recognizing the claims virtue demands in resistance. When she finally is forced to succumb to Lovelace's sexual will, the effect is neither the submission that he desired, nor really her condemnation of his villainy, but her own self-realization that she has been tempted by such an unworthy man. "I hate thee not," Clarissa reports to Lovelace after the rape, "half so much as I hate myself, that I saw thee not sooner in thy proper colours!" With her implacable idealism, Clarissa dooms herself in a world Richardson shows as failing to meet her overly rigid certainties. As her more worldly friend Anna Howe rightly observes, "I am fitter for *this* world than you; you for the next than me." As for Lovelace, Richardson delineates a psychologically rich portrait of a rake far more motivated by hate than love, more by the chase than the consummation. Despite the pleas of Richardson's first readers to rehabilitate Lovelace and work out the novel's plot to allow for marriage in the end, the novelist resisted, convinced that the man who proclaimed it was "REVENGE, which I love. Love which I hate" was incapable of reform and unworthy of any outcome other than the destruction that engulfs him. Both Clarissa and Lovelace emerge, therefore, in Richardson's handling as multidimensional characters in a world of mixed motives where values such as family loyalty, constancy, love, and morality are given a complex interpretation.

By locating narrative interest in the workings of human consciousness itself, Richardson discovered one of the novel's great and continual subjects. Although Richardson's epistolary method would not survive, his rejection of the omniscient narrator in favor of the closely followed perspective of the characters would emerge as the dominant mode for the modern novel, a legacy that *Clarissa* skillfully established.

51

PERSUASION

(1818)

by Jane Austen

You may remember how Lord Tennyson
Once paid a visit to the town of Lyme,
They thought he'd want to see the spot whereon
The Duke of Monmouth landed—so sublime
A souvenir from that historic time,
The poet cried, "On Monmouth do not dwell;
But show me where Louisa Musgrove fell!"

—Mary Corringham, *I, Jane Austen*

Persuasion, the last written of Jane Austen's six completed novels, was composed after the illness (Addison's disease) that would take her life had worsened, sapping her strength and turning the 42-year-old writer into an invalid. That *Persuasion*, published posthumously, was written between 1815 and 1816 in the certain knowledge of impending death adds pathos to a love story about a second chance and self-renewal as well as wonderment about the new departure and the sense of new beginnings that it so unmistakably signals. *Persuasion* is the most contemporaneous and historically grounded of Austen's novels. It is set precisely between Napoleon's exile on Elba in 1814 and the consequent peace treaty that sends Admiral Croft and Frederick Wentworth from their naval commands to shore leave and the resumption of war in 1815. *Persuasion* is, therefore, meant to reflect a specific and crucial moment of English history: the changing of the guard in which a meritocracy, represented by the naval officers that secured the peace, is supplanting an ineffectual and self-indulgent aristocratic oligarchy, typified by Sir Walter Elliot of Kellynch Hall. A great public question of who should best lead English society, therefore, is interwoven with the private drama surrounding Sir Walter's second daughter, Anne. If *Pride and Prejudice* is Austen's most brilliantly witty comedy and *Emma* her most wide-ranging and accomplished, *Persuasion* is her most beautiful and romantic novel, suffused in an autumnal note of Keatsian "mellow fruitfulness." Like all of Austen's books, it is the story of its heroine's entry into the wider world based upon contending with the complications leading to marriage. All of Austen's central female protagonists are forced to negotiate the knotty demands and pressures of self, family, and society, correcting previous views under the tutelage of experience while discovering a proper moral and emotional basis for actions. There are some startling differences, however, between *Persuasion* and Austen's prior novels: Anne Elliot, is 27 when the novel begins, not 20 or 21, like all of Austen's previous heroines. She is eight years removed from the courtship/romance experience that constitutes the action of the other novels. Anne accepts that her time for love and marriage as deemed by convention is most likely over. She will play the piano for others to dance and watch her returned former suitor now court younger women. Anne, unlike Elizabeth Bennet, does not need to overcome her prejudices, or, like Emma, her delusions. They must discover prudence to complete their education. The sensible Anne must rediscover the power of love and the heart's greater claim over caution, class status, and parental authority. Anne is neither the self-confident Elizabeth nor the imperious Emma; she is instead a version of Cinderella, the overlooked and undervalued. She is "Nobody" and "Only Anne."

Persuasion will arrange a second chance for its unconventional romantic heroine. The novel explores what might happen if we could undo past errors based on our present understanding. Lady Russell, the Elliots' sensible family friend and Anne's surrogate mother, following the dictates of common sense, has persuaded Anne at 19 not to follow her heart and to reject the proposal of the naval officer Frederick Wentworth "who had nothing but himself to recommend him, and no hopes of attaining affluence, but in the chances of a most uncertain profession, and no connexions to secure even his farther rise in the profession." Frederick, however, gains a command and a fortune in prizes taken in combat, and Anne has come to regret her decision: "She did not blame Lady Russell, she did not blame herself for having been guided by her; but she felt that were any young person, in similar circumstances, to apply to her for counsel, they would never receive any of such certain immediate wretchedness, such uncertain future good." However, Anne will be given an opportunity to amend her past when Frederick reenters her life. If Anne lacks the looks, status, and superficial brilliance to command the conventional romantic stage, Jane Austen asks us to look beneath the surface, beyond our own prejudice about what a love story or a novel should be about, to discover one of the greatest heroines in English literature and one of the most absorbing and moving dramas of love and renewal.

Originally called "The Elliots," and retitled by Austen's brother Henry when it was brought out following her death in four volumes along with Austen's earliest completed novel, *Northanger Abbey*, *Persuasion* opens with a family in economic crisis brought on by its patriarch, Sir Walter Elliot, whose vanity and narcissism are perfectly encapsulated in the novel's first paragraph:

> Sir Walter Elliot, of Kellynch Hall, in Somersetshire, was a man who, for his own amusement, never took up any book but the Baronetage; there he found occupation for an idle hour, and consolation in a distressed one; there his faculties were roused into admiration and respect, by contemplating the limited remnant of the earliest patents; there any unwelcome sensations, arising from domestic affairs changed naturally into pity and contempt as he turned over the almost endless creations of the last century; and there, if every other leaf were powerless, he could read his own history with an interest which never failed. This was the page at which the favourite volume always opened:
>
> ELLIOT OF KELLYNCH HALL.

The head of an old, titled family, Sir Walter has through self-indulgent extravagance squandered his patrimony and can no longer maintain his place and responsibilities as the area's principal landowner. Convinced to take up less expensive lodgings in Bath, Sir Walter agrees to let Kellynch to Admiral Kroft and his wife, the sister of Anne's former suitor, Frederick Wentworth. Anne, whose sensible schemes for retrenchment are ignored, is left behind to attend to whatever is onerous concerning the estate and its tenants, while Sir Walter, his oldest daughter, Elizabeth, and her companion, Mrs. Clay, depart for the pleasures of Bath. Before the Crofts' arrival, Anne is relieved to be called for a visit to her other sister Mary at nearby Uppercross, the residence of the gentry family, the Musgroves.

At Uppercross, Anne's value as confidante and peacemaker between her petulant sister, Mary's husband, Charles, his parents, and his young sisters, Henrietta and Louisa, is both acknowledged and demonstrated. The Crofts pay their respects to their neighbors and are soon followed by the visiting Frederick Wentworth. Meeting him again, Anne struggles to control her reignited emotions with polite pleasantries. She learns, however, from her sister that Frederick had found her so much changed that she seems almost unrecognizable, and he willingly submits to the attentions of Anne's flirtatious sisters-in-law. Frederick's main interest appears to be Louisa, and, on a walk in the country, Anne overhears Frederick praise Louisa's declared resoluteness in matters of the heart. Decrying "too yielding and indecisive a character," Frederick declares, "Let those who would be happy be firm." Implied is a criticism of Anne's inconstancy and willingness to be persuaded to reject his proposal. At Lyme Regis, where the Uppercross party goes to enjoy the sea and the hospitality of Frederick's naval friends, Captain Harville and Captain Benwick, he will learn the difference between true firmness of character and dangerous self-will when Louisa insists on jumping from a steep flight of steps along the Cobb into his arms. Ignoring his cautions when she insists on repeating her rashness, Louisa asserts, "I am determined I will," and falls to the stone pavement unconscious. Only Anne keeps her wits and sensibly manages Louisa's assistance. Louisa's fall serves as a lesson for Frederick in the danger of resolve unalloyed by good sense and discretion. As Anne wonders on their journey back to Uppercross, "whether it ever occurred to him now, to question the justness of his own previous opinion as to the universal felicity and advantage of firmness of character; and whether it might not strike him that, like all other qualities of the mind, it should have its proportions and limits. She thought it could scarcely escape him to feel that a persuadable temper might sometimes be as much in favour of happiness as a very resolute character." With Frederick's greater reliance on Anne's judgment as a gesture of renewed closeness and trust, they are brought to the brink of a renewed understanding, but Anne and Frederick part again as Anne is delivered to yet another domicile in Bath as the values of Sir Walter reassert themselves.

In the novel's second volume, the romantic tangle is reversed. Instead of Anne contending with rivals for Frederick, he must now compete with another for Anne. At Lyme, the Elliots' cousin and Sir Walter's heir, William Elliot, is encountered, on his way to Bath, and his pursuit of Anne there will provide Anne's ultimate test of her love for Frederick and all it implies, personally and socially. Bath is Sir Walter's vanity and obsession with rank and privilege writ large. In Bath, it is not the house that matters but the street it is on, and all must give way to the Vicountess Dalrymple, though her only claim for deference is her title. Bath shows a society dedicated to the superficial and inauthentic in which motive is often disguised and all is not what it appears. As Anne is pulled into her family's orbit in Bath, she encounters Frederick there in a series of near-misses as Anne's family obligations and the unexpected attentions of William Elliot block the pair from coming together and achieving the confidence needed to reveal themselves fully to one another. Moreover, her cousin's flattering attention and proposal put within Anne's grasp all that she seems to deserve: the possibility of succeeding her mother as Lady Elliot and becoming mistress of her beloved Kellynch Hall, triumphantly securing her name, place, and fortune. However, Anne will not be tempted by his offer or persuaded to accept her cousin, who is exposed as a fortune- and title-hunting schemer. If Elizabeth Bennet comes to realize "that to be mistress of Pemberley might be something!" Anne Elliot reaches a very different conclusion and fate.

In Austen's first attempt at concluding *Persuasion*, the rumor of Anne's engagement to her cousin reaches the Crofts who send Frederick as their emissary to ascertain whether the future mistress requires their departure from Kellynch. Anne contradicts the rumor and reveals her faithfulness, clearing the way for Frederick's proposal. Dissatisfied, Austen tried again, constructing a dramatic scene in which Frederick overhears Anne's conversation with Captain Harville on the topic of the superior constancy in men or women. To Harville's insistence on women's fickleness and men's greater devotion, Anne asserts:

> "I should deserve utter contempt if I dared to suppose that true attachment and constancy were known only by woman. No, I believe you capable of everything great and good in your married lives. I believe you equal to every important exertion, and to every domestic forbearance, so long as—if I may be allowed the expression—so long as you have an object. I mean while the woman you love lives, and lives for you. All the privilege I claim for my own sex (it is not a very enviable one; you need not covet it), is that of loving longest, when existence or when hope is gone."

Anne's confession of an undiminished and constant love convinces Frederick that she still loves him as he does her, and their engagement is happily settled. In accepting him, Anne rejects the dictates of family, name, and place for an uncertain future as "a sailor's wife," becoming the only heroine in Austen's novels with no fixed residence at the end of the novel. Her domain will be the sea, emblematic of constant change, movement, and possibilities. The core values in Austen's previous novels—rank, property, authority, and tradition—are radically reevaluated in *Persuasion* and ultimately deemed irrelevant as Anne declares her independence from them and embraces not the past but the future, not security but potential. Instead of instructing its heroine in the necessity of limitations and the value of self-restraint, *Persuasion* offers a lesson in self-assertion and liberation. Anne Elliot's fictional descendents will include Jane Eyre, Dorothea Brooke, and Isabel Archer, women like her who must surmount crippling social values based on their own sense of self and autonomy. *Persuasion* shows Jane Austen moving from the stable and orderly Augustan world to the expansive, if uncertain, contours of the modern. At the end of her career, Jane Austen redresses her assumptions that had formerly privileged sense over sensibility, head over heart, rootedness over risk. As Virginia Woolf observed, in her last novel, Jane Austen "is beginning to discover that the world is larger, more mysterious, and more romantic than she had supposed."

52

JANE EYRE

(1847)

by Charlotte Brontë

Charlotte Brontë was surely a marvellous woman. If it could be right to judge the work of a novelist from one small portion of one novel, and to say of an author that he is to be accounted as strong as he shows himself to be in his strongest morsel of work, I should be inclined to put Miss Brontë very high indeed. . . . Therefore, though the end of the book is weak, and the beginning not very good, I venture to predict that Jane Eyre *will be read among English novels when many whose names are now better known shall have been forgotten.*

—Anthony Trollope, *Autobiography*

Modern readers of *Jane Eyre* must inevitably filter their view of Charlotte Brontë's achievement through celluloid and video images. With at least 13 film and television adaptations (at least one in every decade of the 20th century since 1914), *Jane Eyre* shares with Dickens's *David Copperfield* and *Great Expectations*, Flaubert's *Madame Bovary*, Hugo's *Les Misérables*, and Twain's *Adventures of Huckleberry Finn* the distinction of being one of the most filmed novels. Regarded as a feminist, romantic, and psychological classic, *Jane Eyre* is the literary fountainhead of the modern gothic suspense novel that has inspired such imitators as Daphne du Maurier's best-selling *Rebecca* as well as countless sentimental romance novels featuring an unassuming though plucky heroine and a dark, Byronic bad boy ultimately redeemed by love. However, imitations and distortions should not obscure the achievement of the original: a novel that in fundamental ways revolutionized the art of fiction. First popular in the eventful year of 1848, when Europe exploded in revolution, *Jane Eyre* likewise mounted an assault on established social hierarchies, conventional morality, and the novel's accepted methods.

Born in 1816, Charlotte Brontë was the third daughter of the vicar of Haworth in the West Riding of Yorkshire, a picturesque but isolated region of impassable roads and desolate moors. After their mother's death in 1821 the six Brontë children were raised by an aunt and their severely puritanical father. After the two eldest Brontë daughters died of tuberculosis contracted at school, Charlotte and her sister Emily were brought home and, with their younger sister, Anne, and brother, Branwell, were largely left to themselves. They filled their time together constructing elaborate fantasies involving the imaginary kingdoms of Gondal and Angria that the four populated with invented and historical figures. Charlotte's first creative work, written in minuscule script in tiny homemade books, records the various lives and adventures in these invented kingdoms and forms an essential key to her artistic vision.

The siblings' imaginative play continued well beyond childhood, but economic pressure forced the Brontë children to break out of their tight family circle and fantasy world of wish fulfillment to make their way in the actual world. Both Charlotte and Emily worked as teachers, and Anne became a governess. Branwell, whom it was hoped would succeed as a portrait painter, became instead the family disgrace, succumbing to drink and opium. To keep the family together, the sisters hatched a plan to open their own boarding school and to perfect their French. Charlotte and Emily left Yorkshire to attend a school in Brussels. Left on her own when Emily's homesickness drove her back to Haworth, Charlotte developed an emotional attachment to the school's owner, whose wife quickly stepped in and stopped the infatuation. Charlotte returned to Yorkshire, where she and her sisters collaborated on a volume of poetry, but only two copies were sold. The sisters next turned to the commercial possibilities of the novel.

Charlotte Brontë's first attempt, *The Professor*, a one-volume realistic story based on her time spent in Brussels, was rejected by at least seven publishers. One sympathetic reader had, however, suggested that "a work in three volumes would meet with careful attention," and she recast some of the elements of her childhood fantasy stories into a new novel in which, as she later recalled, she "endeavored to import a more vivid interest." A year after it was begun, *Jane Eyre* was published in August 1847, and it became the London season's literary sensation. A second edition was published three months after the first, and a third two months after that, an extraordinary success for the first book of an unknown author. The novel was published under the pseudonym Currer Bell to match her sisters Anne and Emily's Acton and Ellis Bell because, as Charlotte explained, "we had a vague impression that authoresses are liable to be looked on with prejudice." Anne's *Agnes Grey* and Emily's *Wuthering Heights* had been accepted for publication before *Jane Eyre*, but did not appear until December 1847, when their publisher, hoping to profit from Charlotte's success, suggested in advertisements that their works were by Mr. Bell, "the successful New Novelist." Both novels were ignored, mistakenly believed to be the cruder, apprentice efforts of Currer Bell.

Contemporary readers were captivated by the novel's daring story, in which a governess falls in love with her employer, accepting him despite his rake's history and sensational secret, as well as by the book's unique style and intense exploration of the narrator's private thoughts and feelings, previously the province of poetry, not the novel. The popularity of Charlotte Brontë's first-person narrative of development was no doubt a factor in Dickens's decision to launch his own first-person bildungsroman, *David Copperfield*, and influenced Thackeray's similar attempt in *Pendennis*. For Thackeray, *Jane Eyre* hit even closer to home when Charlotte Brontë, who greatly admired the novelist, dedicated the second edition to him. Thackeray's wife was known to be mentally incapacitated, and it was widely rumored that Thackeray was Brontë's model for Rochester and that Charlotte Brontë was Thackeray's mistress.

Not all of the novel's first readers, however, were delighted with the book. Jane's frank avowal of love for the morally suspect Rochester, as well as her rejection of the conventional role of the passive, relenting female in favor of an independent heroine with a self-determined morality that challenged and overturned orthodoxy and authority, appalled some readers. Some found the book's sentiments, in the words of a contemporary reader, "un-Christian or worse." With revolutionary events at home and abroad very much on his mind, one reviewer fumed that "We do not hesitate to say that the tone of mind and thought which has overthrown authority and violated every code human and divine abroad, and fostered Chartism and rebellion at home, is the same which has also written *Jane Eyre*." Another delivered the ultimate Victorian coup de grâce, charging that the book "might be written by a woman but not by a lady."

Jane Eyre, the story of a heroine, "as plain and small" as herself, in Charlotte Brontë's words, traces the title character's development from her troubled childhood to independence as a governess. In the care of her widowed aunt, Mrs. Reed, Jane is mistreated and neglected in favor of the three spoiled Reed children until a violent outburst delivers her to the equally oppressive charity school where her repression and rebellion recur. Eventually she learns to harness her egoism and passion, establishing the novel's dominant conflict between assertiveness and restraint, love and duty. Jane makes friends at the school and eventually becomes a teacher there before accepting a position as governess at Thornfield Hall, the country estate of Edward Rochester, caring for his illegitimate daughter. Despite Jane's homeliness and lack of status and sophistication, Rochester's brusque, cynical, world-weary manner, and a series of alarming occurrences, including the sounds of maniacal female laughter, the burning of Rochester's bed, and the wounding of a mysterious visitor, Jane and Rochester fall in love. At the altar Rochester's sensational secret is revealed: He is already married to Bertha Mason, a madwoman concealed in Thornfield's attic. Crushed by Rochester's deception, Jane departs Thornfield, and, after nearly perishing on the moors, is taken in by the Reverend St. John Rivers and his sisters. Jane returns to teaching but rejects Rivers's proposal of a loveless marriage and a life as a missionary's wife. The claims of her former love prove stronger than her sense of duty to the honorable but emotionally shallow Rivers. After a telepathic vision in which she hears Rochester call her name, Jane returns to Thornfield to find the mansion burned, Bertha dead, and Rochester blinded and maimed. With the moral and legal obstructions conveniently eliminated and Rochester sufficiently punished and penitent, the pair are reunited, and in one of most famous lines in fiction that begins the novel's final chapter, Jane records, "Reader, I married him."

The remarkable power of *Jane Eyre* derives as much from its intimate exposure of the narrator as from its melodramatic plot with its sensational central secret and its deviations from reality through signs, presentiments, coincidences, and the heightened aura of the uncanny and the supernatural that lends the novel a poetic, symbolic expressiveness. Rejecting the restriction of the novel to a surface imitation of life, Charlotte Brontë grafts onto her novel a poetic method and intensity to reach a depth of feeling and interior awareness in the stages of Jane's moral and psychological development, linking each stage, as in a poem, through association, imagery, and symbolism. In the process, Charlotte Brontë turns the novel inward, exploring fiction's subjective landscape and discovering the means to bring consciousness to vivid life. Assessing Charlotte Brontë's contribution to the novel in his groundbreaking study *Early Victorian Novelists* (1934), the literary historian David Cecil convincingly asserts that "As Thackeray was the first English writer to make the novel the vehicle of a conscious criticism of life, so she is the first to make it the vehicle of personal revelation. She is our first subjective novelist, the ancestor of Proust and Mr James Joyce and all the rest of the historians of the private consciousness." In dramatizing the moral and psychological development of her central heroine in an intimacy unprecedented in the novel, Charlotte Brontë brings into fictional play for one of the first times the inner world of the psyche and the heart's private longing.

DAVID COPPERFIELD

53

(1849–1850)

by Charles Dickens

If you sift the world's prose literature . . . Dickens will remain; sift Dickens and David Copperfield *will remain; sift* David Copperfield, *the description of the storm at sea will remain.*

—Leo Tolstoy, quoted in *Charles Dickens: The Critical Heritage*

David Copperfield occupies the central position in Dickens's canon, coming at the midpoint of his career with seven novels preceding and seven completed novels following. It is central as well in Dickens's own ranking of his works. "Of all my books," Dickens stated in 1869, a year before he died, "I like this the best . . . like many fond parents, I have in my heart of hearts a favorite child. And his name is DAVID COPPERFIELD." On completing it, Dickens confessed that "I seem to be sending some part of myself into the Shadowy World." For the first time in his fiction, he directly confronted long-buried secrets and traumas from his past. Accordingly, there is an intimacy and confessional quality to *David Copperfield* that is unique in Dickens's fiction. In his previous novels, Dickens had mastered picaresque comedy in *The Pickwick Papers*, social satire in *Oliver Twist*, *Nicholas Nickleby*, and *Dombey and Son*, pathos in *The Old Curiosity Shop*, the historical past in *Barnaby Rudge*, and thematic consistency linking many of these elements in *Martin Chuzzlewit*. *David Copperfield* shows Dickens laying claim to consideration as a psychological novelist. His initial autobiographical narrative, *David Copperfield* (the Esther Summerson portion of *Bleak House* and *Great Expectations* would follow) is Dickens's first full-scale attempt at a novel of growth and development filtered through the evolving consciousness of his title character from infancy to maturity. "Of all Dickens's novels," his biographer Edgar Johnson observes, "*David Copperfield* is the most enchanting. Few novelists have ever captured more poignantly the feeling of childhood, the brightness and magic and terror of the world as seen through the eyes of a child and colored by his dawning emotions." Accompanying the narrator on his life's journey is as rich a gallery of characters and incidents as Dickens ever created, making *David Copperfield* arguably the most beloved and popular of Dickens's works and, in the view of many, the pinnacle of his art, the book that displays the fullest array of his inimitable talents.

As he began to conceive his autobiographically derived novel, Dickens was 35, secure in his success after a hard-fought struggle for respectability. The 12-year-old boy who had been consigned by his parents to a rat-infested Thames-side warehouse to stick labels on blacking bottles and to fend for himself as they took up residence in debtors' prison had become an admired man of distinction and means. With his success, however, Dickens became increasingly preoccupied with the process of his own development and fortune. He began to toy with the idea of writing his autobiography, perhaps as a way of exorcising still powerfully felt wounds and anxieties. No one outside his immediate family knew the details of his childhood humiliations. These were the "dark places" that Dickens felt compelled to revisit. A chance remark by a mutual friend who reported having seen Dickens as a boy at the factory caused Dickens's friend John Forster to ask the writer about it. Forster reported that

> He was silent for several moments; I felt that I had unintentionally touched a painful place in his memory. . . . It was not however then, but some weeks later, that Dickens made further allusion to my then having struck unconsciously upon a time of which he never could lose the remembrance while he remembered anything, and the recollection of which, at intervals, haunted and made him miserable, even to that hour.

With his silence broken, Dickens wrote out some recollections of his childhood experiences, which he shared with Forster. Dickens would return to this autobiographical material as he cast about for the subject of his next novel to follow *Dombey and Son*. He wanted to try his hand at a first-person narrative, possibly influenced by the immense popularity in 1847 of Charlotte Brontë's autobiographical *Jane Eyre*, and who better to use for his subject than himself and his own experiences? Arriving after several tries at his title beginning with "Mag's Diversions," through "Thomas Mag the Younger, of Blunderstone House," "David Mags of Copperfield Hall," and finally variants surrounding "David Copperfield"—Dickens was shocked when Forster pointed out that David's initials were his own reversed, and attributed the coincidence to the fates. "Why else," he said, "should I have so obstinately kept to that name when once it turned up?"

The Personal History, Adventures, Experiences, & Observations of David Copperfield the Younger of Blunderstone Rookery [Which he never meant to be Published on any account] appeared in monthly installments from May 1849 through

November 1850. Before *David Copperfield*, no novel had ever presented so convincingly and intimately the complex texture of childhood with its unpredictable alteration between bliss and terror. George Orwell reported that when he first began to read the novel at the age of nine, its mental atmosphere was "so immediately intelligible" that he thought it must have been written *"by a child."* Moreover, with its memorable first line—"Whether I shall turn out to be the hero of my own life, or whether that station will be held by anybody else, these pages must show"—Dickens alerts his readers that David will be unlike other conventional novel heroes. David is neither an active adventuring hero such as Nicholas Nickleby or Martin Chuzzlewit, nor a passive paragon of innocence or virtue like Oliver Twist or Little Nell. David will not either by bold action or example defeat the hostile forces aligned against him; he is instead an imperfect character whose neediness, romanticism, lack of discipline, and self-deception lead him (and many of his friends) into disaster. No doubt influenced by Thackeray's "Novel Without a Hero," *Vanity Fair*, Dickens embraces in *David Copperfield* a more realistic conception of character, placing at the novel's center a mixed protagonist, who despite his flaws remains the novel's hero, whose essential goodness outweighs his blindness and foibles, and who through hard experience and suffering reaches a mature conception of himself and the world.

Born six months after his father's death and raised by his tenderhearted, childish mother and their faithful servant Peggotty, David's idyllic childhood abruptly ends when, returning from a visit to Peggotty's sailor brother and his family in Yarmouth, he learns that his mother has married the stern Mr. Murdstone. Rebelling against his stepfather's bullying cruelty, David is sent to boarding school whose harsh regime is alleviated by David's friendship with the aristocratic James Steerforth. After David's mother dies, he is sent to work at Murdstone and Grinby's wine warehouse in London, boarding with the grandiloquent and improvident Wilkins Micawber and his family. Micawber with his famous taglines, forever anticipating "something turning up" and "Annual income twenty pounds, annual expenditure nineteen nineteen and six, result happiness. Annual income twenty pounds, annual expenditure twenty pounds ought and six, result misery," is one of Dickens's most magnificent creations, prompting the claim of the writer J. B. Priestley that "With the one exception of Falstaff [Micawber] is the greatest comic figure in the whole range of English literature." When Micawber is imprisoned for debt, David loses his second, surrogate family, and he resolves to seek refuge with his mythical Aunt Betsey who arrived suddenly on the night of David's birth and departed equally suddenly when she learned her anticipated niece is a nephew.

David's journey on foot to Dover in which he is systematically stripped of all his possessions by a succession of predators is one of the triumphs of Dickens's art that infuses the real and familiar with nightmarish terror and expressionistic elements derived from the fairy tale, universalizing childhood innocence and adult exploitation. An outcast in a merciless world that is distinguished by brutality and aggression toward the innocent and helpless, David finally reaches his goal to claim refuge and kinship with his Aunt Betsey who first appears as a witchlike assailant—"'Go away!' said Miss Betsey, shaking her head, and making a distant chop in the air with her knife. 'Go along! No boys here!'"—but is magically transformed into a fairy godmother who provides for her nephew, vanquishes Mr. Murdstone, and allows David to "make another beginning."

Sharing the picaresque method of Dickens's previous fiction in which, after one adventure concludes, a new set of characters is introduced and new episodes begin, *David Copperfield* at least accounts for the shift to new scenes, characters, and challenges based on David's progress from boyhood through adulthood, with each fresh stage of development testing David's understanding and resources. After the intense subjectivity of its first quarter, the novel widens its perspective to consider a larger world and adult circumstances. The narrative alternates between autobiographical reflection and eyewitness reporting as David often joins the audience as an onlooker, learning key life lessons from associates. Sent to school in Canterbury, David becomes connected with Aunt Betsey's lawyer, Mr. Wickfield, his sensible daughter Agnes, and his clerk, the hypocritically humble and devious Uriah Heep, who will prove to be a more formidable villain than the bullying Murdstone. Before embarking on a legal career (the first of several vocations that he will attempt), David pays a visit to Peggotty and her family in Yarmouth, accompanied by Steerforth. David's friend becomes attracted to Daniel Peggotty's niece, Little Em'ly, who is engaged to the stalwart Ham. Steerforth's seduction and abandonment of Em'ly, followed by Daniel's tireless search to find and redeem his disgraced niece, provide the novel's main plot accelerants. Another is the mysterious rise of Uriah Heep and his growing domination over Mr. Wickfield, whose decline brings about Betsey's financial ruin and the necessity of David's vocational choices. David meanwhile has fallen in love with Dora Spenlow, the daughter of his employer who opposes their match. Undeterred, David and Dora are secretly engaged and marry following Mr. Spenlow's death. Dickens's treatment of young love here, based on his own first, unsuccessful romances, provides some of the most engaging sections of the novel, as love blinds David to the utter impracticality of Dora. She proves to be a disastrous household manager after they marry, and David is forced more and more into the role of Mr. Murdstone to discipline his "child-wife." The consequences of an "undisciplined heart," love aligned only with need rather than with mutual support and practicality, become one of the novel's dominant themes with multiple examples in the several love relationships and triangles—Steerforth-Little Em'ly-Ham, Dr. Strong-Annie-Jack Maldon, and David-Agnes-Heep—on display.

The novel's climax is stage-managed by the most unlikely source, Wilkins Micawber, who as Heep's secretary finally exposes his master's manipulations. Deciding to immigrate to Australia in search of better opportunities, the Micawbers are joined by Daniel and the rescued and forgiven Em'ly. Dickens's sympathetic treatment of the fallen woman in which Em'ly retains the sympathy and devotion of her uncle is groundbreaking, a challenge both to Victorian morality and Dickens's family audience. "I hope," Dickens asserted, "in the history of Little Em'ly (who *must* fall—there is no hope for her), to put it before the thoughts of the people in a new and pathetic way, and perhaps to do some good." Ultimately, the moral and financial problems associated with Em'ly and Micawber are exported rather than resolved at home. Similarly, the hard-fought realistic struggle of Dickens's own career is transformed by wish fulfilment and plot expedients. Dora, as if incapable of growing up, dies, freeing David to transfer his affection to the ever-sensible Agnes, in Dickens's words, "the real heroine." She helps David to recover from his grief and self-pity to discover his true vocation as a writer. Overcome by the "accumulated sadness into which I fell," David is pulled back from despondency by a letter from Agnes:

> She knew that in me, sorrow could not be weakness, but must be strength. As the endurance of my childish days had done its part to make me what I was, so greater calamities would nerve me on, to be yet better than I was; and so, as they had taught me, would I teach others. She commended me to God, who had taken my innocent darling to His rest; and in her sisterly affection cherished me always, and was always at my side go where I would; proud of what I had done, but infinitely prouder yet of what I was reserved to do.

Agnes emerges here as the angelic counterpart to the doll-like Dora, David's guide to a life of practical good work and small domestic pleasures that crown his long journey to adulthood. Subsumed under its fairytale ending in which villainy is thoroughly routed and virtue rewarded is still the dominant tone of threat and peril that haunts *David Copperfield* and persists in the reader's mind long after David settles into a satisfying Victorian domestic prosperity. *David Copperfield* becomes Dickens's rags to riches fable of paradise lost and regained around the fireside. Dickens would spend the rest of his writing career radically reassessing the assumptions of privilege and wealth that David's (and Dickens's) career seemed to celebrate. His next novel, *Bleak House*, imagines the world as fog-bound and contaminated, infecting the just and the unjust alike; *Little Dorrit* presents the world as a prison with no parole; and in *Great Expectations* Dickens essentially rewrites *David Copperfield* with a radically altered conclusion, suggesting that the taint of commonness that David dreads is actually preferable to the gentility than David

54

PETERSBURG

(1916/1922)

by Andrey Bely

Petersburg *is the first modernist city novel, but it is also a monument of symbolist prose. One of the most apocalyptic novels in all Western literature, it draws on the literary myth of St. Petersburg which, most notably, Pushkin, Gogol, and Dostoevsky had sustained and enriched. . . . On a more general level,* Petersburg *embodies the idea that the twentieth-century city is the scene of the crisis of modern life.*

—Peter I. Barta, *Bely, Joyce and Döblin: Peripatetics in the City Novel*

Credit for making the modern city the central character in a novel is usually given to James Joyce for *Ulysses*, but that distinction is more accurately attributed to Andrey Bely's *Petersburg*, the masterpiece of the so-called Silver Age of Russian literature and perhaps the greatest example of Russian modernist fiction. Vladimir Nabokov declared it "one of the four great masterpieces of twentieth-century prose," along with Joyce's *Ulysses*, Kafka's *The Metamorphosis*, and Proust's *In Search of Lost Time*. Fragmentary, contradictory, disorienting, and nightmarish, *Petersburg* attempts to mimic a city in its structure and methods while revealing the complex cultural associations of Saint Petersburg in the Russian national and psychic identities. In a richly elaborate, musically inspired, poetic prose with a dream logic, *Petersburg* presciently explores a modern landscape ruled by terror and tottering on the edge of psychic breakdown. Russian poet and literary critic Osip Mandelstam considered the novel unmatched by any other Russian writer in its evocation of prerevolutionary turmoil and anxiety, while Konstantin Mochulky described it as "a rendition of delirium unprecedented in literature . . . a world—unbelievable, fantastic, monstrous, a world of nightmare and horror, a world of distorted perspectives, of disembodied people and living corpses." Bely's masterpiece would be considered degenerate and decadent by the Soviet victors in the revolution that Bely predicted, and the brief flowering of the Russian symbolist movement that Bely helped to lead would be replaced by far more prosaic social realism. Despite its censure and complexity, *Petersburg* has gained a secure place among the major works of literary modernism.

Born in 1880, Boris Bugaev began publishing poetry under the pseudonym "Andrey Bely" in 1902. A major theorist of Russian symbolism, Bely experimented with the combination of poetry, prose, music, and philosophy in four prose "symphonies." In 1910 he published his first novel, *The Silver Dove*, the first of a planned trilogy to be called *East and West*. The projected second volume became the separate work *Petersburg*, which first appeared in installments in 1913 and 1914 and in book form in 1916. Bely continued to work on the novel, however, and completed a final revision, cutting the novel by a third, in a version of the novel that was published in 1922 in Berlin. Bely's literary contributions may best be understood in a comparison with James Joyce. Born within two years of each other, the Russian and the Irish writer share a number of correspondences. Both employ a strategy of verbal innovation, partially derived by a shared interest in music. Both attempt a combination of realistic and symbolic forms to uncover universal patterns beneath the surface of actuality. Both Bely and Joyce embarked on a campaign to revivify language and the novel while simultaneously confronting the challenges faced by their respective nations to define its identity. For Joyce the nexus for his exploration and reclamation was Dublin; for Bely it was Saint Petersburg, his version of T. S. Eliot's "Unreal City."

Bely has described the novel's genesis in his memoirs in mystical terms of a dream vision that came to him as he tried to visualize one of the novel's two central characters, Senator Ableukhov: "Immediately there flared up before me a picture of the Neva . . . a light silvery night and the square of the black carriage . . . it was as though I began to run after the carriage in my thoughts, trying to make out the one sitting in it . . . I made up nothing; I only spied on the actions of those before me." *Petersburg* captures this sense of dreamy reality in which the tangible and the fantastic reinforce one another. As much a concept as a place, Saint Petersburg is the grand idea of Peter the Great who built his model city as "a window on Europe," laid out in a grid pattern with Italian architects imported to line its boulevards and prospects with beautiful buildings in the European style. Saint Petersburg, therefore, marks an attempt by Peter to turn Russia westward, and his capital city underscores the dynamic tension fighting for dominance in the Russian character between East and West. It is the perfect stage set for the conjunction of forces that creates the novel's psychological, family, and national drama. Saint Petersburg is, therefore, both an actual place and an abstraction, as Bely announces in the concluding words of the novel's prologue:

> But Petersburg is not merely imaginary; it can be located on maps—in the shape of concentric circles and a black dot in the middle; and this mathematical dot, which has no defined measurement, proclaims ener-

> getically that it exists: from this dot comes the impetuous surge of words which makes the page of a book; and from this point circulars rapidly spread.

Symbolically, the city's two separate worlds of aristocrats and workers are conjoined by the city's central mounted statue of Peter the Great, Pushkin's Bronze Horseman, "a symbol of the terrible might of the Russian state, which both defeats its enemies and destroys its children." Saint Petersburg itself replicates on multiple levels the various divisions the novel will explore in the Russian nation, family, and soul.

The novel takes place over a few days in October 1905. It is the year of the disastrous war with Japan, strikes, and various acts of revolutionary terror featuring such figures as Azev, who worked for both the revolutionaries and the secret police, and Popedonostzev, the reactionary politician who was the true power behind the czar. *Petersburg* draws on its era to present a society in which appearances deceive, motivations are suspect, and everything seems to be moving toward an inevitable apocalypse. The novel's central hero, Nikolay Apollonovich Ableukhov, is the dilletantish son of a high-ranking reactionary Petersburg official, Senator Ableukhov. Father and son have a strained relationship that is outwardly cool and dismissive but internally a complex mix of love and hate. The division between father and son takes on a wider cultural significance as their European tastes clash with their Mongol descent, which Bely emphasizes in their appearance. Their volatile and combustible mixture of extremes—East and West, reason and passion, order and revolution—is played out in the suspense plot that connects a large cast and its Petersburg setting. Nikolay is in love with Sofia Petrovna, the wife of the army officer Likhutin. In a fit of pique over his disappointment in love, Nikolay has rashly promised "the party," the revolutionary group he has joined, that he will do anything they require of him, even the assassination of his father. Contacted by another party member, Dudkin, Nikolay is asked to take into his possession a small package, the contents of which are not immediately revealed. He eventually receives instructions that the package contains a bomb that he should use to kill his father. Meanwhile, his father is approached by Morkovin, a police agent, who warns him that an attempt on his life is being planned. Morkovin also reveals to Nikolay that he is a double agent working for both the secret police and the party and that Nikolay has no choice but to complete his assignment or face being arrested as a conspirator.

After father and son meet and quarrel, Nikolay unwraps the package and inadvertently activates the bomb's clockwork mechanism, insuring that it will explode within 24 hours. Grasping the full horror of the situation, Nikolay now seeks the assistance of Dudkin, who is convinced that there must be some mistake, that the party would never make such a cruel demand on one its members. He promises to clarify things and urges Nikolay to throw the bomb into the river. Dudkin learns from Lippanchenko, a party official, that there is no mistake and that Nikolay has been declared a traitor to the party and must be destroyed along with his father. He warns Dudkin that he risks a similar fate unless he abandons all attempts to help Nikolay. After a series of hallucinatory visions, including a visit by the Bronze Horseman, Dudkin decides to murder Lippanchenko, buys a pair of scissors, and disembowels him before going mad.

Nikolay, meanwhile, returns home to retrieve and dispose of the bomb. His father, in growing despair over the rift with his son and Nikolay's suspicious behavior, fails to attend to his responsibilities and retires from his governmental post. Determined to find out what his son is up to, he goes to Nikolay's room and carries off the sardine tin concealing the bomb to his study to examine its contents, but he fails to do so. Nikolay returns to his room to find the bomb missing. It finally explodes in his father's empty study, injuring no one. The novel, therefore, parodies the conventions of the suspense novel and ends with a double anticlimax. All the efforts to prevent the bomb from exploding fail, but when it detonates it kills no one. Its intended target has already relinquished his power, accomplishing what the party had hoped to gain by his assassination. Senator Ableukhov retires to the country to write his memoirs, and Nikolay goes abroad, devoting his time to archaeology and philosophy.

Bely's suspense plot becomes the narrative thread used to join the novel's many characters and relationships while revealing a series of essential divisions that typify Saint Petersburg and its inhabitants. The antagonism between father and son, a central theme of Turgenev and Dostoevsky, here escalates into threatened parricide. However, both father and son embody the same divisions that are precariously balanced in the design of the city with its western architecture and eastern inhabitants. In Senator Ableukhov this split is revealed in his rage for bureaucratic order and his underlying heart disease. In Nikolay it is evident in his abstract philosophizing and his emotional neediness, in his detecting in himself aspects of his father that battle for predominance: "In his study Nikolay Apollonovich performed acts of terrorism upon himself—number one upon number two, the socialist upon the aristocrat and the corpse upon the lover; in his study Nikolay Apollonovich cursed his frail being, and inasmuch as he was the image and likeness of his father, he cursed his father."

Nikolay, like his family, city, and his nation, is coming apart at the seams. It is Bely's genius to capture and embody this theme in a landscape that is simultaneously tangible and dreamlike, surface and symbol, capital of the Russian state and a state of mind.

55

THINGS FALL APART

(1958)

by Chinua Achebe

Things Fall Apart *begins a tradition not only because its influence can be detected on subsequent Nigerian novelists . . . but also because it was the first solid achievement upon which others could build. Achebe was the first Nigerian writer to successfully transmute the conventions of the novel, a European art form, into African literature. His craftsmanship can be seen in the way he creates a totally Nigerian texture for his fiction: Ibo idioms translated into English are used freely; European character study is subordinated to the portrayal of communal life; European economy of form is replaced by an aesthetic appropriate to the rhythms of traditional tribal life. Achebe's themes reflect the cultural traits of the Ibo, the impact of European civilization upon traditional African society, and the role of tribal values in modern urban life.*

—Bruce Alvin King, *Introduction to Nigerian Literature*

Only a precious few writers—Cervantes in Spain, Pushkin in Russia, Dante in Italy, Goethe in Germany—have been credited as progenitors of a national literature; only Chinua Achebe has been recognized as responsible for originating the modern literary history of an entire continent. Achebe's first and greatest novel, *Things Fall Apart* (1958), has become the most famous African novel worldwide and a landmark achievement that initiated an indigenous imaginative repossession of the African past and cultural identity. Although not the first novel by a black African published in English (Amos Tutuola's *The Palm-Wine Drinkard* had appeared to international acclaim in 1952), it was certainly the most formally and thematically accomplished that had yet appeared, and its impact both at home and abroad has not been surpassed. A book with exceptional historical, anthropological, sociological, and psychological insights, *Things Fall Apart* achieves its status as a modern classic fundamentally from its power not as a treatise but as a work of art. Its greatness rests in its providing an alternative to the Western ethnocentric distortions of African experience that Achebe found so inadequate, along with a synthesis of narrative and linguistic forms that would graft onto the novel tradition the power and resources of a rich vernacular language and culture. *Things Fall Apart* is, therefore, one of the great acts of creative repossession and liberation that gives voice to a past and a people with an intellectual and artistic seriousness that refuses to idealize or simplify the legacy that has created a complex African identity and history.

Born in 1930 in the village Ogidi in eastern Nigeria, Chinua Achebe was the son of one of his clan's first Christian converts. Achebe, therefore, grew up balanced between the two conflicting worlds of traditional Ibo tribal life and the new European/Christian beliefs and values that he would chronicle in *Things Fall Apart*. "When I was growing up," Achebe has observed, "we were Christians and in our village you had two sides—the 'people of the church,' as we were called, and the 'people of the world,' the others. Although we were in the same village there was a certain distance which I think made it possible for me not to take things for granted. I say this because some of the people who grew up with me, whose parents were heathen, as we called them, these things did not strike them. At least this is what they tell me today—they took things for granted." In 1953 Achebe graduated from University College, Ibadan, with a degree in English literature and went to work for the Nigerian Broadcasting Service. As Achebe recalled, his novel had begun to form in his mind while an undergraduate: "I was quite certain that I was going to try my hand at writing, and one of the things that set me thinking was Joyce Cary's novel set in Nigeria, *Mr. Johnson*, which was praised so much, and it was clear to me that this was a most superficial picture of—not only of the country, but even of the Nigerian character, and so I thought if this was famous, then perhaps someone ought to try and look at this from the inside." To counter the simplifications and distortions of the African experience and character he found in writers like Joyce Cary, Joseph Conrad, and Graham Greene, Achebe was determined to "teach my readers that their past—with all its imperfections—was not one long night of savagery from which the first Europeans acting on God's behalf delivered them."

Central, therefore, to Achebe's intentions in *Things Fall Apart* is the restoration of an awareness of a rich, complex precolonial cultural history destroyed through the assimilation of Western beliefs and customs. Yet Achebe's assessment of the past resists a simplified nostalgia for a lost way of life that casts the Africans in the role of blameless victims and the Europeans as monolithic victimizers. *Things Fall Apart* instead offers a clear-eyed analysis of the crucial encounter between two imperfect, conflicting value systems, each with strengths and weaknesses that collectively form a destructive dynamic that creates the novel's tragedy.

With its title taken from William Butler Yeats's poem "The Second Coming," *Things Fall Apart* similarly explores the crisis point when one system of belief gives way to another. Yeats's poem in apocalyptic images imagines the end of the Christian era and the emergence of a frightening alternative cycle; Achebe examines the passing of traditional African order and beliefs at the beginning of Africa's Christian cycle. The first two-thirds of the novel details traditional Ibo life around the end of the 19th century, before the arrival of Western missionaries and colonial administrators. Before the coming of the Westerners, who will unalterably disrupt the traditional ways of life and beliefs, Achebe establishes a complex and coherent community that belies any suggestion of its primitivism, while establishing the cracks both in its system and in one of the society's strongest representatives that will contribute to its destruction by the inability to adapt to change. Concerning the clan of Umuofia and centered on the village of Iguedo, the home of the novel's protagonist Okonkwo, *Things Fall Apart* links the disintegration of an individual and a society and the causes of both. To measure the impact of a foreign invasion that will challenge traditional political, economic, and religious institution, Achebe first carefully reconstructs a precolonial way of life, animated by Okonkwo's fierce determination to hold onto the established values at all cost. A figure of legendary strength and iron will, Okonkwo is driven to achieve distinction among his people to compensate for the disgrace of his father, Unoka. Improvident and irresponsible, a lover of music and pleasure, lacking in the admired masculine traits of strength and aggression, Unoka is, in the view of his son, *agbala*, a woman and a disgrace. Throughout his life, Okonkwo suppresses any elements in his nature associated with his father: "Okonkwo never showed any emotion openly, unless it be the emotion of anger. To show affection was a sign of weakness; the only thing worth demonstrating was strength." Driven by his fear of resembling his father and allowing elements of his nature such as compassion and sympathy from surfacing, Okonkwo disrupts by his inflexibility the delicate balance between masculine and feminine that Achebe establishes as essential in this tribal community and sets in motion the conditions that insure his downfall. Okonkwo's emphasis on strength and valor causes him to be respected and brings him material success, but ultimately he fails to achieve his aim of becoming a distinguished, honored village leader through a combination of willful violations of tribal customs and fate that seems to curse him. Given the responsibility to accept into his family a young hostage from another tribe, Ikemefuna, Okonkwo, who grows to love the boy as a son, refuses the advice not to participate in Ikemefuna's eventual tribally-required sacrifice out of fear of appearing weak. Later, at the funeral festivities of a village elder, Okonkwo's gun accidentally misfires and kills the deceased's son, prompting Okonkwo's banishment to his motherland for seven years.

During Okonkwo's exile, the arrival of European missionaries and governing officials poses a threat to traditional customs and beliefs that the Umuofians are ill prepared to meet. Their way of life is a formalized series of ceremonies and laws designed to establish basic harmonies among nature and the clan. However, like Okonkwo, Umuofian values are too narrow and rigid to fuse basic divisions between masculine and feminine, between the ideal and those who are excluded as lacking in value. Christianity slowly takes hold, first among the clan's outcasts and increasingly among those like Nwoye, Okonkwo's son, who disapproves of the seemingly arbitrary and unjust Umuofian practices of killing an innocent boy like Ikemefuna or the consigning of twins to death. Tribal practices are at odds with lessons of kinship and humanity, a deficiency that Christianity will exploit. When one of the native converts desecrates an Umuofian religious ceremony, the response, endorsed by Okonkwo, is characteristically violent and destructive. When Okonkwo and the other clan leaders are seized and punished in retaliation, the clan gathers to determine how to respond. Okonkwo's only available response is a war to annihilate the threat. Before consensus is reached, Okonkwo kills the government agent who orders the meeting to disband, hoping to precipitate the war he desires. When the clan fails to respond, Okonkwo realizes that the traditional values that he has clung to are no longer in force, and he commits suicide, unable finally to cope with a changed world that demands integration and accommodation that he cannot command. Okonkwo's fatal, tragic flaw is rooted in a deep psychological need to compensate for his father's disgrace and simultaneously the inadequacy of the Umuofian way of life whose exacting ideology cannot tolerate weakness and whose forms are too rigid to adjust to change. The District Commissioner, charged with restoring order and supplying justice, is given the last word. In ignorance of what is implied by Okonkwo's death—the internal and external collapse of a system of belief and a way of life—he adds the incident as a curious anecdote to a chapter of a book he intends to write titled *The Pacification of the Primitive Tribes of the Lower Niger.*

If the Westerners are shown as insensitive, militant zealots, uncomprehending of a complex system of beliefs they have not bothered to try to understand, Achebe has not absolved the villagers in their fatal encounter with the forces of change. Okonkwo, "one of the greatest men in Umuofia," is an embodiment of an entire way of life who, like Homer's Achilles, precipitates his own downfall by the denial of his humanity in an increasingly ambivalent world that demands a more balanced response. Achebe has managed both to restore a sense of a complex, nuanced precolonial African identity while subtly detailing the factors that contributed to an equally complex postcolonial consciousness that, like the surviving Umuofians, must integrate and accommodate past and present, traditional beliefs and alternative possibilities.

THE PRINCESS OF CLEVES 56

(1678) *by Madame de Lafayette*

To Madame de Lafayette must go the credit for demonstrating more clearly than anyone before her that the novel, as opposed to the drama, is the perfect vehicle for the presentation of an action in which the conflict is profoundly internal, in which, because their situation requires them to assume a mask, almost nothing can be inferred from what the characters do or say—for the gestures, expressions, tones of voice. Madame de Lafayette is preoccupied directly with the psychology of her characters as it reveals itself in consciousness rather than action.

—Blake Nevius, *Edith Wharton*

If the English novel tradition traces the source of its inward turning to Samuel Richardson, the French have an earlier starting point in Madame de Lafayette and her novel *La Princesse de Cleves*, published in 1678. Called the first modern novel, it shifted the focus of fiction from action and adventure to the characters' thoughts and feelings, thereby claiming the distinction of being the first psychological novel. It marked a shift from the pastoral and chivalric romances that defined prose fiction at the time, and as critic Janet Raitt observes, "We find in it a human truth, a moral complexity and a formal beauty, even a poetry, of which there is no hint in any other novel of the century." It is the first classic French novel, and no other early French fiction has had a comparable impact in influencing subsequent generations of French novelists from Rousseau through Stendhal, Flaubert, and Camus. "This novel," André Maurois observed in 1942 as French culture was threatened by the occupying Nazis, "is a kind of miracle because it maintains a perfect equilibrium between the vigor of the passions and the moderations of its tone. . . . If no other language can paint with as delightful exactness as the French the most delicate shades of love, if amorous conversation has become in France the most charming and the most perfect of art, we owe it . . . to the woman, so keen, so wise, and so modest, who succeeded, without irony and without excess, in bringing the novel back to the plane of reality and who showed that the beauty of the most ardent sentiments can be painted in the simplest language: I am referring to Madame de Lafayette." In the Western novel tradition, *The Princess of Cleves* is a foundation text that helped to establish the novel as a truth-telling instrument.

Madame de Lafayette was born Marie-Madeleine Pioche de la Vergne in 1634. Her father was a member of the minor French nobility, and after his death in 1649, her mother's remarriage to a more socially prominent nobleman afforded her daughter a place in court as a lady-in-waiting to Anne of Austria, the widowed queen of Louis XIII and the mother of Louis XIV. In 1655 Marie-Madeleine married François, comte de Lafayette, a provincial nobleman with estates in the remote region of Auvergne in central France, where she lived for the first four years of their marriage. In 1659, after giving birth to two sons, Madame de Lafayette returned to Paris, where she would live for the rest of her life, occasionally visited by her husband. She became the hostess of a fashionable salon that attracted some of the leading intellectuals and writers of her time and began her own writing career. Her first publication, and the only one that appeared under her name during her lifetime, was a portrait of her friend Madame de Sévigné, in the collection *Divers Portraits*. Her first fictional work, *La Princesse de Montpensier*, depicting court life during the reign of Charles IX, appeared in 1662, and she collaborated with her close friend La Rochefoucauld on the romance *Zaïde*, set in ninth-century Spain, publishing a first volume in 1669 and a second in 1671. In 1672 she began six years of research and writing *The Princess of Cleves*, the last of her books to be published in her lifetime.

When *The Princess of Cleves* appeared in 1678, it was an immediate success. Paris booksellers were unable to meet the demand, and provincial readers were forced to wait months for a copy. The novel sparked both a search to uncover its author and a lively debate over its merits as a work of art and its truthfulness. Madame de Lafayette, after denying that she was the author, weighed in with her own commentary on the book:

> I find it most agreeable, well written without being extremely polished, full of wonderfully fine things that even merit a second reading. What I find in it above all is a perfect imitation of the world of the court and the way one lives there. There is nothing of the romance, nothing extravagant in it. Indeed, it is not a romance: it should properly be regarded as a memoir.

She identifies here the key elements that make *The Princess of Cleves* a turning point in the history of the novel in its break with the prevailing prose fiction model, the romance. In 17th-century France, the *roman* designated a fictional narrative of considerable length, set in a remote historical period, dramatizing, usually with numerous subplots, connected through coincidence, the extraordinary adventures of heroic characters who after many challenges to prove their worthiness finally are rewarded with a happy ending in marriage. By the 1660s, the *roman* had become synonymous with the untruthful, and different narrative forms began to emerge to gratify readers' demand for the *vraisemblable*, for lifelikeness and plausibility. One was the so-called *nouvelle historique*, which blurred the distinction between history and fiction by connecting invented characters and situations with historical settings and actual figures. Another was the quasi-historical narrative known as the memoir that purported to offer the private rather than the public side of historical events. Both more realistic alternatives to the *roman* that anchored invention in verisimilitude would be employed in *The Princess of Cleves* to provide in Madame de Lafayette's view "the perfect imitation of the world of the court and the way one lives there," attesting to the new antiromantic standard of truthfulness. Another radical break from the conventional romance is the brevity of *The Princess of Cleves.* With many subplots and a loosely episodic structure, the typical romance of the period could reach 10 to 12 volumes and exceed 1,000 pages. By contrast, *The Princess of Cleves* is a model of compression and economy in which all of its elements, including its occasional historical digressions, support the central action of its title character's inner battle between love and duty.

The novel begins by locating its action not in the remote past of the romance but in the more immediate past of the previous century and the reign of Henri II: "Never has France seen such a display of courtly magnificence and manners as in the last years of the reign of Henri II. The King was chivalrous, nobly built, and amorously inclined. . . ." By treating not the present but the recent past, Madame de Lafayette achieves a tactical objective distance from which she is able safely to reflect the court world of Louis XIV through its correspondence with the reign of Henri II. With its initial emphasis on the glamorous life of Henri, the reader is led to expect either the elaborate extravagances of the romance or the private scandals of the powerful. Instead emphasis shifts to the arrival at court of Mademoiselle de Chartres and her mother to arrange an advantageous marriage. The preliminary description of the intrigues at Henri's court provides the backdrop to the rather mundane process of wooing that commences. Madame de Chartres is her innocent daughter's guide into a world in which glamour conceals motive and appearance disguises reality. "If you judge by appearances in this place," Madame de Chartres tells her daughter, "you will frequently be deceived: what you see is almost never the truth." The conflict between appearance and reality, the disjunction between how people act and what they truly feel, generates the novel's drama. Mademoiselle de Chartres's test of character will come, not before marriage, as in the romance, but after it, as she accedes to her mother's wishes and agrees to marry the Prince of Cleves, whom she does not love.

Having altered the goal of the romance from marriage to its consequence, Madame de Lafayette further violates romantic conventions by shifting emphasis from a sequence of adventures imposed on her characters to plausible circumstances caused by the characters themselves. The handsome and accomplished Duc de Nemours returns to court, and the dutiful newlywed feels passion for a man for the first time. The danger of unchecked passion is one of the neoclassical age's major themes, and the Princess of Cleves is allied to Racine's Phaedra in the internal conflict that ensues as she attempts to cope with her feelings for Nemours while recognizing her responsibilities to her husband. Her conscience prevents infidelity, and, although she attempts to hide her true feelings behind a decorous public mask, the split that ensues between her outward behavior and her inner feelings forces her to try to resolve her conflict. She confesses to her dying mother who acknowledges that her daughter is "on the edge of a precipice." After her mother dies, the princess relies on the only authority figure available to her, her husband, producing the novel's most controversial scene: her confession of her attraction to the unnamed Nemours, while asserting that she has blamelessly resisted his advances. Whether a wife should admit her passion for a lover to her husband became one of the great ethical debates of the era following the novel's publication. The Paris journal *Mercure Galant* invited its readers to vote on whether the princess was right or wrong. Opinion was overwhelmingly against her. Later the prominent critic Jean de Valincour in his review of the novel would cite the confession scene for particular criticism as overly contrived and incredible. What is most interesting in the debate over the princess's behavior is that it is both a moral question and one of plausibility, underscoring the heightened realistic expectation that Madame de Lafayette had succeeded in establishing in the novel.

The prince's reaction lends weight to the side recommending a wife's deception. Already disappointed by his inability to provoke a passionate response from his wife, the prince becomes increasingly consumed by jealousy, desiring to know the name of his rival, and obsessed with uncovering evidence of his wife's betrayal. He is incapable of believing his wife's protestations of her innocence beyond what she feels for Nemours. Convinced of her infidelity, the prince languishes and dies. The way is now clear for the split between love and marriage to be joined in a happy ending that the romance demands. The Duc de Nemours prevails upon the princess's uncle to intercede on his behalf, and he arranges an interview between the two lovers. To Nemours's proposal, the princess is adamant in her refusal, stating

> I confess . . . that my passions may govern me, but they cannot bind me. Nothing can prevent me from recognizing that you were born with a great susceptibility to love and all the qualities required for success in love. You have already had a number of passionate attachments; you

> would have others. I should no longer be able to make you happy; I should see you behaving towards another woman as you had behaved towards me. I should be mortally wounded at the sight and I cannot even be sure I should not suffer the miseries of jealousy. . . . I must remain in my present state and stand by the resolution I have taken never to abandon it.

Here the princess submits passion to the cold logic of reality. Nemours has deceived before; he will again. The princess recognizes a central duty to herself, not to her lover. Instead of marriage and gratified passion, she chooses retirement from the world to her estate in the Pyrenees, and the novel closes with a brief memorial to her life there: "She spent part of the year in the convent; the rest she spent at home, though in profound retreat and in occupations more saintly than those of the most austere houses of religion. Her life, which was quite short, left inimitable examples of virtue."

If the modern reader is more apt than Madame de Lafayette's contemporaries to accept the moral and psychological inevitability of her confession to her husband, the novel's somber conclusion of self-denial continues to provoke differing interpretations of the work. To what extent is irony in play here? Is the princess to be praised or pitied? Is she unable to resolve the split between heart and head except by self-abnegation, or is she a protofeminist who chooses autonomy over a prescribed, subordinate gender role? The various questions raise yet again the issue of plausibility, sending the reader back to the text for the answers to the princess's psychology and emotions, the values of her society, and the intentions of her creator. It is clear in the enigmatic questions raised by *The Princess of Cleves* that we are no longer in the fantasy domain of the romance but the ambiguous and challenging new world of the novel.

57

THE STRANGER

(1942)

by Albert Camus

The Stranger *is a classical work, an orderly work, composed about the absurd and against the absurd.*

—Jean-Paul Sartre, "An Explication of *The Stranger*"

Albert Camus's *The Stranger*, Voltaire's *Candide*, and Hugo's *Les Misérables*, are France's most famous novels worldwide. Each in their way helped define their eras: Voltaire's novel typifies 18th-century Enlightenment thinking; Hugo's captures the spirit of 19th-century Romanticism, and Camus's masterpiece is in fundamental ways the prototypical novel of the modern sensibility. With its alienated antihero, narrative inversions, stripped-down prose, and thematic ambiguity, this fablelike novel continues to puzzle and provoke. With the possible exception of Kafka's initial sentence of *The Metamorphosis*, there is no more famous opening in modern fiction than the protagonist's deadpan declaration in *The Stranger:* "Mother died today. Or perhaps yesterday, I don't know." Published in 1942, the novel made Camus an international celebrity and a dominant intellectual and artistic force in the post–World War II era. Rightly or wrongly, *The Stranger* established the association between Camus and existentialism and his position as moralist and polemicist of the absurd. It would influence the French New Novel of Alain Robbe-Grillet, Marguerite Duras, Nathalie Sarraute, Michel Butor, and Claude Simon, as well as the American antirealists, such as John Hawkes and Donald Barthleme. Often co-opted as a vehicle to deliver a philosophy, *The Stranger* should be appreciated for its imaginative and technical daring as one of the seminal works of the 20th century that helped determine the methods and preoccupations of the modern novel.

The novel presents the reflections of a French Algerian clerk, Meursault, who kills an Arab on a beach and is tried, found guilty, and condemned to death. Divided in a two-part structure of crime and punishment, *The Stranger* is further patterned by three deaths: the natural death of Meursault's mother in the geriatric home where she has been confined, the violent, ambiguously motivated murder, and the state-sanctioned, anticipated execution of Meursault in which his sentence is really determined by his apparently indifferent response to his mother's death rather than the act that killed the Arab. The novel explores the shocking perspective of Meursault, who cannot express emotions he does not feel and refuses to acknowledge the values and beliefs society holds sacrosanct as he is forced to grapple with the implications of living in an absurd world.

Although identified with the sensibility of occupied France that it seemed to reflect when it was published in 1942, *The Stranger* was actually conceived in Camus's native Algeria before the war. Begun in 1938, *The Stranger* was completed in May 1940, when the German invasion of France started. The novel came out of the ideas and attitudes formed during Camus's frenetic activities and experiences following his earning his *baccalauréat* in 1930, including a series of attacks of tuberculosis, the collapse of his first marriage, his membership and quarrel with the Communist Party, his reading of Nietzsche, Kierkegaard, Dostoevsky, Kafka, Gide, Malraux, and Sartre, his theatrical involvement, and his newspaper work in which he contributed articles under the pen name of Jean Mersault. The novel's major incidents were derived from anecdotes of two of his Algerian friends. One told Camus of another's run-in with an Arab on the beach who after a knife fight had returned with a revolver to pursue his attacker, but no shots were fired. The other incident came from the painter Sauveur Galliero, whom Camus met at a café shortly after the death of Galliero's mother. He informed Camus that after burying his mother he had gone to the movies with his girlfriend, prompting Camus to declare, "Now I have the second panel for *L'etranger*." The novel would connect both elements: the murder of an Arab and the implications of Camus's friend's curious impassivity over the death of his mother into a remarkable exploration of a disturbing modern sensibility and its implications.

What sets *The Stranger* apart from other novels is its compressed, economical style and minimalist elements used to capture the narrative consciousness of Meursault. The first part of *The Stranger* delineates the routinized, reactive responses of a man who lives instinctively in the present. Concentrating exclusively on surface elements, the novel achieves its character analysis indirectly, through the details Meursault chooses to notice and by what he refuses to acknowledge. Uninvolved and uncommitted, Meursault lacks any ethical or moral viewpoint beyond a positive reaction to physical stimuli. The news of his mother's death prompts no emotional response as he goes through the motions of the expected vigil before her coffin and her burial. Dozing, smoking, and drinking coffee, without expressing any conventional signs of grief, Meursault displays a shocking passivity, concentrating exclusively on externals. His behavior following his mother's death will eventually become the deciding factor for the jury at his trial for murder. Camus observed, "In our society, a man who does not cry at the funeral of his mother is likely to be sentenced to death." Burying his mother is only a brief interruption in Meursault's routine, a set cycle of work, swimming, and seeing his girlfriend, Marie Cardona. Described in an unsubordinated, declarative style that Camus modeled on Hemingway and American hard-boiled detective fiction, Meursault's narrative is an undifferentiated succession of present occurrences without causality or consequences whose significance is usually unreflectively dismissed with the verbal equivalent of the Gallic shrug in the repeated statement, "It's not important." Meursault has no interest in a job promotion and a transfer to Paris, accepts Marie's marriage proposal although he refuses to acknowledge any reciprocal claim of love, and passively becomes an accomplice in his neighbor Raymond's brutal beating of his Arab girlfriend. It is this act that leads to the climax of the first part of *The Stranger.* An initial confrontation with the girl's brother on the beach is followed by Meursault's chance encounter with Raymond's attacker. Under the blazing midday sun that seems to attack him, Meursault pulls the trigger of Raymond's revolver and then "fired four more times at the motionless body where the bullets lodged without leaving a trace. And it was like knocking four quick times on the door of unhappiness."

In prison and on trial for his life, Meursault is forced to evaluate his relationship with the world. Confined in a cell, Meursault represents what Camus would identify in his contemporaneous essay, "The Myth of Sisyphus," as *l'homme absurde:* an individual increasingly conscious of life as a prison and forced to confront the denial of everything that gave his life meaning. Yet Meursault accommodates himself to prison life, replacing the old routine with the new prison one: "I managed pretty well. At the time, I often thought that if I had had to live in the trunk of a dead tree, with nothing to do but look up at the sky flowering overhead, little by little I would have gotten used to it. I would have waited for birds to fly by or clouds to mingle, just as here I waited to see my lawyer's ties and just as, in another world, I used to wait patiently until Saturday to hold Marie's body in my arms."

Meursault's next challenge is dealing with his death. Relentlessly and damnably honest in his responses to his examiners, Meursault only gradually recognizes his guilt. However, unable to offer any defense for his crime beyond that he killed "because of the sun," Meursault is prosecuted for his lack of remorse, for his refusal to offer any acceptable mitigation, and ultimately for his reaction to his mother's death. From society's perspective, Meursault is an unfeeling monster whose death validates his accusers' beliefs in moral absolutes that he denies. In this sense, Meursault is the ultimate outsider, the stranger in our midst who outrages conventional faith in life's significance and human obligations. In Camus's analysis Meursault is one who "refuses to play the social game, who refuses to lie, who agrees to die for the truth as he sees it" and "the only Christ that we deserve." Condemned to death, Meursault rejects the chaplain's consolation and accepts the inevitability of his end and the reality of human mortality. He denies the false dream of futurity that negates the sole fact of present existence that Meursault is able in the end joyfully to affirm. Meursault finally recognizes and accepts the "gentle indifference of the world" and his extinction as a precondition for an enhanced, authentic engagement in life as the novel shifts from an indictment of Meursault's alleged callousness to the world's blindness and self-serving preservation of illusions that mask the underlying absurdity of existence.

Readers continue to dispute the degree to which Meursault should be regarded as a rebellious, admirable hero or a radically flawed egoist, as well as Camus's thematic assumptions. In critic Germaine Brée's reading of the novel, Meursault before he kills "answers but never asks a question." His murderous act "jolts Meursault out of his purely negative state" and at the end he is "defiant and lucid" in his appreciation of being. Others have denied this therapeutic reading of Meursault's development, suggesting that there is not so much a change in Meursault as a crystallization and intensification in his essential dilemma and attitudes. Still other critics have stressed that the progress of the novel is to take Meursault and the reader to the essential first step in recognizing the value of what is left when false hope and artificial consolations are left behind. Camus continued to explore the implications of *The Stranger* in his essays, plays, and later novels. All share his brilliant assault on conventional assumptions. The essential questions raised in *The Stranger*—how do we live our lives, what is the purpose of our existence, what is sin and salvation in a world devoid of God where traditional moral or spiritual imperatives no longer operate—would become constants in Camus's writings but were never better expressed than in this initial imaginative probing for meaning in an irrational world.

58

THE RED BADGE OF COURAGE

(1895) *by Stephen Crane*

But Crane's work detonated on the mild din of that attack on our literary sensibilities with the impact and force of a twelve-inch shell charged with a very high explosive. Unexpected it fell amongst us: and its fall was followed by a great outcry.
—Joseph Conrad, in a preface to an edition of *The Red Badge of Courage*

Few other novels show as clearly the audacious, transformative power of the imagination to animate experience and to force the reader to see things in a fundamental and defining new way as Stephen Crane's *The Red Badge of Courage.* Taking up the challenging theme of warfare at the age of 21 in 1893, without the aid of firsthand experience, choosing as his subject a Civil War battle that had taken place nearly a decade before his birth, Crane managed a interpretation of combat and the ambiguity of heroism that has altered our understanding ever since. Civil War veterans were convinced that Crane must have been a participant. Historian and novelist Shelby Foote even identified one former Union officer who proudly claimed, "I was with Crane at Antietam." Future veterans of other wars, instructed by Crane, saw their own experiences vividly reflected in Crane's illumination. Although Ernest Hemingway, with the condescension of the eyewitness, dismissed Crane's view of combat as "a boy's dream of war," he conceded that Crane's perspective was "truer to how war was than any war the boy who wrote it would ever live to see," and that *The Red Badge of Courage* was "one of the finest books of our literature." The truth and resonance of Crane's depiction have withstood even the technical skill and graphic authenticity of Steven Spielberg's riveting cinematic version of the D-Day landing in *Saving Private Ryan.* As truthful as this opening sequence is in conveying the horrors of war to the senses, Crane adds what the film cannot so easily or so satisfactorily portray: what combat feels like to an ordinary soldier. As one early reviewer observed, Crane "stages the drama of war . . . within the mind of one man, and then admits you as to a theatre." In rendering the successive impressions of the sensitive Henry Fleming as he is tested under fire, Crane achieved a radical refinement of the novel's methods, conjoining external details and interior states into a heightened totality, and as a result, in the view of novelist Robert Stone, "American literature entered the modernist age."

That Crane could accomplish so much at such an early age in defiance of prevailing literary taste and of the conventional fictional wisdom that one should write only what one knows has contributed to the mystique surrounding the novelist's brief career that ended with his death in 1900 when he was 28. A New Jersey native and dropout from two colleges, Crane mounted his assault on literary fame first with *Maggie: A Girl of the Streets* in 1893. Published at his own expense using a pseudonym, the novel drew on his journalistic experience chronicling New York's lowlife. His clinically realistic tale of a young woman's squalid upbringing, seduction, and descent into prostitution connected Crane with literary naturalists such as Zola and the narrative objectivity of Flaubert. When the novel failed to find an audience, Crane set out to write a potboiler, a war novel, the first draft of which he composed in 10 nights in the spring of 1893. With a working title, "Private Fleming, His Various Battles," the much-revised manuscript that would become *The Red Badge of Courage* was based in part on Crane's reading of veterans' stories collected in the popular four-volume set *Battles and Leaders of the Civil War*, which ultimately disappointed him, causing him to remark that "I wonder that *some* of these fellows don't tell how it *felt* in those scrapes." His research into others' war experiences was supplemented by his own background as a military school student and from undergraduate athletics. Crane would later observe, "I believe I got my sense of the rage of conflict on the football field." His manuscript was read by novelist and editor Hamlin Garland, who helped arrange for publication by *McClure's*, but the book languished for six months as the publisher delayed publication, suspecting that the Civil War had ceased to be a popular subject. Retrieving his manuscript, Crane finally arranged for a newspaper syndicate to bring out an abridged version in 1894, with its book publication in 1895. Although it was reviewed favorably and achieved respectable sales, *The Red Badge* became a best-seller as a result of what H. G. Wells described as the "orgy of praise" for the English edition of the novel that recognized that Crane had "something new to say, and consequently, with a new way of saying it." By the end of 1896, the novel had gone through nine editions, and Crane could justifiably observe that he was "no longer a black sheep but a star."

From the novel's opening sentence, "The cold passed reluctantly from the earth, and the retiring fogs revealed an army stretched out on the hills, resting," Crane follows his central aesthetic principle by presenting, in his words, "a succession of sharply outlined pictures which pass before the reader like a panorama, having each its definite impression." Vivid close-ups, less distinct wider views, and personification reflect the perspective and shifting feelings of the novel's protagonist, Henry Fleming, as word reaches his encamped, untested regiment that the battle is finally to be joined. His apprehensions and doubts about his performance dominate his thoughts and cloud his view. The details of the coming engagement are based on the Battle of Chancellorsville, but Crane keeps the focus on his ordinary soldier's limited perspective with a deliberate vagueness of time, place, and character. The armies are identified only by the details of the "blue-clothed men" and talk of "gray, bewhiskered hordes," without the Civil War even being mentioned, except in a late addition of the subtitle: "An Episode of the American Civil War." As Crane noted, "It was essential that I should make my battle a type and name no names." The surname of the protagonist, who is most often referred to as simply "the youth," is not identified until the novel's midpoint. Others are typified as "the tall soldier" (Jim Conklin) and "the loud soldier" (Wilson). The effect is to universalize the war experience and to join the limited perspective of Fleming with the detached, ironical viewpoint of the narrator, who refuses to arbitrate and clarify Fleming's progress. Crane's contention was that "Preaching is fatal to art in literature. I try to give readers a slice out of life, and if there is any moral or lesson in it, I do not point it out. I let the reader find it for himself."

The trajectory of Fleming's experiences begins with his anxiety over the coming engagement. He is forced to resolve his previous "visions of broken-bladed glory" that led him to enlist with the mundane reality of army life with its depersonalized training and the monotony of camp life. He attempts "to prove to himself mathematically that he would not run from battle." When his initial testing under fire comes, "The youth perceived that the time had come. He was about to be measured. The flesh over his heart felt very thin. He was in a moving box. There were iron laws of tradition and law on four sides." Relying on the power and protection of his unit, Fleming at first stands and fights, like those around him, engulfed by the "war atmosphere—a blistering sweat, a sensation that his eyeballs were about to crack like hot stones. A burning roar filled his ears." Crane fills the atmosphere with vivid and evocative sensory details in which battle flags "jerked about madly in the smoke . . . furiously slit and slashed by the knife-like fire from the rifles." Around Fleming, men drop "here and there like bundles," to become corpses "twisted in fantastic contortions" as if "they had fallen from some great height, dumped upon the ground from the sky." Fleming's fear grows as the scene expressionistically reflects his panic: "To the youth it was an onslaught of redoubtable dragons. He became like the man who lost his legs at the approach of the red and green monster. He waited in a sort of a horrified listening attitude. He seemed to shut his eyes and wait to be gobbled." When those around him begin to break, "He ran like a rabbit."

Fleming's terrified flight and its aftermath show his emotional shift from wide-eyed frenzy to save himself to shame as he learns that the line has held.

He rationalizes the wisdom of his flight as he had previously attempted to convince himself he would not run. He embraces peaceful Nature, seen as a "woman with a deep aversion to tragedy," as the sustaining alternative to the "swollen war god" of violent death, a consolation that is shattered by his confrontation with a decaying corpse in the bosom of Nature. He next confronts personalized death, not of an unknown soldier, but that of his friend Jim Conklin, the tall soldier, the significance of which has been much debated in the religious tonality of Jim's sacrificial acceptance of death, Fleming's rededication to the fight that eventually follows, and Crane's famous description of the red sun "pasted in the sky like a wafer."

Fleming ironically receives his ennobling and face-saving wound, his "red badge of courage," from the rifle butt of a fellow Union soldier who has likewise cut and run and finds Fleming blocking his escape. Finding his way back to his regiment, with his cowardice unchallenged, Fleming gains a second chance to display his courage, which Crane presents as an ambiguous complex of ferocious, instinctive aggression, pride, shame, and "a temporary but sublime absence of selfishness." Carrying the regiment's flag in an assault, Fleming, along with his regiment of "fresh-fish," prove their mettle, capturing their opponent's battle flag, and coming face to face with their enemy in the person of four prisoners who ironically mirror the attitudes and situations of Fleming and his regiment. The foes are revealed as neither the "gray hordes" of the imagination nor very chivalric opponents whose defeat is needed to sustain personal glory, and the novel's climax modulates between ironic reality and Fleming's feelings of triumph and vindication. As the engagement ends, Fleming attempts unsuccessfully to reconcile the joy of his success and the shame of his past failure but does at least manage to "look back upon the brass and bombast of his earlier gospels and see them truly." Compared to the falsity of his previous view of heroic combat, Fleming has been instructed, along with the reader, in a deeper view of human nature and experience: "He felt a quiet manhood, nonassertive but of sturdy and strong blood. He knew that he would no more quail before his guides wherever they should point. He had been to touch the great death, and found that, after all, it was but the great death. He was a man." The issue of Henry Fleming's maturation and the significance of his final revelation, like the meaning of the novel's final sentence—"Over the river a golden ray of sun came through the hosts of leaden rain clouds"—have been the subject of a continuing critical debate. Is the reader expected to regard Fleming's growth and development as affirmative or as ironic, reflecting the author's view or only Henry's limited, deluded perspective, in which another illusion has replaced a former one, misreading the equally clear signs of nature's indifference and the destructive pointlessness of Fleming's experience? The achievement of *The Red Badge of Courage* stems from Crane's remarkable willingness to treat his subject in a manner that opens up these questions imaginatively rather than closing them

59

THE COUNTERFEITERS

(1926)

by André Gide

In The Counterfeiters *Gide overcame his difficulties and facilities as a writer. The antiromantic yet poetic stylization of all the elements of the novel, the orchestration of the diverse voices, the lively pace of the story, the concern with permanent human values, the stringency of the language—all contribute to make* The Counterfeiters *an unusual book. To the ordinary pleasures of novel reading it adds, for the sensitive amateur, the "pure" pleasure of aesthetic understanding. No novel ever written was more "literary" and yet more free of literary influences. What Gide really investigated in his novel is what happens to all forms of "literature," in contact with life. It was perhaps the only real adventure that he himself had fully lived, and as a result,* The Counterfeiters *is the only one of his novels which fully expresses him.*

—Germaine Brée, *Gide*

The Counterfeiters, along with the other great European novels published in the 1920s—Proust's *In Search of Lost Time*, Joyce's *Ulysses*, Mann's *The Magic Mountain*, and Woolf's *Mrs Dalloway* and *To the Lighthouse*—is one of the great innovations of the novel form, renewing its power through daring experimentation. *The Counterfeiters* is the prototypical metafiction that problematizes how we see and express the world. It is one of the modernist wonders that rewrites the rules for the novel and liberates its procedures for a more complex and challenging exploration of experience and consciousness. It is also the first of Gide's many fictions that he called a novel, a complex and expansive work that is simultaneously a novel of ideas, a meditation on the psychology of literary creation, and a comprehensive portrait of manners and morals in the period immediately before and after World War I.

For Gide the novel must present reality from multiple vantage points, replicating the profusion and formlessness of actuality, while exploring the artistic, psychological, social, and philosophical means for its understanding. Begun in 1919 and completed in 1926, *The Counterfeiters* was conceived, in Gide's words, as a novel to "make people say: 'Ah yes! we understand why he claimed not to have written any before this'." Compared to his previous *récits*, short personal accounts illustrating a single perspective and theme, *The Counterfeiters* would contain multitudes. "I can conceive of a novel in the same manner as Dostoevsky," Gide remarked, "[as] a struggle between points of view." His novel would be "an intersection—a *rendez-vous* of problems." To capture multiple themes based on the gap between experience and its perception, Gide arranges multiple reflections of several facing mirrors through the experience of Édouard, a novelist in the process of writing a novel called *The Counterfeiters* about a novelist writing a novel called *The Counterfeiters*, and so on. The dizzying reflexiveness becomes the means for Gide to make his book "the critique of the novel . . . in general." He explained that in *The Counterfeiters* "There isn't one center to my novel, there are two, as in an ellipse: the events on the one hand and their reaction in 'Edouard.' Ordinarily, when one writes a novel, one either starts with the characters and makes up events to develop them, or starts with the events and creates characters as needed to explain them. But 'Edouard,' who holds the psychological strings of a series of beings who confide in him, rather than writing a novel, dreams of making them act in reality, and he doesn't succeed in substantiating the characters by the events. These characters give him events, that he can't do anything with and that becomes part of the subject."

The Counterfeiters juggles two main narrators, a third-person perspective confined to present-time reporting and commenting on events, and Édouard's reflections in his journals (about half the novel) in which he considers the same events while evaluating their use in the novel that he struggles to compose. Other characters mimic the role of narrator through their conversations and the intelligence they provide, and the novel makes use of multiple narrative means, including dramatic monologues, letters, and diary entries. Form is fitted to content so that the novel's structure replicates the fragmented, multivalent nature of existence through several interlocked plots that reveal an elaborate, shifting, and a nearly always deceptive pattern of relationships. The multiple stories never quite cohere into a satisfying, single linear plot but are allowed to shift in and out of focus, trailing off and lost from view, forcing the reader to assume a role like Édouard himself sifting the fragments of experience for a pattern of meaning and significance. Eventually, Édouard realizes that his frustration as a novelist with the act of creation, with the struggle between experience and perception, provides him with the core idea for his projected novel, and the ultimate lesson of *The Counterfeiters*, in "the rivalry between the real world and the representation that we make of it. The way in which the world of appearances imposes itself on us and in which we try to impose on the outer world our particular interpretation constitutes the drama of our life. The resistance of the facts invites us to transport our ideal constructs into dreams, hope, the future life, our belief in which is nourished by all our disappointments in this one." Gide, therefore, has shifted the center of gravity in the novel from experience to its perception, uncovering the drama in the gap between appearances and reality, thought and action, desire and fulfillment.

The incidents of the novel center on the activities and relationship among three families: the Profitendieus, Moliniers, and Azaïs-Vedels. The action starts when 17-year-old Bernard Profitendieu discovers letters proving his illegitimacy. He leaves home to stay with his school friend Olivier Molinier, who has two brothers, Vincent and Georges. Olivier tells Bernard that Vincent has abandoned his mistress, Laura, one of the children of the Azaïs-Vedel family who run a boarding school, and of the imminent arrival of his Uncle Édouard, a writer and discreet homosexual. At the Paris train station, Édouard drops the checkroom ticket for his bag. It is picked up by Bernard, who retrieves the suitcase, finds and reads the writer's diary, and discovers a supplicating letter from Laura that Bernard uses to meet her. Encountering Édouard, Bernard admits the theft of his bag, charms the writer by his impudence and succeeds in convincing Édouard to take him on as his secretary. Bernard accompanies the writer to Switzerland where Édouard takes Laura to conceal her pregnancy and to retrieve an old friend's grandson, Boris, to bring him to the Azaïs-Vedels' boarding school.

In the meantime, Vincent becomes connected with a cynical English woman, Lady Griffith, and her novelist friend Passavant, Édouard's literary rival, while Olivier is jealous of his friend's relationship with his uncle. Back in Paris, Bernard goes to work at the Azaïs-Vedels' school, where several of the students, including Georges Molinier, Olivier's younger brother, are passing counterfeit coins. A party attended by Bernard, Édouard, and Olivier climaxes in Olivier's attempted suicide. Boris is invited to join the gang of counterfeiters if he will complete the initiation, which involves standing before the class at school and pretending to shoot himself with a gun with blank cartridges. The prank goes tragically awry, and Boris is killed. It is one of the novel's three climaxes. In the others Bernard is reconciled with his family and returns home better able to cope with the ambiguity between appearance and reality; while Édouard finds happiness in nursing his nephew and achieving the vision necessary to compose his novel.

Such a summary misses much of the complexity and significance of *The Counterfeiters*, which is organized by juxtaposition and counterpoint. More central than its plot as a unifying element is its theme signaled by the novel's title. Gide's original inspiration for the novel came from a newspaper account of a counterfeiting ring that survives in the story of the gang at the Azaïs-Vedels' boarding school. At a much wider and deeper level, all of the characters are involved in varying degrees in forms of counterfeiting, and the novel assembles a kind of catalog of the ways people live an inauthentic life. The boarding school becomes a prime nexus for this theme. It is run along rigid moral principles based on fidelity to family, church, and country, and those in charge are incapable of seeing the hypocrisy of their teaching or that the student club, the Society of Strong Men, celebrating conventional values, actually deals in extortion and counterfeit currency. A similar duplicity of hiding actual, spontaneous, instinctual feelings under the mask of acceptable behavior afflicts all of the characters, with both comic and tragic results. The novel, therefore, displays variations on the theme of counterfeiting in the progress of its many adolescent characters. As Germaine Brée argues, *The Counterfeiters* is "a novel of orientation which depicts young people emerging from various forms of myth into the reality of life. For the first time Gide's work has really deep social implications. He portrays the struggle of the young to discover through trial and error the genuine forces and limits of their personalities, in the face of obsolete social forms and ethics which tend to impose stereotyped feelings and attitudes upon them. Experience teaches Édouard nothing, since he ignores it, whereas Georges, shaken by Boris's death, alters his disastrous course. For Gide, to live, as to write a novel, is to undergo the test of reality."

The core example of counterfeiting in the novel is Édouard's attempt to create the novel within the novel. Édouard himself is a "counterfeit" author who explains his theory of the novel to Bernard by displaying a counterfeit 10-franc piece. Value, he asserts, depends on whether the coin is believed to be genuine. It is a matter of perception alone, and has nothing to do with reality. Édouard's realization leads him into the labyrinth of subjectivity that complicates his attempt to compose his novel. Claiming he wants to treat all of his actual experiences in his novel, he "edits" out experiences that he does not understand or because they do not conform to preconceived notions. He chooses not to include Boris's death in his book because "I already have enough difficulty understanding it. And, then, I don't like 'news items.' They have in them a bit of the peremptory, the undeniable, the brutal, the outrageously real. . . . I allow reality to support my thought as a proof, but not to precede it. I don't like being surprised." He is, like all artists, therefore, engaged in the creation of a counterfeit reality, a substitute that misses a far more complicated reality that either eludes us or deludes us.

The Counterfeiters acknowledges the ultimate impossibility of achieving authenticity and reassuring objectivity. Both are subjective inventions dependent on the perception of validity. Truth is not absolute but relative, and the best the individual or the author can do is to consider experience in all its infinite refractions, as suggested in Gide's dizzying but finally liberating narrative mirrors.

THE GRAPES OF WRATH

60

(1939)

by John Steinbeck

Along with such works as Upton Sinclair's The Jungle *and Harriet Beecher Stowe's* Uncle Tom's Cabin, The Grapes of Wrath *has achieved a place among those novels that so stirred the American public for a social cause as to have a measurable political impact. Although thus associated with this class of socio-protest fiction,* The Grapes of Wrath *continues to be read, not as a piece of literary or social history, but with a sense of emotional involvement and aesthetic discovery. More than any other American novel, it successfully embodies a contemporary social problem of national scope in an artistically viable expression. It is unquestionably John Steinbeck's finest achievement, a work of literary genius.*

—Peter Lisca, *John Steinbeck: Nature and Myth*

Like the other great landmark novel that came out of America in the 1930s, Richard Wright's *Native Son*, Steinbeck's *The Grapes of Wrath* is an unavoidable, contentious American classic. Both books have been criticized for their message and their method in which, according to some, social protest is pushed to propaganda. However, few readers have been able to resist either book's power or sheer conceptual daring. Along with Dorothea Lange's photographs, *The Grapes of Wrath* has become the defining artistic embodiment of the depression years as Wright's *Native Son* has typified the racial divide in America. Certainly, those too young to have lived through the 1930s draw on Steinbeck, or at least on the film images of John Ford's adaptation of the novel, in their mind's eye for essential images to comprehend the time and place. *The Grapes of Wrath* has become in many ways America's *Les Misérables*, as much a popular testament of humanity as a work of fiction, grandiose in its conception and reckless in its artistic violations that disturb the critic but do not trouble a worldwide popular audience. Criticized on publication in 1939 for its factual distortions and condemned for its "obscene sensationalism," *The Grapes of Wrath* was banned and burned throughout the United States. Critics more concerned with the novel's literary qualities than its social message have been equally harsh, condemning Steinbeck's turning his characters into dogmatic, sentimental sounding boards. Edmund Wilson complained, "It is as if human sentiments and speeches had been assigned to a flock of lemmings on their way to throw themselves into the sea." Others found the novel's structural alternation between narrative and choral, expository interchapters "too shrill, too evangelistic" (Malcolm Cowley) and "perhaps some of the most wretched violations of aesthetic taste observable in modern American fiction" (Frederick J. Hoffman). Despite all the charges leveled against it, *The Grapes of Wrath* has persisted as more than a work of propaganda, with more than historical interest as a defining period piece. Like Whitman's poetry, Steinbeck's novel, with all its lapses, claims the reader's respect as one of the few works of the American imagination that manages the breadth and totality of the epic.

Steinbeck's wrestling with his subject, the plight of the dust bowl refugees in California, which he recognized in 1936 was "like nothing in the world," would be expressed in a number of preliminary responses. The miserable conditions of the migrant camps near Salinas and Bakersfield prompted Steinbeck to write a seven-part investigative report, "The Harvest Gypsies," which appeared in 1936 in the San Francisco *News.* An unfinished novel, *The Oklahomans,* followed. In the fall of 1937, while working in New York to turn *Of Mice and Men* into a stage play, Steinbeck bought a car, drove to Oklahoma, and followed the migrants' path along Route 66 to California. Vigilante strikebreaking tactics used on the Salinas lettuce workers prompted a virulent satire, "L'Affaire Lettuceberg," in 1938. Finally, between late May and October 1938, Steinbeck completed his novel in a rush of inspiration and focus. His title was supplied by his wife, Carol, borrowed from a phrase of "The Battle Hymn of the Republic," which Steinbeck valued for its biblical symbolic possibilities and American association. "I like it," he observed, "because it is a march and this book is a kind of march—because it is in our own revolutionary tradition and because in reference to this book it has a large meaning."

It is this "large meaning" that suffuses the novel, lifting it beyond the level of journalistic reporting or satire of Steinbeck's previous attempts to comprehend the bitter legacy of the dust bowl, the Great Depression, and the fate of the migrants in California in the widest possible contexts. The adventures of the Joads are forced to serve a dual focus, particular and universal, and *The Grapes of Wrath* is constructed with a mixture of intimate close-ups and wider generalizations, much in the manner of Tolstoy's *War and Peace,* in which the domestic story of the Rostóvs, Bolkónskis, and Bezúkhovs alternates with Tolstoy's speculations about the historical forces at play during Napoleon's invasion. Steinbeck's naturalism that attempts to explain the economic and social forces that trapped the Joads and the other migrant families is additionally extended by a persistent symbolism that enriches a social analysis in a complex pattern of universal archetypes. "I have set down what a large section of our people are doing and wanting," Steinbeck declared, "and symbolically what all people of all time are doing and wanting. The migration is the outward sign of the want." Patterned as an American version of the biblical exodus, as well as an ironic echo of the push westward by the American pioneers, the novel is divided into three major sections: the scenes in Oklahoma that illustrate the causes that set the Joads in particular and a people in general in motion west, the trip along Route 66 to California, and what the Joads and others encountered there. During composition Steinbeck conceived of his plan as dealing with "three related longer novels," the connection among the parts fashioned by correspondences of details and symbols, as well as the novel's 16 interchapters, experiments in perspective and point of view that serve to amplify, contextualize, and typify the Joads' adventures.

Part one begins with a masterly evocation of the drought that destroys the tenuous hold of those living on the land. Like the opposite natural forces of the rains and flood that close the novel, the drought is an elemental challenge exacerbated by the political, economic, and social forces that will similarly batter a community and impede its will to live and prompt its wrath. If, however, the novel is meant to illustrate only the pounding the long-suffering Joads take, then the charges of sentimentality and propaganda that have been leveled at the novel may well apply. In such a limited reading, the Joads and their fellow victims are mainly interesting for the humanity they evince through their degradation. The "Okie" is thereby given a human and ultimately elevated face. However, Steinbeck presents a much more complex dynamic for the Joads. Their transformation is marked by the contrasting symbols that open and close the novel. The first is the indomitable land turtle, moving irresistibly southwest, a metaphor for the Joads' own journey as well as their initial self-containment and indestructibility. The other is the controversial final image of the decimated and destitute family and Rose of Sharon's offering her breast milk to feed an unknown starving man. By the novel's end the Joads have reconstituted themselves around an altered concept of the family of man. How this family will deal with the changes that are forced on them dramatizes Steinbeck's central social message that goes considerably further than any dogmatic sociological or economic analysis.

The novel begins with Tom Joad's return from prison on parole, having served his sentence for killing a man in self-defense, an instinctive act, which will be paralleled with the far more significant, altruistic retaliation over the killing of the itinerant preacher turned labor agitator Jim Casy at the novel's close. Suspicious of others and self-contained, Tom retreats back to the protective support of his family only to find the homestead abandoned and his family dispossessed. The Joads' response to their plight is to dream a better life for themselves in California, supported by images of bounty and security, prompted by a bogus handbill promising good jobs in California. For Grampa Joad, California is represented by the grapes he will let soak his beard, for Ma Joad it is a "little white house" as a new setting for the family. On the journey west, circumstances diminish the family and force it to break apart. Their dreams are exposed as delusions to be replaced by other, more practical goals, while offering an alternative kinship in a wider conception of relationships. Casy joins the family for the journey west. Grampa dies of a stroke before leaving Oklahoma in the tent of another family, the Wilsons, whom Ma acknowledges with "almost a kin bond," and the two families merge. The Wilsons will later be left behind, along with Noah, the eldest Joad son, before the desert crossing into the fertile valleys of California that Granma will not live to enter. Later, Connie Rivers, Rose of Sharon's husband, will desert her, and Casy will be arrested and killed by strikebreakers. The group of 12 who set out from Uncle John's farm will finally be reduced to six as Tom is forced into flight. On the novel's sociological level, the fate of the family by the novel's end is suspended, with little hope to be expected through the coming winter as the flood drives them from their boxcar home, swamps their truck, and maroons them to an uncertain future.

This grim version of the corruption of the American dream in which the biblical land of Canaan is a sham is counterbalanced by the moral redemption of the Joads through a conversion to a wider conception of their fate and their response. Increasingly, their experiences force the Joads to accommodate previous attitudes of selfish isolation and exclusive family loyalty to communal claims. The Weedpatch government camp suggests the ways in which cooperation strengthens and ennobles. Ma Joad, "the citadel of the family," who tries to preserve and protect her clan with a jack handle, eventually must persuade Tom to leave them, arguing, "They was the time when we was on the lan'. They was a boundary to us then. . . . We was always one thing—we was the fambly—kinda whole and clear. An' now we ain't clear no more. . . . We're crackin' up, Tom. There ain't no fambly now." In place of the former narrow boundary of clan emerges a sustaining sense of a wider allegiance of sympathy and responsibility. Tom, in hiding, has contemplated Casy's ideas and concluded:

> "Well, maybe like Casy says, a fella ain't got a soul of his own, but on'y a piece of a big one—an' then. . . . Then it don't matter. Then I'll be aroun' in the dark. I'll be ever'where—wherever you look. Wherever they's a fight so hungry people can eat, I'll be there. . . . An' when our folks eat the stuff they raise an' live in the houses they build—why, I'll be there."

Tom breaks out of his isolation for activism, sustained by a greater good that transcends family loyalty and personal protection. It is a sentiment that Ma eventually endorses as well: "Use' to be the fambly was fust. It ain't so now. It's anybody. Worse off we get, the more we got to do." In the social allegory that Steinbeck constructs from the particulars of his migrants' fate, ultimate victory is glimpsed in the transition from I to We that crystallizes in the novel's concluding image of Rose of Sharon's sacrificial gift of breast milk to an unknown fellow sufferer.

Ultimately, Steinbeck's achievement in *The Grapes of Wrath* rests on his ability to generate universal meaning out of material that could easily have been treated as a simplified melodrama of heroic victims and brutal victimizers, a direct statement of social protest asking only outraged indignation on the part of its reader. Although this response dominated the initial reception of the novel, and the strategy by which it is evoked has led to an undervaluing of Steinbeck's artistry, a more balanced view is possible that values the novel's considerable achievement, both its message and manner, in which the particularity of a time and place is skillfully and compellingly orchestrated into an expansive, sustaining, American proletarian epic. If Steinbeck's plan of merging the sociological, historical, and spiritual occasionally falters with his portentousness, sometimes overwhelming the humanity of his characters and their individual stories, *The Grapes of Wrath* remains one of the novel's definitive attempts to comprehend human experience by extending the reader's sympathy and understanding, linking regional and historical issues to fundamental questions that continue to reverberate and elicit a powerful response.

61

THE GOLDEN NOTEBOOK

(1962)

by Doris Lessing

The most considerable single work by an English author in the 1960s has been done by Doris Lessing, in The Golden Notebook *(1962). It is a carefully organized but verbose, almost clumsily written novel, and if we were to view it solely as an aesthetic experience, we might lose most of its force. The book's strength lies not in its arrangement of the several notebooks which make up its narrative and certainly not in the purely literary quality of the writing, but in the wide range of Mrs. Lessing's interests, and, more specifically, in her attempt to write honestly about women. To be honest about women in the sixties is, for Mrs. Lessing, tantamount to a severe moral commitment, indeed almost a religious function, in some ways a corollary of her political fervor in the fifties.*

While the English novel has not lacked female novelists, few indeed—including Virginia Woolf—have tried to indicate what it is like to be a woman: that is, the sense of being an object or thing even in societies whose values are relatively gentle.

—Frederick R. Karl, "Doris Lessing in the Sixties: The New Anatomy of Melancholy"

Doris Lessing's masterpiece has been viewed as the protypical postmodernist self-reflective text, a feminist manifesto, an anatomization of contemporary culture, and one of the most thorough probings of a woman's consciousness in literature. The novel's contradictions and multiplicity, its evasion of simple categories (and responses) are central sources of its power, influence, and still vital relevance. It is hard to imagine a subsequent intensely introspective novel treating identity, society, and gender issues that does not refer back to *The Golden Notebook.*

Lessing objected to *The Golden Notebook* being read as an autobiographical confession or as a chronicle of contemporary "sex wars." Instead she insisted that the novel be seen in the context of the great European works of the 19th century that attempted a synthesizing portrait of the intellectual and moral climate of their times. "For me the highest point of literature," Lessing declared, "was the novel of the nineteenth century, the work of Tolstoy,

Stendhal, Dostoevsky, Balzac, Turgenev, Chekhov." Yet the modern world is dominated by fragmentation and chaos that resists summation. As Matthew Arnold observed in predicting the challenge to come, "the calm, cheerfulness, the disinterested objectivity have disappeared; the dialogue of the mind with itself has commenced." Gone, in D. H. Lawrence's words, is "the old stable *ego* of the character." Lessing's solution is to turn the novel inside out, breaking up and realigning its component parts, shattering chronology and narrative sequence, and rendering her protagonist in multiple narrative voices and alter egos. In her 1971 introduction to the novel, Lessing explains the plan of the novel:

> There is a skeleton, or frame, called *Free Women*, which is a conventional short novel, about 60,000 words long, and which could stand by itself. But it is divided into five sections and separated by stages of the four Notebooks, Black, Red, Yellow and Blue. The Notebooks are kept by Anna Wulf, a central character of *Free Women*. She keeps four, and not one because, as she recognises, she had to separate things off from each other, out of fear of chaos, of formlessness—of breakdown. Pressures, inner and outer, end the Notebooks; a heavy black line is drawn across the page of one after another. But now that they are finished, from the fragments can come something new, *The Golden Notebook*.

Described by Joseph Hynes as a "five-layered sandwich," *The Golden Notebook*, set in London during the 1950s, breaks up a conventional narrative describing Anna Wulf and her friend Molly Jacobs with the intense interior views recorded in Anna's four notebooks, each concerned with a different aspect of her life (or its projection), so that a section of *Free Women* is followed by an excerpt from Anna's black, red, blue, and yellow notebooks. This pattern is repeated four times. A fifth, golden notebook follows recording Anna's breakdown and recovery, in which it is learned that she has been given the first line of *Free Women*—"The two women were alone in the London flat."—by her lover Saul Green. By the end of the novel, therefore, the reader reaches the present moment of the commencement of the embedded novel that is then concluded. Like Joyce's *Finnegans Wake*, *The Golden Notebook* is circular, without a conventional beginning, middle, or end. As with Proust's *In Search of Lost Time*, we reach by the end of the novel the protagonist's developmental state that allows her to write the novel we have just read. Like Gide's *The Counterfeiters*, Lessing's novel is simultaneously a narrative and a reflection on its own creation: Anna Wulf, like Édouard, lives through her experiences while at the same time turning them into a novel. What distinguishes *The Golden Notebook* from other examples of metafictional self-reflection is its ambition to convert its formal challenges into summary statements that encompass the widest possible exploration of its sexual, political, psychological, and authorial themes, depicting a woman protagonist for one of the first times in the multidimensions of lover, mother, writer, individual, and political activist. "It is a novel about certain political and sexual attitudes that have force now," Lessing observed; "it is an attempt to explain them, to objectivize them, to set them in relation with each other. So in a way it is a social novel, written by someone whose training—or at least whose habit of mind—is to see things socially, not personally." The novel's several social points are made through its form. It would be, in Lessing's words, "a book which would make its own comment, a wordless statement: to talk through the way it was shaped." Anna Wulf's inner crisis, her search for wholeness, mirrors a world in chaos in which identity is co-opted and undermined by various personal and public forces. The novel articulates these points of pressure on its central protagonist and the process by which they operate and can be managed. "If I had used a conventional style, the old-fashioned novel," Lessing observed, "I would not have been able to do this kind of playing with time, memory, and the balancing of people."

In the initial segment of *Free Women*, Anna Freeman Wulf is a blocked writer visiting her friend Molly Jacobs. Both are technically "free women" since they are in between relationships, but beneath the surface they are both prisoners of forces that they cannot control. Anna's dilemma of balancing emotional and sexual fulfillment while retaining personal autonomy has paralyzed her. As she tells her friend, "As far as I can see, everything's cracking up." The *Free Women* section serves to introduce simplified versions of the experiences and aspects of Anna's psychic distress that her notebooks will treat in complex detail. In order to cope with her existential crisis as a woman, intellectual, and activist, Anna compartmentalizes her life and reflections into her four color-coded notebooks. Lessing explained that she divided Anna's reflections and different narrative forms into "four parts to express a split person. I felt that if the artist's sensibility is to be equated with the sensibility of the educated person, then it is logical to use different styles to express different kinds of people." When asked by Molly why she bothers with her notebooks, Anna responds, "Chaos, that's the point," meaning that collectively her experiences are spinning out of control and to keep formlessness at bay, by managing the parts, perhaps the whole truth about herself and her life, its purpose and point, might be discovered.

Anna's black notebook records her transactions with film and television agents who want to adapt her novel, *Frontiers of War*. These circumstances prompt her to consider the occurrences on which her novel was based, her own past in Rhodesia and her relationships with a group of communist intellectuals there during the war. These formative details that she has converted into her successful first novel now seem to her a distortion and a simplification of her past. What she perceives as an indulgence in a nostalgia for death and destruction leads her to despair about the ability of writing ever to deliver the truth, the cause of her current inability to write. The red notebook treats Anna's disillusionment with the British Communist Party, based on the inability of either ideology or activism to cope with the conflicts Anna feels as an individual and a woman and the moral collapse of the party as the news of the Stalinist purges come to light. If writing distorts, political solutions equally fail to respond to personal and private imperatives or halt violence and chaos, and the notebook breaks down into a series of newspaper clippings about such events as the execution of the Rosenbergs and the hydrogen bomb tests.

The yellow notebook shows Anna's response to her experiences in a narrative about a women's magazine writer named Ella, Anna's fictionalized alter ego, and her unsatisfying relationship with Paul Tanner, a married psychologist. It is, in the words of critic Jean Pickering, "analysis through the hypothetical," the attempt to set Anna's public and private selves into fictional perspective. Ella is, therefore, a projection of Anna, whose self-destructive tendencies and emotional dependency on her lover mirror her creator's dilemmas. The narrative eventually unravels into a series of story ideas, exploring various possible relationship scenarios. The blue notebook is a diarylike record of daily events, including Anna's psychotherapy sessions with her Jungian analyst, Mrs. Marks, who provides the basis of Anna's eventual recovery by having her relive her experiences. It also records her affair with the American writer Saul Green, which leads to the breakdown and recovery recorded in the concluding golden notebook. The reader now has the interior view and context to understand the character "Anna Wulf" introduced in the novel's opening pages. Alienated from her past, from her former political convictions, from those she has loved, Anna is unable to write or unify her world, shattered into parts that do not cohere.

To achieve some semblance of psychic unity, Anna and her lover go through a cathartic experience that expands the normal limitation of "individuality." The route to Anna's recovery is through confronting the source and implication of the various selves that she has kept carefully separated in her notebooks. By risking madness, by recognizing a central principle that "we must not divide things off, must not compartmentalize," Anna moves from destruction to control, from fragmentation to unity, encouraged by her lover to face her demons and confront her fears. "They 'break down,'" Lessing explains, "into each other, into other people, break through the false patterns and formulas they have made to shore up themselves and each other, dissolve." If the individual notebooks represent a defeat of integration and unity, the inner "Golden Notebook" shows the various elements of Anna's past and psyche reassembled. Anna refuses the role of victim (in love, politics, or art) and accepts the conditions of her past and present circumstances, breaking the spell that has incapacitated and silenced her. She provides the first sentence for Saul Green's next novel, and he provides the first line of hers, the initial sentence of *Free Women* and *The Golden Notebook*. *Free Women*, therefore, is a demonstration of what her experiences have taught Anna, converted

62

SONS AND LOVERS

(1913)

by D. H. Lawrence

For Lawrence the writer, the experience behind Sons and Lovers *served as poetic matrix and paradigm. The novelist who gives voice to the rage of Lady Chatterley's gamekeeper at a boyhood sweetheart; the essayist who fulminates against the murder of a child's "warm, swift, sensual self" by aggressive "Parent Love"; the poet praising death, pansies, and Indians, and battling the middle class, machines, and egoistic lovemaking, are all the Lawrence who created Paul Morel, with his virginal and Oedipal anxieties, enamored of "night, and death, and stillness, and inactions," interested in primitive tribes, believing in the wholesomeness of flowers and the common people, convicted in the book itself of a caddish, angry, yet wistful sexuality. Lawrence's chief theme, which he summarized as "the relation between men and women," expresses itself in* Sons and Lovers, *as in superficially dissimilar works like* The Rainbow, Kangaroo, *and* The Escaped Cock, *as a search for tenderness between parent and child, friends of each sex, lovers, races, man and nature, man and God.*

—Judith Farr, Introduction to *Twentieth Century Interpretations of* Sons and Lovers

D. H. Lawrence's *Sons and Lovers* is distinguished by remarkable firsts and often perplexing contradictions. Lawrence's third novel is his first major work, his first "great book," in its creator's view, and remains his most popular and widely read. It is one of the earliest and best examples of the British proletarian novel, detailing life in a small Nottinghamshire mining community with an insider's familiarity. It has also been claimed as the "first Freudian novel in English"—one of the most extensive case studies of the Oedipus complex in fiction and one of the earliest applications of Freud's emphasis on the roles played by subconscious and the irrational in human experience. Its naturalistic and psychological concerns are joined through the traditional structure of the novel of growth and development, the bildungsroman, or more precisely its subcategory, the *Künstlerroman*, the formation drama of an incipient artist. Like Joyce's *A Portrait of the*

Artist as a Young Man, which followed it in book form two years later and to which it is inevitably compared, *Sons and Lovers* radically reformulated the conventional novel of education and development, by dramatizing the inner, subjective, contradictory, and fragmentary contours of self-development. Like Joyce, Lawrence became an artist by writing about the process of becoming an artist. By contending with his own background and psychic formation, Lawrence discovered his unique subject and focus on subjective experience that would dominate his career and define his contribution to modern literature.

The contradictions that bedevil *Sons and Lovers* stem from issues regarding Lawrence's control over his autobiographical material. Is *Sons and Lovers* a fictionalized autobiography or an autobiographical fiction? Is the novel best read as Lawrence described it, as "a great tragedy. . . . the tragedy of thousands of young men in England" in which the personal is objectified into universal patterns of meaning and significance? Or is it confession, therapy, or purgation? Lawrence would later advise those interested in him to "read *Sons and Lovers*, the first part is all autobiography" and that "one sheds one's sicknesses in books—repeats and presents again one's emotions, to be master of them." A persistent criticism of *Sons and Lovers* is that, despite an often unflinching honesty in probing his own family background and past self, there are, in the words of the critic Mark Shorer, "confusions between intention and performance," in which Lawrence is at times overmastered by his intense identifications with his characters and vacillating in his sympathies and conclusions regarding them. Psychological tension, Shorer argues, "disrupts the form of the novel and obscures its meaning, because neither the contradictions in style nor the confusion in point of view is made to right itself. Lawrence is merely repeating his emotions, and he avoids an austerer technical scrutiny of his material because it would compel him to master them. He would not let the artist be stronger than the man." It is, however, the contradictory battle between man and artist that makes *Sons and Lovers* so fascinating and compelling, as Lawrence wages one of the great literary struggles to convert his past and the psychic and sexual traumas it created into artistic form and universal relevance.

In 1905 Lawrence left the Nottinghamshire mining community of Eastwood where he was raised and became a teacher in South London, work that he abhorred and compensated for by writing poems, stories, and his first two novels. *The White Peacock* (1911) is set in Nottinghamshire, though its mines and miners are not central. It concerns a group of young people whose aspirations for fulfillment, professionally and sexually, are frustrated by aspects of their own nature and impulses that they cannot control. *The Trespasser* (1912) is another tragic novel in which a young woman's affair with a married man leads to his suicide. As Lawrence began to conceive *Paul Morel*, the working title for his third novel, he planned to move from the symptoms of the various social and emotional impasses that destroyed the lives of the characters of his first two novels to their causes, using his own background as the test case. In 1910, Lawrence wrote to his publisher about his new work: "*Paul Morel* will be a novel—not a florid prose poem or a decorated idyll running to seed in realism, but a restrained, somewhat impersonal novel. It interests me very much." Work on the book halted as Lawrence helped nurse his mother through the cancer that took her life in December 1910. By March 1911 Lawrence reported that "I have begun *Paul Morel* again. I am afraid it will be a terrible novel. But, if I can keep it to my idea and feeling, it will be a great one." Committed to exposing more directly his own experiences and feelings than in his previous novels, while coping with the loss of his mother whom he confessed to having loved "almost with a husband and wife love," Lawrence sent his manuscript to Jessie Chambers, the model for Miriam in *Sons and Lovers*, his childhood soul mate and Lawrence's mother's longtime rival for his emotional allegiance. She found the manuscript "story-bookish" and advised him, as she recalled, to "write the whole story again, and keep it true to life." Urged on to an honesty that he declared, "The British public will stone me if it ever catches sight [of it]," Lawrence rewrote the novel for a third time, by 1912, under the influence of Frieda Weekley, the wife of Lawrence's former French professor and mother of three with whom he eloped to the Continent. Frieda, who would serve as a model for Clara Dawes in the novel, encouraged Lawrence's interest in Freud's theories. They helped Lawrence detect universal patterns in the particulars of his autobiography and buttress the novel's eventual title, *Sons and Lovers*, as well as the novel's "ruling idea," that Lawrence explained as follows:

> A woman of character and refinement goes into the lower class, and has no satisfaction in her own life. She has had a passion for her husband, so the children are born of passion, and have heaps of vitality. But as her sons grow up she selects them as lovers—first the eldest, the second. These sons are *urged* into life by their reciprocal love of their mother—urged on and on. But when they come to manhood, they can't love, because their mother is the strongest power in their lives, and holds them. . . . As soon as the young men come into contact with women, there's a split.

The novel would trace this split in the two sons—William and Paul—while diagnosing the sources—psychological and social—of their mother's frustrations and its consequences on the Morel family.

William Heinemann, Lawrence's previous publisher, refused the novel, reportedly calling it "the dirtiest book he had ever read." It received a sympathetic hearing, however, from Edward Garnett, editor at the publishing firm Duckworth that agreed to bring it out under Garnett's guidance. He is responsible for cutting nearly 10 percent of the original manuscript, shortening scenes and censoring others, in many instances without consultation or approval from Lawrence. (It would not be until 1992 that Cambridge University Press finally published *Sons and Lovers* in its original manuscript form.) Initial reactions to *Sons and Lovers* were decidedly mixed. Praised for its "interest and power," the novel was charged with a lack of form and a consistent or objective point of view. Lawrence, in the view of many, failed to efface himself sufficiently. "The men and women," one reviewer complained, "use words which are his and not their own; their reading is in the literature for which he cares; often they express thoughts which belong to him and not to them." The novelist John Galsworthy, who admired the novel's domestic scenes, disapproved of "the love part . . . It's not good enough to spend time and ink describing the penultimate sensations and physical movements of people getting into a state of rut; we all know them too well." The hostility over the book's form and content suggests the extent that *Sons and Lovers* fundamentally challenged basic assumptions about the novel.

Sons and Lovers does have a conventional and reassuring chronological arrangement, beginning a few months before Paul Morel's birth and proceeding through his childhood, love affairs, and final departure following his mother's death. The narrative is controlled by an omniscient narrator who sees and understands all and whose commentary guides the reader's interpretation. Compared to the radical time shifts of Joseph Conrad or the stream of consciousness methods that would be employed by Joyce and Woolf, Lawrence's novel justifies a description as the "last 19th-century novel," closer in method to Thomas Hardy and George Eliot. It expresses its innovations in other ways, however, by radically abandoning conventional plot for naturalistic episodes. Nothing happens in the novel out of the ordinary and plausible events in the lives of a miner's family. Scenes are joined through a network of suggestive imagery as well as by the causal logic of the evolving psychic dilemma and growth of the protagonist. Each episode is made to contribute to the reader's growing understanding of the various forces affecting the characters. Perhaps the novel's greatest modernist innovation is Lawrence's locating dramatic conflict in the working of unconscious desires and environmental forces so that psychology, naturalism, and symbolism unite into a complex thematic whole.

Part one of *Sons and Lovers* treats the early married life of Paul's parents to establish the basis for the family's oppositions and their consequences. The cultured Gertrude has married down in class to wed Walter Morel, and her initial passion for the vital and handsome young miner has turned to bitterness over his vulgarity, brutality, and drunkenness and to despair over the "struggle with poverty and ugliness and meanness." In one of the finest depictions of working-class English life, one of the first to be written with an insider's authority, the opening section of the novel documents a "battle between the husband and wife—a fearful, bloody battle that ended only with the death of one. She fought to make him undertake his own responsibilities, to make him fulfill his obligations. But he was too different from her. His nature was purely sensuous, and she strove to make him moral, religious." The main casualties are the children—eventually four, William, Annie, Paul, and Arthur—who side with their mother and her values that cost them the qualities their father possesses even in his excesses and failures. She desperately clings, particularly to her sons, as substitutes and compensations for her loveless marriage. The pattern of crippling dependence that defines the Morel sons' relationships with their mother and its psychic-sexual scars is played out first with the eldest, William. His mother's ambitions for him push him away from home to a respectable position as a clerk in London, and William becomes engaged to a girl Lily, whose beauty attracts him but whose shallowness repels him, repeating the disjunction between the physicality of his father whom he scorns and the intellect of his mother on whom he depends. William's dilemma, trapped between his mother's aspirations for him and a love-hate relationship with a frivolous girl, ends with his death from pneumonia, and Mrs. Morel's and the novel's focus shifts to the second son, Paul.

Paul's sensitivity that is expressed in an artistic ability as a painter, an even greater dependence on his mother, and a growing alienation from his father and his community creates a similar mind/body duality crisis as the one that afflicted his brother. Leaving boarding school, Paul, at 16, takes a clerical post in Nottingham with a manufacturer of surgical appliances and meets a farmer's daughter Miriam Leivers, who becomes his first love. Miriam is the polar opposite of the shallow beauty Lily. Where Lily's relationship with William was based almost entirely on sexual attraction, without any spiritual communion, Miriam more closely resembles Paul's mother in her earnest idealism and resistance of the sensual, and Paul's attraction to her sets in motion what Lawrence referred to in a letter as "a battle . . . between the mother and the girl with the son as object." Miriam offers Paul only "sex in the head" and a denial of any richer sense of life based in spontaneous feeling. After she eventually gives herself sexually to him as a "sacrifice," Paul remains unfulfilled and turns to Clara Dawes, a freethinking, older factory worker who is separated from her blacksmith husband. With Clara, Paul experiences his true "baptism of passion," but Clara's independence and guilt over her husband as well as Paul's continuing emotional bond with his mother doom their affair. "The son decides to leave his soul in his mother's hands," Lawrence summarizes the climax of the novel, "and, like his elder brother, go for passion. He gets passion. Then the split begins to tell again. But, almost unconsciously, the mother realises what is the matter, and begins to die. The son casts off his mistress, attends to his mother dying. He is left in the end naked of everything, with the drift towards death." The novel ends with Paul's registering the loss of his mother to begin an ambiguous future, poised ambiguously between defeat and resistance:

> Now she was gone abroad into the night, and he was with her still. They were together. But yet there was his body, his chest, that leaned against the stile, his hands on the wooden bar. They seemed something. Where was he?—one tiny upright speck of flesh, less than an ear of wheat lost in the field. He could not bear it. On every side the immense dark silence seemed pressing him, so tiny a spark, into extinction, and yet, almost nothing, he could not be extinct. Night, in which everything was lost, went reaching out, beyond stars and sun. Stars and sun, a few bright grains, went spinning round for terror, and holding each other in embrace, there in a darkness that outpassed them all, and left them tiny and daunted. So much, and himself, infinitesimal, at the core a nothingness, and yet not nothing.
>
> "Mother!" he whispered—"mother!"
>
> She was the only thing that held him up, himself, amid all this. And she was gone, intermingled herself. He wanted her to touch him, have him alongside with her.
>
> But no, he would not give in. Turning sharply, he walked towards the city's gold phosphorescence. His fists were shut, his mouth set fast. He would not take that direction, to the darkness, to follow her. He walked towards the faintly humming, glowing town, quickly.

Readers have long debated what to make of this ending. Is Paul drifting to death, as Lawrence suggested, or moving away from the darkness toward the city and a future life made possible by self-understanding? In a sense, these become the central questions of all of Lawrence's subsequent novels, as heart and head, soul and body, life and death battle for supremacy, and Lawrence explores the roots of psychic paralysis and the routes away from extinction toward affirmation and fulfillment.

THE GOOD SOLDIER

63

(1915)

by Ford Madox Ford

I happened to be in a company where a fervent young admirer exclaimed: "By Jove, The Good Soldier *is the finest novel in the English language!" whereupon my friend Mr John Rodker, who has always had a properly tempered admiration for my work, remarked in his clear, slow drawl: "Ah, yes. It is, but you have left out a word. It is the finest French novel in the English language!"*

—Ford Madox Ford, letter to Stella Ford, 1927

When Ford Madox Ford began *The Good Soldier* on his 40th birthday, in 1913, he was determined "to show what I could do" as a writer. Known as an acolyte and collaborator with his older friend, Joseph Conrad, as the founding editor of the *English Review*, and as an indefatigable supporter of literary talent, Ford regarded this book as his first serious novel. "I have never really tried," he observed, "to put into any novel of mine *all* that I knew about writing. I had written rather desultorily a number of books—a great number—but they had all been in the nature of *pastiches*, of pieces of rather precious writing, or of tours de force." In a career that included more than 80 books, most written too hastily to claim lasting importance, Ford managed to craft at least one masterpiece, the one work in his immense oeuvre besides the formidable World War I tetralogy, *Parade's End* (1925–28), which continues to be read today and is commonly regarded as one of a handful of the greatest novels of the 20th century. *The Good Soldier* is in many ways the defining Georgian novel of the pre–World War I era. Like the war itself, it can be regarded both as the end and a beginning: the culmination of the nuanced moral comedy of manners of Henry James, and in the novel's endlessly refracting indirectness and suggestiveness, its subtle display of consciousness and narrative unreliability, a forecast of how novels would increasingly be written in the postwar era.

The Good Soldier is a study of sexual intrigue, betrayal, obsession, madness, and destruction lurking just below the surface in the seemingly placid, respectable lives of a few "good people." It is an ironic comedy of manners that attempts to summarize a world on the brink of collapse, rotting from the inside and ready for the destruction of the war that on a domestic, personal level the novel anticipates and explains. When he began to write his novel, Ford must have felt his own life was spiraling out of control. His first wife, Elsie Martindale, whom Ford left in 1909, refused to divorce him. In a highly publicized libel suit, she had received damages from a magazine that had connected Ford's name to the writer's mistress, Violet Hunt, whom he had bigamously married and had subsequently replaced with another lover. To this marital and sexual tangle was added a bitter quarrel with Ford's close friend Arthur Marwood that precipitated a break with Conrad, who sided with Marwood in the dispute. Abandoned by his closest friends, embroiled in a sexual rondel that showed no signs of ending, Ford found himself in a characteristic personal muddle that prompted Ezra Pound to remark about his friend, "I once told Fordie that if he were placed naked and alone in a room without furniture, I would come back in an hour and find total confusion."

That Ford would be able to achieve such masterful control over his personal torments, channeling them into the subject of his novel, is one of the remarkable achievements of *The Good Soldier.* By the time he had finished his book, World War I had begun. In one of the truly eerie coincidences in literary history, August 4, which Ford uses as the pivotal date for the novel's significant action—Florence Dowell's birth, her first sexual affair, her marriage, the start of her affair with Edward Ashburnham, and her suicide—would also become the date that England declared war on Germany, making explicit the connection between Ford's fiction and historical events that the novel prefigures. Ford's publisher, recognizing that there was no wartime market for the book's original title, *The Saddest Story,* accepted the cynically offered, ironically consoling substitute, *The Good Soldier,* instead.

The germ of Ford's novel was an incident recorded in his impressionistic study of the English national character, *The Spirit of the People* (1907). In it, Ford notes the "true story" of a married man of his acquaintance who fell in love with his young ward and to prevent further scandal, sent the girl on a trip around the world. Ford was asked to accompany the unhappy couple to the station for their parting to help forestall a "scene." The writer regarded the lack of emotion of the pair as "a manifestation of a national characteristic that is almost appalling." The brutal, pathetic lack of tenderness turned tragic when the girl died en route at Brindisi, and Ford concludes that "at the moment of separation a word or two might have saved the girl's life and the man's misery without infringing eternal verities." *The Good Soldier* would work toward this same parting as Edward Ashburnham separates from his ward, Nancy Rufford, an act that destroys them both, but to get there Ford must first penetrate the "eternal verities" that conceal the worst kinds of infringement.

The Good Soldier announces in its first sentence that "This is the saddest story I have ever heard." Narrated by an American gentleman of leisure, John Dowell, it is the story of two couples—John and his wife, Florence, and Edward and Leonora Ashburnham, scions of the English gentry. They meet at the fashionable German spa town of Nauheim, where both Florence and Edward treat their heart conditions, and the couples form a "little four-square coterie," companionably linked over a span of nine years. On the surface, they are "good people," unimpeachably respectable, seemingly the distinguished end products of an elaborate social refinement. "We were, if you will," as Dowell ruefully observes, "one of those things that seem the proudest and the safest of all the beautiful and safe things that God has permitted the mind of men to frame. Where better could one take refuge? Where better?" As the story unfolds, the refined, civilized veneer of the Dowells and the Ashburnhams will eventually be penetrated. Appearances will give way to a shocking reality that their tranquil companionship is actually "a prison full of screaming hysterics." All will be exposed as the reverse of what they appear to be: Florence, the helpless invalid who seemingly must be guarded against any undue emotional strain is an active, unfaithful libertine; Edward, the good soldier of the title, is far from the noble, heroic type he appears but a sentimentalist, consumed by passion he is expected but unable to control; Leonora proves to be a dutiful, supportive wife in the most sinister sense; and finally the narrator is revealed as severely limited in his capacity for understanding, his sense of the world collapsing under the weight of the revelations that his story dramatizes.

Ford's innovation in telling their sad story is to forgo a chronological account for a complex, shifting narrative perspective that only gradually connects the various pieces of the puzzles that fully reveal the characters and their true relationships. "I have, I am aware," the narrator confesses, "told this story in a very rambling way so that it may be difficult for anyone to find their path through what may be a sort of maze. . . . And, when one discusses an affair—a long, sad affair—one goes back, one goes forward. One remembers points that one has forgotten and one explains them all the more minutely since one recognizes that one has forgotten to mention them in their proper places and that one may have given by omitting them, a false impression. I console myself with thinking that this is a real story and that, after all, real stories are probably told best in the way a person telling a story would tell them. They will then seem most real." Dowell reconstructs his story in a series of impressions, reflecting how things first appeared as well as how viewpoints and understanding shift as a result of revelations that emerge. Ford was convinced that "Life did not narrate, but made impressions on our brains," and he therefore constructs his novel using the restricted perspective of his narrator's consciousness. In such a dynamic, indirect strategy, the reader must play an active role in assessing the narrator's observations, alert for clues that foreshadow eventual developments and for hints that the narrator either overlooks or misinterprets. Dowell's reliability has become one of the novel's most debated aspects, and *The Good Soldier* encourages an intriguing double focus both on the events and personalities that are revealed and on Dowell's own culpability in the story's sad progress.

At least one part Dowell is forced to play is that of the deceived, naive husband who will gradually and painfully become aware of his wife's unfaithfulness, her affair with the admired Edward Ashburnham, and the truth of all that has been overlooked and misperceived, including the reasons behind the suicides of both Florence and Edward. Lies define virtually all the novel's relationships. Florence's innocence and illness are masks, and the marital relationship between Leonora and Edward is a battleground of jealousy and control on the part of Leonora and a string of sexual violations on the part of Edward. Florence eventually kills herself, possibly out of fear that her sexual past has been revealed to her husband, possibly because she has learned that Edward, her lover, has fallen in love with his ward, Nancy Rufford. Leonora, in despair of ever commanding her husband's love, vindictively urges Nancy to give herself sexually to Edward, using her knowledge of her husband's dalliances as a weapon to destroy him and her rival. The result is Nancy's madness and Edward's eventual suicide. As Dowell struggles to discover the significance of their story, he observes, "I call this the Saddest Story, rather than 'The Ashburnham Tragedy,' just because it is so sad, just because there was no current to draw things along to a swift and inevitable end. There is about it none of the elevation that accompanies tragedy; there is about it no nemesis, no destiny. Here were two noble people—for I am convinced that both Edward and Leonora had noble natures—here then, were two noble natures, drifting down life, like fireships afloat on a lagoon and causing miseries, heartaches, agony of the mind and death. And they themselves steadily deteriorated? And why? For what purpose? To point what lesson? It is all darkness." The hell that *The Good Soldier* explores is a distinctly English version: the self-inflicted torment of souls who self-destruct under the force of desires they are ill-fitted to control and who have nothing but the props of their social role to rely on, forms of behavior that indeed are revealed as prisons for hysterics.

In the end, Dowell has acquired the Ashburnham estate, from which he surveys the wreckage of their lives, and has gone from a loveless relationship as the caretaker of a sham invalid to the caretaker of the genuinely mentally incapacitated Nancy Rufford. Love, marriage, friendship all have been exposed and found wanting in Ford's version of Conrad's *Heart of Darkness:* a trip into the abyss found much closer to home than in the Belgian Congo.

64

A PASSAGE TO INDIA

(1924)

by E. M. Forster

[A Passage to India] *is the last and best of Forster's attempts in that most difficult genre, the novel of ideas. It is an almost-successful attempt at an all-but-impossible task: an attempt to fuse the real world of social comedy and human conflict with the meaning and value of the universe which that world mirrors; to impose on experience the pattern of a moral vision; and out of these disparate elements to create a satisfying aesthetic whole. The wonder is not that it fails of complete success, but that it so nearly succeeds completely.*

—Gertrude M. White, "*A Passage to India:* Analysis and Revaluation"

When *A Passage to India* was published in 1924, Forster broke a 14-year silence since his last novel, *Howards End,* had appeared in 1910. A more prolonged creative silence lay ahead. At the age of 46, with exactly half of his life before him, Forster wrote no more novels. Tied intellectually and emotionally to the stability and order of the Victorian era in which he was born and had disappeared, Forster was also allied by artistic temperament to the realistic tradition derived from Jane Austen that seemed quaintly inadequate from the perspective of literary modernism. Forster admitted in *Howards End* that "It is impossible to see modern life steadily and see it whole," and he deferred persistent questions about his next novel, asserting that he had nothing more to say about a world he no longer really understood. Although far from inactive after 1924 as a writer of essays, biography, and criticism, Forster, as the saying went, became more and more famous with every book that he did not write. *A Passage to India,* therefore, stands as the capstone of Forster's career as a novelist, easily the most ambitious novel he ever attempted, as well as the most artistically patterned and satisfying. It is also one of the great justifications that the comedy of manners can be employed to reach an unsurpassed integration of social, political, spiritual, and moral themes. *A Passage to India* has consequently been called by critic Malcolm Bradbury "Forster's *Moby Dick*" and described by Norman Page "as if a novel of Jane

Austen had become embedded in one by Albert Camus or William Golding. Without quitting the English tradition of realism and even social satire and domestic comedy, Forster moves in his last novel beyond that tradition to examine, as Dostoevski and Kafka do, the nature of man and of the universe." All of Forster's novels in a sense are variations on the theme of division, explorations of the social, moral, and spiritual divides among individuals, classes, nations, between thought and feeling, the inner and outer world, with, "Only connect," the motto of *Howards End*, serving, as Cyril Connolly has argued, as "the lesson of all his work." *A Passage to India* presents Forster's most expansive inquiry of the fault lines that separate East and West, the British from the Indians, the beliefs of Muslims, Christians, and Hindus, as well as the factors that confound human relationships and ultimately undermine mankind's search for spiritual and moral redemption.

The multiple ironies and contradictions of India under British rule offered Forster the ideal subject to dramatize the essential fractures of life, but he struggled with his focus through two Indian trips over a period of a dozen years. "I began the book after my 1912 visit," he recalled, "wrote half a dozen chapters of it and stuck. I was clear about the chief characters and the racial tension, had visualized the scenes, and had foreseen that something crucial would happen in the Marabar Caves. But I hadn't seen far enough." He subsequently put the manuscript aside for nearly 10 years, resuming work on it after a second visit to India in 1921. Serving as the private secretary to the maharajah of Dewas Senior, Forster continued to gather material for his novels, in particular, experiencing the Hindu Krishna festival of Gokul Ashtami, which Forster regarded as "the strangest and strongest Indian experience ever granted me." Between his two visits, World War I had intruded, inevitably forcing a reassessment of previous views, as had the gap that Forster experienced between the India remembered from his first visit and the India experienced on the second. As Forster recalled,

> When I returned in 1921 to stay with the Maharajah I took chapters with me and expected that the congenial surroundings would inspire me to go on. Exactly the reverse happened. Between the India I tried to create and the India I was experiencing there was an impassable gulf. I had to get back to England and see my material in perspective before I could proceed. Perhaps the long wait was to the good and the religious atmosphere of Dewas certainly helped to establish the spiritual sequence I was seeking, particularly in the last section of the book.

The juxtaposition of Forster's two encounters with India between a major historical shift produced by the war eventually led Forster to see far enough into and beyond the Marabar Caves, which would serve as the novel's climactic scene, to fashion the complex social and moral design of *A Passage to India*.

Its title is a reference to a poem by Walt Whitman that celebrates the opening of the Suez Canal as a mystical union of East and West. With a three-part structure, corresponding to the three seasons of the Indian year (cool, hot, and wet), each part named for a different place—Mosque, Caves, and Temple—and each associated with alternative understandings of the world: Muslim, Christian, and Hindu, Forster's intricate patterning of thematic and symbolic associations derives from the fairly straightforward plot of an initiation journey. A young British woman, Adela Quested, comes to the fictional Indian city of Chandrapore accompanied by the elderly Mrs. Moore to finalize her engagement with Mrs. Moore's son by her first marriage, Ronny Heaslop, the city's magistrate. Liberal and humane in their sympathies, both women are anxious to "know India," and are appalled and disoriented by the lack of coherence and sympathy they encounter. India is a muddle of conflicting religious and social values. The only thing that unites the Indians is their distrust of their British masters, and the British make no attempt to diffuse tension or further understanding. Segregated in their compound, the Anglo-Indian community is condescending and uncivil to those they rule, and the best the British Raj can muster is a misnamed "bridge party" that serves only to underscore division, as their invited Indian guests are coldly treated and neither side coalesces. On her own, Mrs. Moore ventures into a mosque and makes the acquaintance of a young Muslim doctor, Aziz. Their encounter, marked by mutual respect and sympathy, suggests a positive alternative response in which disharmony can be overcome and unity achieved. The undermining of difference through communication and understanding is continued when Mrs. Moore and Adela accept an invitation by Mr. Fielding, the principal of the Government College, to take tea at his house. Included at the party is Dr. Aziz and the Hindu professor Godbole. The mercurial Aziz, emboldened by the group's camaraderie, invites the English ladies to his home, and when they readily accept, counters to avoid the embarrassment of their visiting his shabby home with an alternative excursion to the Marabar Caves.

The experience of the two Englishwomen in the Marabar Caves serves both as the novel's central plot action and metaphysical center, as the novel reaches after a broader conception of the source for the divisions that separates individuals from each other and from nature itself. In a novel concerned with the question of achieving sympathy and understanding to resolve difference, the cave experience represents an existential challenge that neither Adela nor Mrs. Moore are equipped to handle. For Mrs. Moore, the confinement and emptiness of the cave with its sinister echo, reducing all human communication to "ou-boum," is a glimpse of nothingness and an occasion for despair:

> The echo began in some indescribable way to undermine her hold on life. . . . It had managed to murmur: "Pathos, piety, courage—they exist,

> but are identical, and so is filth. Everything exists, nothing has value." If one had spoken of vileness in that place, or quoted lofty poetry, the comment would have been the same—"ou-boum." If one had spoken with the tongues of angels and pleaded for all the unhappiness in the world, past, present, and to come; for all the misery men must undergo whatever their opinion and position, and however much they dodge or bluff—it would amount to the same. . . . But suddenly at the edge of her mind, religion reappeared, poor little talkative Christianity, and she knew that all its divine words from "Let there be Light" to "It is finished" only amounted to "boum."

The muddle of India has shifted to a mystery too oppressive to be reconciled by Mrs. Moore's Christian precepts. Adela experiences the cave in a far different way, as a sexual rather than a spiritual violation. Although what precisely happens to her in the cave remains the novel's great unsolved ambiguity, Adela flees in terror from her encounter, setting in motion the machinery of British justice that charges Aziz with assault.

At the trial the latent hostility and deep suspicion that have divided Chandrapore threaten to explode in riot and its containment by force that has, despite professed principles of justice, defined British control all along. As in the novel's first section, it is Mrs. Moore who helps to break the escalating cycle of misunderstanding and hostility. Her departure from India is interpreted as a conspiracy on the part of the English to obstruct justice by the mob of Aziz's defenders who begin to chant her name. It is subsequently revealed that Mrs. Moore has died on her voyage back to England, giving her summoned presence a ghostly, providential aspect. Mrs. Moore's confidence in Aziz's goodness helps Adela recant her story of her attack and leads to the dropping of all charges against him. In the trial's aftermath, the English community abandons Adela as a traitor, and the one positive friendship between the races, that of Fielding for Aziz, is compromised in Aziz's increasing suspicion of the English and Fielding's presumed sympathy for Adela, who has at least withstood the pressure of her countrymen that demanded Aziz's conviction.

The novel closes with a coda, set two years after the previous events in the Indian-controlled city of Mau. During the celebration of the Krishna festival, supervised by Professor Godbole, with a suggestion of the Hindu acceptance and affirmation of life's seemingly intractable oppositions between good and evil, past and present, time and space, Aziz is finally reconciled with Fielding, with Mrs. Moore again the agent of reconciliation. Aziz is convinced that Fielding has married his betrayer, Adela. Fielding has actually married Mrs. Moore's daughter, and hostility gives way to a tentative, temporary resolution of differences. As Fielding and Aziz ride on horseback together before their final parting, which ends the novel, the Englishman asks of his friend:

> "Why can't we be friends now? . . . It's what I want. It's what you want."
>
> But the horses didn't want it—they swerved apart; the earth didn't want it, sending up rocks through which riders must pass single file; the temples, the tank, the jail, the palace, the birds, the carrion, the Guest House, that came into view as they issued from the gap and saw Mau beneath: they didn't want it, they said in their hundred voices, "No, not yet," and the sky said, "No, not there."

Although Forster has forecast the inevitable process in which British rule must give way to Indian independence, the novel finally is less about English attitudes toward India and Indians toward the English than the essential questions of what can sustain us in a chaotic world in which nothingness always threatens and all seems to conspire to disunite. Despite a philosophical conclusion that threatens to overpower the novel's drama and characters, *A Passage to India* is a marvel of close observation, ironic social comedy, and ultimately a profound moral and spiritual exploration. In the many levels of *A Passage to India* the social question of England's responsibility to India serves to launch a much grander, more profound inquiry of how the universe and those factors that unite and divide humanity can be understood.

65

DANIEL DERONDA

(1876)

by George Eliot

In great Victorian fiction . . . there is an unprecedented density and convergence of psychological, moral, and visual detail. Eliot's masterpiece, Daniel Deronda, *is subtler, richer, more rapidly notated, and more challenging intellectually than anything that preceded or followed it.*

—Edward White, "*Introduction: George Eliot's Intelligence,*"
in *Daniel Deronda,* Modern Library Edition

George Eliot's final novel is both a culmination and a radical departure. Easily one of the most ambitious and intellectually daring of Victorian novels, *Daniel Deronda,* in its break with fictional conventions, anticipates the innovation and experimentation of modernism in the novels of James Joyce, Marcel Proust, Virginia Woolf, William Faulkner, and others. Eliot's popularity and acclaim during her lifetime were based on her ability to animate and anatomize English rural and provincial life, but in *Daniel Deronda* she offered a European novel, beginning and ending it abroad and relating a sharp satire of the English upper classes to the widest possible contexts of European history. Set in the 1860s, *Daniel Deronda* is the only one of Eliot's novels that does not rely either on a regional grounding or a distancing in the historical past. It is Eliot's version of *The Way We Live Now,* her engagement with the contemporaneous. In its twinned double plot following the growth and development of Gwendolen Harleth and Daniel Deronda, Eliot offers her final and most ambitious version of the novel of moral education, producing in the case of her heroine a female character as great as Flaubert's Emma Bovary, Tolstoy's Anna Karenina, and James's Isabel Archer. In telling Gwendolen and Daniel's stories, Eliot continually challenges her reader to think and understand more, making *Daniel Deronda* an ultimate test and reward of Eliot's avowed mission of aesthetic teaching. It is inevitably compared to its immediate predecessor, *Middlemarch,* and found wanting, but as the critic Barbara Hardy has observed, "As an experimental novel, *Daniel*

Deronda is a work of peculiar excitements and certain difficulties. It pushes beyond the achievement of its predecessors, and the very nature of its push makes it less easy and less entertaining than these predecessors. . . . It is one of those works of art whose greatness is inextricably bound up with imperfection." If its ambitious reach at times exceeds its grasp, *Daniel Deronda* is still an unavoidable novelistic experience opening up new fictional dimensions and fittingly capping a great novelist's career.

The origin of *Daniel Deronda* can be traced back to 1872 to Hamburg where George Eliot completed the finale of *Middlemarch* and rested from her labors. At the casino, Eliot reported back to her publisher John Blackwood that "The saddest thing to be witnessed is the play of Miss Leigh, Byron's grand-niece, who is only 26 years old, and is completely in the grasp of this mean, money-making demon. It made me cry to see her young fresh face among the hags and brutally stupid men around her." The incident would trigger the opening of *Daniel Deronda* in which the headstrong, self-willed Gwendolen Harleth gambles recklessly under the disapproving eye of the title character and the beginning of their crossed paths and connection. The novel's Jewish theme surrounding Daniel's development, which some readers have judged an unneeded distraction from the main interest of Gwendolen's story (the critic F. R. Leavis famously suggested that the novel should be split in half and the good part published separately as "Gwendolen Harleth"), was an essential part of Eliot's plan from the start. Returning from Germany, she began extensive reading in Jewish history and resumed her association with the scholar and Jewish nationalist Emanuel Deutsch, with whom she studied Hebrew and listened to his advocacy of a Jewish homeland. Deutsch's death from cancer on a journey to the Middle East in 1873 occurred just as Eliot began planning her new novel, and he would serve as the model for the character Mordecai who inspires Daniel to embark on his mission as a Zionist leader.

Daniel Deronda was written between 1874 and its serialization in eight monthly installments from February to September 1876. Initial sales were strong, and reception was generally favorable, though reviewers soon began to confirm Eliot's fear that "the Jewish element seems to me likely to satisfy nobody." Although Jewish readers were vocal and effusive in their praise for Eliot's sympathetic handling of Jewish customs and aspirations, others regarded the Jewish characters as "personages outside our interest" and their world "completely foreign to us," in the words of one reviewer. The high-minded, earnest Daniel was dubbed the "Prince of Prigs" and dismissed as unlikable and unbelievable; particularly in contrast to the fascinating vividness most readers regarded the treatment of Gwendolen. Eliot chaffed at "readers who cut the book into scraps and talk of nothing in it except Gwendolen," insisting that she intended "everything in the book to be related to everything else there." In Eliot's patterning of the novel, Deronda's embracing his identity as a Jew and his vocation as a leader of his people is inextricably connected to Gwendolen's own journey of self-discovery and eventual engagement with a world larger than her self-interest. The novel's penetrating satire of upper-class English life is directly related to English attitudes to Jews that Eliot intended to expose. As she explained to the American novelist Harriet Beecher Stowe, "As to the Jewish element in 'Deronda,' I expected from first to last in writing it, that it would create much stronger resistance and even repulsion than it has actually met with. But precisely because I felt that the usual attitude of Christians toward Jews is—I hardly know whether to say more impious or more stupid when viewed in the light of their professed principles. I therefore felt urged to treat Jews with such sympathy and understanding as my nature and knowledge could attain to." Anti-Semitism, Eliot insisted was only one manifestation of English moral blindness and their undeserved sense of superiority "towards all oriental people," "a spirit of arrogance and contemptuous dictatorialness" that Eliot was determined to challenge, a symptom of the larger dilemma of moral blindness and selfishness that thematically connects the novel's double plot. Integration of the novel's two worlds—upper-class English and Jewish—and the novel's two plots became in Eliot's mind, the point of the story, testing the reader's own moral capabilities of sympathy and self-assessment.

Other sources of resistance to the novel are attributed to Eliot's structural and stylistic innovations that challenge both Victorian novel conventions and her own reputation as a realist. The novel's action covers two years, between 1864 and 1866, and it daringly, and potentially confusingly, opens at its midpoint, at the casino in the German spa of Leubronn and the first of the several meetings between Gwendolen and Daniel that knit together their two stories and different circles. Beginning in medias res and plunging the reader directly into the consciousness of her characters without background exposition, Eliot anticipates subsequent modernist dislocation of narrative sequence. The novel's first three books are mainly flashbacks tracing how the pair came to Leubronn and the conditions that explain their attitudes and behavior. Gwendolen, a high-spirited and imperious young beauty, described in the first book as "The Spoiled Child," is determined to reign supreme over all around her and marry well to secure her independence and privilege. Resisting intimacy and "determined to be happy—at least not to go on muddling away my life as other people do . . . not to let other people interfere with me as they have done," Gwendolen enters the Victorian marriage market and eventually chooses the coldly aristocratic Henleigh Grandcourt, whom Gwendolen declares, compared to other suitors, "is not ridiculous." Recognizing his haughty selfishness, Gwendolen is confident in her beauty and charm to manage him. The result is the equivalent of irresistible force meeting an immovable object, as Gwendolen soon discovers. On the brink of receiving Grandcourt's anticipated proposal, Gwendolen confronts his discarded mistress, Lydia Glasher, who has borne Grandcourt's children and who extracts Gwendolen's promise to reject his proposal. Gwendolen flees to Leubronn to avoid him but is summoned home to attend to her family's financial crisis before he arrives in pursuit. Instead, Grandcourt encounters his distant relative Deronda, and the narrative loops backward again to describe Deronda's past as the ward of the upper-class Englishman Sir Hugo Mallinger. Adrift and without focus, Daniel abandons his studies at Cambridge to travel abroad. Before departing, while rowing on the Thames, he prevents a desperate young Jewess, Mirah Lapidoth, from drowning herself. In despair at her failure to find her lost brother, Mirah recovers with Daniel's assistance at the home of his friends the Meyricks, and his mission to assist her further will eventually lead Daniel to Mordecai Lapidoth and London's Jewish community after his return from Germany.

In the aftermath of Leubronn, in the third book, "Maiden's Choosing," Gwendolen rejects taking a humble post as a governess due to her family's financial distress and accepts Grandcourt's offer of a fashionable marriage, repressing both her promise to Lydia Glasher and her clear money motive in her decision. Eliot, who complained that popular convention dictated that novels must be love stories, here challenges that convention in unexpected ways. In a standard romantic novel, the heroine may learn of the other woman in time to reconsider her choice; certainly never does the heroine after such a revelation go on to marry the villain as Gwendolen does. Hoping to secure her independence in marriage and the means to gratify her self-interest, "She had found a will like that of a crab or a boa-constrictor which goes on pinching and crushing without alarm at thunder." Theirs is one of the most sinister marriages in Victorian fiction in which Grandcourt's demand for total mastery and Gwendolen's complete subordination to his will are a study in sadism. Gwendolen's misery in which a few months of marriage seemed "half her life" begins her painful process of self-knowledge and self-understanding. She turns to Daniel, whose sympathetic understanding was demonstrated at Leubronn by returning to her the necklace Gwendolen had sold to recoup her gambling loses, to confess her misery and to seek relief in his pity. Daniel, however, is increasingly preoccupied by events and revelations that overshadow Gwendolen's designated role for him as sympathetic confessor and supporter. Meeting Mordecai, a consumptive scholar and Zionist visionary, Daniel is embraced by him as the disciple for whom he has been waiting. Book 6, "Revelations," includes the realization that Mordecai is Mirah's long-sought brother and the announcement by Sir Hugo that Daniel's mother, whom he thought was dead, is alive and wishes to see him. Daniel travels to Genoa to learn that his mother, Princess Halm-Eberstein, a Jew who renounced her heritage to succeed as a singer, had consigned her son to the care of a devoted suitor, Sir Hugo, to be raised as an English gentleman in ignorance of his background. Gwendolen and Grandcourt also arrive at Genoa on a yachting holiday. While sailing in a small boat, Grandcourt is drowned, and Gwendolen is rescued. Consumed by guilt at having done nothing to save her husband because secretly wishing him dead, Gwendolen is comforted by Daniel. Ready now to depend on Daniel to validate her self-worth, Gwendolen is shocked to hear his intention to marry Mirah and accept the vocation that Mordecai had predicted for him as a leader to his fellow Jews. "Before the bewildering vision of these wide-ranging purposes in which she felt herself reduced to a mere speck," Gwendolen felt "for the first time dislodged from her supremacy in her own world, and getting a sense that her horizon was but a dipping onward of an existence with which her own was revolving." Gwendolen has journeyed far in the novel from "Princess in exile" to "banished soul," whose genuine remorse for her past behavior "was the precious sign of a recoverable nature; it was the culmination of that self-disapproval which had been the awakening of a new life within her." Expecting the logical conclusion of this new life to lead to her marriage to Daniel, the reader is disappointed. Gwendolen's growth into maturity and awareness of a larger sense of the world beyond her claims of supremacy are shown not ending by her reliance on another but beginning with full reliance on and acceptance of herself. So too, Daniel's future is left open and unsure, on his way to Palestine with Mirah and an uncertain future but one predicated on service in a cause greater than self, matching Gwendolen's liberation from the tyranny of ego, Eliot's precondition of moral worth and adult responsibility.

In working out the moral calculus of the novel in which vocation and self-awareness trump romance, Eliot has reinterpreted herself as a novelist. Having previously defined her philosophy and method by her realistic treatment of the ordinary life of nonidealized characters, Eliot in *Daniel Deronda* shows her willingness to expand and alter her methods. Secrets, coincidences, and sensational actions, more the province of Dickens and Wilkie Collins, play a much more prominent role in Eliot's last novel, serving a psychological and thematic purpose in pushing her characters to extremes and circumstances that underscore Eliot's moral of sympathy and self-awareness. She alternates between the careful psychological realism that defines Gwendolen's story and a more abstract and idealizing method in which Daniel, Mirah, and Mordecai become more abstract types, more the subject of romance than realism. So jarring and unexpected are the romantic elements in *Daniel Deronda* that one critic, R. S. Francillon, titled his review of the novel, "George Eliot's First Romance." In his view, Eliot's reliance on the sensational and the improbable caused *Daniel Deronda* to seem "practically a first novel by a new author," and either "a parenthesis" or "a brilliant display in a foreign field." The end of George Eliot's writing career closed the parenthesis at this juncture, with the realistic paradigm that Eliot had established widened to include other elements such as symbolism, philosophical speculation, melodrama, and moralizing in competition with her usual psychological realism. The result is a challenge to the capacity of the novel itself that links *Daniel Deronda* with other hybrid and expansive works like *War and Peace*, *Anna Karenina*, *The Brothers Karamazov*, *Ulysses*, and *The Magic Mountain*. Readers may prefer Eliot's realism over her didacticism, but *Daniel Deronda* offers a new paradigm for the Victorian novel: as wide as it is deep, suggesting new directions that the novel might follow. As Virginia Woolf observed, George Eliot "was one of the first English novelists to discover that men and women think as well as feel, and the discovery was of great artistic moment. Briefly, it meant that the novel ceased to be solely a love story, an autobiography, or a story of adventure. It became . . . of much wider scope."

GERMINAL 66

(1885) *by Émile Zola*

With Germinal, *Zola reached the top of the ladder of success and achieved his greatest literary triumph. Powerful, extremely poetic in its way, compassionate, indignant, dominated, in spite of the conflict between workers and management, by a strong sentiment of human solidarity, it consecrated Zola's reputation not only in France but in Europe.*

—Elliott M. Grant, *Émile Zola*

It is perhaps the angriest book ever written, relentless in its depiction of individuals and a community locked in an epic struggle with natural, social, and economic forces beyond their control that threaten to obliterate what little humanity is left when all is reduced to the grim calculus of labor alone. Few novels deal as extensively or as intimately with the world of work, and, despite Zola's reputation as an objective, naturalistic clinician who simply recorded what he saw, the greatness of *Germinal* is a result of Zola's masterful documentation processed by a mythic imagination that reaches the level of universal human experience. Zola himself would describe his method as "a leap to the stars on the springboard of the exactly observed." The sheer force of Zola's imaginative leap and the compelling nature of its drama prompted André Gide to declare that *Germinal* was one of the 10 greatest novels ever written. When Zola died, he was celebrated in France as a national hero, a crusading truth-teller, called by Anatole France in his eulogy "a moment of the conscience of man." At his funeral procession, miners shouted "Germinal! Germinal!" as their tribute.

Germinal is the 13th volume of Zola's massive 20-novel Rougon-Macquart cycle, subtitled *A Natural and Social History of a Family under the Second Empire.* With the series Zola updated and refined the massive realistic documentation of Balzac's *La Comédie humaine* by tracing the forces of heredity, environment, and history in a multigenerational saga. Balzac had used repeated characters in his series to establish a network of connections. Zola would further unify Balzac's scheme by treating an extended family over time whose two branches—the shopkeepers and petty bourgeois Rougons and the laboring and criminal Macquarts—allowed for the fullest possible depiction of a complex social panorama both in breadth and depth. In an attempt to extend to fiction the empirical method of science, Zola developed a fictional approach that formed the main tenets of literary naturalism. "The novelist," he wrote, "is part observer, part experimenter. As observer he collects the facts, sets the point of departure, establishes the solid ground on which the characters will walk. . . . Then the experimenter appears and institutes the experiment. I mean, causes the characters to move in a given story in order to show that the succession or order of facts will be such as is required by the determination of the phenomena under study." Combining the methods of the biological and social scientist, Zola was determined to become the first novelist to study systematically a single historical period: France's Second Empire, from the December 1851 coup to its fall in Franco-Prussian War of 1870 to 1871. Unlike Balzac, Zola intended to document the entire social hierarchy, particularly the working class, which Balzac often ignored. Zola's first exploration of the urban poor was *L'Assommoir* (translated variously as *The Dram Shop*, *The Gin Palace*, and *Drink*) in 1877. Before Zola, if working-class individuals appeared in fiction at all they were invariably idealized and caricatured, with their language sanitized and discretion preventing a fully authentic, convincing portrait. Zola's realistic, documentary approach was a shocking revelation, and readers were taken into an unfamiliar environment with an unprecedented intimacy. After *L'Assomoir* Zola intended to return to the working class as a subject, and he cast about for a venue that could best display the impact of industrialization on a community. In 1884 coal miners of Anzin in northern France began a 56-day strike, and Zola conducted his characteristic methodical research there, posing as an engineer to descend into the pits, attending workers' meetings, and interviewing miners. He supplemented his direct observations with extensive reading of technical source material on mining and newspaper accounts of past strikes.

Originally conceived as a self-contained novel independent of the Rougon-Macquart series, *Germinal* establishes its links to the previous books in the cycle by casting Étienne Lantier, an offspring of the Macquart line, the son of the heroine of *L'Assommoir*, as the novel's chief eyewitness and moral conscience. In search of work, Lantier arrives at Montsou, in northern France, where he meets miner Vincent Maheu and is given a job in the Le Voreux mine. An outsider, Lantier becomes a surrogate for the reader, introduced to the customs and routines of underground life and its aboveground impact on the extended Maheu family and their neighbors. Because he is an outsider, Lantier questions what the miners take for granted, reacts with horror and outrage to conditions the miners accept, and begins to search for an ideology to explain the forces at work and the means for changing them. Lantier's developing awareness of the plight of the miners and his growing commitment to improving working conditions help to shape Zola's documentation into a tragic drama as Lantier gradually convinces the miners to strike. The novel's early chapters establish the background for this evolving drama. It is a period of severe economic depression and high unemployment with no system of worker benefits and no collective bargaining system to inhibit wage and labor abuses. The miners compete with one another for subsistence and are virtual prisoners of management, living in company housing and shopping in company-owned stores. Zola is masterful in rendering the dehumanized scene that begins to blur the distinction between life above ground and below. The blighted landscape has reduced humanity into cogs of a rapacious machine. "There was no sign of dawn to relight the dead sky," Lantier observes on his first morning in Montsou, "only the blast-furnaces burning alongside the coke ovens. And Le Voreux lay lower and squatter, deep in its den, crouching like a vicious beast of prey, snorting louder and longer, as if choking on its painful digestion of human flesh."

Before the novel's climactic strike, Zola carefully presents both opposing sides. The workers are seen from the perspective of the large Maheu family, with whom Lantier eventually lodges. Patriarch Vincent, known as "Bonnemort" for having escaped death numerous times in his 45 years in the mines, is an invalid living on a meager pension. His son Toussaint and his wife Constance now are the heads of a family of seven children, including Zacharie, who will be killed in a firedamp explosion, Catherine, the 14-year-old cart tender, who becomes the mistress of the brutish Chaval, Lantier's rival and nemesis, and Alzire, their hunchbacked fourth child who dies of starvation during the strike. The Maheu family is contrasted with the well-to-do Grégoire family, headed by Leon, a shareholder in the Montsou Mining Company, typifying the idle capitalist who lives on his dividends and is completely out of touch with the harsh realities of the mine. As in Dickens's novels of the social group, such as *Bleak House* and *Little Dorrit,* Zola contrives to connect through plot the various social classes, insisting on an unavoidable mutuality. Their assured self-destruction is made starkly clear when the debilitated and addled Vincent Maheu strangles the Grégoires' pampered daughter, Cecile. Other representatives of ownership and management are Monsieur Hennebeau, the director-general of the Montsou Company, running the mine for absent stockholders in Paris, and Monsieur Deneulin, a small independent owner of the Jean-Bart mine. Finally, Zola represents three different political responses to the miners' plight in the characters of Rasseneur, the former miner and now innkeeper-proprietor of L'Avantage, a moderate, gradualist reformer; Souvarine, a nihilistic Russian émigré who advocates a violent overthrow; and Lantier himself, who tries to arrive at some middle ground between the extremes represented by Rasseneur and Souvarine.

The mining company's cost-cutting measure changes the wage structure of the workers and provokes the strike. Condemned to starve anyway,

Maheu justifies the strike decision to Monsieur Hennebeau, declaring that they "prefer to die doing nothing." Strike funds raised by Lantier are soon depleted, and the miners and their families slowly but steadily starve. Without the support of their fellows at other pits, the Montsou miners are isolated and powerless, and the novel traces the increasing violence that results when the strikers try to force others to join them and begin to destroy property to insure that the mines stay closed. When strikebreakers are brought in, protected by soldiers, the strikers are fired upon, and Maheu is among the 14 who are killed. The violence forces an end to the conflict, and the miners return to the pits, having achieved nothing. Lantier, Catherine, and Chaval are among those who go back to work, but Souvarine has sabotaged the works, and the mine collapses in an apocalyptic implosion, slowly becoming flooded. The three are trapped below ground, and the long simmering animosity of the two men over Catherine explodes as Lantier kills Chaval. Catherine dies before she can be rescued, and Lantier, after recovering, sets out for Paris and an uncertain future.

Although nothing has changed positively for the Montsou miners, Zola ends the novel with the language of an inevitable future rebirth and revolution, contained in the novel's title, suggestive of a recurrent life cycle of germination and death. *Germinal* chronicles a year in the life of the mining community, and Zola chooses to end not with a direct moral or political message, not with a practical solution to the conflict between management and labor, but with a lyrical explosion of the life force that ultimately survives the rapacious monster of the mine:

> High in the sky the April sun now shone down in its full glory, warming the bountiful earth and breathing life into her fertile bosom, as the buds burst into verdant leaf, and the fields quivered under the pressure of the rising grass. All around him seeds were swelling and shoots were growing, cracking the surface of the plain, driven upwards by their need for warmth and light. The sap flowed upwards and spilled over in soft whispers; the sound of germinating seeds rose and swelled to form a kiss. Again, and again, and ever more clearly, as if they too were rising towards the rays of the sun, in that morning of new growth, the countryside rang with song, as its belly swelled with a black and avenging army of men, germinating slowly in its furrows, growing upwards in readiness for harvests to come, until one day soon their ripening would burst open the earth itself.

MY ÁNTONIA

67

(1918)

by Willa Cather

No romantic novel ever written in America, by man or woman, is one-half so beautiful.
—H. L. Mencken, "The Novel," *Prejudices: Third Series*

"If, as is often said," Wallace Stegner observed, "every novelist is born to write one thing, then the one thing that Willa Cather was born to write was first fully realized in *My Ántonia*." It remains Cather's most beloved book and the novel that best demonstrates her considerable talent for resurrecting the past and revivifying a region. *My Ántonia*, however, carries additional significance as the last great celebration in the American novel of the frontier past and its heroic archetypal pioneers. Cather observed that the world "broke in two in 1922 or thereabouts," and she found herself philosophically and emotionally on the distant side of the divide, allied with America's agrarian past rather than with its industrialized, urban future. That split forced Cather farther and farther back in time to find the heroism and ideals she most admired in such novels as *Death Comes for the Archbishop* (1927) and *Shadows on the Rock* (1931) or to confront the collapses and compromises that the modern world forced on the individual in such works as *A Lost Lady* (1923) and *The Professor's House* (1925). In *My Ántonia*, though change is measured between prairie and town life, between the innocence and limitless possibility of childhood and the inevitable diminishment of adulthood, there is a precarious, hard-fought equipoise. The American novels following *My Ántonia* would increasingly deal with the betrayal and collapse of the American dream with the nation's frontier past and heroism more an absence than a vital presence. Cather's novel succeeds as one of the grandest pastoral elegies in American literature celebrating all that is elemental and prototypical in its central figure, Ántonia, one of a core group of essential female characters in American literature along with Hawthorne's Hester Prynne, James's Isabel Archer, Chopin's Edna Pontellier, Dreiser's Carrie Meeber, Hurston's Janie Crawford, and Mitchell's Scarlett O'Hara.

Published in 1918, when Willa Cather was 45, *My Ántonia* was her fourth novel but the first that most completely reflected Cather's realization that "Life began for me when I ceased to admire and began to remember." Like Jim Burden, the novel's narrator, with whom Cather shares key biographical correspondences, Cather came to Nebraska from Virginia as a child, lived on the prairie and in the town of Red Cloud (the Black Hawk of the novel) before leaving for schooling at the university in Lincoln and her professional career in the East. Also like Jim, Cather remained fascinated by the Nebraska prairie and the intensity and idiosyncracies of its inhabitants, particularly the immigrants who first carved homes from the unforgiving wilderness. In 1916, on a visit to her family in Red Cloud, Cather was reunited with her childhood friend, Annie Pavelka (formerly Sadilek), a Czech immigrant whose father's suicide was one of the earliest stories Cather recalled hearing as a child. Annie, now middle-aged, surrounded by her children at the center of a thriving domestic world, served as the model for Cather's protagonist and the means for Cather's processing of her memories of her Nebraskan childhood into a mythic expression of American life and character.

Unquestionably, the biographical elements in *My Ántonia* contribute to the emotional intensity and vividness of the novel. Another contributing factor is the novel's curious structure, which departs from many of the accepted narrative conventions, replacing linear plotting with the disjointed though impassioned workings of memory itself. In the introduction, the narrator (presumably Cather herself) meets a childhood friend from Nebraska, Jim Burden, now a successful New York attorney in an unhappy marriage. The two recall their mutual friend, Ántonia Shimerda, who continues to exert a powerful hold on their affection and imagination. Months later, Jim delivers a manuscript of his recollections of Ántonia, apologizing that his effort "hasn't any form." He says, "I simply wrote down pretty much all that her name recalls to me." Jim's prefatory comments alert the reader to expect not a conventionally plotted novel but a series of episodes, or rather images, of Ántonia and evidence of her impact. She is "My" Ántonia in the sense of her significance for Jim Burden in his attempt to clarify his feelings about the past and its role in forming his present identity and fundamental values. The novel, therefore, provides a multiple focus, what critic Charlotte Goodman has appropriately called a "double bildungsroman," interweaving the lives of its two central protagonists—Jim and Ántonia—with the logic of memory in which years contract and scenes expand as the past is reassessed for significance. As Jim admits, "Ántonia had always been one to leave images in the mind that did not fade—that grew stronger with time. In my memory there was a succession of such pictures, fixed there like the old wood cuts of one's first primer." Ántonia, therefore, is as much a catalyst as a subject, the means by which Jim can penetrate the "precious, the incommunicable past," and unlock its treasures. The narrative logic of *My Ántonia* is shaped, therefore, less by a tightly conceived dramatic progression than by the actual workings of memory, full of occasional sidetracks, shifting perspective, and altered focus, in which Ántonia is allowed to recede from view and is recalled, as if in an echo, by the reports of others, while gathering the symbolic associations of another's needs and desires.

Cather described her unconventional method in dealing with her heroine in the following terms, recorded in Elizabeth Shepley Sargeant's *Willa Cather: A Memoir* (1953). The writer had placed an apothecary jar filled with flowers on a bare table and observed that "I want my new heroine to be like this—like a rare object in the middle of a table, which one may examine from all sides. . . . I want her to stand out—like this—like this—because she *is* the story." At the core of the book, therefore, is the symbolic center of gravity, Ántonia, whom Jim will come to appreciate as the organizing principle to redeem his past and sustain his present.

Ántonia is first encountered along with the Nebraskan prairie when Jim comes, orphaned at age 10, to live on his grandparents' farm. There he confronts for the first time the vastness of the surroundings, the elemental landscape that will make or break its inhabitants. "There seemed to be nothing to see;" Jim recalls, "no fences, no creeks or trees, no hills or fields. If there was a road, I could not make it out in a faint starlight. There was nothing but land: not a country at all, but the material out of which countries are made." It is a landscape so vast and featureless that the land seems to obliterate the individual. In presenting the new arrivals—Jim and the Shimerda family—along with a diverse collection of Nebraskans, Cather suggests that one must either grow in heroic dimensions to deal with the land or be diminished or destroyed by it. Safely sheltered on his grandparents' well-regulated farm, Jim watches the challenges faced by Ántonia's family through a seasonal cycle that will cause Ántonia's father, a sensitive former musician ill-prepared and unconditioned for the poverty and grinding work they face or the blank and to him pointless countryside, to commit suicide. The forces that break her father, however, strengthen Ántonia. Generous, empathetic, and vital, Ántonia meets the challenge that defeats her father. His death, however, sets in motion the different courses Jim and Ántonia will take. As she remarks to her friend, "Things will be easy for you. But they will be hard for us." Ántonia is forced to take on farm chores like a man, forgoing the possibility of refinement and cultivation that she lost with her father's death. She will begin to recede from Jim's view, excluded from the possibilities that education and travel open up for him. Finally, the elemental relationship between Jim and Ántonia and the land that created a kind of vivid pastoral symbiosis in the opening chapters of the novel will also be tested as the scene shifts from the prairie to the town of Black Hawk.

With Jim's grandparents too old to take care of their farm, the Burdens move to Black Hawk, where social custom and prejudice relegate Ántonia to the lowest rung of the social ladder as one of the "hired girls," the immigrant daughters forced off the farm to work as domestics for the more established citizens of Black Hawk. As pioneer life gives way to town life, there is a clear loss of stature among the townspeople and a confusion of assessment that undervalues as primitive those who have subdued the prairie and created the conditions out of which the prairie towns were created. Although Jim's sympathy is clearly with the hired girls, whose instinctive openness and vitality contrast with the drearily respectable, supercilious townspeople, Jim's career as a student will break his close association with Ántonia, who will be glimpsed only occasionally through reports from her friends. He learns that she has been deceived by a lover and left pregnant and unmarried. Meeting her again working in the fields, Jim finds that despite all that she has suffered, Ántonia retains her sympathy with others and affection for her life. Their meeting prompts Jim's crucial statements, "The idea of you is part of my mind," and "You really are a part of me," evidence that Ántonia has secured a symbolic place in Jim's imagination that the conclusion of the novel will help to clarify.

It is 20 years before Jim sees Ántonia again. Married to Anton Cuzak, Ántonia is the Demeter-like organizing principle of a prosperous farm and her large family. Toothless, gray-haired, and flat-chested, she is "battered but not diminished." For Jim, Ántonia possesses the "fire of life"; she has become the indomitable spirit of the land itself. By the end of the novel Jim completes a reunion with his childhood soulmate, a vital linkage with his past, and a return to his spiritual home. Ántonia, in turn, has been grandly appreciated as a principle of fertility and goodness, an indestructible, redeeming impulse to set against the counterforce of time's destruction and the inauthenticity of civilization. There is a sense of almost overwhelming culmination in the novel's concluding paragraph:

> This was the road over which Ántonia and I came on that night when we got off the train at Black Hawk and were bedded down in the straw, wondering children, being taken we knew not whither. I had only to close my eyes to hear the rumbling of the wagons in the dark, and to be again overcome by that obliterating strangeness. The feelings of that night were so near that I could reach out and touch them with my hand. I had the sense of coming home to myself, and of having found out what a little circle man's experience is. For Ántonia and for me, this had been the road of Destiny; had taken us to those early accidents of fortune which predetermined for us all that we can ever be. Now I understood that the same road was to bring us together

68

AN AMERICAN TRAGEDY

(1925)

by Theodore Dreiser

In the first task of the novelist, which is to create an imaginary social landscape both credible and significant, Dreiser ranks among the American giants, the very few American giants we have had. Reading An American Tragedy *once again, after a lapse of more than twenty years, I have found myself greatly moved and shaken by its repeated onslaughts of narrative, its profound immersion in human suffering, its dredging up of those shapeless desires which live, as if in fever, just below the plane of consciousness. How much more vibrant and tender this book is than the usual accounts of it in recent criticism might lead one to suppose! It is a masterpiece, nothing less.*

—Irving Howe, Afterword to the New American Library edition of *An American Tragedy*, 1964

Theodore Dreiser's *An American Tragedy* is a full-frontal assault, a hammer blow directed at still-vulnerable sore points of American society and identity. Published in 1925, the same year that Fitzgerald's *The Great Gatsby* appeared, both novels, so different in method and mastery, similarly attempt a groundbreaking definition and diagnosis of the American dream. Dreiser's novel would prove to be the climax of his career, the last of his novels to be published during his lifetime and the first that brought him success and recognition (though with qualifications) of his standing at the front ranks of American literary artists. *An American Tragedy* is certainly Dreiser's most ambitious and accomplished creation that synthesizes years of grappling with the phenomena of American experience after opening the floodgates of American realism in *Sister Carrie* (1900). In the words of director Sergei Eisenstein, who struggled in vain to bring a faithful version of the novel to the screen, *An American Tragedy* is an "epic of cosmic veracity and objectivity" that is "as broad and shoreless as the Hudson . . . as immense as life itself."

It is Dreiser's pioneering truthfulness that Sinclair Lewis, having bested Dreiser in 1930 by a single vote to become the first American to receive the Nobel Prize in literature, acknowledged when he declared that "Dreiser, more than any other man, is marching alone. Usually unappreciated, often hounded, he has cleared the trail from Victorian, Howellsian timidity and gentility in American fiction to honesty, boldness and passion of life. Without his pioneering I doubt if any of us could, unless we liked to be sent to jail, express life, beauty and terror." *An American Tragedy* is still capable of delivering all three, while relentlessly holding the reader's gaze on the implications of American life and disturbing its reader in the same ways that Clarence Darrow, no stranger to the darker recesses of human motivation and the vagaries of American justice, identified in an initial review:

> I finished Theodore Dreiser's latest story just before going to bed last night. I assumed that I must have had some sleep during the troubled hours through which I tossed and dreamed after laying it down. But the haunted face of a helpless boy, strapped to an iron chair at Sing Sing, and the wan form of a dead girl floating on a lonely black lake surrounded by tall pine trees in Northern New York still were haunting me when I awoke. I presume the feeling will slowly fade from my consciousness and be blended with the other experiences, painful and pleasant, which make up life. I hardly can think of the eight hundred pages of "An American Tragedy" as a book. It does not leave the impression that goes with reading a story; the feeling is rather that of a series of terrible physical impacts that have relentlessly shocked every sensitive nerve of the body.

Dreiser's immediate source for *An American Tragedy* was a murder committed in 1906 by Chester Gillette, the nephew and employee of a collar factory owner in Cortland, New York. Gillette's fellow worker and lover, Grace Brown, demanded Gillette marry her after she became pregnant or she would expose him to his "fine friends." Taking Grace rowing on Big Moose Lake, Gillette apparently struck Brown with the tennis racket he had brought along before she fell into the lake. Found guilty of her murder after a highly publicized trial, Gillette was executed in 1908. Dreiser would draw on, change, and amplify the documentary evidence of the Gillette case, compelled by what the writer was convinced was its archetypal, representative qualities. The Gillette case was, in the novelist's mind, a version of an essential, uniquely American phenomenon. "I had long brooded upon the story," Dreiser later recalled about the origin of his novel, "for it seemed to me not only to include every phase of our national life—politics, society, religion, business, sex—but it was a story so common to every boy reared in . . . America. It seemed so truly a story of what life does to the individual—and how impotent the individual is against such forces." It was only one of several similar crimes that attracted Dreiser's attention, all murders committed by ambitious American youths to remove obstacles to more socially and financially desirable matches. They typified a uniquely American phenomenon, and as Dreiser's wife recalled, he realized that "the most interesting American story of the day concerned not only the boy getting the girl, but more emphatically, the poor boy getting the rich girl. Also, he came to know that it was a natural outgrowth of the crude pioneering conditions of American life up to that time, based on the glorification of wealth which started with the early days of slavery and persisted throughout our history." The Gillette case grew into an embodiment of a full-scale American myth of success and its consequences. In Dreiser's view, the murder was only a symptom, and his novel would attempt to decipher and document the causes.

To do so, Dreiser accumulates an extensive developmental background for his future condemned murderer, Clyde Griffiths, detailing the forces that shape him and foreshadow his crime. Drawing on his own impoverished background, Dreiser chronicles Clyde's assault on American success, beginning with the 12-year-old's unwilling participation in a street religious service conducted by his missionary father. The faith of his parents eludes Clyde, who finds in it no consolation for the family's chronic poverty. Clyde chooses instead the particularly American faith in upward mobility, the Horatio Alger myth that with sufficient pluck and determination anyone in America can succeed and gain a heart's desire. In Dreiser's analysis, the inalienable life, liberty, and pursuit of happiness that once typified American imperatives have in modern America crystallized into the last of the three, defined exclusively in terms of material success. Clyde, described by Dreiser as "a soul that was not destined to grow up," succumbs to what critic F. O. Matthiessen has called the "overwhelming lure of money-values in our society." Clyde is, as critic Ellen Moers indicates, "the Everyman of desire. A poor, simple boy who pursues neither honor nor glory nor distinction" but "pretty girls, nice clothes, sweet foods, good times, and the money and leisure to procure them." Drawn to a symbol of opulence, a luxury hotel in Kansas City, Clyde works as a bellhop "insanely eager for all the pleasures which he imagined he saw swirling around him." Unable to see through the shallow emptiness of his surroundings, Clyde becomes a prisoner of them, mastered by forces he cannot control.

The first of the novel's three books ends foreshadowing the conclusion of the second with Clyde forced to flee a crime as the car he joy-rides in runs down a child. Moving on to Chicago, Clyde by chance encounters his uncle, a well-to-do collar manufacturer from Lycurgus, New York. Impressed by Clyde's good looks and determination to get on, secretly guilty over his neglect of his brother's needy family, Samuel Griffiths gives his nephew a job in his mill. There, Clyde meets Roberta Alden, who has come from a hardscrabble life on her family's farm to work in the mill and is infected by the same "virus of ambition and unrest" that afflicts Clyde. The two form an attachment, and their relationship proves to be a liability when Clyde manages to succeed with the well-to-do debutante Sondra Finchley. On the threshold of Clyde's achieving everything he had ever wanted—entry into the charmed world of the materially blessed and powerful—Roberta's pregnancy threatens everything. Forced to act, Clyde plots her murder based on a boating accident that he reads about in the newspaper. As the novel begins to correspond to the Gillette case, Dreiser significantly alters aspects of his source material, going to great lengths to mitigate, or at least put into question, Clyde's guilt. Unlike Charles Gillette, Clyde brings into the rowboat not a potential weapon (Gillette's tennis racket), but a more plausible camera, muddying the question of premeditation. Despite Clyde's murderous intentions, Roberta's death is in fact an accident with Clyde's crime one of omission by not attempting to rescue her when she falls into the lake. The issue of Clyde's guilt became one of the significant controversies surrounding the novel. Dreiser's publisher seized on the issue by running an essay contest on the question of whether Clyde committed murder in the first degree. Dreiser's treatment of Clyde's crime is, therefore, far more ambiguous than Gillette's crime, helping to shift the emphasis from Clyde's guilt to the system that misses any distinction and hence judges Clyde so poorly.

Book three of the novel recounts in minute detail the inexorable workings of the judicial system leading up to Clyde's execution in the electric chair. It is clear that Clyde's blunders in disguising his involvement with Roberta are meant to underscore his ineptitude, with the ironic conclusion inescapably demonstrated that Clyde is actually on trial for his incompetence. Since Clyde lacks the means to evade responsibility for his "indiscretion" with Roberta, murder proves an inevitable solution. The deeper message that the American mania for success is partially to blame for the tragedy is missed by everyone but narrator and reader. As critic Donald Pizer helpfully summarizes, *An American Tragedy* is "not merely a story of crime and punishment but of how a young man's life is frozen by his nature and experience into an inflexible pattern and how society ignores the reality in judging him." In the escalating irony of the novel, blame shifts from the criminal to his judges. Clyde's crime stems more from the banality of his existence, inculcated with the American consumer values of pleasing surfaces without substance. It is Dreiser's singular achievement in *An American Tragedy* to compel the reader's interest and identification with his protagonist while eliminating any claims for his heroism. He is more a victim than a villain. Ruled by a series of accidents—from the automobile accident that leads him to Chicago where he by chance encounters his uncle, to the series of happenstances that leads to Roberta's death—Clyde is shown as lacking the will to determine his own destiny. The tragedy of the title is, therefore, ironic, with social and environmental determinants replacing an individual's will as the agents of destiny. It is ultimately the emptiness and unreality of his insatiable desires that mark Clyde as one of modern fiction's most disturbing antiheroes. As Robert H. Elias has argued, "Clyde Griffiths is the creature of fate, the captive of desire, the consequence of capitalism. He is the successor to Raskolnikov, the forerunner of Bigger Thomas, the anticipator of Meursault."

Dreiser closes his novel with a reprise of his opening with the Griffiths family on another city street, doing the Lord's work with Clyde's part now filled by his young nephew, ambiguously suggesting a repetition. The forces that determined Clyde's short career remain, and the reader has gained an unprecedented awareness of their operation.

69

HUNGER

(1890)

by Knut Hamsun

The whole modern school of fiction in the twentieth century stems from Hamsun.
—Isaac Bashevis Singer, preface to *Hunger*

Knut Hamsun's *Hunger* represents an important dividing line between 19th-century naturalism and the evolution of something radically different that turned the novel inward to explore the recesses of human needs and desires in ways that predict the deep psychological probing of Kafka and Beckett. If Goncharov first suggested the comic possibilities of an immobile, self-divided, and alienated hero in *Oblomov*, Hamsun, similarly restrictive in his concentration, manages one of the first full-scale existential dramas in the novel with his story of a young writer's survival battle. Hamsun, one of the groundbreaking psychological novelists, produced, in the words of his biographer Robert Ferguson, "perhaps the first novel to make consciousness itself a hero." *Hunger* is, therefore, one of the formative works of European modernism whose literary techniques, including the stream of consciousness and the interior monologue, anticipate the innovations of Proust, Joyce, and Woolf, while his subject of nightmarish torment and phantasmagoric introspection forecast the preoccupations of writers such as Kafka, Camus, and Beckett. "Twenty-five years before Kafka created Gregor Samsa, man as insect," scholar Sverre Lyngstad points out, "and more than fifty years before Camus popularized the absurd hero as a modern Sisyphus, Hamsun in *Hunger* did both."

Since *Hunger* draws extensively on Hamsun's biography, some details of his life are in order. Born Knut Petersen in 1859 to an impoverished family in central Norway, Hamsun moved in 1862 to northern Norway above the Arctic Circle to live on his uncle's farm named Hamsund. From the age of nine to 14, Hamsun was separated from his family, working as a kind of indentured servant for his frequently abusive uncle. He received no more than a grade school education and later lived a nomadic existence, working as a peddler, shoemaker's apprentice, sheriff's assistant, and schoolteacher while reading widely and nursing literary aspirations. He published two juvenile narratives in the 1870s and lectured on literature while working as a road builder. In the 1880s he immigrated to America, struggling as a farmhand and store clerk. In 1884 he was diagnosed by an American doctor with "galloping consumption" and given only a few months to live. He returned to Norway resigned to his death from an illness that turned out to be nothing more than a severe but not life-threatening case of bronchitis.

Back in Norway, Hamsun wrote stories, articles, and reviews that brought in only a meager income, and he experienced many of the deprivations and incidents that occur in *Hunger.* An article on Mark Twain for a weekly paper, signed Hamsund after his uncle's farm, became the work of "Hamsun" by a compositor's error, giving him the name he would go by for the rest of his life. Another sojourn in America followed, during which he worked as a streetcar conductor in Chicago and a farm laborer in the Dakotas. By 1888 he was in Copenhagen, where he struggled in desperate conditions to complete *Hunger.* In a letter he described his winter quarters: an "attic where the wind blows through the walls; there is no stove, almost no light, only a single small pane in the roof." In the summer he wrote, "A couple of times I was quite done for; I had pawned all I owned, I didn't eat for four days on end, I sat here chewing dead matchsticks." When he delivered a section of his manuscript to a journal, its editor reported that "I have seldom seen anybody so down and out. Not just that his clothes were tattered. But that face!" He read through the manuscript Hamsun had given him when "it struck me that the author was walking about town hungry. I was overcome by a sense of shame and ran like crazy to the post office and mailed him ten kroner."

Published first anonymously in the Copenhagen journal *Ny Jord* in November 1888, *Hunger* created a sensation for its unrelenting realistic depiction of the lower depths and for its unconventionality. Hamsun addressed this in an 1890 article, "From the Unconscious Life of the Mind," in which he argued that the conventional plot and standard character types in fashionable novels were no longer important. What mattered was revealing the conscious and subconscious mind of the individual:

> Now what if literature on the whole began to deal a little more with mental states than with engagements and balls and hikes and accidents and such? Then one would, to be sure, have to relinquish creating types, as all have been created before, "characters" whom one meets every day at the fish market . . . But in return . . . we would experience a little more of the secret movements which are unnoticed in the remote places of the soul, the capricious disorder of perception, the delicate life of fantasy held under the magnifying glass, the wandering of these thoughts and feelings out of the blue; motionless, trackless

> journeys with the brain and the heart, strange activities of the nerves, the whispering of the blood, the pleading of the bones, the entire unconscious life.

Hamsun's theory and its application in *Hunger* mark a break with the strategies and subject matter of previous novels, replacing idealization and social criticism with an introspection that pointed the way for a radically new psychological novel. Hamsun's departure is evident in the preoccupations and structure of *Hunger*. Narrated in the first person, the novel thrusts the reader inside the consciousness of its anonymous young protagonist: "It was in those days when I wandered about hungry in Kristiania, that strange city which no one leaves before it has set its mark upon him." The speaker is a writer without means, unable to find work, whose eclectic and often arcane writing—an appreciation of Correggio, denunciations of Kant, and a verse drama set in the Middle Ages—are predictably valueless to the various newspaper editors to whom he tries to sell them. Immediately, the novel establishes its fundamental tension between the speaker's lofty and energized imagination and the sordid reality of his situation as the claims of the body battle for control of the mind. Hamsun replaces plot with a central situation—the speaker's contention with his dire circumstances—in which the protagonist is shown scrambling to relieve his condition, encountering various individuals, and when all seems hopeless, managing to find the means to continue. This cycle is repeated in each of the novel's four sections. Responding to a complaint that his subject and treatment of it would prove "monotonous," Hamsun observed to a friend, "I have avoided all the usual stuff about suicidal thoughts, weddings, trips to the country and dances at the mansion house. This is too cheap for me. What fascinates me is the endless motion of my own mind, and I thought I had described in *Hunger* moods whose total strangeness, would not be likely to tire the reader by its monotony." The emphasis, therefore, is not on what happens, but on the impact of circumstances on the narrator's consciousness.

In the first section, the narrator leaves his shabby room and walks the streets, shunned by his friends who suspect that he will try to borrow money from them. What strikes him as most distinctive in his plight is that he now cannot afford to give even the smallest coin to another in need. When he manages to pawn his vest, he relieves his shame by giving most of the money to a passing beggar. His condition stimulates erratic behavior in which he gratuitously lies to strangers and accosts two unfamiliar women on the street. Back in his apartment, he finds a letter from his landlady demanding the rent. The next day he is even hungrier but inspired to write a sketch. He moves out of his room, carrying his few belongings to a newspaper editor to sell his story. With a promise from the editor that he will at least read the story, the narrator spends the night in a nearby woods. The next day he fails to borrow money from friends and is unable to find work. He plans to sleep on a park bench, but a policeman hurries him along and he returns to his room to find a letter from the editor informing him that he will pay 10 kroner for the story.

In the second section, two weeks have passed. The money is gone, and the narrator is starving again. His obsession with food distorts his vision, and he begins to hallucinate. Growing more and more emaciated and ill, he is found by a policeman who puts him in jail for the night. When he is released the next day, the narrator has had nothing to eat for three days, and his mental disorientation becomes more severe. Finally he meets an old friend who pawns his watch and shares some of the money with him.

In the third section, a week has passed and his condition has caused him to lose much of his hair, and he is afflicted with severe headaches. Efforts to place some of his work are futile. When he goes to a store to get a candle on credit, the clerk mistakenly gives him five kroners, which he uses to buy food. In his starved condition, he is unable to keep the food down. On his way back to his room he meets one of the women he had previously accosted on the street, and the affection he feels for her momentarily replaces his hunger pangs. The next day he meets an old friend who invites him to have a beer. A small amount, given his empty stomach, makes him drunk, and the narrator goes to the homes of strangers asking for fictitious people and returns to the store where he had received the money from the clerk to complain. He finally meets the editor, who advances him money for his article, and sees again the girl from the previous evening, but his hope for romance is frustrated.

As winter comes, the narrator reaches the desperate end of his circumstances, subsisting in the worst part of town, unable to write, his health in a steady decline. He decides that his only alternative is to defer his writing to find work on board a ship bound for England.

At one level, *Hunger* is one of the great novels of modern urban alienation, portraying realistically the dire circumstances of the urban poor. However, on another level, Hamsun is far more interested in the psychological aspect of his story, using the narrator's grinding poverty to reach levels of psychological truths opened up by his adversity and ensuing alienation. The narrator displays symptoms that psychologists today might label manic-depressive, sadomasochistic, and psychotic, while his hunger also produces an uncanny sensitivity. "Nothing escaped my eyes," he remarks. "I was sharp and my brain was very much alive, everything poured in toward me with a staggering distinctness as if a strong light had fallen on everything around me." This "strong light" produces a surrealistic and expressionistic rendering of the narrator's surroundings, projecting his desperate condition and the trauma it causes. At still another level, the novel makes less a psychological point than a symbolic one concerning the artist and his quest. "As the hero's vivid torment continues," Robert Ferguson asserts, "we begin gradually to suspect something that Hamsun undoubtedly wanted us to suspect; namely that what looks at first like a dogged *inability* to do anything about his plight is in reality a dogged *refusal* to act. He does not in fact want release, and is in some perverse way enjoying his predicament, savouring to the full the bizarre sensations of homelessness, hunger, insecurity, and the attendant forms of isolation, social, cultural, sexual, economic. We get the curious feeling that the whole thing is willed; a life-game that the hero is playing, to see how far it can go, how far he can let it go." Like Kafka's Hunger Artist, Hamsun's protagonist turns himself into his greatest creation, willfully exploiting the one heroic struggle he has left: the ultimate battle between body and soul, between his animal needs and his intellectual aspirations. In Hamsun's meditation, writing becomes a form of self-annihilation. *Hunger*, therefore, does not so much end as adjourn, with its cycle of desperate physical need and psychological pressure continuing as the steady state of the human condition.

70

BERLIN ALEXANDERPLATZ

(1929)

by Alfred Döblin

You will find him unsettling; he will make your dreams weigh heavily upon you. There will be much for you to stomach; you will find him unpalatable: he is indigestible and at times unwholesome. His readers will find themselves changed by him. Whoever is self-sufficient is warned against reading Döblin.

—Günter Grass: *On My Mentor, Döblin*

Berlin Alexanderplatz is one of the wonders of modernism, a demanding, technically innovative novel that became a popular success. It is the first German novel to deploy the stream-of-consciousness technique and to feature an urban metropolis as its setting and central theme. In it Döblin captures the spirit of the modern city, with its masses of people, noise, fast-moving traffic, crime and violence, and indifference toward the individual, in a style related to such contemporary films as *Berlin: Chronik einer Großstadt* (*Berlin: Chronicle of a Metropolis*) and Fritz Lang's *Metropolis*. Following the adventures and misadventures of Franz Biberkopf, a working-class protagonist who has just been released from jail as the novel begins, Döblin shows how the "little man" gets caught in the wheels of a society that no longer offers a sense of community, while his sophisticated narrative technique brilliantly conveys the complexity and harshness of modern urban life. Its story of the criminal underworld and the denizens of the complex, sinister urban jungle is noteworthy, according to critic Felix Bertreaux, because "for the first time in Europe a novel of the masses has the true popular accent—the language of the people, reproduced with the fidelity of a phonograph recording the hum of the city crowd." Bertreaux goes on to declare that the novel's "sheer massive power gives the work value, as well as the scalpel strokes with which the author lays bare hitherto fibers in the tissue of man."

Döblin's background made him particularly suited to probe the recesses and the implications of the modern metropolis on human consciousness. He was born to a Jewish family in Stettlin, Germany (now Szczecin, Poland), in

1878. His father, a tailor, abandoned the family, and Döblin's mother relocated them to a working-class section of Berlin. Döblin earned his medical degree from the University of Freiburg and worked in psychiatric clinics and hospitals until 1911, when he began to practice family medicine and neurology in the working-class district of Berlin's Alexanderplatz. In 1913 his first collection of short stories, *The Assassination of a Dandelion and Other Stories*, was published, followed by his first full-length work, *The Three Leaps of Wang-lun*, based on an 18th-century Chinese rebellion, which sounded Döblin's characteristic theme of the individual forced to contend with social forces beyond his control. A second novel, *Wadzek's Struggle with the Steam Engine*, appeared in 1918, depicting events in the life of an industrialist and reflecting the breakdown of the social order in Germany following the war. A similar theme is explored in his next novels, *Wallenstein*, a historical novel set during the turmoil of the Thirty Years' War, and *Mountain Seas and Giants*, a futurist dystopia. While publishing a steady stream of plays and fiction, Döblin also began working out a narrative theory to support a new conception of the novel, summarized in the lecture "The Structure of the Epic Work," which he delivered in 1928 as he worked on *Berlin Alexanderplatz*. In the lecture he calls for a new open form for the novel, blending lyrical, dramatic, and philosophical elements that echo the methods and concerns of Homer, Cervantes, and Dante. "There one finds powerful basic situations," Döblin argues, "elementary situations of human existence, being worked out." Instead of predetermined plot, Döblin suggests that the epic writer begins with a subject and "works his way toward the theme by writing. Thus the reader experiences the production process along with the author." Döblin's desired epic novel, therefore, aspires to a direct confrontation with experience, a collaborative exploration in which the reader must become a cocreator in uncovering the overall significance.

Applying his theories to *Berlin Alexanderplatz*, Döblin creates a vast network of relationships and shifting perspectives that mimics the complex, multilayered texture of the modern city. At the center of the web is Felix Biberkopf, a transport worker of great physical strength but limited intelligence who at the novel's outset emerges from prison after serving a four-year sentence for murdering his girlfriend in a drunken, jealous rage. Biberkopf is determined to start afresh, to "stay respectable" and keep to himself. His intention to resist temptations by force of will alone is tested in a series of setbacks that erodes his strength and sense of identity, while challenging his conception of the world and his place in it. The reader, like Biberkopf, is bombarded by a welter of data—snatches of hit songs, advertising, news reports, weather forecasts, theater programs, statistics—directly presenting the buzzing multiplicity of the metropolis that Biberkopf must make sense of and negotiate. An exemplary figure, Biberkopf is representative of a class that fascinated Döblin. "I am interested in the social problem of people who," he observed, "for one reason or another, have been torn from their own inner sphere and cannot easily join another class, the problem of people who stand 'between the classes.'" The novel will challenge Biberkopf's independence and autonomy, forcing a widened recognition in him and the reader of the various connections among the atomistic forces in the apparently chaotic modern city.

Biberkopf first goes to work as a street vendor of tie clasps and Nazi newspapers, detached from the implications of their message. He later becomes a door-to-door shoelace salesman, and the first blow to his conception of the world comes when he boasts of the generosity of a widow he has met to his uncle, Otto Lüders, who betrays his confidence by robbing the widow and assaulting her. Deeply hurt and disturbed by the duplicity of someone he has trusted, Biberkopf retreats into isolation and drink, intent on avoiding further complications. Through his friend Meck he is introduced to members of a burglary ring, the Pums gang. One of its members, Reinhold, employs Biberkopf in taking girlfriends off his hands once he has tired of them. When Biberkopf refuses to continue complying with Reinhold's "spirited white slavery," he antagonizes Reinhold, who seeks his revenge by recruiting Biberkopf to participate in a burglary. As their getaway car speeds away, Biberkopf is pushed out and run over by the pursuing car. For a second time, Biberkopf's naiveté results in a blow, this one physical, as Biberkopf's right arm is amputated at the shoulder.

In the novel's final sequence, Biberkopf reestablishes contact with his old friends Herbert and Eva, a pimp and a prostitute, whom he had previously avoided. Biberkopf has abandoned his former intention to live a respectable life but still is confident that his strength will ensure his survival. That last illusion will be tested in the novel's final blow to his confidence: "Now the hammer crashes down, it crashes on Franz Biberkopf." Through Eva he meets a young country girl, Mieze, who becomes a prostitute for him. Although he genuinely loves Mieze, he boasts about her faithfulness to Reinhold and arranges to conceal him in his apartment so that Reinhold can witness her devotion. Instead Mieze confesses her attraction to another man, and Biberkopf almost kills her in a jealous rage. Reinhold decides to complete his revenge on Biberkopf through Mieze and lures her into a woods outside Berlin, where he tries to rape her and then kills her. Suspected in Mieze's murder, Biberkopf briefly eludes capture disguised with an artificial arm and wig. Finally cornered in a seedy nightclub, he shoots a policeman while resisting arrest.

In the novel's final book, Reinhold is brought to justice, having confessed his crime to a fellow prisoner who betrays him. Biberkopf is then confined to a mental hospital where he has been reduced to a state of catatonia. Wrestling with the specter of death in the form of Reinhold, he manages to regain his will to live by recognizing his hubris and guilt. "The world," Biberkopf realizes, "is made of sugar and dirt," and his vulnerability has come from his isolation. The chaos around him, Biberkopf finally decides, is only comprehensible and manageable when he joins the community: "Much unhappiness comes from walking alone. When there are several, it's somewhat different. I must get the habit of listening to others, for what the others say concerns me, too. Then I learn who I am, and what I can undertake. Everywhere about me my battle is being fought, and I must beware, before I know I'm in the thick of it."

Released from the asylum, he emerges with a new name and identity: Franz Karl Biberkopf, finding a job as an assistant doorman in a factory: "He is no longer alone on Alexanderplatz. There are people to the right, and people to the left of him, some walk in front of him, others behind him." Biberkopf's story closes with the narrator declaring that there is "nothing further to report at this point." It is implied that Biberkopf, by undergoing his mental and physical tests, is now better able to cope with the internal and external forces that have buffeted him, less dependent on his separate strength but relying on the shared power of others:

> But it is also nicer and better to be with others. Then I feel and I know twice as well. A ship cannot lie in safety without a big anchor, and a man cannot exist without many other men. The true and the false I will know better now. Once I got myself into trouble for a single word and had to pay bitterly for it, this shan't happen to Biberkopf again. The words come rolling up to us, we must be careful not to get run over; if we don't watch out for the autobus, it'll make apple-sauce out of us. I'll never again stake my word on anything in the world. Dear Fatherland, be comfort thine, I'll watch and use these eyes of mine.

The ambiguity of the novel's ending, however, concerning the nature of Biberkopf's recognitions and insights, and what is implied by the theme of solidarity sounded at the end, has been much debated. What is implied by the marchers Biberkopf hears outside his window? Their political allegiance is unclear. Are they a sign of communal strength that sustains the fragmented and isolated individual or an emblem of the mindless conformity offered by the Communists or the Nazis? Döblin offers no clear solution, providing instead an open rather than a closed narrative structure. In fact, the suggestion of Biberkopf's redemption has been called a "mock catharsis," with the conclusion echoing the novel's opening in its suggestion of a continual cycle of idealistic intentions followed by testing circumstances.

In a sense Biberkopf disappears back into the collective fate of the inhabitants of *Berlin Alexanderplatz*. It is fundamentally a novel structured less by the career of its central protagonist than spatially by its setting. Like Bely's *Petersburg*, Dos Passos's *U.S.A.* trilogy, Joyce's *Ulysses*, and Woolf's

Mrs Dalloway, *Berlin Alexanderplatz* is a polyphonic narrative that replaces the novel's standard convention of the individual hero and a central plot with an elaborate network of relationships in which all the characters attain equal importance. Biberkopf's story, one of many that intersect in the working-class district of Berlin, is a dominant base note in an elaborately scored symphony that captures the fragmentary, alienating, baffling, and finally exhilarating experience of modern city life.

71

MIDNIGHT'S CHILDREN

(1981)

by Salman Rushdie

In the diverse and fragmented world of India—in the postcolonial, postmodern world in general—the epic hero is no longer universally applicable and has no place in the individual formation of identity. Midnight's Children *above all emphasizes the importance of the individual, and the individual's relationship to history. Saleem's story represents the process of self-, not epic, definition. Rushdie presents an alternative to the epic hero: the anti-epic hero, whose process of self-definition—his self-narration—is accessible and applicable to all. Rushdie insists that the individual, too often subsumed by colonizers, the idea of the nation-state, or national mythology, must be understood as part of history. . . .* Midnight's Children *and Saleem explode the notion of epic, offering the reader a personalized view of the individual and his or her relationship to history.*

—Michael Reder, "Rewriting History and Identity: The Reinvention of Myth, Epic, and Allegory in Salman Rushdie's *Midnight's Children*"

Salman Rushdie's postcolonial picaresque, *Midnight's Children,* his second and breakthrough book, has become a classic of modern world literature, a novel that both invites and sustains comparison with such works as Voltaire's *Candide,* Sterne's *Tristram Shandy,* Grass's *The Tin Drum,* and Márquez's *One Hundred Years of Solitude.* Awarded the Booker Prize in 1981, it was in 1993 named the Booker of Bookers, the best of the winning novels during the prize's first 25 years. In July 2008, it was once again voted the Booker of Bookers to celebrate the 40th anniversary of the prize. Refracting India's struggle for independence and nationhood through the years between 1915 and 1979 from the uncanny and unreliable viewpoint of Saleem Sinai, one of the 1,001 magic children born during the first hour of August 15, 1947, when India received its independence from Britain, *Midnight's Children* is a virtuoso verbal performance orchestrating allegory, political satire, magic realism, the grotesqueries of the Western comic tradition of Aristophanes, Rabelais, and Sterne, as well as Joycean and postmodern self-reflexivity. Drawing equally on the Indian oral, folk storytelling tradition, *Midnight's Children* has been described by the writer Anita Desai as a "modern epic" of the subcontinent, masterfully combining "the 'great' and the 'little' traditions of India," that is, both Sanskrit masterpieces, the *Rāmayana* and the *Mahābhārata*, and vernacular legends and customs in a synthesis of "the classical and the folk, the learned and the popular, the parochial and the universal." *Midnight's Children* is both heterodox in its approach and provocative in its imaginative reassessment of both India's past and present. It is a transformative work that signaled the arrival of a major figure on the world literature stage.

Like his protagonist, Saleem Sinai, Salman Rushdie came in with Indian independence. "There's a joke in my family," Rushdie has said, "about how I was born in 1947 and two months later the British ran away. I suppose the joke gave me a sort of notion that you could connect a child and a historical event." The son of well-to-do Muslim parents in Bombay—now Mumbai—Rushdie was raised bilingually in English and Urdu. A self-described bookworm as a child and an Anglocentric youth, Rushdie was strongly influenced by his Cambridge-educated barrister father, who had a passion for books and a talent for storytelling, and his maternal grandfather, a doctor who held progressive social and religious views. "Although I came from a Muslim family background," Rushdie recalled, "I was never brought up as a believer, and was raised in an atmosphere of what is broadly known as secular humanism." After attending an English mission school in Bombay, Rushdie left for England in 1961 to attend the prestigious Rugby School. There he reported having "a pretty hideous time from my own age group: minor persecutions and racist attacks which felt major at the time," but managed to distinguish himself as a student of history, which he continued to study at King's College, Cambridge, gaining an M.A. in 1968. After graduation, he rejoined his family who had immigrated to Karachi, Pakistan. "I am an emigrant from one country (India)," Rushdie would later comment, "and a newcomer to two (England, where I live, and Pakistan, to which my family moved against my will)." Finding the political and intellectual atmosphere in Pakistan uncongenial and repressive—his initial literary efforts: a television adaptation of Edward Albee's play, *The Zoo Story*, and a magazine article on first impressions of Pakistan were both censored by the government—Rushdie refused to help run the family's towel factory, returning instead to England to pursue an acting career. Struggling as a professional actor, Rushdie supported himself as a freelance advertising copywriter, while devoting evenings and weekends to writing. He produced a first novel in 1971, which he abandoned ("I've still got the typescript, and I look at it to horrify myself."). His first published novel, *Grimus*, a futuristic quest narrative, combining elements of science fiction, fantasy, philosophy, and political satire, appeared in 1975. Although a commercial and critical failure, Rushdie gained some attention as a new writer worth watching and encouragement to undertake his ambitious second novel, *Midnight's Children*.

Completed in 1979 from successive drafts, *Midnight's Children* owes much of its daring originality and reach to what Rushdie has called his "stereoscopic vision" as a writer coexisting in the two different cultural worlds of India and the West. "In a sense I'm both inside and outside both the cultures," Rushdie has explained. "There are ways in which I'm no longer Indian. There are ways in which I've never been English. It gives you . . . stereoscopic vision so that you can simultaneously look at two societies from both the inside and the outside. And I think the tensions in that are quite useful; they strike sparks." *Midnight's Children* was "partly conceived as an opportunity to break away from the manner in which India had been written about in English, not just by Indian writers but by Western writers as well." Drawing on an insider's view of Indian folk elements and customs and an outsider's view that is equally at home with the Western literary tradition to comprehend and encapsulate Indian history and experience, *Midnight's Children* also claims kinship with the great antirealist comic tradition. "Displaced writers," Rushdie has observed, ". . . select, partly consciously and partly not consciously, a family of writers to belong to. And it just seems to me that there is another great tradition in world literature which really hasn't been discussed in the way that the realistic tradition has been. In almost every country and in almost every literature there has been, every so often, an outburst of this large scale fantasized, satiric, and anti-epic tradition, whether it was Rabelais or Gogol or Boccaccio. . . . That simply was the literature that I liked to read. So it seemed to me that it was also the literature that I would like to write."

Rushdie's original impetus in writing *Midnight's Children* was to chronicle and celebrate the Bombay of his boyhood and the consequences of Indian independence on his postcolonial generation. "When I began it was more autobiographical, and it only began to work when I started making it fictional. The characters came alive when they stopped being like people in my own family." After initially producing an unwieldy manuscript of nearly a thousand pages, Rushdie discovered the key to controlling his "mess of material" by telling the story in the first person, as recalled by Saleem Sinai, one of the children born during the first hour of Indian nationhood. By this means, *Midnight's Children* "became a novel of memory, which is why the narrator is so suspect and makes all kinds of mistakes, some of which he perceives and some of which he does not. . . . It tries to recognize the way in which memory operates: it exalts certain things which may be unimportant in themselves and become very important because they have lodged in your mind. And then history seen through that obviously becomes a rather odd thing: it becomes distorted."

Midnight's Children opens significantly with Saleem's struggle to fit his story and his memories into some kind of narrative order and in the conflict between a fable and facts, private and public history:

> I was born in the city of Bombay . . . once upon a time. No, that won't do, there's no getting away from the date: I was born in Doctor Narlikar's Nursing Home on August 15th, 1947. And the time? The time matters, too. Well then: at night. No, it's important to be more . . . On the stroke of midnight, as a matter of fact. Clock-hands joined palms in respectful greeting as I came. Oh, spell it out, spell it out: at the precise instant of India's arrival at independence, I tumbled forth into the world. There were gasps. And, outside the window, fireworks and crowds. A few seconds later, my father broke his big toe; but his accident was a mere trifle when set beside what had befallen me in that benighted moment, because thanks to the occult tyrannies of those blandly saluting clocks I had been mysteriously handcuffed to history, my destinies indissolubly chained to those of my country.

Awaiting death in a corner of a Bombay pickle factory where he works, the 30-year-old Saleem—prematurely aged, impotent, and damaged by a personal history that parallels his country—tells his life story in flashbacks and flashforwards to Padma, an illiterate factory worker who loves and tends him. Saleem, like all of the children born during the fateful first hour of Indian independence, has a unique magical power making him one of the nation's marvels and a mirror reflecting his subsequent history as symbolic and representative of the promise and betrayal of India following nationhood. In Saleem's often digressive and frequently distorted recollections, the great events of modern Indian history unfold, from the Amritsar massacre in 1919, through Partition in 1947, Nehru's first five-year plan in 1956, the coup in Pakistan in 1958, the India-China war of 1962, the India-Pakistan war of 1965, the creation of Bangladesh in 1971, and the "Emergency" of 1975 when Indira Gandhi declared martial law and suspended civil liberties. "Handcuffed to history," Saleem interweaves his family and personal history. "To understand me," he declares, "you'll have to swallow a world." Like Sterne's *Tristram Shandy*, to which *Midnight's Children* invites comparison, much of the first part of Saleem's story precedes his birth, beginning in 1915 with his maternal grandparents. Establishing the novel's dominant tone of loss and disillusion in the wake of Indian modernity, Aadam Aziz, Saleem's grandfather, is a Western-trained doctor in Kashmir whose loss of faith leads to a God-shaped hole "in the middle of me the size of a melon." Saleem recounts Aziz's extended courtship with Naseem Ghani, the daughter of a fundamentalist Muslim family whom Aziz can only observe in parts, through small holes in a perforated sheet. After their marriage, the couple is in Amritsar on the day in 1919 when British troops fired on a crowd of Indian nationalists. Doctor Aziz survives when, sneezing, he bends down just as the troops fire. Saleem's narrative next jumps forward to 1947 and the conflict over Partition and its impact on the courtship and marriage of Saleem's mother, Mumtaz, later

Amina, Aziz, who eventually marries a leather merchant, Ahmed Sinai, and moves with him first to Delhi and then to Bombay where Saleem is born.

More than magic is attendant on Saleem's fateful birth. At the same moment that Amina gives birth, another woman named Vanita, the Hindu wife of a street musician, delivers a baby she names Shiva. The father is a British gentleman named William Methwold, Vanita's lover, and the hospital's midwife switches the babies. Saleem, therefore, though raised in privilege and renown while Amina's actual son sinks into obscurity, is not Muslim but Hindu, not from an upper-class but from a lower-class background, and the bastard son of an English gentleman: a true hybrid and anomaly of modern India. Shiva will become Saleem's alternative mirror image through the course of the novel with the rivalry between the two establishing key themes in the opposition between capitalism and socialism, pacifism and belligerence, and internationalism and nationalism that constitute modern India.

Book two treats Saleem's childhood, which is a series of humiliations interrupted by the revelation of his magical power. Saleem's overlarge nose gives him the power of "seeing into the hearts and minds of men," and the discovery of his gift when Saleem is nine leads him to create a network connecting all of the children of midnight (only 581 of the 1,001 have survived). Shiva, who believes that he, not Saleem, should be the midnight's children's conference leader, vies for control while advocating violent resistance. Domestically, despite the revelation of his true identity, Saleem is still accepted as a member of the Sinai family. Their fortunes, affected by shifting historical events, cause them to move between Bombay and Pakistan. The climax of book two is the war between India and Pakistan in 1965 during which Saleem loses his home, family, and memory.

Book three, covering the period between 1970 and 1978, describes events in East Pakistan that led to the formation of Bangladesh. With his uncanny sense of smell, Saleem is employed as "a human dog," by a West Pakistan hit squad during the Bangladesh war. Saleem's experiences there, one of the most powerful and disturbing portions of the novel, is a phantasmagoria of the horror of war and brutality. "It seemed to me that if you are going to write an epic," Rushdie has stated, "even a comic epic, you need a descent into hell. That chapter is the inferno chapter." Regaining his memory, Saleem is magically returned to Bombay by Parvati-the-witch, another of the children of midnight. In India, the "Widow" (Indira Gandhi) declares the Emergency, ending Nehru's promise of freedom he proclaimed on the night of independence. The surviving children of midnight are condemned to be sterilized, and Saleem, impotent and anticipating death, abandons his former illusion of his responsibility for India's history based on his special gift and birth and faces his helplessness and defenselessness. In despair over the perceived betrayal of what was promised with nationhood, Saleem, in Rushdie's analysis "is cracking and he's going to crumble to pieces." *Midnight's Children* is finally a novel of displacement, alienation, and the world seen by the dispossessed. Reacting to charges of nihilistic pessimism in the conclusion of the novel, Rushdie has stated, "I don't think the end of the book suggests a negative view. Saleem's personal destiny does lead to despair, but Saleem does not represent the whole of India but only one particular historical process, a certain kind of hope that is lost and which exhausts itself with the death of Saleem. But in the way the book is written I am suggesting also reserves beyond this the multitudinous possibilities that India generates. I think I have shown that although the possibility that Saleem represents is finished, a new and tougher generation is just beginning."

Saleem's picaresque comic adventures over the first three decades of India's national history and his family's history through the three decades preceding independence, despite a dominant tone of loss, betrayal, and disillusion, are ultimately a liberation and a release of the inexhaustible potential and marvels inherent in the Indian experience. "Behind all my writing," Rushdie has observed, "is the idea of *crowd* . . . India's turbulent multiplicity . . . a throng not only of people but also of dreams, memories, fears, hopes, portents, fictions, and gods."

72

U.S.A. TRILOGY

(1930–38)

by John Dos Passos

Dos Passos is the only major American novelist of the twentieth century who has had the desire and the power to surround the lives of his characters with what Lionel Trilling once called "the buzz of history" in the actual, homely, everyday sounds of current events and politics, of social ambitions and the struggle for money, of small pleasures and trivial corruptions, amidst which we all live. He has given us an image of a major aspect of our experience that has hardly been touched by any other novelist of our time.

—Arthur Mizener, *Twelve Great American Novels*

John Dos Passos's *The 42nd Parallel*, first published in 1930, *1919*, issued in 1932, and *The Big Money*, in 1936, collected as the U.S.A. trilogy in 1938, constitute one of the most challenging and ambitious works of modern American literature. In it Dos Passos attempts an unprecedented panoramic depiction of American life during the first three decades of the 20th century that comes as close as any American novel to approximating a national epic. To capture the range and complexity of America, Dos Passos pioneered the use of innovative narrative techniques that make the U.S.A. trilogy both a historical chronicle and a compendium of modernist fictional strategies that have influenced subsequent novelists both in America and abroad. For his vision, Jean-Paul Sartre called Dos Passos in 1938 "the greatest writer of our time," while critic George Steiner declared that he had been "the principal American literary influence of the twentieth century." Only a select few American novels—Melville's *Moby-Dick*, Faulkner's Yoknapatawpha novel sequence, and Pynchon's *Gravity's Rainbow*, for example—provide such a comparable reach and innovative narrative strategies.

Departing from more traditionally structured novels in his *Manhattan Transfer* (1925), Dos Passos translated his interest in avant-garde painting and film technique into a verbal collage capturing a cross section of New York City through a series of juxtaposed vignettes constituting what critic George J. Baker describes as "a kind of mosaic, or, better, a revolving stage that presents a multitude of scenes and characters which, taken together, convey a sense of the life of a given milieu and by extension give the tone of contemporary life generally." Beginning around 1927, Dos Passos took up a far vaster challenge in both time and space exploring the various political, economic, and social patterns that emerged out of the seeming chaos of modern American experience. Concerned with the impact of history on American identity and values, Dos Passos set out to diagnose how the present emerged out of the events of the first three decades of the 20th century. The U.S.A. trilogy represents the stages of America's modern development beginning with the innocence and confidence of the pre–World War I years but with the forces of change predicted in the title, *The 42nd Parallel*, the North American continent's most frequent storm track. The second book, *1919*, treats the moral and political disruptions following World War I, and *The Big Money* presents the collapse of the American dream under the crushing weight of materialism and spiritual and moral bankruptcy. In the trilogy's 52 narrative sections Dos Passos tells the stories of 12 representative American figures who appear and reappear in one or more of the novels and in some cases interact with one another. Juxtaposed to the fictional narratives are "Newsreel" documentary sections made up of contemporary newspaper articles, verses of popular songs, and advertisements. There are also "Camera Eye" sequences of the author's own impressions, reactions, and memories, what critic Donald Pizer calls "a form of autobiographical symbolic poetry" in which Dos Passos reveals "his state of mind, feeling, or spirit at a specific moment of his development." Finally, Dos Passos provides a series of biographical profiles of such figures of the era as Henry Ford, William Randolph Hearst, Rudolph Valentino, Isadora Duncan, Eugene Debs, Thomas Edison, Big Bill Haywood, Thorstein Veblen, and Woodrow Wilson. Pizer speculates that Dos Passos worked on each narrative segment separately and then artfully combined the elements in a strategy of ironic juxtaposition. The overall effect, described by Pizer as a "kind of cubistic portrait of America," of Dos Passos's complex mix of narrative styles and elements is the creation of a rich American panorama from multiple angles in which history, fact, and fiction reinforce one other.

As the trilogy opens with *The 42nd Parallel*, the new century commences with America triumphant after the Spanish-American War, anticipating its wider role on the world stage. In a sense, the trilogy will document the loss of American innocence when it seeks to become a world power. The first fictional narrative begins the story of Fenian "Mac" McCreary from his Connecticut childhood (juxtaposed with contrasted scenes from Dos Passos's own childhood) through his travels across the country as a printer and his involvement in radical and revolutionary politics. Next Janey Williams is introduced, a young woman from a lower-class background who becomes the private secretary of advertising mogul J. Ward Moorehouse, who will emerge as the central character in the evolving moral drama of the corruption and collapse of the American dream. Moorehouse, born on the Fourth of July, a self-made man who rises from a humble background, typifies a perverted Horatio Alger story. He is the new man of the new century: opportunistic, hypocritical, and self-important who gains power as an advertising executive and public relations wizard from the manipulation and corruption of language itself. The volume ends with the introduction of another eventually major figure in the trilogy, Charley Anderson, another self-made man, who joins an ambulance corps in France as the war threatens to test core American values, while disrupting the lives of the novel's cast of fictional characters.

1919 traces the impact of the war while introducing a number of new characters, including Joe Williams, Janey's brother, a merchant seaman who is killed on Armistice Day in a barroom brawl; Anne Elizabeth Trent, known as Daughter, a Texas socialite who goes to Europe at the end of the war and is killed after a drunken spree with a French aviator in an airplane crash; and Ben Compton, a Jewish radical, jailed for refusing to be conscripted. Dominating the scene, however, is Moorehouse, who has capitalized on the war to enhance his power and turns up at the Versailles Conference to ensure that American money interests are well protected. The thematic patterns that begin to emerge in Dos Passos's diagnosis are the hollowness of capitalism, the destructive power of greed and self-indulgence, and the betrayal of the ideals of the American republic by self-interest and a moral hollowness. Characters begin to be grouped as exploiters, the exploited, and frustrated idealists caught between the two. As Alfred Kazin summarizes, *1919* is written with "fury behind it . . . a picture of waste, hypocrisy, and debauchery."

The Big Money treats the 1920s as the ultimate disintegration of social order and moral values in pursuit of wealth. Charley Anderson, having become a flying ace in the war, returns home to pursue success in the aviation business. His is a morally empty achievement, and both his marriage and his finances collapse. Charley's rise and fall intersect with the triumph of actress Margo Dowling, whose image will be manufactured and exploited in Hollywood. Moorehouse appears as well, in decline, a shadow man of little more than windy rhetoric. The final important character accounted for is Mary French, an idealist whose love affairs with Ben Compton and another leftist activist end badly when neither man is able to combine his public lives with his private concerns. She works in vain in the unsuccessful defense of Sacco and Vanzetti, whose execution becomes the symbolic death knell of the American promise of freedom and justice. As Alfred Kazin observes, "out of the bitter realization that this society . . . could grind two poor Italian anarchists to death for their opinions, came the conception of the two nations, the two Americas, that is the scaffolding of *U.S.A.*" The seemingly unbridgeable gap between the haves and have-nots and the ultimate betrayal of the American dream are glimpsed in the trilogy's final chapter, which describes a jobless, hungry young hitchhiker during the Great Depression, watching a plane filled with the rich and powerful fly overhead as cars speed by him:

> The young man waits on the side of the road; the plane has gone; thumb moves in a small arc when a car tears hissing past. Eyes seek the driver's eyes. A hundred miles down the road. Head swims, belly tightens, want crawls over his skin like ants:
>
> went to school, books said opportunity, ads promised speed, own your own home, shine bigger than your neighbor, the radiocrooner whispered girls, ghosts of platinum girls coaxed from the screen, millions in winnings were chalked up on the boards in the offices, paychecks were for hands willing to work, the cleared desk of an executive with three telephones on it;
>
> waits with swimming head, needs knot the belly; idle hands numb, beside the speeding traffic.
>
> A hundred miles down the road.

As the trilogy concludes, fiction, history, and autobiography conjoin to form America's present, having achieved a symphonic blending of American voices and experiences. As effective as the representative fictional narratives are, as impressive is the mixing of them with Dos Passos's own reactions and memories and the assembled documentary evidence, perhaps his greatest achievements in U.S.A. are the brilliant biographical portraits that contextualize and deepen the novel's vision of American possibilities and betrayal. Included are such politicians as Theodore Roosevelt, Woodrow Wilson, and Robert La Follette; such inventors as Thomas Edison and the Wright Brothers; such artists as Frank Lloyd Wright and Isadora Duncan; such heroes as Luther Burbank and Eugene Debs; and such villains as J. P. Morgan. Like the story of the fictional characters, the lesson of their lives is also the battle between exploiter and exploited and the division of America in the hands of a powerful few.

Although savage indignation and fury drives U.S.A., its experimental aesthetic helps to prevent it from descending into the merely polemical. There is a richness here in subject and style that makes the trilogy one of the most daring and significant works by an American novelist.

73

LES LIAISONS DANGEREUSES

(1782)

by Pierre Choderlos de Laclos

If this book burns, it burns as only ice can burn.

—Charles Baudelaire, *Notes on Les Liaisons dangereuses*

One of the most notorious novels ever written, *Les Liaisons dangereuses* was an instant succès de scandale when it was published in 1782, transforming an obscure artillery captain and first-time novelist, Pierre Choderlos de Laclos, into an overnight celebrity. Decried as "four volumes of seduction" and "a veritable pack of horrors and infamies," *Les Liaisons dangereuses* quickly sold out as many as 16 editions in 1782 alone and went on to become the most famous and esteemed French novel in the 18th century. Laclos's singular and sole contribution to French fiction would subsequently fascinate France's greatest writers, including Stendhal, Baudelaire, Proust, Giraudoux, Gide, and Malraux, as well as English writers as various as Arnold Bennett, Virginia Woolf, and Aldous Huxley. Successful stage and film adaptations of the novel have demonstrated its undiminished capacity to shock and captivate. One of the most ironic and diabolically clever novels ever constructed, *Les Liaisons dangereuses* has seduced its audience as well as its characters, while posing fundamental questions about the arts of seduction, reading, and interpretation.

The enigmatic and elusive Pierre-Ambrois-François Choderlos de Laclos was born in 1741 at Amiens, the second son of a recently ennobled family. Sent to military school, Laclos joined a less-than-fashionable artillery regiment in 1762. The Treaty of Paris that ended the Seven Years' War thwarted Laclos's ambition for wartime service, and he began a 25-year career in the peacetime army posted to various provincial garrison towns throughout France. Regarded as an able and steady, if unspectacular, officer, Laclos managed only to reach the rank of captain. With free time to read, write, and socialize with the fashionable in the cities in which he was stationed, Laclos wrote poetry and drew some attention with the anonymous publication of "Epistle to Margot," in 1776, which was read as a satire on Louis XV's mistress Madame Du

Barry. Following a six-year posting in Grenoble, where he would later declare that the local aristocracy's salons provided him with the inspiration for *Les Liaisons dangereuses*, Laclos was in 1779 seconded to the Marquis de Montalembert who was charged with fortifying the Île d'Aix, off La Rochelle. It is believed that during his stay on this rugged and uninhabited island, Laclos conceived and wrote *Les Liaisons dangereuses.* When the scandal broke following its publication in 1782, Laclos was recalled to his regiment in Brest, presumably to better monitor his activities and to prevent further embarrassing publications. Montalembert, however, intervened on Laclos's behalf, and he was allowed to return to La Rochelle to resume his duties. There he met and married Marie-Soulange Duperré in 1786. Laclos's subsequent writings include a review of Fanny Burney's novel *Cecelia*, three unfinished essays on the education of women, and a negative critique of popular French military strategist Vauban, which nearly cost him his military career. In 1788, Laclos was granted a leave of absence to serve as secretary to the Duke of Orlèans, the king's cousin. In 1790, Laclos joined the Jacobin Club, became editor of its newspaper, and participated in the debates that followed the king's flight to Varennes in 1791. During the Reign of Terror, Laclos was imprisoned and barely escaped the guillotine. Released in 1794, he applied to rejoin the army but was rejected. Rewarded for his services in assisting Napoleon's rise to power, however, Laclos was reinstated in the army and promoted to the rank of general in 1800. Under Napoleon, Laclos saw action in Germany and Italy, where he died of dysentery and malaria in 1803.

That a professional soldier with a somewhat checkered career should produce one of the uncontested masterworks of French fiction is one of the exceptional stories in the history of the novel. Ralph Ellison's *Invisible Man* comes to mind as a comparable "one-book wonder." Exerting an oversized impact on the history of the novel, *Les Liaisons dangereuses* helped to redefine two important subgenres of the novel—the epistolary and the libertine—and became a precursor, like Sterne's *Tristram Shandy*, of another: self-reflective metafiction or novels about the nature and status of the novel itself.

Epistolary narratives are as old as Ovid's *Heroides* (ca. 15 B.C.) and the 3rd-century Greek author Alciphron. Proto-novels in letters include Abbé d'Aubignac's *Novel of Letters* (1667), Gabriel de Lavergne Guilleragues's *Letters from a Portuguese Nun* (1669), and Aphra Behn's *Love-Letters Between a Nobleman and His Sisters* (1683–87), commonly regarded as the first epistolary novel in English. Samuel Richardson's mastery of the epistolary form, particularly in *Pamela* (1740) and *Clarissa* (1747–48) would establish the vogue of epistolary fiction in the 18th century, setting the form for many imitators, including Jean-Jacques Rousseau's *Julie; or, The New Eloise* (1761), Goethe's *The Sorrows of Young Werther* (1774), and the work frequently cited as the first American novel, William Hill Brown's *The Power of Sympathy* (1789). Novel readers of Richardson and his imitators had never before encountered anything like the directness and immediacy of these letter narratives in which emotions were so straightforwardly and powerfully expressed so that human consciousness itself seemed to be revealed for the first time. Laclos's contribution to the epistolary tradition was both to widen its range, symphonically orchestrating a collection of 13 correspondents, each with a distinctive voice and perspective, while complicating the form's reliability. Previous epistolary novels offered an assumption of honesty and authenticity in which correspondents confessed and revealed their innermost thoughts and feelings. In *Les Liaisons dangereuses,* however, letters take on a far more sinister and deceptive quality in which not honesty but disguise and manipulation define correspondence. It becomes a challenge in the novel to untangle motive from expression, confession from exploitation, and to know for sure what each writer truly believes, feels, or wants. The letters in *Les Liaisons dangereuses* are not windows into the soul, though they may appear to be, but verbal traps, carefully laid to disguise the truth and to direct their reader's response. Laclos's demonstration of the subversive power of the letter undermines and explodes the epistolary conventions so that the reader can no longer trust the truthfulness of individual letters or letter writers, and narrative transparency is replaced with an opaque and distorted hall of mirrors.

Laclos would also draw on another important 18th-century novel tradition, the libertine novel, a French literary form that called into question and flaunted commonly accepted social and ethical standards. Marked by a freethinking attitude that opposed the precepts of the church and established morality while insisting on the supremacy of reason and the individual will allied with an unalienable right to pleasure and sexual gratification beyond restrictive social codes, the libertine novel took various forms. There were fictional memoirs of young aristocrats' adventures in society such as Charles Pinot-Duclos's *The Confessions of Count * * ** (1741) and Claude Joseph Dorat's *The Sacrifices of Love* (1771), erotic libertine novels such as Crébillon fils's *The Sofa* (1746) and Diderot's *Indiscreet Jewels* (1746), as well as pornographic works such as *The Philosophical Thérèse* (1748), attributed to Boyer d'Argens. The culminating figure of the libertine tradition is the Marquis de Sade, in such works as *Justine* (1790) and *Juliette* (1797). All, in varying degrees, exploit the erotic for its shock value and overturn established codes of behavior and belief. *Les Liaisons dangereuses* displays the characteristic setting of the libertine novel among the aristocracy whose preoccupations with sexual conquest and revenge are stage-managed by the novel's striking cynical freethinkers, the Vicomte de Valmont and the Marquis de Merteuil. Supreme analysts and iconoclasts, Valmont and Merteuil manipulate by their words and their recognition of the potency of desire beneath the poses of morality. Sex in the novel is less an exercise in eroticism than a display of power politics. Laclos's version of the libertine novel demonstrates, in a memorable phrase by André Malraux, "an eroticization of the will," or what Baudelaire described as "the love of war and the war of love." Forerunners of the revolutionaries who would bring down the ancien régime, Valmont and Merteuil, as libertines, herald a new breed of fictional protagonists, as witty, attractive, and irresistible as they are lethal and destructive.

Laclos's strategy in *Les Liaisons dangereuses* deliberately assaults reader expectation from the outset. The novel begins with contradictions. A Publisher's Foreword (penned by Laclos) opens the book with a warning that "despite the title and the editor's comments in his preface, we cannot guarantee the authenticity of these letters. We even have strong reasons to suspect that this is a work of pure fiction." Reversing the standard 18th-century assertion of a novel's verisimilitude and moral utility, Laclos immediately calls attention to the novel's artifice and lies. The Editor's Preface (also written by Laclos) that follows contradicts the publisher, insisting both on the letters' authenticity and their moral purpose. "It seems to me, at least," writes Laclos in his editor's guise, "that morality is served by unmasking the methods used by those with bad morals to corrupt those whose moral standards are high, and I think that these letters can contribute effectively to this aim." The complication of untangling truth from deception, sounded from the beginning of the novel, will be carried through the 175 letters that follow. Alerted to the contradictions, the reader is forced to take an active role in assessing the truth, of reassembling the narrative from multiple, limited, and unreliable viewpoints by reading between the lines of correspondence which, as even the editor admits, "almost all the feelings expressed in it are contrived or disguised."

In *Les Liaisons dangereuses* two linked seduction plots metastasize. The Marquise de Merteuil is a young widow with a reputation for virtue despite numerous clandestine affairs. She enlists her former lover, the Vicomte de Valmont, a well-known womanizer, to seduce the young Cécile de Volanges, who has recently been taken out of her convent school to be married to the Comte de Gercourt, another of Merteuil's former lovers. Valmont initially refuses to assist Merteuil's revenge on Gercourt because corrupting the virginal Cécile offers too little a challenge. Valmont instead has set his sights on "the most ambitious plan I have yet conceived," to seduce Madame de Tourvel, a judge's wife, well known for her religious fervor and respectability. Valmont desires not just another conquest but to snatch Tourvel "from the bosom of the God she worships. . . . I want her to have these high principles—and to sacrifice them for my sake! I want her to be horrified by her sins yet unable to resist sinning; to suffer endless terrors which she overcomes and forgets only in my arms." He blasphemously aspires to become "the God whom she loves best." An obstacle to achieving his end is Cécile's mother (one of Valmont's former conquests) who alerts Tourvel about his reputation. To revenge himself on Madame de Volanges, Valmont finally agrees to aid Merteuil while he awaits Tourvel's capitulation. Sent away from his aunt's country home where he has been ingratiating himself with Tourvel, Valmont produces one of the novel's most striking letters to Tourvel using the nude body of courtesan Emilie as his writing desk. Tourvel reads Valmont's impassioned words of love for her, while the reader comes to understand that Valmont's arousal comes from a very different source:

> Everything seems to add to my delight: the air I am breathing is full of joy and pleasure; even the table on which I am pressing as I write, which has never before been devoted to such a purpose, has been turned into a holy altar of love in my eyes. . . . I shall have written down on it my pledge to love you for ever! I must beg you forgive me: my senses are in disarray. Perhaps it is wrong for me to abandon myself so utterly to delights which you cannot share yourself. I must leave you a moment to relieve the frenzy which is overtaking, nay, overpowering me. . . .

Seemingly overcome by his passion for Tourvel, Valmont breaks off to make love to Emilie, as he later confesses to Merteuil, forcing the reader to reassess his words of devoted love from our privileged insider's position with access to the two strategists comparing notes. Their finely tuned plot is set in motion when Valmont, under the pretext of serving as an intermediary between Cécile and the young music teacher she fancies, the Chevalier Danceny, gains access to her room and beds Cécile, while Tourvel admits that she can withstand Valmont's pleas no longer. Merteuil and Valmont achieve their intended goals, but their scheme goes tragically awry: Merteuil manipulates Valmont into sending Tourvel a letter she concocts confessing that he has grown tired of her, sending a shattered Tourvel to a convent where she breaks down and dies. The pregnant Cécile miscarries, and Merteuil betrays Valmont to Danceny who challenges Valmont to a duel and kills him. Rumors spread about Merteuil's role in the affair, and she is publicly humiliated, contracts smallpox, loses her looks and her fortune, and flees from Paris to obscurity in Holland.

Why do the two proto-Nietzschean supermen who so successfully prey on the vulnerabilities and desires of their victims fail in the novel? And what are we to make of their failure? It can be argued that Valmont and Merteuil's elaborate plot simply collapses under the weight of its own complexity: There are just too many moving parts that even the master-manipulators cannot ultimately control. The arbitrariness of the denouement, however, suggests more poetic justice than naturalism: Is it likely, for example, that the experienced Valmont would be out-dueled by the untested, ineffectual Danceny? Is it necessary, except as moral punishment, to destroy Merteuil so utterly? The didacticism of a retributional reading of the conclusion is contradicted by Laclos's scrupulous avoidance of moral censure through all that has preceded it, an intention signaled clearly in Laclos's alteration of his original, edifying title, *Le Danger des liaisons*, to its more neutral final title. There is, however, another possible reading of the novel that considers the conclusion in psychological, rather than naturalistic or moralistic terms. It can be argued that Valmont's genuine love for Tourvel and Merteuil's jealousy over it destroys them both. Valmont's description of Tourvel's capitulation lets slip what Merteuil had suggested all along, that Valmont has fallen deeply in love with Tourvel, and in his own words, "might somehow be dependent on the very slave whom I've just subjugated." He writes: "And so, with an innocence in all her beauty, sharing my pleasure until it ended in simultaneous ecstasy. And for the first time, mine outlasted my pleasure. I left her arms only to fall at her feet and swear eternal love. . . . after we'd parted, I kept thinking of her and had to make a great effort to put her out of my mind." In Merteuil's case, jealousy provides the most plausible motive for her insistence that Valmont break off the affair and her making Danceny aware of the part Valmont played in Cécile's ruin. In such a reading, Valmont's death at the hands of Danceny is more like assisted suicide brought on by despair over Tourvel's fate and their doomed love. To reach these conclusions, the reader must contend with the fact that the seemingly frank correspondence between the two strategists—Valmont and Merteuil—is as full of disguise and deceit (self- and otherwise) as their artfully designed letters to their victims. In the relativist and polyphonic *Les Liaisons dangereuses*, paradox and indeterminacy become the novel's operating principles. Ultimately, the novel is less about the art of physical seduction than it is about verbal seduction, the ways in which language and writing conceal and reveal, in which the reader becomes its 14th silent correspondent with our interpretation of the other 13 the unsent synthesizing letter that makes sense of them all.

74

THE CHARTERHOUSE OF PARMA

(1839)

by Stendhal

One may say roughly that his subject is always Italy. He had a number of affectations but his passion for Italy is evidently profoundly sincere and will serve to keep his memory sweet to many minds and his authority unquestioned. This subject he treated under a number of different forms; most successfully, toward the end of his life, in a novel which will always be numbered among the dozen finest novels we possess. . . .

—Henry James, "Henry Beyle," in the *Nation*, September 17, 1874

Stendhal's *La Chartreuse de Parme (The Charterhouse of Parma)* stands in marked contrast with *The Red and the Black*. If the earlier book is Stendhal's French novel, dissecting the obsession with money, rank, and conformity in post-Napoleonic France, *The Charterhouse of Parma* is Stendhal's Italian novel offering an alternative worldview and take on human passion and possibilities. *The Red and the Black* serves as one of the foundation texts of realism in the novel; romance, however, is the dominant tone in the later novel, evoking critical analogies to the opera and fairy tale rather than the "mirror in the roadway." So contrasting are the two novels in matter and method that they have long divided critical opinion into opposing camps of *rougistes* ("Red and Blackers")—admirers of Stendhal's satire and innovative realism in his first masterwork—and "Carthusians" (a charterhouse is a monastery of the Carthusian order) who prefer *The Charterhouse of Parma*'s lyricism and visionary power that extends the narrower focus of the earlier novel into a massive social panorama and human fable. Zola, who declared *The Charterhouse of Parma* to be the first French novel to portray another nationality convincingly, still found it less successful than *The Red and the Black* in which a "work of analysis" had been succeeded by "a novel of adventure." Balzac, one of the earliest Carthusians, offers an opposing view, declaring that *The Charterhouse of Parma* went far beyond *The Red and the Black* to become a "masterpiece of the literature of ideas," "a book in which the sublime shines forth from one chapter to the next . . . the novel that Machiavelli would have written had he lived, banished from Italy in the 19th century," in which "One finds perfection in every detail." Henry James, who regarded *The Red and the Black* as "absolutely unreadable," was also a dedicated Carthusian. André Gide ranked *The Charterhouse of Parma* as the greatest French novel, and, with Laclos's *Les Liaisons dangereuses*, the sole French novels he ranked in the world's top 10. My own ranking reveals me as slightly more *rougiste* than Carthusian, though it seems unnecessary to take an either/or approach, trumpeting one of the novels only at the expense of the other. If I prefer Julien Sorel to Fabrice del Dongo as a central protagonist and *The Red and the Black*'s satire and psychological realism over the operatic expressionism of *The Charterhouse of Parma* that does not diminish appreciation for what is by any measure one of the world's great novels and a culminating work by a pioneering novelist that has influenced later novelists as diverse as Tolstoy, Proust, and Hemingway.

The Charterhouse of Parma is Stendhal's summary statement of his love affair with Italy and its passionate hold on his imagination. Born Marie-Henri Beyle in 1783 in provincial Grenoble whose bourgeois conservativism and pious hypocrisy he despised, Stendhal escaped first as a student to Paris and then in 1800 as a commissioned officer in the French army joining Napoleon's Italian campaign. Crossing the border on horseback, Stendhal was immediately entranced by Italy and its culture, discovering there a liberation of spirit and an emotional release that he found sorely lacking in France. Writing of his initial stay in Milan and his first encounter with Italian opera and art, Stendhal declared that "it was the most beautiful time of my life . . . an interval of mad and complete happiness." He would return for an extensive tour of Italy—to Parma, Florence, Rome, and Naples—in 1811, and, after participating in the retreat from Moscow in 1812, settled in Milan from 1814 to 1821, during which he completed his first three books—*The Lives of Haydn, Mozart, and Metastasio* (1815), *The History of Italian Painting*, and *Rome, Naples, and Florence* (1817). Suspected as a French spy and political subversive by the Austrian authorities, Stendhal left Milan for Paris where he spent the next nine years, publishing *On Love* (1822), his first novel, *Armance* (1826), and *The Red and the Black* in 1830, the year King Charles X abdicated and the Bourbon monarchy fell. Under the new regime, Stendhal applied for a diplomatic position and was offered the consulate at Trieste. However, the Austrian government rejected the appointment, based on his past history in Milan, and Stendhal was reassigned to Civitavecchia, the main port of the Papal States, 30 miles from Rome. Stendhal found both the work and the town dreary and in 1836 began a three-month medical leave in Paris that he managed to extend to almost three years.

During this period, Stendhal began publishing short narratives based on manuscripts he collected in Italy recounting the exploits of the great Italian families of the 15th and 16th centuries. One of these, *Origine delle grandesse della famiglia Farnese*, chronicled the colorful career of Alessandro Farnese

(1468–1549), who, after a string of reckless love affairs, aided by his aunt Vandozza Farnese, the former mistress of Rodrigo Borgia (Pope Alexander VI from 1490 to 1502), became a cardinal and subsequently Pope Paul III in 1534. In one of the more outlandish of Farnese's adventures, after abducting a young woman and killing one of her attendants, Farnese was imprisoned in the Castel Sant'Angelo in Rome before escaping by means of a long rope. Stendhal regarded Farnese's career and the other stories from the Italian Renaissance as emblematic of lives lived dangerously, passionately, and without regard for timid moral conventions and in August 1838 resolved to "make of this sketch a romanzetto." On 4 November, he shut himself in his Paris apartment and gave orders that he was not to be disturbed. In an extraordinary creative burst, Stendhal dictated *The Charterhouse of Parma* in its entirety over the next 52 days, completing six "enormous notebooks" on 26 December that were dispatched to a publisher. Stendhal would later tell Balzac, no stranger to Herculean literary labors himself, that he composed "20 or 30 pages" at a time between breaks for "a little love-making when I can, or a spot of orgy." His method was to achieve an effect of breathless and artlessly improvised narrative movement, "more natural and worthier to find favor in 1880," Stendhal observed, than the more deliberately constructed contemporary novels written in the grand manner with conventional characters and situations.

The Charterhouse of Parma achieves a striking immediacy and momentum, as well as a radical break with established novelistic conventions. Its unconventionality extends to its evasion of traditional restrictions of genre and character focus. Nominally a novel of formation that chronicles the development of its youthful, naive hero—Fabrizio Del Dongo—from childhood to retirement, the novel's focus frequently departs from him and shifts to others, most notably to Fabrizio's aunt, Gina, duchess of Sanseverina, and her lover, Count Mosca, the prime minister of Parma. Stendhal's alternating multi-focus establishes compound narrative centers forming a collective novel of the social group, organized less by a single character's progress than thematically by shared concerns of love and power. Deeply psychological and nuanced in its portraits of persons and accomplished in its sociological rendering of place and era, *The Charterhouse of Parma* is also a pastiche of romantic adventure elements in which its characters are pushed in extraordinary ways. Moreover, a persistent irony pervades the novel with full disclosure existing only between the all-knowing narrator and the reader, producing a genre-bending narrative that has been described by the literary historian Martin Turnell as "a study of tragic individuals who find themselves in comic situations," which "explains the mixture of levity and seriousness." As a historical novel, *The Charterhouse of Parma* is equally defiant. More than one critic has demonstrated the justice of Benedetto Croce's statement that the novel shows only "the Italy of Stendhal," not a reliably authentic portrait of 1830s Italy. The critic Matthew Josephson has suggested that as a historical novelist, Stendhal "reverses the procedure of Walter Scott," and that "instead of writing really of modern people dressed in antique costumes, he writes of sixteenth-century characters and events as they appeared in his own time." Ultimately, it is the novel's sheer captivating vitality and multiplicity that best recommend it. As the novelist Italo Calvino has observed, *The Charterhouse of Parma* is "one novel that contains many novels."

Its opening sentence, "On 15 May 1796 General Bonaparte entered Milan at the head of that youthful army which a few days earlier had crossed the bridge at Lodi, and taught the world that, after so many centuries, Caesar and Alexander had a successor," sets an initial heroic tone that successive details and events will deflate. Throughout the novel, the ideal—private and public aspirations for love and liberty—will collide with reality in the overall educative process of the novel. The exhilaration and release experienced by the Italians with the arrival of Napoleon the liberator will be followed politically and socially by repression and disillusion. A similar pattern of disappointed fulfilment forms the arc of the characters' experiences as the private and public spheres interpenetrate. Opening before the birth of "our hero," Fabrizio del Dongo, the novel reveals in its initial pages the crucial central irony of the book, namely that Fabrizio is the illegitimate son of the marquise del Dongo and a French officer. This revelation, known only to the marquise, the narrator, and the reader, exposes as false the resistance both Fabrizio and his "aunt" feel in their longing for one another that they fear is incestuous. In a novel consumed by the question of how happiness is possible, this central irony will set nephew and aunt on a course of misunderstanding and disappointment as each tries to find other alternatives to love and passion in other partners.

Raised by the miserly and reactionary marquis del Dongo, the idealistic Fabrizio rebels by traveling in disguise to France to join the French army in support of the admired Napoleon. Managing to find his way onto the Waterloo battlefield, Fabrizio anticipates a crowning attainment of heroism and comradeship with the French troops, seeing "springing up between himself and them that noble friendship of the heroes of Tasso and Ariosto." Instead he encounters the vulgar reality of soldiers who take advantage of him and abandon him under fire. By rendering the battle from the isolated combatant's limited and naïve perspective, Stendhal achieves one of the most striking effects in the novel in which the chaos and confusion of warfare contradict other battlefield accounts of strategic and coherent maneuvers rationally stage-managed by the generals from on high. Fabrizio's experiences on the ground are so random and confused that he wonders, "Have I really taken part in a battle? It seemed to him that he had, and he would have been supremely happy if he could have been certain of this."

Stendhal's inglorious treatment of combat, relaying its trivia along with its terror, would have a major influence on Tolstoy when he sent his own illegitimate naïf, Pierre Bezukov, onto the Borrodino battlefield in *War and Peace*, as well as on Hemingway in his description of the Capporetto retreat in *A Farewell to Arms*.

Fabrizio eventually makes his way back to Italy to continue his search for authentic heroic fulfillment in the church, aided by his aunt, and as a lover in a succession of affairs. The novel's focus shifts and expands to include the relationship of Gina and her lover, Count Mosca, and the world of power politics and intrigue in the state of Parma. In Gina, Stendhal creates one of his finest characters, a woman of great depth and complexity who prompted Simone de Beauvoir to praise Stendhal's rare gift of capturing a woman "without mystery." That same sense of penetration extends to the microcosm of Parma. In so brilliantly depicting a total world in miniature, Stendhal manages not only to produce one of the greatest of all political novels but an unprecedented realistic social texture in which no detail is insignificant or fails to contribute to the reader's deepening understanding of a richly complex society. As the great theorist of literary realism, Erich Auerbach, has explained, "Insofar as the serious realism of modern times cannot represent man otherwise than as embedded in a total reality, political, social, and economic, which is concrete and constantly evolving—as in the case today in any novel or film—Stendhal is its founder." Count Mosca's maneuvering for power and his struggle for dominance with the despotic ruler of Parma, Prince Ernesto Ranuccio IV, becomes entwined with his passion for Gina and her protection of her beloved nephew who is charged with the murder of a jealous rival for the affection of a young actress. Tried and convicted in absentia, Fabrizio is imprisoned on his return to Parma. Clélia Conti, the daughter of Fabrizio's jailer, next attracts Fabrizio's passion, and his subsequent contentment in confinement (one of Stendhal's repeated themes) is ended with Gina's arrangement of her nephew's escape. Back in Parma where a new prince has assumed power, the now reformed and chaste Fabrizio eventually becomes an archbishop, noted for his inspiring sermons. Hearing him preach, Clélia, who has complied with her father's wishes and married another, cannot resist Fabrizio, and the two become lovers. Clélia gives birth to a son fathered by Fabrizio, whom he kidnaps. The infant dies, and the remorseful Clélia soon follows him. At last aware of what his passions have wrought, Fabrizio withdraws from the world to the monastery of the book's title, finally explained in the novel's last pages.

An operatic fable of love and power, *The Charterhouse of Parma* explores the central preoccupations of all of Stendhal's works: the imperatives of love and its inevitable defeat at the hands of time, human nature, and social concerns that overvalue ambition, rank, and wealth. At the end of the novel, Count Mosca has attained all that his pursuit of power could imagine, but after the death of Gina, following shortly after that of her nephew, he is bereft and alone, a prisoner in a way that Fabrizio had not been in his jail cell, nor Gina had been in her unbreakable devotion to the man she thought was her nephew. Ultimately, the liberation of *The Charterhouse of Parma* is the reader's alone, made possible through the educative process of the novel to transcend the contradictions and limitation of human existence with understanding and compassion.

75

THE SORROWS OF YOUNG WERTHER

(1774)

by Johann Wolfgang von Goethe

In the Sorrows of Werther, *besides the interest of its simple and affecting story, so many opinions are canvassed and so many lights thrown upon what had hitherto been to me obscure subjects that I found in it a never-ending source of speculation and astonishment. . . . I thought Werther himself a more divine being than I had ever beheld or imagined; his character contained no pretension, but it sank deep. The disquisitions upon death and suicide were calculated to fill me with wonder. I did not pretend to enter into the merits of the case, yet I inclined towards the opinions of the hero, whose extinction I wept, without precisely understanding it. . . . Who was I? What was I? Whence did I come? What was my destination? These questions continually recurred, but I was unable to solve them.*

—Mary Shelley, *Frankenstein*

After Samuel Richardson's *Pamela* (1740), Goethe's *The Sorrows of Young Werther* (1774) was the novel's second great international success in the 18th century. One of the defining works of European Romanticism, it is a book that both diagnosed and defined a cultural era and sensibility while turning the novel inward to expose the subjective and emotional basis of consciousness and motivation. The tormented, hypersensitive Werther and the story of his hopeless love for Lotte that leads to his suicide captivated Europe, producing not only a sensational, controversial best-seller but a fashion and a cult. Werther sequels, dramatizations, artistic representation of scenes from the novel, and merchandise were enthusiastically consumed. Young men imitated Werther's characteristic dress—blue frock coat and yellow waistcoat and trousers—as well as his world-weariness and, in some cases, his demise. Cases of suicide associated with reading *Werther* were reported, and complaints that the book condoned suicide prompted Goethe in 1775 to add to the opening of the novel's second book these warning lines:

> You bemoan him, you love him, dear soul
> You salvage his memory from disgrace;

> Behold, his spirit signals to you from his cavern:
> *Be a man and do not follow after me.*

Goethe would revise *Werther* in 1786 to underscore his protagonist's pathology, eliminating mitigation for his passion for Lotte and his behavior, but Werther's hold on the popular imagination, which established Goethe's European reputation, continued unabated well into the 19th century. Napoleon is said to have read the novel at least seven times, and his 1808 conversations with the author that produced Napoleon's memorable exclamation, "There is a man!" consisted mainly of discussions of the novel. Werther's inwardness and his testing of the limits of experience influenced the creation of Byron's Romantic heroes as well as anticipated such fictional characters as Mary Shelley's Victor Frankenstein, Charlotte Brontë's Rochester, and Melville's Ahab. *The Sorrows of Young Werther* is one of the essential landmarks in the history of the novel, defining the ways autobiography, private consciousness, and the cultural moment can unite to produce a memorable and still disturbing psychological and moral drama.

After Goethe completed his legal studies in Strasbourg in 1771, he went to Wetzlar, the seat of the Supreme Court, where he made the acquaintance of Christian Kestner, the secretary to the Hanoverian legation, and Kestner's fiancée, Charlotte Buff, with whom Goethe fell in love. Goethe would recast their triangular relationship to form the core of Werther's dilemma in his passion for Lotte, who was "as good as betrothed" to the stalwart Albert. After Goethe left Wetzlar in 1772, he learned of the suicide of Karl Wilhelm Jerusalem, a secretary to the Brunswick legation, to whom Kestner had lent his pistols. Jerusalem was despondent over his love for another's wife, and Kestner provided Goethe with Jerusalem's written communications with him and his own account of Jerusalem's suicide. The writer would draw on and fuse this material with his own recollected emotional turbulence during the Wetzlar period to create Werther's drama. In February 1774 Goethe began work on the novel, which he finished in four weeks. He later recalled, "I myself was in this case and know best what anguish I suffered in it and what exertion it cost me to escape from it." The power of *Werther* stems from Goethe's unflinching reproduction of his own feelings and attitudes cast in a wider context in which Werther's private sorrows can be traced to cultural and universal sources. As Goethe later recalled about his hero, seen as a representative of his generation, "We are not here talking of such persons as led an active and significant life, employed their days in the service of some great kingdom or in the cause of freedom. . . . We are dealing here with those who lost the taste for life essentially from want of action, in the most peaceful state imaginable, through exaggerated demands upon themselves." Werther is the prototypical romantic overreacher in conflict with essential dualities—subject/object, body/spirit, will/duty—cut off from useful channels for his energies and emotions, which Goethe saw as a chief affliction in himself and his generation. He would attribute the success of the novel to its timely embodiment of the zeitgeist. "I am weary of bewailing the fate of our generation of human beings," Goethe wrote, "but I will so depict them that they may understand themselves, if that is possible, as I have understood them." The novel provided an explosion of sympathetic self-recognition. "The effect of this book was great," Goethe recalled in assessing the impact of his novel, "indeed immense, and principally because it hit exactly the right moment. For just as little priming is needed to detonate a powerful bomb, so the explosion which ensued among the public was so violent because the young people had already undermined themselves, and the shock was so great because each erupted with his own exaggerated demands, unsatisfied passions and imagined sufferings."

To detonate the powerful cultural and private recognition that the novel set off, Goethe radically refined the inwardness, immediacy, and intensity inherent in the epistolary narrative. Richardson in *Pamela* (1740) and *Clarissa* (1747–48) and Rousseau in *La nouvelle Héloise* (1759) had earlier exploited the psychological and emotional directness to be derived from an exchange of letters in which the reader overhears the mind in the act of forming its ideas and feelings. Goethe's innovation in *Werther* is having all of the letters written by the same person: Werther provides a one-sided account of his affairs to his friend Wilhelm, whose replies are not given. Except for the intrusion by the editor to summarize the events of Werther's final days, the novel stays exclusively within Werther's sensibility, the shifts of which form the novel's central drama. As Karl Viëtor has argued, "Among European novels *Werther* is the first in which an inward life, a spiritual process and nothing else, is represented, and hence it is the first psychological novel. . . . The scene is the soul of the hero. All events and figures are regarded only in the light of the significance they have for Werther's emotion. All that happens serves but to nourish the absolution of Werther's emotions—a fatal propensity which swells to a demonic possession and engulfs all other inward forces and possibilities."

Werther's monodrama offers an illustration of the novel's second sentence: "My dear friend, what a thing is the heart of man!" Werther is a young man of accomplishment and culture who has come to a south German town to settle some family business. There, in spring, amid a refreshing natural setting and simple country folk, Werther finds much to delight him, including Lotte, the daughter of the local bailiff, encountered in one of the most famous scenes in the novel, cutting bread for her siblings, a symbol of domestic tranquility and simplicity that Werther craves. The source of Werther's pathology, however, is glimpsed in the novel's early idylls, what Goethe called the "white-hot expression of pain and joy, irresistibly and internally consuming themselves." Lotte is intended for another, and Werther, narcissistically striving to sustain the intensity of his feelings, requires a correspondence between his soul's yearnings and the external world. In attempting to merge his spirit with the world, Werther breaks down the boundary between subject and object in a passionate intensity that results in a growing disintegration of Werther's connection with others and his world as his mood changes to one of despair. Breaking away from his unrequited love, Werther seeks an antidote to his private torments in public life, taking up a diplomatic post, but the tedium of the work and the social humiliation he experiences in the snobbish court world cause him to resign within a year. Lotte and Albert are now married, and with winter approaching, Werther inevitably and fatally returns to the scene of his passion where everything that had once reflected his joy now mirrors his gloom. Suicide becomes Werther's only available option in dealing with the frustration of his emotions and the intractability of experience that fails to gratify his desires. Borrowing Albert's pistols, Werther shoots himself, isolated and solitary, his attempt to live intensely, guided by his feelings alone, leading to self-destruction and a crippling solipsism.

Goethe's drama, though very much an expression of a particular time and place in its overwrought gestures of sentimental excess, derived from the German Sturm und Drang movement, still has the ability to provoke and to reflect universal dimensions of human nature and experience. Goethe treats his protagonist with both sympathy and irony. Werther can be simultaneously viewed as a noble victim of his hopeless passion, venturing deeply, like the greatest romantic and tragic heroes, in search of transcendence, and as a self-deluded, doomed neurotic, enclosed in sterile self-projection. *The Sorrows of Young Werther* challenges its reader to face the human predicament glimpsed in the protagonist's internal battleground between self and object, heart and head, love and duty. Goethe also sustains in the novel form for one of the first times in fiction the intensity and profundity usually reserved for the lyric poem in the delineation of the heart's capacities and human consciousness itself.

CITIES OF SALT

76

(1984–89)

by 'Abd al-Rahman Munīf

As the novel progresses, seismic social and economic changes open chasms so wide that Mr. Munīf's characters are always scrambling to keep from tumbling in. Their fates suggest the convolutions of a Victorian novel transcribed into Arabic calligraphy, or perhaps The Arabian Nights *as retold by Stendhal—with Sinbad driving a white Rolls-Royce and the Grand Vizier jetting off to Atlanta for counterintelligence training.*

—Francine Prose, *New York Times Book Review*, October 27, 1991

Munīf's monumental novel quintet, named for the first novel in the sequence, *Cities of Salt*, has been described as the epic contemporary Arabic novel that helped to initiate a new Arabic literature. It is certainly the most ambitious project ever attempted in Arabic fiction since *The Arabian Nights*, encompassing the entire modern history of a region that has evoked comparisons to Hardy's Wessex and Faulkner's Yoknapatawpha County. Beginning with *Al-tīh* (1984; *Cities of Salt*), through *Al-ukhdūd* (1985; *The Trench*), *Taqāsīm al-layl wa-al-nahār* (1989; *Variations on Night and Day*), *Al-munbatt* (1989; *The Uprooted*), and *Bādiyat al zulumāt* (1989; *The Desert of Darkness*) Munīf chronicles the impact of the oil boom on Arabia's inhabitants, economy, politics, and customs. The novel cycle is both an elegy for a departed way of life and a complex portrait of a transformed world, exposing the internal dynamics shaping the modern Middle East. As the Arab world increasingly presents a perplexing challenge to the West, Munīf's novel cycle is one of the best fictional resources to help readers come to grips with the region, its tensions, and values.

Munīf drew on his background and extensive knowledge of the Arabian Peninsula to create his epic work. Born in Jordan in 1933, Munīf is the son of a Saudi father and an Iraqi mother. He studied law in Baghdad and Cairo before completing a doctorate in petroleum economics at the University of Belgrade in 1961. He then worked as an oil economist in Baghdad and for OPEC, while editing the industry journal *Oil and Development*. His political activism resulted in his having his Saudi citizenship revoked in 1963. In Baghdad he became a close colleague of Palestinian literary figure Jabrā Ibrāhim Jabrā who encouraged Munīf to begin a writing career. Munīf's first novel, *The Trees and the Assassination*, appeared in 1973, sounding many of the dominant themes that would recur throughout his work: the falsification of Arab history and the struggle for freedom of expression and the discovery of authentic literary forms. Coming to the novel relatively late in a career that has forced him to consider the wide-ranging impact of economic change on an entire region, Munīf conceived his role as a novelist to fill in the gap in the unwritten history of Arabia. In Munīf's view, the history of the region has either been distorted by Westerners or by Arabs who have viewed their history from the misleading perspective of the powerful social elite. The story of ordinary Arabs and their culture has been consequently misunderstood or inadequately treated, and Munīf set out as a novelist to supply "the history of those who have no history, the history of the poor and the oppressed, as well as those who dream of a better world." The nexus of that history is the discovery of oil, which forced an unprecedented shift in a way of life, values, and beliefs. "As a sphere and a topic," Munīf has declared, "oil may help uncover some novelistic aspects in our contemporary life in the Arab world." The oil economy changed unalterably traditional Arabic culture, and, like Chinua Achebe in *Things Fall Apart*, who treated the impact of Western missionaries on African tribal life, Munīf registers what happened politically, economically, and psychically when the desert began to give up its buried treasure.

To chronicle the history of modern Arabia, Munīf puts at center stage for the first time in Arabic fiction ordinary characters caught between traditional values and the transformation brought by Western technology. Like Dos Passos in his *U.S.A.* trilogy, Munīf abandons the single protagonist hero for a collective protagonist made up of dozens of individual stories narrated in flashbacks, flash-forwards, and multiple perspectives conforming to Arabic oral tradition. Time and place in *Cities of Salt* are, in a sense, the central characters, and the reader must adjust expectations to deal with a writing style in which myth and history contend, joining the particular to the universal. In the first volume, Munīf begins by lovingly recreating the bucolic desert oasis of Wadi Al Uyoun in the years immediately following World War I. It is a society that values the collective and the traditional, and hence is ill prepared for the ethical dilemmas that come with the Westerners who begin to explore beneath the desert's surface. At first their activities merely baffle the inhabitants, but soon the Westerners begin to buy land and bulldoze the oasis to create an oil field. Munīf presents the transformation from the viewpoint of the Arabs who have no understanding of the technology the Westerners bring with them: "With the first light of dawn, huge iron machines began to move. Their deafening noise filled the whole wadi. So gigantic and strange were these iron machines that no one had ever imagined such things existed."

The emotional core of the entire novel sequence is the destruction of Wadi Al Uyoun as registered by the choral figure Miteb Al Hathal, one of the first to feel the threat posed by the Westerners:

> For anyone who remembers those long-ago days, when a place called Wadi Al Uyoun used to exist and a man named Miteb Al Hathal, and a brook, and trees, and a community of people used to exist, the three things that still break his heart in recalling those days are the tractors which attacked the orchards like ravenous wolves, tearing up the trees and throwing them to the earth one after another, and leveled all the orchards between the brook and the fields. After destroying the first grove of trees, the tractors turned to the next with the same bestial voracity and uprooted them. The trees shook violently and groaned before falling, cried for help, wailed, panicked, called out in helpless pain and then fell entreatingly to the ground, as if trying to snuggle into the earth to grow and spring forth alive again.
>
> The butchery of Wadi Al Uyoun had begun, and it continued until everything was gone. Miteb Al Hathal witnessed the beginning of the butchery but not the end, for the men who came when they heard the sounds of the maddened machines and stood watching what was taking place before them, after they recovered from the daze that possessed them, looked around and saw Ibn Hathal and made many sad comments. They said it was the first time in their lives that they had ever seen a man like Miteb Al Hathal cry.

Miteb Al Hathal disappears from the scene into legend, reappearing periodically as a reminder of a receding past and the increasingly antagonistic present. "He is a symbol of the great heroism of the past and also the hope for the future," Munīf has explained. "Miteb had children and his children will have children, meaning that hope is always there."

Keeping hope alive becomes the challenge as the oasis inhabitants are forced into the nearby town of Harrān ("the overheated") that is subdivided between the luxurious residences of the foreigners and the few Arabs who have profited from the oil boom and a teeming slum housing workers who swarm to the region along with prostitutes brought in to service the Western workers. As employees of a foreign oil company, Arab men are required to give up their camels, adopt Western-style dress, and relinquish their autonomy and cultural identity for a dubious kind of prosperity. Inevitably cultural discord, alienation, and social dislocation result. However, Munīf avoids a simplistic assignment of villainy and victimage. As writer Ivan Hill observes, "It is in his treatment of futile and destructive good intentions that Munīf excels." Westerners are more often than not naive blunderers rather than malicious, and the prime moral blame is usually assigned to Arab characters who exchange social responsibility for self-interest. At the center of the changes that *Cities of Salt* chronicles is the foreign-educated Syrian doctor Subhi Mahmilji, whose rise and fall through the modernization that he helps to implement will dominate the action of the entire sequence.

In the second volume, *The Trench*, the scene shifts to the capital, Mūrān ("the changeable"), and forward in time to the 1950s. Dr. Mahmilji has become the principal adviser of Sultan Khazael, characterized as an indolently corrupt leader more interested in appeasing his CIA contacts than in benefiting his people. The scheming Mahmilji is gradually undone by the forces of corruption and bribery by which he has profited when the sultan is deposed and succeeded by his brother, Sultan Fīnār. The third volume, *Variations on Night and Day*, provides a wider historical context for the political intrigues in the Arab state by chronicling the creation and expansion of the sultanate of Mūrān. Sultan Khazael's father is shown consolidating his power by eliminating his tribal rivals through the tacit support of the Westerners who prefer to deal with one strong leader rather than several contending powers. The novel introduces one of the sequence's strongest characters, the British adventurer Hamilton, modeled in part on T. E. Lawrence, who provides an outsider's perspective on a complicated series of palace intrigues and tribal conflicts. In the fourth volume, *The Uprooted*, narrative interest returns to Sultan Khazael, living in exile in Germany, and the final undoing of Dr. Mahmilji and his increasing isolation. The sultan, who has married one of Mahmilji's daughters, divorces her, and the doctor moves to Switzerland. His daughter commits suicide, and Mahmilji's wife abandons him for Mūrān and their son, who has sided with Sultan Fīnār. The fifth volume, *The Desert of Darkness*, chronicles Fīnār's reign up to his assassination at the hands of one of his relatives.

Cities of Salt is a remarkable use of the novel as a means of reinterpreting history that taps into the crucial dynamics underpinning modern Arabic society, not only on the geopolitical and cultural levels but on linguistic and narrative levels as well. Munīf's novel cycle provides a synthesis, much like the cultural clash he portrays between the Arabs and the West, by combining indigenous methods of an earlier oral tradition of storytelling and borrowings from experimental Western modernism. The result is both a more authentic history of a people and a region and a masterly demonstration of how traditional resources of Arabic culture can be resuscitated and reclaimed.

77

A FAREWELL TO ARMS

(1929)

by Ernest Hemingway

The Hemingway of Farewell to Arms, *the Joyce of* Dubliners, *the Keats of "The Eve of St. Agnes" [and] "The Grecian Urn," the* Daisy Miller *of Henry James, the Kipling of* The Drums of Fore and Aft *are great English classics.*

—F. Scott Fitzgerald in a letter to Martin Kroll, 1939

On the theory that only what is most fundamental will survive, the Hemingway of posterity may well be Hemingway the short story writer, not the novelist. His greatest strength is in the short form, the remarkable precision of what Barbara Kingsolver has called the main attribute of the short story: the telling of "large truths delivered in tight places." Hemingway revolutionized the modern short story with his vernacular and tight-lipped cadences and a strategy of indirection that suggests depths through omission. Such a narrative plan is less effective in the novel, a form that depends on continuity and amplitude. Hemingway's is an art of intensification by a lyrical narrative artist who shunned the epic. With this said, it still seems a grave omission to exclude Hemingway the novelist from consideration here. I have chosen *A Farewell to Arms* from his three novels that deserve a hearing among the best (the others being *The Sun Also Rises* and *For Whom the Bell Tolls*) for its historical significance as well as its artistic importance as the work that more than any other defines Hemingway's conception of the human condition and the dilemma of surviving with dignity faced by his protagonists. It is undeniably, along with Ford Madox Ford's *Parade's End*, one of the best fictional treatments of World War I. Moreover, it challenges Stephen Crane's *The Red Badge of Courage* as the essential American novel of warfare. It is also one of the defining modern love stories in which both romance and tragedy are radically reconceptualized in the context of contemporary experience.

There are few better depictions of the values that defined the post–World War I generation than Hemingway's. *A Farewell to Arms* unequivocally announces the writer's essential themes of war and survival that he will return to again and again, whether on the battlefield or in symbolic or ritualized versions in bullfighting, fishing, or big-game hunting. Hemingway's essential strengths are also unmistakably on display here: the vivid scenes and the brilliantly authentic dialogue. However, not all readers have joined in a chorus of praise for the novel's achievement. Even Holden Caulfield in J. D. Salinger's *A Catcher in the Rye* dismisses *A Farewell to Arms* as "phony," while others have resisted both its protagonists and its tragic theme. For Wyndham Lewis, Frederic Henry, the novel's narrator, is a "dull-witted, bovine, monosyllabic simpleton." Undoubtedly the greatest scorn has been heaped on Henry's lover, the English nurse Catherine Barkley, who has variously been described as a "passionate priestess," a "divine lollipop," an "inflated rubber doll woman," and condemned as a sorry excuse for Hemingway's fantasy, a pliant dream girl. Others, such as critic Edmund Wilson, have found in the novel melodramatic pathos rather than tragedy, with Catherine and Frederic seen as only "innocent victims with no relationship to the forces that torment them . . . merely an idealized relationship, the abstractions of a lyric emotion." It may be impossible to meet and defeat all these charges, but the novel survives the assault with Hemingway's considerable strengths undiminished, derived from the writer's insistence that war is the permanent, universal condition of modern life, that human existence is a battle with an indifferent Nature that "can have only one end." In such a conception neither tragedy nor romance can ever have the same meaning again.

The autobiographical coordinates for *A Farewell to Arms* matter, if only to underscore the degree of Hemingway's invention and artistic control. First and subsequent readers have assumed that the novel's eyewitness quality and remarkable authenticity must have derived from firsthand experience. Like Frederic Henry, the novel's narrator, Hemingway served on the Italian front in an ambulance corps, though under the Red Cross, not the Italian army. The novel commences in the summer of 1915 with Italy's entry into the war and covers the 1917 Caporetto retreat through the spring of 1918 and Catherine Barkley's death in childbirth. This precedes Hemingway's summer 1918 arrival in the war zone. Hemingway's much-admired reconstruction of the Caporetto debacle, regarded by many as one of the most authentic depictions of war in literature, was based, therefore, not on firsthand observation of the actual event but imagined with the help of details Hemingway derived from his coverage of the Greek retreat in the Greco-Turkish War of 1922. Like Frederic Henry, Hemingway was wounded in a trench mortar explosion and hospitalized in Milan, where he began an affair with a nurse. Hemingway's autobiographical experiences, however, are closer to what he revealed in "A Very Short Story" in the collection *In Our Time* (1925) in which a wounded officer is humiliatingly dumped by his nurse lover. The writer, therefore, had no direct knowledge of the Italian front from 1915 through the spring of 1918, nor did his own experience in love or war suggest the tragic shape that he refashioned from the bits and pieces of his own war experience to create *A Farewell to Arms.*

Tragedy in fact dominates Hemingway's conception of his novel. He referred to *A Farewell to Arms* as his *Romeo and Juliet* and observed, "The fact that the book was a tragic one did not make me unhappy since I believed that life was a tragedy and knew it could only have one end." Hemingway's initiation of Frederic Henry into a full realization of the tragic dimensions of existence supplies the novel's considerable power, derived from a universalization of the war experience and its painful cost. As Hemingway's editor, Maxwell Perkins, summarized, the novel shows "how everything is conditioned, and indeed contaminated, by war—and how a purely physical attempt at seduction grew, in spite of everything, into love."

As in a conventional tragedy, the novel is arranged into five act-like books. The first introduces the narrator, Frederic Henry, an American architecture student, who joins the Italian army's ambulance corps when Italy enters the war in 1915. Henry's motivation for his participation is unstated or unknown. "There isn't always an explanation for everything" is the best he can manage, and his initial reaction to his circumstances is as a detached observer, sustained by drinking and whoring. The war, he remarks, "did not have anything to do with me. It seemed no more dangerous to me myself than war in the movies." Henry has safely retreated behind a protective shell of indifference. His conscience may be briefly stirred by the idealism and faith of the young priest in the officer's mess, but he follows the example of the hedonistic nihilism of Doctor Rinaldi, who introduces him to Catherine Barkley. At first Henry intends only a seduction and regards his pursuit of Catherine as play: "I knew I did not love Catherine Barkley nor had any idea of loving her. This was a game, like bridge, in which you said things instead of playing cards. Like bridge you had to pretend you were playing for money or playing for some stakes. Nobody had mentioned what the stakes were. It was all right with me."

The stakes escalate both in love and war, forcing the formerly callow Henry to become an intimate participant in both. At the front Henry is wounded in an explosion that forces a recognition about the terrifying human cost of the war. Choosing life over death as he recuperates in the hospital in Milan, Henry consummates his affair with Catherine in Book Two, and the pair manages a brief, idyllic, life-affirming alternative to the fighting. Catherine becomes pregnant, and Henry, now fully committed to her, returns to the front in Book Three, only to experience an escalating disillusionment. He is thrust into the chaos of the Caporetto retreat in which every semblance of military order and purpose beyond elemental survival breaks down. Henry fails to save his ambulance crew, and he is seized by the Italian authorities and marked for execution for cowardice. Betrayed by his own side, Henry escapes by jumping into a river and swimming to safety, making his separate peace. The experience is transformative, and Henry must develop a new language and a new set of values to comprehend the change that his experience of combat has forced:

> I was always embarrassed by the words sacred, glorious, and sacrifice and the expression in vain. . . . I had seen nothing sacred, and the things that were glorious had no glory and the sacrifices were like the stockyards at Chicago if nothing was done with the meat except to bury it. There were many words that you could not stand to hear and finally only the names of places had dignity. . . . Abstract words such as glory, honor, courage, or hallow were obscene beside the concrete names of villages, the numbers of roads, the names of rivers, the numbers of regiments and the dates.

Henry responds by reducing all to the barest essentials: "Eat and drink and sleep with Catherine . . . and never going away again except together."

To act on his desire, Henry reunites with Catherine at Stresa, and the two escape by boat across the lake to Switzerland with Henry's separate peace now expanded into a union, sustained by his commitment that his highest value, as he explains to Count Greffi, is "Some one I love." However, the lovers are allowed only a few months of peace in the alpine winter. When spring comes, so too does the rain, the novel's leitmotif for disaster, and the couple moves to Lausanne to be near the hospital when the baby is due.

In the novel's shattering conclusion, Catherine dies delivering a stillborn child, making Hemingway's point clear that there can be no such thing as a separate peace, no safe neutrality, and that war and the threat of sudden death are part of the steady state of human existence. As Henry bitterly insists, "If people bring so much courage to this world the world has to kill them to break them, so of course it kills them. The world breaks every one and afterward many are strong at the broken places. But those that will not break it kills. It kills the very good and the very gentle and the very brave impartially. If you are none of these you can be sure it will kill you too but there will be no special hurry." Hemingway's Romeo and Juliet are not star-crossed but war-crossed lovers, and love is conceived as not an opposite of war but related with the threat of extinction expanded to include battlefield and bedroom. Stripped of poetic justice, without the ability to reap any bounty from his hard-earned lessons in engagement, Frederic Henry is left at the end of the novel a casualty of an ongoing conflict that will have no armistice: "After a while I went out and left the hospital and walked back to the hotel in the rain." Having developed from someone who tries to live as if nothing very much matters to someone made to care passionately about life and love, Frederic Henry must now begin the characteristic process of all Hemingway's protagonists, learning how to live with the inevitable pain of the vulnerable.

78

THE DEATH OF ARTEMIO CRUZ

(1962)

by Carlos Fuentes

The Death of Artemio Cruz *had an immediate influence upon younger writers in the rest of Latin America as well as in Spain. Its experimental structure influenced the nascent movement that would eventually be called the Boom in Latin American literature and the "New Novel" in the Iberian Peninsula.* The Death of Artemio Cruz, *arguably one of the first truly postmodernist novels in the Hispanic world, will remain in the canon for generations to come.*

—Genaro J. Pérez, "*The Death of Artemio Cruz* by Carlos Fuentes," in *The Encyclopedia of the Novel*

If it is true, as many have claimed, that the history of the novel in the second half of the 20th century has been essentially written by Latin American and Hispanic writers, then Carlos Fuentes's *The Death of Artemio Cruz* is one of the era's first undisputed modernist Hispanic masterworks. It is generally regarded, in the words of Genaro J. Pérez, as "the first successful literary portrait of the geography, history, ethnic configuration, and social makeup of Mexico." The work is further significant and influential in its treatment of its social, historical, and psychological themes with an experimental method incorporating elements from European and American modernists, including Proust, Joyce, and Faulkner. Fuentes helped redirect sophisticated linguistic structures to explore significant social themes, while tapping the rich vein of history, myth, and customs that would help to create an unprecedented revitalization of Hispanic literature.

The Death of Artemio Cruz treats the life experiences of one man to explore Mexican identity and reflect modern Mexican history from the Revolution of 1910–20 through its contemporary aftermath. In 1959 the 71-year-old, powerful, and corrupt Mexican business tycoon Artemio Cruz has been stricken by a gastric attack. He regains consciousness as the novel opens and gradually becomes aware of those surrounding his deathbed, including his wife, Catalina, and his daughter, Teresa, both of whom hate him. Cruz's life story will unfold in nonchronological flashbacks of 12 pivotal days in his life, ranging from 1889 to 1955, coinciding with the 12 hours of life that Cruz has remaining. His physical deterioration and moral, spiritual, and psychological dissolution are reflected by the novel's unusual and challenging narrative method, which alternates first, second, and third person perspectives to objectify Cruz's fragmentation and self-division. The "I" of Cruz's present and the "he" of a third person perspective on the past, linking Cruz's experiences with the wider historical scene, are joined with a "you" narrator that Fuentes has called "a third element, the subconscious, a kind of Virgil that guides [Cruz] through the twelve circles of hell, and that is the other face of his mirror, the other face of Artemio Cruz: the you that speaks in the future tense. It is the subconscious that clings to a future that the I—the dying old man—will never know. The old I is the present while the He digs up the past of Artemio Cruz." A kind of symphony of voices or a narrative fugue results that Fuentes characterizes as "a dialogue of mirrors between three people, the three times that constitute the life of this hard and alienated character. In his agony, Artemio tries to regain through memory his twelve definitive days, days which are really twelve options." Having reached his terminal point, Cruz is therefore forced to revisit the key crossroads in his life that brought him to his dying present. The result is a rich and varied exploration of a complex character of whom critic John Brushwood has stated that "I doubt that there is anywhere in fiction a character whose wholeness is more apparent than is the case of Artemio Cruz." Fuentes raises the idealist turned corrupt power broker to the level of a national and universal symbol representing the human forces that betrayed the revolution and reflect what Mexico has become: moribund and corrupted.

Since the novel's title announces Cruz's death, narrative suspense is generated by forcing the reader to reassemble the dying man's nonsequential past life into a coherent and cohesive pattern of meaning. The episodes shift back and forth in time and alternating viewpoints, but when chronologically ordered, they reveal the remarkable career of an illegitimate son of a plantation owner and a mulatto servant. Artemio's father was a wealthy hacendado who raped his mother and then ran her off his estate. Born on the *petate*, the mat symbolic of the peon's condition, Cruz's only friend is the mulatto servant Lunero, his mother's brother who raises him until Artemio is 13. In an attempt to prevent Lunero's being taken away by a neighboring tobacco grower, Artemio kills a man and Lunero is shot dead. Artemio flees to Veracruz, where he is educated by a schoolmaster who inspires him with revolutionary ideals. When the revolution begins, in 1910, Cruz joins the rebels. He unexpectedly falls in love with the Indian woman he rapes during the fighting, Regina, who becomes his first and greatest love. In 1913 federal troops kill all the inhabitants of a village in which rebels have taken refuge. Included among the victims is Regina. In 1915 Cruz is captured by a rival revolutionary force and imprisoned along with a young lawyer, Gonzalo Bernal. He reveals that his father owns a hacienda and that he has a sister named Catalina. Before Bernal is shot, Cruz bargains with his captors for his own safety by providing the intelligence they seek. Cruz's complicity in Bernal's death and his betrayal of his comrades become defining turning points, or in Fuentes's word, "options," in Cruz's life that will have far-reaching implications. The incident also marks the severest violation of Cruz's ideals and virtues that will alienate him from aspects of himself, and which will remain repressed until revisited through memory on his deathbed.

In 1919, discharged from the army as a colonel, Cruz conceives the scheme to introduce himself to the landowning family of Gonzalo Bernal, ingratiate himself as Bernal's dying companion, and marry Gonzalo's sister Catalina to achieve the respectable background he requires to further his ambitions. Catalina, though skeptical of Cruz's story and motives, eventually relents and marries him. She will love him physically but comes to loathe him for using her dead brother, her family, and ultimately herself to advance his willful rapaciousness. In violation of the ideals of the revolution, Cruz builds a financial empire by seizing others' land through deception and manipulation. With wealth comes power, and Cruz is elected to congress largely on the strength of his bogus contribution to agrarian reform. He will deal in bribes and corrupt business schemes with U.S. firms anxious to exploit the unstable Mexican political circumstances. Taking his family to live in Mexico City, Cruz, in a loveless marriage, surrounds himself with sycophantic friends and associates in a grand mansion decorated with Mexican antiques, suggesting that the culture he has violated has been translated into a commodity for display to gratify Cruz's high conception of himself.

Fuentes presents his central character with considerable subtlety and complexity. Despite his venality and ruthlessness, Cruz's humanity and affection for others are in evidence, particularly in Cruz's loyalty to the peon Lunero, his great love, Regina, and especially for his son Lorenzo. Cruz eventually triumphs in the battle of control over Lorenzo with Catalina and creates an alternative version of his own background for his son to fulfill the idealistic aspirations Cruz has betrayed, as Lorenzo goes to fight for the Republican cause in Spain, where he is killed.

Cruz is offered a final option to choose love over gain and power by his mistress Laura, who cares little for his money and presents him with an ultimatum: Leave his loveless marriage or forgo Laura's love. Cruz opts for the status quo.

By the end of the novel, it is clear that Artemio Cruz's life has been a betrayal of everything and everyone he once held dear: his principles, his family, his lovers, his country. At various points Cruz consistently rejected love, selflessness, and ideals for self-gain. The revolutionary has become a bourgeois captain of industry and power in post-revolutionary Mexico that is a corrupt sham. Cruz is forced to confront his bitter legacy: "You will bequeath the futile dead names . . . men despoiled of their names that you might possess yours." To achieve his ambitions, Cruz has had to violate, deny, and destroy aspects of himself, and by reassembling his memories as his life ticks down to death he finally integrates his experiences into a totality that demonstrates who he is and what he has become. His final memory is that of his birth, coinciding with his death, in which the three divided voices—past, present, and future—finally merge into one in a cacophony of accusation before subsiding into silence:

> I don't know . . . I don't know . . . if I am he . . . if you were he . . . if I am the three . . . You . . . I carry you inside me and you are going to die with me . . . God. . . . They say . . . Eat, gnaw . . . The hemorrhaged substance runs out of your open stomach . . . They say, repeat . . . "Useless" . . . "useless" . . . all three . . . the coagulation wrenches itself from the black blood . . . will run, will stop . . . stopped . . . your silence . . . your open eyes . . . which cannot feel . . . your black, blue nails . . . your shuddering jaws . . . Artemio Cruz . . . name . . . "Useless" . . . "Heart" . . . "Massage" . . . "Useless" . . . You will no longer know . . . I carried you within and I shall die with you . . . all three . . . We shall die . . . You . . . are dying . . . have died . . . I shall die

The Death of Artemio Cruz is a tour de force of historical reexamination that achieves through its demanding though accomplished experimental methods a brilliant verbal texture of both breadth and depth, a panorama of Mexican political and social history that never loses its human focus, helping the reader understand the human motives behind great events and their damaging human costs.

79

HERZOG

(1964)

by Saul Bellow

In Herzog *one could say that Bellow is attempting to combine what he discerned as the separate strands of the American novel, but depicting a sensibility oppressed by too much information. The single sensibility cannot hope to triumph over the waves of incoming information . . . but it is the effort of the book not to let the information completely annihilate that part of the sensibility which is in fact the core of the self. Thus it is a book about a man breaking down . . . but also seeking to arrive at a new form of integration; the energy of the book is aimed at recomposing the "decomposing" self.*

—Tony Tanner, *City of Words*

When *Herzog* was published in 1964, it was immediately acclaimed a triumph. Called by Brendan Gill "a well-nigh faultless novel" and by Malcolm Bradbury the author's "most conclusively expressed and densest book" and one of "the fullest and most explored presentations of modern experience we have," *Herzog* became what a dense presentation of modern experience usually is not: a best-seller. The novel, with its assault on victimhood, on the "cheap mental stimulants of Alienation," with its attempt to find a way out of the morass of self-obsession and cultural nihilism, struck a popular chord among readers wearied by a persistent modernist ethos of pessimistic defeat. The book was in turn attacked by some as sentimental, confused, and pretentious, with critic John W. Aldridge, for example, charging the novel with "heaving a fatty sigh of middle-class intellectual contentment." Others objected to the novel's affirmation being imposed rather than earned. Despite complaints about Bellow's methods and his meaning, *Herzog* is unavoidable, one of the most challenging novels of ideas written by an American in the second half of the 20th century. It is a daring, ironic comedy about a man overwhelmed with ideas struggling to fashion a code to halt his decline. It casts the intellectual in the role of the schlemiel and universalizes the fate of the modern individual in the disintegration and regeneration of Moses Herzog.

The novel begins with one of the great opening lines in modern fiction: "If I am out of my mind, it's all right with me, thought Moses Herzog." Herzog is a 48-year-old Jewish-American academic, alone in his dilapidated country house in Ludeyville, Massachusetts. Twice married and twice divorced, Herzog is trying to cope with the betrayal he feels after his second wife, Madeleine, has become the lover of his best friend, Valentine Gersbach, and is living with him and Herzog's daughter June in Chicago. The trauma has forced Herzog to reexamine his life and his failures as a son, husband, father, friend, citizen, and scholar: "Late in the spring Herzog had been overcome by the need to explain, to have it out, to justify, to put in perspective, to clarify, to make amends." The novel proceeds by flashback as Herzog examines his past and the more recent series of events that has led to his coming to rest in his Berkshire retreat and the precarious balance he has managed to achieve between madness and sanity, despair and hope, collapse and reconstruction.

Herzog's ambition to complete a grand cultural synthesis by writing the definitive account of Romanticism has floundered. Intending to expose "the last of the Romantic errors about the uniqueness of the self," in which the drive for self-supremacy inevitably results in despair, Herzog has fallen into that very morass of self-obsession and self-pity. Having gained a foothold in "White Anglo-Saxon Protestant America," he finds himself an outcast and outsider. Now on the fringe of academic life, Herzog teaches adult education courses. His lectures have degenerated into obsessive rambles and rants expressive of his feelings of betrayal by his family, friends, and an ever growing list of contemporary or historical figures, including Martin Luther King, Willie Sutton, Pierre Teilhard de Chardin, Jawaharlal Nehru, Friedrich Nietzsche, Adlai Stevenson, Baruch Spinoza, and many others to whom he communicates in a series of unmailed letters. Herzog's overall theme is his disappointment in contemporary life and the failure of any system of value, order, and belief that can serve to resolve the chaos he experiences or relieve the despair he feels. Balancing his self-pity is a self-lacerating streak that is fully conscious of what he calls his "victim bit." Characteristically, in Shelleyan overdramatization, Herzog recognizes his tendency toward self-indulgence: "And then? I fall upon the thorns of life, I bleed. And what next? I get laid, I take a short holiday, but very soon after I fall upon those same thorns with gratification in pain or suffering in joy—who knows what the mixture is!"

Intimately connected with his intellectual disappointments are his domestic, emotional failures that point up his neuroses, which cycle between order and chaos. Herzog's first wife, Daisy, offered him stability and support, but Herzog found her dull and uninspiring. "What happened? I gave up the shelter of an orderly, purposeful, lawful existence because it bored me, and I felt it was simply a slacker's life." Instead he winds up with Daisy's antithesis, Madeleine, who is disorderly and destructive in the extreme. Having betrayed

Herzog, she sets the terms for his victim role in their domestic melodrama: "The knife and the wound asking for each other."

Herzog, therefore, has reached a crisis point in which no intellectual or emotional answer is able to relieve the combined guilt and distress he feels over the wreckage of his life. In Yeatsian terms, "the center cannot hold." Herzog flees the ministrations of his current mistress, Ramona, by train to friends on Martha's Vineyard, only to return to New York as soon as he arrives: "Have to go back," he writes his hosts. "Not able to stand kindness at this time. Feeling, heart, everything in strange condition. Unfinished business." One piece of that unfinished business is to try to regain custody of his daughter, and Herzog arranges to meet his lawyer at the courthouse to discuss his chances. While there, Herzog witnesses a series of court hearings, all comically and tragically confirming his view of the degradation of modern life and the inability of any philosophical system to understand and cope with it. One case in particular, the trial of a mother charged with the beating death of her three-year-old child, triggers Herzog's fear for his own daughter's safety, and he departs for Chicago assuming the role of avenger and rescuer. Going to his stepmother's house, Herzog retrieves his father's pistol and sets out to kill his betrayer, Valentine Gersbach. He finds, however, not the scene he requires to complete the melodrama he has constructed with himself as the heroic savior of his imperiled daughter but a loving domestic scene of Valentine giving Junie a bath: "To shoot him!—an absurd thought," Herzog realizes: "As soon as Herzog saw the actual person giving an actual bath, the reality of it, the tenderness of such a buffoon to a little child, his intended violence turned into *theater*, into something ludicrous." Herzog is finally shocked into the recognition that paves the way for his recovery. Herzog has failed as a father and a husband, both roles Gersbach has now assumed, and his former friend has been cast in the role of a scapegoat, concealing the true nature of Herzog's dilemma: "Moses refused to know evil. But he could not refuse to experience it. And therefore others were appointed to do it to him, and then to be accused (by him) of wickedness." Evading the true source of his torment, Herzog faces the recognition that "Only self-hatred could lead him to ruin himself because his heart was 'broken.' How could it be broken by such a pair?" The insight proves crucial for Herzog's recovery. Valentine Gersbach, Madeleine, Herzog's life and identity have proven to be far more complex than Herzog previously admitted. This insight becomes the first step in Herzog's halting his slide into confusion and despair and forging a new sense of coherence and a revitalized identity. Bellow would later observe in an interview:

> My novel deals with the humiliating sense that results from the American mixture of private concerns and intellectual interest. That is something which most readers of the book seem utterly to have missed. . . .

> To me, a significant theme of *Herzog* is the imprisonment of the individual in a shameful and impotent privacy. He feels humiliated by it; he struggles comically with it; and he comes to realize at last that what he has considered his intellectual "privilege" has proved to be another form of bondage. Anyone who misses this misses the point of the book. Any *Bildungsroman* . . . concludes with the first steps. The first *real* steps. Any man who has rid himself of superfluous ideas in order to take that first step has done something significant.

After a traffic accident and an arrest for carrying a concealed weapon, Herzog is bailed out by his brother and retreats to his country house in the Berkshires. In its ruined garden, a tangle of weeds and blossoms that symbolically mirrors his life and mind, Herzog sheds his "superfluous ideas," accepts the conditions of his untended garden, and makes his peace with the past and the world. "We love apocalypse too much," he observes, "and crisis ethics and florid extremism with its thrilling language. Excuse me, no. I've had all the monstrosity I want. We've reached an age in the history of mankind when we can ask about certain persons, 'What is this Thing?' No more of that for me—no, no! I am simply a human being, more or less." Herzog has learned the lesson that the drive toward self-supremacy results in self-hatred and an accompanying puerile whine when the world inevitably does not conform to the ego's massive needs. Chaos is life's order, and the individual and the intellectual can do little to resist its processes. As Tony Tanner ably summarizes, "The will to deny the universal truth of the law of entropy is what drives Herzog on, even though in his own disintegrating state he is an ambiguous witness against it. He feels the presence of something in the sheer fact of life which is more positive and more important than the bleak though undeniable fact that even in life we are in the midst of death. Life is not only about its own inevitable decline." Herzog ultimately finds a way out of his nihilistic box by embracing and affirming experience without the need for resolving matters. Ultimately his is a lesson in self-awareness and self-acceptance: "Myself is thus and so," Herzog realizes, "and will continue thus and so. And why fight it? My balance comes from instability."

Herzog mounts a counteroffensive against the conventional wisdom that "the human being is through," in Bellow's phrase. "We have had," he writes, "a bellyful of a species of wretchedness which is thoroughly pleased with itself." Herzog's recovery, then, is Bellow's more universal prescription for coping in a modern world that refuses to make sense, in which responsibility is far too easy to evade, and self-deception is at the core of the individual's tendency to claim little other than victimhood. Bellow has asked "After absurdity, what . . .?" *Herzog* represents one possible response.

CANDIDE

80

(1759)

by Voltaire

With so much sunshine at command,
Why light with darkness mix?
Why dash with pain our pleasure?
—Edward Young, *Resignation*, 1762, addressing Voltaire's *Candide*

If, as is often contended, all novels derive from a handful of archetypal stories, then surely *Candide* is one of these: the adventures of a young naive hero introduced to the ways of the world and forced to reassess his inadequate worldview. Voltaire takes the convention of the picaresque novel and grafts onto its episodic comedy and satire an intellectual seriousness that was new to the novel in the 18th century. Goethe described his *Faust* as a "very serious jest," a characterization that certainly applies to Voltaire's book as well. *Candide* is a synthesis of fiction and philosophy linked with such earlier narrative hybrids as François Rabelais's *Gargantua and Pantagruel* (1532–34), Thomas More's *Utopia* (1516), Francis Bacon's *New Atlantis* (1626), John Bunyan's *The Pilgrim's Progress* (1678), and Jonathan Swift's *Gulliver's Travels* (1726), as well as the writings of Voltaire's contemporaries, such as Montesquieu, Diderot, and Samuel Johnson, whose own philosophical narrative fable, *Rasselas*, appeared the same year as *Candide*. Voltaire's *contes philosophiques*, the greatest of which is *Candide*, supplied an alternative route for the emerging realistic novel, provoking the reader's thoughts rather than feelings, replacing an identification with character and scene with an ironical, critical distancing that foregrounds the novel's clash of ideas. Echoes of Voltaire's reconception of the novel as secularized allegory and intellectual fable in *Candide* can be found in the works of authors as different as Kafka, Mann, Sartre, Beckett, Camus, and Rushdie. H. N. Brailsford contended that *Candide* "ranks in its own way with *Don Quixote* and *Faust*," as one of the world's great moral fables. It is ironic that the work Voltaire regarded as a mere "bagatelle," judged inferior to his plays, poetry, and essays, would become the only one of his works that continues to be regularly read and maintains his place as a literary giant.

Voltaire's remarkable rise to become Europe's preeminent intellectual force in the 18th century spans the entire Enlightenment period, from the reign of Louis XIV to the years immediately preceding the French Revolution. A confidant of kings and emperors and an inspiration of revolutionaries, Voltaire spent a lifetime on the attack as an instigator against the irrational, superstitious, and hypocritical and a proponent of intellectual freedom, social reform, and religious tolerance. Like Candide, Voltaire was a man displaced in his search for truth. A frequent exile, condemned as well as courted, Voltaire pursued an often elusive safe haven from France to England, Prussia, and Switzerland before eventually coming to rest, like Candide on his farm near Constantinople, at a large estate at Ferney in France, near the Swiss border, purchased in 1759, the year *Candide* was published. Interestingly, Voltaire's own life search for an ideal residence and way to live amid the evil of the world patterned both the philosophical journey of his protagonist and his resting point.

Several factors contributed to the creation of *Candide* and the darkening of Voltaire's worldview from the moderate, rational optimism of his first important philosophical statement in his *Lettres philosophiques* (1734). In 1749 Voltaire's patron and mistress, Madame du Châtelet, died suddenly. Forced out of her chateau at Cirey, Voltaire moved on to the Prussian court of Frederick II at Berlin from 1750 to 1753 before quarrels caused Voltaire to relocate to Geneva. This Calvinist stronghold promised a sympathetic reception for Voltaire's anticlerical sentiment, but again he was disappointed and soon on the move. In 1755 an earthquake struck Lisbon, and the perishing of some 100,000 people in the disaster prompted Voltaire to meditate on the nature of evil in the world and specifically the benign optimistic philosophy that attempted to rationalize it away. His long philosophical poem, *Poème sur le désastre de Lisbonne* (1756) carried the subtitle: "Examination of the Axiom: *All is Well*," and targeted both the philosophy of Gottfried Leibnitz and Alexander Pope's famous sentiment from his *Essay on Man:*

> All Nature is but Art, unknown to thee;
> All Chance, Direction which thou canst not see;
> All Discord, Harmony not understood;
> All partial Evil, universal Good:
> And, spite of Pride, in erring Reason's spite,
> One truth is clear, "Whatever is, is Right."

In 1756 the outbreak of the Seven Years' War between England and France added human evil to natural manifestations, and Voltaire began in 1758 to envision his response to both. While staying at a castle belonging to the Margrave of Baden-Durlach in Karlsruhe, Voltaire conceived *Candide.* Locked in his room for four days, Voltaire reputedly emerged with his manuscript, handing it over to his niece with the words, "Here, curious Madame, is something you may read." Published anonymously in 1759, *Candide* became a sensation throughout Europe. Before the end of the year, at least 17 editions had appeared, in Paris, Geneva, London, and Amsterdam. Through the initial controversy that greeted the novel as subversive (it was denounced in Geneva as "full of dangerous principles concerning religion and tending to moral depravation") Voltaire coyly pleaded innocence to the charge of authorship. "It is said that some people are brazen enough to claim that I am the author of this work," he wrote to a friend, "which I have never laid eyes on." He would subsequently acknowledge ownership and in 1761 issued a revised and augmented edition.

Candide, or Optimism is a rollicking, ironic tour de force that chronicles the adventures of a naive young hero who is expelled from the novel's initial utopia, the castle of the baron of Thunder-ten-Tronckh, for being caught in the embrace of the baron's daughter, Cunégonde. Forced into the wider world where he is beset by a crushing array of human vice and corruption, Candide is initially armed only with the philosophical principles of his tutor, Pangloss, who reduces the optimistic sentiment, "All is well," to a rationalized absurdity:

> —It is clear, said he, that things cannot be otherwise than they are, for since everything is made to serve an end, everything necessarily serves the best end. Observe: noses were made to support spectacles, hence we have spectacles. Legs, as anyone can plainly see, were made to be breeched, and so we have breeches. Stones were made to be shaped and to build castles with; thus My Lord has a fine castle, for the greatest Baron in the province should have the finest house, and since pigs were made to be eaten, we eat pork all year round. Consequently, those who say everything is well are uttering mere stupidities, they should say everything is for the best.

Pangloss's concept that this is best of all possible worlds, his optimism that is later defined by Candide as "the mania for asserting that all is well when one is not," is put to the test as Candide is tricked into the army, beaten, abused, and learns that the baron and his family have been murdered, their castle destroyed, his beloved raped, and his tutor ravaged by a sexual disease. Pangloss is unfazed and continues to justify the worst kinds of evil as benevolence and utility in disguise. Such a facile approach to human experience, used to justify a wide range of human misery and atrocities, is effectively demolished by Voltaire's plot, which tests optimism under increasingly more trying circumstances and exposes the various dogmas and fanaticism that insulate the individual from dealing honestly with reality. Voltaire's catalog of human misery includes natural disasters, human ailments, war, religious persecution, and their accompanying social and personal ideologies of religious superstition, nationalism, and colonialism. Neither the idea of the progress of civilization nor the Rousseau-like faith in primitive innocence offers any lasting consolation.

Candide becomes a witness of the Lisbon earthquake, a victim of the auto-da-fé that apparently claims Pangloss's life to prevent further disasters, but is happily reunited with the miraculously resurrected Cunégonde. They sail to South America, where Candide experiences three versions of utopian societies: the Jesuit theocracy in Paraguay, the primitive land of the Oreillons, and the ideal, fantastical realm of Eldorado. Each is found wanting. The Jesuits rule through oppression of the native populace; the noble savage Oreillons are cannibals who cohabitate with monkeys. Even Eldorado, which is free from want and ruled by reason, ultimately fails to content Candide for long. Armed with the worthless gold and precious stones of Eldorado, he returns to Europe. Having shown Candide as a victim of his poverty, Voltaire now dramatizes what happens to a wealthy Candide, whose victimization continues unabated. He is now possessed of a new mentor, the Manichean pessimist Martin, who regards this as the worst of all possible worlds, a philosophy as untenable as Pangloss's optimism because it paralyzes through fatalism and despair.

In the end, Candide forms his own philosophy between the equally unworkable extremes of optimism and pessimism. Finally reunited yet again with his old tutor Pangloss and his beloved Cunégonde, who has lost her beauty and turned into a shrew, Candide comes to rest on a small farm near Constantinople. Candide is determined "to take care of his garden," offering a modest solution of meliorism based on human labor, cooperation, and an acceptance of the duality of good and evil that forms the totality of human experience. Suspended between a limited engaged activism and a tragic awareness of moral and social shortcomings, Candide reaches Voltaire's ideal and articulates the author's realization that man and society, although far from perfect, are perfectible, at least in the hope that positives can develop from facing the truth.

Voltaire's message is delivered in his brilliantly witty ironic arrangement of situation and characters' reactions that leave few illusions about man's fate or capabilities intact. Both the novel of growth and development—the classic bildungsroman—and the novel of sentiment of the hero's adventures in love are pressed into service as a vehicle to engage the reader in the pursuit of truth and a widened conception of the world and human nature. Ultimately, *Candide* operates as a kind of extended shock therapy to restore Voltaire's version of mental health, the liberation from crippling delusions and codes of behavior that enslave.

THE SLEEPWALKERS

81

(1932)

by Hermann Broch

There is . . . a radical difference between The Sleepwalkers *and the other great twentieth-century "frescoes" (those of Proust, Musil, Thomas Mann, etc.): In Broch, it is continuity neither of action nor of biography (a character's or a family's) that provides the unity of the whole. It is something else, something less apparent, less apprehensible, something hidden: the continuity of one theme (that of man facing the process of a disintegration of values).*

—Milan Kundera, "Notes Inspired by *The Sleepwalkers*"

Of all the great, experimental European modernist masters, Hermann Broch is perhaps the most unexpected and the least known. He began writing at the age of 45 after a 20-year career in his family's textile business. Intellectually drawn to the study of philosophy, Broch came to literature only because he felt that the logical positivism that dominated the Viennese school at the time had abandoned an exploration of metaphysics that Broch came to believe could best be accomplished by the novel. Described by Hannah Arendt as "a writer malgré lui," Broch rejected the notion of "art for art's sake" and deprecated his own "temptation to tell stories" for an "ethical art" that followed literature's "mission toward a cognition that embraces totality." His first major work is the trilogy *Die Schlafwandler* (1931–32), translated as *The Sleepwalkers* (1932), one of the most intellectually ambitious and innovative novels of the 20th century that invites comparison with the other great synthesizing and encyclopedic modernist texts, including Joyce's *Ulysses*, Proust's *In Search of Lost Time*, Mann's *The Magic Mountain*, Musil's *The Man Without Qualities*, Dos Passos's *U.S.A. Trilogy*, and Döblin's *Berlin Alexanderplatz*. According to the critic Theodore Ziolkowski, "It was to be the first attempt at an 'epistemological' novel, in contrast to the psychological novel that was currently fashionable." In it Broch intended to delve "back behind psychological motivation to basic epistemological attitudes and to the actual logic and plausibility of values." *The Sleepwalkers* ambitiously attempts nothing less than a comprehensive account of the intellectual and moral forces in Germany that culminated in World War I and a diagnosis of the metaphysical patterns underlying the modern age. Although its intellectual complexity and stylistic innovation initially failed to find a popular audience, *The Sleepwalkers* was immediately appreciated by fellow writers. Thomas Mann described it as "intellectually rich and stimulating"; Hermann Hesse ranked *The Sleepwalkers* among the greatest of contemporary fiction. In its English translation, *The Sleepwalkers* gained the attention and respect of T. S. Eliot, Stephen Spender, Thornton Wilder, and Aldous Huxley, who reported that "I read the trilogy with steadily increasing admiration. It is the work of a mind of extraordinary power and depth, and at the same time of extraordinary subtlety and sensitivity—of a philosopher who is also an artist of exceptional refinement and purity. It is a difficult book that makes great demands of the reader—nothing less than his whole mind at the highest pitch of attention. Not at all a book for tired business men! But I hope, all the same, that it will be widely read; for it is manifestly a work of first-rate importance." Wider recognition of his achievement would come only after Broch's death in 1951 when the stature of *The Sleepwalkers* was secured as one of the landmark novels of the 20th century.

Born in Vienna in 1886, Broch was the son of a Jewish wholesaler of textiles who acquired a textile factory at Teesdorf, outside of Vienna, in 1906. Broch was designated by his imperious father for a business career in the family firm, despite his son's interests in humanistic studies. After graduating from the Imperial and Royal State Secondary School, Broch attended a textile institute in Vienna, while, against his father's wishes, registering for courses in mathematics and philosophy at the University of Vienna. Broch continued his training as a textile engineer in Alsace and made a six-week trip to the United States to inspect cotton mills there. He returned to work at the Teesdorf factory, becoming its director in 1909. Broch converted to Catholicism before marrying the daughter of a well-to-do sugar manufacturer, Franziska von Rothermann, with whom he had a son in 1910 and divorced in 1923. After his father retired in 1915, Broch took control of the family business and for the next decade became, in his words, "a captain of industry," supervising mills, directing a local military hospital during the war, serving on various government advisory councils, and gaining a reputation as a skilled labor mediator.

During this period, however, Broch also engaged in what he called his "double profession" that combined his business activities with his intellectual interests and involvement with the Viennese literary and intellectual circles that included Robert Musil, Franz Blei, and Alfred Polgar. Beginning a rigorous self-directed study in philosophy and a systematic analysis of modern culture, Broch during the 1920s developed an aesthetic theory and a philosophy of history and culture that would provide the foundation upon which *The Sleepwalkers* would be constructed. The metaphysical question that absorbed him was the nature of reality, and Broch concluded that the reality of a given historical period could be determined by its predominant values. Seeing history as a cycle of value formation and decay, Broch viewed the Christian era, which had emerged from the declining pagan era, as reaching its end point in the modern period, deteriorating from the cultural unity of the Middle Ages through a "process of the five-hundred-year dissolution of values." Contemporary man, Broch argued, was caught between the old system of values that is no longer adequate and a future value system that has yet to take hold. Like a sleepwalker suspended between two states, modern man finds himself trapped between, in Broch's terminology, "no longer" and "not yet"—no longer served by the ethical codes of the past but still bound by them, whose deficiencies are revealed by the intrusion of the irrational, or what Broch calls "irruption from below." For Broch, the novel, not modern philosophy with its emphasis on mathematical proofs, offered access to explore these subjective states. As he recalled his eventual shift from philosophical inquiry to literature, Broch explained, "those areas of philosophy that are inaccessible to mathematical treatment—primarily ethics or metaphysics—become 'objective' only in the realm of theology. Otherwise they become relativistic and, ultimately, 'subjective.' It was this subjectivity that forced me into the area where it is radically legitimate, namely into literature."

In 1927, to the shock of his family, Broch sold the family business so that he could commit full time to his studies and work on *The Sleepwalkers* beginning in 1928. Constructed as a trilogy—*Pasenow oder die Romantik 1888* (translated as *The Romantic [1888]*), *Esch oder die Anarchie 1903* (translated as *The Anarchist [1903]*, and *Huguenau oder die Sachlichkeit 1918* (translated as *The Realist [1918]*)—*The Sleepwalkers* reflects three critical stages in the historical and cultural development of Germany, which Broch characterizes by the predominant value systems: romantic, anarchistic, and objective. Its three protagonists—Joachim von Pasenow, August Esch, and Wilhelm Huguenau—each from a different socioeconomic class and background, represent contrasting aspects of the sleepwalker state and the conflict between "no longer" and "not yet" over the period 1888 to 1918.

In volume one, the young Prussian lieutenant Joachim von Pasenow, the second son of a landed-gentry Junker family, depends on the conventions, traditions, and trappings of his class, family, and a military code, symbolized by his dependence on his uniform, to provide him with his sense of identity and stability that will be disrupted by "the irruption from below" of the irrational force of love that Pasenow feels for the barmaid Ruzena. Pasenow is "romantic" for clinging to past values that prove inadequate to contain or control his feelings of guilt, loss, anxiety, and self-doubt that are released by his passion for Ruzena and mounting family pressures when his eldest brother's death in a duel requires Pasenow to give up military service to run the family estate. He eventually retreats to his established place as dutiful son and his expected class role by marrying the socially accepted Elizabeth whom he admires rather than loves. The novel ends on their wedding night with Pasenow lying fully dressed beside his bride adjusting his uniform jacket, impotent and unable to break through his romantic glorification of Elizabeth to treat her as woman rather than an icon to be worshipped, unable to overcome the gap between the romantic ideal that he strives for and a disturbing reality that he cannot control.

In volume two, a similar pattern of disruption of established values is explored 13 years later in a shift of milieu to the petty bourgeois bookkeeper August Esch who responds to the increasingly anarchic contention of values by a dominant "business is business" philosophy and an accountant's precise balancing of debits and credits. When, without warning, however, he is fired from his job to cover up the embezzlement of a superior, his worldview collapses and the disruption releases Esch's rage and irrationality in a mission to set cosmic accounts right by apportioning punishment and reward wherever he sees violations. The helplessness which Pasenow felt in the face of outmoded values is here intensified by Esch's frustrations and fury, symbolic of the release of the irrational in the breakdown of value systems. He finds employment as a clerk in the Mannheim dockyards and at a cabaret encounters Ilona, the partner of a knife-thrower, whom he tries to "redeem." Like Pasenow, Esch finds himself drawn between the spiritualized Ilona and his landlord's more earthly sister, Erna, a conflict eventually resolved by marriage with tavern-keeper Mutter Hentjen as a form of simplified erotic union. Linking the first two books is the character Eduard von Bertrand, an acquaintance of Pasenow, who leaves military service for business and becomes the owner of the shipping firm that employs Esch. Compared to Pasenow's romantic clinging to the past and Esch's rage at the present, Bertrand represents an alternative response in accepting the contradictions of contending values and attempting to steer clear of the consequences, which he ultimately fails to do when Esch's exposure of his homosexuality drives him to suicide.

In the third volume, both Pasenow and Esch are residents of a small Mosel village in the final months of the war. Pasenow is the town's aged commandant, and Esch is the owner and editor of its local newspaper. Their lives are disrupted by the arrival of Huguenau who has deserted from the army in Flanders. Broch described Huguenau as "the truly 'value-free' person and therefore the adequate child of his times. He alone is able to endure, he alone lives in the 'autonomy of these times,' which harbor a revolutionary struggle for freedom. . . . He is ethical only by virtue of the form of the autonomy, but otherwise completely amoral." Attaining a full break with the past and a dispassionate objectification of values, Huguenau manages to manipulate the residents to rise to prominence, swindling Esch out of his newspaper and bullying Pasenow so that the commandant will not report him as a deserter. During the revolution that breaks out in the closing weeks of the war, Hugenau murders Esch by stabbing him in the back, rapes Esch's wife, and transports the injured and insane Pasenow to a military hospital. By the end of the novel the irrational has overwhelmed and swept away all remnants of the past, preparing the way for a new society and a new system of values to emerge.

Broch's analysis of the progression from romanticism to anarchism and objectivism is reflected in stylistic shifts in each of the trilogy's volumes, from the realism in the first, naturalism in the second, and expressionism in the third. The final volume further replicates fragmentation by adding to the central story complementary subplots and contrasting narrative methods from lyrical passages to 10 essays that expound on the underlying themes of the work. "The book," Broch explained, "consists of a series of stories which are all variations of the same theme, i.e., man's confrontation with loneliness—a confrontation due to the disintegration of values. . . . These individual stories, interwoven like tapestry, present various levels of consciousness: they rise out of the wholly irrational (story of the Salvation Army Girl) to the complete rationality of the theory (disintegration of values). The other stories take place between these two poles on staggered levels of rationality." In this way, Broch widens and universalizes his focus while breaking apart his previously continuous narrative with bits and pieces of stories, lyrical prose and poetry, drama, and essays that must be reassembled into meaning, much in the same way as the search for new sustaining values must be undertaken by shifting through the wreckage of the past.

The efforts on his behalf by James Joyce and other influential writers due to their appreciation for his achievement in *The Sleepwalkers* helped Broch escape Nazi Austria in 1938 after a time in prison under suspicion as a Marxist (his Jewish background had not come to the attention of the authorities). Exiled first to England and then to the United States where he lived the rest of his life, Broch completed two further major works: *Der Tod des Vergil* (1945; translated as *The Death of Virgil*), a brilliantly sustained interior monologue of Virgil's last hours of life; and *Die Schuldlosen* (1950; translated as *The Guiltless*, 1974), an exploration of the rise of the Nazis in Germany. They, along with *The Sleepwalkers*, confirm Broch's stature as a writer of great complexity, brilliance, and artistic integrity who deserves a respected place among the great European modernist novelists.

THE LAST CHRONICLE OF BARSET

82

(1866–67)

by Anthony Trollope

"What am I to do without ever meeting Archdeacon Grantly?" a man said the other day; "he was one of my best and most intimate friends, and the mere prospect of never hearing his 'Good heavens!' again when any proposition is made touching the dignity of Church or State, is a bewilderment and pain to me. It was bad enough to lose the Old Warden, Mr. Septimus Harding, but that was a natural death, and we must all bow to blows of that kind. But to lose the Archdeacon and Mrs. Grantly in the prime of their life, is more than I can bear. Life has lost one of its principal alleviations."

—Quoted in an unsigned notice in the *Spectator*, July 13, 1867

An argument can be made that Anthony Trollope, long overshadowed by his fellow Victorian novelists Dickens, Thackeray, and Eliot, in fact wrote far more good novels than they or indeed than any novelist in his era or in any other. Trollope's dogged, workmanlike approach with his quota of 10,000 words of fiction a week throughout his long career, and his avoidance of the poetic and the profound for minutely observed ordinary life have kept him from being included in the rank of the greatest literary artists. However, his reputation over the last 25 years has risen dramatically with more of his impressive production back in print and the full depth of his achievement finally being critically explored. It seems more and more clear that future generations will turn to Trollope for the clearest insights into the life of the Victorians, as we now turn to Jane Austen for our view of the Regency period. Trollope's novels are of more than historical interest, however: There are some genuine masterpieces as well. Of his 47 novels, there were several candidates for inclusion in this ranking—*Orley Farm*, *The Way We Live Now*, *Barchester Towers*, *Phineas Redux*, *The Eustace Diamonds*, *The Prime Minister*, *The Duke's Children*, and several more. I have decided, however, to select *The Last Chronicle of Barset*, the novel that Trollope himself considered his best, as the single work that best displays Trollope's multiple gifts and achievements as a novelist.

Trollope's 19th novel was written in 1866 and appeared in weekly installments from December 1866 to July 1867. *The Last Chronicle of Barset* concluded his cycle of six novels set in his imagined English country setting of Barsetshire that began with *The Warden* (1855) and continued with *Barchester Towers* (1857), *Doctor Thorne* (1858), *Framley Parsonage* (1861), and *The Small House at Allington* (1861). In the five years between *The Small House at Allington* and *The Last Chronicle* Trollope had written seven other novels, including the first in the Palliser series, signaling his shift of focus from ecclesiastical and country life to London and politics. *The Last Chronicle* serves, therefore, as a wrapping-up of what many of his contemporaries and subsequent readers regard as the best set of sequels in English literature, as well as a transition to contemporary themes that would increasingly command his attention. In building a series of novels with repeated characters in a common setting Trollope had introduced the *roman fleuve* pioneered by Balzac in *La Comédie humaine* into the English novel, and *The Last Chronicle* is both a summation and a culmination of Trollope's efforts as a social panoramist, as the faithful recorder of a complex web of relationships joining multiple characters into a fully realized community and social order. Nathaniel Hawthorne wrote that Trollope's novels "precisely suit my taste,—solid, substantial . . . and just as real as if some giant had hewn a great lump out of the earth and put it under a glass case, with all its inhabitants going about their daily business, and not suspecting that they were being made a show of." Like Chaucer, Trollope numbered the classes of men, chronicling nuances of behavior among his collection of clerics and country gentry families, needing only the slightest of narrative stimulant to set his dense and expansive web in motion to provide the desired animation and illumination.

For all the other things that *The Last Chronicle* is—Trollope's most massive social panorama, his finest character portrait, and his tying up of the many strands of his Barsetshire series—it is also a detective story that opens with a mystery involving an apparent theft: How did the eccentric, poverty-stricken curate of Hogglestock, Josiah Crawley, acquire a misplaced check for £20 used to pay his butcher's bill? This is admittedly a slender thread upon which to hang such an immense narrative, and Trollope remained throughout his career conscious of his defects as a contriver of highly energized plots, preferring to concentrate not on the vehicle but on the passengers. "A weekly novel," Trollope observed, "should perhaps have at least an attempt at murder in every number. I never get beyond giving my people an attack of fever or a broken leg." That a clergyman may be guilty of theft, however, is a sufficient sensation that Trollope required to draw out his characters' reactions as the Barsetshire community aligns itself into pro- and anti-Crawley factions, with the implications of the possible crime on Crawley, his family, and his neighbors followed through a series of interrelated subplots and groups of characters.

The exceptional allows Trollope to animate the normal, as the incident causes individuals to reveal themselves and to test their values under the pressure of heightened circumstances. For Major Henry Grantly, son of the archdeacon, the suspicion surrounding Crawley becomes a test for his love for Crawley's daughter Grace. A match with the daughter of a thief proves to be a considerable challenge as well for Archdeacon Grantly's liberality. The accusation also becomes the ultimate test for one of Trollope's greatest creations, the bishop's wife, Mrs. Proudie, who continues her campaign of interference in diocesan business by insisting on Crawley's guilt and dismissal from his position. Although the novel's situation spreads an impact throughout the Barsetshire community, for Trollope proximity alone is often sufficient to introduce an additional circle of characters and incidents. When Grace visits Lily Dale, the heroine of *The Small House at Allington*, this intersection is enough to continue the story of her complicated relationships with Adolphus Crosbie, who jilted her, and her ever-faithful suitor Johnny Eames. Johnny's activities take him to London, where the painter Conway Dalrymple and the parvenu Dobbs Broughton and their circle are introduced. Illustrating Tom Stoppard's line that "Every exit is an entrance someplace else," in expanding circles of characters and relationships, Trollope sets a conservative society at odds with itself, revealing the forces at play beneath the surface quiet of country life, as well as the new money ethic of the town that increasingly relegates Barsetshire to quaint irrelevance. At issue in the notion that a clergyman and a gentleman would be capable of theft is the moral claim of an entire way of life.

The novel opens with the first chapter's title, "How Did He Get It?", that is, how did Crawley come by Lord Lufton's check for £20. The answer will come nearly 70 chapters later. Although for the reader there is little doubt about Crawley's innocence, it is his reaction under the pressure of circumstances that matters. A man of immense learning and dignity who is consigned to grinding poverty by an inability to get on, Crawley is revealed as a complex mixture of strengths and weaknesses in which excessive humility alternates with excessive pride. Crawley courts his own martyrdom with extreme bitterness and an alienating isolation that leads him to the edge of madness. He is Trollope's most masterful portrait of a tragic outsider, a living denial of all the complacent assumptions that undergird Barsetshire society: that moral worth is more valuable than material worth, that gentility is its own reward. In this regard, Crawley is made to serve both a psychological and a social function. It is as if King Lear had been allowed to wander throughout the Barsetshire community. Like the mystery of the check, Crawley also is an enigma that must be "solved" before the novel's conclusion.

Crawley is given one grand heroic moment before being reconciled with society in a conversion that is far less convincing than his resistance to the established norms. His "Peace, woman" breaks the spell of Mrs. Proudie's tyrannical rule in Barsetshire when he opposes her meddling in clerical business: "Madam . . . you should not interfere in these matters. You simply debase your husband's high office. The distaff were more fitting for you." Crawley routs Mrs. Proudie, and initiates her eventual fall from power. Her demise is the occasion for one of the most famous of Trollope's anecdotes, recorded in his *Autobiography.* Having overheard at his club two clergymen complaining about his practice of reintroducing in his novels characters such as Mrs. Proudie, Trollope recounts that "I got up, and standing between them, I acknowledged myself to be the culprit. 'As to Mrs. Proudie,' I said, 'I will go home and kill her before the week is over.' And so I did."

The other crucial death, which balances Mrs. Proudie's departure, is that of Mr. Harding, one of the saintliest figures Trollope ever conceived. Harding's career, the subject of Trollope's initial Barsetshire novel, *The Warden*, is brought to a benign conclusion in an affirmation of a life of devotion and virtue that is part of the restoration of order of the novel's climax. All the confusion and discord produced by the suspicion of Crawley as a thief gives way to the appropriate restoration of harmony and balance that comedies traditionally assert. Crawley, finally exonerated, is granted a comfortable preferment; Mrs. Proudie's reign is over, and sensible moderation is restored. The world as he found it is Trollope's great subject, in which life's essence is discovered not among extremes of undue saint or sinner but in the mixed middle of ordinary strengths and weaknesses. As Henry James asserted, Trollope's "first, his inestimable merit was a complete appreciation of the usual," and *The Last Chronicle of Barset* in its amplitude and clarity makes a convincing argument that actuality is more absorbing than artifice and that the novelist who can populate his imaginary world with the living possesses the essential fictional magic.

83

THE AWAKENING

(1899)

by Kate Chopin

The Awakening *was the most important piece of fiction about the sexual life of a woman written to date in America, and the first fully to face the fact that marriage, whether in point of fact it closed the range of a woman's sexual experiences or not, was but an episode in her continuous growth. It did not attack the institution of the family, but it rejected the family as the automatic equivalent of feminine self-fulfillment, and on the very eve of the twentieth century it raised the question of what woman was to do with the freedom she struggled toward. . . . [Edna Pontellier] was an American woman, raised in the Protestant mistrust of the senses and in the detestation of sexual desire as the root of evil. As a result, the hidden act came for her to be equivalent to the hidden and the true self, once her nature awakened in the open surroundings of Creole Louisiana. The new century was to provide just such an awakening for countless American women, and* The Awakening *spoke of painful times ahead on the road to fulfillment.*

—Larzer Ziff, *The American 1890s*

It was Willa Cather in her review of Chopin's masterpiece, *The Awakening*, who first noted the link with Flaubert when she called the novel a "Creole Bovary." Like Flaubert's incendiary *Madame Bovary*, Chopin's novel similarly traces a woman's dissatisfaction with her conventional life, and the tragedy that follows when its heroine insists on a different course than what propriety allows. What makes Chopin's novel even more daring and rebellious than Flaubert's is Chopin's refusal to condemn her protagonist, Edna Pontellier, as she eventually sacrifices her husband, her place in society, her children, and even her life in pursuit of an expanded sense of self-identity and self-determination. Flaubert may have extended his sympathy to Emma Bovary wide enough to claim identification ("Madame Bovary, c'est moi."), but Emma's moral transgressions are still unmistakable. With *The Awakening* the reader is not so sure how to interpret its heroine's fate, and the novel's avoidance of the didactic and its ambiguous ending helped consign it to half a century of critical neglect. Published in 1899, it is in a sense the last great 19th-century

American novel and the first major novel of the next century, establishing some of the key themes and methods that would dominate modern fiction.

Chopin was born Katherine O'Flaherty in Saint Louis, Missouri, in 1850. Her father was an Irish immigrant who became a successful businessman and married into a socially prominent French-American family. When her father died suddenly in 1855, Chopin was reared in a matriarchal household run by her mother, her grandmother, and great-grandmother. Educated at a Catholic girls' school, she entered the fashionable world of the debutante upon graduation in 1868, marrying French Creole Oscar Chopin of New Orleans in 1870. Between 1871 and 1879 the Chopins had five sons and one daughter while living in New Orleans, where Oscar worked as a cotton broker, and vacationing each summer at Grand Isle, an important setting for *The Awakening*. In 1879, to save money as a result of a poor cotton crop, the family moved to French-speaking Cloutierville in north-central Louisiana, where Oscar ran a general store, and his wife often waited on customers, absorbing incidents and character types that she would eventually draw on in her novels and stories. Oscar died suddenly of malaria in 1882, leaving his family in debt, and Chopin eventually moved her family back to Saint Louis, beginning a period of self-assessment. During this period, Chopin declared, she "made her own acquaintance." She also studied Darwin, who impressed her with the concept that women cannot avoid their "biological fates." At the age of 39, motivated by her need to support her large family, Chopin launched her writing career. She began to sell her short stories to leading periodicals, published her first novel, *At Fault*, at her own expense in 1890, and eventually brought out two well-received story collections, *Bayou Folk* in 1894 and *A Night in Acadie* in 1897. With these works, she secured a rising reputation as a gifted and prolific writer of southern regional life who unsentimentally emphasized the nuances of human psychology and the various challenges faced by women.

When her second novel appeared in 1899, *The Awakening* proved to be both the culmination of a decade of artistic and intellectual development and the effective end of her literary career. Like Byron's overly dramatic elegy to Keats alleging that he "was kill'd off by one critique, / Just as he really promised something great," subsequent Chopin advocates have attributed the hostile reaction to *The Awakening* with silencing Chopin and hastening her death. The evidence is far less dramatic. The book was indeed harshly attacked by many reviewers, who judged Edna Pontellier's behavior immoral and dismissed her tragic end as good riddance. As one reviewer moralistically intoned, had Edna "flirted less and looked after her children more, we need not have been put to the unpleasantness of reading about her and the temptations she trumped up for herself." However, the novel was neither extensively banned nor uniformly condemned, as some have alleged. Neither did the book's reception completely silence its author, who continued to write poems and stories up to her death. Declining health more than the hostile reception to *The Awakening* is the more plausible, if less striking, determining factor in ultimately ending Chopin's life and career. Returning from a visit to the Saint Louis World's Fair, Chopin died of a massive cerebral hemorrhage in 1904, at the age of 54.

Although never completely forgotten, Chopin's works were relegated after her death to the marginal category of the regionalist and local colorist. Her literary reputation, however, was significantly resurrected in the 1950s and 1960s, and *The Awakening* began to be reclaimed as an overlooked American masterpiece. In his literary history, *The Confident Years* (1952), Van Wyck Brooks called the novel "one small perfect book that mattered more than the whole life-work of many a prolific writer." His opinion was increasingly shared by other critics, particularly as the 1960s women's movement accelerated, and gender issues prompted new assessments. *The Awakening* was heralded as a fundamental protofeminist text, as a powerful fictional rendering of the social, biological, and psychological dilemma women face as well as the consequences of a raised consciousness. Subsequent critics have emphasized not the novel's ideology but its considerable artistry, and an appreciation of Chopin's luminous, painterly style, her intricate weaving of images and symbols, and her brilliant psychological penetration has helped secure her place as a key literary figure and *The Awakening* as an essential American novel.

The novel's considerable power derives from the simplicity and economy of its story as well as the tragic momentum that it rapidly generates. Edna Pontellier is a 28-year-old wife of a wealthy Creole businessman, Léonce Pontellier, and the mother of two sons. As the novel opens, she is vacationing with her family at a summer resort on Grand Isle in the Gulf of Mexico. Viewed conventionally, Edna's marriage is ideal. Léonce is judged by all as a model husband who has provided Edna with a comfortable life of material ease and a place of distinction in society. For Edna, however, "a certain light was beginning to dawn" about the inadequacy of her existence. She is treated by her husband as a "valuable piece of personal property," in which submission to her husband's will and sacrifice for her children's sake are all that are expected of her. Edna gradually awakes to an expanded sense of her individuality and sexuality, as well as to her corresponding need for autonomy. Experiencing an almost overwhelming aesthetic joy through music, reveling in the physical pleasure of swimming, Edna "was beginning to realize her position in the universe as a human being, and to recognize her relations as an individual to the world within and about her." Her recognition as an individual rather than a possession or in the role predetermined for her by her gender and class as a wife and a mother inevitably begins a process in which her relationship with Léonce deteriorates and her sympathy with the admiring Robert Lebrun escalates into a passionate affection. Robert, however, is unable to cope with the implications of his feelings for Edna and flees to Mexico.

Returning to New Orleans, Edna translates her growing dissatisfaction with her life into abandoning her previous routine, cultivating her aesthetic interest in painting, and, in the eyes of her husband, neglecting her assigned duties in his household: "Mr. Pontellier had been a rather courteous husband so long as he met a certain tacit submissiveness in his wife. But her new and unexpected line of conduct completely bewildered him. It shocked him. Then her absolute disregard of her duties as a wife angered him. When Mr. Pontellier became rude, Edna grew insolent. She had resolved never to take another step backward." Unable to comprehend or cope with the changes in his wife, Léonce follows the advice of the family doctor to bide his time, and he leaves on an extended business trip. While he is away, Edna moves out of their home into a smaller dwelling that she can finance independently, and begins an affair with the rakish Alcée Arobin. Gratifying Edna's heightened sexuality, Arobin proves to be as proprietary as her husband. When Robert suddenly returns and declares his devotion, the possible culmination and combination of Edna's sexual desires and love are thwarted by his inability to accept her autonomy. Left alone, without a satisfying role for her expanded sense of self, neither as a wife, mother, or lover, Edna can foresee only a succession of affairs and scandal that will ruin her children. Instead, she acts to protect their reputation by ending her life in a way that could be viewed as accidental by swimming out to sea and drowning.

It is, in the words of critic Barbara C. Ewell, "perhaps the most ambivalent conclusion in all American literature," in which Chopin connects Edna's selfless sacrifice on behalf of her children with her desire to preserve the inviolability of her essential self. The ending has been viewed both as a triumphant act of self-assertion, a liberation from the confines of unbearable constriction, and as a tragic failure, the self-deluded, regressive act of an individual unable to translate her desires and identity into any meaningful relationship in a world blind to the implications that the novel has so effectively displayed. Chopin's novel marks out the battleground in an ongoing and escalating gender discussion, between individuality and defining roles, between self-assertion and determinism. The many novels that would follow *The Awakening* in a sense either document the same oppositions or attempt to find the way for Edna to regain the shore rather than extinction.

84

ROBINSON CRUSOE

(1719)

by Daniel Defoe

Few will acknowledge all they owe
To persecuted, brave Defoe.
Achilles, in Homeric song,
May, or he may not, live so long
As Crusoe, few their strength had tried
Without so staunch and safe a guide.
What boy is there who never laid
Under his pillow, half afraid,
That precious volume, lest the morrow
For unlearnt lesson might bring sorrow?
But nobler lessons he has taught
Wide-awake scholars who fear'd naught:
A Rodney and a Nelson may
Without him not have won the day.

—Walter Savage Landor, *Daniel Defoe*

The achievement of *Robinson Crusoe* rests on its pride of place as England's first significant novel and on its mythmaking power. Crusoe in his goatskins surveying his deserted island domain is one of the most recognizable characters in fiction, and his story of shipwrecked survival one of the most captivating, familiar even to those who have never actually read the original. Rousseau went so far as to claim that *Robinson Crusoe* was "the one book that teaches all that books can teach," while Samuel Johnson considered it, along with *Don Quixote* and *The Pilgrim's Progress,* the only books he regretted were not longer. "*Robinson Crusoe* falls most naturally into place," Ian Watt argues in his classic study, *The Rise of the Novel,* "not with other novels, but with the great myths of Western civilization, with *Faust, Don Juan,* and *Don Quixote.* All these have as their basic plots, their enduring urges, a single-minded pursuit by the protagonist of one of the characteristic desires of Western man."

Defoe reached in his central character and his imaginatively reconstructed experiences the level of the archetype and created by harnessing the primary truth-telling resources of the novel a fictional prototype, setting the novel on the realistic course that it has followed ever since.

Coming to fiction late in a varied and multiple career that included business ventures as a trader and a manufacturer and political activities as a pamphleteer and a domestic intelligence agent, Defoe faced down bankruptcies and imprisonment before settling in as a journalist. He eventually became associated with 26 periodicals, writing on domestic and foreign affairs, religious controversies, and the political issues of the day. In 1719, at the age of 59, while still busy with daily and weekly journalism, Defoe launched a new career as a fiction writer with *Robinson Crusoe.* Partially based on the actual story of Scottish sailor Alexander Selkirk, who was marooned for four and a half years on the island of Juan Fernandez off the coast of Chile, *The Life and Strange Surprizing Adventures of Robinson Crusoe, of York, Mariner* capitalized on the popular interest in Selkirk's adventures and on travel narratives with a fictional equivalent, disguised as truth. *Robinson Crusoe* is a radically new narrative form in which Defoe asks his readers to accept the truthfulness of his imagined story and helps us to accept his account by treating Crusoe's adventures as possible, bolstered by a representation of actuality that allows the reader to visualize Crusoe's world as if it were the reader's own.

Defoe, like Cervantes, formulated his revolutionary narrative art based on a rejection of what readers had come to expect in earlier prose romances involving the fantastical adventures of idealized characters in exotic or generic locations. Crusoe's situation ostensibly provides the perfect material for an expected romantic treatment. Like the questing knight's forest, Crusoe's unnamed island is a remote and unfamiliar place, as far from the actual world of the novel's readers as possible. Defoe has only to employ a potentially inexhaustible supply of marvels to hold the reader's attention. The novel Defoe chooses to write, however, could not be further from the prose romance standard. Reversing what Dickens would later identify as his fictional formula of the "romantic side of familiar things," Defoe supplies the familiar side of romantic things. *Robinson Crusoe* is still an adventure story, but one defined not by the remarkable but by the particular. Faced with the challenge of survival on his island, Crusoe domesticates the wilderness with the skills of a middle-class homemaker, raising his living standard through ingenuity and industry. What grips readers are the practical challenges Crusoe faces—how he will bake his bread, mend his clothing, or make a pot—described with a relish for the mundane details of daily activities. Crusoe gains the reader's sympathy not because of his excellence as an exemplary hero, like Lancelot or Galahad, but by his ordinariness, by his modest accomplishments, dogged persistence, and understandable human limitations. Coleridge rightly called him "the universal representative, the person for whom every reader could substitute himself." Defined by his class and customs, Crusoe builds an equivalent English home on the island, and the reader can identify with how he faces his humble but compelling challenges in a new kind of adventure story that reflects the reader's experiences and capabilities even in its exotic locale and exceptional circumstances.

Besides the truthful representation of actuality in which the readers can see their own world and themselves mirrored in Crusoe's experiences, Defoe's other major innovation is to join Crusoe's physical adventures with his moral and spiritual development, thus translating Crusoe's experiences into universal significance and charging the mundane with symbolic resonance. Readers acquainted with Crusoe's story but not with the Defoe original may be surprised by the attention the novelist gives to his protagonist's pre- and post-island life and the degree to which his adventures follow an allegorical Christian pattern of disobedience, punishment, and deliverance. Crusoe's life story begins with his "original sin" of filial disobedience stemming from his inability to control his "rambling thoughts," rejecting the stay-at-home, modest, deferential way of life recommended by his father for a life of ambition, travel, and adventure. Crusoe ignores or rationalizes away providential warnings of storms at sea and temporary enslavement until he is faced with his ultimate punishment, fit for a restless wanderer. "I was a prisoner lock'd up with the eternal bars and bolts of the ocean," Crusoe realizes, "in an uninhabited wilderness, without redemption." Crusoe's eventual redemption is his transformation from prisoner to liberated master of his domain and is based on the eventual realization of his dependence on God's will and grace. Crusoe's reassessment of his identity and his gradual acceptance of his human limitations order the events and details of the novel's account as he is forced to deal with the basic, essential relationships that the isolated island setting allows while anticipating all the conflicts that future novels will examine: man versus nature, man versus self, man versus God, man versus man.

First, Crusoe must confront his solitude, and Defoe equips him with stores from his wrecked ship, just enough to make his struggle a challenge. Defoe's greatness as a novelist is his exceptional ability to enter imaginatively into Crusoe's dilemmas, allowing the reader to see through Crusoe's eyes and vicariously participate in his day-to-day existence. Crusoe faces his practical tests and his loneliness with the sensibility of an accountant, meticulously calculating gains and losses. The fears and setbacks that undermine his self-sufficiency inevitably draw him toward a recognition of his ultimate dependence on God's true deliverance, not from his island captivity, but from his sinful pride. Following his conversion experience, Crusoe rests easier in his captivity and develops the will and the resources to deal with the next challenge: his relationship with others who invade his solitude. In the most dramatic event in the book and one of the most memorable in fiction, after 15 years of isolation, Crusoe discovers the uncanny single footprint of another human. Given time to reflect on the implication of the footprint before encountering the cannibal visitors to his island, Crusoe again goes through a developmental process from irrational terror to practical competence aided by his trust in God's guidance. Crusoe deals with both the cannibals and a group of mutineers sensibly. He is able to secure a companion in Friday, a native whom he rescues and names based on the day on which Friday becomes useful to him. Very much the English colonist of his own time, he extends to Friday the blessings of civilization as Crusoe understands them, teaching him "every thing that was proper to make him useful, handy, and helpful," including converting Friday to Christianity.

After 28 years Crusoe is finally delivered from his island. Chastened by his past sins, he has become through his island experiences more capable in judgment and action. His post-island history, including a winter passage over the Pyrenees pursued by 300 wolves, strains credibility and lacks the clear focus of Crusoe's island existence, but these scenes, along with his pre-island activities, serve to frame the tale and to show the full cycle of his maturation and development, now demonstrated in the greater world and full of the same emblematic, allegorical qualities that structured and unified his history from the start.

Defoe's narrative is marred by careless writing, repetition, and contradictions that suggest the novel's improvised character. Crusoe also lacks a convincing inner life, and Defoe's allegorical method owes more to Bunyan's *The Pilgrim's Progress* than to any resemblance with the psychological exploration of later novels. However, in discovering the novel's essential elements—the believable representation of actual experience and the mining of man's most basic existential relationships—*Robinson Crusoe* is one of fiction's great originators, enduring and unavoidable both on the level of literary history and myth.

85

CALL IT SLEEP

(1934)

by Henry Roth

Transposed Yiddish and Joycean constructions; David Schearl's uncorrected apprehensions of the East Side, a mixture of stony realism and ecstatic phantasmagoria; and the discipline of a man who, in re-creating the experience of a boy he once was, cuts himself off forever from that boy—this nervous union of perspectives is not only the ground of the book's artistry, it is also the term of survival for a serious writer breaking away from immigrant Jewish life. The whole experience is here, rendered with a luxuriant fullness: the quarrelsome grownups, marauding toughs, experiments in voyeurism and precocious sex, dark tenements with rat-infested cellars, the oppressive comedy of Hebrew school where children learn to torment an enraged rabbi, and, above all, the beauty of his mother, tall and pale, glowing with feminine grace and chastened sexuality, that sexuality always present in the Jewish world but rarely acknowledged. A writer possessed by his material, driven by a need to recapture the world of his youth, does not choose his setting: it chooses him. And here it chooses him through the purity of discovery and terror which forms the boy's vision, through the warmth of a mother whose lap is heaven, through the strange accents and rasping consonants of that other language, the speech of childhood repressed and recaptured.

—Irving Howe, *World of Our Fathers*

When it was published in 1934, Henry Roth's intensely lyrical account of David Schearl's childhood psychological and emotional development in New York City in the second decade of the 20th century—Roth's first and for 60 years his only novel—earned both respectable sales and reviews eliciting favorable comparisons to Theodore Dreiser and James Joyce. However, the book (and its author) quickly disappeared from view. Its publisher was bankrupted by the Great Depression, and Roth's interior family saga seemed at odds with what the era demanded in social realism and proletarian propaganda. *Call It Sleep* was dismissed in the communist press as too introspective and febrile, the narcissistic obsessions of a "six-year-old Proust." After trying unsuccessfully to write a proletarian novel, Roth slipped into silence and obscurity, abandoning writing for work as a precision metal grinder, as an aide at a mental hospital, and as a raiser of waterfowl on a farm in Maine.

In 1956 *The American Scholar* published a special feature inviting scholars and critics to select books that were the "most undeservedly neglected." *Call It Sleep* was the only work mentioned twice, by Leslie Fiedler and by Alfred Kazin. "If you can imagine the patient sensibility of Wordsworth and the unselfconscious honesty of Dreiser brought to the shock of this environment [the Lower East Side] upon the senses," Kazin observed, "you may have some inkling of the slowness, the patience and the strange inner serenity of this book—as of something won, very far deep within, against the conventional cruelties of modern city life." The attention helped to bring the novel and its author back from obscurity. When *Call It Sleep* was reissued in paperback in 1964, it prompted Irving Howe, in an unprecedented front page review for a paperback reprint in the *The New York Times Book Review*, to assert that it was "one of the few genuinely distinguished novels written by a 20th-century American." *Call It Sleep* went on to sell more than 1 million copies in one of the greatest reclamations in literary history. It has been described as the greatest Jewish-American novel published in the 20th century, the finest depiction of Jewish-American immigrant and ghetto life, the greatest achievement in the use of the interior monologue by an American, and the richest mining of the vernacular and dialect since Mark Twain's *Adventures of Huckleberry Finn.* The book is now deservedly secure as an American and world literary classic.

Born in Galicia, then part of Austria, in 1906, Henry Roth came to America when he was 18 months old, living first in the Brownsville section of Brooklyn, then on Manhattan's Lower East Side, and finally, when he was eight, in a predominantly Irish-American neighborhood of Harlem. Attending New York's City College, Roth intended to become a biology teacher or zoologist. However, after publishing a first story during his freshman year, an expository writing exercise, "Impressions of a Plumber," in the college's literary journal, Roth was launched on a writing career. Through a friend he met Eda Lou Walton, a New York University professor and poet who encouraged Roth's literary aspirations and with whom Roth lived from 1928 until 1938. In the summer of 1930 Roth accompanied Walton to a New Hampshire art colony where he began work on what would become *Call It Sleep.* It began as a straightforward autobiographical account of his childhood, but the story's fictional and universal possibilities were soon evident as Roth began to reconceptualize his narrative. Many of the details of the novel are derived from fact. Like David's father, Albert Schearl, Roth's father, Herman, preceded his family to America, working to earn the passage for his wife and infant son. As in the novel, Roth's parents were emotionally estranged with the question of Roth's paternity, like that of David's, a prominent source of family strife. However, unlike Albert Schearl, Herman Roth was a diminutive man, not the monstrously powerful figure of David's imagination, and Roth's mother, Leah, combined features that Roth splits between Genya Schearl, David's nurturing, long-suffering mother, and her more vulgar, extroverted sister, Bertha. Also excluded from the Oedipal triangle of the Schearl home is Roth's younger sister, Rose, who became her father's favorite. In these details and many others, Roth adapted his circumstances to present a more dramatically unified portrait of the Schearl family with an emphasis on archetype and symbol that gives *Call It Sleep* its impressive thematic resonance and universal significance.

Structured by a prologue and four sections, the novel opens with Albert Schearl's reunion with his wife and infant son. He has come to collect them from Ellis Island and take them to their new American home. Facing an alien environment, mother and child are received coldly by their protector and guide, with hostility that culminates when Albert snatches David's hat and throws it into the harbor. The source of Albert's disapproval of his wife and child is unexplained, but his gnawing resentments and his volatile temperament establish the dominant forces that will shape David's upbringing and set in motion David's quest for the source of personal power and understanding.

Book I, "The Cellar," takes place four years later, when David is six years old. Responding to his father's coldness, contempt, and unpredictable rages, the hypersensitive David clings to his mother as his only solace in a world that terrifies him. Critic Walter Allen has praised *Call It Sleep* as the "most powerful evocation of the terrors of childhood ever written," and like two other masterpieces of the child's perspective—Dickens's opening chapters of *David Copperfield* and Joyce's initial section of *A Portrait of the Artist as a Young Man*—Roth holds his focus firmly on the expressionistic perspective of the young David, whose view of the world is distorted by his fears. These and David's accompanying sense of helplessness are objectified by the tenement's dark, terrifying cellar, which David must pass to enter and exit the family's apartment. It represents the unknown, mortality (with its associations of rats and corruption), and female sexuality. Invited by a lame neighbor girl to "play bad" with her in a dark closet, a variant of the cellar, David is sickened by what he finds beyond the maternal protection of his mother, and the novel chronicles David's struggle to come to terms with experience, with the physical world that both attracts and repels him, frequently at odds with the spiritual and emotional support derived from his relationship with his mother.

In Book II, "The Picture," the family moves to the Lower East Side as Albert Schearl takes a new job as a milkman, and the family circle increases with the arrival of Genya's sister, Bertha. The section's title refers to a picture of a field of green stalks and tiny blue flowers that David's mother buys. David overhears Genya's confession to her sister that the picture's significance derives from the memory it evokes of her former life in Austria and her scandalous, unhappy affair with a Gentile. The revelation of his mother's sexuality forces David to readjust his understanding that must now connect the associations derived from the cellar to his angelic, nurturing mother. A possible means of enlightenment to resolve the contradictions of David's experience with the world is suggested in Book III, "The Coal," which describes David's career at Hebrew school. There he learns the story of an angel's touching Isaiah's lips with a fiery coal, which allows the prophet to hear God. David is fascinated with how coal, an object of darkness associated with the cellar, can produce light, that is, how corruption can cleanse. A version of the Isaiah story is later symbolically enacted as David is tricked by two street toughs into touching a metal sword to the power source of the tramline: "Like a paw ripping through all the stable fibres of the earth, power, gigantic, fetterless, thudded into day! And light, unleashed, terrific light bellowed out of iron lips." David associates the electric flash with the mystical source of power and revelation that he seeks for an answer to his helplessness and confusion.

The event prefigures the book's climax in Book IV, "The Rail," in which David comes under the influence of a Polish Catholic boy, Leo Dugovka, a free spirit who possesses all the confidence that David so sorely lacks. Leo is willing to exchange another source of mystical power, a rosary, for an introduction to David's Aunt Bertha's stepdaughters. As Leo and David's cousin Esther "play bad" in the cellar, David is once again revolted and overwhelmed with guilt in an escalating sequence of events that culminates with a final, violent confrontation with his father in which the long-festering source of Albert's resentment is finally clarified. Made aware of his wife's affair, Albert suspects that David is another man's child: "All these years my blood told me!" Albert finally confesses. "Whispered to me whenever I looked at him, nudged me, told me he wasn't mine!" Albert's rage climaxes in a rejection of both his wife and child, and his violent outburst is momentarily halted by the shock caused by the rosary that falls to the floor. David escapes into the street and concludes his quest—"*Now I gotta make it come out*"—in a crescendo of street voices and symbolic significance that has been called by critic Albert Guttmann "among the most remarkable [passages] in American literature." Picking up a steel milk dipper, David returns to the source of power and illumination at the tramline. Touching that source David feels

> Power! Incredible, barbaric power! A blast, a siren of light within him, rending, quaking, fusing his brain and blood to a fountain of flame, vast rockets in a searing spray! Power! The hawk of radiance raking him with talons of fire, battering his skull with a beak of fire, braying his body with pinions of intolerable light. And he writhed without motion in the clutch of a fatal glory, and his brain swelled and dilated till it dwarfed the galaxies in a bubble of refulgence—Recoiled, the last screaming nerve clawing for survival.

Electrocuted, David goes through a spiritual death and rebirth. Reencountering all the images of evil, death, corruption, and threat that have haunted him, David survives, and the experience literally shocks him out of his crippling dependency and connects him to the vast energies beyond his home and family. Like Isaiah, David achieves a cleansing and an illumination that breaks his sense of powerlessness and dispels the animosity that has wracked his family. David's almost fatal mishap results in a reconciliation with his father, who acknowledges David's preciousness threatened by his loss. For his part, the terror David has felt is replaced by "a vague, remote pity" he now feels for his father. The spell that has cursed the Schearl family is broken. David's initiation into experience has been accomplished, and the novel closes with his review of the insight he has gained. Asked by his mother whether he is sleepy, David thinks:

> He might as well call it sleep. It was only toward sleep that every wink of the eyelids could strike a spark into the cloudy tinder of the dark, kindle out of shadowy corners of the bedroom such myriad and such vivid jets of images. . . . It was only toward sleep one knew himself still lying on the cobbles, felt the cobbles under him.

David, in tapping into his conscious and unconscious thoughts and emotions, finds inside himself the third rail and Isaiah's burning coal, the inner source of his own power and illumination. He, therefore, feels "not pain, not terror, but strangest triumph, strangest acquiescence. One might as well call it sleep. He shut his eyes." David achieves through his hard-fought encounter with experience the means to break through his pain and terror, to accept the multiplicity of life and his own capacity to make sense of his world. What David realizes in the semiwaking dream state that unites contradictions and contrasts, Roth has achieved in his novel, a revealing blend of subject and object, body and soul, the potential for spiritual rebirth in the midst of sordid, chaotic tenement life.

WAVERLEY

86

(1814)

by Sir Walter Scott

Walter Scott has no business to write novels, especially good ones—It is not fair. He has fame and profit enough as a poet and should not be taking the bread out of other people's mouths. I do not mean to like Waverley *if I can help it—but I fear I must.*

—Jane Austen, letter to her niece, 1814

Walter Scott was 42 years old and one of the preeminent poets of his day when his first novel, *Waverley*, was published anonymously in 1814. It launched the most popular and influential series of novels ever written and opened up, as no other novel had accomplished before, history as an imaginative resource for the novelist. Moreover, *Waverley* is generally regarded as one of the first best-selling novels, with an unprecedented 6,000 copies sold in its first six months. The novel and its many successors, collectively known as the Waverley novels, made Scott a phenomenon and ushered in, in the words of Richard Altick, "a new era in fiction," that turned novel readers into novel buyers. That one of the age's most celebrated writers should turn to the novel moreover enhanced the form's respectability rivaling poetry and drama as a vehicle for both beauty and truth. Scott would help to make the novel the dominating literary form in the 19th century. When Scott died in 1832, after more than two dozen novels, he was eulogized as the "Columbus of fiction," and it is almost inconceivable to the modern reader who may associate Scott only with *Ivanhoe* in its many film and television reincarnations to appreciate Scott's massive impact on the novel in the 19th century worldwide. Each of the major Victorian novelists—Dickens, Thackeray, and Eliot—worked to emerge from the long shadow he cast, while the novel tradition in several countries, including Russia, France, Italy, the United States, and Spain, can be traced at least in part to the powerful influence of Scott.

It is a commonplace of literary history to credit Scott with "inventing" the historical novel. In *Waverley*, Scott captivated his audience with a colorful depiction of Scottish life at the time of the Jacobite Rebellion of 1745. What was new about the 18th-century novel tradition that Scott inherited was the replacement of prose romance's conventions—exotic and vague settings, generic character types, and idealized situations—with realistic, recognizable details of ordinary life in which readers could see themselves and their world imaginatively reflected. The novel substituted the romance's interest in the general and the ideal with a concern for the particular. As 18th-century novelist Clara Reeve observed, "The Novel is a picture of real life and manners, and of the times in which it was written. The Romance, in lofty and elevated language, describes what has never happened nor is likely to." The long ago and the far away of romances was replaced by the here and now of the novel. What Scott added to the mix was the redirection of the novel back in time from the contemporary to the historical past, explored not as the romantic netherworld of the gothic and romance writers but as believable and recognizable a place as the reader's contemporary world—familiar yet strange. Scott labored to provide an accurate historical setting and to equip his distant characters with plausible motives and behavior. As Pushkin observed, from Scott, "we get to know the past times as though we were living a day-to-day life in them ourselves." In *Waverley*, Scottish customs, speech, and geography, as well as historical events, are all carefully and plausibly rendered, shaped by Scott's intention to reveal a drama of actual individuals and "those passions common to men in all stages of society, and which have alike agitated the human heart, whether it throbbed under the steel corselet of the fifteenth century, or the blue frock and white dimity waistcoat of the present day." Nothing like it had ever been done in the novel—the historical past exposed with the immediacy and verisimilitude of the present.

Waverley began to take shape in Scott's imagination as early as 1805. After the success of *The Lay of the Last Minstrel*, set in the Scottish Borders, Scott began to conceive of a "Highland romance," and seized on the Jacobite Rebellion of 1745 as an appropriate subject. The doomed attempt by Prince Charles Edward Stuart, or "Bonnie Prince Charlie," and his Scottish followers to claim the English throne that culminated in defeat at the Battle of Culloden, the last battle fought on British soil, exercised a powerful hold on Scott's imagination as a crucial turning point dividing the feudal and modern world. The prose work, however, stalled and was set aside, until in a search for fishing tackle, Scott rediscovered his manuscript in 1813 and completed the novel's final two volumes in a rush of concentrated effort. In his preface Scott describes his intention to write a historical adventure novel in imitation of a gothic romance. "I had nourished the ambitious desire," he admits, "of composing a tale of chivalry, which was to be in the style of the 'Castle of Otranto,' with plenty of Border characters and supernatural incident." The novel that he eventually wrote, however, is strikingly different from his intention, indicated by Scott's settling on a subtitle, "'Tis Sixty Years Since," that announces his dual goal to tell the story of his title character, Edward Waverley, and his era. Scott explains that

> Had I, for example, announced in my frontispiece, "Waverley: A Tale of Other Days," must not every novel-reader have anticipated a castle scarce less than that of Udolpho, of which the eastern wing had long been uninhabited, and the keys either lost, or consigned to the care of some aged butler or housekeeper, whose trembling steps, about the middle of the second volume, were doomed to guide the hero, or heroine, to the ruinous precincts? . . . Had my title borne, "Waverley: A Romance from the German," what head so obtuse as not to image forth a profligate abbot, an oppressive duke, a secret and mysterious association of Rosicrucians and Illuminati, with all their properties of black cowls, caverns, daggers, electrical machines, trap-doors, and dark-lanterns? Or if I had rather chosen to call my work a "Sentimental Tale," would it not have been a sufficient presage of a heroine with a profusion of auburn hair, and a harp, the soft solace of her solitary hours, which she fortunately finds always the means of transporting from castle to cottage, although she herself be sometimes obliged to jump out of a two-pair-of-stairs window, and is more than once bewildered on her journey, alone and on foot, without any guide but a blowzy peasant girl, whose jargon she hardly can understand?

What began in imitation of the gothic and sentimental romances took shape in Scott's mind as a realistic reaction to them. Although located in the romantic past, Scott's historical drama attempted to illustrate what links the reader with the past, how former values, customs, and events, as much as human nature itself, shape individuals. It is this realization that Scott biographer Edgar Johnson has called "Scott's revolutionary insight as an imaginative writer." By setting his novel just outside the reach of individual memory, Scott also establishes a key distinction for the historical novel, that its concern is the created past, not the remembered past, presented in such a way that does full justice realistically to what in the past is different *and* similar to the present. The Marxist critic Georg Lukács has summarized that "Scott's greatness lies in his capacity to give living human embodiment to historical-social types. The typically human terms in which great historical trends became tangible had never before been so superbly, straight-forwardly, and pregnantly portrayed. And above all, never before had this kind of portrayal been consciously set at the center of the representation of reality."

Scott's medium for presenting his tour of the past is his title character, Edward Waverley, a young, inexperienced Englishman much given to the romantic fiction that Scott parodies in his preface. Edward's susceptibility to romantic fantasy causes him on his arrival in Scotland to misperceive reality and contributes to his participation in the ill-fated Jacobite cause, which will force a reassessment of his values. The novel, therefore, is the story of Edward Waverley's maturation and education in learning to see things clearly. He is also the reader's proxy, and the reader is thereby also instructed in clear vision.

Edward joins the army and is sent to Scotland. There he visits his uncle's friend Baron Bradwardine, a Jacobite sympathizer. Venturing into the Highlands for the first time, Edward is entranced by its rugged beauty and soon comes under the influence of the clan chieftain Fergus MacIvor and his beautiful and spirited sister Flora. Brother and sister are ardent Jacobites, committed to restoring the English throne to Prince Charles and anxious to recruit Edward to their cause. Circumstances conspire to prevent Edward's return to his unit, and his loyalty comes under suspicion, culminating in his being relieved of his command and charged with treason. On his way to Edinburgh to try and clear his name, he is arrested. Rescued by Highlanders, he eventually finds himself at Prince Charles's temporary court at Holyrood. Carried away by romantic enthusiasm, by his hope of winning Flora's love, and by his resentment over his treatment by the Hanoverians, Edward pledges fealty to the prince and participates in the Jacobite victory at Preston. The sobering and deadly reality of civil war and revolution, however, is disillusioning. "The plumed troops and big war used to enchant me in poetry;" Edward observes, "but the night marches, vigils, couches under the wintry sky, and such accompaniments of the glorious trade, are not at all my taste in practice."

During the Jacobite invasion of England, Edward is separated from the army in the ensuing retreat and forced into hiding. Few of Edward's previous chivalric notions remain untested, and he is forced into recognizing what the rebellion is in fact: a bloody and senseless mistake. Through the efforts of the English officer Colonel Talbot, whose life Edward saved at Preston, Waverley gains a pardon. After the Jacobite forces are decisively beaten at Culloden, Fergus is tried and executed. Flora rejects Edward's marriage proposal and enters a French convent. Edward turns instead to the less glamorous but more sensible, domestic Rose Bradwardine, whom he eventually marries. With her Edward settles into a quiet and respectable life as the revolutionary turmoil gives way to a more placid, secure future. Edward's maturation is marked by his acknowledgment that "He felt himself entitled to say firmly, though perhaps with a sigh, that the romance of his life had ended, and that its real history had now commenced."

In a sense, with *Waverley*, novel readers could say the same thing about the form. Scott allows his readers to see the exotic Highlands and the past not romantically but realistically, as complex, ambiguous, and revealing in its display of human nature under the pressure of time and circumstance. It is this quality that prompted Georg Lukács to call Scott the "great poet of history" because "he has a deeper, and more genuine and differentiated sense of historical necessity than any writer before him."

87

OBLOMOV

(1859)

by Ivan Goncharov

No other novel has been used to describe the ever-so-elusive "Russian mentality" or "Russian soul" as frequently as Oblomov *by Ivan Goncharov, published in 1859. This is quite an achievement for a book in which the main protagonist spends most of his time asleep, thus mocking the very notions of plot, suspense, and character development that were the cornerstones of many other nineteenth-century Russian and European novels.*

—Galya Diment, "The Precocious Talent of Ivan Goncharov"

Few other novels make such a virtue out of limitation as Goncharov's *Oblomov.* Featuring one of the most immobile characters in all of literature, *Oblomov* is one of the great tragicomic novels and a landmark in the development of the novel in Russia. As scholar David Magarshack asserts, "*Oblomov* occupies a unique place among the great masterpieces of the nineteenth century. Goncharov's great novel lacks Dostoevsky's violence, Turgenev's brilliance and compactness, and Tolstoy's monumental force. And yet Goncharov did something that none of these great creative writers was able to do: he transformed the humdrum life of his totally insignificant and uninteresting hero into a great tragi-comedy, and he did it not by any tricks from the novelist's bag, but by a painstaking accumulation of seemingly insignificant details and by a completely detached and, at the same time, sympathetic analysis of his hero's character." In Margarshack's view, *Oblomov* initiates the realistic potential of the Russian novel. For critics Alexandra and Sverre Lynstad, *Oblomov* is the first Russian novel to claim the status of epic, "by its magnitude, complexity, national relevance, and poetic quality." They argue, "Compared to Goncharov, Turgenev becomes a writer of novelettes. And though Tolstoy worked on a much broader scale, his novels are less poetic." This is high praise indeed for a novel in which virtually nothing happens to rouse the protagonist from his sofa. Goncharov's innovation was to restrict the novel to an essential core of psychological, social, and moral truths and create out of the idiosyncratic traits of his hero a figure who unites class, national, and universal characteristics. *Oblomov*, like Knut Hamsun's *Hunger*, is one of the great protomodernist texts that moves the focus of the novel inside to the desires, dreams, and phobias of its central character. In its diagnosis of fragmentation, alienation, and Pynchonesque entropy, *Oblomov* predicts the themes and the landscapes of much of modern literature in writers as different as Kafka and Proust. It is interesting to note that Samuel Beckett read *Oblomov* some time before he composed his own masterpiece of suspended animation, *Waiting for Godot*, which may have a tribute to the Russian author in that one of his characters is named Vladimir. Beckett, who has been called the "Irish Oblomov," fashions his groundbreaking play by reducing his drama down to the anticipation of something happening. *Oblomov* manages the same in a novel about a protagonist, who, like Melville's Bartleby, "prefers not to," and retreats into a comforting alternative world of sleep, a dressing gown, and slippers.

Goncharov was born in Simbirsk, the son of a prosperous grain merchant. After his father's death in 1819, Goncharov was raised by a member of the provincial gentry. Like Oblomov, therefore, Goncharov grew up on a provincial estate. Both studied at Moscow University and entered the Russian civil service. Also like Oblomov, Goncharov was disappointed in love, but unlike his alter ego never married. His first novel, *A Common Story*, which appeared in 1847, was heralded as a precursor of the new Russian realistic novel. In 1849 Goncharov published "Oblomov's Dream," a prose poem describing the idyllic country estate of Oblomovka. It would serve as the germ of the novel that would be published 10 years later. Appearing three years before the emancipation of the serfs in a period of radical reassessment of traditional Russian society and national values, *Oblomov* created a sensation and was initially interpreted as a blatant social critique. The radical critic Nikolai Dobrolyubov in his famous article "What Is Oblomovism?" treats Oblomov as representative of his class, alienated and corrupted by serfdom, and praises the novel as an important social fable. "Oblomovism" thereafter entered the Russian lexicon to define a key aspect of the national character, describing a particularly Russian fatalism and lack of dedication and perseverance. In 1922 Lenin would rail at the Oblomovs in Russian society:

> Russia has made three revolutions, and still the Oblomovs have remained, because Oblomov was not only a landowner, but also a peasant; and not only a peasant, but also an intellectual; and not only an intellectual, but also a worker and a Communist. . . . the old Oblomov has remained, and he must be washed, cleaned, pulled about, and flogged for a long time before any kind of sense will emerge.

Clearly, Goncharov had touched a nerve with his character who typifies not simply a class but a national character trait. As notorious as his novel was, Goncharov never repeated the success of *Oblomov*. His next novel, *The*

Precipice (1869), which Goncharov regarded as his masterpiece, received only a lukewarm reception. Increasingly embittered, Goncharov engaged in a series of intemperate battles with fellow writer Turgenev, whom Goncharov accused of plagiarism. In an instance of life following art, Goncharov eventually retreated from the public scene as an Oblomov-like recluse, dying virtually alone in 1891, attended only by his servants. Goncharov, therefore, drew on his own experiences or what was clearly latent in his own temperament to fashion his most famous character, helping to establish a sympathetic though ironic view of his slothful dreamer that manages to broaden the reach of his novel from mere social or political commentary to a more expansive universal portrait of the human condition.

As *Oblomov* opens, Ilya Ilyitch Oblomov is a 32-year-old member of the Russian landowning class who has retired from a government job to his Saint Petersburg apartment, where his world has contracted to the irresistible routine of eating and sleeping. Flabby and unkempt, Oblomov is attended by his equally indolent though loyal valet Zahar. Having left his position as work unseemly for a gentleman, Oblomov has managed to reduce his activities to the key question of whether or not he should get out of bed. A succession of visitors fails to rouse him. His estates in southern Russia are being mismanaged by his bailiff, but Oblomov cannot summon the energy to travel so far to set things right. The reasons behind Oblomov's apathy and inactivity are glimpsed in the chapter derived from Goncharov's earlier published "Oblomov's Dream," the evocation of his childhood experiences on his family's country estate. Pampered by his parents and relieved of the responsibility of doing anything for himself, Oblomov has been infected by self-indulgence and a fatal dissatisfaction between the perfectly satisfying world of his childhood and a disappointing present. Oblomov is, therefore, both a neurotic and a dreamer whose desire for the lost past world clashes with the actual that always fails to meet his expectations.

Oblomov's only goad to a more active life comes from his childhood friend, Andrey Stolz, who has been raised by his German father to be practical and ambitious. Stolz, a successful businessman, is emblematic of the European vigor lacking in the Russian character. When he visits his friend, Stolz is shocked by Oblomov's state and aghast when he learns that Oblomov's doctors have warned him that he will not long survive unless he changes his habits. Stolz takes control of his friend and tries to pique Oblomov's active involvement in life. He introduces Oblomov to Olga Ilyinsky, a vivacious and sensitive young woman, who seems to be exactly what Oblomov needs to energize him. They fall in love; Oblomov eventually proposes, and he is for a time stimulated into activity as they plan their wedding and married life together. Soon, however, as the wedding approaches, Oblomov's torpor returns, and a frustrated Olga finally is compelled to break off their engagement, despairing that Oblomov will never become more than an idler.

Following Olga's dismissal, Oblomov reclaims his bed and his routine of doing nothing, shamefully labeling his apathy "Oblomovism," He is both painfully aware of his shortcomings and unable to break the hold of his lethargy. He is also unable to resist the manipulations of the parasitical Tarantyev, who finds him a new apartment in a suburban home run by the widowed Agafya Mateyevna. Oblomov slips deeply into the seductive routine of petit-bourgeois indolence. Meanwhile, on a trip abroad Olga has met Stolz in France, and they marry. Years pass, and Stolz looks up his old friend and finds that he has married Agafya and has fathered a son, whom Oblomov asks Stolz to raise. As the doctors predicted, Oblomov's health has declined from his routine of inactivity. Oblomov dies, fittingly, in his sleep shortly after Stolz's visit.

What are we to make of this story that violates virtually every conventional rule for the novel up to its time? At its center is a protagonist who seemingly lacks any heroism at all. To tell his story Goncharov has slowed the usual forward narrative momentum to a crawl, eliminating any series of actions beyond the daily routine, forcing a concentration on Oblomov's mannerism and oddities. Readers must adjust their focus to observe Oblomov's minutely observed consciousness and milieu, the necessary accoutrements to Oblomov's superficiality and stagnation. On one level, Oblomov's is the story of a wasted life, an allegory of a will broken and corrupted by his class. This is Stolz's diagnosis; he comments that his friend's fatal susceptibility to indolence began "with your not knowing how to put on your socks and ended with your not knowing how to live." Ironically, however, Oblomov, who is freed from doing anything by his reliance on others, becomes everyone's slave and victim. Yet Oblomov exerts a much greater resonance than merely as a victim of the serf-holding class. For V. S. Pritchett, Oblomov "seems to symbolize the soul, now he is the folly of idleness, now he is the accuser of success." Oblomov's perverse refusal to accept adult responsibility becomes a critique of those responsibilities. From the Stolz perspective Oblomov is a parasitical sluggard, but what of Oblomov's perspective on Stolz, whose frantic activities make as little sense? From the perspective of the sofa, the world seems to miss the point, and there remains something of the romantic hero in Oblomov, whose "non serviam" links him with the great opponents of self-denying intractable actuality, with Satan, Prometheus, Ahab, and others. On still another level, Oblomov is a pre-Freudian casebook study on infantile regression and the death wish. Denied the perfect fulfillment of protected, childish freedom and irresponsibility, Oblomov opts out of adulthood and retreats into his womblike sofa and Agafya's mothering. Oblomov, therefore, is ultimately multiple and contradictory, a victim, romantic hero, *and* neurotic, a mirror by which readers can read themselves and their values.

Beyond the importance of *Oblomov* as a key novel in the history of Russian literature, its wider significance rests in its exploration of the theme

THEIR EYES WERE WATCHING GOD

88

(1937)

by Zora Neale Hurston

Reading Their Eyes Were Watching God *for perhaps the eleventh time, I am still amazed that Hurston wrote it in seven weeks; that it speaks to me as no novel, past or present, has ever done; and that the language of the characters, that "comical nigger 'dialect'" that has been laughed at, denied, ignored, or "improved" so that white folks and educated black folks can understand it, is simply beautiful. There is enough self-love in that one book—love of community, culture, traditions—to restore a world. Or create a new one.*

—Alice Walker, *I Love Myself When I Am Laughing . . . And Then Again When I Am Looking Mean and Impressive: A Zora Neale Hurston Reader*

With the exception of Herman Melville's literary resurrection, there is no more impressive reclamation of a writer's reputation in American literature than that of Zora Neale Hurston and the concurrent recognition of her masterpiece, *Their Eyes Were Watching God.* Along with the rediscovery and canonization of Kate Chopin's *The Awakening,* no other American novels have risen so far from obscurity. Few college courses on African-American literature, women's literature, or 20th-century American literature fail to include Hurston's novel. It has earned the distinction, as Hurston's biographer Robert Hemenway summarizes, "as one of the most poetic works of fiction by a black writer in the first half of the twentieth century, and one of the most revealing treatments in modern literature of a woman's quest for a satisfying life." The novel's protagonist, Janie Crawford, has joined a select group of emblematic American heroines that includes Hawthorne's Hester Pyrnne, James's Isabel Archer, and Dreiser's Carrie Meeber. However, Janie Crawford is the first great black woman protagonist in American literature, and her story, along with the techniques used in its telling, would prove to be a fountainhead for subsequent novelists such as Alice Walker, Toni Morrison, and many others who have followed Hurston's example in giving voice to African-American experience from the long-overlooked woman's perspective.

A central figure of the Harlem Renaissance, Zora Neale Hurston was an innovator, a provocateur, and a contrarian. She was a pioneer in recording and incorporating black folktales and traditions into her work, invigorating American writing, as Twain had done earlier, with the power and expressiveness of the vernacular. Hurston was born in Eatonville, Florida, the first incorporated all-black community in the United States. Her father was the town's mayor and a Baptist preacher. The town's vibrant folk tradition with its frequent "lying" sessions of tall tales stimulated Hurston's anthropological and creative interests. When her mother died and her father remarried, Hurston was passed around from boarding school to friends and relatives. At 16 she worked as a wardrobe girl for a traveling light-opera troupe. She quit the show in Baltimore and went to work as a maid for a white woman who arranged for her to attend high school.

From 1918 to 1924, Hurston studied part time at Howard University in Washington, D.C., while working as a manicurist. Her first writing appeared in the African-American magazine *Opportunity*, whose founder, Charles Johnson, encouraged her to come to New York City to develop her writing and to finish her college degree. While studying anthropology at Barnard College, Hurston wrote poetry, plays, articles, and stories, and in 1925 received several awards given by *Opportunity* to promising black writers. She went on to study with the eminent cultural anthropologist Franz Boas and conducted field research in Eatonville, Haiti, and Jamaica, which was incorporated in two important folklore collections, *Mules and Men* (1935) and *Tell My Horse* (1938). Her first novel, *Jonah's Gourd Vine*, appeared in 1934, and her masterpiece, *Their Eyes Were Watching God*, in 1937. Two final novels—*Moses, Man of the Mountain* (1939) and *Seraph on the Suwanee* (1948)—along with her autobiography, *Dust Tracks on a Road* (1942), failed to halt a declining reputation, and her later years were spent in extreme poverty and obscurity. She worked for a time as a maid and a librarian before dying as an indigent, buried in an unmarked grave.

A complex woman, Hurston is described by Hemenway as "flamboyant yet vulnerable, self-centered yet kind, a Republican conservative and an early black nationalist." Some African-American critics reacted to her ideological independence and contrariness by complaining that the folk elements in her work were demeaning and one-dimensional. Seeking acceptance by mainstream literary standards, other black writers feared that Hurston's evocation of rural black experience marginalized and diminished wider acceptance of African Americans. Richard Wright dismissed her work as outside the central protest tradition that he insisted serious black literature should embrace. Reviewing *Their Eyes Were Watching God*, Wright ridiculed the novel as a "minstrel-show turn that makes the 'white folks' laugh" and could detect in Hurston "no desire whatever to move in the direction of serious fiction." Even Ralph Ellison, in whom many subsequent critics have detected influences from Hurston in the expressionistic, folk-rich, black-comic makeup of *Invisible Man*, complained about Hurston's "blight of calculated burlesque." Few initially credited Hurston's work as a major source of poetic and intellectual strength. However, as critic Judith Wilson has observed, Hurston "had figured out something that no other black author of her time seems to have known or appreciated so well—that our homespun vernacular and street-corner cosmology are as valuable as the grammar and philosophy of white, Western culture." It would take the women's movement of the 1970s and the particular advocacy of writer Alice Walker to cause readers and critics to look again at Hurston's achievement in *Their Eyes Were Watching God*, and to recognize it finally as a complex and controversial, groundbreaking work combining central issues of race, gender, and class in ways that had never previously been attempted in American literature. It is a novel that continues to stir controversy and has successfully resisted relegation to a narrow critical niche, whether as an exclusively feminist or racial text.

Hurston wrote her second novel in 1936, when she was in Haiti doing fieldwork for her second folklore collection. *Their Eyes Were Watching God* is, therefore, suffused with the exoticism of the Caribbean setting, transposed to the American landscape of Hurston's youth. Hurston identified the central impetus in writing the novel as the failed love affair she had had in 1931 with a younger West Indian student, in which she attempted to capture the "emotional essence of a love affair between an older woman and a younger man." The novel is patterned by Janie Crawford's quest for identity, by her search to transcend the restrictions imposed by others as well as the seemingly immutable laws of gender, economics, and race in the discovery of her authentic self. As the novel opens, Janie has returned to her all-black Florida community after having buried her younger lover, Tea Cake Woods, and after going on trial for his murder. She is an affront to the black community. Forty years old, she wears her hair swinging down her back like a much younger woman. A woman of means, she dresses as a man in muddy overalls. She is relegated by the community's scorn to typicality: an older woman who should know better, undoubtedly abandoned by her younger lover, returning home in shame. Nothing could be further from the truth, and Janie confesses her full story to her best friend, Pheoby Watson, chronicling her three marriages and the stages of her development that she has accomplished.

Janie's story begins with her teenage sexual awakening, prompted by her noticing the organic process of bees pollinating a pear tree. The image suggests to Janie an exalted natural concept of marriage and the beginning of her quest for a human equivalent. "Oh to be a pear tree—*any* tree in bloom!" she exclaims. "With kissing bees singing of the beginning of the world! She was sixteen. She had glossy leaves and bursting buds and she wanted to struggle with life but it seemed to elude her. Where were the singing bees for her?" Her vitalism and desire for expansion will be countered by the restrictions of others with a very different concept of a woman's place and marriage. Janie's poetry will be translated into other's prose; her sense of spirit into hard, material facts. Janie's grandmother, a former slave, imposes on her granddaughter a marriage of security with an aging farmer, Logan Killicks, to prevent Janie becoming "de mule uh de world," the inevitable fate of the unprotected black female. However, that is precisely what Janie becomes as Mrs. Killicks, property to serve her husband's economic ambition, destined to drive a second mule and enhance his acquisitiveness. Instead, Janie runs away with the similarly restless and ambitious Jody Starks, heading to the newly formed black community of Eatonville to make his fortune. Although Janie recognizes that Jody "did not represent sun up and pollen and blooming trees," he "spoke for far horizon," of expansive opportunity compared to her restricted fate as Killicks's drudge. Jody pampers his "lady-wife" with new clothes and luxuries while restricting her direct involvement in the black community that he begins to dominate. Starks desires not a mule but a "doll-baby," a precious ornament to be admired as a sign of his distinction and power. Their marriage eventually collapses, shifting its locus from the bedroom to the parlor. Locked in a stagnant existence in which she "got nothing from Jody except what money could buy, and she was giving away what she didn't value," Janie gains her liberation following Starks's death when Tea Cake Woods, 18 years her junior, comes into her life.

Tea Cake, a musician and a gambler, totally absorbed in the present, is indifferent to social conventions. Unlike Janie's first two lovers, he is also free from their class consciousness and gender notions, uninterested in her inherited fortune from Starks and unconcerned by their age difference. Tea Cake is "a bee for her bloom," making Janie feel alive, vital, truly offering the unlimited horizon that Starks once promised. Tea Cake loves her for what she is, neither a mule nor a doll-baby but an autonomous equal, and thus Janie is reborn. Their life together defies conventions of age and class, and the first lady of Eatonville dons overalls to go "on the muck" into the primitive depths of the Florida Everglades for the bean-picking season. As critic Mary Helen Washington has observed, "Here, finally, was a woman on a quest for her own identity and, unlike so many other questing figures in black literature, her journey would take her, not away from, but deeper into blackness, the descent into the Everglades with its rich black soil, wild cane, and communal life representing immersion into black traditions." Their lyrical, pastoral honeymoon there does not come unalloyed with threat. Tea Cake fears that Janie will abandon him for a lighter-skinned rival, and the couple is crucially tested in a hurricane. Here Hurston explains the significance of the novel's title as the hurricane suggests a sign of God's intention that must be anticipated and interpreted, an existential moment that forces self-definition. During the storm, Tea Cake is bitten by a rabid dog while trying to save Janie's life. In his subsequent derangement, his jealousy overpowers him, and he tries to shoot Janie, who kills him in self-defense. Forced to kill the one man she truly loves, Janie is pressed to an ultimate test, like the hurricane, that demands understanding. As a key passage in the novel makes clear, the incident, though painful, makes a crucial spiritual point: "All gods dispense suffering without reason. Otherwise they would not be worshipped. Through indiscriminate suffering men know fear, and fear is the most divine emotion. It is the stones for altars and the beginning of wisdom. Half gods are worshipped in wine and flowers. Real gods require blood."

Janie's story has now cycled back to the novel's beginning, to her return to Eatonville. Janie confesses to her friend, "So Ah'm back home agin and Ah'm satisfied tuh be heah. Ah done been tuh de horizon and back and now Ah kin set heah in mah house and live by comparison." By embracing the intensification, the immersion in experience that Tea Cake afforded her, Janie Crawford has fashioned a self-determined identity, one more organic, expansive, and vital than that prescribed by race, gender, or class. As Janie explains in her final declaration, "It's uh known fact, Pheoby, you got tuh *go* there tuh *know* there. Yo' papa and yo' mama and nobody else can't tell yuh and show yuh. Two things everybody's got tuh do fuh themselves. They got tuh go tuh God, and they got tuh find out livin' fuh theyselves."

Janie has moved from dependence to self-reliance largely through embracing experience, by not settling for the commonly imposed definition of possibility, whether as an African American or as a woman. At its thematic core, *Their Eyes Were Watching God* pushes the concept of race beyond the narrower range of equity and tolerance, protest and prejudice, into a much more expanded celebration of essential humanity that dissolves established distinctions. The conventional dichotomies of male/female, white/black, rich/poor are shown to have no real sway in the lyrical, spiritualized consciousness of Hurston's novel—hence the novel's power and its undiminished capacity to unsettle and challenge.

89

UNDER THE VOLCANO

(1947)

by Malcolm Lowry

The Volcano is a mountain. We must climb. And it is difficult to maintain a foothold at first. Yet soon we begin to feel the warmth at its core, and few books will finally flow over us so fully. . . . Of novels, few are so little like life, few are so formal and arranged; there are few whose significance is so total and internal. Nonetheless, there are scarcely any which reflect the personal concerns of their author more clearly, or incline us as steeply to a wonder and a terror of the world until we fear for our own life as the Consul feared for his, and under such pressures yields to the temptation to say what seems false and pedestrian: that this book is about each of us—in Saint Cloud, Oil City, or Bayonne, N.J.—that it is about drunkenness and Mexico, or even that it is about that poor wretch Malcolm Lowry.

—William H. Gass, "In Terms of the Toenail: Fiction and the Figures of Life"

Malcolm Lowry's reputation, like Ralph Ellison's, rests on a single novel, *Under the Volcano*, which like *Invisible Man* is one of the certain enduring achievements of the novel in the 20th century. This view is by no means uncontestable, even though considerable critical muscle can be called on for support: from Stephen Spender ("an authentic modern tragedy"), Granville Hicks ("one of the major novels of our time"), and perhaps most extravagantly by Alfred Kazin in 1969, who called Lowry's novel "the last thoroughly successful instance" of a fictional masterpiece. Yet qualification is also part of the novel's critical heritage. Viewed by some as a cult favorite of readers more interested in the doomed author than his creation or consigned to the academics who have turned the novel into a cryptic, coded message of esoteric allusions and arcane correspondences, *Under the Volcano* has been undervalued as a self-indulgent, confessional "regurgitation" of *Ulysses* (Jacques Barzun) and dismissed as "a rather good imitation of an important novel" (J. H. Jackson). Ultimately, the test for greatness in *Under the Volcano*, as with any novel, is the degree to which the reader responds to the human drama represented based on the novelist's success in converting private matter into universal significance. By my reckoning, *Under the Volcano* succeeds as few modern novels have as a daring, rich, and finally breathtaking achievement that accomplishes what Lowry set out to do: to tell the reader "something new about hell fire."

It is the Day of the Dead, November 1938, in Quauhnahuac, Mexico. Two volcanoes—Popocatépetl and Iztaccíhuatl—are in view in the distance, while a deep ravine, the barranca, cuts through the town near the ruined palace of the ill-fated Maximillian and Carlotta, and the alcoholic former British consul Geoffrey Firmin's home. In the plaza there is a fiesta. Crowds come and go to the cemetery, while children eat chocolate skulls and marzipan coffins. Yvonne, the consul's ex-wife, has this morning unexpectedly returned, offering Firmin the hope of a reconciliation and, after a desperate separation, the possibility of salvation from his torments. The consul's younger brother, Hugh, is also visiting before departing aboard a ship loaded with arms for the Loyalist forces in Spain who are being defeated at the Battle of the Ebro. Hugh is attempting to salvage his brother's life by giving him a strychnine cure to cut down his drinking. The three will take a bus trip to the Tomalin bull-throwing, and in 12 hours the consul will be officially dead, tossed into the barranca after a run-in with a group of fascist thugs. On its most basic level, *Under the Volcano* offers one of the most convincing fictional depictions of drunkenness ever recorded, but as Lowry observed, "you will be right to suspect that drinking is a symbol of something else." Lowry epically inflates his story of a drunken British expatriate caught up in a failed marriage as the "universal drunkenness of mankind during the war." Through symbol and allusion Lowry takes the reader on a guided tour of internal and external damnation, an unrelenting and moving record of the author's own experiences, patterned into archetypal and representational significance.

Lowry's decade-long struggle to convert his experiences into *Under the Volcano*, finally published after many revisions in 1947, is one of the great compositional sagas in literary history. After graduating from Cambridge in 1932 and completing an apprentice novel, *Ultramarine* (1933), about his previous seafaring adventures and a brief commitment to Bellevue Hospital in New York due to his drinking, Lowry and his first wife, Jan Gabriel, settled in Cuernavaca, Mexico, from 1936 to 1938, where he lived through most of the incidents depicted in *Under the Volcano*. Inescapably autobiographical as a writer, Lowry observed that "I do not feel so much as if I am writing this book as that *I am myself being written*." According to his fictionalized memoir in the posthumous volume, *Dark as the Grave Wherein My Friend Is Laid* (1968), Lowry traced the origin of the novel to an incident that occurred in 1936:

> We were going to a bullthrowing. . . . About halfway there we stopped beside an Indian who seemed to be dying by the roadside. We all wanted to help but were prevented from doing so . . . because we were told it was

> against the law. All that happened was that in the end we left him where he was, and meanwhile, a drunk on the bus had stolen his money out of his hat, which was lying beside him on the road. He paid his fare with it, the stolen money, and we went to the bullthrowing. . . . The whole story grew out of that incident. I began it as a short story. It then occurred to me . . . that nobody had written an adequate book upon drinking, and so while the first short version of the book was getting turned down by publisher after publisher, I began to elaborate upon that theme of drunkenness, both in my life, and in the book too, if you understand me. There's far more to it of course than that, but out of this . . . came the character of the Consul.

Eventually, his short story "Under the Volcano," was incorporated into Chapter VIII of the expanded novel with the story's consul, his daughter, and her fiancé changed to Firmin, his ex-wife, Yvonne, and his younger brother, Hugh. His principal theme—later described as "the forces in man which cause him to be terrified of himself . . . with the guilt of man, with his remorse, with his ceaseless struggling toward light under the weight of the past, and with his doom"—would be reworked and expanded through five separate drafts and a continual accretion of experiences and developments reflecting Lowry's relocation to British Columbia in 1939, his second marriage, to Margerie Bonner, in 1940, the fire in 1944 that almost destroyed his manuscript, and a return to Cuernavaca in 1945. In 1946 Lowry responded to British publisher Jonathan Cape's demand for revisions of the novel with a remarkable chapter-by-chapter defense that clarified his intentions. In it Lowry describes the novel's structure, its 12 chapters ("like that of a wheel, with 12 spokes, the motion of which is something like that, conceivably, of time itself"), reflecting the 12 remaining hours of the consul's life. Chapters alternate from the internal perspective of the major characters, and the novel begins with a risky opening chapter, set a year later on the anniversary of Yvonne and the consul's deaths, robbing the novel of a certain kind of suspense about the pair's fate but establishing an ominous foreboding of the doom that awaits in flashback. To the charge that Mexican local color is "heaped on in shovelfuls" Lowry insisted that "all that is there is there for a reason." His Mexican landscape, described as "good place to set our drama of a man's struggle between the powers of darkness and light," as well as his network of associations and allusions, are intended to generate the epic and tragic tone that the novel aspires to reach. Challenging many of the novel's conventions, Lowry explained that

> The novel can be read simply as a story which you can skip if you want. It can be read as a story you will get more out of if you don't skip. It can be regarded as a kind of symphony, or in another way as a kind of

> opera—or even a horse opera. It is hot music, a poem, a song, a tragedy, a comedy, a farce, and so forth. It is superficial, profound, entertaining and boring, according to taste. It is a prophecy, a political warning, a cryptogram, a preposterous movie, and a writing on the wall. It can even be regarded as a sort of machine: it works too, believe me, as I have found out. In case you think I mean it to be everything but a novel I better say that after all it is intended to be and, though I say so myself, a deeply serious one too.

Lowry's three epigraphs, from Sophocles, Bunyan, and Goethe, establish the serious intention surrounding the consul's demise while offering an additional key to the novel's intentions in the interconnection of three aspects of damnation—classical, Christian, and romantic—that will help delineate the consul's struggle. *Under the Volcano* is on one level a modern equivalent of Hades, visited by Odysseus and Aeneid in Homer's and Virgil's epics, in which the spirits of the dead are restored to consciousness by drinking blood. Here the living-dead consul is fueled by alcohol, which is taken like an "eternal sacrament," that grants him intense perceptions but also paralyzes him with despair, like the lost souls in the heroic epics. A second version of hell comes from Dante, and the novel can be read as a kind of *Divine Comedy* in reverse, beginning with the reunion with the consul's Beatrice and the glimpse of paradise Yvonne offers, followed by Firmin's purgation and final damnation as he is finally unable to accept the salvation that is offered him. The consul's defiance of salvation, a naturalistic condition of his alcoholism, also echoes the self-assertion of the romantic overreacher, such as Satan, Faustus, Ahab, and Kurtz, who willfully affirm the supremacy of self even at the ultimate cost of death or damnation. Given a final chance of deliverance, the consul finally rejects all aid, determined "to disintegrate as I please."

By the novel's end the consul's multiple damnations are played out in the Babel-like confusion of the Farolito cantina, where the Consul's private torments collide with reality exploding into violence and destruction. Despite the grim fate that destroys both the consul and his wife, Lowry asserted, "I don't think the chapter's final effect should be depressing: I feel you should most definitely get your katharsis, while there is even a hint of redemption for the poor old Consul at the end, who realizes that he is after all part of humanity . . . what profundity and final meaning there is in his fate should be seen also in its universal relationship to the ultimate fate of mankind." Lowry has converted his firsthand view of torment into an infernal machine to produce pity and terror in a remarkably new way: cinematic, symbolically expansive, and finally utterly convincing in its delineation of a modern soul's complex and compelling battle against disintegration.

90

SNOW COUNTRY

(1937, 1948)

by Kawabata Yasunari

It would be hard to name a work of classical Japanese literature to which Kawabata was specifically indebted, but the prevailing impression one received from Snow Country *is a work that is close to the spirit of the Heian writings. It is unmistakably modern in its manner, especially the free associations that skip from one perception to the next, but the ending of the work is as tantalizingly obscure and as aesthetically satisfying as any creation of traditional Japanese art.*

—Donald Keene, *Dawn to the West: Japanese Literature of the Modern Era*

"As the train emerged from the long border tunnel, they were in the snow country. The earth turned white under the night sky. The train stopped at a signaling station." The opening lines of Kawabata Yasunari's *Snow Country (Yukiguni)*, transporting the reader into a symbolically rich landscape, are perhaps the most famous in all modern Japanese literature. For many years college applicants in Japan were required to memorize them in preparation for their entrance examinations. Kawabata's remarkable novel, one of the masterpieces of Japanese fiction, more than any other of Kawabata's works helped win its author the first Nobel Prize in literature awarded to a Japanese writer, in 1968. *Snow Country* is likely the most-read modern Japanese novel in the West, one of the essential texts to help define modern Japanese consciousness and modern fictional expression in its subtle interplay of traditional and experimental elements.

Kawabata Yasunari (1899–1972) first emerged on the Japanese literary scene in the 1920s as one of the chief theorists of the New Perception or New Sensualist movement of loosely affiliated writers influenced by European modernism and opposed to the dominant naturalistic conventions of contemporary Japanese fiction. Kawabata's evolving aesthetic combined the compression, elimination of transitions, and presentation through image of a European modernist such as James Joyce with Japanese *renga*, traditional linked-verse poetry in which a longer poem evolves by successive additions that responds to the verse that came before, joined by association. All of Kawabata's novels somewhat follow this accretion method, beginning as diminutive works that he called "palm-of-the-hand stories" of only two or three pages. *Snow Country* commenced as a short story in 1934 and became Kawabata's first fictional work to reach novel length. He had no intention of writing an extended work when he began and no clear conception of the direction his story would take as successive scenes were added, producing a longer work, which he said "could be cut off at any point." "One could say," Kawabata later observed about his narrative method in composing *Snow Country*, "that only while I was writing the first part did the material for the later part begin to take shape. This means that while I was writing the first part, the materials from the conclusion still did not actually exist." His first story of the Tokyo dilettante Shimamura and the geisha Komako, whom he meets in Japan's snowy northern province at a hot-spring inn, appeared in a literary magazine in 1935. The characters, setting, and circumstance, however, continued to haunt his imagination, and additional scenes appeared from 1935 to 1937, when the linked stories were first collected in book form. It proved a popular success, and Kawabata issued additional sections in magazines in 1939 and 1940, revising the whole work for a final edition in 1948. Ironically, one of the last works Kawabata ever wrote was a distillation of his most famous novel back into one of his "palm-of-the-hand stories" from which it had first originated, entitled "Gleanings from Snow Country." In a sense, *Snow Country* proved to be a continuously evolving work whose resonance and significance fascinated Kawabata for nearly 40 years, until his suicide in 1972.

Alternatingly spare and direct and complexly elusive, *Snow Country* describes three visits by the wealthy, middle-class Tokyo resident Shimamura to a hot-spring resort in northern Japan over a period of nearly three years. Cut off from modern Japan by snowfalls of as much as 15 feet and its rugged mountains, "snow country" represents a retreat into a revivifying natural setting and a way of reconnecting with traditional Japanese customs and values by Shimamura, who is described as living "a life of idleness," who "tended to lose any sense of purpose, and he frequently went out into the mountains to recover something of it." Allied (and contrasted) to the purifying, regenerating quality of snow country is the somewhat tawdry sexual allure provided by the hot-spring geishas to gratify unaccompanied male visitors to snow country. Unlike city geishas ennobled by their accomplishments as singers, dancers, and great beauties, hot-spring geishas are closer in association to common prostitutes, doomed to fade with their looks. At its core, therefore, *Snow Country* considers the role and nature of beauty, its necessity and sacrifice, embodied in the landscape and in particular in the woman, Komako, whom Shimamura meets.

The novel opens with Shimamura's second visit in early winter (his first, during the previous spring, is related by flashback). Wiping condensation from the window as the train arrives in snow country, Shimamura sees the reflection of a young woman, Yoko, who is caring for an invalid, and he is struck by her "inexpressible beauty." Shimamura, a specialist in Western ballet, which he has never seen performed, is a quester after such ideal beauty who resists direct contact with the things he loves. His quest and its inevitable compromises when translated into reality will set the conflict for the novel's tragedy. Captured by his first appearance, Shimamura is depicted as a detached observer threatened and repelled by the corruption he finds in the world. His relationship with Komako will test his capacity to connect the beautiful and the real and to accept the consequence. When he first meets her, Shimamura is struck by Komako's cleanliness, vibrancy, and freshness. Not yet a geisha, she serves as a temporary fill-in hostess when needed and retains her virginal quality despite evidence of a clear animal sexuality. Komako is one of the Kawabata's triumphs in psychological portraiture and one of the great fictional depictions of a Japanese woman. Kawabata would later respond to persistent questions about the sources for his fiction by stating that "The events and the emotions recorded in *Snow Country* are products more of my imagination than of reality. Especially with respects to the emotions attributed to Komako, what I have described is none other than my own sadness. I imagine that this is what has appealed to readers."

When she first meets Shimamura, Komako is somewhat precariously balanced between girlish innocence and the reality of her situation as a prospective geisha. Although the pair intends to be only "friends," they make love on the night of their second day of acquaintance following Komako's drunken return from a party. Shimamura responds to their intimacy by leaving the hot-spring town the next day and not returning until six months later. Attracted to Komako's beauty and passion, Shimamura is incapable of combining his aesthetic vision of her with her more complex and difficult reality, in the conjunction of spirit and body.

A change in Komako is evident on his return. She has become a geisha, now available to any man on request, and the subtle changes in Komako's looks and temperament form the psychological and emotional core of the novel. The couple resumes their affair, which progresses through intimacy and familiarity to a kind of married life. Their closeness, however, results in Shimamura's second departure, as he is unable to cope with his ideal in human form. Instead, he is increasingly taken with the disembodied image of virginal beauty glimpsed at his arrival in the form of the girl Yoko.

The final, third visit is two years later in early autumn, concluding with the first snow. Caught between the lush green foliage of spring and summer and the purifying winter snow, the landscape takes on aspects of decay and corruption, which are reflected in Komako's increasingly faded beauty. The decisive collapse of their relationship hinges on a slip of the tongue. In the climactic scene of the novel, Shimamura praises Komako by calling her a "good girl" but, when he repeats his compliment, he changes his phrase to a "good woman." It is a subtle, but crushing blow, suggesting the phrase made to a prostitute by her client on the morning after. Shimamura suggests that Komako's days of fresh, unspoiled beauty are over, and that their relationship is now associated with Komako's trade as a fading prostitute. The novel has through a series of sharply etched scenes and nuanced conversations shown their relationship shift from virginal to married, and finally to the debased transactions between prostitute and client.

The cycle of the rise and fall of love and beauty is hauntingly concluded in the novel's much interpreted close. The cocoon warehouse catches fire, and Komako attempts to rescue Yoko from the burning building. Yoko is an embodiment of the virginity that Komako has lost. It is this vision of Komako, in a sense cradling her lost self, that prompts Shimamura's final epiphany: a recognition of the painful and inexorable cycle of life and death, the conjunction of the ideal and the real, as "the Milky Way flowed down inside him with a roar." Like James Joyce's brilliant use of the symbol of snow at the conclusion of "The Dead," Kawabata's concluding images of Komako holding Yoko before the blazing fire and the cold white of the first snow and the Milky Way produce a reverberating series of suggestions that gathers up the novel's many themes into an expansive totality. Implied is Shimamura's connection with the universe that he has long resisted. He at last moves from detachment to direct contact with the world that contains both great beauty and its opposite. Implied as well is Komako's acceptance of the woman she has become, a fusion of ideal qualities and inevitable realities.

Kawabata has achieved a remarkable presentation of some of the central issues of human existence captured in precise, lyrical, and symbolically powerful language and scenes that draw on his snow country setting and combine great beauty and the transient and tragic quality of life and existence.

91

NINETEEN EIGHTY-FOUR

(1949)

by George Orwell

Nineteen Eighty-Four *is a book that goes through the reader like an east wind, cracking the skin, opening the sores; hope has died in Mr. Orwell's wintry mind, and only pain is known. I do not think I have ever read a novel more frightening and depressing; and yet, such are the originality, the suspense, the speed of writing and withering indignation that it is impossible to put the book down. The faults of Orwell as a writer—monotony, nagging, the lonely schoolboy shambling down the one dispiriting track—are transformed now as he rises to a large subject. He is the most devastating pamphleteer alive.*

—V. S. Pritchett, review of *Nineteen Eighty-Four*, 1949

Nineteen Eighty-Four is the unavoidable nightmare of the 20th century. It is the warning that still haunts our consciousness now that this singular novel about the future has become a novel about the past. As critic Irving Howe has perceptively observed, *Nineteen Eighty-Four* is a book that is rarely reread because no reader is likely ever to forget it. Despite the passing of the chronological 1984, there is little that seems anachronistic in Orwell's vision. It remains a crucial fictional measure of how far our civilization has come in realizing its potential horrors. (Moreover, as we now have another date, 9/11, to gauge what we were and what we have become, as we have been asked to ready ourselves for an open-ended war on terrorism and as issues of patriotism and recrimination suggest our own version of "Hate Week," Orwell's vision offers strikingly urgent correspondences.) If the prophecy of *Nineteen Eighty-Four* remains unfulfilled, the threat is still believable. O'Brien's statement—"If you want a picture of the future, imagine a boot stamping on a human face—forever"—retains its chilling relevance. In so many essential ways, Orwell's novel has given us the means to imagine a worst-case scenario and the vocabulary to name it. It is unlikely that any other novel has provided so many words and concepts that have entered our cultural consciousness—"doublethink," "Newspeak," "Big Brother," "Thought Police," "proles," "unperson"—abstract concepts made concrete, unforgettable, and referable to our world through the skill and daring of Orwell's vision.

Nineteen Eighty-Four is Orwell's last work, completed shortly before his death. Its despairing, bleak tone is clearly attributable to his grief over his wife's death in 1945 and his own intermittent attacks of tuberculosis that would take his life in 1950. In a sense, however, *Nineteen Eighty-Four* is less a response to Orwell's painful present than a synthesis of the crucial events and issues of the first half of the 20th century that Orwell witnessed and documented throughout his writing career. Born in 1903, Orwell grew up in a version of Winston Smith's "Golden Country," before the disruption caused by World War I, when Britain's imperial power was unrivaled and its hierarchical class structure unchallenged. Orwell's first exposure to life under a totalitarian regime that forecast his depiction of tyranny in *Nineteen Eighty-Four* was his tormented prep school days. Reflecting on the beatings and abuse he received in the essay, "Such, Such Were the Joys . . ." Orwell observes, "This was the great abiding lesson of my boyhood: that I was in a world where it was not possible for me to be good. . . . It brought home to me for the first time the harshness of the environment into which I had been flung." Orwell would further experience that environment, first as a member of the British civil service in Burma and then as a common laborer from 1927 to 1933, in a descent to the lowest depths of poverty. Political solutions to the inequities he experienced disappointed him as well. Volunteering to fight for the Republican cause during the Spanish Civil War, Orwell observed at first hand the brute power of the Fascists under Franco and betrayal by the Communists. During World War II, Orwell worked for the British Broadcasting Corporation as a propagandist, continually beset by the fear that to combat totalitarianism, humanity, integrity, and individuality were being compromised and sacrificed, and that there was no way out. He would write in 1944 that "Capitalism leads to dole queues, the scramble for markets, and war. Collectivism leads to concentration camps, leader worship, and war." Amid the harsh postwar rationing and the emerging cold war among the former Allies, Orwell set to work on what he called "a novel about the future—that is, it is in a sense a fantasy but in the form of a naturalistic novel." Set in the future, the date of which was arrived at by inverting the year it was written, *Nineteen Eighty-Four* is one of literature's greatest anti-utopias, less a prophecy than a warning of where society is headed unless disturbing aspects of contemporary life are corrected. He would later publicly repudiate efforts to use the novel as part of antisocialist propaganda, claiming that

> My recent novel is NOT intended as an attack on socialism or on the British Labour Party (of which I am a supporter) but as a show-up of the perversions to which a centralized economy is liable and which have already been realized in Communism and Fascism. I do not believe

> that the kind of society I describe *necessarily* will arrive, but I believe (allowing of course for the fact that the book is a satire) that something resembling it *could* arrive.

Beginning with the novel's memorable opening sentence—"It was a bright cold day in April, and the clocks were striking thirteen"—*Nineteen Eighty-Four* initiates its imaginative displacement of recent world history into a logical terrifying conclusion. The world is controlled by three superpowers—Eurasia, Eastasia, and Oceania. London, called Airstrip One, is a province of Oceania, a totalitarian state in which the populace is grouped into three classes: the Inner Party (the ruling elite), the Outer Party (the party functionaries), and the proles, the vast, ignorant class of laborers. The symbol of power, the leader of the state, is Big Brother, a figurehead who may or may not be an actual person but whose pictures and statues are omnipresent, as are the three central party slogans: "War Is Peace," "Freedom Is Slavery," "Ignorance Is Strength." In 1984, since war is continual as the means for insuring the Party's control and hence social stability, it is in a sense peacetime. Control is maintained by four monolithic ministries: the Ministry of Truth (involved in falsification), the Ministry of Peace (concerned with war), the Ministry of Love (maintaining law and order), and the Ministry of Plenty (responsible for chronic shortages). Individuality has been replaced by an absolute conformity to the rules of the Party, with compliance monitored by the ever observant telescreens, in which even thoughts that differ from party orthodoxy are fatal crimes. Objective truth has disappeared since the past is continually being rewritten to conform with current events and policies.

Orwell's nightmare state, combining elements of communism, fascism, and wartime social engineering and propaganda, is dramatized through the rebellion of the novel's protagonist, Winston Smith, an Outer Party member who works for the Ministry of Truth revising the historical record. Winston begins to keep a diary, a record of private thoughts and his opposition to the Party and its objectives. It is an act of defiance that he realizes is fatal. "Thoughtcrime does not entail death," he observes; "thoughtcrime is death." The novel will record his brief rebellion and inevitable downfall. He begins an equally fatal affair with another worker in the Ministry of Truth, Julia, and the pair eventually retreat to an upstairs room above Mr. Charrington's antique shop, unequipped with a telescreen, for moments of intimacy and privacy. Their conspiracy widens to include O'Brien, another functionary at the Ministry of Truth whom Winston believes is sympathetic and is involved in the force of opposition to the Party known as the Brotherhood. O'Brien gives Winston and Julia a copy of the analysis of the operating principles of the Party, "The Theory and Practice of Oligarchical Collectivism," presumably written by the leader of the Brotherhood, Emmanuel Goldstein. In it Orwell makes clear that the maintenance of perpetual power alone is the purpose of the Party, and all is designed to eliminate opposition to the Party's will. This includes continual war to focus the populace on external enemies while justifying privation, reducing the function of love to procreation to insure that loyalty is only given to the Party, and reengineering language itself so that undesirable concepts will be inconceivable.

When Winston has answered his questions regarding the whys of the Party, he is made to feel its full power and authority. His and Julia's private room has been a trap; the kindly Mr. Charrington turns out to be a member of the Thought Police, and O'Brien is in charge of a long-term investigation to convict Winston of thoughtcrimes. Taken to the Ministry of Love, Winston goes through both physical and mental torture designed to destroy his sense of moral superiority and reeducate him in the absolute power of the Party. He is compelled to accept not only that two plus two equals five, but that he must not simply submit but love his torturer. As O'Brien declares, "I shall save you, I shall make you perfect." The one last shred of Winston's independence and self-respect is his selfless love for Julia. In the most chilling scene in the novel, that, too, is destroyed as Winston faces the worst thing in the world for him in Room 101: a cage of starving rats attached to a face mask. Before the rats are released, Winston screams, "Do it to Julia! Not me! Julia!"

Winston's reeducation is now complete. The one thing he has loved he has symbolically killed, destroying himself in the process. No longer a threat to the Party, Winston is released and given a new job. He spends his off-hours drinking synthetic "Victory Gin." He meets Julia again, and they admit to having betrayed each other. They feel nothing except relief when they separate. As the novel ends, the telescreen in the dingy Chestnut Tree café announces a decisive military victory, while Winston contemplates the face of Big Brother silently watching him:

> Forty years it had taken him to learn what kind of smile was hidden beneath the dark mustache. O cruel, needless misunderstanding! O scented tears trickled down the sides of his nose. But it was all right, everything was all right, the struggle was finished. He had won the victory over himself. He loved Big Brother.

Orwell's fable is ultimately so unforgettable and so powerful due to its creator's remarkable ability to translate the abstractions of politics and culture into the physical reality of a compelling human story that strikes at our deepest fears about privacy and personal identity and our tenuous autonomy in a world beyond our control.

92

AS I LAY DYING

(1930)

by William Faulkner

When Faulkner was questioned on As I Lay Dying, *he invariably replied that it was a tour de force. As much by the speed with which it was written as by the audacity of its technique and the superb virtuosity of its art, the novel is precisely that. It charms like a brilliant impromptu, dazzles like a perfectly executed trapeze exercise. Of all Faulkner's novels, it is perhaps the most agile, the most adroit, the one in which the writer's mastery of his craft and the versatility of his gifts reveal themselves in the most spectacular way. It is also, beneath its guise of an improvisation, one of his most complex and most intriguing works.*

—André Bleikasten, *Faulkner's As I Lay Dying*

Compared to the long and often tortuous delivery of Faulkner's other great masterpieces—*The Sound and the Fury* and *Absalom, Absalom!*—his fifth novel, *As I Lay Dying*, came to him fully formed at its inception and was completed in a great sprint of imaginative intensity. "Before I began I said," Faulkner declared, "I am going to write a book by which, at a pinch, I can stand or fall if I never touch ink again." Faulkner's grotesquely heroic account of the hardscrabble Bundren family's attempt to bury its matriarch, Addie, while contending with what Faulkner described as "the two greatest disasters known to man: flood and fire" on their journey through the blazing heat of midsummer Mississippi is fractured into 59 alternating monologues by 15 witnesses, from the four Bundren brothers—Cash, Jewel, Darl, and Vardaman—their sister Dewey Dell, and their father Anse, to a chorus of eight neighbors and those encountered along the way, as well as the dead Addie herself. In Faulkner's daring, Cubistlike structure of multiple, juxtaposed perspectives, narrative coherence and a full understanding of the family's past and motives emerge only gradually, reassembled by the reader out of often conflicting, subjective, and biased testimony. With such a book, Faulkner asserted, "the finished work is simply a matter of fitting bricks neatly together, since the writer knows probably every single word right to the end before he puts the first one down. This happened with *As I Lay Dying*. It was not easy. No honest work is. It was simple in that all the material was already at hand." The result is one of Faulkner's greatest technical achievements and one of his most profound explorations of the human condition. With *As I Lay Dying* Faulkner dissolves the fundamental polarities of human existence: life and death, the individual and the group, language and actuality, private and public, comedy and tragedy in pursuit of a new synthesis that expresses a fuller truth. As much a metaphysical and ontological quest as a family's internment drama, *As I Lay Dying* is in every sense the tour de force that Faulkner habitually described it, a masterpiece in which the vernacular and its regional setting buttress a profound, universal human drama.

In 1928, Faulkner was in New York City revising the final draft of *The Sound and the Fury* and working with an editor on the cuts that turned *Flags in the Dust* into his third novel, *Satoris*, the first with a Yoknapatawpha County setting and the first of his works in which Faulkner contended he had discovered his fictional voice. Spent over the long and painful composition of *The Sound and the Fury*, Faulkner returned home to Oxford, Mississippi, determined to address his dire financial situation by writing a commercial success. He recalled a story he had heard from a young prostitute in a Memphis nightclub who had taken up with an impotent gangster nicknamed Popeye who had raped her with a corncob and kept her as virtual captive in a brothel. In January 1929, Faulkner set out to turn this story into a popular "shocker." In February, his publisher rejected *The Sound and the Fury* because it was judged incomprehensible and not likely to find "a profitable audience," to which Faulkner replied, "That's all right. I did not believe that anyone would publish it." Faulkner's editor, Harrison Smith, however, had formed his own publishing company, Smith and Cape, and was willing to gamble on Faulkner's brilliant, experimental novel. In May 1929, Faulkner submitted *Sanctuary*, a novel with seven violent murders, rape, and incest. Smith wrote back, "Great God, I can't publish this. We'll both be in jail." (A revised version would be eventually published in 1931 and become the popular sensation that Faulkner had intended, bringing him his first national attention and financial success.) In the summer of 1929, Faulkner married his childhood sweetheart, Estelle Oldham, a divorcee with two children. After a honeymoon on the Gulf Coast, Faulkner returned to Oxford and to support his new family took a job working the 12-hour night shift at the university's power station. From six to 11, he delivered coal to the fireman who shoveled it into the dynamo's boiler. Between 11 and four, when power demand was lowest, as the fireman dozed in a chair, Faulkner overturned his wheelbarrow in the coal bin and used it as a desk, writing to the sound of the dynamo, which he called "the finest sound to work by I have ever heard." In six weeks beginning October 25, 1929, just a few weeks after the publication of *The Sound and the Fury* and a few days after the stock market crash that began the Great Depression,

Faulkner completed *As I Lay Dying.* He described his new work to Smith as "a son bitch sho enough," with its title taken from Homer's *Odyssey* in which Agamemnon describes the calamity that occurred on his return to the House of Atreus ("As I lay dying the woman with the dog's eyes would not close my eyelids for me as I descended into Hades."). "How's that for a high?" Faulkner wrote to his editor.

As I Lay Dying represents both a complication and a simplification of the theme and method of *The Sound and the Fury.* As in the earlier novel, Faulkner presents a family drama of inadequate parents and their damaged children from multiple viewpoints within the family. However, instead of the four narrative divisions of *The Sound and the Fury*—of the three Compson brothers and a third-person narrator centered on the family's servant, Dilsey—*As I Lay Dying* multiplies both the number of viewpoints (all seven Bundrens and eight "outsiders") and narrative sections (59). Despite this increase in perspectives and fragmentation, *As I Lay Dying* is considerably easier to follow than *The Sound and the Fury.* Instead of the flashbacks and flashforwards before and during the period 1910 to 1928 in the earlier novel, time in *As I Lay Dying* contracts to a 10-day, straightforward chronological sequence, beginning with an account of Addie Bundren's death and the family's subsequent journey, in fulfillment of her wishes, to bury her with her people in the cemetery at Jefferson, 40 miles away. Less a disjointed series of interior monologues that *The Sound and the Fury* sometimes resembles, *As I Lay Dying* employs clearly identified alternating first-person narration, with each of the various narrators advancing the action in a logical, chronological sequence shaped dramatically and suspensefully by the Bundrens' goal of completing their delivery mission. The monologues here more closely resemble soliloquies, and as Faulkner's biographer Frederick Karl has stated, *As I Lay Dying* can be regarded as "Faulkner's first play." Like *The Sound and the Fury,* key secrets relating to family relationships that the Bundrens repress are withheld from the reader and are only gradually clarified. Finally, although both novels share a nihilistic tone, established by Faulkner's reference to Shakespeare's lines—life "is a tale/Told by an idiot, full of sound and fury,/Signifying nothing"—the tragic resonance of *The Sound and the Fury* is in *As I Lay Dying* complemented with a greater emphasis on the comic absurdity and grotesqueness of life's meaninglessness. The Bundrens' heroism as they doggedly contend, Job-like, with the punishing forces aligned against them is continually undercut by the ludicrousness of their situation and their behavior, transporting a putrefying corpse in the Mississippi summer heat in defiance of all common sense and propriety. Absurdist comedy is juxtaposed with existential tragedy, complicating the reader's assessment of the Bundren family and the significance of their actions.

The literal and figurative center of the novel is Addie herself, both dead and alive. Introduced on her deathbed as her son Cash constructs her coffin outside her window, presenting each board for her approval before nailing it in place, Addie suggests someone in a liminal state, suspended between life and death, symbolic of the contradictory role she will play throughout the novel, as well as Faulkner's interest in overturning or, more precisely, interpenetrating rigid categories of human experience. Married to the shiftless Anse, who is convinced that sweat is fatal and who has managed mainly by having others work for him, Addie has endured a kind of living death with her unresponsive husband. Now in death she assumes a more vital and central role than she ever played in life. The Bundrens, riven by resentments, instinctual needs, and divisive compulsions, will be brought together as a family to carry out Addie's final request for burial in Jefferson. Yet each is far from selflessly devoted to their task. Anse, called by the critic Cleanth Brooks, "one of Faulkner's most accomplished villains," wants to take advantage of the visit to Jefferson to obtain "store-bought teeth." Cash, the cool-headed, practical craftsman, would like to buy a "graphophone." The pregnant Dewey Dell wants to procure medicine that will induce an abortion. The youngest, Vardaman, the Benjy-like innocent who, struggling to comprehend his mother's death, drills holes into her coffin (and Addie's face) to give her air, wants a toy train. The visionary, intuitive Darl, the Hamlet-like figure in this domestic drama, is jealous of his mother's favorite, self-centered, cruel Jewel, who refuses to let his mother go and blames everyone else for her death. As the critic Harold Bloom has observed, "The Bundrens manifestly constitute one of the most terrifying visions of the family romance in the history of literature." Faulkner devises for them a mythic journey to deliver Addie "home" for burial, setting in motion the means to unbury the various family secrets and traumas that have crippled them, while turning the Bundrens' alternately ludicrous and heroic efforts into a universal and existential drama.

With the bridges down by flood, the six-day journey to Jefferson takes on the quality of an epic challenge causing the family and several onlookers to confront its meaning. Faced with the rapidly decomposing corpse they are transporting, each faces the question to what extent the coffin holds mother, wife, neighbor, human being, or only noxious matter that should be disposed of as quickly as possible. Vital spirit or memento mori, Addie in her coffin is the still center of the novel's swirling action that culminates in the two biblical tests of flood and fire. Forced to ford the swollen Yoknapatawpha River, the Bundrens are forced into an elemental immersion described by Darl:

> It is as though the space between us were time: an irrevocable quality. It is as though time, no longer running straight before us in a diminishing line, now runs parallel between us like a looping string, the distance being the doubling accretion of the thread and not the interval between. The mules stand, their fore quarters already sloped a little, their rumps high. They too are breathing now with a deep groaning sound; looking

> back once, their gaze sweeps across us with in their eyes a wild, sad, profound and despairing quality as though they had already seen in the thick water the shape of the disaster which they could not speak and we could not see.

Struck by a log, the wagon overturns, the mule team is lost, but the coffin is rescued. Anse, stripped now of the means of continuing the journey, sells Jewel's most prized possession, his horse (a displaced substitute for his mother), for another team. Undercutting the Bundrens' heroic resistance to the flood and their stubborn determination to accomplish Addie's last wishes at all costs is Addie's own testimony that makes clear that she has set her family their task out of sheer vindictiveness and penance for the life she has led with Anse. In the tour de force monologue of this tour de force novel, unlocking the family secrets and the philosophical core of the book's meditation on the link between sex and death, being and nonbeing, words and actuality, Addie offers an interpretation of her father's saying "that the reason for living was to get ready to stay dead a long time." For Addie, living requires a vital sexual drive to break through one's isolation—"my aloneness had to be violated over and over each day." Anse, who "did not know that he was dead," fails her, and, after giving birth to her two sons, Cash and Darl, Addie achieves the violation she requires in an affair with the preacher Whitfield, the father of Jewel. "I gave Anse Dewey Dell to negative Jewel," Addie confesses. "Then I gave him Vardaman to replace the child I had robbed him of. And now he has three children that are his and not mine. And then I could get ready to die." Addie makes clear that failed autonomy and mutuality are at the core of the novel's existential drama, and their breakdown is the source of the family's disintegration. Anse, who was incapable of apprehending Addie's vital existence in life, must now contend with the reality of her corpse in death, as her children, damaged by too much or too little love from their needy, bereft mother, struggle for a sustaining grasp on their reality.

As the burial journey continues, buzzards circle the wagon attracted by the stench emanating from the coffin that appalls all they pass. On the fifth day of their journey, the Bundrens stay the night at Gillespie's farm. Darl, who insists on bringing an end to the family's painful and pointless mission, sets fire to the barn where the coffin is being stored. Jewel, however, manages to save his mother's coffin, riding it out of the burning barn like a horse. Finally arriving at Jefferson the next day, they manage to bury Addie, but the successful completion of their quest mixes tragedy and black comedy. Darl, who is turned in by his siblings as a barn burner, is taken away to a prison for the criminally insane; Cash's broken leg, set grotesquely in concrete by his family, is treated, but he will be permanently crippled. Dewey Dell is deceived and seduced by a soda jerk pretending to be the druggist, and the toy train that Vardaman had been promised would be in the drugstore window is gone. Only Anse emerges from the ordeal unscathed. Acquiring his new teeth by appropriating the money Dewey Dell had saved for her abortion drug, Anse returns to his family ready for the return home with a new acquisition, introducing the duck-shaped woman from whom he had borrowed the spades to bury Addie, saying "Meet Mrs. Bundren."

Managing what Cash the craftsman calls "on a balance," *As I Lay Dying* unites tragedy and comedy, unavoidable death and irrepressible life, private selves and public actions, soul and body, heroism and absurdity, naturalism and symbolism. It aspires, like all Faulkner's great works, to the widest possible truth in which limited and simplistic categories of experience and expression are made to reveal the greatest mysteries and meanings of our existence.

93

THE PICKWICK PAPERS

(1836–37)

by Charles Dickens

It is doubtful if any other single work of letters before or since has ever aroused such wild and widespread enthusiasm in the entire history of literature.

—Edgar Johnson, *Charles Dickens: His Tragedy and Triumph*

What is initially striking about Charles Dickens's remarkable achievement in his first novel is the sense of the collision of the accidental with the incendiary genius of a 24-year-old, relatively obscure journalist and parliamentary reporter. *The Pickwick Papers* launched Dickens's career as a novelist to unrivaled heights, helped to establish the novel as the dominant literary form of the Victorian period, and set the model for the ways fiction would be published for a significant portion of the 19th century. All because Dickens, who was not the first choice of publishers Chapman and Hall, was hired to supply the text for a series of Cockney sporting sketches for a picture book to be published in monthly installments by the popular illustrator Robert Seymour. Most established writers would have rejected both the use of their words as a mere accompaniment to the book's illustrations and the installment form of publication, a method previously reserved for cheap reprints of standard works, religious tracts, and vulgar comedies. Dickens, however, who had begun to get noticed for his series of views of London street life, *Sketches by Boz*, jumped at the chance to earn £14 for each monthly installment. He could marry his intended, Catherine Hogarth, and begin in earnest his career as a full-time writer.

What happened next is one of the great publishing stories of all time. Dickens convinced Chapman and Hall to modify Seymour's original concept of views of the sporting misadventures of a group of townsmen to give the writer "freer range of English scenes and people." Dickens was no sportsman, but he was fresh from his travels reporting on provincial elections and filled with details about contemporary customs and characters that he wanted to exploit through the travels of Samuel Pickwick and his fellow club members—Nathaniel Winkle, the amateur sportsman, Augustus Snodgrass, the aspiring poet, and Tracy Tupman, the romantic bachelor. As Dickens's control over the project increased, Robert Seymour watched his own part in what had been his concept shift to a secondary position by the sheer force of the young writer's imagination and ambition. The illustrator dutifully completed the revision of his drawings demanded by his young collaborator for the series' second number and then committed suicide.

Seymour's death caused Chapman and Hall to consider abandoning the project, but Dickens offered a plan to alter it, putting the onus on his imagination to save the situation. Dickens proposed increasing the monthly text from 24 to 32 pages and reducing the number of illustrations in each installment from four to two. *The Pickwick Papers* was thereby transformed into a novel, giving Dickens more space to develop his characters and situations. With his introduction of Sam Weller, Mr. Pickwick's Cockney servant in Number 4, sales of the series exploded. Number 1 had an initial printing of 1,000 copies, and Number 2 and 3 half as many, but with Number 4, sales increased to more than 20,000 per month. By the conclusion of the novel's installment run, monthly sales had risen to 40,000 copies, and the novel had become not just a success but a phenomenon. Pickwick merchandise flooded the market. There were Pickwick hats, canes, cigars, jest books, and china figurines, Pickwick songs, dances, stage productions, and unauthorized sequels. Judges read parts during breaks in trials, while the poor pooled their pennies to share each installment, with the illiterate having each number read to them. The book's initial audience was drawn to Dickens's comic inventiveness and was transfixed by the young author's ability to craft a fresh, comic masterpiece out of stock characters and situations. As a result of the success of *The Pickwick Papers*, the installment form of publication was established as one of the principal ways Victorian novels would appear (all of Dickens's following 13 novels would appear in either monthly or weekly installments, either separately or part of a periodical offering), increasing the novel's appeal by putting book ownership into the hands of individuals who previously could not afford novels. *Pickwick* allowed readers to extend payments for novels over a 19-month period, made it possible for publishers to recoup their costs regularly during the same period, and established an unprecedented relationship between novelist and audience as monthly sales immediately gave the writer a clear reaction to a work in progress.

It is not surprising, given the inherited conception and improvisational nature of publication, that *The Pickwick Papers*, or more precisely *The Posthumous Papers of the Pickwick Club Containing a Faithful Record of the Perambulations, Perils, Travels, Adventures and Sporting Transactions of the Corresponding Members*, begins as a series of picaresque episodes and interpolated tales. Samuel Pickwick and his companions set out from London to Rochester, where they fall in with the rascally, though irresistible, Alfred Jingle, who gets Winkle involved in a duel. They move on to Dingley Dell and the home of the Wardles, where Jingle reappears and elopes with Mr. Wardle's sister. Jingle is pursued, and Mr. Pickwick, ever in need of a practical guide, engages the irrepressible, street-smart Sam Weller as his servant, providing a Cockney Sancho Panza for the idealistic and naive Quixote-like Pickwick. Together they visit Eatanswill during a parliamentary election and Bury St. Edmunds, where Jingle and his servant Job Trotter resurface. Both are again pursued to Ipswich, where at an inn Mr. Pickwick accidentally enters the bedroom of a middle-aged lady during the night, provoking a conflict with her admirer. The novel proceeds, therefore, to new locations, situations, and characters with little unity beyond the episode, nor with much depth of characterization beyond comic types. However, the novel's episodic structure finally develops into an actual plot, when Mrs. Bardell, Pickwick's London landlady, confused over Pickwick's intentions, falls into the hands of lawyers and brings a suit against Mr. Pickwick for breach of promise. The trial, one of the novel and literature's comic triumphs, results in a judgment for the plaintiff, and Mr. Pickwick, who refuses to pay the damages, is imprisoned. Pickwick by this time has been transformed in Dickens's handling from a comic cliché to a moral force and archetype of innocence and benevolence. In the Fleet, Pickwick begins to see himself and his world clearly for the first time, and the novel's exuberant comedy begins to reflect real-world concerns and consequences. The novel concludes with a satisfying resolution, including the regeneration of Jingle, the long-delayed marriage of the perennial bachelor Winkle, and Pickwick's retirement from his travels into a small community of fellowship and good intentions.

The Pickwick Papers is a triumph of Dickens's ability to animate characters and scenes, and is a rich, exuberant catalog of unforgettable situations and dialogue. It is also the beginning of the novelist's pantheon of remarkable fictional portraits, including the coachman Tony Weller, medical students Bob Sawyer and Benjamin Allen, the Fat Boy, the rapacious lawyers Dodson and Fogg, Mr. Sergeant Buzfuz, and a host of others. The novel allowed Dickens to develop his imaginative muscle while learning to control his powers under the pressure of serial publication. At this early stage of his career, Dickens apologetically observed in the preface written after the novel's installment run that "no artfully interwoven or ingeniously complicated plot can with reason be expected." He would go on to write the most artfully interwoven and ingeniously complicated plots imaginable in this "detached and desultory form of publication," producing mystery novels, such as *Bleak House*, *Little Dorrit*, *Great Expectations*, and *Our Mutual Friend*, that are also massive social and moral fables. *The Pickwick Papers* announced the arrival of a writer whom Edmund Wilson called the "greatest dramatic writer the English had

had since Shakespeare." If *The Pickwick Papers* lacks the artistry, the daring social themes, and accomplishment of Dickens's later works, such as *Bleak House*, *David Copperfield*, and *Great Expectations*, it is still one of the comic treasures of English and world literature, the beginning of his incredible ability to reshape the world imaginatively in ways that continue to be described as "Dickensian."

94

THE BETROTHED

(1827, 1840)

by Alessandro Manzoni

If Manzoni had been thinking of the public's wishes, he would have had the formula handy: the historical novel with a medieval setting, with illustrious characters as in Greek tragedy, kings and princesses . . . great and noble passions, heroic battles, and a celebration of Italian glories from a period when Italy was a land of the strong. . . . But what does Manzoni do instead? He chooses the seventeenth century, a period of servitude, and lowly characters, and the only swordsman is a scoundrel. Manzoni tells of no battles, and dares weigh his story down with documents and proclamations. . . . And people like him, everyone likes him, learned and ignorant, old and young, devout and anticlerical, because he sensed that the readers of his day had to have that, even if they did not know it, even if they did not ask for it, even if they did not believe it was fit for consumption. . . . Manzoni did not write to please the public as it was, but to create a public who could not help liking his novel.

—Umberto Eco, *Postscript to The Name of the Rose*

Umberto Eco's point that the greatest writers create their own readers is well taken as applied to Alessandro Manzoni's single fictional achievement, *The Betrothed (I promessi sposi).* In it, in fundamental ways, Manzoni altered fictional expectation, helping to initiate reader demand for the real rather than the ideal. By doing so, Manzoni contributed significantly to the redefinition of the novel in the 19th century as a truth-telling instrument of great delicacy and sophistication. Perhaps no other work of fiction, with the exception of Cervantes's *Don Quixote,* has proven to be such a dominating native cultural icon as Manzoni's novel, and no other work in Italy other than Dante's *Divine Comedy* has done more to establish the literary language of Italian. Having begun the modern novel tradition in Italy with *The Betrothed,* Manzoni labored in his revisions of his novel to create out of the Tuscan dialect a national language that as much as any political movement helped to unify his homeland.

Manzoni devoted nearly 20 years to the creation and revision of his single masterwork. The author of a few previous poems and essays as well as two verse tragedies, Manzoni conceived the idea for his novel in 1821, while reading extracts from Italian proclamations during the Counter Reformation of the 17th century. "The memoirs that we have of that period," Manzoni wrote to a friend as he was starting his novel, "show a very extraordinary state of society; the most arbitrary government combined with feudal and popular anarchy; legislation that is amazing in the way it exposes a profound, ferocious, pretentious ignorance; classes with opposed interests and maxims; some little-known anecdotes, preserved in trustworthy documents; finally a plague which gave full rein to the most consummate and shameful excesses, to the most absurd prejudices, and to the most touching virtues . . . that's the stuff to fill a canvas." Like the Jacobite Rebellion of 1745, which animated Walter Scott's imagination and produced *Waverley*, Manzoni seized on a similar pivotal era that illustrated the clash of ideology and values between the aristocracy and peasantry, intellect and faith, revolution and order. To fill his canvas and perfect his portrait, Manzoni spent two years conducting research and writing the first version of his novel published in 1827; three more for a revised edition; and 12 more for the final, definitive edition of 1840.

Located in the Duchy of Milan in 1628, *The Betrothed* is set in motion by the interruption of the marriage ceremony of two young peasants, Renzo Tramaglino and Lucia Mondella, by the nobleman Don Rodrigo, who desires to seduce Lucia. Eluding a kidnapping attempt by Don Rodrigo's henchmen, the couple seeks help from the saintly Capuchin monk, Fra Cristoforo, who directs Lucia and her mother to the safety of a convent in the city of Monza and sends Renzo to a monastery in Milan. The novel thereby divides its interest between what happens separately to Lucia and Renzo before their reunion at the novel's conclusion.

Arriving at Monza, Lucia is put in the care of Sister Gertrude, a nun who years before had been sent there against her will by her family to avoid paying her bridal dowry. Gertrude, sometimes called the Nun of Monza, is one of the novel's most intriguing characters. Frequently compared with Flaubert's Emma Bovary, she is a complex individual beset with romantic delusions in the grip of external forces she cannot control. Don Rodrigo eventually learns of Lucia's sanctuary and recruits the aid of the powerful, mysterious aristocrat called the Unnamed (L'Innominato) to capture her. A Byronesque romantic hero, the Unnamed is driven to evil and destruction by a conviction that life is absurd, and he is, therefore, freed from any moral constraints. The Unnamed uses the intelligence of Sister Gertrude's complicity in a murder to compel the nun to send Lucia out of the convent; he then takes her to his mountain retreat. Lucia's great beauty and virtue, however, regenerates the Unnamed, who decides not to return her to Don Rodrigo, repents his former evil ways, and converts to Catholicism. Through the agency of the historical Cardinal Federigo Boromeo, Lucia is reunited with her mother and sent to the home of a charitable noblewoman for their protection.

Meanwhile, Renzo never reaches the Capuchin monastery in Milan but instead becomes swept up in a bread riot that grips the city. Arrested by the police as an instigator, Renzo is freed by the mob and flees into Venetian territory, where he works in a silk mill under an assumed name. More than a year passes, and Renzo learns from Lucia by letter that she had vowed during her captivity that if she survived she would never marry. Renzo returns to Milan to find Lucia and persuade her to relent, but while searching for her in the plague-ridden city, Renzo is stricken. He recovers and learns that Lucia has also become a plague victim and has been sent to a *lazaretto* with other plague survivors. There Renzo meets Fra Cristoforo, who is ministering to the sick, as well as the cause of the couple's long distress, Don Rodrigo, who is near death from the disease. At Fra Cristoforo's urging, Renzo pardons the nobleman and promises to pray for his soul. Renzo is finally reunited with Lucia, and Fra Cristoforo solves the couple's dilemma by insisting that their betrothal vow supersedes Lucia's vow of chastity. The couple, once again betrothed, returns to their village where they are at last married before moving on to Venice, where Renzo returns to the silk mill, and the couple raises a large family.

The drama of separated lovers has been a convention of prose romances from the Greeks through Shakespeare's dramas. In two regards, however, Manzoni revolutionized the romantic standard. Manzoni's ill-fated lovers are not nobles (or nobles in disguise) but are in fact peasants, and by placing such ordinary characters at the center of his novel, Manzoni signals his shift toward realism. One contemporary reviewer immediately perceived that *The Betrothed* was "a dangerous book because the peasants cut such a better figure than the nobles." Renzo and Lucia become in a sense the novel's first proletarian heroes. Peasants before Manzoni rarely claimed center stage or the moral high ground compared to the aristocracy. Secondly, their travails also are not set in a romantic netherworld but in an elaborately presented actuality, refined by minute research to an authenticity rarely previously attempted in fiction. "I do what I can to become imbued with the spirit of the time I am to describe," Manzoni observed about his method of historical reconstruction, "in order to live in it." The scenes of mob violence in Milan and the graphically described impact of the plague are high points of the novel and hallmarks of new standard of fictional realism. Renzo and Lucia encounter not a series of marvelous adventures as much as a host of psychologically complex characters, including Gertrude, Fra Cristoforo, and the Unnamed, whose interpolated stories widen the novel's focus and help to shift the emphasis from the pathos of the forlorn lovers to a panoramic depiction of an entire culture and its values. It is certainly something of this realistic texture that Edgar Allan Poe noted in his review when he called the novel "a work which promises to be the commencement of a new style in novel-writing. . . . It might be too much to say that the novel is every sense original." That originality points the way for the massive realism that would follow in the wake of *The Betrothed* in novels such as Dickens's *Bleak House*, George Eliot's *Middlemarch*, and Tolstoy's *Anna Karenina*. As critic Richard Maxwell observes, these novels "owe much to *The Betrothed* in their presentation of related but distinct actions through intricately woven back-and-forth narratives. Such contrapuntal structures create the impression of a society miraculously represented in its completeness—seen from every side. Decades earlier than these other books, Manzoni showed how this feat could be accomplished. Paradoxically, then, *The Betrothed* is a romance that made possible the major works of realistic fiction."

It is for this reason that more than a few critics have described the novel as the greatest prose work produced in 19th-century Europe. If Walter Scott opened the territory of history for the novelist, certainly Manzoni, exploiting Scott's innovation, widened the realistic range for the novel. Scott's appreciation of his protégé's achievement is captured in an apocryphal account of the two authors' meeting (there is no evidence that they ever met) in which Scott congratulated Manzoni on *The Betrothed* and Manzoni responded that he was the other's debtor for everything he had written. Scott then replied, "In that case, this is my finest work."

95

PALE FIRE

(1962)

by Vladimir Nabokov

Pale Fire, *written after half a century of violent revolution, world war, totalitarian terror, and the genocidal slaughter of millions, . . . is very much a self-conscious novel of our times. Its display of the writer's blue magic of word-and-image play is a dazzling delight; its affirmation of the abiding beauty of life in the imagination is brilliantly enacted in the fiction; but after the last glitter of the prestidigitator's implements, it is the shadow of the assassin that falls on the final page. . . . Our vision of the imagination, through the history-haunted quixoticism of this self-conscious novel, has been both enlarged and subtly, somberly transformed; and that is precisely what the novelistic enterprise, from the seventeenth century to our own age, has at its best achieved.*

—Robert Alter, "Nabokov's Game of Worlds"
in *Partial Magic: The Novel as Self-Conscious Genre*

In one of the earliest and still one of the best critiques of Vladimir Nabokov's *Pale Fire*, Mary McCarthy called it "a jack-in-the-box, a Fabergé gem, a clockwork toy, a chess problem, an infernal machine, a trap to catch reviewers, a cat-and-mouse game, a do-it-yourself kit." She concludes her assessment by asserting that "this centaur-work of Nabokov's, half-poem, half-prose, this merman of the deep, is a creature of perfect beauty, symmetry, strangeness, originality, and moral truth. Pretending to be a curio, it cannot disguise the fact that it is one of the very great works of art of this century, the modern novel that everyone thought was dead and that was only playing possum." Often cited as postmodernism's exhibit A in its undermining of realistic illusion by ingeniously and originally calling attention to the artifice of language, literary form, and the problematic workings of the imagination, *Pale Fire* is actually linked to the novel's great alternative tradition of antirealism and the genre defined by the critic Robert Alter as the "self-conscious novel," that "systematically flaunts its own condition of artifice and that by so doing probes into the problematic relationship between real-seeming artifice and reality." Originating with Cervantes's *Don Quixote*, the self-conscious novel would be continued in the works of Fielding, Sterne, Laclos, Gogol, Proust, Joyce, Bely, Musil, Gide, and many more. *Pale Fire* is one of the form's triumphs, a masterwork of reflectivity and a hall of mirrors that achieves far more than dizzying disorientation and gamesmanship. "In sheer beauty of form," Nabokov's biographer Brian Boyd contends, "*Pale Fire* may well be the most perfect novel ever written." Simultaneously a metafiction, an ontological and epistemological meditation, a case study of delusion and paranoia, and a murder mystery, *Pale Fire* is also a compellingly profound drama of human desire and the imagination's daring and dangerous remaking of the world.

Nabokov's earliest inkling of what would become *Pale Fire* occurred in 1957 after he had completed his follow-up to *Lolita*, one of his most delightful and accessible novels, *Pnin*, the story of a bumbling Russian émigré scholar's coping with life at an upstate New York college, reflecting Nabokov's own teaching experiences at Cornell. In the synopsis of a new novel called *Pale Fire* that he sent to his publisher, there is no reference to poem or commentary that would eventually supply the novel's structure. The only components of the eventual work are an exiled ex-king from a mythical country and an assassin who is tracking him:

> The story starts in Ultima Thule, an insular kingdom where a palace intrigue and some assistance from Nova Zembla clear the way for a dull and savage revolution. My main creature, the King of Thule, is dethroned. After some wonderful adventures he escapes to America. . . . He lives more or less incognito, with the lady he loves, somewhere on the border of Upstate New York . . . The book is regularly interrupted, without any logical or stylistic transition, right in the middle of a sentence . . . by glimpses of an agent . . . whose job is to find and destroy the ex-king.

Nabokov set aside this idea for a novel for the next three years to tackle his monumental translation of Pushkin's *Eugene Onegin*. Ironically, Nabokov's own proliferating and contentious commentary that dwarves the text of Pushkin's poem would serve as the structural foundation for his novel when the success of *Lolita* allowed Nabokov to resign his teaching position at Cornell and move to Europe in 1960 where he took it up again. In New York, before departing, Nabokov reported that he had "thought up something big," recording in his diary, "*The Theme* a novel, a life, a love—which is only the elaborate commentary to a gradually evolved short poem." Now the basic machinery was in place for his novel which would eventually consist of four interrelated parts: a 999-line poem of four cantos in heroic couplets, written by the American poet John Shade during the final month of his life, along with an editor's foreword, commentary, and index, supplied by Shade's faculty colleague and next-door-neighbor, Charles Kinbote. Settled in Nice, Nabokov tackled the poem first, describing it as "the hardest stuff I ever had to compose," and Shade its fictional creator, "by far the greatest of *invented* poets." Shade teaches at Wordsmith College in New Wye, Appalachia. The poem, "Pale Fire," is an autobiographically based meditation filled with the poet's childhood memories, his art, reflections on death, and the grief he feels over the suicide of his daughter, Hazel, and its implication for meaning and purpose in the universe. Managing an affirmation by the poem's conclusion, Shade declares:

> I feel I understand
> Existence, or at least a minute part
> Of my existence, only through my art,
> In terms of combinational delight;
> And if my private universe scans right,
> So does the verse of galaxies divine
> Which I suspect is an iambic line.
> I'm reasonably sure that we survive
> And that my darling somewhere is alive,
> As I am reasonably sure that I
> Shall wake at six tomorrow, on July
> The twenty-second, nineteen fifty-nine,
> And that the day will probably be fine . . .

Moments after writing these lines asserting an order in the universe, Shade is shot to death as he walks with his next-door neighbor, the émigré scholar Charles Kinbote, on the way to a drink celebrating the completion of his poem.

Kinbote, a refugee from Zembla, a country somewhere north of Russia, who has managed since his recent arrival on campus as a faculty member to ingratiate himself with the admired, renowned Shade, seizes the poem and flees to a cabin in the Southwest where he completes his scholarly edition of Shade's poem—with foreword, extensive commentary, and index. Within the first paragraphs of Kinbote's foreword, the reader confronts a critic whose massive ego and obsessions betray any expected scholarly objectivity or detachment by continual insertions of his own personality, perspectives, and ideas at every turn. Invited at the outset to consider several of his notes, the reader who departs from the linear reading of foreword-text-commentary-index is immediately assaulted by the disjunction between Shade's verse and Kinbote's interpretation, signaling Kinbote's unreliability and the reader's need to "interpret" Kinbote as he is interpreting Shade's poem. At its most basic level, *Pale Fire* works as a diabolically comic parody and satire on academic exegesis, exposing the ways in which a scholar can misappropriate a text, insinuate himself into it, and force it to mean what he would like it to say. Kinbote's obsessions and delusions go well beyond those of the overzealous self-aggrandizing scholar, however. As he insists, "without my notes Shade's text simply has no human reality at all since the human reality of a poem such as his (being too skittish and reticent for an autobiographical work), with the omission of many pithy lines carelessly rejected by him, has to depend entirely on the reality of its author and his surroundings, attachments and so forth, a reality that only my notes can provide." Kinbote's bullying and daft gloss on Shade's poem constitute an alternative narrative or, rather, one of several alternative narratives that begin to emerge in the collision between poem and commentary.

Kinbote believes he has provided Shade with his poem's subject based on Kinbote's tales of his native Zembla and its exiled king, Charles the Beloved, who has been ousted in a revolution. Having pressed his Zembla story on Shade "with a hypnotist's patience and a lover's urge," Kinbote is undeterred after acquiring the poem when he finds few explicit references to any aspect of the Zembla saga he was expecting. His gloss, however, "corrects" Shade's discretion and the suspected censorship from Shade's wife, Sybil, interpreting the poet's autobiographical work as a coded text chronicling the fall of Charles the Beloved and his flight from Zembla, landing in disguise as an émigré professor at an American college campus. Eventually admitting to be Charles the Beloved himself, Kinbote also reveals that the Shadows, the Zembla secret revolutionary police, have dispatched a gunman named Jakob Gradus to assassinate him, and that Kinbote-Charles was the killer's actual target when Shade was murdered.

Penetrating beneath the surface of Kinbote's commentary, attuned to his hints and slips (as he has read between the lines of Shade's poem), the reader eventually realizes that there is even a greater disparity between Kinbote's assertions and the truth with yet another narrative line emerging here: Our commentator is not just delusional, he is mad and is neither Charles the Beloved nor Charles Kinbote but actually a much mocked teacher in the Russian department with halitosis named Vseslav Botkin. He has invented the imaginary kingdom of Zembla to reign over as Charles the Beloved to compensate for his dislocation from his Russian homeland and his present campus reality that has relegated him as a despised nobody and whose paranoia is behind both his delusions of grandeur and persecution complex that cause him to believe that he is an assassin's target. Shade's killer is not Jakob Gradus but who he says he is, Jack Grey, an escaped criminal lunatic, who is after Botkin-Kinbote-Charles the Beloved's landlord, Judge Goldsworth, who committed him to his asylum. Shade who resembles the Judge is the victim of mistaken identity, suffering the same fate as his poem that is misinterpreted to death by the mad Botkin-delusional Kinbote-king in exile.

Like a series of false bottoms and fun house mirrors, *Pale Fire* scrambles perspective and causality. Shade's American pastoral meditation on his life and family is hijacked to reveal a royal drama in faraway exotic Zembla expressing the needs and desires of the poem's commentator as the poem has expressed the needs and desires of its creator. Shade's harnessing his memories and grief in his orderly couplets contrasts with Kinbote's wildly imaginative transformation of similar needs into the scholarly apparatus of foreword, commentary, and index. In their congruence, Nabokov offers a master class on art's power both to consume and redeem. Kinbote and Shade are mirrored opposites: Shade, the American, family man, poet reflects a more sinister double in Kinbote—Zemblan, homosexual, isolated, prose writer. Shade's expressions of love, hope, and lucidity contrast with Kinbote's loneliness, despair, and madness: two sides of the same imaginative coin. Each reflects the other and the imaginative process they share. Reflection, indeed, is encoded in virtually every aspect of the novel, becoming its central theme. It is part of the novel's title drawn from Shakespeare's *Timon of Athens*, Act IV, scene 3, in which the moon is indicted "an arrant thief, / And her pale fire she snatches from the sun," producing illumination through reflected light. Reflection is the basis of Zembla itself, as Kinbote explains "the name Zembla is a corruption not of the Russian zemlya [land], but of Semblerland, a land of reflections, of 'resemblers.'" Mirror images and reflections sound the keynotes at the opening of Shade's poem in the image of a bird killed by flying into a window deceived by its reflection of sky and the nighttime reflection of the room's interior projected on the outside wintry landscape:

> I was the shadow of the waxwing slain
> By the false azure in the windowpane;
> I was the smudge of ashen fluff—and I
> Lived on, flew on, in the reflected sky,
> And from the inside, too, I'd duplicate
> Myself, my lamp, an apple on a plate:
> Uncurtaining the night, I'd let dark glass
> Hang all the furniture above the grass,
> Covered my glimpse of lawn and reached up so
> As to make chair and bed exactly stand
> Upon that snow, out in that crystal land!

That crystal land, Kinbote insists, is a coded reference to Zembla. What it really is is an invocation to the entrancing and ever elusive domain of the imagination that exists always at a remove from the thing it is after, reality. As Nabokov commented in an interview given when he was composing *Pale Fire*, "You can get nearer and nearer, so to speak, to reality, but you never get near enough because reality is an infinite succession of steps, levels of perception, false bottoms, and hence unquenchable, unattainable." *Pale Fire* dramatizes this pursuit of the unquenchable and unattainable and the imagination's extraordinary capacity to reflect the world in the order and lucidity of art and in the obsessive compulsions and delusions of madness.

THE LAST OF THE MOHICANS 96

(1826)

by James Fenimore Cooper

It is easy to find fault with The Last of the Mohicans; *but it is far from easy to rival or even approach its excellences. The book has the genuine game flavor; it exhales the odors of the pine woods and the freshness of the mountain wind. Its dark and rugged scenery rises as distinctly on the eye as the images of the painter's canvas, or rather as the reflection of nature herself. But it is not as the mere rendering of material forms, that these wood paintings are most highly to be esteemed. They are instinct with life, with the very spirit of the wilderness; they breathe the sombre poetry of solitude and danger. In these achievements of his art, Cooper, we think, has no equal.*

—Francis Parkman, "The Works of James Fenimore Cooper"
in *The North American Review*, January 1852

Few today dare to claim artistic greatness for Cooper, particularly after Mark Twain's tour de force indictment of his "Literary Offenses": "A work of art? It [in this case *The Deerslayer*, but certainly Twain would say the same of *The Last of the Mohicans*] has no lifelikeness, no thrill, no stir, no seeming of reality; its characters are confusedly drawn and by their acts and words they prove that they are not the sort of people the author claims they are; its humor is pathetic; its pathos is funny; its conversations are—oh! Indescribable; its love-scenes odious; its English a crime against the language." Yet Cooper persists, despite all his "offenses" as America's first great mythmaking novelist, like Twain himself, initiating a national literature and an indigenous imaginative landscape that continues to haunt us. *The Last of the Mohicans* is Cooper's most popular work, the second of the five Leatherstocking Tales, which proved to be Cooper's principal legacy. It is his one unavoidable novel that, like Stowe's *Uncle Tom's Cabin*, claims iconic status, having seeped into our collective consciousness whether we have read the original or not. In it, the protagonist, Nathaniel "Natty" Bumppo, introduced in *The Pioneers* (1823) as a 70-year-old fading figure of America's frontier past, is shown in his prime as the intrepid, self-reliant, quintessential hero of early America.

Hawkeye, his name in *The Last of the Mohicans*, is the first great American hero, the prototype either to be imitated or reacted against by virtually every native hero that has followed. He is, in the words of Edwin Fussell, "that new man, the generic American, the metaphor of the western frontier fleshed out as a human being."

The Last of the Mohicans shifts its action back in time to the mythopoetical realm when the future of America hung in the balance between the primitive and the civilized, between the French and the British, between white men and red men. It is the first novel to treat this decisive cultural moment, and the first novel to consider in depth the humanity and psychology of Native Americans and their place in American culture and conscience. If there is truth to Hemingway's assertion that the source of all American literature is Twain's *Huckleberry Finn*, a comparable argument could be made that another progenitor is *The Last of the Mohicans.* Both novels open up the great mythic resources of the American landscape; both embed in their dramas essential questions of race and the American identity. Cooper's importance as a novelist has perhaps been best appreciated by D. H. Lawrence, who, granting all the offenses that Twain alleges, still claims Cooper as the Homer of American literature. For Lawrence the Leatherstocking Tales "go backwards, from old age to golden youth. That is the true myth of America. She starts old, wrinkled and writhing in old skin. And there is a gradual sloughing of the old skin, towards a new youth. It is the myth of America." In his adventure story in the wilderness of America, Cooper provides a myth of renewal and rebirth and, in Lawrence's view, a "new relationship" that promised a "new society": "a stark, stripped human relationship of two men [Hawkeye and Chingachgook] deeper than the deeps of sex . . . the two childless, womanless men, of opposite races. They are the abiding . . . [and represent] the inception of a new humanity." Subsequent critics have considered this relationship—the prototype for Ishmael and Queequeg, Huck and Jim, the Lone Ranger and Tonto—and the other racial, social, and gender patterning of *The Last of the Mohicans* as establishing the essential metaphors for an understanding of American history and the American psyche. "If Cooper is of only secondary importance as an artist," scholar Richard Chase argues, "he is of the first importance both as a creator and critic of culture. In his novels and other writings he was both the analyst and the visionary of American conditions."

The Last of the Mohicans blends the historical novel elements inherited from Scott's Waverley novels with indigenous American forms, such as the captivity narratives and biographical accounts of frontiersmen such as Daniel Boone. The time is 1757. The place is near Lake George, in northern New York State, during the French and Indian War. Cora and Alice Munro travel through the wilderness from Fort Edward to Fort William Henry, where their father is the English commanding officer. Half sisters, Alice is blond and in need of protection; while Cora is dark, showing traces of her mother's

West Indian background, and more practical and vital. They are accompanied by Major Duncan Heyward, a young British officer from Virginia, who is in love with Alice, and David Gamut, a Connecticut singing-master. Their guide through the woods is a renegade Huron named Magua, who claims that he knows a shortcut to their destination. Hawkeye and his companions, Chingachgook and his son Uncas, the last descendants of the once mighty Mohican tribe, fall in with the group and point out that Magua has been leading them in a circle. Suspected of treachery to expose the party to attack by the Iroquois, Magua escapes, and Hawkeye agrees to guide the party to safety.

They seek shelter at Glenn's Falls in a cave on an island in the middle of the river, with the falls on either side. Under attack by a hostile Indian band led by Magua, and with their ammunition gone, Cora convinces Hawkeye and his companions to escape for help in order to rescue them later. After the remaining party is captured by Magua, Heyward tries to convince him that he should betray his comrades and deliver them to Colonel Munro for a large reward. Magua agrees, but only if Cora consents to be his wife. Cora refuses, and just as the enraged Indians prepare to kill their captives, Hawkeye and his friends rescue them.

They arrive at Fort William Henry, which is under siege by the French. Challenged by a young French sentinel, Heyward fools him by conversing in French, and the party then passes through enemy lines, following the trail left by a cannonball at Hawkeye's suggestion to find their way in the dense fog. To break the siege, Hawkeye is dispatched to Fort Edward for assistance, which is refused (a satirical thrust at English military incompetence that predicts the English defeat in the Revolutionary War). Fort William Henry is forced to capitulate, and Montcalm, the French commander, agrees to a safe passage for the garrison and its inhabitants back to the protection of the English. However, when one of the Indian allies of the French kills a mother and her child, it sparks a massacre, which the French do nothing to halt. During the carnage and chaos, Magua seizes Alice and flees, pursued by Cora and David Gamut. On the third day following the massacre, Hawkeye, his two Indian friends, Heyward, and Munro search for signs of the sisters. Cora's veil and a trinket owned by Alice point out the correct trail to them.

They eventually reach a Huron camp and meet the singing-master, who is allowed to wander about on his own because the Indians think he is feebleminded due to his spontaneous habit of psalm singing. He reports that Alice is in the Huron camp nearby, while Cora is with a tribe of Delawares some distance away. Heyward, disguised as a French doctor, enters the Huron camp in the hope of saving Alice. Aided by Hawkeye, dressed in an Indian conjurer's bearskin, Heyward carries away Alice wrapped in a blanket. Uncas, who has also been captured, escapes wearing the bearskin with Hawkeye dressed in the singing-master's clothes while Gamut impersonates Uncas.

They seek the protection of the Delawares. The next day, Magua visits the Delawares and demands the prisoner he left with them. Indian custom compels compliance, but Uncas, who is recognized as a descendant of a great chief who was once a friend of Tamenund, the ancient leader of the Delawares, pledges to pursue Magua to rescue Cora, whom he loves. The Delawares, led by Uncas, Chingachgook, and Hawkeye, win a victory over the Iroquois in a climactic forest battle. However, Cora is fatally stabbed by a Huron; Magua kills Uncas; and Hawkeye shoots Magua.

The novel concludes with the Delawares' solemn burial of Cora and Uncas. Cora's body is interred on a small knoll near some "young and healthy pines." Uncas, arrayed "in his last vestments of skins," is placed "in an attitude of repose, facing the rising sun, with the implements of war and of the chase at hand, in readiness for the final journey." Chingachgook eulogizes his lost son as "good . . . dutiful . . . brave," and grieves that he is now alone. Hawkeye interrupts him to say that Chingachgook is not alone since his friend remains with him. The two companions stand over the grave of Uncas, with their "scalding tears" watering it "like drops of falling rain." Tamenund concludes the funeral with his declaration that he has "lived to see the last warrior of the wise race of the Mohicans."

Cooper instructed his readers in his first preface to concentrate on the narrative and not to seek within *The Last of the Mohicans* "an imaginary and romantic picture of things." Part of the novel's appeal is certainly its irresistible power as a fast-moving, exciting adventure tale. With its two captivity sequences and rescues balanced by the historical Fort William Henry massacre, the novel's narrative momentum and suspense carry the reader forward, in the words of an early reviewer, "as through the visions of a long and feverish dream. The excitement cannot be controlled or lulled, by which we are borne through strange and fearful, and even agonized scenes of doubts, surprise, danger, and sudden deliverance." Yet the novel's romance and mythic dimension are equally responsible for the persistence of *The Last of the Mohicans,* derived from the idealization that Twain and others have deplored. Beginning with Cooper's remarkably evoked wilderness of great beauty and menace, the novel deals ultimately with the archetypal. Cooper's Indians fool no ethnologist. Even Francis Parkman, who admired the book, concedes that his "Indian characters . . . it must be granted, are for the most part either superficially or falsely drawn." Yet they represent a considerable advance in humanity over previous depictions of the "red savages." Magua, in particular, although assuming the role of the novel's satanic villain, is given a clear and compelling motivation for his villainy in his degradation at the hands of Colonel Munro. Cooper also allows him to mount a telling case against the whites for the dispossession of the Indians based on white "gluttony": "God gave him enough, and yet he wants all. Such are the pale faces." Magua's charge is difficult to dismiss, as is the sentiment derived from

Uncas's death and Tamenund's moving elegy that converts the last of the Mohicans into a memorial to the doomed Indian in civilized America. Magua and Tamenund, impossibly villainous and noble in turn, provoke the reader at a deep level about American justice, equality, and racial identity. In one of the dominating interpretations of the novel, Leslie A. Fiedler has isolated its secret theme as miscegenation. In his reading, *The Last of the Mohicans* derives its power from exploring threats to racial purity. Uncas and Cora, deviants from the white norm, threaten to cross racial lines and must be killed, and Cooper compensates his guilt over their demise (and its implication) with the sexless, homoerotic love between Hawkeye and Chingachgook.

Ultimately, it is the appeal of the frontiersman Hawkeye that establishes the novel's core mythmaking power. A border figure caught between the civilized and the primitive, Hawkeye represents the essential American character traits that have persisted: strong, steadfast, and deadly, a man of multiple identities, fated to keep moving west just ahead of the forces of civilization that threaten to destroy the wilderness from which he has derived his exceptional powers. We know where he is heading and what will become of the Eden-like forest of *The Last of the Mohicans*, and therein resides a crucial element of the novel's power and pathos.

97

LES MISÉRABLES

(1862)

by Victor Hugo

With his seemingly unrepresentative life, his egocentrism, his isolation and his bizarre, patchwork religion, Hugo had produced the most lucid, humane and entertaining moral diagnosis of modern society ever written. For all the sniggering about his cranky predictions and self-serving idealism, it should now be said, 135 years after the novel appeared, that he was as close to being right as any writer can be, that a society based on the principles dredged by Hugo out of the sewers of Paris would be a just and a thriving society, and that, were biographers not far more prone to the petty professionalism commonly ascribed to Hugo, readers should be advised immediately to put down this book and go and read Les Misérables.

—Graham Robb, *Victor Hugo: A Biography*

What a magnificent mess *Les Misérables* is! One can only wonder how Hugo's masterpiece would fare if submitted today for critique at any writer's workshop. Hugo's incomparable account of the battle of Waterloo, his disquisitions on historical forces, convent life, street slang, and the Paris sewer system would almost certainly be marked for excision as irrelevant. And what of Hugo's dependence on coincidence for his narrative glue or the operatic crescendos of sentiment and exclamations, his unabashed reaching toward the grandiose symbol? More an anthem than a realistic novel, *Les Misérables*, like Tolstoy's *War and Peace*, which it resembles, defies any conventional novel category. Part detective story, part historical chronicle, social, philosophical, and religious treatise, *Les Misérables* mixes the lyrical and dramatic, comedy and tragedy, romance and realism, analysis and prophecy into what can only be described as a prose epic so expansive that selectivity gives way to an unprecedented inclusiveness. Testing the limits of the novel's form and any standard of artistic decorum, *Les Misérables* has been scorned critically but read avidly by an immense worldwide audience, making it, in Graham Robb's view, "one of the last universally accessible masterpieces of Western literature." *Les Misérables* has become what only a handful of other literary works—Homer's epics, Virgil's *Aeneid*, the *Divine Comedy*—have achieved, a mythic summation of a culture's history and values. Among novels, only a very few continue to resonate throughout the world on stage and in film adaptations like *Les Misérables.* The wretched criminal Jean Valjean and his implacable pursuer, Inspector Javert, have become instantly recognizable archetypes whose duel has entered the collective unconscious. Yet those who have made their acquaintance outside the pages of Hugo's massive text have encountered only their trimmed-down shadows. For a full appreciation of Hugo's achievement there is no substitute for the original.

In literary history Victor Hugo is incomparable. A dominating force through most of the 19th century, the seminal figure of French romanticism as a poet, playwright, and novelist, Hugo owned an outsized ego that caused him to regard himself as the conscience of his age and the displaced soul of the French people in exile during the reign of Napoleon III. It is Hugo's prophetic side, his call for social and spiritual reform, that illuminates *Les Misérables* and gives his novel its remarkable visionary power. As he intoned in the book's preface, "So long as there shall exist, by reason of law and custom, a social condemnation, which, in the face of civilization, artificially creates hells on earth, and complicates a destiny that is divine, with human fatality; so long as the three problems of the age—the degradation of man by poverty, the ruin of woman by starvation, and the dwarfing of childhood by physical and spiritual night—are not solved; so long as, in certain regions, social asphyxia shall be possible; in other words, and from a yet more extended point of view, so long as ignorance and misery remain on earth, books like this cannot be useless." Hugo first conceived his story of a convict and a fallen woman as a modern myth of social redemption and natural justice in the 1840s. His first novel since *Notre-Dame de Paris* (1831) had the initial working title of *Jean Tréjean*, then *Les Misères,* but the project was set aside as Hugo devoted his creative energy to poetry and politics.

Having been attracted to the cult of Napoleon Bonaparte around 1831, to liberalism between 1832 and 1835, and to the July Monarchy of Louis-Philippe (1830–48), Hugo's political ideals shifted to accommodate the times. In 1845 he was named a Peer of France, and during the Second Republic (1848–51), Hugo, as a member of the Legislative Assembly, was a committed republican whose opposition to the restoration of the empire under Louis Napoleon Bonaparte, nephew of Napoleon I, led to his expulsion from France in 1851. In partially self-imposed exile on the Channel Islands that was to last 19 years, Hugo was the Javert-like, dogged opponent of the emperor he branded "Napoleon the Little," the enemy of progress and social justice. As he took up his earlier manuscript, surveying contemporary French affairs under what he regarded as a repressive regime, the revised *Les Misérables* was expanded to serve a widened purpose, not just to affirm humanity under institutional assault through the oppression of the Second Empire but to trace French history from the fall of Napoleon through the Restoration to the revolutionary forces that toppled the Bourbons and by implication could oust Napoleon III as well. His novel would become the summa of Hugo's understanding of human nature and social institutions, a kind of bible of self- and social liberation. Highly anticipated through a massive advertising campaign, *Les Misérables* was released in parts throughout Europe and abroad during 1862. The sensation it caused as an immediate international best-seller was unparalleled in publishing history, as individuals from every class queued for copies, consuming entire editions in hours. Hugo's famous succinct inquiry, "?," to his English publisher about how his book was selling, prompted an equally terse and unequivocal response of "!" It was clear that Hugo had met a perceived popular need. As his friend Paul Meurice reported to Hugo about the reception of the novel, "Everyone is raving! Everyone is carried away! There is a complete absence of petty objections and pedantic reservations. The crushing weight of so much grandeur, justice, and sovereign compassion is all that counts. It is quite irresistible."

Not all were bowled over, however. Baudelaire condemned *Les Misérables* as an "unspeakably foul and stupid book," and Lamartine called it "a dangerous book. . . . The masses can be infected by no more murderous, no more terrible, passion than a passion for the impossible." Attacked for its method and message, *Les Misérables* still asserted a hold on the popular imagination that has not yet diminished. The appeal of *Les Misérables* derives from Hugo's ability to combine a skillfully arranged, suspenseful story with a moral and social fable. Covering 17 years of French history from 1815 to 1832, Hugo links the fate of the social outcast Jean Valjean to universal questions of justice and the reclamation of the individual in his wider political, moral, spiritual, and philosophical context. Released from prison after 19 years of hard labor for stealing bread, Valjean has been brutalized and debased by a justice system designed only to punish and a social system that refuses to grant a convict's humanity and worth. At the novel's outset, Valjean is redeemed by the charity and forgiveness of Bishop Myriel, whom he robs. "Jean Valjean, my brother," the bishop declares, "you belong no longer to evil, but to good. It is your soul that I am buying for you. I withdraw it from dark thoughts and from the spirit of perdition, and I give it to God." Reborn as an agent of good, Valjean will be continually tempted to save himself, not others, and will show his moral superiority in his selflessness and charity despite his background as justifying Myriel's confidence in him. Embodied in Valjean's moving story are Hugo's central themes of the perfectibility of mankind through love and good work and the unseen human potential of even the most wretched, whom society represses and ignores to its shame.

It is in this context that Javert's pursuit of Valjean is understood by Hugo, reversing the conventional notion that associates criminality with evil and law and order with good. The police inspector is the agent of a social system that refuses to acknowledge any possibility for Valjean other than his criminality and insists that the letter of the law must be served without mercy or mitigation. In disguise as a prosperous factory owner and mayor, Valjean is suspected by his former prison guard of being the former convict and parole breaker, and the novel follows the pursuer and the pursued as Valjean tries to fashion a meaningful life under threat of exposure of his criminal past. Befriending the prostitute Fantine, another of the novel's wretches shown sympathetically, Valjean adopts her daughter, Cosette, after her mother's death. Safely hidden in a Paris convent while Cosette grows to womanhood, Valjean and Cosette reenter the wider world in which Valjean is forced to relinquish his beloved companion by acknowledging the greater claims of love in Cosette's affection for the revolutionary Marius Pontmercy. The climax of the novel is the doomed Revolution of 1832, in which the forces of history and the themes of authority and liberation followed in the personal story of Valjean collide with their wider, social implications. On the barricades, Valjean risks his life and freedom to save Marius for Cosette while encountering Javert for the last time. A prisoner of the rebels, Javert now is at the mercy of Valjean. Instead of executing him, Valjean sets Javert free, an act of charity that destroys Javert psychologically. After the novel's most famous adventure, the breathless pursuit of Valjean carrying the wounded Marius through the Paris sewers, Javert finally manages to gain his prey, but the reality of who Valjean is and what he has done on the policeman's behalf destroys Javert's rigid notion of criminality and his stark dichotomy of the world as either law abiding or law breaking, an untenable insight that results in his suicide. Now free of the hatred and relentless pursuit of the policeman, Valjean must accommodate himself to his continuing outcast status, excluded from the domestic happiness of the married Cosette and Marius. As his final testimony, Valjean is forced to acknowledge to Marius, "I am of no family. I am not of yours. I am not of the family of men, but they are not for me. I am the unfortunate; I am outside. . . . To be happy, I! Have I the right to be happy? I am outside of life, monsieur." Facing his death stoically, Valjean manages a final affirming benediction and Hugo's canonization of his romantic hero: "It is nothing to die; it is frightful not to live."

Such a hurried summary of the course of Valjean's story by necessity obscures the epic quality of Hugo's masterpiece, ignoring dozens of supporting characters and telling incidents and asides that elevate the drama into a social and historical panorama. Although oversized and overstated, *Les Misérables* justifies its tendency toward melodrama and sentimentality by the sheer force of its narrative power and the courage of its convictions. In defense of melodrama, George Bernard Shaw insisted that melodrama was of "first-rate literary importance, because it only needs elaboration to

Baldwin at nearly the same time considered it "a very bad novel," simplistic and inherently racist, affirming the racial attitudes that made slavery possible. Tom himself has shifted in our collective understanding from a moving paragon of virtuous forbearance—a Christlike martyr willing to sacrifice his body to save his soul—to a code word for subservience. Clearly, the forces Stowe unleashed maintain their power to provoke, and if modern readers are tear-resistant, our reluctance to respond unashamedly to Stowe's spell may say more about our aesthetic coldness than her emotional warmth. Great book or great propaganda, *Uncle Tom's Cabin* is surely one of the greatest novels both for its impact and its powerful and mythic reflection of American (and universal) themes regarding race, gender, and human nature.

Stowe was born in Litchfield, Connecticut, the seventh of nine children of Lyman Beecher, one of the leading clergymen of his time. Her mother died when she was five, and Stowe would later attribute her ability to empathize with black families who were broken up by slavery from her own grief at the death of her mother and, later, her young son. Lyman Beecher remarried and had four more children, and Stowe grew up in a large family circle dominated by her Calvinist-leaning father for whom God was a wrathful though attentive spirit. Like all the Beecher children, Harriet developed an interest in theology and in schemes for improving humanity. As a woman she was denied the pulpit, but would translate the minister's role in her writing. In 1832 the Beecher family relocated to Cincinnati, where Lyman Beecher served as the first president of the Lane Theological Seminary. It was in this border city, across the river from the slave state of Kentucky, that Harriet was first exposed to slavery and first acted on behalf of its victims by aiding fugitives on the Underground Railroad. In 1836 she married Calvin Stowe, a biblical scholar and professor at the seminary, and Harriet began her writing career around her household tasks to supplement their meager income.

In 1850 the Stowes returned to New England, where Calvin Stowe joined the faculty of Bowdoin College in Maine. That year, the Fugitive Slave Act was passed, mandating that slaves who escaped to freedom in the North had to be returned to their masters. All Americans, therefore, were now legally compelled to support the institution of slavery. Stowe's outrage over the act and its implication led her to write *Uncle Tom's Cabin; or, Life Among the Lowly*, first published serially in an abolitionist newspaper, the *National Era*. Stowe began by writing the climactic scene of the long-suffering and devout Tom's beating and death at the hands of Simon Legree and his black henchmen for refusing to reveal the hiding place of the runaway slaves Cassy and Emmeline. She then began to work her way back to the beginning of Tom's travails in a series of vivid scenes of slave life that she read tearfully to her children, who responded in kind. "My vocation," she declared, "is simply that of a *painter*, and my object will be to hold up in the most lifelike and graphic manner possible, slavery, its reverses, changes, and the Negro character, which I have had ample opportunities for studying." Committed to persuading her readers of the evils of slavery, Stowe was also careful not to forsake southern converts to the cause in an unbalanced indictment, presenting "the best side of the thing, and something approaching the worst." Accordingly, she shows benign and thoughtful slave owners as well as brutes, with the worst of all, Simon Legree, a renegade New Englander.

Stowe had only modest expectations for her novel, hoping to earn enough to buy a new silk dress. What she got instead was a publishing phenomenon. Released in book form in 1852, the first edition, 5,000 copies, sold out almost immediately; a second edition was gone in three weeks. The New York *Independent* reported that "Notwithstanding [that] three paper mills are constantly employed making the paper, and three of Adams's power presses are kept running twenty-four hours per day (Sundays only excepted), and 100 bookbinders are unceasingly plying their art, the publishers are still some thousands of copies behind their orders." It is estimated that 3 million copies were sold in the United States alone. The novel appeared in 40 different editions and was quickly translated into 37 foreign languages. Henry Wadsworth Longfellow wrote in his journal: "How she is shaking the world with *Uncle Tom's Cabin*. . . . Never was there such a literary *coup-de-main* as this." English historian Thomas Macaulay called the novel "the most valuable addition America has made to English literature," and Tolstoy considered it the highest achievement of moral art, on the same level as *Les Misérables* and *A Tale of Two Cities*. Dramatizations of the novel proliferated, and *Uncle Tom's Cabin* is almost certainly the most popular American play as well. It is estimated that between 1853 and 1930, dramatic versions of Stowe's story never ceased to be performed. Yet Stowe's novel divided as well as conquered. She was predictably attacked in the South, with one reviewer stating that Stowe has "shockingly traduced the slaveholding society of the United States . . . as the mouthpiece of a large and dangerous faction which, if we do not put down the pen, we may be compelled one day . . . to repel with the bayonet." As events transpired, there is more than a little justification in the comment Abraham Lincoln allegedly made greeting Stowe on a visit to the White House by calling her "the little lady who made this big war." Stowe met criticism of the novel's exaggerations and inaccuracies with a defense published as *A Key to Uncle Tom's Cabin* (1853), documenting the abuses she had described. Her most frequent defense, however, was her continual assertion that God actually wrote the book, and she had merely transcribed His words.

The novel opens with a Kentuckian, Mr. Shelby, forced to sell two of his most capable and valued slaves, his wife's maid, Eliza, and his most trusted hand, Tom, to satisfy his creditors. Eliza flees with her child north to Canada, producing one of the novel's most famous scenes, her flight from slave catchers across the ice floes of the Ohio River. Tom, however, sustained by his Christian faith, accepts his fate and heads downriver, where he is sold to

Augustine St. Clare of New Orleans. Stowe's innovation in *Uncle Tom's Cabin* is the presentation of her black characters in human terms that her white readers could understand. For the first time in literature, slaves were portrayed as possessing basic human emotions, capable of thought and feeling, as committed to husband, wife, and children as any white person. Much of the power of the book is then generated by forcing the reader to exchange places imaginatively with the slaves. Again and again, Stowe asks her readers to think how they would feel uprooted from their family, separated from a child, husband, or wife, treated as unfeeling chattel. The inescapable conclusion is that slavery is a great wrong that every professed Christian must oppose.

Stowe draws her moral by providing one of the grandest panoramas of American life ever attempted in a novel up to that time, offering a wide-ranging portrait of Northerners and Southerners and the details of their religious, domestic, marital, and family lives. This aspect of *Uncle Tom's Cabin*, as social satire, is often underappreciated and obscured by emphasis on the novel's grand theme and theatrical set pieces. One of the most challenging for the modern reader is the tearful death of St. Clare's daughter Eva, who expires with all the sentimental orchestration that Dickens perfected in depicting the deaths of Little Nell in *The Old Curiosity Shop* and Paul Dombey in *Dombey and Son*. The scene seems the height of manipulative emotionalism, a wallowing in grief that Stowe's contemporaries responded to but which mostly embarrasses modern readers. However, a thematic case can be made that Eva's death, like the death of Uncle Tom, redirects the reader to spiritual questions that become the true locus of the novel's response to the institution of slavery. Affirming the worth and sanctity of the human soul (black and white), Stowe argues that the true solution to the dehumanizing and destructive power of slavery is a William Blake-like inner reform of spiritual faith and belief. Eva's death redeems the life of the abused and self-hating Topsy, and Tom's death, like Christ's, offers the same valuable lesson in salvation and redemption. It is interesting to note that the future Stowe imagines for her central characters—Eva, Tom, Topsy, George, Eliza, and Cassy—is either in the afterlife or outside of America, in Canada or Africa. There is something otherworldly about the direction that the book takes, reflected at its conclusion in which Stowe addresses directly the question of what one person can do in the face of the horrors of slavery:

> There is one thing that every individual can do—they can see to it that *they feel right.* An atmosphere of sympathetic influence encircles every human being; and the man or woman who *feels* strongly, healthily and justly, on the great interests of humanity, is a constant benefactor to the human race. See, then, to your sympathies in this matter! Are they in harmony with the sympathies of Christ? Or are they swayed and perverted by the sophistries of worldly policy?

The central lesson of *Uncle Tom's Cabin* is in feeling, in the extension of sympathy and empathy that serves both the purpose of destroying the conditions that make slavery possible and potentially enslave every individual. Critic Kenneth Lynn called the novel "the greatest tear-jerker of them all," but a tear-jerker with a difference: "It did not permit its audience to escape reality. Instead the novel's sentimentalism continuously calls attention to the monstrous actuality which existed under the very noses of its readers. Mrs. Stowe aroused emotions not for emotions sake alone—as the sentimental novelist notoriously did—but in order to facilitate the moral regeneration of an entire nation." It may be that *Uncle Tom's Cabin* serves today primarily to measure the emotional and spiritual gap between Stowe's world and our own. However, the novel that first gave slavery and the issues of race in America a living dramatic reality and a mythic force continues to disturb and provokes a reaction. "Viewed at a distance," cultural critic Constance Rourke observed, "apart from its inevitable association with a cause, its worth becomes that of the typical and the prototypical; subtract it from literary history, and a certain evaluation of human experience would be gone."

99

DOCTOR ZHIVAGO

(1957)

by Boris Pasternak

Doctor Zhivago *is ultimately about the paradox that death can produce new life and that meaning can come from the debris of existence. Many Russian novels are structured like rivers: their plots flow in one direction—toward victory, say, as in* War and Peace, *or toward suicide, as in* Anna Karenina. *But* Doctor Zhivago *is more like an ocean. The very evident climaxes that do occur are nonlinear. Rather, they are really moments of revelation that happen when out of this "mess and chaos" one finds a pattern, a series of images, and an "immediate perception" that leads to the effect of transcendence, of self-overcoming.*

—Edith W. Clowes, "*Doctor Zhivago* in the Post-Soviet Era: A Re-Introduction"

Considered by many the greatest Russian novel of the 20th century, Boris Pasternak's *Doctor Zhivago* is certainly the most famous fictional treatment of the defining moments of modern Russian history at the outset of the 20th century, inviting a comparison with Tolstoy's similar effort in *War and Peace* to dramatize the crucial events of the Napoleonic era. *Doctor Zhivago* shares with *War and Peace* an epic tonality; both attempt to encapsulate a national history, culture, and philosophy of human nature and experience in the stories of individuals caught up in the maelstrom of history. Depicting pre-revolutionary Russian culture, the revolution, and the ensuing civil war from a decidedly subjective viewpoint, *Doctor Zhivago* broke with the enforced literary dictates of socialist realism and party doctrine at a time when such a challenge demanded enormous courage and conviction. "A miracle of non-conformity," the Russian scholar Victor Frank has called Pasternak's novel, "full of supreme indifference to all the official taboos." Refused publication in the Soviet Union, the novel was surreptitiously sent to an Italian publisher who brought it out in 1957, with an English translation appearing in 1958. Hailed by the critic Edmund Wilson as "one of the great events in man's literary and moral history . . . a great act of faith in art and the human spirit,"

Doctor Zhivago became a worldwide popular and critical sensation that culminated in Pasternak being awarded the 1958 Nobel Prize in literature "for his notable achievement in both contemporary poetry and the field of the great Russian narrative tradition." Regarded by the Soviet state as a political rather than a literary judgment on behalf of a novel it considered unpatriotic and subversive, *Doctor Zhivago* provoked a barrage of hostile reviews and resolutions in Russia that branded it "literary trash" and a "malicious lampoon of the socialist revolution." Pasternak was expelled from the Writers' Union and condemned as "worse than a pig" because "a pig never befouls where it eats or sleeps." Pasternak's deportation from the Soviet Union was averted only by the writer's refusal of the Nobel Prize and by his impassioned appeal to Nikita Khrushchev in which Pasternak equated banishment from Russia to a death sentence. *Doctor Zhivago* would not be officially published in Russia until 1988 to great acclaim and acceptance into the post-Soviet literary canon as a landmark and unavoidable masterpiece.

Despite its undisputed importance as a social document chronicling a crucial period in Russian and world history, *Doctor Zhivago* continues to divide critics at the most basic level of how it works, its affinity to the novel tradition in the 19th and 20th centuries, and even the genre to which it belongs. Described as both one of the greatest political novels and one of literature's great love stories, *Doctor Zhivago* has also been called "a fairy tale," "a kind of morality play," "an apocalyptic poem in the form of a novel," "one of the most original works of modern times," and "a nineteenth-century novel by a twentieth-century poet." Compared to predecessors like Tolstoy and Dostoevsky in the great 19th-century Russian realistic novel tradition, Pasternak has been found wanting in his failure to provide believable, rounded characters. Compared to modernist innovators like Joyce, Woolf, and Faulkner, he has been viewed as old-fashioned and outmoded. To appreciate fully Pasternak's achievement in *Doctor Zhivago,* it is necessary to recognize that its nonconformity extends beyond its unorthodox and unsanctioned ideas to its formal challenges to established narrative assumptions. *Doctor Zhivago* is neither a failed 19th-century nor a disappointing modernist novel, but a radical synthesis of both traditions in a daringly original construct.

Aspects of Pasternak's life and career provide crucial contexts for his single novel published three years before his death. Born in Moscow in 1890, Boris Leonidovich Pasternak was the eldest child of the painter Leonid Pasternak and the concert pianist Rosa Kaufman and was raised in the midst of Moscow's intellectual and artistic community. Tolstoy was a household visitor, and the distinguished composer Alexander Scarabin encouraged the 14-year-old Pasternak in his study of music. Convinced that he lacked the necessary technical skills, at age 19, Pasternak abandoned music for poetry and philosophy, eventually enrolling in Germany's prestigious Marburg University until 1912 when he returned to Russia and committed himself exclusively to poetry. Associated with the Russian symbolist and futurist movements, Pasternak began to gain a reputation as a leading figure of a new generation of Russian poets who sought a greater freedom of poetic subjects and expression, more closely tied to actual experience and colloquial language. Declared exempt from military service during World War I because of a childhood leg injury, Pasternak managed a draft board in the Urals. When the revolution came, Pasternak was largely sympathetic, embracing the promise of needed social reform and liberation of the spirit that his poetry advocated. As the new Soviet regime grew increasingly conservative in cultural matters and repressive in silencing dissent, Pasternak, throughout the 1930s, published little, perfecting the delicate art of survival under Stalin, of maintaining core principles while avoiding the fate of fellow writers and artistic colleagues who faced death sentences and banishment to labor camps. Convinced that the Soviet state had betrayed the ideals of the revolution and that the drive for collectivism in Soviet society violated essential imperatives of human nature, sometime during the 1930s Pasternak decided to turn from poetry to prose to tell the story of his generation and its historical fate under the czar, during the Great War, and through the revolution and the establishment of the communist state, in part as an expression of survivor's guilt. Writing in 1948, Pasternak admitted, "I am guilty before everyone. But what can I do? So here in the novel—it is part of this debt, proof that at least I *tried*." Drawing on his earlier interests in musical composition, philosophy, and a career devoted to poetry, Pasternak conceived a novel capacious enough to contain his "views on art, the Gospels, human life in history and many other things." Rejecting the "idiotic clichés" of socialist realism and an edited, sanitized view of the revolution and its aftermath, Pasternak embraced the role as truth teller in which "Everything is untangled, everything is named, simple, transparent, sad. Once again, afresh, in a new way, the most precious and important things, the earth and the sky, great warm feeling, the spirit of creation, life and death, have been delineated." *Doctor Zhivago* began to take final shape during the late 1940s as Pasternak faced increasing government hostility for his "anti-Soviet" views. To punish him indirectly, Pasternak's mistress, Olga Vsevolodovna Ivinskaia, was arrested in 1949 and sentenced to five years in a hard-labor camp "for close contact with persons suspected of espionage." Pasternak would later confess that Olga was the Lara of his novel, which was finally completed in early 1956.

Pasternak's comments about his work in his letters reveal key points about his intentions and methods for *Doctor Zhivago*. Throughout his correspondence, Pasternak refers to his "novel in prose," a nod to Pushkin's "novel in verse," *Eugene Onegin*, and a connection to Pasternak's following the same literary trajectory of Russia's literary fountainhead, Pushkin, from poetry to prose. Regarding his poetry as preparatory work and incapable of supporting his historical and philosophical aspirations, Pasternak claimed, "a poem is to prose as a sketch is to a painting." Yet at the core of *Doctor Zhivago* is Pasternak's insistent lyricism in which narrative elements are joined through imagery, counterpoint, and symbolism. Pasternak's poetic method explains why *Doctor Zhivago*, measured against the standard of the realistic novel, often falls short. Characters, rather than appearing distinct and original, tend to merge together, expressing shared preoccupations and feelings. Defending himself against charges of "not sufficient tracing of characters," Pasternak insisted that "more than to delineate them I tried to efface them." To the charge of the novel's many violations of probability with coincidence, Pasternak claimed, "Realism of genre and language doesn't interest me. That's not what I value. In the novel there is a grandeur of another kind." Underlying the novel's blending of elements from poetry and prose and a manipulation of events that lends a fairy tale or providential aura to the book is Pasternak's contention that "existence was more original, extraordinary and inexplicable than any of its separate astonishing incidents and facts. I was attracted by the unusualness of the usual." Pasternak's subjective, poeticized perspective aligns *Doctor Zhivago* in certain ways with magic realists like Márquez as much as with Tolstoy in his pursuit of "the atmosphere of being," which he described as "the whole sequence of facts and beings and happenings like some moving entireness, like a developing, passing by, rolling and rushing inspiration, as if reality itself had freedom and choice and was composing itself out of numberless variants and versions."

Pasternak's "moving entireness" in *Doctor Zhivago* begins with the 10-year-old Yury Zhivago attending his mother's funeral in a driving snowstorm, imagistically uniting human destiny and the vitality and power of nature that threaten to engulf and overwhelm the individual. This theme of the survival of the individual will be orchestrated throughout the novel, embedded even in the title character's family name, an older Russian form of the word "alive." It is the first of many scenes in which Zhivago's isolation and vulnerability to both natural forces and human events aligned against his aspirations toward selfhood will be emphasized. The novel relies on several traditional structural principles including the novel of development and education of the artist as well as the quest novel in which the artist Zhivago eventually emerges after a succession of tests. Yet *Doctor Zhivago* is a tragically conceived modern *Odyssey* in which not home but isolation and separation from virtually every sustaining relationship and external consolation are his destination. Ultimately, Zhivago's only reward or redemption is his art and the affirmation of the mystery and majesty of existence that his poems assert.

The first portion of the novel dramatizes the last decade of czarist rule and the events leading up to World War I and the revolutions of 1917. Following the suicide death of his father over the loss of his fortune, Yury is raised in the professorial home of Alexander and Anna Gromeko and their daughter Tonya. The novel's catalyst and moral touchstone is the "Girl from a Different World," Lara Guishar, the teenaged daughter of a Belgian hatmaker, whose story connects the comfortable bourgeois world of the Gromekos with Moscow's labor class and incipient revolutionaries. Her seduction by the rich lawyer, Komarovsky, establishes a connection with Yury who is on hand after Lara's mother's failed suicide attempt and at the Christmas party where Lara tries and fails to shoot her lover. They next meet at the front during World War I where Yury, having married Tonya, is serving as a doctor and Lara is working as a nurse, having gone to the front in search of her husband, Pasha Antipov, who has abandoned her and their child, unable to reconcile himself to his wife's past with Komarovsky. As Yury and Lara's attachment grows, news of the revolution reaches them, and both return to their respective homes—Yury to Moscow, and Lara to Yuryatin in Siberia.

Having experienced the dehumanizing conditions of war, Yury returns to similar conditions in Moscow under the Bolsheviks where his family's privileged existence has been transformed to a struggle for survival in which Yury's integrity, individualism, and artistic sensibility are not just valueless but dangerously subversive. Seeking relief, the family travels east to Tonya's former family estate in Siberia, near Yuryatin, Lara's home. The train journey is one of the triumphs of the novel in which the immense Russian landscape is brilliantly evoked and a rich collection of the various classes of Russian society displaced by the revolution are brought together during the dangerous and lawless days of the civil war. Yury barely avoids execution in an encounter with the merciless revolutionary leader Strelnikov, Lara's renamed husband Antipov. Settling at the Varykino estate and subsisting off the land, the family thrives for a year before a chance reunion between Yury and Lara leads to their love affair. Guilt-ridden and determined to reconcile with Tonya, Yury is kidnapped on his way home by Bolshevik partisan fighters in need of a doctor. Serving with them for over a year and experiencing the horrific violence and human debasement of the civil war, Yury finally escapes back to Yuryatin where he is nursed back to health by Lara and learns that Tonya, her father, and their children have returned to Moscow. (They will subsequently be deported to the West.)

The reunited lovers are interrupted by the appearance of Komarovsky who warns Lara of her danger as the wife of the now-condemned Strelnikov. They respond by leaving Yuryatin for Varykino and two weeks of happiness in which Yury resumes his poetry, inspired by Lara. Komarovsky offers Lara and her child safe passage to the East, and Yury, to convince her to take it, lies that he will join them. Left alone, Yury is visited by the hunted Strelnikov who, in despair over the failure of his revolutionary ideals and his betrayal of Lara's love, shoots himself. The novel concludes with Yury's life in Moscow, having been stripped of everything he had formerly relied on to sustain him—his wife, family, and lover. Resuming his medical career and his writing, Yury finally dies of a heart attack, ultimately vindicated by the poems that close the book, testimony of both his heroic resistance to the forces of death and despair and affirmation of the value of life, embodied by the essential human qualities of his muse, Lara. She arrives in Moscow in time for the funeral before disappearing: "She must have been arrested in the street, as so often happened in those days, and she died or vanished somewhere, forgotten as a nameless number on a list which later was mislaid, in one of the innumerable mixed or women's concentration camps in the north."

In the fates of both Lara and Yuri, the reader feels an overwhelming sense of human waste, having been instructed by the author in the value their lives and living has, set beside the necessities of history and ideology that has diminished both. *Doctor Zhivago* attempts to redress the balance, translating the "nameless number on a list" into memorable human terms that never neglects the "unusualness of the usual."

100

NATIVE SON

(1940)

by Richard Wright

The day Native Son *appeared, American culture was changed forever. No matter how much qualifying the book might later need, it made impossible a repetition of the old lies. In all its crudeness, melodrama and claustrophobia of vision, Richard Wright's novel brought out into the open, as no one ever had before, the hatred, fear and violence that crippled and may yet destroy our culture.*

—Irving Howe, "Black Boys and Native Sons" in *A World More Attractive*

For sheer visceral assault few other novels can match Richard Wright's *Native Son*. Published in 1940, *Native Son* is commonly regarded as the culminating novel of American naturalism. It is, along with John Steinbeck's *The Grapes of Wrath*, one of America's greatest social protest novels, and, linked with Dostoevsky and anticipating Camus, a preeminent exploration of existential themes. *Native Son* also represents a watershed in African-American literary expression. Still the best-known and influential novel written by a black American, *Native Son* altered the terms by which racial identity and race conflict are understood in America, exerting an enormous influence on African-American novelists such as Ralph Ellison, James Baldwin, Toni Morrison, and others who followed Wright's pioneering lead. The daring of Wright's conception and the morally chilling implication of his drama still disturb and still challenge more than 60 years later. *Native Son* is an unrelentingly intense study of crime and punishment in which a 20-year-old black man, Bigger Thomas, trapped in Chicago's ghetto, explodes into violence. As the novel's title makes clear, Bigger, whose double murders horrify, must be accommodated in an expanded conception of American life that *Native Son* presents. As one of the first and best expressionistic renderings of the modern American city and the dislocation, alienation, and violence it breeds, the novel dares its reader to see Bigger not just as victim of the environmental forces that shaped him, not just as a new kind of racial stereotype, but, more challenging, as a monster who finally gains his humanity. As one early reviewer observed, *Native Son* is "a book which takes you by the ears and gives you a good shaking, whirls you on your toes and slaps you dizzy against the wall." To achieve this effect, Wright mounts one of the most unremitting assaults on the reader's sensibility in fiction, a strategy that refuses discretion in its presentation or mitigation and sentimentality in its characterization of its protagonist. Wright wrings out the book's truth in defiance of the reader's need for easy consolation. If Wright was correct in declaring that "the Negro is America's metaphor," then *Native Son* is one of America's seminal displays of that metaphor at work, and Bigger Thomas is one of America's most shocking projections.

Wright was, like his central character, a native of Mississippi, brought up in the Jim Crow South that outwardly and inwardly defined the possibility of African Americans as second class and inconsequential. At the age of 15 he went to work for a white family and was befriended by its young daughter until he accidentally entered her room while she was dressing and was reprimanded. The incident would form the dramatic core of *Native Son*. Again like Bigger, Wright migrated north to Chicago in 1927 where he lived on the South Side in a small apartment with his mother, aunt, and brother. In his essay "How 'Bigger' Was Born," Wright traces the origin of his protagonist to a number of black youths he had encountered in the South and the North whom he had both feared and admired for their rebellion against the warping oppression that defined black life in America. All were "shot, hanged, maimed, lynched, and generally hounded until they were either dead or their spirits broken." Detecting a commonality of oppression, hatred, and fear that connected all these Biggers, Wright "became convinced that if I did not write of Bigger as I saw and felt him, if I did not try to make him a living personality and at the same time a symbol of all the larger things I felt and saw in him, I'd be reacting as Bigger himself reacted: that is, I'd be acting out of *fear* if I let what I thought whites would say constrict and paralyze me." Having succeeded with his first published book, *Uncle Tom's Children* (1938) in gaining a response for his interpretation of black life in America, Wright conceived his next work as a necessary challenge to his audience's sympathies. "I swore to myself that if I ever wrote another book," Wright remembered, "no one would ever weep over it; that it would be so hard and deep that they would have to face it without the consolation of tears." Completing the first draft in four months, Wright struggled through successive drafts to forge Bigger Thomas into a "symbolic figure of American life, a figure who would hold within him the prophecy of our future."

When it appeared in 1940, *Native Son* was an instantaneous best-seller. A Book-of-the-Month Club selection, its first edition sold out in three hours and some 250,000 copies were purchased within six weeks. Wright had become the most famous African-American novelist, and the controversy that still surrounds *Native Son* had begun. Critics then and now agree on the novel's extraordinary power and intensity, and Wright has been given credit for his revolutionary treatment of modern urban life and the impact of America's racial divide. However, readers remain split over the effectiveness of Wright's sensationalized method. Some have found the novel's melodramatic collision of extremes gripping and appropriate; others have criticized it as often crude and reductive, the substitution of a different form of racial stereotyping and a protest undermined by marxist propaganda. The core of the debate remains Bigger Thomas, one of fiction's most disturbing creations who, like Heathcliff, Ahab, Meursault, and Humbert Humbert, defies easy solutions and reassuring moral estimation.

Native Son is organized into a three-part dialectical structure—"Fear," "Flight," and "Fate," and the sound of an alarm clock in the Thomases' shabby one-room apartment launches the compressed events of three days that will end with Bigger's imprisonment and impending execution. The killing of a rat that follows is the first of Bigger's escalating acts of violence and a symbolic telescoping of the entire novel's action. Wright in commenting on this opening stated that he struggled to create "the type of concrete event that would convey the motif of the entire scheme of the book, that would sound, in varied form, the note that was to be resounded throughout its length, that it would introduce to the reader just what kind of organism Bigger's was and the environment that was bearing hourly upon it." Ratlike, cornered in a deadening and dehumanized environment that denies his worth and humanity, Bigger is alienated even from his family; his mother insults his manhood for Bigger's failing to relieve the family's plight and predicts that "the gallows is at the end of the road you traveling." Ruled by fear and a product of his environment, Bigger is the ultimate consequence of an oppression that is vented in reflexive violence. "We black and they white. They got things and we ain't," Bigger reflects. "They do things and we can't. It's just like living in jail. Half the time I feel like I'm on the outside of the world peeping in through a knot-hole in the fence."

After the proposed robbery of a white delicatessen owner goes awry and Bigger reacts, covering his own fear, by striking out violently against one of his fellow gang members, Bigger is given a job as a chauffeur in the home of Mr. Dalton, a wealthy white philanthropist. This well-intentioned act of charity misses the mark of Bigger's most basic needs for self-recognition and self-worth and simply exacerbates the helplessness, distrust, and animosity Bigger feels. Disoriented when befriended by the Daltons' daughter, Mary, and her Communist boyfriend Jan, Bigger responds again violently when, having escorted the drunken Mary to her bedroom, he finds himself cornered by the entrance of the blind Mrs. Dalton. Bigger tries to protect himself by stifling Mary's voice, which results in her death. To disguise his crime, Bigger thrusts Mary into the Daltons' furnace, and Wright spares the reader nothing in his graphic account as Bigger must sever Mary's head to consign her to the flames. However, the horror and revulsion of Bigger's actions pale in comparison to the chilling implication of his reaction: "The thought of what he had done, the awful horror of it, the daring associated with such action, formed for him for the first time in his fear-ridden life a barrier of protection between him and a world he feared." In Bigger's devalued world, his murder of a white person is a form of liberation, a defining though damning act of self-creation: "He had murdered and created a new life for himself. It was something that was all his own, and it was the first time in his life he had anything that others could not take from him."

Bigger struggles to gain some control over the forces he has unleashed in the book's second part, "Flight," by recruiting his girlfriend Bessie to join him in a kidnap scheme to extract money from the Daltons, while casting blame for Mary's disappearance on the Communist boyfriend, Jan. When Mary's remains are discovered, Bigger flees a citywide manhunt and the violent racial hatred his crime has generated. Again trapped by circumstances he cannot control, Bigger murders Bessie, who has become a liability in his escape plan. Bigger is eventually captured by an outraged white community. He has become the personification of the monstrous, bestial black man whose crime of murder and assumed rape of a white woman calls for immediate extermination.

By far the most controversial section of Wright's novel is the third, "Fate," detailing Bigger's trial. With Bigger behind bars, the narrative pace slows, and Wright presents different interpretations of the criminal and his crimes. For State Attorney Buckley, who prosecutes the case, playing on the fear and prejudice of the white community, Bigger is a monster, a "black mad dog" and a "rapacious beast." For his sympathetic defense lawyer, Boris A. Max, Bigger is a symptom of America's class and racial hatred: "Multiply Bigger Thomas twelve million times, allowing for environmental and temperamental variations, and for those Negroes who are completely under the influence of the church, and you have the psychology of the Negro people." The attorney's impassioned plea for understanding of the context and compulsion for Bigger's crime has been criticized as Wright's party-line oration in which Max is seen as the author's mouthpiece, with the dramatist giving way to the propagandist. Such a reading misses the crucial point that neither Buckley nor Max adequately capture Bigger and his developing consciousness. Far from settling for a final political answer at the novel's conclusion, Wright attempts an existential one. Faced with his impending death, Bigger gains a final terrifying but ultimately sustaining insight:

> "They wouldn't let me live and I killed. Maybe it ain't fair to kill, and I reckon I really didn't want to kill. But when I think of why all the killing was, I began to feel what I wanted, what I am. . . . I didn't want to kill! But what I killed for, I *am!* . . . What I killed for must've been good!"

> Bigger's voice was full of frenzied anguish. "It must have been good! When a man kills, it's for something. . . . I didn't know I was really alive in this world until I felt things hard enough to kill for 'em. . . . It's the truth, Mr. Max. I can say it now, 'cause I'm going to die. I know what I'm saying real good and I know how it sounds. But I'm all right. I feel all right when I look at it that way."

Bigger's articulation of the meaning of his actions, his acceptance of responsibility for them, is his first important step in reclaiming his humanity and control over his destiny. Wright has managed the impossible: By giving voice to the nearly inarticulate product of oppression and not shying away from the enormity of his crimes, he forces the reader to acknowledge complicity and kinship.

101

ON THE ROAD

(1957)

by Jack Kerouac

Jack Kerouac's On the Road *was the* Huckleberry Finn *of the mid-twentieth century. Kerouac substituted the road for the river, the fast car for the slow raft, the hipster in search of freedom for the black slave in search of freedom. . . . While Huck and Jim were floating down America's mile-wide aorta, while Sal Paradise and Dean Moriarty were roaring across America's heart, they were helping to change the course of American prose.*

—Aaron Latham, review of *Visions of Cody* in *The New York Times Book Review*, 1973

No other American novel written during the second half of the 20th century, with the possible exception of J. D. Salinger's *The Catcher in the Rye*, is so heavily freighted with a cult or cultural significance as Kerouac's revered, reviled, and all too often misunderstood *On the Road*. It is the foundation text of the Beat Generation, which Kerouac named, a catalyst for the counterculture of the 1960s, and a key autobiographical source for an ongoing fascination with its creator and his circle. As his friend William Burroughs (Old Bull Lee in *On the Road*) observed, "After 1957 *On the Road* sold a trillion levis and a million expresso machines, and also set countless kids on the road." It is also, in the estimation of Thomas Pynchon, "one of the greatest American novels," one of the key "centrifugal lures" for later writers that encouraged the "expansion of possibilities" in its themes, subjects, and style. A subversive, liberating counterpoint to the gray-flannel conformity of the 1950s, *On the Road* opened up a range of American experience previously ignored by novelists, while tapping into central sources from the American literary tradition, poetry, and jazz to redirect the energies of the novel for an essential rediscovery of America and its imaginative possibilities.

Legend surrounds the novel's composition. Most have heard the famous story of Kerouac's Benzedrine-assisted, three-week-marathon typing of his manuscript in a single paragraph on a 120-foot-long scroll of paper. The image has encouraged the notion that the novel is a kind of spontaneously generated, undisciplined rhapsody, inspiring Truman Capote's famous dismissal, "That's not writing at all—it's typing." The reality is quite different and leads to an altered conclusion. The April 1951 version of Kerouac's manuscript is only one of several drafts that the writer reworked obsessively beginning in 1948 and long after Malcolm Cowley at Viking Press accepted the book for publication in 1955. *On the Road*, despite its unconventional prose and improvisational feel, is far more skillfully structured and crafted than the legend suggests. It is also not the exuberant ode to the open highway that has inspired countless spring break road trips. It is a novel far closer to tragedy than comedy, as much about despair as ecstasy, haunted by an almost desperate search for transcendence amid an awareness of inevitable failure.

On the Road is structured by four continental journeys, reworking actual travels made by Kerouac and Neal Cassady (his model for Dean Moriarty) between 1947 and 1950. In a sense, the novel is an attempt to answer the question Kerouac's second wife, Joan, had asked: "What did you and Neal really do?" on the cross-country trips the two men had taken before the couple's marriage. Kerouac would later describe the style he eventually employed to capture his experiences directly as "spontaneous prose" or "sketching," a form of jazz riffing in prose, with a feeling of immediacy and emotional intensity like a great jazz solo. "Sketching language," Kerouac explained, "is undisturbed flow from the mind of personal secret idea-words, blowing (as per jazz musician) on a subject of image." It was the opposite of the highly contrived artifices of other modernist novelists. Nor was it the carefully reflective confessional style that Kerouac used for his first novel, *The Town and the City*, modeled on the works of Thomas Wolfe. Kerouac contended that he had "broke loose from all that" and began to write "picaresque narratives. That's what my books are." Kerouac pursued a prose theory of direct, immediate response, modeled on the two men's extended conversations "driving across the old U.S.A. in the night with no mysterious readers, no literary demands, nothing but us telling."

Each of the novel's four journeys is a variation on the theme of confronting the reality of life on the road, of American experience apprehended directly, while reflecting the developing awareness of the novel's narrator, Sal Paradise. The novel opens with a terse introduction:

> I first met Dean not long after my wife and I split up. I had just gotten over a serious illness that I won't bother to talk about, except that it had something to do with the miserably weary split-up and my feeling that everything was dead. With the coming of Dean Moriarty began the part of my life you could call my life on the road.

Sal Paradise is inspired to escape his depression over his illness and failed marriage by Dean, a larger-than-life "sideburned hero of the snowy West," whose boundless energy and constant exuberant movement contrast with the more morose and circumspect Sal, sheltered in his aunt's New Jersey home. Dean infects Sal with the redemptive possibilities of the West, and Sal sets out on his first encounter with American road life. It is a series of missteps and frustrations, beginning with Sal's naive notion that he should follow the straight line of Route 6 to Denver that becomes a hitchhiker's nightmare. "It was my dream that screwed up," Sal realizes, "the stupid hearthside idea that it would be wonderful to follow one great line across America instead of trying various roads and routes." Without Dean, an expert in the art of navigation, as a guide, Sal blunders west, alternatively exhilarated by the expansive, mythologized western landscape and frustrated by the conflict between his expectations and reality. The first journey west establishes the essential pattern of each subsequent trip—high anticipation, frenzied excitement, eventual dissipation and frustration, and the return home. In Denver, Sal is unprepared to deal with the intense self-exploration of Dean and their mutual friend Carlo Marx (Allen Ginsberg), and he moves on to San Francisco, where he sets up house with his friend Remi Boncoeur and his girlfriend while working as a security guard. Eventually Sal realizes that he is no better there than he was on the East Coast: "Here I was at the end of America—and now there was nowhere to go but back." With money wired from his aunt, Sal takes a bus back east after a brief stay with Terri, a Mexican woman, whom he vaguely plans to meet again. In this opening section, Sal is characterized by his shallow unawareness of the impact he has on others or the true cost and implication of life on the road. That lesson will be taught by Dean in the next three journeys.

First in a trip east to west via New Orleans, and then from west to east, Dean takes the wheel, supercharging the road experience as, in the words of a hostile *Newsweek* reviewer in 1957, "a frantic animal-like delinquent . . . a kind of T-shirted Ahab of the automobile." The put-down is actually spot-on. Dean is, in fact, a version of the questing romantic, a searcher for the way to "know time," to live in the moment, to achieve and sustain a liberation from social constraint. Inevitably, he also becomes an Ahab-like obsessive, self-destructive and harmful to the various wives, children, and friends—roadblocks of responsibility—whom he accumulates and cons along the way. Dean's search for transcendent experience, for the expansive possibility of road life, never arriving but always moving, is therefore two-edged. His seemingly limitless vitality inevitably dissipates, and the ideal is eventually compromised by the real. By the end of the second trip to San Francisco, Sal observes, "What I accomplished by coming to Frisco I don't know. We were all thinking we'd never see one another again and we didn't care." By the end of the third transcontinental trip Sal realizes, "I was beginning to cross and recross towns in America as though I was a traveling salesman—ragged by travelings, bad stock, rotten beans in the bottom of my bag of tricks, nobody buying." Dean's manic energy has opened up a magical new world for Sal, discovered by abandoning responsibilities and rules, but each time they run out of road, and the conditions that they need to evade return with a vengeance.

The climactic fourth journey breaks the east-west pattern by sending Sal and Dean south to Mexico. It is planned as "the most fabulous" trip of all, which Dean identifies as "entering a new and unknown phase of things." Outside the United States for the first time, the pair journeys to the continent's primitive source, glimpsed in the peasants they meet who seem to have achieved the act of "knowing time," defeating the cycle of past and future in an eternal present of recurrence. Yet the same old frustrations and disillusionment catch up with the travelers as Dean deserts Sal to "get back to my life." Sal returns as well to the East Coast and a new relationship and stability off the road. The last recorded Dean sighting is Remi Boncoeur's sad refusal of a lift in his Cadillac, and Dean recedes from view, heading west across the continent once again. By now the complexity of Dean's entanglements with girlfriends, present and former wives, and various children have absorbed him almost completely. He becomes a tragic figure, like Fitzgerald's Gatsby, consumed by his dreams as translated in a world hostile or indifferent to his particular brand of heroic striving. "Dean, by virtue of his enormous series of sins," Sal observes, "was becoming the Idiot, the Imbecile, the Saint of the Lost . . . That's what Dean was, the HOLY GOOF."

Images of defeat and loss suffuse the end of the novel. The final lesson of the world as revealed in the experiential test of life on the road is a tragic awareness. The attempt to beat back time and tap into the energy of the eternal American present, inspired by Dean Moriarty, has ultimately failed. The novel ends as Sal looks west and meditates on the full, tragic implication of the landscape and the attempt to know it fully:

> So in America when the sun goes down and I sit on the old broken-down river pier watching the long, long skies over New Jersey and sense all that raw land that rolls in one unbelievable huge bulge over to the West Coast, and that road going, all the people dreaming in the immensity of it, and in Iowa I know by now the children must be crying in the land where they let the children cry, and tonight the stars'll be out, and don't you know that God is Pooh Bear? The evening star must be drooping and shedding her sparkler dims on the prairie, which is just before the coming of complete night that blesses the earth, darkens all river, cups the peaks and folds the final shore in, and nobody, nobody knows what's going to happen to anybody besides the forlorn rags of growing old, I think of Dean Moriarty, I even think of Old Dean Moriarty the father we never found, I think of Dean Moriarty.

Kerouac would continue imaginatively to reconceptualize his own experiences in a cycle of novels variously titled "The Legend of Duluoz" or "The Legend of Kerouac," with the period celebrated in *On the Road* treated again in what Kerouac considered the superior version, *Visions of Cody*, published in its entirety in 1972, three years after Kerouac's death in 1969. Like the four journeys in *On the Road*, all of his other books are in a sense variations on the same theme: the search for transcendence and its defeat by the implacable forces of time and space. As the first of Kerouac's explorations of this theme and the search to find a form and style to contain his unique vision, *On the Road* remains the prototypical Kerouac novel, sustaining its interest by the quality and intensity of Kerouac's writing, which mines the American landscape for its lyrical essence, cultural significance, and personal relevance.

102

FRANKENSTEIN

(1818)

by Mary Shelley

Whenever we attempt to find an image of human aspiration in a technological and scientific world, wherever we attempt to find an image for the failure of that aspiration, the metaphor of Frankenstein comes immediately to hand. . . . Frankenstein *is the perfect myth of the secular, carrying within it all the ambivalence of the life we lead here, of civilization and its discontents, of the mind and the body, of the self and society. It is, indeed, the myth of realism. To find another myth, . . . we must look elsewhere if we can.*

—George Levine, "The Ambiguous Heritage of *Frankenstein*"

What is perhaps most striking about the gothic thriller written by the 19-year-old Mary Shelley is its persistent, now nearly 200-year, grip on culture and the imagination. Is there anyone, reader or nonreader alike, unfamiliar with Frankenstein, or rather with what the collective consciousness and popular culture have made of Shelley's novel? Most immediately think of her unnamed monster, not its creator, Victor Frankenstein, and intuitively make the doubling association between creature and creator that critics have labored to define. *Frankenstein* continues to haunt us even if we are unfamiliar with the Shelleyan prototype. Credit to Shelley's originality and genius has been, however, long in coming. Published anonymously in 1818, the novel created an initial sensation. "There never was a wilder story imagined;" the reviewer of the *Edinburgh Magazine* asserted, "yet, like most fiction of this age, it has an air of reality attached to it by being connected with the favourite projects and passions of the times." *Frankenstein* rejuvenated the flagging stimulants of the gothic romance by adding to its story of a Faustian overreacher aspects of technology that transformed it into the first science fiction novel. It thereby became the prototypical scientist-creates-monster myth, which has persisted ever since. Yet how could such a powerful and original myth be the brainchild of a previously unpublished teenager? Many of Mary Shelley's contemporaries assumed that the novel was the work of her more famous husband, Percy Bysshe Shelley. Even after Mary became known as the author, many located the novel's genius in Percy Shelley's direction and editing. Mary Shelley has long been overshadowed by her famous parents—radical philosopher and novelist William Godwin and groundbreaking women's rights theorist Mary Wollstonecraft—and by her poet husband. Her novels that followed *Frankenstein* never duplicated its unique power and depth, and her respectable maturity as the custodian of her husband's poetic legacy helped to consign her to the reactionary world of Victorian conformity. It was only in the 1960s and 1970s with the emergence of feminist criticism that a reassessment helped refocus attention on Mary Shelley's genius and remarkable literary and intellectual contribution. *Frankenstein* has now entered the canon as the crucial English Romantic novel. Critic J. Paul Hunters has called it "required reading for anyone who wants to understand the nineteenth century or the making of the modern consciousness," and it has been recognized as a complex and sophisticated exploration of some of the central issues that continue to haunt our psyches.

Perhaps no other novel has a more interesting or intriguing origin. *Frankenstein* came about by accident during one of the most famous summer parties in literary history. Weary of the turmoil caused by the scandal of their relationship (Percy Shelley was already married when their affair began), the couple with their infant son and Mary's half sister, Claire Clairmont, embarked on a trip to Switzerland in 1816. On the shore of Lake Lemain, near Geneva, Percy Shelley met Byron for the first time. Their outdoor activities together were halted by rain, forcing the small group indoors to amuse themselves by reading ghost stories together. It was proposed that they should have a ghost-story contest, each composing their own tale of supernatural terror. As Mary Shelley later recalled in her introduction to the 1831 edition of *Frankenstein*, "I busied myself *to think of a story*—a story to rival those which had excited us to this task. One which would speak to the mysterious fears of our nature, awaken thrilling horror—one to make the reader dread to look round, to curdle the blood, and quicken the beatings of the heart." For inspiration she remembered a recent conversation between Shelley and Byron on "the nature of the principle of life, and whether there was any probability of its ever being discovered and communicated." Following the discussion, Mary experienced a nightmare or a waking dream in which "I saw the pale student of unhallowed art kneeling beside the thing he had put together. I saw the hideous phantasm of a man stretched out, and then, on the working of some powerful engine, show signs of life, and stir with an uneasy, half vital motion. Frightful must it be; for supremely frightful would be the effect of any human endeavour to mock the stupendous mechanism of the Creator of the world." Mary Shelley's terrifying vision of scientifically animated life became her "hideous progeny," first as the short tale she offered as her contribution to the ghost-story contest (and clearly its winner), and then, over the next year, expanded and elaborated into the novel *Frankenstein; or, The Modern Prometheus.*

Those whose knowledge of *Frankenstein* has come only from films and are unfamiliar with Shelley's novel are, upon first encountering it, often shocked by its elaborate narrative frame. Like the other great English 19th-century update of the gothic, Emily Brontë's *Wuthering Heights*, *Frankenstein* is a complex design of enfolding narratives in which several narrators, including creator and creature, offer their perspectives, calling into question issues of reliability that force the reader to suspend judgment while actively assessing motive and meaning. The frame narrator is English explorer Robert Walton reporting to his sister his progress into the Arctic. Walton serves as a kind of "shock absorber" for the reader, a more conventional perspective on the fantastical story he and the reader will learn. Walton also shares a temperamental connection with both Victor Frankenstein, as another Faustian quester into the unknown, and with the monster in his lonely isolation. After Walton and his crew first glimpse on a desolate ice field a dogsled driven by a huge, misshapen man, they encounter his pursuer, Victor Frankenstein, who relates the story of his creation and its horrifying aftermath.

The son of an aristocratic family in Geneva, Victor attends the University of Ingolstadt, where his research in science and the arcane leads him to the discovery of the means for creating life. Constructing a man from body parts derived from butcher shops and dissecting rooms, he assembles a grotesque, eight-foot-tall creature whom he brings to life. Victor is horrified by the result and immediately disowns his creation, fleeing from it in terror. After recovering from a long bout of brain fever, Victor eventually returns home to find that his younger brother has been murdered, and the family's devoted servant Justine has been charged with the crime. Suspecting that his creature is responsible, Victor fails to prevent Justine's execution. Tormented by guilt, Victor hikes into the Alps, where he encounters his creation on Mont Blanc.

Unlike many of the film versions of *Frankenstein*, Mary Shelley's novel endows the monster with articulate speech, and he tells the story of what happened after leaving Ingolstadt. Terrifying all whom he encounters, the creature eventually takes up residence in a hut near a cottage where he learns the ways of humankind by secretly observing the cottagers. After assisting them surreptitiously in their labors, the creature craves the companionship and affection that he witnesses. He shows himself to the family, who are repulsed. He then sets out on a campaign of vengeance on humanity in general and his creator in particular. Encountering Victor's brother, he strangles the young boy, removes a miniature that he wears, and plants it on the family servant. To cease his deadly campaign, the creature demands that Victor fashion him a mate, promising to go with her into the jungles of South America and never trouble mankind again. Victor reluctantly agrees and goes to the Orkneys to complete his work. On the brink of animating his second creature, Victor is horrified by the notion that he will be making possible a new race of monsters and destroys his work. Enraged, the creature seeks revenge, first by killing Victor's best friend, Henry Clerval, and then, visiting his creator on his wedding night, by strangling Victor's bride. Now the pursuer becomes the pursued as Victor follows his creation into the Arctic waste, intent on destroying him.

Walton's final letter to his sister relates his decision to turn back from his quest into the unknown for safety and fellowship. It is a decision that reflects the advice of the dying Victor, who urges Walton in his final words to "Seek happiness in tranquility, and avoid ambition, even if it be only the apparently innocent one of distinguishing yourself in science and discoveries. Yet why do I say this? I have myself been blasted in these hopes, yet another may succeed." Victor's persistent notes of self-pity and self-deception in his confession to Walton suggest that he has learned little from his ordeal or about his own culpability in the horrors he has unleashed. This is the theme of the creature's final soliloquy as he visits Walton and the corpse of his creator. He argues that Victor's crime is greater than his own because Victor has called into being a creature forced to exist without love or friendship and has abdicated his responsibility for his actions. "Am I to be thought the only criminal," he asks Walton to consider, "when all human kind sinned against me?" The monster here achieves a degree of tragic dignity that complicates any simplistic moralizing. The book ends with the creature's promise to destroy himself and his disappearance into the Arctic darkness.

Frankenstein exerts such a strong and intriguing hold on the imagination because it works on so many different interpretive levels. Beyond its appeal as a gripping tale of fascinating horror, it is a myth of technological arrogance dramatizing what happens when man rivals the laws of God and nature. Victor's is the cautionary tale of the unchecked ego whose drive for mastery and power is ultimately self-destructive. On another level it is the exploration of creation itself, both physical birth and the creative act, posing fascinating questions of consequence and responsibility. At a deep, psychological level Frankenstein and his monster may represent twinned aspects of a fractured psychic whole, with the monster enacting murderous desires that the conventional Victor represses. The novel also treats society's sin in turning away from disturbing aspects of human nature that ask us to redefine our conception of the monstrous. Does it reside with the creature or with the denial of love and fellowship that he craves? *Frankenstein* stimulates so many responses that it is clear that the novel is as powerful a vehicle for exploring human nature and the modern world now as it was at the moment of its birth during a rainy summer in 1816.

103

THE LEOPARD

(1958)

by Giuseppe Tomasi di Lampedusa

The Leopard *is a classic because it ignored the fads of a literary generation and concentrated on perennial concerns. Lampedusa once said that London would never die because Dickens had made it immortal, and to many people he has done the same for Sicily. Yet his own immortality will not rest on the evocation of a certain place in a certain epoch—memorable though that is—but on the sensibility and experience he distilled in his writing. Lampedusa's work will survive, long after the last palaces of Palermo have gone, because he wrote about the central problems of the human experience.*

—David Gilmour, *The Last Leopard: A Life of Giuseppe di Lampedusa*

The most popular 20th-century novel in Italy, *The Leopard*, by eschewing technical innovation and ambiguously viewing progress and the unification of Italy, has become a lightning rod for an ongoing debate over Lampedusa's ideology, intentions, and the ways and means of the modern Italian novel. "No novel in Italian literature has caused so much argument," British critic and Lampedusa biographer David Gilmour has observed, or "aroused so much passion and begun so many quarrels as *The Leopard*." Like another great Italian novel, Alessandro Manzoni's *The Betrothed*, Lampedusa's is a historical novel dealing with Italian culture at a crossroad; both works attempt nothing less than a chronicle of a pivotal era in Italian history that serves as a profound meditation on cultural and national identity and the human condition.

Part of the controversy surrounding *The Leopard* comes from the identity and class of its author. Giuseppe Tomasi di Lampedusa was born in 1896 in Palermo, Sicily. The last prince of Lampedusa, he was descended from a distinguished aristocratic family whose title derived from their acquisition in the 16th century of the small, barren island of Lampedusa in the Mediterranean between Sicily and the northern coast of Africa. Powerful grandees in Palermo, the Lampedusa family began to decline in the 19th century. Schooled by private tutors and by his mother, Lampedusa studied law at the University of Genoa and the University of Rome. During World War I he served as an artillery officer. Captured by the Austrians, he managed to escape from a prison camp in Hungary and in disguise made his way back on foot to Italy. He would remain in the military until 1921, thereafter spending the rest of his life traveling throughout Italy and Europe while attempting to restore his family estate. During World War II the Lampedusa palace was bombed and looted by Allied troops, an experience that provoked in Lampedusa a severe depression that lasted for many years. In 1955 his wife suggested that as a form of therapy he begin writing a long-contemplated historical novel reflecting his family history, and he began *Il Gattopardo* while simultaneously working on his autobiography. Completed in 1956, *The Leopard* was rejected by two Italian publishers, with news of one rejection reaching Lampedusa two days before he died of lung cancer in 1957. The novel was eventually published posthumously, in 1958, to international acclaim and controversy. An immediate best-seller, *The Leopard* was attacked on the right for its fatalism and anticlerical views and on the left for its apparent opposition to Italian unification and its nostalgia for the decadent feudal world. Ignoring both the bleak neorealistic style of contemporary Italian fiction and the burgeoning avant-garde experimental movement, Lampedusa's novel seemed to many an anachronism, old-fashioned both in its outlook and its method. It would, however, win the prestigious Strega Prize in 1959 and prompted the French marxist writer Louis Aragon to break ranks with his leftist comrades and call the novel "one of the great books of this century, one of the great books of all time." It would go on to sell an unprecedented 1.6 million copies in Italy up to 1982 and eventually earned a place as one of the most significant of all Italian novels and one of the important works of 20th-century fiction.

In interesting ways, the controversy surrounding *The Leopard* anticipates a similar debate over German novelist Günter Grass's objections to German unification in his novel *Too Far Afield* (2001). Both novels challenge conventional wisdom and assert a far more complex and nuanced view of politics and human possibilities. Despite the conventionality of the structure of *The Leopard*, its tragic, existential view of life, unconsoled by palliatives, suggests a novel with important modern and universal significance.

The core of the novel's power is its divided, struggling central figure, Don Fabrizio Corbera, the prince of Salina, who tries to make sense of the historical changes that engulf him and topple his value system. *The Leopard* covers 50 years, from 1860 to 1910, reflecting the impact of these changes on a Sicilian aristocratic family. As the novel opens, Giuseppe Garibaldi has sailed from Genoa with 1,000 red-shirted volunteers and landed at Marsala, in western Sicily, to liberate the island and topple the reactionary Bourbon dynasty. It would complete the destruction of the ancien régime, leading to the unification of Italy for the first time since the fall of Rome. The reader's first glimpse of Don Fabrizio and his threatened world comes during the daily recital of the rosary in a large elegant room of his palace that typifies tradition and stability.

But the counterpoint of change and death is immediately sounded in the novel's first line, from the Hail Mary: "Nunc et in Hora Mortis Nostrae, Amen" (Now and in the hour of our death, Amen.). Later a disemboweled government soldier is discovered in the prince's garden, making clear the full implication of Garibaldi's arrival, that "That adventurer, all hair and beard . . . would cause a lot of trouble." Don Fabrizio realizes that the hegemony of his class with its privileges and powers is coming to an end. He is intelligent and sensitive enough to accept the inevitability of change and his own extinction, but still laments the passing of the tradition and refinement of the aristocratic way of life. The disjunction between the past and the present, between the prince's feudal values and the new forces of democracy, produces in Don Fabrizio what can be described only as a existential crisis. With his world melting away, caught between an ineffectual past and a unrefined and uncongenial present, Don Fabrizio struggles to define life's meaning and his response. "The real problem," he is forced to realize, "is how to go on living this life of spirit in its most sublimated moment, those moments that are almost like death." Divided and alienated, Don Fabrizio meditates on the social and political questions to reveal their existential implications. Although rooted in a particular historical moment, *The Leopard* shares with other works such as Sartre's *Nausea* and Camus's *The Stranger* an ultimately modern, philosophical orientation surveying the wreckage of absolutes while trying to define what can be believed in the absence of any possibility for belief.

What is abstract and philosophical becomes personal, as Don Fabrizio through his affection for his nephew Tancredi Falconeri is forced to recognize the legitimacy of the new ruling class in the person of Don Calogero Sedora, a self-made man who has capitalized on the moment to amass a fortune and power. Tancredi has opportunistically decided to forsake his love for Don Fabrizio's daughter to woo Don Calogero's daughter Angelica, and Don Fabrizio is persuaded to help make the match. Don Calogero in his greediness, hypocrisy, and crass materialism is the antithesis of the dignity, loyalty, and refined manners that the prince values, but he accepts the inevitability of progress, change, and death of his conception of the world.

Later Don Fabrizio is asked to accept a post of senator in the new regime. His refusal prompts his most public diagnosis of the history of Sicily and the Sicilians, and his despair that any government will ever truly change their essential nature that is typified by a collective death wish:

> Sleep, that is what Sicilians want, and they will always hate anyone who tries to wake them, even in order to bring them, the most wonderful of gifts; and I must say, between ourselves, I have strong doubts whether the new Kingdom will have many gifts for us in its luggage. All Sicilian expression, even the most violent, is really wish-fulfillment: our sensuality is a hankering for oblivion, our shooting and knifing a hankering

> for death; our laziness, our spiced and drugged sherbets, a hankering for voluptuous immobility, that is, for death again; our meditative air is that of a void wanting to scrutinize the enigmas of nirvana. That is what gives power to certain people among us, to those who are half awake: that is the cause of the well-known time lag of a century in our artistic and intellectual life; novelties attract us only when they are dead, incapable of arousing vital currents; that is what gives rise to the extraordinary phenomenon of the constant formation of myths which would be venerable if they were really ancient, but which are really nothing but sinister attempts to plunge us back into a past that attracts us only because it is dead.

For Don Fabrizio the only constants in life are vanity and change, and the only consolations are the various expressions of vitality in the face of death and decay. At a ball Don Fabrizio finds a momentary antidote for his despair in the energy of the dancers: "His disgust gave way to compassion for all these ephemeral beings out to enjoy the tiny ray of light granted to them between two shades: before the cradle, after the last spasms."

In 1888 Don Fabrizio dies, the last survivor of a way of life replaced by a new class defined by money and bourgeois power. The novel's final section, set in 1910, takes us further into that diminished world in Don Fabrizio's absence. Tancredi has died, and Angelica is a stylish widow. Don Fabrizio's spinster daughters live in pious seclusion, surrounded by worthless relics, awaiting the extinction of their line. Concetta, the daughter whose love Tancredi has rejected for the opportunistic match with Angelica, marks her own break with the past by throwing out the stuffed carcass of her father's beloved hunting dog, Bendicò. It is the novel's culminating symbol: "As the carcass was dragged off, the glass eye stared at her with the humble reproach of things that are thrown away, that are being annulled. A few minutes later what remained of Bendicò was flung into a corner of the courtyard visited every day by the dustman. During the flight down from the window his form composed itself for an instant; in the air one could have seen dancing a quadruped with long whiskers, and its right foreleg seemed to be raised in imprecation. Then all found peace in a heap of livid dust." The image of the Leopard, the symbol of the Salina line, is, therefore, consigned to the dust heap of history, valueless in a new world that fails to recognize its connection to the past or an alternative of its own self-interest.

In Lampedusa's important critical essay on the works of Stendhal, whose influence is dominant in *The Leopard*, Lampedusa commends Stendhal's blending of historical facts and the "lyrical outpourings of their author's sentiments." It is the same formula that determines Lampedusa's procedure in *The Leopard:* Grounded in a specific time and place, the novel provides a provocative meditation that is both local and universal.

THE AGE OF INNOCENCE

104

(1920)

by Edith Wharton

[The Age of Innocence] *is a triumph of style, of the perfect adaptation of means to a conception fully grasped from the outset.*

—Blake Nevius, *Edith Wharton*

Edith Wharton is a supreme example of an author who has followed the advice often given to writers of fiction: Write about what you know. In *The Age of Innocence* Wharton offers readers a uniquely incisive portrait of the culture in which she grew up: the aristocratic, fashionable New York society of the 1870s, with all its subtleties, innuendoes, and strict adherence to the manners and mores necessary to maintain one's place in what was a highly stratified world. *The Age of Innocence*, at once loving and satirical, is so precisely rendered it is easy to visualize the characters' chessboard-like movements in and out of the novel's various mise-en-scènes. Wharton, who once said that she "always saw the visible world as a series of pictures, more or less harmoniously composed," created a depiction of a closed, not to say claustrophobic, circle of interrelated families in America's Gilded Age that is virtually unparalleled.

Wharton was already an acclaimed author when *The Age of Innocence* was published in 1920. She had written popular short stories, novellas, and novels, one of which, *The House of Mirth* (1905), was an enormous commercial success. During World War I, she achieved a different kind of fame, when in 1914 she traveled to Europe to establish the American Hostels for Refugees. The organization's various programs provided care facilities for tubercular soldiers and civilians, workrooms for unemployed women, gifts of housing, food, clothing, medical, and child care, and employment opportunities for more than 10,000 refugees. In 1915 Wharton helped found the Children of Flanders Rescue Committee, which established homes providing shelter and training for Flemish children, most of whom were orphans. Throughout the war she continued to initiate rescue efforts, as well as write and publish. In

1917 Wharton was awarded the Order of Leopold and the French Legion of Honor for her war work. By the war's end, writes critic Linda Wagner-Martin, she was "exhausted—mentally, physically, emotionally, and financially. . . . she was in an introspective mood. This mood stemmed partly from her own weariness, but mostly from her immersion in the crucible of war. When she decided to write the novel that became *The Age of Innocence*, she was trying to find relief from the massive sorrow that had, necessarily, enveloped her. . . . Writing about New York in the 1870s gave Wharton a chance . . . to place herself in a time when, and a country where, people saw life as promising." In a letter to a friend written soon after the war, Wharton remarked that "The nineteenth century is such a blessed refuge from the turmoil and the mediocrity of today—like taking sanctuary in a mighty temple." The working title of Wharton's new novel was *Old New York* (she would later use the title for a collection of four novellas); she soon retitled the novel *The Age of Innocence.* Recognized as one of Wharton's finest works, it was a best-seller that brought its author her greatest critical and scholarly attention and was awarded the Pulitzer Prize for fiction in 1921.

Wharton was purposely writing about a safer and more stable era, but her sense of nostalgia was tempered by her acute awareness that the years during which she grew up were also "guarded and monotonous." This secure, if narrow, class-conscious conservatism to which Wharton alluded forms the moral centerpiece of her novel. Wharton's hero is Newland Archer, whose first name resembles the author's middle name, Newbold; his last name is a reference to Isabel Archer, the main character of *The Portrait of a Lady*, by Wharton's close friend Henry James. Newland is a privileged young man of intellect and Victorian masculine vanity, who accepts and sometimes finds amusing the genteel hypocrisies of his class. He is engaged to the lovely, outwardly demure May Welland. There is a passionate side to Newland: He was once attracted to a worldly "married lady whose charms had held his fancy through two mildly agitated years," and "if he probed to the bottom of his vanity (as he sometimes nearly did) he would have found there the wish that his wife should be as worldly-wise and as eager to please." But "how this miracle of fire and ice was to be created, and to sustain itself in a harsh world, he had never taken the time to think out." Staid and correct, May is completely a product of the tribal customs of the New York aristocracy; Newland perceives that she will never surprise him "by a new idea, a weakness, a cruelty, or an emotion." Completing the novel's love triangle is May's cousin, Countess Ellen Olenska, a member of the socially prominent Mingott family, whose matriarch is the formidable and diverting Mrs. Manson Mingott. The attractive, thirtyish Ellen is one of the Mingotts' many "black sheep"; she left the family fold to marry a ne'er-do-well Polish count, then separated from her husband and has returned to New York from Europe. Ellen has a slight French accent and an aura of sophistication and mystery. The family defends her against all outsiders, but she is often treated as a pariah. The clan keeps watch on her and unsuccessfully tries to prevent her from such bohemian behavior as renting a house in a socially unacceptable part of town and consorting with the unconventional and dissipated Julius Beaufort, an unscrupulous businessman considered an outsider despite his marriage to a wellborn New Yorker. Warmhearted, open, and individualistic, Ellen possesses more depth and understanding than any other female character in the novel. Newland, who had known Ellen when both were children, is attracted to her from the start.

Not long after Newland's engagement to May is announced, he begins to send Ellen flowers and to call on her, with the excuse that he wants to make the cousin of his fiancée feel at home. When Newland, a junior attorney in a venerable law firm, is asked to handle Ellen's divorce settlement, he further justifies his attachment to her in a spirit of chivalry: He views her as the victim of a cruel husband and of an equally cruel legal system that treats a wife as the property of her husband. Newland's sense of chivalry soon blossoms into a love that carries with it a newfound perception that the individual matters more than the tribe. Convinced that he is seeing too much of Ellen, Newland goes to Saint Augustine, where May, her mother, and her hypochondriac father are vacationing. There Newland feels a resurgence of affection for the beautiful May despite her lack of response to his wooing. He begs her to advance the date of their wedding, but May and her parents insist that the elaborate preparations make it impossible for the date to be changed and refuse. Unbeknownst to Newland, he achieves his purpose with the aid of Mrs. Mingott, and learns of the changed wedding date in a telegram sent by May to Ellen, which Ellen reads to him just as he is about to advance the intimacy of their relationship. At home, Newland finds a similar telegram sent to him from May. Thus protected from the possibility of further indiscretion, Newland prepares to marry within a month.

After their lavish wedding, Newland and May embark upon a conventional European honeymoon. Back in New York, Newland soon becomes dissatisfied with his sweet and passive wife and feels trapped within his rigid, codified social environment. He continues to see Ellen and proposes that they go away together. Ellen does not want to threaten the tenuous family stability she has found and makes him understand that they cannot consummate their love. Newland feels his lack of courage keenly, especially when he accedes to the family's request that he urge Ellen not to divorce her husband, and she agrees. Next, a crisis erupts when Julius Beaufort's business, built on a shaky framework of financial speculation, fails, ruining him and his duped customers. One of those affected is Mrs. Mingott, who suffers a stroke. She sends for Ellen, who had left New York for Washington, D.C. When Ellen returns, Newland begins to see her again. The family convinces Ellen to return to Paris, and Newland is frozen out of any decisions concerning her.

At a farewell dinner for Ellen given by May, Newland belatedly realizes that his family and members of his social set have long known about his relationship with Ellen and believe them to be lovers. After the dinner, he expresses to May his desire to go on a long trip "away from everything" but May, inferring, probably correctly, that he plans to seek out her cousin, tells him he cannot go because she is pregnant. She reveals that she told Ellen of her pregnancy before telling Newland, even though she "wasn't sure then—but I told her I was." Thus neatly manipulated into correct behavior by May's lie to Ellen, Newland is welcomed back into the family as a prodigal and makes peace with his life.

During the years that follow, Newland dabbles in liberal politics and embraces civic reform; he becomes "what people were beginning to call 'a good citizen.'" He and May have two children, Dallas and Mary. Newland remains a faithful husband through the long years of his marriage, and after May suddenly dies, he "honestly mourned her." At 57 Newland reflects on "something he knew he had missed: the flower of his life. But he thought of it now as a thing so unattainable and improbable that to have repined would have been like despairing because one had not drawn the first prize in a lottery. . . . When he thought of Ellen Olenska it was abstractly, serenely, as one might think of some imaginary beloved in a book or a picture . . . he honoured his own past, and mourned for it. After all, there was good in the old ways." When Dallas, now engaged to Julius Beaufort's daughter, proposes a last father-and-son trip together to Paris, Newland agrees. In Paris, Dallas reveals that he knows about his father's relationship with Ellen and has arranged to visit Countess Olenska at her apartment. When they arrive, Newland sends his son on ahead, sits on a bench opposite the building, and looks up at Ellen's apartment, picturing the scene inside. Deciding that his romantic picture of Ellen is "more real to me here than if I went up," he sits until a servant closes the shutters, then gets up slowly and makes his way alone back to his hotel. To the end he has remained faithful to May and to the "old ways."

Reaction to *The Age of Innocence* upon its publication was varied and interesting. As Linda Wagner-Martin observes, Wharton's first "readers justified Newland Archer and May Welland staying together. Rather than seeing any irony in Archer's living by values that he questions at the beginning of the novel, they accepted his wife's earnest, moral thinking. Many readers overlooked May's lie to Ellen Olenska about her pregnancy, excusing her subterfuge because she is saving her marriage. Ellen, moreover, was thought to be an unsympathetic character, regardless of Wharton's apparent preference for her." Cognizant of Wharton's place in literary history, reviewers compared her to such authors as Jane Austen, Joseph Conrad, and, predictably, Henry James. A. E. W. Mason wrote in the *Bookman* that "On the book's enduring quality it is idle to speculate," referred to the novel's "slight theme," and allowed that "a multitude of readers today will read with a well-justified delight this picture of New York in the 'seventies.'" *The New York Call*, a socialist newspaper, referred to Wharton's "oblique criticism" of the 1870s and asked, "Is New York, or America, so different in the year 1920?" The *Saturday Review* found it "on a level with Mrs. Wharton's best work. As a retrospect of the early 'seventies, it is less satisfactory, being marred by numerous historical lapses." *The New Republic* praised the novel as "a book of unsparing perception" and "verity."

Differing social sensibilities during each era of the 20th century have altered critical perceptions of the novel. Considered a masterpiece during World War II and then largely forgotten during the 1950s, when such modernists as F. Scott Fitzgerald, Ernest Hemingway, and William Faulkner became the literary giants of the American scholarly canon, *The Age of Innocence*, as well as Wharton's other works, enjoyed a revival in the last decades of the century. "Then," observes Wagner-Martin, "feminism rivaled modernism for scholars' attention; in some ways, *The Age of Innocence* satisfied both interests. Not only was it written by a woman, with two strong women characters facing moral dilemmas involving sexual choices; but its style approaches the precise, elliptical, and highly polished modernist narrative."

The Age of Innocence endures in popularity because it is an appealing 19th-century romantic story with interesting characters. But Wharton's novel of manners remains stylistically relevant and thematically and historically significant because of her precise, polished, and elliptical language. Wharton's use of language allows us to understand and dissect the complicated rules of behavior imposed upon Newland Archer, Ellen Olenska, and May Welland, as they express and repress their desires in an age that Wharton shows us was not quite so innocent after all.

105

DOM CASMURRO

(1899) *by Joaquim Maria Machado de Assis*

Machado's seventh novel, Dom Casmurro . . . *is Machado's most nearly perfect single novel and one of the greatest of its time. A masterpiece of psychological portraiture, of ironic inversion, and of symbolically charged narrative,* Dom Casmurro *is a towering human tragedy. With its plot structure paralleling that of* Othello, Dom Casmurro *returns once again to the use of a keenly self-conscious narrator/protagonist, whose powerful but not immediately apparent bias in regard to his telling of the story gradually emerges as the novel's great clandestine theme.*

—Earl E. Fitz, *Machado de Assis*

Inviting comparisons to such literary giants as Laurence Sterne, Henry Fielding, Gustave Flaubert, James Joyce, Marcel Proust, and Samuel Beckett, the Brazilian writer Machado de Assis has long remained a neglected master of the modern novel. Susan Sontag, an ardent admirer, called him "the greatest writer ever produced in Latin America"; while the critic Harold Bloom declared him "the supreme black literary artist to date." Despite such high praise, Machado has only gradually and fitfully gained international recognition for his achievement. One reason is that Machado as a writer in Portuguese has suffered the fate of expressing himself in what has been called the "cemetery of literary languages." "Though it is currently the sixth most widely spoken language in the world, ranking well ahead of such better-known tongues as German, French, Italian, and Japanese," the scholar Earl Fitz has argued, "Portuguese is not commonly studied. As a consequence, its literature remains a terra incognita to the vast majority of readers and critics, including those who pride themselves on being knowledgeable about the Western literary tradition." Moreover, Machado, whose career overlapped several literary movements, including romanticism, realism, naturalism, symbolism, and impressionism, resists being contained by any one. Rather Machado's works constitute a challenging hybrid of aesthetic tenets and characteristics. If exceptions make for bad laws, exceptional writers like

Machado fare poorly in canon formation. One hundred years after his death, however, more and more of his works are being translated, read, and studied, and Machado is finally being recognized as a preeminent master of the modern novel.

Dom Casmurro is the consensus choice for his masterpiece. An innovative psychological study of desire, jealousy, paranoia, and delusion, it is, in the view of the Machado scholar Helen Caldwell, "the finest novel ever written in the Americas, North or South" and should be regarded as his culminating work: "Not only does it surpass the others as an artistic work, but elements of the first six novels appear here in more perfect form: composition of characters, narrative structures, theme development—the whole novelist's art." For readers new to this remarkable writer, *Dom Casmurro* is the ideal starting point to begin an appreciation of Machado's considerable achievement.

Joaquim Maria Machado was born in Rio de Janeiro in 1839. His father, who worked as a housepainter, was the son of freed slaves; his Portuguese mother emigrated from the Azores and helped support the family as a washerwoman. Machado lost his mother and his only sister at an early age and was looked after by his more well-to-do godmother, who is credited with introducing him to literature. Much about Machado's early years is unknown, but it is believed that he was mainly self-taught. Afflicted with chronic illnesses and a speech impediment, Machado went to work at age 15 as a printer's apprentice, proofreader, and bookstore clerk. Journalistic and literary contacts formed through his work led to the publication of his first poems, stories, and essays. In the 1860s, Machado entered the civil service, married a socially prominent Portuguese woman, and settled into a stable domestic life from which he advanced his career, eventually attaining the directorship of the Ministry of Agriculture, while enhancing his reputation as one of Brazil's leading literary figures. Caldwell provides this summary of Machado in his maturity: "an intellectual; a courteous gentleman; a patriot; a devoted husband; a hard working, steady, law-abiding citizen and public servant; drank tea instead of something stronger; an honest man in every sense of the word; a great reader but also gregarious; a 'joiner' of both political and literary societies; a man given to warm friendships, fond of animals, children, whist, chess, dancing, music, theater and conversation; and above all a man of infinite good taste." He was also immensely prolific. It is calculated that between the ages of 15 and 30, Machado "composed some 6,000 lines of poetry, 19 plays and opera librettos, 24 short stories, 182 columns and articles, and 17 translations into Portuguese from French and Spanish." His early published works include the poetry collections *Chrysálidas* (1864; *Chrysalises*), *Phalenes* (1870; *The Moths*), and *Americanas* (1875; *Americana*), the story collections *Contos fluminenses* (1869; *Stories of Rio de Janeiro*) and *Histórias da Meia-Noite* (1873; *Midnight Stories*), and the novels *Resurreição* (1872; *Resurrection*), *A mão e a luva* (1874; *The Hand and the Glove*), *Helena* (1876), and *Yayá Garcia* (1878).

In 1878, exhausted from overwork and suffering from severe illnesses including epileptic seizures, eye trouble, and intestinal infections, Machado left Rio to recover at a nearby mountain resort. He returned in 1879 rejuvenated and recommitted to his literary career. His most important and innovative writing followed, and scholars have long divided Machado's works into pre- and post-1880, with the first period characterized by a predominant romanticism and formal conventionality and the second by a radical break with established conventions and the narrative innovations that have secured his international reputation. Although such a view overlooks the innovative qualities of Machado's early stories and essays, it does suit a comparison between Machado's early and later novels. His initial novel in this second phase is the strikingly experimental *Memórias póstumas de Brás Cubas* (1881; *Epitaph of a Small Winner*). Nothing like the kind of mordant satire of social conventions or the anatomy of a contradictory egotist had featured in his previous novels. Machado employs an unreliable narrator for the first time as well as the striking conceit of a posthumous memoir, not one published after death but composed after death. The life story of the privileged and spoiled Brás Cubas proceeds in a flood of associative digressions, in "the free form of a Sterne or of a Xavier de Maistre." Moving beyond the romanticism of his previous novels and the attraction of realism and naturalism that was entering Brazilian literature at the time, whose strict objectivity and excessive accumulation of details he rejected, Machado instead found a more congenial narrative form in the associative and self-reflective style of 18th-century writers. Machado, thereby, began to inhabit the narrative domain that would be occupied decades later by the modernists. As Susan Sontag observed, "*Epitaph of a Small Winner* is probably one of those thrillingly original, radically skeptical books which will always impress readers with the force of a private discovery." In his next novel, *Quincas Borba* (1891; *Philosopher or Dog?*), Brás Cubas's mentor, the mad philosopher Quincas Borba, bequeaths all his wealth, his dog, and his philosophy to a simple provincial schoolmaster, launching him into the upper reaches of Brazilian society for an attack on its pretensions and hypocrisy. The picaresque narrative is continually being interrupted by the omniscient narrator to address the reader and to call attention to the artifice of storytelling, elements that confirm Machado's status as a proto-modernist.

The triumph of Machado's innovations in his mature phase is the third novel he completed after 1880, *Dom Casmurro*, that brings together the obsessively self-conscious and unreliable narrator/protagonist of *Epitaph of a Small Winner* with the freewheeling satire and self-reflexive characteristics of *Philosopher or Dog?* Organized into 148 titled sections, some as short as a single paragraph, *Dom Casmurro* immediately strikes the reader as a direct challenge to accepted realistic novel conventions, offering what the narrator describes as a "book with gaps," in which the reader must fill in the blanks and read between the lines. In the opening section, "The Title," the narrator introduces himself using his acquired nickname, "Dom Casmurro," meaning "Lord Taciturn" or "Lord Stubborn." "Don't consult your dictionaries," he warns, however. "*Casmurro* is not used here in the meaning they give for it, but in the sense in which the man in the street uses it, of a morose, tight-lipped man withdrawn within himself . . . Well, I have found no better title for my narrative. . . ." In the second section, "The Book," the narrator, whose actual name is Bento Santiago, states his purpose "to tie together the two ends of my life, to restore adolescence in age." Having constructed in the suburbs of Rio a house exactly like the one in which he grew up, the middle-aged Bento similarly constructs the story of his life as an act of repossession. As the two opening sections make clear, the reader is immediately put on notice to assess the extent that the narrator lives up to his nickname as a misanthropic egoist and is providing a truthful confession or a compensating justification. His recollections commence when he is 16 and overhears a conversation between a household retainer, José Dias, and his widowed mother, Dona Glória, accusing him of "getting into corners" and flirting with a neighborhood girl Capitolina, known as Capitú. This is problematic because before Bento was born, his mother vowed that he would become a priest. The conflict that ensues, between Bento's desire for Capitú and his resistance to fulfilling his mother's vow while gaining approval to court the less socially prominent Capitú, dominates the first portion of the novel. The resourceful and intelligent Capitú proves to be "more of a woman than I was a man," in this courtship battle, and the early scenes make clear Bento's insecurities and inadequacies that will later manifest themselves in the irrational outbursts of jealousy that will doom their relationship. Bento eventually agrees to enter the seminary but with the understanding that he will not be forced into the priesthood against his wishes. There he meets and befriends another resistant seminarian named Escobar, for whom "commerce is my real vocation," who devises the means to satisfy Dona Glória's vow by sponsoring another young man who wants to become a priest as a substitute for Bento. Both Escobar and Bento leave the seminary—Escobar to succeed in business and Bento to enter the law—and the way is clear for him to marry Capitú. Like *Othello*, which *Dom Casmurro* clearly echoes, the lovers' initial complications are overcome, but the tragedy proceeds after the usual comic conclusion in marriage. In *Dom Casmurro*, however, the noble Othello and the destructive Iago come together in the same character.

Initially, Bento and Capitú's happy marriage is marred only by a lack of children. Finally a son, Ezekiel, is born. Escobar dies in a drowning accident, and at his funeral Bento sees Capitú wiping away tears. This leads to Bento's growing jealous suspicions that his wife has been unfaithful, culminating in his apprehension that Ezekiel looks more and more like his friend, supporting the conclusion that "it was the will of destiny that my first girlfriend and my best friend, so affectionate as well as so beloved, got together and tricked me." Bento finds more circumstantial evidence for his suspicion, and the marriage collapses under his certainty of Capitú's guilt. Exiled to Switzerland, Capitú dies, followed by the death of Ezekiel from typhoid on a trip to Egypt financed by his father. Bento is left alone, in retirement in his reconstructed house where, after his reconstruction of his past, he plans to write a *History of the Suburbs.*

The first readers of *Dom Casmurro* accepted the narrator's perspective at face value, viewing the novel as a straightforward story of adultery in which Capitú was clearly guilty. Later readings of the novel have stressed Bento's unreliability and the ambiguity concerning the actual facts. Unlike other 19th-century treatments of adultery, such as Flaubert's *Madame Bovary* and Tolstoy's *Anna Karenina*, as critic Earl Fitz has argued, "*Dom Casmurro* is probably the first novel about adultery where the facts of the matter are dubious." Mounting his case against his wife, Bento lets slip views and circumstances that undermine his proofs, forcing the reader to assess the degree to which Bento's own insecurities and inadequacies allied with his controlling and jealous temperament produce the novel's tragedy. Whether Bento is the put-upon Othello or the destructive Iago, betrayed victim or betrayer, *Dom Casmurro* finally leaves that judgment to the reader, suggesting that any kind of certainty in contending with experience or human nature and behavior is problematic. Othello's tragedy results from his incapacity of living with doubt and uncertainty. "To be once in doubt/ Is once to be resolved," Othello asserts. Bento similarly destroys what he once loved, refusing to accept the ambiguity that the narrative offers its readers. The controversy over Bento's case against Capitú has made *Dom Casmurro* the most popular of Brazilian novels, and one of the great examples of a domestic drama that becomes an epistemological inquiry into what can be known and trusted. With its fragmented, associative form, unreliable narrator, and tolerance of ambiguity and paradox, *Dom Casmurro* anticipates the style and methods of modern and postmodern novels and earns Machado's place as one of the form's master innovators.

A HERO OF OUR TIME

106

(1840)

by Mikhail Lermontov

A Hero of Our Time *represents a crucial moment in the development of the Russian novel and of the realist technique with which it becomes identified in the course of the 19th century. Paradoxically the first-person narrative, with its romantic-confessional overtones, which is used in all the constituent parts of the novel, yields in its plurality a realistic, since unprivileged, point of view. Moreover the experimental structure of the work—a novel that is a congeries of autonomous stories rather than organically subordinate chapters—forms an important bridge between the tentative short prose works of the earlier part of the century and the mature novels that began to appear toward the middle of the 19th century. These structural features, coupled with the three-dimensional portrait of the novel's hero, combine to make* A Hero of Our Time *one of the single most important Russian prose works of the 19th century.*

—Robert Reid, "*A Hero of Our Time*," in *Reference Guide to Russian Literature*

Critically regarded as the first major Russian novel, Mikhail Lermontov's *A Hero of Our Time* is a pioneering and innovative work that initiated the great age of the Russian novel, exerting an enduring influence on subsequent Russian literature. Only Pushkin is esteemed more highly as Russia's greatest 19th-century poet, but Lermontov's singular contribution is his one completed, extended work of fiction. In *A Hero of Our Time*, Lermontov established the tradition of psychological realism in the Russian novel that would become the defining legacy for the writers that followed him—for Turgenev, Goncharov, Dostoevsky, Tolstoy, and Chekhov. Moreover, in its central character, Grigory Pechorin, Lermontov embodied for the first time in prose fiction a dominant Russian character type, the so-called "superfluous man"—disaffected, alienated, and doomed—introduced in the eponymous character of Pushkin's narrative poem *Eugene Onegin* (1831) and christened in Turgenev's short story, "Diary of a Superfluous Man" (1850). Embodying contradictions and paradoxes, Pechorin is one of fiction's first great antiheroes, Lermontov's version of Russia's representative modern man, a distillation of, in his creator's words, "all the vices of our generation." Pechorin would serve as precedent to some of the most famous characters in Russian literature from Turgenev's Bazarov *(Fathers and Sons)*, Goncharov's Oblomov, Dostoevsky's Underground Man *(Notes from the Underground)*, to Tolstoy's Andrei Bulkonski and Pierre Bezukhov *(War and Peace)*. In penetrating the depths of Pechorin's character while reflecting the zeitgeist of the age that could claim him as the hero of its time, Lermontov started the Russian novel on its dual course: inward into the heart of a complex psychology and outward to depict the social world that formed and affected such a character. To render Pechorin in multiple dimensions, Lermontov would radically redefine prose narrative form, violating chronology and juxtaposing conflicting perspectives, while demonstrating for one of the first times in modern literature how the intensity and compression of the short story could be put to service in a longer narrative, how disjointed parts could be artfully united to form a greater whole. Formally, *A Hero of Our Time* is a forerunner both of the modern short story sequences, such as James Joyce's *Dubliners* and Hemingway's *In Our Time* and the modern novel's fragmented narrative in which the reader is forced to play an active role assembling and synthesizing the whole from its parts.

Lermontov's own persona as Russia's Byron fostered by a reckless life and an early death rivals Pechorin as an influential Russian archetype. Born in Moscow in 1814, Lermontov claimed descent from a Scottish mercenary who entered the czar's service in the 17th century. His father was a handsome though unconnected officer who retired from the army in 1811 and married Lermontov's mother over her family's objections. Her death when Lermontov was two and a half provoked a contentious custody battle between his father and his maternal grandmother who succeeded in buying off her son-in-law and taking control of her grandson's upbringing at her grand provincial estate. Childhood illnesses stunted Lermontov's growth and left him stoop-shouldered and bowlegged. Recuperative trips to the Caucasus in southern Russia started Lermontov's passionate attachment to the area. Its dramatic mountainscapes and untamed native population would dominate Lermontov's imagination, embodying a longed-for "lost paradise" he would celebrate in his poetry. In one early poem, Lermontov imagines the Caucasus speaking to him with his dead mother's voice:

In my childhood years I lost my mother,
But it seemed, in the rosy hour of evening,
That the steppe repeated that memorable voice.
For this I love the summits of those cliffs,
  I love the Caucasus.

At the age of 13, Lermontov went to Moscow to attend the preparatory school for Moscow University, which he entered in 1830. Beginning to write his first poetry in boarding school, he discovered a kinship with Byron who supplied him with the prototype of the brooding, alienated rebel that Lermontov began to imitate. Bored and restless at the university, Lermontov transferred to the Guards Cadet Academy in St. Petersburg and was commissioned as an officer in the Life Guard Hussars in 1834, serving the next three years at Czar Nicholas I's summer palace outside St. Petersburg. While fully engaged in fashionable court circles, Lermontov produced in addition to a steady stream of lyrics the play *Masquerade* (1835), a satire on Petersburg society that was rejected for performance by the censor, and an unfinished short novel, *Princess Ligovskaya*, in which Lermontov introduced the character of Pechorin, that would form the basis of the "Princess Mary" section of *A Hero of Our Time*. In 1837, after Pushkin was killed in a duel, Lermontov wrote "The Death of a Poet," an angry elegy alleging official complicity in the poet's death that came to the attention of the czar who ordered Lermontov's arrest and exile to active duty in the Caucasus. Allowed to return to Petersburg and his regiment after a year, Lermontov began work on *A Hero of Our Time*, which was published to acclaim in 1840. That same year, Lermontov fought a duel with the son of the French ambassador, provoking a second banishment to a combat regiment in the Caucasus, where Lermontov distinguished himself. In 1841, Lermontov, returning from leave in St. Petersburg and while heading to an assignment in a Black Sea regiment, quarreled with a retired army officer at Pyatigorsk. In the ensuing duel, the 27-year-old Lermontov was killed instantly, ironically, in one of the most eerie and perverse cases of life imitating art, at the same location where Pechorin, his alter ego, had met his death in a duel. Nothing burnishes a reputation better than a meteoric career and an early death, and Lermontov has persisted in the Russian consciousness as the embodiment of Russian romanticism: the hypersensitive, tormented rebel, both passionately creative and empathetic and willfully self-destructive.

The enigmas surrounding Lermontov's character and career are reflected in *A Hero of Our Time* in which the reader confronts through multiple perspectives the puzzling protagonist, Grigory Pechorin, an army officer posted to the Caucasus, with many of the same contradictions and paradoxes as his creator. Made up of five linked sections, three of which had been published separately in 1839 and 1840, *A Hero of Our Time* opens with a foreword in which Lermontov defends his subject against criticism of immorality and inutility: "*A Hero of Our Time*, my dear sirs, is indeed a portrait, but not of one man; it is a portrait built up of all our generation's vices in full bloom. . . . You say that morality will gain nothing by it. I beg to differ. People have been fed enough sweetness to upset their stomachs; now bitter remedies, acid truths, are needed." Insisting on a truthfulness missing from previous books in portraying "the modern man as he sees him and as he so often, to his own and your misfortune, has found him to be," Lermontov concludes by declaring: "Suffice it that the disease has been diagnosed, how to cure it the Lord alone knows!" What follow are five instances of the author's diagnosis of his representative modern man.

The first, "Bela," is narrated by a nameless officer who, while traveling in the Caucasus along the Military Georgian Highway in 1837, meets a veteran officer, Maksim Maksimych who tells the story of a former comrade, a young officer, Pechorin, who five years earlier had kidnapped a Circassian princess named Bela. Pechorin convinces her brother to abduct her in exchange for a horse stolen from a Circassian bandit, Kazbich. Pechorin eventually compels Bela to fall in love with him only to tire of her. Kazbich, to avenge himself on Pechorin, kidnaps Bela and stabs her to death to evade his pursuers. The story ends with Maksimych's attempts to console Pechorin, whose behavior shocks him: "'It angered me to detect no sign of emotion on his face, for in his place I should have died of grief. Finally, he sat down on the ground in the shade and began to trace some design in the sand with a stick. I began to speak, wishing to console him, more for the sake of good form than anything else, you know, whereupon he looked up and laughed. . . . That laugh sent cold shivers running up and down my spine.'" The reader, like the nameless narrator, is left with many unanswered questions and Pechorin's perplexing laugh undercutting Maksimych's sentimentality and any conventional response to the violent death of a loved one. Lermontov's innovation here stems from his departure from omniscient narration, giving the reader almost nothing about Pechorin's background or motivation, presenting him at two removes that fail to make sense of Pechorin's baffling behavior, while stimulating an interest in resolving it.

The second section, "Maksim Maksimych," records the narrator's second encounter with Maksimych in the town of Vladikavkaz where it is learned Pechorin is also staying. Maksimych's enthusiasm about meeting his former comrade is coldly rebuffed, and the scorned older officer disposes of Pechorin's papers that had been entrusted to him by giving them to the narrator before they separate. The narrator fleetingly glimpses Pechorin and notes his eyes as his one distinctive feature, which "never laughed when he was laughing," a characteristic which the narrator understands as "either the sign of a wicked nature or of a deep and constant melancholy." Like the earlier laugh that closes "Bela," Pechorin's behavior toward Maksimych, defies expectation and further extends the enigma of his character and the narrator's (and by extension, the reader's) desire to solve it. If the eyes truly are the windows of the soul, what do they reveal: Pechorin's wickedness or deep melancholy? The reader can base an answer on Pechorin's own words in the three sections that follow. They are preceded by a foreword in which the narrator reveals that he had recently learned that Pechorin has died, freeing him to publish extracts "bearing on Pechorin's stay in the Caucasus" that reveal the "sincerity of this man who so mercilessly exhibited his own failings and vices."

The first extract from Pechorin's journal is "Taman," which both Tolstoy and Chekhov esteemed as the finest short story in Russian literature. Named for a seacoast town that Pechorin visits as a young officer around 1830, the story describes his encounter with smugglers, including a young woman who lures him into a boat and attempts to drown him. On display is the opposite of the Byronic Pechorin the reader anticipates meeting from the first two sections. Instead, he appears as a naïve young man, more clueless than in control, with the gender/power relationship of "Bela" reversed. Here the woman is the aggressor, and he is her victim. "Taman" establishes a baseline to measure the behavioral and developmental changes that chronologically follow it, in the preceding two sections and the following two. In "Princess Mary," an older and more seasoned Pechorin records in diary entries an earlier seduction like that in "Bela," but set in Pyatigorsk, a fashionable spa in the Russian-occupied area of the Caucasus. Pechorin competes with a young cadet named Grushnitski for the attention of Princess Mary, and, when she prefers the younger man, sets out to avenge himself on both of them. Pechorin is successful in humiliating Grushnitski and manipulating Princess Mary's attachment. She, unlike Bela, however, survives her encounter with only a broken heart, while Grushnitski is killed in a duel in which Pechorin offers as confirmation of his now firmly established pose of perverse indifference, *"Finita la commedia!"* ("The comedy is ended!"). Pechorin concludes his account with this self-diagnosis: "I am like a mariner born and bred on board a buccaneer brig whose soul has become so inured to storm and strife that if cast ashore he would weary and languish no matter how alluring the shady groves and how bright the gentle sun." The story shows the process of Pechorin's formation and condition—his recognition of the emptiness of society's moral codes, his philosophical nihilism, and his willful courting of destruction to test its truths—that helps to explain his behavior in the opening two sections and is finally clarified in the novel's final one, "The Fatalist," a disquisition on whether fate or will principally rules the human condition. Pechorin records how a fellow officer Vulich tests his confidence in the power of fate by surviving Russian roulette, only to be killed in the street by a drunken Cossack. The lesson Pechorin draws from this is that any human action—good or ill—is ultimately trumped by fate, leaving him morally unanchored and adrift, indifferent to any human claims, trapped in a self-destructive campaign to prove human futility.

In Pechorin, Lermontov offers an intriguing diagnosis of the Byronic pose of cynical self-detachment that he often imitated, finding in the romantic rebel the symptoms of modern alienation, dislocation, and angst that anticipate Nietzsche and the existentialist, making *A Hero of Our Time* strikingly up-to-date and still disturbingly powerful and relevant.

THE CATCHER IN THE RYE 107

(1951)

by J. D. Salinger

What, finally, is left to be said about this novel that variously has been called "great" and "true" as well as "perverse" and "immoral"? In secondary schools, colleges, and universities, it may well be the most widely read post–World War II American novel—and the most banned. For a few years critics and scholars seemed as interested in Salinger's fiction as did undergraduates . . . Yet despite his dismissal by some critics, his failure to publish anything in the last twenty-five years, and the competing popularity of such writers as Toni Morrison, Thomas Pynchon, and Kurt Vonnegut, Jr., The Catcher in the Rye *retains a remarkable hold on our cultural imagination.*

—Jack Salzman, Introduction, *New Essays on The Catcher in the Rye*

An enduring classic of American literature, *The Catcher in the Rye* is one of the most significant—and controversial—novels to appear after World War II. J. D. Salinger's only novel, published in 1951, arrived at a telling moment in American history—a prosperous postwar period that gave rise to suburban conformity and teenage angst (the novel was so influential in the 1950s that the decade has sometimes been called "the Age of Holden Caulfield," in reference to the novel's 17-year-old main character). *The Catcher in the Rye* has remained a favorite for the more than 50 years since it was first published because of its scathing indictment of middle-class values, its irreverent, caustic humor, the precision with which Salinger captured colloquial speech, and above all, because of its narrator and main character, Holden Caulfield, perhaps the most sensitive and sorrowful adolescent in all of postwar 20th-century American adult fiction.

As a young writer in his early 20s, Salinger had been, writes his biographer Paul Alexander, "searching for that special character or milieu . . . he came to understand that the vehicle through which he was destined to examine the world in such a way as to make his fiction distinctly his own was Holden Caulfield." Holden made his first appearance in a 1941 Salinger short story, "Slight Rebellion Off Madison," which was accepted by *The*

New Yorker magazine but not published until 1946. The magazine's editors, writes Alexander, "did not feel it was appropriate to publish—so soon after Pearl Harbor—a story about a neurotic teenage boy whose 'slight rebellion' is prompted by the fact that he had become disenchanted with the life he leads as the son in a wealthy family in New York. Holden's problems were trivial compared to world developments." Salinger served as a staff sergeant in an army counterintelligence unit during World War II, took part in the D-day invasion, and fought in the Battle of the Bulge. From 1942 to 1945 he published several short stories in such magazines as *Collier's* and *The Saturday Evening Post.* A character named Holden Caulfield appears in some of the stories Salinger wrote during this period. In 1945 *Collier's* published "I'm Crazy," the first story to feature Holden as narrator and to include material later incorporated in *The Catcher in the Rye.*

By 1950 *The New Yorker* had published six of Salinger's short stories, including the popular "A Perfect Day for Bananafish" (1948) and "For Esmé—With Love and Squalor" (1950). In the fall of 1950 he completed *The Catcher in the Rye*, which was turned down by Harcourt Brace, the publishing house that had solicited it, because the senior editor could not determine whether or not Holden Caulfield was crazy. It was then sold to Little, Brown and shortly thereafter, to the British publisher Hamish Hamilton. Editors at *The New Yorker* declined to publish excerpts from the novel because they felt that the precocity of Holden and his three siblings was not believable and that Salinger's writing style was too self-consciously clever. *The Catcher in the Rye* was published by Little, Brown in July 1951, and simultaneously appeared as a Book-of-the-Month Club selection. It was an immediate best-seller, and has sold more than 60 million copies to date.

The Catcher in the Rye is mainly set in New York City in the late 1940s and takes place over a three-day period in December. Holden, "a demon of verbal incision," as critic Louis Menand has characterized him, begins by informing the reader not to expect "all that David Copperfield kind of crap." Holden is chronicling his account from a sanitarium in California, where he was sent after "this madman stuff that happened to me around last Christmas just before I got pretty run-down and had to come out here and take it easy." The first scenes of the novel are set at Pencey Prep, a boarding school in Pennsylvania. Holden has been expelled from Pencey for failing all his subjects except English. It is the third school from which he has been expelled. Holden knows that his parents will be infuriated with him, and he does not look forward to returning to New York to face them. He articulates his disgust with Pencey—"a terrible school, no matter how you looked at it"—and with his classmates, and is impatient even with a favorite history teacher, whom he visits to say good-bye. He provokes altercations with another student, the annoying, pimply Robert Ackley, and with his roommate, the handsome, glib Ward Stradlater. A disagreement over a composition Holden had agreed to write for Stradlater escalates into a fight between the two over Stradlater's treatment of his weekend date, a girl named Jane, whom Holden knows and likes. Bleeding from the fight, Holden decides to leave Pencey before the official start of the Christmas vacation, take the train to New York, and use his savings to "rest up" in a hotel until his parents have "digested" the news of his expulsion.

Once in New York, Holden has several encounters that increase his disillusionment, disaffection, and despair at the "phoniness" of the world, and bring him to a point of crisis and partial reconciliation. His first experiences are disappointing: He cannot engage a predictably dour cabdriver in conversation concerning where the ducks go in Central Park when the lake "gets all frozen over"; the unintelligent young women out-of-towners he picks up in the hotel bar are "dopes." Later, while drinking in a club, he runs into a "strictly phony" ex-girlfriend of his older brother, who is accompanied by a starchy naval officer, "one of those guys that think they're being a pansy if they don't break around forty of your fingers when they shake hands with you."

Holden's downhill slide begins when he returns to the seedy hotel in which he has chosen to hole up and agrees to have Maurice, the elevator operator, send a hooker up to his room. The girl's youthful hardness makes him feel "more depressed than sexy, if you want to know the truth," and he finds himself too dispirited to do anything other than suggest they talk. As she is leaving, a disagreement over the fee for her services results in Holden being punched in the stomach by Maurice. Holden finally drags himself to bed after fantasizing that he is a movie hero who has "plugged" Maurice for punching him.

The next afternoon, Holden meets a girlfriend, Sally Hayes, and the two go to the theater, where Sally gushes over the "marvelous" Lunts. Even though Holden is irritated with Sally's self-conscious pseudo-sophistication, he decides that he is in love with her and begs her to run away with him. When she refuses, he insults her, calling her "a royal pain in the ass." After Sally's angry departure, Holden joins an older ex-schoolmate at a bar and soon alienates him with his excessive drinking and mocking comments. Finally, drunk and broke and wandering around in the rain, Holden goes home to see his 10-year-old sister, Phoebe, the only person he has felt close to since the death from leukemia of his gifted younger brother, Allie. He attempts to explain to Phoebe his dissatisfaction with school and tells her that he would like to be a "catcher in the rye," who would stand "on the edge of some crazy cliff" and catch children before they fall over it. Forced to sneak out of the apartment when his parents return home, he finds refuge with a favorite English teacher, Mr. Antolini, and his wife. Despite his emotional and physical exhaustion, he tries to listen attentively to the drunk and garrulous Antolini as he warns him that Holden is riding for "a special kind of fall, a horrible kind" and lectures him on the necessity of living humbly for a cause rather than dying for one. Holden settles down for the night on the Antolinis' sofa but awakes abruptly to find his teacher sitting beside him and stroking his hair. Confused as to whether or not Antolini is a "flit," Holden makes a hasty exit from the apartment and spends the night in Grand Central Station.

The next day, despite feeling increasingly physically and emotionally debilitated, Holden resolves to hitchhike out West, where "people didn't know me and I didn't know anybody," and where he could "pretend I was one of those deaf-mutes. That way I wouldn't have to have any goddamn stupid useless conversations with anybody." He arranges to meet Phoebe at the Museum of Natural History to say goodbye to her, but when she arrives with a suitcase and forcefully announces her intention to go with him, Holden realizes he has to go home. He takes his sister to Central Park, where he reaches a reconciliation of sorts as he watches Phoebe happily ride the carousel. Although he worries that his sister will fall while reaching out to grab the gold ring, he understands, in contrast to his earlier desire to "catch" children before they fall, that "the thing with kids is, if they want to grab for the gold ring, you have to let them do it."

The Catcher in the Rye has been interpreted variously as a quest narrative, a religious metaphor, a scornful critique of American capitalism and conformity, and a bildungsroman. Although popularly considered an explication and indictment of 1950s society, it is really, Louis Menand contends, a novel of the 1940s, "a book about loss and a world gone wrong." Salinger, observes Menand, "wasn't trying to expose the spiritual poverty of a conformist culture; he was writing a story about a boy whose little brother had died. Holden, after all, isn't unhappy because he sees that people are phonies; he sees that people are phonies because he is unhappy." This does not make Holden's cultural insights and observations any less real or true, as evidenced by the countless students over the years who have taken Salinger's teenager to their hearts when the book has been assigned to them, often together with *Huckleberry Finn*. The two novels are strikingly similar in many respects: like Huck, Holden uses idiomatic and frequently vulgar language; both characters feel trapped by adults, who want to "sivilize" them. Despite the separation of time and geography, they are, observes critic Charles Kaplan, "true blood-brothers, speaking to us in terms that lift their wanderings from the level of the merely picaresque to that of a sensitive and insightful criticism of American life." For contemporary adolescent readers, the most definitive difference between the two novels may be accessibility: Twain was writing about a 19th-century character and society in a 19th-century style; it is easier for teenagers to identify with Holden's grief and pain, if not always with his cultural mordancy.

For many adolescents in the decades following its publication, *The Catcher in the Rye* was the most influential novel they had ever read. In a 1959 issue of the *Saturday Review*, the critic Granville Hicks noted that, to students in his college course in contemporary fiction, "Holden Caulfield meant more than Jake Barnes or Jay Gatsby or Augie March or any other character we encountered in the course, and in the discussion of the novel there was a direct involvement such as I felt on no other occasion." In one later notable—and notorious—case, Mark David Chapman, a disturbed loner, claimed identification with Holden Caulfield so strong that it prompted him to murder rock star John Lennon in 1980.

It is not surprising that such an exceptional novel would raise a storm of reaction from critics and reviewers. Most seemed not quite sure what to make of Salinger's story. Another *Saturday Review* writer, Harrison Smith, acknowledged that readers who might be shocked by *The Catcher in the Rye* "should be advised to let the book alone," but suggested that it was "a book to be read thoughtfully and more than once." *The Nation*'s Ernest Jones allowed that the novel was "ingenious" but "though always lively in its parts" was, as a whole, "predictable and boring." Subsequent critics have had a field day deconstructing every aspect of the novel, from its use of language to the psychology of its main character to its place in the context of the socioliterary American tradition. Praise and condemnation have followed *The Catcher in the Rye* almost from the start. In a 1962 issue of *Ramparts*, Robert O. Bowen spoke for those who found the novel objectionable when he wrote, "Far from being a kind and gentle and above all wise book, *The Catcher in the Rye*, like all of Salinger's fiction, is catty and snide and bigotted [sic] in the most thorough sense. It is crassly caste-conscious . . . it is religiously bigotted [sic] . . . it is vehemently anti-Army and even anti-American. . . . All of these things are the reasons for the book's success, for its success lies in its utility as propaganda." The sensibilities cited above, plus uneasiness concerning the vulgar language and discussion of sex in the novel have led to accusations of perversity and immorality and resulted in frequent attempts to ban *The Catcher in the Rye* from school curricula and from libraries, another distinction it shares with *Huckleberry Finn.*

Such attempts at censorship only serve to parody the society Salinger criticized in the novel—and most teenagers know it, because, like Holden Caulfield, they are struggling with the pain of leaving behind an idealized childhood to enter the deeply flawed world of adulthood. Salinger's novel, observes Louis Menand, provides adolescents "with a layer of psychic insulation." Critic Harold Bloom speaks to the novel's enduring influence when he states, "*The Catcher in the Rye* struck a nerve for one generation, but it seems to appeal to sensitive young people in later generations as well. Its sensitivity fits the sensitivity of young people who are going to develop a consciousness and distrust of the adult world. Probably it will survive."

108

MOLL FLANDERS

(1722)

by Daniel Defoe

The great fame of the book [Robinson Crusoe] *has done its author some injustice; for while it has given him a kind of anonymous glory it has obscured the fact that he was a writer of other works which, it is safe to assert, were not read aloud to us as children. Thus when the Editor of the* Christian World *in the year 1870 appealed to "the boys and girls of England" to erect a monument upon the grave of Defoe, which a stroke of lightning had mutilated, the marble was inscribed to the memory of the author of* Robinson Crusoe. *No mention was made of* Moll Flanders. *Considering the topics which are dealt with in that book, and in* Roxana, Captain Singleton, Colonel Jack *and the rest, we need not be surprised, though we may be indignant, at the omission. We may agree with Mr. Wright, the biographer of Defoe, that these "are not works for the drawing-room table". But unless we consent to make that useful piece of furniture the final arbiter of taste, we must deplore the fact that their superficial coarseness, or the universal celebrity of* Robinson Crusoe, *has led them to be far less widely famed than they deserve. On any monument worthy of the name of monument the names of* Moll Flanders *and* Roxana, *at least, should be carved as deeply as the name of Defoe. They stand among the few English novels which we can call indisputably great.*

—Virginia Woolf, "Defoe"

Daniel Defoe, the English novel's great originator, in *Moll Flanders* further extends the boundaries of fictions he mapped out in *Robinson Crusoe.* Having domesticated the exotic and replaced romance with realism, Defoe's follow-up to his autobiography of a marooned mariner is a confession of a woman, cut adrift from conventional class, gender, and moral imperatives and forced to survive not on a deserted island but in the contemporary urban jungle. The full title warns the reader that Moll's story is as remarkable, exciting, and ultimately edifying as that of any questing knight or modern male adventurer:

> *The Fortunes and Misfortunes of the Famous Moll Flanders, &c. Who was Born in Newgate, and during a Life of continu'd Variety for Threescore Years,*

besides her Childhood, was Twelve Year a Whore, *five times a* Wife *(whereof once to her own Brother), Twelve Year a* Thief, *Eight Year a Transported* Felon *in Virginia, at last grew* Rich, *liv'd* Honest, *and died a* Penitent, *Written from her own Memorandums.*

It is safe to say that Moll Flanders—Whore, Wife, Thief, Felon, Rich, Honest, and Penitent—is the most multiple and complex heroine who had ever taken center stage in a novel before. Not since Chaucer's Wife of Bath had a woman with a comparable earthy vitality and authenticity been celebrated in literature. Challenging the gender convention of the passive and virtuous disembodied female, Moll would initiate a new conception of the empowered heroine—willful, ambitious, contradictory, and resourceful—the literary progenitor for later female protagonists like Thackeray's Becky Sharp in *Vanity Fair*, the title characters in Charlotte Brontë's *Jane Eyre* and Zola's *Nana*, Carrie Meeber in Dreiser's *Sister Carrie*, Lilly Briscoe in Wharton's *The House of Mirth*, and Scarlett O'Hara in Mitchell's *Gone with the Wind.* Moreover, with her frankly rendered consciousness in which her narrative reads like an extended interior monologue, Moll Flanders claims kinship with her namesake—Joyce's Molly Bloom. In what E. M. Forster called a "masterpiece of characterization," Defoe initiated in *Moll Flanders* what would become a dominant tradition of the English novel: a narrative of growth and development in which the historical moment, social conditions, and gender assumptions all contribute to the making of an individual. Moll is the first great heroine of the English novel with a mythic dimension, composed in equal measure of particularity and universality. In discussing *Robinson Crusoe*, Coleridge famously attributed to Defoe the power to make "me forget my specific class, character, and circumstances" and to raise "me into universal man. Now that is Defoe's excellence. You become a man while you read." In the case of *Moll Flanders*, you become a woman.

After a long and turbulent career as a struggling businessman and journalist, Daniel Defoe, at the age of 60, followed up the enormous success of his first novel, *Robinson Crusoe* (1719), with his first fully developed fictional account of a criminal, *The Life, Adventures, and Pyracies, of the Famous Captain Singleton* (1720). Defoe's fascination with London's criminal underworld was stimulated when, also in 1720, he began writing for *Applebee's Weekly Journal* whose specialty was the biographies of criminals and their gallows confessions. Throughout 1721, Defoe was a regular visitor to Newgate prison. There he likely met the notorious convict, Moll King, and from her heard accounts of the adventures of her friend, thief and whore "Callico Sarah." (Sarah's nickname, after a kind of cloth targeted by thieves, may have suggested to Defoe another, Flanders, or Flemish lace, to serve as Moll's surname.) As the scholar Gerald Howson suggests, "It seems likely that Defoe sought [Moll King] out when she was under sentence of death, as a suitable subject for a criminal pamphlet. . . . After her reprieve, the pamphlet grew into the novel, the first of its kind in English." If *Robinson Crusoe* was based on Defoe's reading of Alexander Selkirk's memoir, *Moll Flanders* originated from Defoe's firsthand research and direct knowledge of the ways and means of contemporary urban life and its demimonde. Beyond its contemporaneousness and authenticity, the uniqueness of *Moll Flanders* rests in Defoe's ingenious and original amalgam of previously incompatible narrative forms.

Ballads, broadsides, and chapbook biographies and confessions of notorious criminals constituted a major part of the popular literature of the time. Fictional accounts of crimes and criminals go back to the picaresque narratives that first appeared in 16th-century Spain, a series of loosely connected episodes in the life of a picaro, a rogue, outlaw, or transgressor of established social and moral values. As the critic Martin Halliwell has argued, "Written within and set against the backdrop of a society in transition from fixed feudal relationships to a more flexible social structure in which the middle classes began to have significant economic and moral influence, the picaresque foreshadows the novel, charting the rise of bourgeois individualism in its exploration of the tensions between oppressive societies and disaffected individuals." The methods and subjects of the picaresque would be put to use by Defoe in the emerging English novel and subsequently employed by his novelist successors, most notably Henry Fielding and Tobias Smollett. Defoe's contribution to the picaresque tradition would be to feature a female picaro. Moll's gender and the inclusion in her adventures of love as well as crime link Defoe's narrative further to another proto-novel form, the so-called amatory tale, as practiced by Defoe's contemporary Eliza Haywood in one of the period's best sellers, *Love in Excess* (1719–20). Derived from the earlier prose romances, the amatory tale selects love and sexual passion as a principal narrative focus, while retaining the romance's idealized, stock characters and generalized settings and situations. Defoe's version of the amatory tale in *Moll Flanders* adds the specificity and concreteness that would define the transition from romance to novel. Love in Defoe's novel is firmly rooted in the particularity of place and personality. Never before in fiction had the amatory been shown in its full practical and commercial contexts, as experienced by a new kind of lover who is alternatively victim and transgressor, passionate and calculating.

Moll's account of her life begins with what little she knows about her birth and infancy. Her mother was a petty thief who escaped hanging by "pleading her belly," giving birth to Moll in Newgate, before being transported to America when her daughter was six months old. Somehow having fallen in with a tribe of gypsies (Moll's recollections are plausibly vague), she was abandoned or escaped at Colchester at the age of three and is put into the care of a poor woman paid for maintaining parish orphans. At the age of eight when she is intended to go into service, Moll resists, asserting instead that she desires to become a gentlewoman, which she defines as being able "to work for myself, and get enough to keep me without that terrible bugbear going into service." Moll here announces her life's mission: to gain independence and autonomy. Hers is a radical redefinition of gentility as not a matter of birth or breeding, but as self-sufficiency, within the reach of even someone with no fixed social position and limited financial possibilities but with drive, natural resources, and determination. At the outset of Moll's story, Defoe establishes an intriguing social, class, and gender conundrum: How is survival and self-actualization possible for a person like Moll; what are her options for contending with the seemingly insurmountable limitations of class, economics, and gender, without the leg up of birth, background, and means? Defoe's response comes in the series of subsequent survival challenges Moll faces that collectively demonstrate a complex nexus of sexual, economic, and moral necessity in the formation of an individual's character and destiny.

After her guardian dies when Moll is 14, she is taken in as the companion of two daughters of a local gentry family. Learning by "imitation and enquiry," Moll proves to be naturally superior in intelligence than these privileged girls, but it is her physical assets that most directly affect her future as she is seduced and becomes the mistress of the family's eldest son. When he gratifies Moll with both sex and money, the essential pattern of Moll's career is established in her association of sexuality with profit and social advancement. When her lover accedes to his younger brother's proposal of marriage to Moll, his betrayal steels her to control her emotional attachments and to use her physical attractions as the means to gain the independence and sustenance she requires. Married for five years to the brother of her seducer, Moll frankly confesses, "I never was in bed with my husband, but I wished my self in the arms of his brother . . . I committed adultery and incest with him every day in my desires. . . ." After her husband's death, Moll conducts the first in a series of accountings that follows all her subsequent marriages and affairs in which she calculates profit and loss, like a periodic quarterly report. Consigning her two children to her in-laws, Moll sets out with her accrued savings for London determined to remarry profitably. "I had been tricked once by that cheat called love," she insists, "but the game was over; I was resolved now to be married or nothing, and to be well married or not at all." Entering the London marriage market, Moll learns the value of disguise, role-playing, and adapting one's identity to attract suitors. Her next husband is a tradesman who squanders both his and Moll's savings, goes bankrupt, and abandons her. Moll's third husband is a sea captain, whom she accompanies to America. There, to her horror, Moll discovers that her mother-in-law is her mother, and she has married her own half brother. Concealing this anguishing secret for several years, Moll finally returns to England where she becomes the mistress of a married gentleman who maintains her and the son she bears him until, repenting his immorality, he ends their relationship. Next, agreeing to marry a banker after he has divorced his wife, Moll, portraying a gentlewoman of means on a visit into Lancashire, becomes infatuated with a man she believes is a rich Irish peer. Jemmy in fact turns out to be a penniless fortune-hunter like Moll, and they marry, each convinced that the other is rich. When the truth is discovered, they agree to separate, reluctantly on Moll's part as her passion for Jemmy for the first time overpowers practical necessity. Back in London, Moll disposes of the child Jemmy fathered and bigamously marries the now-divorced banker with whom she lives happily until his investments fail and he dies from despair.

Now at the age of 48, destitute and "past the flourishing time . . . when I might expect to be courted," Moll begins to steal to survive, justifying her actions by asserting that "a time of distress is a time of dreadful temptation, and all the strength to resist is taken away; poverty presses, the soul is made desperate by distress, and what can be done?" Despite an initial reluctance and pangs of guilt, Moll, resourceful as ever, soon masters and ascends to the top of her new profession, whose ways and means Defoe elaborately documents. Eventually, she is caught and taken back to where she began, to Newgate. Defoe's vivid description of prison life is one of the high points of the novel; another is Moll's dramatized process of self-assessment and repentance brought on by her incarceration. Having over a lifetime successfully evaded the limiting circumstance of her lot with inventiveness and ingenuity, Moll must now contend with the intractable reality of prison that causes her to "degenerate into stone; I turned first stupid and senseless, and then brutish and thoughtless, and at last raving mad. . . ." Moll's self-recovery and renewal begin with her discovery that Jemmy is a prisoner as well, awaiting execution as a highwayman. Moll blames herself for Jemmy's descent into crime, and her compassion and sympathy for the afflictions of another are transformative: "I bewailed his misfortunes and the ruin he was now come to, at such a rate, that I relished nothing now, as I did before, and the first reflections I made upon the horrid detestable life I had lived, began to return upon me, and as these things returned my abhorrence of the place I was in, and of the way of living in it, returned also; in a word, I was perfectly changed, and became another body." Condemned to death, Moll achieves a spiritual conversion, aided by a visiting minister who leads her to repentance, not from fear of punishment, but for her offense to God and others. The minister secures a commutation of her sentence to transportation to America, and Moll manages to convince Jemmy to seek the same fate and to accompany her. There, with the aid of an inheritance from Moll's mother, the pair becomes successful planters in Carolina, returning eventually to England "where we resolve to spend the remainder of our years in sincere penitence for the wicked lives we have lived."

By the end of her story, Moll completes the accepted pattern of the spiritual biography—from innocence, to sin, repentance, and redemption (morally and financially). It has been argued that her reclamation, in the words of the critic G. A. Storr, the "gradual, fairly systematic development of the heroine's spiritual condition," unifies the novel's episodic structure. Such a view is contested by another that asserts that the power of the novel derives not from its morality but from its sins, not from Moll's repentance but from her transgressions. In such a view, Moll's is the story of an irrepressible, clear-eyed individualist who manages to circumvent a hostile environment and expand her possibilities by her adaptability and continual self-invention. The critical debate over how to interpret Moll and her career centers on Defoe's handling of his volatile and often contradictory protagonist whose moralism is frequently at odds with her actions and attitudes. Is the pride Moll expresses in her criminal accomplishments and the obvious relish she expresses in narrating some of her sinful ways that contrasts with the insights of her conversion meant to be ironic or evidence of Defoe's mishandling, of forgetting his spiritual theme in the face of a more compelling actuality? Ultimately, it is not the novel's consistency but its contradictions that have fascinated readers for nearly four centuries. The power and persistence of Moll Flanders as one of the greatest characters of the English novel derive from her rich mixture of virtue and villainy. Combining cupidity and conscience, Moll offers novel readers for the first time access to a unique heroine, one who evades and expands simple moral and psychological distinctions. *Moll Flanders* points the ways in which the emerging novel with all its complexity of characterization and context exceeds the limits of either the romance or the spiritual fable.

THE GOOD SOLDIER ŠVEJK

109

(1921–23)

by Jaroslav Hašek

What happens, however, when the Leporellos, the Falstaffs, and the Sancho Panzas begin to inherit the earth? When the remaining masters are in fact more egregious Falstaffs and Leporellos and Sancho Panzas, and all that Don Quixote and Prince Hal and Don Giovanni once stood for is descredited or dead? What happens in a time of democracy, mass culture, and mechanization, a time when war itself is transformed by the industrial revolution? The Good Soldier Schweik *addresses itself to answering, precisely and hilariously, this question. And the answer is: what happens is what has been happening to us all ever since 1914, what happens is* us.

We inhabit for the first time a world in which men begin wars knowing their avowed ends will not be accomplished, a world in which it is more and more difficult to believe that the conflicts we cannot avert are in any sense justified. And in such a world, the draft dodger, the malingerer, the gold brick, the crap-out, all who make what Hemingway was the first to call "a separate peace," all who somehow survive the bombardment of shells and cant, become a new kind of anti-heroic hero. Of such men, Schweik is the real ancestor.

—Leslie A. Fieldler, "The Antiwar Novel and the Good Soldier Schweik"

Subversive is the operative term for Czech writer Jaroslav Hašek's career and his masterpiece, *The Good Soldier Švejk and His Fortunes in the World War.* Anarchist, hoaxer, and rabblerouser, Hašek, to the chagrin and embarrassment of many of his countrymen, produced the most internationally famous Czech novel, one of the paradigmatic antiwar novels, and the archetypal modern Everyman. Josef Švejk, with his benign, vapid smile and childish blue eyes, who may be an idiot or a con man, manages to provoke and expose the hypocrisy and stupidity of those responsible for the madness of war and the lunacy of a dehumanizing social system. Švejk's response is not rebellion or confrontation but adaptability and compliance. With an uncanny knack for gratifying (and subverting) the needs and desires of those in authority, he manages to improvise his survival while his literal-minded obedience to orders becomes the means for Hašek to reveal the absurdity of the Austrian empire, its military bureaucracy, and the ultimate futility of war. Unlike Kafka's characters who are destroyed by authority, Švejk manages to turn the system to his advantage, blundering along, disarming the authorities and exposing their imbecilities while they try to cope with his. His strategy anticipates the instructions Ralph Ellison's Invisible Man receives from his grandfather: "Son, after I'm gone I want you to keep up the good fight. I never told you, but our life is a war and I have been a traitor all my born days, a spy in the enemy's country ever since I give up my gun back in the Reconstruction. Live with your head in the lion's mouth. I want you to overcome 'em with yeses, undermine 'em with grins, agree 'em to death and destruction, let 'em swoller you till they vomit or bust wide open." It takes the Invisible Man the entire novel to decipher the rationale of his grandfather's subversive strategy, which Hašek clearly demonstrates in the picaresque adventures of his remarkable protagonist.

Hašek's biography provides both a model for his hero's adventures and the source of the book's satirical attitudes. Born in 1883 in Prague, the Czech capital of Bohemia that had been annexed to the Austrian Hapsburg empire and dominated by its Germanic minority, Hašek from an early age developed a contempt for authority that he acted out in disruptive behavior and his writing. Attending Prague's Commercial Academy, he produced his first literary work attacking the school's principal. By the time he left the academy he was already publishing poetry and comic sketches in periodicals. Dismissed from a job as a bank clerk for unexcused absences, Hašek soon developed a reputation as a hard-drinking vagabond and anarchist, defiant of both the Austrian establishment and the ideals of the Czech nationalists. Supporting himself fitfully as a writer, editor, and cabaret performer, Hašek was drafted into the Austrian army in 1915 and saw action at the front in Galicia. In September 1915 he was captured by the Russians (it is thought he deliberately allowed his capture), and, after serving time in a Ukrainian prison camp, he volunteered to join the Russian-sponsored Free Czechoslovak Legion to fight the Austrians. During the Russian Revolution he changed sides yet again to join the Red Army. He finally returned to Prague in 1920, having alienated the Bolsheviks. From 1915 to 1920, therefore, Hašek changed sides five times, from the Austrians to the Czechs to the Russians to the Bolsheviks back to the Czechs. It is a pattern of accommodation that Josef Švejk would imitate on a more mundane scale.

Deemed a traitor by his countrymen for deserting the Czech Legion and a subversive for joining the Red Army, Hašek remained an irritant in the new Czech Republic by setting to work collecting and expanding earlier sketches into his masterwork *The Good Soldier Švejk*, one of the earliest ironical fictional reassessments of World War I. The first appearance of Švejk dates from 1911 in Hašek's first volume of prose works, *The Good Soldier Švejk and Other Strange Tales.* His origin is traceable from a note Hašek made under the heading "The Idiot in the Company," about a Czech who, instead of following the customary practice of doing whatever possible to avoid serving in the Austrian army, "had himself examined to prove that he was capable of serving as a regular soldier." Švejk's defiance of all logic makes him a ludicrous projection to expose the equally absurd Austrian bureaucracy. His essential character feature is his ever-present smile and acquiescence that disturb the authorities whom he encounters. The world is so absurd, Hašek suggests, that obeying its rules can only be a sign of idiocy or provocation.

By 1920, Hašek revised his character to reflect the war experience, and his "good soldier" began to take on the mythic lineaments of a modern Everyman, as announced in the Author's Preface to the novel:

> Great times call for great men. There are unknown heroes who are modest, with none of the glamour of a Napoleon. If you analyzed their character you would find that it eclipsed even the glory of Alexander the Great. Today you can meet in the streets of Prague a shabbily dressed man who is not even himself aware of his significance in the history of the great new era. He goes modestly on his way, without bothering anyone. Nor is he bothered by journalists asking for an interview. If you asked him his name he would answer you simply and unassumingly: "I am Švejk."
>
> And this quiet, unassuming, shabbily dressed man is indeed that heroic and valiant good old soldier Švejk. In Austrian times his name was once on the lips of all the citizens of the Kingdom of Bohemia, and in the Republic his glory will not fade either.

The reader is, therefore, primed for the mock-heroic adventures to follow in which Hašek's devaluation of the heroic is embodied by his shabbily dressed goof-off whose entire military career is a combat against his superiors.

The novel opens with the news that Archduke Franz Ferdinand has been killed. Švejk, a dog trader, discharged from the army as "feebleminded," comments that war is inevitable, and he is promptly arrested for subversion by a police spy, initiating the novel's opening circular movement that shuttles Švejk from police headquarters, to jail, to a medical board, to an insane asylum, back to police headquarters before he returns to his home. It is a circuit that allows the various authorities to try to cope with Švejk's behavior that is interpreted as either devious or idiotic, qualities also revealed in their reactions. Despite his presumed deficiencies and transgressions, Švejk is called up as the slaughter escalates and arrives for processing in a wheelchair, complaining of a rheumatic condition. His infirmity is ignored, and he is sent to a military prison for a quick recovery of his fighting spirit. There the former Jewish army chaplain, Otto Katz, engages Švejk as his batman but soon loses him in a card game to Lieutenant Lukáš. Švejk's gift of a dog, which actually belongs to the commanding officer, to his new superior results in both men being assigned to frontline duty. The rest of the novel is made up of the Švejk's long-delayed and circuitous route to the battlefield.

On the train, Švejk manages to insult a fellow passenger who turns out to be the inspector general, and Švejk is eventually thrown off the train. Arrested by the military police for not having the proper papers, he is ordered to set off to the front on foot. Švejk, however, proceeds in the opposite direction and is arrested as a spy. Eventually he is returned to his regiment, where he either causes or is the victim of a series of blunders that frustrates the regiment's progress to the fighting. While assisting the quartermaster in finding billets and supplies, Švejk comes across an escaped Russian prisoner of war taking a bath in a pond. Švejk tries on the Russian's uniform and is promptly seized as the escaped man and assigned to repair a railroad that leads to the Russian front. At this point, the novel breaks off with its fourth of a projected multivolume series interrupted by Hašek's death in 1923. Švejk's adventures are suspended rather than concluded, fittingly in a novel whose central theme is futility and the frustration of any plan, design, and control.

If Shakespeare in *Henry IV, Part 1* established the ultimate dichotomy of the response to war between the honor-obsessed Hotspur and the braggart survivalist Falstaff, Švejk represents a third alternative, a downsized Everyman, a ranker for whom self-preservation is the only value of importance, who may be a holy fool or the ultimate manipulator. In him Hašek defines the modern landscape in which it is impossible to distinguish friend or foe, front line or home front, war from peace. The only reasonable response is Švejk's idiotically indifferent smile. Švejk anticipates Beckett's comic tramps who fill in the vacuum with a torrent of words and stories while never actually reaching any destination. Švejk, in a sense, is the first mythic antihero of the 20th century.

Initial reaction to *The Good Soldier Švejk* among Czech intellectuals was generally hostile. The book's (and its creator's) vulgarity and crudeness represented a slander to Czech national identity, and its vernacular language and unshapely episodic structure were viewed as embarrassingly unliterary. The novel was banned in army barracks in 1925. The first Hungarian translation, published in Paris, was not allowed into the country. Likewise, a Polish translation was confiscated in 1928. What international recognition *The Good Soldier Švejk* gained generally came from its German translation, but the book was burned by the Nazis in 1933. When the Communists gained control of Czechoslovakia after World War II, *The Good Soldier Švejk* was proclaimed a great work of proletarian literature, and Hašek was declared a Czech folk hero. This began a reassessment that has led to *The Good Soldier Švejk* being placed in the canon as one of the singular imaginative works of the 20th century. One wonders what the ultimate antiestablishment writer Hašek would make of his canonization. Perhaps he would echo Groucho Marx, refusing membership in any club that would have him as a member. Certainly, Švejk's reaction would be the same placid, indifferent smile.

THE MASTER AND MARGARITA 110

(1967) *by Mikhail Bulgakov*

> Follow me, reader! Who told you that real, true, eternal love does not exist? Cut out the liar's vile tongue!
> Follow me, my reader, and only me, and I shall show you such a love!

These are the words that open Part II of the novel and introduce the 'love story.' The devil, officially declared non-existent, disproves this theory by appearing with all his old costumes and props, fulfilling his traditional role of mockery and retribution. This literary outlaw expresses the outlawed intellectual mode of scepticism. At the heart of the work stand the Jerusalem chapters, presenting the original 'positive hero,' the entry into history of a new concept of humankind, an image built into the foundations of the 'old' culture. And laughter too is here, defying smug complacency and transcending the terror that was the true face of the decade behind the optimistic double created by its official literature. This was the 'old' culture displayed in brilliant parade in Mikhail Bulgakov's 'last sunset novel.'

A quarter of a century later the laughing word of the novel was released from the darkness of the drawer into the echo chamber of 'great time.' The reception of The Master and Margarita *and its assimilation into the mainstream of Soviet literature marked moments in slow dawn, as the new culture began to lose its arrogance and apply its best energies to remaking its links with the old.*

—Lesley Milne, *Mikhail Bulgakov: A Critical Biography*

Mikhail Bulgakov began writing *The Master and Margarita* at a time when the sovietization of Russian literature, marked by socialist realism as the only officially acceptable literary style, had eclipsed the poetry of Russia's silver age during the first years of the 20th century and the postrevolutionary avant-garde prose literature that followed. In defiance of the conformity imposed by the Soviet state, Bulgakov boldly produced works in which fantasy, realism, the absurd, satire, and metaphysics combined to explore the plight of the intellectual in conflict with communist society and to ridicule the Soviet system. Bulgakov's works were censored during his lifetime, and the majority remained unpublished until after his death. But when *The Master and Margarita* finally came to light, decades of neglect ended for its accomplished author, and his last work was recognized as one of the greatest novels of 20th-century Russian literature.

Mikhail Bulgakov (1891–1940) did not leave memoirs or substantive autobiographical information, and he destroyed all but four pages of a three-notebook diary written from 1921 to 1926 after his apartment was searched by Soviet authorities. Bulgakov's third wife, Elena Sergeevna, preserved his archives and manuscripts and was responsible for making his works available for publication in the 1950s. What is known about Bulgakov's life is that he was born in the Ukrainian city of Kiev, the eldest of 10 siblings, six of whom survived and helped inspire characters in his works. Born into a family of priests and theologians, Mikhail's father, Alfanasy, was a professor at the Kiev Theological Seminary, and his mother, Varvara, was a bishop's daughter. Nicknamed "Misha," young Bulgakov grew up in a household that stressed the importance of music, literature, and the theater. Also emphasized were spirituality and a belief in God, qualities that would remain with Bulgakov throughout his life and inform his work. From 1901 to 1904, Bulgakov attended the prestigious First Kiev Gymnasium, where he became interested in Russian and European literature and was known for telling stories to classmates that adroitly combined fantasy and reality. He began to write seriously when he was 15, composing farcical stories for family and friends he called "humoresques," and which he presented as stories, plays, satiric verse, and caricatures. Bulgakov's early development as a writer was influenced by the work of Nikolai Gogol. In 1907, Bulgakov's father died from sclerosis of the kidneys, the disease that would eventually claim his son's life. To help support Mikhail and his siblings, Bulgakov's mother went to work, first as a teacher and then as a treasurer for an educational society.

In 1909, Bulgakov entered the medical school of Kiev University, where, along with his medical studies, he continued writing stories and performing in theatrical sketches. In 1913, he married the first of his three wives and three years later graduated from medical school with distinction in 1916. Bulgakov was assigned to noncombat duty in the Russian army during World War I and after working for several months in frontline military hospitals was assigned to a village in the province of Smolensk, where he served as the only physician for the entire district. His experiences tending to the peasants in the area are recorded in an autobiographical story collection, *A Country Doctor's Notebooks*. He was discharged in 1918 and returned to Kiev, where he saw patients, worked on his writing, and witnessed the power struggles and violent changes in government caused by the White Army, Red Army, and Ukrainian nationalists in the aftermath of the Russian Revolution. Bulgakov's first novel, *The White Guard* (1925), chronicles the suffering of a family in Kiev under the Bolsheviks during this time. In 1919, Bulgakov, hoping to find news of his brothers who were serving with the Russian Volunteer Army, went to the Caucasus region as a field physician. His search was unsuccessful (both brothers had been wounded and later went to Romania), and in December Bulgakov resigned from military service. He abandoned medicine to devote his time to writing, publishing stories for local newspapers and writing plays for local theaters in the Caucasus cities of Vladikavkaz, Tiflis, and Batun. He also gave lectures on literature art, and music and taught drama.

In 1921, Bulgakov went to Moscow, where he wrote stories and sketches for newspapers and magazines and worked on *The White Guard* and part of the semiautobiographical *Notes on Shirt-Cuffs*, which was published in *Nakanunne*, a journal in Berlin founded by Russian émigrés. Bulgakov's works during the early 1920s include the novelette *Heart of a Dog*, the satirical story "The Fatal Eggs," and *Diaboliad*, a collection of five short stories, a few of which stressed the instability of the new communist bureaucracy in the style of grotesque fantasy. He found his greatest success in the theater, however, with the 1926 production of *The Days of the Turbins*, an adaptation of *The White Guard*, at the famed Moscow Art Theatre. Despite its critical themes, the play won favor with Soviet audiences, and Bulgakov continued writing plays for other theater companies in Moscow. Bulgakov's creative and ideological nonconformity aroused the suspicion of the communist government, however, and by 1929 his works were banned from publication and performance. In desperation, he wrote an appeal directly to Joseph Stalin, secretary-general of the Communist Party and an admirer of *The Days of the Turbins*. Through Stalin's influence, Bulgakov began work as a literary consultant for the Theatre of Working Youth (TRAM) and was reinstated in the Moscow Art Theatre as an assistant producer. Bulgakov wrote, directed, and acted for the Moscow Art Theatre from 1930 until his fatal illness. His second novel, *Black Snow*, also known as *A Theatrical Novel*, concerns Bulgakov's experiences in the theater world with a subplot that is a satirical view of life in Moscow. Unfinished at his death, the novel was published in 1966.

Bulgakov began writing *The Master and Margarita* in 1928. Titled variously "A novel on the Devil," "A Black Magician," "The Hoof of the Engineer," and "The Consultant with a Hoof," the novel received its official title in 1937. He produced eight manuscript versions in all, continuing to revise the novel on his deathbed. Bulgakov remained largely unknown until the publication of *The Master and Margarita* in bowdlerized installments in the journal *Moskva* in 1966–67, at a time when experimental fiction was gaining favor in the Soviet Union. He was hailed as the link between the past tradition of Gogol and Dostoevsky and the postmodern new wave of literature.

Set in Moscow during four days in May sometime in the 1930s, *The Master and Margarita*, combining satire and realism, speculations on art and religion, history and metaphysics, operates on three interconnected narrative lines: a visitation by the devil to contemporary Russia; the story of the love between the Master, who has been languishing in a mental asylum, and Margarita; and the Master's fictional account of the crucifixion. The novel begins with a sunset meeting at a lake called Patriarch's Ponds between Mikhail Alexandrovich Berlioz, a famous Moscow editor, and Ivan Nikolayevich Ponyryov, a poet who writes under the pseudonym "Bezdomny" (Homeless). Ivan has written a poem for Berlioz on Jesus, a historical figure Berlioz insists never existed. The two are joined by the mysterious Professor Woland, who "looked to be a little over forty. Mouth somehow twisted. Clean-shaven. Dark-haired. Right eye black, left—for some reason—green. Dark eyebrows, but one higher than the other. In short, a foreigner." Woland assures them that Jesus did exist and predicts that Berlioz will be decapitated before the day is over. He begins the story of Pontius Pilate and Yeshua (Jesus), at which point the scene shifts to Yershalaim (Jerusalem), where Jesus is condemned to death. Back in Moscow, Berlioz is decapitated by a streetcar, prompting Ivan to confront Woland and chase him and his retinue, consisting of Korovyov, an ex-choirmaster, and a large tomcat named Behemoth. No one believes Ivan's story, and he is taken to a psychiatric clinic, where he is diagnosed with schizophrenia.

Woland abducts Styopa Likhodeyev, Berlioz's flatmate and director of the Variety Theatre, to Yalta. When the theatre's manager attempts to find Styopa, Woland's creature, Hella, turns him into a vampire. Woland and his gang, which now includes the sinister, single-fanged devil, Azazello, install themselves in Styopa's apartment, where they play diabolical tricks on the tenants and the manager. In the evening, they give "Séances of Black Magic" at the theater, during which the master of ceremonies is decapitated. Meanwhile, at the asylum, Ivan receives a visit from a man who reveals that Woland and his gang are Satan and his minions. The man tells him that he has written a novel about Pontius Pilate:

> "You're a writer?" the poet asked with interest.
>
> The guest's face darkened and he threatened Ivan with his fist, then said:
>
> "I am a master." He grew stern and took from the pocket of his dressing-gown a completely greasy black cap with the letter "M" embroidered on it in yellow silk. He put this cap on and showed himself to Ivan both in profile and full face, to prove that he was a master. "She sewed it for me with her own hands," he added mysteriously.
>
> "And what is your name?"
>
> "I no longer have a name," the strange guest answered with a gloomy disdain. "I renounced it as I generally did everything in life. Let's forget it."

The Master, who is the hero of the story, tells Ivan of his secret love for Margarita, who, like himself, is married, and of his novel, which was lambasted by critics before it was published and rejected by the editor, causing the Master to fall into a depression and burn his manuscript. Later, Ivan dreams of Yeshua's execution. Book One ends with Woland and his crew continuing to wreak havoc in Moscow and at the theater: "What other prodigies occurred in Moscow that [Friday] night we do not know and certainly will not try to find out—especially as it has come time for us to go on to the second part of this truthful narrative. Follow me, reader!"

Book Two introduces Margarita:

> Margarita Nikolaevna was not in need of money. . . . Margarita Nikolaevna knew nothing of the horrors of life in a communal apartment. In short . . . she was happy? Not for one minute! Never, since the age of nineteen, when she had been married and wound up in this house, had she known any happiness. Gods, my gods! . . . What did this woman need, in whose eyes there always burned some enigmatic little fire? What did she need, this witch with a slight cast in one eye, who had adorned herself with mimosa that time in the spring? . . . she needed him, the Master, and not at all some Gothic mansion, not a private garden, not money. She loved him, she was telling the truth.

Desperate to learn the fate of the Master, Margarita allows Azazello to make her a witch. She flies naked over the city to the river to meet with Woland and on the way destroys the home of the critic who had ruined the Master. She agrees to preside over Woland's satanic ball, for which she is granted one wish: to be reunited with the Master. Woland causes the Master's manuscript to magically rise from the ashes, and the lovers return to the Master's apartment. There, Margarita rereads the last two chapters of the Master's novel, which recount events concerning Pilate in Jerusalem on a Friday night. On Saturday evening, the Master sets free his hero, Pontius Pilate, from his immortal insomnia; Pilate, accompanied by his dog, then seeks to join Yeshua. Woland's crew carries out more pranks that leave many areas burning in Moscow. Azazello poisons the Master and Margarita, who leave with Woland and his entourage for their last peaceful refuge. In the epilogue, only Ivan, now a professor of history, remembers the tale of Pilate and the Master. The lovers appear before Ivan, and Margarita kisses him on the forehead, so that "everything with you will be as it should be. . . . It is then that Ivan Nikolaevich sleeps with a blissful face."

Brilliantly imaginative and inventive, *The Master and Margarita* boldly reinterprets the traditional conception of the devil and the story of Jesus in the context of contemporary Soviet life for a radical reassessment of good and evil, guilt and innocence, freedom and servitude. Bulgakov has sometimes been compared with Boris Pasternak, the author of *Doctor Zhivago*. Both authors were physicians who wrote about the upheavals caused by the Russian

Revolution; both resisted and challenged official communist ideology in their works; both were censored and victimized by the Soviet state (Pasternak was forced to decline the 1958 Nobel Prize in literature). But *Zhivago*, a heartbreaking chronicle of love and loss at a time of chaos, at least in part, belongs to 19th-century literary tradition. In contrast, *The Master and Margarita*, with its deep exploration of ethical and social issues and its artistically adept blend of satire, the absurd, the fantastical, and the real, is an experimental masterpiece that rightfully deserves a place beside the great avant-garde novels of the 20th century.

111

BRIDESHEAD REVISITED

(1945)

by Evelyn Waugh

In 1946, when asked to summarize the theme of Brideshead Revisited *for Hollywood movie producers who were considering adapting the novel to film, Waugh wrote a faintly patronizing memorandum in which he stressed the theology, and by implication, the use of the novel rather than its entertainment value: "Grace is not confined to the happy, prosperous and conventionally virtuous. . . . God has a separate plan for each individual by which he or she may find salvation. The story of 'Brideshead Revisited' seeks to show the working of several such plans in the lives of a single family." Sykes* [Waugh's biographer] *believes that Waugh knew he had written a novel in which theology and story had not been successfully united, and that he was all the more impelled, therefore, to stoutly defend the work.*

—Calvin Lane, *Evelyn Waugh*

The best known and most popular of Evelyn Waugh's novels, *Brideshead Revisited* deserves a place in this listing for its accurate evocation of English undergraduate life of the 1920s and English upper-class society between the 20th century's two world wars. It also presents, observes Calvin Lane, a "gallery of sharply drawn minor characters . . . nowhere surpassed in the novels Waugh wrote at the outset of his career." Finally, despite an awareness among critics that Waugh's joining of theology and story was not entirely convincing, *Brideshead Revisited* remains a valiant attempt by an author known primarily for producing satiric novels of savage and sophisticated wit to use his famous sense of the ironic together with a greater richness of language to present an earnest, thought-provoking, and singular account of an English Catholic family for whom the world and the spirit are ultimately—and often tragically—interrelated.

Brideshead Revisited is framed by a prologue and an epilogue, both of which are set during World War II. In his preface to the revised edition, published in 1960, Waugh wrote that the novel was "offered to a younger generation of readers as a souvenir of the Second War rather than of the twenties or of the thirties, with which it ostensibly deals." Waugh had been commissioned as an officer in the Royal Marines in 1939, served with commando forces in the Middle East, and in 1942 transferred to the Royal Horse Guards. The following year he became injured during parachute training in Manchester and, early in 1944, while on a leave of absence, wrote *Brideshead Revisited*, which was published in 1945. The novel greatly increased Waugh's readership, especially in the United States, where it was offered as a Book-of-the-Month Club selection. In the 1980s *Brideshead Revisited* gained an even greater audience when it was made into a popular television miniseries that was extremely faithful to the novel.

It should be noted that *Brideshead Revisited* was written by a convert to Catholicism. Waugh had become a Catholic in 1930, the same year *Vile Bodies*, his darkly comic satire on the witless excesses of England's post–World War I upper-class Bright Young Things, was published. After finishing *Vile Bodies*, Waugh, who had discovered that his wife had been having an affair, wrote to his brother, Alec, that "The trouble about the world today is that there's not enough religion in it. There's nothing to stop young people doing whatever they feel like at the moment." In *Brideshead Revisited* Waugh pits agnosticism against the twin principles of religious faith and obligation to explore the possibility that religion is the means to a moral, as well as spiritual, end, especially in a world in which aristocratic and esthetic grace and opulence have ceased to matter.

Subtitled *The Sacred and Profane Memories of Captain Charles Ryder*, the novel is narrated by Ryder, and tells the story of his association with the Marchmains, an old, aristocratic Catholic family, from 1923 to 1939. In the prologue, Ryder, an infantry captain, a painter, and a divorced man, describes the soldiers as "a race of the lowest type," epitomized by his subordinate, Lieutenant Hooper, a lazy, uncouth, lower-class young man who has no attachment to recent English history. In the mid-20th century, Waugh, through Ryder, informs the reader in the epilogue, that Britain has, "in sudden frost," entered "the age of Hooper." When Ryder and his men arrive at a new training camp, he discovers it is Brideshead Castle, a large country house in Wiltshire and the ancestral home of the Marchmains. He is reminded of his earlier experiences with the family and it is that story which follows.

Book One, entitled "Et in Arcadia Ego" ("I, too, was in Arcadia"), is a pastoral reminiscence of Charles Ryder's attendance at Oxford and his first encounters with the Marchmains and Brideshead. At Oxford, Charles meets and becomes close friends with Sebastian Flyte, the younger Marchmain son, a beautiful, sensitive young man, whose attitude of weary sophistication and affinity for childhood attachments (evidenced by the constant presence of his teddy bear, Aloysius, and his fondness for his old nanny) mask a deep, unacknowledged despair. The first memory Charles relates is of a drive he and Sebastian took to Brideshead Castle to visit Nanny Hawkins one day during term. They stop along the way to picnic on champagne and strawberries. Charles recalls that it was "a cloudless day in June, when the ditches were creamy with meadowsweet and the air heavy with all the scents of summer; it was a day of peculiar splendour, and although I had been there so often, in so many moods, it was to that first visit that my heart returned on this, my latest." Nineteen-year-old Sebastian characterizes the pastoral setting as "Just the place to bury a crock of gold," and goes on to say, "I should like to bury something precious in every place where I've been happy and then, when I was old and ugly and miserable, I could come back and dig it up and remember."

At luncheon in Sebastian's rooms, Charles is introduced to Anthony Blanche, one of the novel's most entertaining minor characters. The impeccably dressed Anthony, with his affected stutter, is described as a young man of indeterminate continental origin: "part Gallic, part Yankee, part, perhaps, Jew; wholly exotic . . . the 'aesthete,' par excellence." Later Anthony tells Charles that Lord Marchmain, a convert to Catholicism who has rejected his religion, separated from his beautiful, pious wife shortly after the end of World War I and went to live in Venice with his mistress, Cara.

During the college vacation, Charles, who has overdrawn his account because of the expensive tastes he acquired through his association with Sebastian and his set, returns to London to spend his vacation at home with his eccentric, unloving widowed father. A respite from this stifling atmosphere arrives in the form of a telegram from Brideshead, which announces that Sebastian has been injured. Charles rushes off to Brideshead, where he is met at the station by Sebastian's 18-year-old sister, Julia. She tells him that Sebastian is merely recovering from a cracked ankle bone. Beautiful and restless, Julia has just made a successful debut and although she is not particularly religious, she knows that her Catholicism will hinder her expected goal, which is to marry well.

Charles is entranced by the vast estate, described by Waugh in lush detail. As Lane observes, Brideshead and the Marchmains represent "a closed world to the outsider, rendered even more complex to the nonbelieving Ryder by the family's Catholicism." At Brideshead, Charles meets Sebastian's serious and impassively dogmatic older brother, Lord Brideshead, called "Bridey," and his vivacious 12-year-old sister, Cordelia, a convent-school girl of untroubled and refreshingly undogmatic religious faith. Sebastian has rebelled against the strictures of his religion, but when he remarks in passing that "It's very difficult being a Catholic," there is a suggestion of the tenacious hold Catholicism continues to have upon him. Charles and Sebastian spend the rest of their vacation in Venice with Lord Marchmain and Cara. There, Cara, a practical and observant woman, provides Charles with insight on Lord Marchmain and Sebastian. She speaks of the hatred both Lord Marchmain and Sebastian have for Lady Marchmain, and declares, "Sebastian is in love with his own childhood. That will make him very unhappy."

Charles meets Lady Marchmain during the next school term, when she visits Sebastian at Oxford. Her famous charm captivates him, and he agrees to spend the Christmas holiday with the family. Charles, Sebastian, and another college friend, Boy Mulcaster, are invited to a dinner in London given by Rex Mottram, Julia's suitor. Rex, a vulgar, opportunistic Canadian, is a wealthy businessman turned politician, who later marries Julia. After the dinner and a sojourn in a nightclub, the three young men are arrested for drunkenness and disorderly conduct. The competent Rex obtains their release, but the result of this escapade is that Lady Marchmain, in an attempt to keep Sebastian from sliding into alcoholism, appoints the odious Mr. Samgrass, a history don, who is doing some literary work on the Marchmain family, to watch closely over her son at Oxford. Despite Mr. Samgrass's efforts, Sebastian spoils Christmas and Easter for the family with his constant drinking, which continues upon his return to Oxford. He is finally sent abroad with Mr. Samgrass, who is charged with seeing that he has no access to alcohol.

Book Two, "Brideshead Deserted," begins during the Christmas vacation at Brideshead. There, Charles learns that Sebastian managed to escape Mr. Samgrass abroad and upon their return, had pawned some valuables and borrowed money, and had spent a "happy Christmas" in complete drunkenness. Charles is torn between his loyalty to his friend—he is sympathetic to the idea of "Sebastian *contra mundum*"—and his attachment to Sebastian's family. After giving Sebastian money, which he knows will be used for drink (Charles later learns that Cordelia has done the same), he is chastised by Lady Marchmain. When Sebastian tells him that he does not want him to stay, Charles leaves Brideshead in disgrace.

Charles decides to study art in Paris rather than return to Oxford. There, he learns through Rex that Sebastian has slipped away from him in Paris, while en route to a clinic in Switzerland. When Charles comes back to London during the General Strike of 1926, he discovers from Anthony Blanche that Sebastian, now a confirmed alcoholic, is living in Morocco with a young German named Kurt, who has shot himself in the foot to escape the Foreign Legion. Charles is next summoned to Marchmain House, the family's London home, by Julia, who informs him that Lady Marchmain is dying. She wants to apologize to Charles for her behavior to him at Brideshead and hopes he can bring Sebastian home to see her before she dies. Charles travels to Morocco, where he finds Sebastian ill and suffering from progressive alcoholism. Sebastian prefers to stay in Morocco with the injured Kurt, telling Charles, "it's rather a pleasant change, when all your life you've had people looking after you, to have someone to look after yourself." When the news of Lady Marchmain's death arrives, Sebastian remarks, "Poor mummy. She really was a *femme fatale*, wasn't she? She killed at a touch." Charles arranges an allowance for Sebastian and returns to England. Bridey commissions him to paint several portraits of Marchmain House, which is being torn down to make way for a block of flats.

In the opening lines of Book Three, "A Twitch Upon the Thread," Charles Ryder reminds the reader that "My theme is memory, that winged host that soared about me one grey morning of wartime. These memories, which are my life—for we possess nothing certainly except the past—were always with me." Sebastian is dropped from the center of the narrative, and the story focuses on the relationship between Charles and Julia. In the 10 years after Book Two ends, Charles has become a successful and wealthy architectural painter, married Boy Mulcaster's sister, Celia, and fathered two children. After returning from a two-year painting journey to Latin America, he meets his wife in New York, and, while returning to England, encounters Julia on board ship. The two become lovers and eventually live together for some two years, mostly at Brideshead. They make plans to divorce their respective spouses and marry. One evening, Bridey arrives, announces that he is engaged to be married, and shocks Julia by informing her that he cannot bring his fiancée to the house, because his sister and Charles are living in sin. In a scene of high emotion, Julia becomes hysterical over what she characterizes as the "little sin" of religious imperfection she has carried about with her since childhood. Charles, the unbeliever, cannot begin to understand Julia's crisis of faith and has no comfort to offer other than pat psychological clichés.

Later, Cordelia comes home from tending the wounded and displaced during the Spanish Civil War with the news that Kurt has hanged himself after he was forced to return to Germany and that Sebastian has found his way back to the church by becoming an underporter at a monastery in Tunis. In the final event of the memoir, Lord Marchmain arrives at Brideshead with Cara to spend his last months. Despite Charles's hopes, Lord Marchmain repudiates his years of apostasy at death by crossing himself during the last rites. Julia then confirms what Charles has known for nearly a year: She cannot marry him. She tells Charles, "It may be a private bargain between me and God, that if I give up this one thing I want so much, however bad I am, he won't quite despair of me in the end."

In the epilogue, the reader is back with Charles Ryder at Brideshead during wartime. Charles brings the story full circle by visiting Nanny Hawkins, the only member of the household in residence, whose presence represents the constancy and childlike quality of faith. There is an exchange with Hooper in which Charles confesses to his subordinate that he is "homeless, childless, middle-aged, loveless," which Hooper takes to be a joke. Charles then visits the Brideshead chapel. In this last scene, the reader discovers that Charles, now estranged from everything that once had value to him, has become a Catholic convert. As Calvin Lane observes, "Neither the vacuousness of Hooper, nor the fierce tensions of the Flytes finally matter to him, for the altar lamp of the Brideshead chapel is once more relit, and the flame the Crusaders saw now 'burns again for other soldiers, far from home. . . .'"

Brideshead Revisited initially received mixed critical reaction. Some critics regarded the novel as an artistic failure. In England the *Times Literary Supplement* found the novel "often extremely amusing," but felt it lacked "detachment or disinterestedness of mind" and suffered from "a too obviously preconceived idea." The *New Statesman* felt it was flawed but also saw in the novel "a fine and brilliant book." Waugh worried that it would not be understood in the United States; its status there as a best-seller proved him wrong. The *New York Times Book Review* was positive, declaring that the novel had "the depth and weight that are found in a writer working in his prime." However, the eminent critic Edmund Wilson, writing in *The New Yorker*, sharply criticized Waugh for bringing to the work a lack of common sense, banality, snobbery, and a deteriorating style. "In these reviews and many others," writes Lane, "the praise or blame sprang from political or sectarian bias, rather than from a reasoned critical evaluation."

Brideshead Revisited represents an ambitious effort by Waugh to move in a new direction in writing a realistic novel with a religious theme. Even if the author's reach exceeded his grasp, *Brideshead Revisited* "must be considered," writes critic Patrick Adcock, "one of literature's most magnificent failures."

THE UNBEARABLE LIGHTNESS OF BEING

112

(1984)

by Milan Kundera

What is fine and valiant in Mr. Kundera is the enormous struggle not to be characterized as a writer by his exile and by his nation's disenfranchisement, even though they are the conditions his nose is rubbed in by Czechoslovak history. He works with cunning and wit and elegiac sadness to express "the trap the world has become," and this means he wants to reconceive not only narrative but the language and history of politicized life if he is to accord his experience the dimensions of its tragedy.

—E. L. Doctorow, "Four Characters under Two Tyrannies: *The Unbearable Lightness of Being*"

The Czech writer Milan Kundera in his collection of critical essays *The Art of the Novel* (1988) offers a definition of the novel as "a meditation on existence as seen through the medium of imaginary characters," while providing "my personal conception of the European novel." In Kundera's analysis, European novelists, beginning with Cervantes, "discovered the various dimensions of existence": in the nature of adventure (Cervantes), "what happens inside" (Richardson), man's rootedness in history (Balzac), the terra previously incognita of the everyday (Flaubert), the impact of the irrational on human behavior (Tolstoy), the force of the present and past (Joyce and Proust, respectively), and the role of ancient myth plays in shaping present action (Mann). Under pressure of the Great War, which "unbalanced forever an enfeebled Europe," writers— particularly Kafka, Hašek, Musil, and Broch, whom Kundera calls "the pleiad of great Central European novelists"—"saw, felt, grasped the *terminal paradoxes* of the Modern Era." According to Kundera, all existential categories suddenly changed their meaning:

> What is *adventure* if a K's freedom of action is completely illusory? What is *future* if the intellectuals of *The Man without Qualities* have not the slightest inkling of the war that will sweep their lives away the next day? What is *crime* if Broch's Huguenau not only does not regret but

> actually forgets the murder he has committed? And if the only great comic novel of the period, Hašek's *Schweik*, uses war as its setting, then what has happened to the *comic?* Where is the difference between *public* and *private* if K., even in bed with a woman, is never without the two emissaries of the Castle? And in that case, what is *solitude?* A burden, a misery, a curse, as some would have us believe, or on the contrary a supremely precious value in the process of being crushed by the ubiquitous collectivity?

With these questions still unanswered, Kundera rejects the notion that the novel has "already mined all its possibilities, all its knowledge, and all its forms" and identifies the novel's four continuing appeals "to which I am especially responsive": the appeal of play, which originated in the works of Laurence Sterne and Denis Diderot, providing an alternative novel tradition contrary to the "imperative of verisimilitude"; the appeal of dream, in which the novel can break through that imperative; the appeal of thought, in which "all the means—rational, and irrational, narrative, and contemplative—that could illuminate man's being" might be employed; and the appeal of time, beyond the "Proustian problem of personal memory to the enigma of collective time, the time of Europe, Europe looking back on its own past, weighing up its history like an old man seeing his whole life in a single moment." All of these appeals emanate from Kundera's best-known work, *The Unbearable Lightness of Being*, a radical repossession of the intellectual and emotional possibilities of the novel that challenges the "imperative of verisimilitude," offering an alternative sense of thematic and structural possibilities conforming to what Kundera would later call the "novel as a debate." In Kundera's handling of the novel's conventions, ideas dominate over plot and psychology, orchestrated as in music through counterpoint and variation. Narrative chronology and coherence are violated while Kundera insists on calling attention to the compositional process itself and the continual struggle to reflect life by language.

Kundera is uniquely positioned to respond to the impact of modern history on existence and consciousness. He was born in Brno, Czechoslovakia, in 1929, a decade after the collapse of the Habsburg Empire after World War I and a decade before the Nazi takeover signaling the beginning of World War II. His father, Ludvik Kundera, was a prominent musicologist and pianist who taught him to play and helped his son to discover in music what Kundera would later call his first great revelation of art. Music would remain a fascination even as he abandoned it as a prospective vocation during his teenage years. In secondary school during the Nazi occupation, Kundera was forced to learn German, but as a protest secretly studied Russian. As a student, Kundera also began translating and writing poetry. In 1945, Czechs greeted the Red Army as liberators, and, like many idealistic, reform-minded young Czechs, Kundera enthusiastically joined the Communist Party in 1947. "Communism enthralled me," Kundera has remarked, "in much the way Stravinsky, Picasso and Surrealism had. It promised a great, miraculous metamorphosis, a totally new and different world." Kundera would eventually discover that as Czechoslovakia was absorbed into the Soviet bloc, the state had little patience for the individualism, freedom, and nonconformity that he demanded as an avant-garde writer. Studying film at the Prague Film and Music School, Kundera would be expelled from it and the party for a lack of seriousness and "hostile thoughts." Working as a manual laborer and occasional jazz musician during the 1950s, Kundera published his first book of poetry *(Man, the Vast Garden)* in 1953 and a second *(The Last May)* in 1955 before being reinstated by the Communist Party and returning to his former school as a member of the faculty teaching world literature. After a third volume of poetry *(Monologues)* in 1957, Kundera abandoned poetry for drama, fiction, and literary theory. During the 1960s, his first play *(The Owners of the Keys)*, about young idealistic students in Czechoslovakia during the Nazi occupation, was performed in 14 countries, including the United States and Britain. He published three volumes of short stories, collectively titled *Laughable Loves.* His first novel, *The Joke* (1967), drew on his own expulsion experience, showing its protagonist's life transformed when authorities react to his playful parody of Marxist slogans. During the Prague Spring of 1968, the novel, which his publisher initially considered "diametrically opposed to the official ideology," became an enormous popular success. With the Russian invasion and clampdown on dissent later that year, Kundera was expelled from the party again and released from his teaching position. His books were banned, and he lost the ability to publish. In 1975, however, Kundera was permitted to travel outside Czechoslovakia to accept a teaching position at France's University of Rennes. In 1979, Kundera published *The Book of Laughter and Forgetting*, a novel that the critic John Leonard has described as "part fairy tale, part literary criticism, part political tract, part musicology and part autobiography." The Czechoslovak government responded by revoking his citizenship. In 1980, Kundera accepted a professorship at L'École des hautes études en sciences sociales in Paris, where he has lived ever since. In 1985, Kundera insisted, "My stay in France is final, and therefore I am not an émigré. France is my only real homeland now. Nor do I feel uprooted. For a thousand years Czechoslovakia was part of the West. Today, it is part of the empire to the east. I would feel a great deal more uprooted in Prague than in Paris." Dislocated by history and ideology, Kundera has resisted defining himself as a dissident and his work as predominantly political. Instead, he has summarized his past and its impact by saying, "The events we have lived through in the last thirty years were no milk and honey, but they gave us a tremendous working capital for artistic exploitation. . . . Our experience may thus enable us to ask more basic questions and to create more meaningful myths than those who have not lived through the whole political anabasis."

The Unbearable Lightness of Being, published in 1982 to international acclaim, in characteristic Kundera fashion combines a love story, political commentary, and aesthetic exploration with a meditation on the paradoxes of human existence. The novel opens with a consideration of Friedrich Nietzsche's concept of the "eternal return." If life is only a sequence of transitory events, Nietzsche suggests, then everything becomes "a shadow, without weight, dead in advance, and whether it was horrible, beautiful, or sublime, its horror, sublimity, and beauty mean nothing." If, however, every act and moment are seen as recurring ad infinitum, everything becomes "a solid mass, permanently protuberant, its inanity irreparable." In the world of eternal return, "the weight of unbearable responsibility lies heavy on every move we make. That is why Nietzsche called the idea of eternal return the heaviest of burdens." Offering two different conceptions of existence—transitory or eternally present—lightness or weight, Kundera asks "What then shall we choose?" If lightness liberates, it also makes man "soar into the heights, take leave of the earth and his earthly being, and become only half real, his movements as free as they are insignificant." With eternal return, responsibility "crushes us, we sink beneath it, it pins us to the ground." This central dichotomy, between lightness or weight, in the novel is embodied in the temperaments of its four central characters—Tomas, a womanizing Prague surgeon, Tereza, his wife, Sabina, one of his many lovers, and Franz, a Swiss professor who has an affair with Sabina. Set before, during, and after the 1968 Soviet invasion, the novel tests its opening thesis about existence in the lives of this quartet.

In the opening of the novel's seven sections, Kundera introduces Tomas and Tereza. Embodying the concept of lightness, Tomas has engaged in a countless series of "erotic friendships" with other women. However, he finds himself falling in love with Tereza, who represents the opposing principle of weight and responsibility, and they marry, celebrating their union by acquiring a dog they name Karenin. By coming together, each begins to experience the attraction and repulsion of the other's opposite condition: Tomas, weight, and Tereza, lightness. Tomas, however, continues his compulsive pursuit of women, which Tereza accepts as the burden she must bear to claim his love. Sabina, Tomas's regular mistress (another personification of lightness whose avoidance of commitment and responsibility will lead her to abandon her numerous lovers and her country), helps Tereza find direction as a photographer, and Tereza enjoys a sense of purpose in her life documenting the Soviet invasion. Sabina, by contrast, immigrates to Switzerland, to Geneva, eventually followed by Tereza and Tomas, who is given a position at a hospital in Zurich. After several months, Tereza learns that Tomas is once again seeing Sabina, and she returns to Prague. Within days Tomas follows her, experiencing the unbearable lightness of being of the novel's title.

The second section, Soul and Body, retells their story from Tereza's point of view, filling in details of her family background that explain her neediness in her love for Tomas and her troubling dreams about him. The third section, Words Misunderstood, focuses on Sabina and her relationship with a married Swiss professor, Franz, who, like Tereza, is a figure of weight and responsibility, attracted to his opposite in Sabina. After trying to balance his relationship with his wife and his affair with Sabina, Franz decides to leave his wife, but, after telling Sabina, he arrives at her apartment to find her gone. Documenting the mismatch of Franz and Sabina are interspersed excerpts from "A Short Dictionary of Misunderstood Words," such as *Woman*, *Fidelity and Betrayal*, *Music*, *Light and Darkness*, that underscore their opposite understanding of reality that dooms their affair. In Paris, Sabina receives a letter informing her that Tomas and Tereza have been killed in a road accident. The fourth and fifth sections, Body and Soul and Lightness and Weight, return to Tomas and Tereza's life in Prague after their return. When Tomas refuses to sign a retraction for an article that he had earlier published critical of Soviet authorities that is now deemed subversive, he loses his job as a surgeon and works as a window washer. Tereza tends bar. Ironically, both learn that when they believe that they were acting to oppose the regime, they were actually helping it. Tereza discovers that her photographs of the invasion are being used by the secret police to identify dissidents. Tomas, refusing to identify the editor of his article, lies about his appearance and unwittingly implicates another editor who resembles his made-up description. To understand Tomas's appetite for extramarital sex, Tereza has sex with a man from the bar whom she learns may be part of a blackmail plot by the secret police. The couple responds to their increasing anxiety under the repressive Czech government by moving from Prague to a collective farm in the country where Tomas works as a truck driver and Tereza as a cowherd.

The two final sections, The Grand March and Karenin's Smile, resolve all four of the protagonists' stories, while providing additional contexts to understand the varying attractions and limitations of lightness and weight. In The Grand March Sabina's commitment to lightness is positively presented as a strategy for contending with the falsification of communist kitsch, which "causes two tears to flow in quick succession. The first tear says: How nice to see children running on the grass! The second tear says: How nice to be moved, together with all mankind, by children running on the grass!" Sabina resists state-sponsored optimism and idyllic imagery that are little more than "folding screens that curtain death." Her advocacy of lightness thereby assumes a political dimension. Her rejection of kitsch, commitment, and responsibility, however, reaches a nihilistic dead end. As she wonders in Words Misunderstood, "Her betrayals had filled her with excitement and joy, because they opened up new paths to new adventures of betrayal. But what if the paths came to an end? One could betray one's parents, husband, country, love, but when parents, husband, country, and love were gone—what was left to betray?" In Franz's case, responsibility is equally futile. Traveling to Thailand to protest Cambodian human rights violation, Franz is senselessly killed by muggers, and in death, as a martyr to the cause, "Franz at last belonged to his wife." In both cases, neither Sabina's lightness nor Franz's weight of commitment and responsibility offer much consolation.

In contrast, the novel ends with Tomas and Tereza reconciled to each other and the contrary condition of existence—light or weight—that has caused them so much distress and unhappiness. As Karenin, suffering from cancer, is put down by Tomas, Tereza speculates that her love for the dog has been superior to her love for Tomas because she never demanded anything of Karenin. For Tomas's part, he concedes that being faithful to Tereza while living in the country has been the happiest time of his life. The novel, therefore, closes on a note of mutual recognition and acceptance of the appeal of the other's condition, lightness interpenetrates weight. The couple dances in a concluding image of movement, music, and harmony as Kundera's debate ends in a precarious, and, since the reader already knows the couple's fate, short-lived balance of overcome oppositions:

> On they danced to the strains of the piano and violin. Tereza leaned her head on Tomas's shoulder. Just as she had when they flew together in the airplane through the storm clouds. She was experiencing the same odd happiness and odd sadness as then. The sadness meant: we are at the last station. The happiness meant: we are together. The sadness was form, the happiness content. Happiness filled the space of sadness.

Like Tomas and Tereza's final dance, *The Unbearable Lightness of Being* is a brilliant act of intellectual choreography, setting in motion a compelling human story that is also a provocative meditation on the meaning of existence, human destiny, and desire.

113

AMERICAN PASTORAL

(1997)

by Philip Roth

Seymour Levov is no paragon of perfect virtue, and his father can seem shrill and forbidding in his vehemences. But these are men who continue to display thoughtfulness, however much reason they have to be disappointed and to flee in bitterness from the decencies that make them seem irrelevant to their contemporaries. The father may have absurd ideas about how to deal with disorder—"I say lock [the kids] in their rooms"—but he is strangely appealing in his insistence that "degrading things should not be taken in their stride." That is right. And the son, who suffers greatly, who does not have enough, who takes "to be good" everyone "who flashed the signs of goodness," retains in Roth's hands the capacity to be appalled—not thrilled, but appalled—by transgression, to be tormented by the spectacle of needless suffering, and to think, ever to think, about "justification" and "what he should do and . . . what he shouldn't do." His humanity is intact. And it is, Roth seems to be saying, the only thing we can rely on.

—Robert Boyers, "The Indigenous Berserk,"
in the *New Republic*, July 7, 1997

Since publishing his first book, *Goodbye, Columbus and Five Short Stories* in 1959, Philip Roth has been a persistent and unavoidable presence in contemporary American letters, producing an astounding range of imaginative works that has generated outrage, controversy, and continual fascination for their intellectual and moral complexity and artistic skill. As the critic David Lehman has written, "Roth is our Kafka: a Jewish comic genius able to spin a metaphysical joke to a far point of ingenuity—the point at which artistic paradox becomes moral or religious parable." Describing his own career as "a self-conscious and deliberate zigzag" in which each of his books veers "sharply away from the one before," Roth has modulated between low comedy and high seriousness, as he explained in *Reading Myself and Others* (1975) "to find the means to be true to these seemingly inimical realms of experience that I am strongly attached to by temperament and training—the aggressive, the crude, and the obscene, at one extreme, and something a good deal more subtle and, in every sense, refined at the other." Deciding which of Roth's many novels and modes deserves a place in this ranking is no easy matter considering a writing career that has been so prolific and so diverse. I have selected *American Pastoral* as Roth's mature summary statement, a novel that draws on themes from five decades of his writing but still manages a fresh and original synthesis. Voted by critics and reviewers among the five greatest American novels in the second half of the 20th century, *American Pastoral* is Roth at his best: provocative, dissecting, and comprehensive. It is a capstone work in a series of fictional explorations of the American psyche and society. *American Pastoral* is the achievement of an American novelist at the top of his game who continues to surprise and evade attempts to contain him by a single genre or set of attitudes and mannerisms.

Born in 1933, Philip Milton Roth was raised in a working-class Jewish neighborhood in Newark, New Jersey, the second child of parents born to immigrants with roots in Galicia. Roth graduated from Weequahic High School in 1950 and attended Newark College of Rutgers University and Bucknell University in Pennsylvania. At Bucknell, Roth cofounded and edited a literary magazine, *Et cetera*, in which his first story, "Philosophy," was published. After graduating magna cum laude and Phi Beta Kappa from Bucknell in 1954, Roth went on to the University of Chicago, where he received a master's degree in English in 1955. At the university, Roth met his first wife, Margaret Martinson Williams, from whom he separated in 1963 after four years of marriage. Martinson, who died in an automobile accident in 1968, inspired several of Roth's female characters, including Lucy Nelson in *When She Was Good* (1967) and Maureen Tarnapol in *My Life as a Man* (1974). After serving for a few months in the U.S. Army, Roth was discharged because of a back injury. He returned to the University of Chicago to pursue a doctorate, but he withdrew from graduate school in 1957 to follow a writing career. By then, he had published several stories, four of which had won awards. Roth's first book, *Goodbye Columbus and Five Short Stories* (1959), written with help of a grant from the National Institute of Arts and Letters, a Houghton Mifflin Literary Fellowship, and a Guggenheim Fellowship, was a critical success and earned Roth the National Book Award in 1960. The title novella concerns the tenuous love affair between Neil Klugman, a lower-middle-class Jewish librarian from Newark, and Brenda Patimkin, a Radcliffe student from a wealthy suburban Jewish family.

During the 1960s, Roth taught at the Writers' Workshop at the University of Iowa and at Princeton University, where he was writer-in-residence. His first full-length novel was *Letting Go* (1962), which chronicles the experiences of a graduate student in literature. Roth was able to leave his teaching post and devote himself to writing full time following the financial success of his third novel, *Portnoy's Complaint* (1969). Perhaps Roth's most popular and controversial novel, *Portnoy's Complaint* is structured as a monologue in which the guilt-ridden Alexander Portnoy relates his sexual adventures and complexes to his psychiatrist. Roth's novels of the 1970s include *Our Gang* (1971) and *The Great American Novel* (1973). In the same decade, Roth introduced two ongoing characters: David Kepesh, a professor and the protagonist of three novels, *The Breast* (1972), *The Professor of Desire* (1977), and *The Dying Animal* (2001); and Nathan Zuckerman, a novelist, who first appeared in *The Ghost Writer* (1979) and was subsequently featured in such novels as *Zuckerman Unbound* (1981), *The Anatomy Lesson* (1983), *The Counterlife* (1986), *I Married a Communist* (1998), and *The Human Stain* (2000), and whose most recent appearance was in *Exit Ghost* (2007). Roth is also the author of two memoirs, *The Facts: A Novelist's Autobiography* (1988) and *Patrimony: A True Story* (1988). In 1990 Roth married his longtime companion, the British actress Claire Bloom, from whom he separated in 1994. Bloom's memoir *Leaving a Doll's House* (1996) is an unflattering account of her marriage to Roth. Some critics view certain elements of *I Married a Communist* as veiled responses to the accusations in Bloom's memoir.

It is Roth's alter ego, Nathan Zuckerman, who narrates the events of *American Pastoral.* The novel is divided into three parts, "Paradise Remembered," "The Fall," and "Paradise Lost." The now-aging Zuckerman, a prostate cancer survivor, looks back on his happy childhood and high school years in the Newark neighborhood of Weequahic in an era when the promise of the American dream infused the lives of the Jewish immigrants and their children. He recalls in particular one Jewish boy, the loved and admired Seymour Levov, who was seven years older than Zuckerman and Weequahic High's star athlete during the early 1940s. Seymour's handsome blond Nordic appearance earned him the nickname "the Swede." After serving in the Marines as a drill instructor, he declined a baseball contract to enter the family's leather-goods firm after graduating from college. His Edenic life is further enhanced by his marriage to an Irish Catholic beauty queen, Dawn Dwyer, and the birth of a much-loved daughter, Meredith, known as "Merry." Swede is the perfectly assimilated American Jew, at home in Jewish and gentile society. In contrast, his unassimilated, rough-hewn, but loving and loyal father, Lou Levov, has retained his Old World respect for religion and a strict ethical code that dictates right from wrong.

In 1995, Zuckerman receives a letter from Swede inviting him to meet for dinner in New York, ostensibly to talk about the recent passing of Seymour's father at the age of 96. Lou Levov, Swede writes, had "suffered because of the shocks that befell his loved ones." However, at dinner, Swede, ever polite and bland, intentionally focuses the conversation on his three sons with his second wife and does not mention his father, to Zuckerman's frustration. Sometime later, Zuckerman attends an enjoyable 45th high school reunion. There, Zuckerman meets his classmate, Jerry Levov, Swede's younger brother, who tells Zuckerman that Swede died of prostate cancer only a few days earlier.

He reveals that Swede's happy and charmed life ended in 1968, when his 16-year-old daughter, in a protest against the war in Vietnam, planted a bomb in the post office at Old Rimrock, a village near where the family lived. One person was killed in the explosion. Known as the Rimrock Bomber, Merry went into hiding, although Jerry is convinced that his brother always knew where she was. Two years earlier, Jerry found Swede in his car outside a restaurant, sobbing, and was told that Merry was dead. Zuckerman learns from Jerry that Swede's wife, Dawn, was never satisfied with her marriage, and that Merry, afflicted with a stutter and emotional problems that were never resolved despite the intervention of therapy, grew to hate her father. Intrigued by what Jerry has told him about Swede, Zuckerman decides to write a book about Swede, to explore the man's life in the context of post-war America and the cultural upheavals caused by the Vietnam War. The focus will be on Swede's particular "American pastoral" and the dystopian "violence, and the desperation of the counterpastoral." He begins Swede's story in Deal, New Jersey, at a seaside cottage, where, on their way back from the beach, Swede kisses 11-year-old Merry passionately on the mouth, at her request to be kissed like he kisses her mother. Zuckerman goes on to describe Merry as developing into an unhappy, overweight teenager who rejects her family's middle-class values and rebels against the constraints placed upon her regarding her antiwar activities.

The bombing and Merry's subsequent disappearance spark a series of events. Swede becomes involved with Rita Cohen, a young woman radical posing as a graduate student to whom he gives some of Merry's belongings as well as $10,000 in the hope that she will take him to see his daughter. She agrees, if he will have sex with her first. A disgusted Swede runs out of the hotel room at the New York Hilton where they have met and contacts the FBI. Agents arrive, but Rita has fled. Several years later, Swede mistakenly thinks he has found Merry, first as a young woman he sees staggering out of a Greenwich Village house that has been destroyed by a bomb, then as one of the dead women found in the house. He subsequently begins to carry on an imaginary dialogue with black radical Angela Davis, during which he cites the loyalty of his black employee during the 1967 Newark riots and his refusal to move his factory away from the inner city as an examples of his liberalism, which he hopes Merry will appreciate. In 1973, Swede receives a letter from Rita, who writes that Merry is working at a dog and cat hospital in Newark, not too far from Swede's factory, and has taken the name Mary Stolz. When Swede and Merry are reunited, Merry, who wears a surgical mask over her mouth because she does not want to hurt the microscopic organisms in the air, tells him that she has joined a small Indian religious sect, the Jains, who embrace asceticism and self-denial. She refuses to come home but tells her father about her odyssey as a fugitive after the bombing, including episodes in which she planted more bombs that killed three people and a brief sojourn in Chicago where she was robbed and raped. This last fact deeply distresses Swede, who later appeals to his brother for help in bringing Merry home. Jerry responds with a catalogue of criticism focusing on Swede's inability to show his real feelings and his flawed sense of passive diplomacy. He urges Swede to assert himself and get Merry or put her out of his mind. Swede rejects the notion that he is in some way responsible for the tragedy that has occurred.

"Paradise Lost," the third section of the novel, is primarily set at a dinner party hosted by Swede and Dawn, and brings Zuckerman's narrative to its dénouement. Neither Swede's parents, who are visiting from Florida, nor Dawn, know what has happened to Merry since the bombing, a deliberate strategy on the part of Swede to protect his family. Among the party guests are the Levov's neighbors, Bill and Jessie Orcutt. Bill is an architect who is designing a new home for the Levovs, and Jessie drinks too much. Bill's family has lived in the area since the 18th century, and he possesses a historical sense of ancestry and belonging that Swede, as a Jew, can never hope to emulate. During the party, Swede witnesses Dawn and Bill together in the kitchen, and it becomes clear to Swede that they are lovers. At the dinner table, the guests discuss the Watergate scandal and the pornographic film, *Deep Throat*, which Lou Levov roundly condemns, prompting a response from Bill that banning such movies would be impossible, since permissiveness has become culturally ingrained in American society. Other guests include Barry and Marcia Umanoff, Columbia University professors, and Sheila Salzman, Merry's speech therapist, and her husband Shelly. Swede has recently learned that the Salzmans harbored Merry after the bombing; it also develops that Sheila was Swede's mistress for four months after Merry's disappearance. Swede had once gone to her husband's office intending to confess the affair, but he could not bring himself to do it. Swede comes to realize that Bill and Dawn will live in the house Bill is designing for the Levovs.

After Swede takes an abusive phone call in his study from Rita Cohen, Sheila enters the room and Swede confronts her with the fact that she sheltered Merry and did not tell him. The conversation ends with an angry Swede pulling a picture off the wall and throwing it at Sheila. Later, while talking with Bill on the terrace, Swede is consumed with hatred for him. He feels distressed at the prospect of losing Dawn, but he considers the possibility that he should never have married her at all. The narrative goes back to the early days of their marriage, when Lou Levov insisted on knowing from Dawn whether their children would be raised as Catholics or Jews. A compromise was struck, whereby the children would have limited exposure to Catholicism; however, Dawn had Merry secretly baptized. Back at the party, Swede and Dawn hold hands as they recall a trip they made to Switzerland with the then six-year-old Merry. Swede continues to think obsessively about Merry and becomes convinced that his brother has contacted the FBI concerning her whereabouts. Zuckerman's narrative concludes with a drunken Jessie Orcutt stabbing Lou Levov near the eye with a fork and the party ending in confusion.

In tracing the reality behind the American dream life represented by Swede Levov and his family, *American Pastoral* is one of the defining social and moral chronicles of post–World War II America in which Jewish and American identity and values intersect in the context of the breakup of traditions and the moral relativism of the radicalized 1960s. As in most of Roth's fiction, the private and public spheres collide within the battleground of family dynamics. Swede's quest in *American Pastoral,* as in all of Roth's greatest works, is a search for authenticity and meaning in a world that continually denies both. As the critic Philip Hensher observes, "Like many of [Roth's] books, it examines love, and the rejection of love; in taking on a terrorist who rejects the love of her family, and the love of the country which nurtured her, he has found an ideal, satisfying subject for his recurrent obsession." In contending with the contradictions of Swede's life and times, Zuckerman realizes "The fact remains that getting people right is not what living is all about anyway. . . . It's getting them wrong that is living, getting them wrong and wrong and wrong and then, on careful reconsideration, getting them wrong again. That's how we know we're alive: We're wrong." Replacing the simplistic with the complex, surface with depth, Roth in *American Pastoral* releases the messiness of American life with all its capacity for wonder and compassion, an exercise in cultural and human reanimation to which Roth's entire writing career has been devoted.

114

THE HANDMAID'S TALE

(1985)

by Margaret Atwood

The Handmaid's Tale *is Atwood's most popular novel, which is perhaps surprising given its bleak futuristic scenario. . . . A great deal of critical attention has been paid to it as dystopian science fiction and as a novel of feminist protest. Certainly Atwood's abiding social and political concerns are evident here in her scrutiny of structures of oppression within public and private life, as well as her concerns with the environment, and her nationalist engagement with Canadian-American relations. Yet the novel exceeds definitions of political correctness and has provoked much unease in its critique of second wave North American feminism. . . .*

—Coral Ann Howells, *Modern Novelists: Margaret Atwood*

In contemporary literature, Margaret Atwood is exceptional: a writer of the highest literary distinction whose books have found a wide readership. Of all her many works, *The Handmaid's Tale*, which has been translated into more than 20 languages, secured her international reputation as a writer of great power and vision. Her presentation of a future America has been deservedly ranked along with the greatest of the 20th century's dystopian novels—H. G. Wells's *The Time Machine*, Aldous Huxley's *Brave New World*, George Orwell's *1984*, Ray Bradbury's *Fahrenheit 451*, and Anthony Burgess's *A Clockwork Orange*. Although rooted in Atwood's feminism, *The Handmaid's Tale* exceeds expectations as a controversial work of consciousness-raising to become both a page-turning thriller and an incisive, prophetic, and profound social, ethical, and gender commentary by an astute and synthesizing cultural critic.

When Margaret Atwood began her writing career in the 1960s, Canadian literature was beginning a decadelong surge of popularity that would mark it as a literary topic worthy of critical study. Atwood would come to exemplify the importance of what has been called Canlit. The second of three children, Margaret Eleanor Atwood was born in Ottawa, Canada, in 1939 and spent much of her childhood in northern Ontario and Quebec, where her father, Carl, an entomologist, conducted research. Although the family moved to Toronto in 1946, Atwood did not attend school regularly until 1951. She began writing poetry in high school and, while attending Victoria College of the University of Toronto, published stories and poems in the college literary journal and had a poem published in *The Canadian Forum.* At her graduation, in 1961, Atwood won the school's E. J. Pratt Medal for a privately published chapbook of poems titled *Double Persephone* and was awarded a Woodrow Wilson Fellowship to attend Radcliffe College. She received her M.A. from Radcliffe in 1963 and, after a year of doctoral studies at Harvard, returned to Toronto, where she worked for a market research company and began a first novel. From 1964 to 1965, she taught English literature at the University of British Columbia in Vancouver. There, she composed numerous short stories and poems and competed a draft of her novel, *The Edible Woman*, which she wrote on examination booklets. Atwood then completed her doctoral coursework at Harvard but did not finish her thesis. In 1967, she married James Polk, a fellow graduate student and an American novelist. The couple divorced in 1973, and since then Atwood's partner has been the Canadian novelist Graeme Gibson, with whom she has a daughter, born in 1976.

Atwood's career in the late 1960s and 1970s included teaching positions at various colleges and universities, as well as a stint on the board of directors of the House of Anansi Press and writer-in-residence posts at Massey College in Toronto and the University of Edinburgh. Her first published work was *The Circle Game* (1966), a collection of poems for which Atwood won the Governor-General's Award for Poetry in 1967. Her first novel, *The Edible Woman* (1969), concerns a woman's identity crisis and liberation from the feminine mystique, explored through the baking of a cake for the two men in her life. Prior to *The Handmaid's Tale*, she published the novels *Surfacing* (1972), in which an unnamed protagonist struggles with madness and metamorphosis when she returns to her home in Quebec to try to solve the mystery of her father's disappearance; *Lady Oracle* (1976), a study of duality, duplicity, and multiplicity, whose protagonist, a successful romance novelist and feminist poet, must discover her authentic self; *Life Before Man* (1979), a character study told from the perspective of each of the novel's three main protagonists; and *Bodily Harm* (1981), which chronicles the experiences of a breast cancer survivor who is drawn into the politics of a Caribbean island through her romance with a man involved in the island's uprising.

The Handmaid's Tale, Atwood's fifth novel, is set in Cambridge, Massachusetts, in a United States at the beginning of the 21st century. The president and members of Congress have been killed in a terrorist attack, after which a military coup deposed the government, abolished the Constitution, and set up the Republic of Gilead, a totalitarian, patriarchal theocracy based on the Old Testament, 17th-century Puritanism, and 1980s right-wing ideology. Nuclear, chemical, and biological pollution and AIDS have devastated the country and left many women infertile. The ruling class is known as Commanders of the Faithful. Women have been stripped of their jobs and financial and sexual independence and forced into prescribed roles. Fertile women, called "handmaids," are tattooed with a number and have babies for the sterile wives of the elites; those who rebel or who fail to produce a child after three unsuccessful two-year posts are threatened with deportation to the colonies to spend the rest of their lives as Unwomen, cleaning up toxic waste. The status of women is identified by the color of the clothes they wear: handmaids wear red; Commanders' wives wear blue; and girls wear virginal white. Secret police, called Eyes, drive black vans, which they use to round up undesirables and enemies of the state. The regular police are called Guardians.

The novel is narrated by the handmaid, Offred (a patronymic of Of Fred), who characterizes her narrative as "this limping and mutilated story," in reference to her fragmented recollections of the fates of other handmaids and of the violent, repressive society that controls her experiences. Placed in the home of a Commander named Fred, Offred's forbidden real name remains unknown to the reader: "I keep the knowledge of this name like something hidden, some treasure I'll come back to dig up, one day. I think of this name as buried . . . the name floats there behind my eyes, not quite within reach, shining in the dark." Offred, once illegally married to a divorced man, was arrested for trying to leave the country with her husband and daughter. She recalls her handmaid training at the Rachel and Leah Re-Education Center, also known as the Red Center, where she was taught by the Aunts, who use electric cattle prods: "No guns, though, even they could not be trusted with guns. Guns were for the guards, specially picked from the Angels [soldiers]." The members of the household to which she has been assigned include the Commander's wife, Serena Joy, once a performer on a television program Offred watched as a child; Nick, the attractive chauffeur; and two Marthas (household servants). One afternoon, Offred sees a mysterious message scratched into her floor: "Nolite te bastardes carborundorum." That evening, in a ceremony derived from the biblical story in which Jacob sires a child with his wife's maid, Offred lies on Serena's bed between her legs, while the Commander tries to impregnate her. Offred and the Commander form a relationship of sorts, and two or three nights a week Offred visits him in his study, where he allows her to read forbidden books and magazines, plays Scrabble with her, lets her use forbidden hand lotion in his presence, and has her kiss him good night. The message, he tells her, means, "Don't let the bastards grind you down." The handmaid who wrote it hanged herself in Offred's room. During Offred's daily task of purchasing food for the household with Ofglen, another handmaid who is her shopping partner, Ofglen reveals that she is a member of the resistance movement. She invites Offred to join the movement and tells her the password: "May Day."

Offred has not become pregnant by the Commander, and Serena, fearing her husband is sterile and desperate for a child, suggests that Offred secretly mate with Nick. She offers to try to obtain a picture of Offred's daughter and gives her a cigarette; after getting a match, Offred contemplates the possibility of burning down the house with it and escaping. One evening, the Commander dresses Offred as a prostitute and takes her to a brothel called Jezebel's to have sex with her in a different setting. There, Offred encounters Moira, a former handmaid who escaped on the Underground Femaleroad but was caught and forced to become a prostitute. At home, Offred, although ashamed of her unfaithfulness to her husband, meets Nick frequently for lovemaking. In midsummer, the women of the district are forced to attend a Salvaging, during which two handmaids and a wife are executed for unknown crimes. This is followed by a Particicution, in which the handmaids, goaded to action by an Aunt, kill a condemned rapist. Ofglen reveals to Offred that the man is part of the May Day resistance and was falsely accused; she kicks him in the head and knocks him unconscious to spare him further pain before he is beaten to death. Ofglen subsequently hangs herself after she sees the black van coming to take her away. Serena finds the prostitute costume and confronts Offred with the knowledge of Offred's affair with the Commander. Offred waits for the black van to come for her, but instead Nick arrives, accompanied by the Eyes, to arrest Offred for a "violation of state secrets." He whispers "May Day" to Offred and explains that she should leave with them under the guise of an arrest. Offred steps into the van, her fate uncertain.

An epilogue to the novel, titled "Historical Notes," jumps ahead to the year 2195, after the Republic of Gilead has fallen and is now the subject of historical dissection. A professor from Cambridge University has read a transcript of Offred's story for a panel of the Giladean Research Association. The account has been transcribed from tapes found near Maine, suggesting that Offred may have managed to escape. But questions remain: "We may call Eurydice forth from the world of the dead, but we cannot make her answer; and when we turn to look at her we glimpse her only for a moment, before she slips from our grasp and flees." Although there is hope to be found in her account, Offred's true fate ultimately remains unknown.

An international best seller, *The Handmaid's Tale* won numerous awards, including Canada's Governor General's Award, the Los Angeles Times Award for fiction, and the Arthur C. Clarke science fiction award. It was made into a popular 1990 film with a screenplay by Harold Pinter. Atwood has continued to publish impressive and important books of poetry, fiction, and criticism, including novels *The Robber Bride* (1993), *Alias Grace* (1996), and the Booker Prize winner, *The Blind Assassin* (2000). All are marked by Atwood's superb artistry and rare ability to conjure imaginatively fundamental issues of abiding personal, political, and social relevance.

MANON LESCAUT

115

(1731)

by *Abbé Prévost*

Prévost reflects his age, and, at the same time, illuminates the tradition of the humanist and moralist that has characterized every century of French literature. His inherent skepticism and perception of human instability and change recall Montaigne. His understanding of man's aversion to self-contemplation and need for diversion evokes Pascal. Prévost the psychologist foreshadows Proust's analysis of love's pathology whereas Prévost the chronicler of man's fundamental solitude and inability to control and understand his destiny anticipates the twentieth-century absurdists.

—Richard A. Smernoff, *L'Abbé Prévost*

One of the world's greatest love stories, *Manon Lescaut* is the only work still popularly read by Antoine-François Prévost d'Exiles, better known as the Abbé Prévost, whose real-life adventures and the legends that have grown up about him rival any of the extravagant inventions of his fiction. His collected works extend to more than 100 volumes, but it is *Manon Lescaut* that has secured his reputation and importance in the history of the novel. As the literary historian George Saintsbury has observed, Prévost "is really a pilgrim of novel-writing, who finds the object of his quest once and once only, but in so finding achieves, for that once, amazingly." In *Manon Lescaut*, Prévost establishes two of the enduring fictional archetypes: the femme fatale title character and her doomed and fated lover, des Grieux. In telling their story, Prévost transformed the treatment of sexual passion in the novel, recasting the romance as a psychologically believable phenomenon in a realistic, contemporary setting. His narrative has gone on to inspire countless imitations and adaptations, including Prosper Mérimée's *Carmen* (1846), Dumas fils's *Camille* (1848), George Sand's *Leone Leoni* (1855), operas by Auber, Massenet, and Puccini, and numerous ballets, melodramas, and films based on Prévost's story and lovers or echoing the novel's central themes. If Shakespeare's *Romeo and Juliet* provided drama with its prototypical tragic romantic lovers, Prévost did something similar for the novel. *Manon Lescaut* takes up the story of star-crossed lovers, replicating Shakespeare's notion of the transformative power of love, but extending his focus to consider not just what love does to individuals but all that one is capable of doing for love—robbery, betrayal, even murder. Prévost also for one of the first times in fiction transports romance from its conventional pastoral setting to an urban habitat hostile to the transcendent claims of the lovers who must be nourished not just by the overflow of their sensibilities but with cold, hard cash. Prior to Prévost, money figures slightly in the budget of love, but his lovers will be shown fully enmeshed in a calculating and crippling social and economic network. Moreover, in its first-person narrative, derived from the French memoir-novel tradition, by the transfixed des Grieux, Prévost provokes his readers to consider strikingly modern issues: how perception and desire distort reality and how a lover remakes the loved one in his own image to gratify deep-seated needs and compulsions. *Manon Lescaut* continues to exert an influence and power, whether directly or as echo, based on Prévost's demonstration of love's apparently bottomless contradictions and paradoxes.

That the notorious author who famously demonstrated the imperatives of absolute sexual longing was an ordained priest is consistent with the multiplicity and contradictions that are the dominant elements in his life and career. A contemporary offers this unflattering summary:

> Having been a soldier, then a Jesuit, a soldier for a second time and again a Jesuit, he made himself a soldier once again, then an officer, a Benedictine and at last either a Protestant or a Gallican, I doubt if he himself knows which. . . . Finding it difficult to live out his own romances in his Order, he had the kindness to retreat to England, whence he was banished for practicising them too much. He then took himself to Holland . . . [where] he has had the humor of becoming bankrupt and of letting himself be kidnapped by a young girl or woman. . . . This author takes the name sometimes of M. Prévost, sometimes of M. d'Exiles . . . according to his needs.

Like his protagonist des Grieux, Prévost similarly oscillated between the secular and the religious, frequently in conflict with a moral and social code that demanded containment, and which his life as a soldier, scholar, priest, best-selling novelist, lover, and occasional fugitive clearly defied. Born in 1607 at Hendin, in northern France, Prévost was the younger son in a large well-to-do family. Educated by the Jesuits and intending to enter the Society as a priest, Prévost twice enlisted in the army only to return both times to the sanctuary of the Jesuits, who dismissed him shortly after his second return. In 1720, as a result of what he would later describe as "the unhappy conclusion to an all too tender attachment," he entered the Benedictine order, taking his monastic vows in 1721. Assigned to the monastery of Saint Germain-des-Prés in Paris, Prévost was ordained a priest, taught, and assisted in writing an important work of historical scholarship, the *Gallia Christiana*, while secretly completing the first four volumes of a picaresque novel, the *Memoirs and Adventures of a Man of Quality*. In 1728, the year it was published, Prévost petitioned Rome to transfer to a less restrictive monastery so that he could devote more time to his writing. Leaving before securing the Pope's written approval, which he eventually received, Prévost fled to England to avoid arrest. There he converted to Anglicanism as a practical expedient to obtain a post as tutor to the son of Sir John Eyles, a prominent London politician and businessman. After two years, Prévost was dismissed from his position, probably because of an affair with Sir John's daughter.

Prévost landed in Holland where he finished the last three volumes of *Memoirs and Adventures of a Man of Quality*, which concluded with *The Story of Chevalier des Grieux and Manon Lescaut*. In 1731, Prévost published the first four volumes of his second novel, *The Story of Cleveland, Cromwell's Natural Son*, and in an instance of life imitating art began a ruinous relationship with the Manonlike extravagant and demanding Lenki Eckhard. In 1733, to avoid his creditors, he fled back to England where he was imprisoned for forging a promissory note for 50 pounds. Prévost managed to evade punishment on this capital offense, possibly through the intervention of the Eyles family, and he returned secretly to France, eventually obtaining permission to rejoin the Benedictines. He produced a third long memoir-novel, *The Dean of Killerine*, the last two volumes of *Cleveland*, and, in 1740, a shorter novel, the *Story of a Modern Greek Woman*. Continuing financial difficulties led to another departure from France and a nearly two-year exile in Belgium and Germany before returning and settling in to his most productive period of literary activity, producing biographies, travel books, and translations from English, most notably, in 1751, Richardson's *Clarissa*. Prévost's translation contributed greatly to Richardson's reputation and influence in France. Jean-Jacques Rousseau who knew Prévost during his later years, records in his *Confessions* that he was "a very likeable, very simple man, whose works, deserving immortality, sprang straight from the heart, and in whose temperament and society there was none of that somber coloring he gave to his writings." On a visit to neighboring Benedictine monks in 1763, the Abbé Prévost suffered a stroke and died. One of the many rumors circulating about the writer that conflated the man and his fiction was that he had not quite died when the autopsy was performed, a rather macabre confirmation that Prévost represented to many, for good or ill, a life force too strong for death.

Like its creator, contradictions define *Manon Lescaut*. The narrative frame of the novel is the concluding installment of the memoirs of M. de Renoncourt, a much traveled *homme de qualité* whose narratives of his own and others' experiences in love are presented as monitory lessons in the workings of passion in human behavior and nature. *Manon Lescaut* opens with a foreword in which Renoncourt makes clear his moral purpose in illustrating "a terrible example of the power of the passions":

> The portrait I have to paint is of a young man who, in his blindness, rejects happiness in order to plunge voluntarily into the uttermost depths of misfortune; who, possessing all the qualities that mark him out for brilliance and distinction, prefers, from choice, a life of obscurity and vagrancy to all the advantages of fortune and nature, who forces his own misfortunes without having the will to avoid them; who feels and is oppressed by them, without benefiting from the remedies that are continually offered him and which could at any moment end them; in short, an ambiguous character, a mixture of virtues and vices, a perpetual contrast between good impulses and bad actions.

Renoncourt's condemnation of his protagonist is undercut at the outset when in the novel's opening pages he relates his chance encounter with the young Chevalier des Grieux who is escorting a cartful of women being deported to Louisiana for their sexual misconduct and is clearly fascinated by one of the prisoners, Manon Lescaut. Renoncourt reports that "I have never seen a livelier image of grief" in des Grieux, whom he describes "in all his movements so refined and so noble an air that I instinctively felt disposed to wish him well." His sympathy causes him to intervene on des Grieux's behalf with money and support. Renoncourt's fascination and empathy guide the reader's response and prepare the ground for his second encounter two years later with the now solitary, grieving des Grieux who takes over the narrative to tell the story of his passion for Manon and its consequences. In contrast to Renoncourt's opening assessment that des Grieux's sexual passion for Manon is willful and destructive, the lover insists that it is unconquerable and the greatest happiness known to man. As he tells Renoncourt at the outset of his story, "You'll condemn me but you'll pity me too, I'm sure of that. You won't be able to help yourself."

The novel, therefore, offers the reader two contradictory perspectives: that of Renoncourt's conventional moralistic disapproval and des Grieux's escalating challenge to it as the details of Manon's nature and the circumstances of their affair are described. Prévost here alters the Cinderella myth, describing not how the low-born female is rescued and restored to respectability by the prince, but how the prince is degraded to her survivalist level, all in the name of an innocent and transformative love.

Des Grieux describes how as a prudent and responsible student of philosophy he accidentally met the beautiful but common Manon as she was being escorted by an elderly gentleman to a convent. Instantly smitten, des Grieux conspires with her to escape to Paris. What is striking here is that Manon from the outset becomes the projection of des Grieux's desires: "Her charms were beyond description. There was an air about her, so delicious, so sweet, so appealing—the air of Love itself. Her whole person seemed to me an enchantment." The enchantment that des Grieux desires to perpetuate in his idealized image of Manon will become harder and harder to support as evidence begins to emerge of Manon's true self as a woman driven by pleasure and ever ready to exploit her charms to make her way in the world. That world is a vividly described Paris populated by a full range of its denizens from dissipated young aristocrats to wealthy financiers, monks, innkeepers, policemen, prostitutes, petty thieves, and gamblers. *Manon Lescaut* becomes one of the first great Paris and city novels in which urban ways and means and Paris's thoroughfares and pleasures are minutely recorded. The lovers' idyll there comes to an abrupt end after three weeks when des Grieux learns that Manon has also bestowed her affection on a Monsieur de B—, and he allows himself to be convinced by his father and his sensible friend Tiberge to abandon Manon to enter the Seminary of Saint-Supplice as a theology student. One of the novel's great dramatic moments is when Manon attends his public disputation at the Sorbonne. Following the ceremony, Manon's single kiss causes des Grieux to abandon his vocation and resume their affair.

What follows is a steady decline into crime and scheming to support an extravagant and riotous lifestyle far beyond the lovers' means aided by Manon's opportunistic brother who does not hesitate to suggest that Manon should sell herself to the highest bidder. Des Grieux initially resists this option, becoming himself a professional gambler and card cheat to support Manon. Des Grieux's luck holds for a time, but necessity causes Manon to agree to her brother's suggestion by becoming the mistress of the old and wealthy Monsieur de G— M—. Duping the old man of his money and jewels, they are apprehended by the police and imprisoned. With a pistol he receives from Manon's brother, des Grieux escapes, killing a turnkey in his flight, and manages to secure Manon's release, seeking refuge at an inn. There they encounter the son of Monsieur de G— M—, and their plan to rob him of his money is foiled by the father who learns of the plot, and the lovers are arrested again. Des Grieux secures his release with his father's intercession, but Manon is sentenced to exile to the penal colony of Louisiana. It is des Grieux's commitment to sacrifice everything to follow her there that finally transforms Manon's attachment to him from expedience to devotion. Ironically, their desire to legitimize their relationship by marriage results in their undoing. In New Orleans, petitioning the governor for permission to marry, they attract the attention of the governor's nephew who falls in love with Manon. Des Grieux fights him in a duel and believing that he has killed him flees with Manon into the Louisiana wilderness. There, ill with fatigue, Manon dies. Des Grieux is persuaded by his friend Tiberge to return to France as a penitent. In a final irony, Manon's death makes her finally the object of her lover's worship without the contradictions of reality that expose her as less than ideal.

Despite the novel's moralism and melodrama, it is ultimately the magnetism of Manon herself that persists in the reader's imagination, despite the fact that we rarely view her beyond the romantic nimbus in which des Grieux surrounds her. Fascination with Manon is the reason that the novel titled *The Story of Chevalier des Grieux and Manon Lescaut* was almost immediately popularly shortened to *Manon Lescaut,* by which it has been known ever since, shifting Prévost's emphasis from the young nobleman and his moral progress to his obsession. Manon has remained a kind of blank screen upon which readers, like des Grieux himself, project their own desires for a passion so total and absolute that nothing else—neither practicality nor morality—matters. Inevitably such an inspiration is both sanctifying and destructive. Manon as angel and a temptress offers transcendence even as she degrades. Prévost's discovery of these contradictions is his singular contribution to the novel's treatment of love and sexual passion.

THE WOMAN IN WHITE 116

(1860)

by Wilkie Collins

To Mr. Collins belongs the credit of having introduced into fiction those most mysterious of mysteries, the mysteries which are at our own door.

—Henry James, "Miss Braddon," in *The Nation*, 1865

In what is surely the most seamless and irresistible grip on an audience's attention in literary history, readers of page 95 of the November 26, 1859, issue of Dickens's newly launched weekly *All the Year Round* reached by the bottom of column one the conclusion of Dickens's own serialized novel, *A Tale of Two Cities* (with Sydney Carton's noble final words: "It is a far, far better thing that I do, than I have ever done; it is a far, far better rest that I go to, than I have ever known."). In column two they were presented with the opening words of Wilkie Collins's *The Woman in White* ("This is the story of a what a Woman's patience can endure, and of what a Man's resolution can achieve.") before being thrust into Walter Hartright's account of his moonlit encounter with a mysteriously dressed woman in Hampstead fleeing an unknown threat. Dickens called the scene one of the two best he had ever read in fiction in the 19th century. Collins's novel concluded 39 weeks later, on August 25, 1860, having created one of the greatest sensations since *The Pickwick Papers* (1836–37).

Collins's biographer Nuel Davis called *The Woman in White* "probably the most popular novel written in England during the nineteenth century," and critic Henry Peter Sucksmith has hailed it "the greatest melodrama ever written." It is, arguably, the first and best thriller ever conceived, the first mystery novel to feature private investigators (Walter Hartright and Marian Halcombe), what literary historian John Sutherland has suggested may be "the first Mafia novel (with Fosco as the proto-Godfather)," and the archetypal page-turner that added to the experience of novel reading almost unbearable suspense. The hold on the contemporary readers was so great that crowds assembled at the *All the Year Round* offices to secure each weekly installment as soon as possible. Merchandisers offered *Woman in White* perfume, cloaks, and bonnets; men fell in love with Marian, and at least one wrote Collins for the identity of the original so he could propose to her. Walter became a fashionable name for babies, and Fosco served as Oscar Wilde's undergraduate nickname. Dickens responded to his friend's success with his own weekly serial of secrets and suspense, *Great Expectations* (1860–61), and it, along with *The Woman in White*, helped establish the fictional genre of the "sensation novel," the thrilling manipulation of mysteries and crimes in a believable contemporary setting. Collins and Dickens, as well as a host of subsequent imitators, updated and relocated gothic thrills next door.

There are many versions of the origin of Collins's novel, with the most plausible explanation the one Collins offered to a friend:

> I was in Paris wandering about the streets with Charles Dickens, amusing ourselves by looking into the shops. We came to an old bookstall. . . . and I found some dilapidated volumes of records of French crimes, a sort of French *Newgate Calendar*. I said to Dickens, "Here is a prize!" So it turned out to be. In them I found some of my best plots. The Woman in White was one. The plot of that has been called outrageous: the substitution and burial of the mad girl for Lady Glyde, and the incarceration of Lady Glyde as the mad girl. It was true, and it was from the trial of the villain of the plot—Count Fosco of the novel—I got my story.

Collins's sourcebook has been identified as Maurice Méhan's *Recueil des causes célèbres* (second edition, 1808–14) and the crime a 1788 conspiracy against Madame de Douhault, the daughter of a marquise. Her greedy, unscrupulous brother seized her inheritance by confining her in a Parisian lunatic asylum under a false name. Collins gives this past French crime a contemporary English setting in the story of Laura Fairlie and Marian Halcombe, Laura's marriage to Sir Percival Glyde, and her resemblance to the woman the young artist Walter Hartright meets before becoming the two sisters' art tutor. It would be churlish to say too much more and rob anyone who has not read the book one of the great treats of suspense and surprise in literature. Let me concentrate instead on defending Collins's innovations and strategies in arranging his material into an unsurpassed exercise in provoking bated breath that warrants his inclusion among the greatest novelists of all time.

Rarely have critical appraisals of Collins's sensational and melodramatic method gone much further than to grant him mastery of what he does best: the invention of lively and fast-paced stories of suspense and mystery. Even then his achievement has been qualified as not really the stuff out of which great novels or novelists are made. One critic has complained that Collins was "a writer for tired minds," and his appeal has been denigrated as mere entertainment for the nondiscriminating reader more interested in a "good read" than what the greatest novels offer in the way of a rich, complex depiction and criticism of life. Even T. S. Eliot, who defended Collins's artistry and his melodramatic method, placed Collins's appeal on the level of the perennial literary craving that we all suffer from, as if from an addiction to sweets. Critic Bradford Booth has qualified his admiration for Collins's "brisk narrative pace, intricate and ingenious plotting and tremendous dramatic force" by explaining that "There is an hour when we prefer Verdi to Schonberg, Grant Wood to Braque, *John Brown's Body* to *Paradise Lost.*" While Booth is no doubt correct that Collins's narrative art *is* deliberately or inevitably set at a lower register of greatness than that of Dickens, Eliot, Hardy, Conrad, and others, Collins certainly deserves inclusion here as one of the formidable practitioners of a fictional element that is assumed but rarely discussed, that is, the power of plot in the novel. In this one area of the fictional arsenal, Collins reigns supreme.

The Woman in White is built upon "the interest of curiosity, and the excitement of surprise," which Collins considered the main attraction of all novels. "I have always held the old-fashioned opinion," Collins observes, "that the primary object of a work of fiction should be to tell a story." The novel's pivot is a central secret, or more precisely, a series of secrets, artfully designed to detonate like a string of firecrackers. "We are commanded to be silent," the reviewer for the London *Times* complained about the author's injunction not to reveal his plot, "lest we should let the cat out of the bag. . . . There are in this novel about a hundred cats contained in a hundred bags, all screaming and mewing to be let out. Each new chapter contains a new cat. When we come to the end of it out goes the animal, and there is a new bag put into our hands which is the object of the subsequent chapter to open."

Joined to Collins's skill in withholding or revealing information is a dramatist's mastery in devising a series of exciting confrontations and plot-turns (Walter's meeting with Anne Catherick, the deed-signing scene, Marian on her balcony, the church burning) that propel the reader breathlessly forward. Aiding suspense is Collins's decision, which he described as an "experiment . . . which has not (so far as I know) been hitherto tried in fiction," to present his story from a variety of eyewitnesses "as the Judge might once have heard it." By doing so, Collins attempts "to present the truth always in its most direct and most intelligible aspect; and to trace the course of one complete series of events, by making the persons who have been most closely connected with them, at each successive state, relate their own experience, word for word." Collins dramatizes, therefore, not only the action of *The Woman in White* but its narration as well, offering testimony that provides immediacy of viewpoint, controlling also what is revealed and when by silencing his narrators when they threaten to tell too much.

With his emphasis on plot, Collins is rarely appreciated for his characterization, but he provides two of his most interesting and innovative characters as the central opponents in *The Woman in White.* The first is Count Fosco, the "Napoleon of crime" and mastermind of the conspiracy, who is surely one of the greatest villains in literature. Collins casts against type by making him fat and giving him a full array of peculiarities. His fondness for animals and sweets are realistic touches that make Fosco so unusual and so memorable. He is both diabolical and juvenile, a monster and a great favorite—a clouding of the obvious moral distinctions expected in conventional melodrama. Fosco's ambiguous nature is also suggested by Collins's putting so much of himself into his villain. Fosco's "theories concerning the vulgar claptrap that 'murder will out,'" Collins confessed, "are my own." Considering the count's massive ego, the reader may not be surprised to hear him say that "the fool's crime is the crime that is found out; and the wise man's crime is the crime that is not found out." It is unusual, however, to hear the novel's villain speak so convincingly about the crimes condoned by respectable English society. Fosco points out that an honest man goes to debtors' prison because his friends refuse to lend him money; the philanthropist goes to relieve misery in prisons, "where crime is wretched—not in huts and hovels where virtue is wretched too"; a woman marries for her husband's money, "and all your friends rejoice over you; and a minister of public worship sanctions the base horror of the vilest of human bargains." Out of the mouth of Collins's devil, therefore, issues the novel's social criticism.

The other unconventional character at the center of the novel is Marian Halcombe. If Sir Percival Glyde is the conventional stage villain, whom Fosco towers over by comparison, then Laura is the novel's conventional heroine and Marian her anti-type. The reader is rather cruelly made aware of the stepsisters' differences in Walter's first meeting with Marian. Standing with her back to Walter, she appears "tall yet not too tall; comely and well-developed." But when she turns to face him, we discover that she is "ugly" in Walter's view: "Never was the fair promise of a lovely figure more strangely and startlingly belied by the face and head that crowned it." A masculine woman, Marian is swarthy, and "on her upper lip was almost a moustache." She is the complete opposite of her stepsister in both looks and temperament: perceptive, impulsive, and active. Marian is, therefore, in Fosco's own estimation, his match. "With that woman for my friend," he declares, "I would snap these fingers of mine at the world. With that woman for my enemy, I, with all my brains and experience—I, Fosco, cunning as the devil himself . . . I walk . . . upon egg-shells!"

With an ever-accelerating narrative vehicle and at least two fascinating passengers, *The Woman in White* moves irresistibly forward. But to what purpose beyond entertaining thrills? One way of justifying Collins's sensational method is by its thematic resonance. Collins's emphasis on crime next door, beneath the respectable surface of society, does make a satirical point. Even more, the novel's villains manipulate conventional values, playing on what we would like to believe of ourselves: that a gentleman does not lie, that a lady who goes to church cannot be a sinner, that sisterly love cannot be subverted. In this way, Collins's attention on the seamier side of Victorian life, on the chinks in the social armor, makes an important thematic point overlooked from much of realistic fiction by its concentration on the ordinary and commonplace.

Ultimately, however, the justification of greatness for *The Woman in White* rests neither on Collins's characters nor his themes. His achievements in both are sporadic, an added bonus from his fundamental appeal in delivering thrilling narrative puzzles. Collins's ability to arouse in his reader the desire to know what happens next is a crucial fictional skill. Scheherezade is Collins's mentor in the art of the novel, and she and Collins have much to teach the novelist in the art of arranging incident to produce the necessary forward pressure to compel a reader through many pages. Collins's lesson has largely been forgotten or ignored by writers of the literary novels of our time, who have mostly abandoned plot as a means of unifying a novel. Collins challenges this concept, insisting that to teach or move readers, one must first engage and delight them, and *The Woman in White* offers valuable lessons about how an audience may be effectively entertained and captivated. Ultimately Collins's sensational and melodramatic method needed greater literary artists, such as Dickens, Hardy, and Conrad, to push it to another level of truth and tragedy. *Great Expectations* is not a better story than *The Woman in White*, but it is a greater novel, using the same sensational techniques that Collins originated and perfected.

117

SOME PREFER NETTLES

(1929)

By Tanizaki Jun'ichirō

Everywhere in Tade kuu mushi [Some Prefer Nettles] *characters dress themselves to express cultural postures. This emphasis on costume is so prevalent as to suggest a certain view of man's relationship to culture: in* Tade kuu mushi *Tanizaki depicts a world where cultural identity has become a suit of clothes, something that can be worn, taken off, changed. His protagonist Kaname not only participates in this masquerade, he finds the objects of his desires among women costumed to represent cultural fantasies, in O-hisa's case a fantasy not even his own. The fate of passion in a world where the "past" has become as malleable and as ephemeral as the "West" is the pursuit of disguises.*

—Ken K. Ito, *Visions of Desire: Tanizaki's Fictional Worlds*

Tanizaki Jun'ichirō's *Some Prefer Nettles* has been described by the literary critic Van C. Gessel as "one of the most concise and intriguing studies of infatuation in Japanese literature." The novel explores the cultural basis of desire in the dynamics of a failed marriage set along the fault lines of Japanese modernity with its push and pull between the old and the new. Compared to other admired modern Japanese novelists, Tanizaki has the reputation of the outlaw whose obsession with "lust, cleptomania, sadomasochism, homosexuality, foot-fetishism, [and] coprophilia," in a list compiled by the critic Anthony Chambers, has marked him as a connoisseur of the unsavory who has been charged with a lack of intellectual substance and moral seriousness. "There is virtually no chance," Gessel asserts, "it seems safe to venture, that the likeness of Tanizaki Jun'ichirō will ever appear on any denomination of Japanese currency," as did the celebrated naturalist writer Natsume Sōseki. Yet a strong case can be made for Tanizaki's central position as one of the preeminent authors of the Japanese modern novel. According to the literary historian Donald Keene, "If any one writer of the period will stand the test of time and be accepted as a figure of world literature, it will be Tanizaki." Few other writers in any language have probed the dark recesses of human identity and desire so deeply, nor has any Japanese writer better placed the private in the wider public context of the cultural and historical moment. Of all his works, *Some Prefer Nettles* serves as his most representative novel, detailing both Tanizaki's private obsessions and his culture's conflicts between a seductive Western future and a consoling traditional Japanese past.

Born in Tokyo, Tanizaki grew up in a family crippled by financial distress largely the fault of his father, an unsuccessful businessman who failed at every venture he undertook. Tanizaki's mother was a great beauty, her son's inspiration for the ideal of Japanese womanhood that haunts his writing. A precocious and talented student, Tanizaki was introduced by a teacher to the classics of the East and West. In 1901, when he graduated from elementary school, his father was anxious that he should go to work to help support the family, but a teacher persuaded him to allow Tanizaki to continue his education at middle school. A version of this incident is dramatized in Tanizaki's first story published in 1903, "Shumpu Shuu Roku" ("Account of Spring Breezes and Autumn Rain").

Tanizaki financed his education by serving as a *shosei*, a houseboy and tutor in the family of a restaurant owner, an experience he bitterly resented. In 1908, he enrolled at the Tokyo Imperial University but neglected his studies and largely ignored his family's financial distress to pursue his writing and indulge in a lifestyle of flamboyant sexual experimentation, from which his early writing is drawn. He began to publish his work in 1909, rejecting the prevailing fashion of naturalism for an interest in private desires and unusual characters and events. Once declaring that only lies interested him, Tanizaki would throughout his career advocate on behalf of invention in fiction. His story, "Shisei" ("The Tattooer"), a haunting tale of an artist enslaved by a girl he has helped transform by tattooing a spider on her back, established his reputation and taste for the perverse and the sinister. The story gave the title to his first short story collection, published in 1911. Nicknamed the diabolist, Tanizaki shocked readers with his sexual candor, indulgence in the abnormal, and defense of masochism and other deviance. His work during this "bad period" would embarrass Tanizaki in maturity, and much of his writing from it has not been collected or reprinted. In 1916, he commented on the relationship between his life and his art during this time:

> For me art came first and life second. At first I strove to make my life accord, insofar as possible, with my art, or else to subordinate it to my art. At the time I was writing "The Tattooer," "Until One Is Deserted," and *Jotaro*, this seemed possible. And I managed to carry on my pathological life of the senses in the greatest secrecy. When eventually I began to feel that there was a gap between my life and art that could not be overlooked, I planned how I might, at the very least, make as advantageous use of my life as possible for my art. I intended to devote the major part of my life to efforts to make my art complete.

Tanizaki's literary reputation has been negatively shaped by his early dissolute lifestyle. Despite his excesses and the artistic weakness of many of his efforts at this time, his early work remains an important indicator of his analysis of hidden longings and motivations that he discovered in himself and would resurface in his later masterpieces. During this period, Tanizaki indulged an exorbitant taste for everything Western. He moved to Yokohama to enjoy its large foreign enclave, dressed in brown suits and played the guitar, ate roast turkey and kidney pie, seeming to obliterate from himself any traces of Japanese customs and the past. As Tanizaki admitted, "I discovered that, as a modern Japanese, there were fierce artistic desires burning within me that could not be satisfied when I was surrounded by Japanese. Unfortunately for me, I could no longer find anything in present-day Japan, the land of my birth, which answered my craving for beauty."

A turning point, however, occurred as a result of the great earthquake of 1923 that devastated Tokyo. Tanizaki, away from the city when it hit, greeted the news with a perverse joy. He later recalled thinking that "Now Tokyo will become a decent place!" He hoped the city would be rebuilt along modern, Western lines more to his taste, with Western customs finally replacing Japanese ways. Temporarily relocating to the Kansai region near Kyoto, in the heart of traditional Japan, Tanizaki, however, began to reassess his earlier enthusiasm for the West and his rejection of Japanese tradition. He would remain in the area for the next 20 years, and the experience of rediscovering the Japanese past and customs would be reflected in his mature works, through their more complex blend of past influences with modern ideas and concerns.

In 1925, Tanizaki published *Chijin no ai* (A fool's love, translated as *Naomi*, 1985), his first post-earthquake novel that confronted directly the conflicts of Japanese cultural identity enthralled by the West. In the novel, a Japanese engineer, named Jōji, who "imitated the Western style in everything," encounters Naomi, a young bar girl with an uncanny resemblance to American film star Mary Pickford. Jōji attempts to support the illusion by Westernizing her. Installing her in a Western-style cottage and giving her lessons in English and dressing her in Paris fashions, Jōji succeeds so well in her makeover that Naomi begins to despise Jōji for being too Japanese. Despite her rejection, his obsessions prove too strong to break, and the novel ends with Jōji's masochistically procuring for Naomi the Western men she now only desires. A fable about the ways culture intersects with desire and fantasy and the consequences of breaking with the past, in confusing Eros with the West, *Naomi* anticipates similar concerns in *Some Prefer Nettles* in which the lure of Western modernity is opposed by an equally strong attraction to the Japanese past and tradition that Tanizaki increasingly was drawn to after his move from Tokyo. An important indicator of Tanizaki's position during this period can be glimpsed in a famous essay, *In'ei raison* (1939, *In Praise of Shadows*). Ostensibly a treatise on aesthetics, the essay is also a heartfelt evocation of the past and the power of the Japanese sensibility in the formation of identity and taste. While acknowledging the cultural innovations of the West and modernity, Tanizaki argues on behalf of a counter lesson to be derived from Japanese traditions, from its architecture, dress, and arts. In tracing the difference between East and West, Tanizaki writes, "We Asians tend to seek our satisfactions in whatever surroundings we happen to find ourselves, to content ourselves with things as they are; and so darkness causes us no discontent, we resign ourselves to it as inevitable. . . . But the progressive Westerner is determined always to better his lot. From candle to oil lamp, oil lamp to gaslight, gaslight to electric light—his quest for a brighter light never ceases, he spares no pains to eradicate even the minutest shadow."

Tanizaki's appreciation of what is uniquely and essentially Japanese and its implications on psychic development are at the center of his most famous novel. The Japanese title of *Some Prefer Nettles (Tade kuu mushi)* literally translates as "insects that eat *tade*," a bitter herb often served with raw fish. It is part of a Japanese expression suggesting "to each his own," that is, some insects prefer *tade* to a sweeter plant. The title suggests the direction of the story as its protagonist, Kaname, comes to appreciate the special flavor of Japanese traditions for which he had previously no taste. The novel's cultural clash is interconnected with Kaname's marital conflict that mirrors Tanizaki's own experience in his first marriage. Like Kaname's relationship with his wife Misako, a woman who is superficially modern in much the same way that he is, Tanizaki, during his Western period, grew sexually indifferent to his first wife, Chiyo, and, like Kaname who permits or even encourages Misako's taking a lover, Tanizaki was complicit in Chiyo's affair with his friend and fellow writer Sat Haruo. Again, like Kaname, Tanizaki was similarly indecisive about the fate of his marriage. Initially agreeing to divorce Chiyo to allow the lovers to marry, Tanizaki abruptly changed his mind and withdrew his offer. Unlike *Some Prefer Nettles*, however, which ends with Kaname still suspended between a desire for a new life and his failed marriage, Tanizaki eventually resolved his marital impasse in 1930 by approaching Sat Haruo and urging him to marry Chiyo after divorcing her, which was accomplished. The two themes of marital and cultural conflict, both strong elements of Tanizaki's own background, are, therefore, connected in *Some Prefer Nettles* as its domestic drama equally serves to illustrate a wider cultural search for an authentic identity in the face of modernity.

The novel opens with an introduction of Kaname and Misako's dilemma: no longer sexually interested in the other, they lack the will to alter their circumstances. Kaname's question "What would you like to do?" results in a Beckett-like impasse:

> Today was not the first time they had been faced with this difficulty. Indeed, whenever they had to decide whether or not to go out together,

> each of them became passive, watchful, hoping to take a position according to the other's manner. It was as if they held a basin of water balanced between them and waited to see in which direction it would spill.

Kaname, indecisive and unwilling to accept consequences for his feelings, prefers to "be drifting into a divorce and hardly knowing it." He has encouraged Misako's affair in the hope that it will lead her to a new marriage of her choosing, absolving him of guilt over emotionally and sexually abandoning his wife and initiating the resolution he cannot manage himself. The couple eventually accedes to an invitation from Misako's father, Koharu, to join him and his mistress, O-hisa, for a performance at an Osaka Bunraku puppet theater. The old man, who "in his earlier years indulged in foreign tastes of the most hair-raising variety," has transformed himself into a model "old-style gentleman of taste," having moved into a traditional residence in Kyoto, trained O-hisa to be a mistress in the traditional style, and devoted himself to playing the samisen, collecting antiques, and attending Bunraku. Kaname, alienated from his wife and displaced from his past, will increasingly be attracted to the old man's lifestyle and all it implies as a means of reintegrating a basis for self-understanding and behavior.

The novel is structured around a series of journeys representing Kaname's search for meaning derived from the past. The first is his trip to the puppet theater, which suggests "the quiet, mysterious gloom of a temple, something of the dark radiance that a Buddha's halo sends out from the depth of its niche. It was far from the brightness of a Hollywood movie. Rather, it was a low, burnished radiance, easy to miss, pulsing out from beneath the overlays of the centuries." Drawn by the harmony between puppet and puppeteer in the performance, Kaname sees the parallels with that of the old man and O-hisa, who has been trained and dressed to become an extension of the male will, an ideal that is the opposite of his relationship with Misako. Following a visit by his cousin, a businessman working in Shanghai, who in his decisiveness and energy is Kaname's opposite, Kaname next travels to Awaji with Koharu and O-hisa to see the island's puppet theater. The experience deepens Kaname's reopened channel to his past and reawakens a connection to the Japanese past and cultural heritage. After a less than satisfying visit to his longtime Eurasian mistress and alternative Western attractions, Kaname finally travels with Misako to her father's home in Kyoto to discuss their pending divorce. In a setting in which all conforms to old-style tastes, Kaname realizes that "Deep down he may have had unsuspected motives, it occurred to him, for seeking out the company of the old man these last few months. He had cherished a dream in secret, an extraordinary dream, and he had neither cautioned himself nor reproved himself for it." This dream about reestablishing the vital link between the present and past has a final apotheosis. Having successively regarded O-hisa as the old man's puppet and as an embodiment of the "eternal woman," Kaname, for whom a woman "had to be either a goddess or a plaything," begins to move beyond this dichotomy. Having previously seen O-hisa as a disembodied "shade left behind by another age," he is suddenly struck that she is a woman of flesh and blood, an ideal made real. In one of the most suggestive and lyrical passages in Tanizaki's work, Kaname in the garden cottage of the Kyoto house where he is to spend the night awaits the arrival of O-hisa's return with books for him to read:

> For an instant he thought he saw O-hisa's face, faint and white, in a shadowy corner beside the bed. He started up, but quickly caught himself. It was the puppet the old man had brought back from Awaji, a lady puppet in a modest dotted kimono.
>
> A gust of wind came through the open window and the shower began. Kaname could hear large drops falling against the leaves. He raised himself on an elbow and stared out into the wooded depths of the garden. A small green frog, a refugee from the rain, clung halfway up the fluttering side of the net, its belly reflecting the light from the lamp.
>
> "It's finally begun."
>
> The door slid open, and this time, half a dozen old-style Japanese books in arm, it was no puppet that sat faintly white in the shadow beyond the netting.

For Kaname his dream has begun, a sudden manifestation of a now reintegrated life in which past and present, body and soul, self and other, ideal and reality come together in a fragile yet redemptive harmony. The novel ends abruptly with implication rather than resolution, so it is unclear whether the dream can be sustained, but Tanizaki has offered at least a glimpse of an alternative to the paralysis of will and breakdown brought on by cultural infatuation.

118

A BEND IN THE RIVER

(1979)

by V. S. Naipaul

The notation of Africa in Bend *is not dissimilar from that found in the disillusioned postcolonial novels of Achebe, Armah, Ngugi wa Thiong'o, Soyinka and others. Unlike the African novelists, however, Naipaul does not have a commitment to Africa. His deepest sympathies are with the Indians threatened by African nationalism and political disorder. But such disorder is found to be universal, partly the result of the withdrawal of the older imperial order, partly a continuing process throughout history. Is the instability really African if all history consists of change, of peoples struggling against peoples, tribes against tribes, individuals against individuals? Salim learns from reading an encyclopaedia that the universe may be nothing more than fragments of the Big Bang that created it. This then is Naipaul's big bang novel, although the immediate focus is on Africa that resulted from the collapse of imperial order.*

—Bruce King, *V. S. Naipaul*

A Bend in the River is V. S. Naipaul's masterwork of displacement and dispossession, a summary statement from a distinguished writing career documenting what John Updike has called "one of the contemporary world's great subjects—the mingling of its peoples." In his fiction, travel writing, and essays, Naipaul has embraced his role as an uprooted, homeless global wanderer reporting on the collapse of the past imperial order and the uncertain postcolonial future, seeking evidence supporting his contention offered in his 2001 Nobel Prize lecture that "The world is always in movement. People have everywhere at some time been dispossessed." None of his many works better expresses this theme than *A Bend in the River*, Naipaul's postcolonial repossession and revision of Joseph Conrad's *Heart of Darkness*. It is a return to Africa as a symbolic center that cannot hold, where things continue to fall apart, the novel that Naipaul's biographer, Patrick French, has asserted, "brought together all his experience and the uniqueness of his perspective, a late twentieth-century global narrative that could have been written by no one else." More than a century after Joseph Conrad and his fictional surrogate Marlow journeyed upriver into the center of Congo to confront the lies of the colonial mission and the paltriness of civilization in the face of an overwhelming wilderness and human evil, Naipaul stages a return visit into the heart of a newly independent African nation by Salim, an Arab-African of Indian descent whose family has lived on the eastern coast of Africa for generations. What Salim discovers about himself and the world as he sets up shop in a partially revolution-ravaged interior town at the bend in the river constitutes Naipaul's disturbing assessment of the postcolonial experience and modern angst. As Salim observes, "The political system we had known it was coming to an end, and that what was going to replace it wasn't going to be pleasant." *A Bend in the River* is, according to the literary scholar Bruce King, "perhaps the last modernist epic, using Africa as a symbolic wasteland for the collapse of a universal European order."

Naipaul's perspective of global dispossession and alienation is informed by his background, which has contributed to what Salman Rushdie has identified as a "stereoscopic vision" of the insider who is also an outsider. Vidiadhar Surajprasad Naipaul was born in the small rural town of Chaguanas, Trinidad, in 1932, a third-generation descendant of Indian laborers who had gone to Trinidad as indentured servants to find work on the island's plantations after slavery had been abolished. "My background is at once exceedingly simple and exceedingly confused," Naipaul has commented. ". . . Trinidad is not strictly of South America, and not strictly of the Caribbean. It was developed as a New World plantation colony, and when I was born in 1932 it had a population of about 400,000. Of this, about 150,000 were Indians, Hindus and Muslims, nearly all of peasant origin, and nearly all from the Gangetic plain." Growing up as a member of the Asian-Indian minority in black-dominated Trinidad, a former British colony that was not quite Caribbean and not quite South American, half a world away from an ethnic and cultural homeland, contributed to Naipaul's sense of a global identity under pressure by the forces of history and modernity. Naipaul's father, Seepersad Naipaul, was a journalist and short story writer who encouraged his son's literary ambitions. "At really quite an early age," Naipaul has observed, "I thought of myself as a writer . . . because of this overwhelming idea of its nobility as a calling." In 1938, his family settled in the capital of Port of Spain, and, after attending Queens Royal College, Trinidad's leading secondary school, Naipaul won a government scholarship to study abroad, which led him to University College, Oxford, in 1950. His time at Oxford was not happy. Missing his home and struggling to find a place in England, Naipaul would later confess that the only reason he did not commit suicide was that the gas meter in the flat where he was living was too low. After graduating in 1954, Naipaul worked as a writer and editor for the BBC program, *Caribbean Voices*, for which he produced his first short stories based on his childhood in Trinidad, many of which would be collected in *Miguel Street* (1959). His first published work was the novel *The Mystic Masseur* (1957), about a Hindu in Trinidad who progresses from masseur to pundit and politician while gradually losing his hold on his community and his identity. The search for autonomy and a sustaining habitation would become the dominant theme of Naipaul's third novel and early masterpiece, *The House of Mr. Biswas* (1961), a tragicomic life story, based partly on Naipaul's father, of a Trinidadian Hindu's determined effort to achieve his dream of owning a home and thereby repossessing his own life and place.

The House of Mr. Biswas gained Naipaul worldwide recognition while it brought to a close the initial phase of his career that drew on his recollections and experiences of his upbringing on Trinidad. Increasingly, Naipaul would widen his perspective through extensive travel as his writing began to reflect a global assessment of the postcolonial world and a shared sense of loss and alienation he had dramatized locally in his fiction. *The Middle Passage* (1962), *An Area of Darkness* (1964), *India: A Wounded Civilization* (1977) are nonfiction works based on his travel to and observations of postcolonial conditions in the Caribbean, Africa, and India. Naipaul's fiction would keep pace with his travels as well. *Mr. Stone and the Knight's Companion* (1964), Naipaul's first novel without a Trinidad setting, is the story of a Caribbean man living in England. After a 1966 appointment to teach at Makerere University in Uganda, Naipaul published *The Mimic Men* (1967), the search of a migrant from the Caribbean living in London for authenticity and a usable past. Naipaul's next novel, *In a Free State* (1977), which won the Booker Prize, is an innovative, mixed-genre work combining short fiction and travel narratives linked by common themes of colonialism and migration set around the world. The title novella with its African setting in particular enhanced Naipaul's reputation as a dissenter from Western liberal notions of an optimistic postcolonial African future and an "intrepid and brutally honest chronicler of the Third World." Following *Guerrillas* (1975), set on a Caribbean island recently liberated from colonial rule, Naipaul returned to an African setting for *A Bend in the River.*

Drawing upon his stay in East Africa in the 1960s and an extensive 1975 visit to Zaire under the autocratic rule of Mobutu Sese Seko who came to power in 1965, the novel was inspired, as reported by his biographer French, by "a chance encounter in Kisangani, his [Naipaul's] plane had been taken out of service, and he found himself at the airport talking to a young Indian man." "The hotels were closed because Mobutu was in town," Naipaul recalled, "and he said come and sleep at my flat. Everything that happened over the next two days, I used in *A Bend in the River.* He was a businessman running a shop, and his 'Jeeves' talked a lot of rubbish about going to Canada. He told me about his private life, that there was a woman, and took me to look at her house. She was a Vietnamese woman; that disappears in my narrative. We can call him

Salim. The essence of the book is: what is this man doing here?" Naipaul's answer to that question would be shaped not just by his field observations but by two essays Naipaul produced based on his Congo experience, "A New King for the Congo: Mobutu and the Nihilism of Africa" and "Conrad's Darkness," republished in the essay collection *The Return of Eva Perón* (1980). Zaire, formerly the Belgian Congo and the setting for Joseph Conrad's great anti-imperial novella, *Heart of Darkness*, based on Conrad's own experiences there as riverboat captain, had overthrown its colonial rule but remained, in Naipaul's bitter assessment, one of the "dark places on earth." As Naipaul writes in "A New King for the Congo," "To Joseph Conrad, Stanleyville—in 1890 the Stanley Falls station—was the heart of darkness. It was there, in Conrad's story, that Kurtz reigned, the ivory agent degraded from idealism to savagery, taken back to the earliest ages of man, by wilderness, solitude and power, his house surrounded by impaled human heads. Seventy years later, at this bend in the river, something like Conrad's fantasy came to pass. But the man with 'the inconceivable mystery of a soul that knew no restraint, no faith, no fear' was black, and not white; and he had been maddened not by contact with wilderness and primitivism, but with the civilization established by those pioneers who now lie in Mont Ngaliema, above the Kinshasa rapids." Naipaul finds correspondences to Conrad's anatomy of the hollowness of the colonial venture in the postcolonial reign of Mobutu, depicted as a corrupt and violent sham, an exemplum with strong associations to Naipaul's biography and aspirations as a writer. In "Conrad's Darkness," Naipaul summarizes:

> To be a colonial was to know a kind of security; it was to inhabit a fixed world. And I suppose that in my fantasy I had seen myself coming to England as to some purely literary region, where, untrammeled by the accidents of history or background, I could make a romantic career for myself as a writer. But in the new world I felt that ground move below me. The new politics, the curious reliance of men on institutions that were yet working to undermine, the simplicity of beliefs and the hideous simplicity of actions, the corruption of causes, half-made societies that seemed doomed to remain half-made: these were the things that began to preoccupy me. There were not things from which I could detach myself. And I found that Conrad—sixty years before, in the time of a great peace—had been everywhere before me. Not as a man with a cause, but a man offering, as in *Nostromo*, a vision of the world's half-made societies as places which continuously made and unmade themselves, where there was no goal, and where always "something inherent in the necessities of successful action . . . carried with it the moral degradation of the idea." Dismal, but deeply felt: a kind of truth and half a consolation.

A Bend in the River revisits one of these Conradian half-made places that barely conceals the void beneath its surface. As the novel opens, the narrator, Salim, describes his weeklong journey into the interior of an unnamed revolution-ravaged central African state to take over management of an abandoned shop in a settlement at the bend in the river partially destroyed in the violence that preceded independence. "Africa was my home," Salim observes, "had been the home of my family for centuries. But we came from the east coast, and that made the difference. The coast was not truly African. It was an Arab-Indian-Persian-Portuguese place, and we who lived there were really people of the Indian Ocean. True Africa was at our back. . . . These were also the lands of our ancestors. But we could no longer say that we were Arabians or Indians or Persians, when we compared ourselves with these people, we felt like people of Africa." A dispossessed, alienated African outsider, Salim decides to leave the coast and his settled Muslim community for a self-made, uncertain future in the interior. "To stay with my community," Salim acknowledges, "to pretend that I had simply to travel along with them, was to be taken with them to destruction. I could be master of my fate only if I stood alone."

Salim's fate, however, is far from masterful. His shop and most of the town is in shambles, and Salim doggedly awaits the prosperity promised by the Big Man, the former military strongman turned tribal leader, modeled on Mobutu. Agreeing to look after Ferdinand, the son of an African trader and magician named Zabeth so he can attend the local lycée run by a Belgian priest Father Huismans, a collector of African antiquities, Salim also takes in one of his family's slaves, Ali (later Metty), displaced in the persecution of the coastal Muslim community. Father Huismans will be found mutilated with his head cut off and displayed on a spike, a victim of efforts to purge the state of European influences. Through his childhood friend, Indar, Salim is introduced to some of the residents of the huge government complex outside the city called the Domain, most notably a European historian named Raymond, known as "The Big Man's White Man," an adviser to the regime whose influence is waning, and his wife Yvette. Complying with Indar's philosophy that "You trample on the past, you crush it," Salim begins a passionate affair with Yvette. Initially liberating and fulfilling the promise of his self-made future, the relationship breaks down in disillusionment and violent rage as Salim comes to realize that he is simply being used by Yvette, and the supposedly glamorous world of Raymond and Yvette and its proximity to power are exposed as tawdry and illusory.

New insurrections are followed by bloody reprisals that drive Salim out of Africa for a time to London where instead of escape he finds "neither the old Europe nor the new. It was something shrunken and mean and forbidding. . . . In the streets of London I saw these people, who were like myself, as from a distance. I saw the young girl selling packets of cigarettes at midnight, seemingly imprisoned in their kiosks, like puppets in a puppet theatre. They were cut off from the life of the great city where they had come to live, and I wondered about the pointlessness of their own hard life, the pointlessness of their difficult journey." Finding no satisfying place for himself in Europe, Salim returns to discover his shop, like all property owned by "foreigners," has been nationalized and handed over to a drunken, incompetent African manager. Now working in the shop he formerly owned, Salim begins dealing in gold and ivory to amass as much money as possible out of the country. Jailed, Salim is released through the intercession of Ferdinand, who has progressed from culturally shocked schoolboy to a government official with authority over the town. Ferdinand convinces Salim that he has no future there and that "we're going to hell and every man knows this in his bones," and Salim departs on the steamer with its towed passenger barge carrying a full cargo of the similarly displaced. The closing paragraph is a descent into the darkness and equivalent of Kurtz's recognition of the "horror" in Conrad's masterpiece:

> At the time what we saw was the steamer searchlight, playing on the riverbank, playing on the passenger barge, which had snapped loose and was drifting at an angle through the water hyacinths at the edge of the river. The searchlight lit up the barge passengers, who behind bars and wire guards, as yet scarcely seemed to understand that they were adrift. Then there were gunshots. The searchlight was turned off; the barge was no longer to be seen. The steamer started up again and moved without lights down the river, away from the area of battle. The air would have been full of moths and flying insects. The searchlight, while it was on, had shown thousands, white in the white light.

In Naipaul's sobering assessment, the world is caught between a collapsed imperial order and a dehumanized, adrift postcolonial future. Only Salim's persistent adaptability and survival instinct oppose the social and historical forces aligned against him and his search for authenticity and a sustainable existence.

119

COLD NIGHTS

(1947)

by Ba Jin

Cold Nights *is firmly grounded in physical and everyday reality. To watch the gradual but inevitable disintegration of the hero's body is in itself a shattering experience. All the tender and pathetic scenes establish their immediate authority by virtue of their almost unbearable closeness to ordinary Chinese family life. With this novel Pa Chin has become a psychological realist of great distinction. And because he is solely concerned with the presentation of truth as he knows it and makes no bid for ambitious philosophical meanings, he also succeeds to a remarkable degree in giving his novel symbolic dimensions: the fate of the three principal characters is not only a parable of China in her darkest hour of defeat and despair but a morality play about the insuperable difficulties facing Everyman walking the path of charity.*

—C. T. Hsia, *A History of Modern Chinese Fiction, 1917–1957*

Cold Nights, the final novel by Ba Jin (1904–2005), the most popular Chinese novelist of the 20th century, is his masterpiece. The author of more than 30 volumes of novels, novellas, and short stories, Ba Jin's vivid depiction of contemporary Chinese life and unsparing attack on greed, poverty, war, and social injustice, in the assessment of the critic Olga Lang, "helped to create among the intellectuals an emotional climate that induced them to accept the Chinese revolution." While his idealistic, rebellious heroes' search for truth found a sympathetic audience among the young who, like Ba Jin himself, had come of age under the influence of the revolutionary May Fourth Movement (1919), *Cold Nights*, a harrowing treatment of a family's dissolution during the close of the Sino-Japanese War, represents a new direction in Ba Jin's works, a departure from the panoramic method of social realism and tone of revolutionary fervor of his previous novels for a focus on "Little people and Little Events," as he titled a wartime collection of essays and short stories. If revolutionary and humanitarian sentiment predominates over artistry in his earlier novels, *Cold Nights* is a more masterful blending of theme and technique, a shift from a deductive to an inductive approach and from external to internal states, in which imagery, characterization, symbolism, and setting all unite to anchor a story that is at once a precise documentation of a particular place and time, "a parable of China," in the words of the literary historian C. T. Hsia, and a universal study of humanity.

Ba Jin was born Li Fei-kan to a wealthy family in Chengtu, Sichuan, in 1904. He was raised in an extended family compound of uncles, aunts, and cousins under the rule of his grandfather or in the *yamen*, the official walled compound in Kuang-yuan in northern Sichuan where his father served as a magistrate. Receiving a traditional Confucian education at home, Ba Jin was greatly influenced by his mother, a practicing Buddhist, who fostered his love of literature and sensitivity to the experiences and feelings of others. She died when he was 10, followed by the death of his father three years later. As Ba Jin matured, he became more and more aware of the internal frictions within his extended family under the traditional patriarchal rule of his grandfather, the abuses of the family's servants, and of the injustice of the outside world, particularly in the discrepancy between his privileged life and the common lot. A self-described "product of May Fourth," the intellectual reform movement that spread Western humanitarian ideas through China, Ba Jin became an avid reader and translator of European writers and, in the words of his biographer Lang, would be influenced by "three Western ideological complexes . . . international anarchism, Russian populism, and, to a lesser extent, the Great French Revolution." Of these, anarchism, which Ba Jin understood as "a new social order based on liberty unrestricted by man-made law," had the greatest impact, and he would become the preeminent authority among Chinese writers on the revolutionary and anarchistic literature of the West. His pen name was derived from the first and last syllables of the names of two admired Russian anarchists, *Ba*kunin and Kropot*kin*.

After studying in Shanghai and Nanking, Ba Jin traveled to Paris in 1927 to further his study of European literature and economics. He wrote his first novel, *Destruction* (1929), there as a form of self-therapy to contend with his feelings of being cut off from the intellectual ferment and activities that were happening in China. A revolutionary romance exposing the discrepancy between social ideals and reality that advocated an urgent need for political and cultural reform, *Destruction* found an enthusiastic audience among the young and intellectuals. It would be followed by a succession of popular novels that were published on his return to China in 1929, documentary-based melodramas with a strong social message, including *Love: A Trilogy* (1931–33) and the *Turbulent Stream Trilogy* (1931–40). Despite acclaim as the best-loved and admired Chinese novelist during the 1930s and 1940s, Ba Jin insisted that "I am not a literary writer, nor do I understand art. The fact that I write does not indicate that I have talent, but that I have passion." For Ba Jin the purpose of art was to "bring some light to the masses and strike a blow at darkness," in which the message predominates over the medium or the messenger. In characteristic fashion, Ba Jin viewed himself as a kind of unconscious receptor and transmitter of the consequences of social injustice:

> I lack the temperament of an artist. I cannot compose a novel as if it were a work of art. When I write, I forget myself and become practically an instrument. I have really neither the leisure nor the detachment to choose my subject and form. . . . At the time of writing I myself no longer exist. Before my eyes looms a dark shadow, and it expands until it becomes a series of pathetic pictures. My heart becomes as it were whipped by a lash; it palpitates, and my hand moves rapidly along the paper. . . . Many, many people are taking hold of my pen to express their sorrows. . . . Do you think I can still pay attention to form, plot, perspective and other trivial matters? A power drives me on, forcing me to find satisfaction in "mass production": I have no way of resisting it and it has become a habit with me.

During the Sino-Japanese War, Ba Jin completed a trilogy, *Fire* (1940–43), which patriotically celebrated Chinese resistance to the Japanese invasion. His next three novels, however, *Garden of Rest* (1944), *Ward Number Four* (1946), and *Cold Nights* (1947) represent a shift in focus from grand patriotic or revolutionary themes to more local and intimate studies of ordinary characters and events. In the *Garden of Rest*, the corrupting power of money divides and destroys a family; *Ward Number Four* is a detailed, realistic first-person description of a badly run wartime hospital. Both novels imply their social themes through the stories' details while demonstrating a deepening of psychological subtlety and nuance in characterization, both advances that culminate in the artistry and achievement of *Cold Nights.*

Cold Nights reflects Ba Jin's growing despair and hopelessness based on his wartime experiences that included after his return from France the destruction of his home on the outskirts of Shanghai by Japanese bombers and frequent dislocations during the Japanese advance. Initially buoyed by a patriotic fervor and solidarity with the resistance to Japanese aggression, Ba Jin increasingly viewed the war as divisive rather than unifying, with the chasm between the haves and the have-nots exacerbated under wartime threat. In 1944, Ba Jin married, and the couple was forced to move to Chongquing, the capital of the provisional capital of the Nationalist government, where they lived until the end of the war in a single room while they witnessed the death of many friends from rampaging tuberculosis and cholera outbreaks. When the Japanese surrendered in August 1945, victory brought Ba Jin little relief, and his mood is expressed in a dramatized essay, "No Title," describing Chongquing a few months after the war's end, while he was writing *Cold Nights:*

> It was reported that repairs were still being made, and therefore there was no electricity in the city. It rained in the afternoon and turned cold in the evening. Walking on the slightly wet pavement, I went to visit a friend. The sky was dark, and the stores' acetylene lamps on both sides of the street were so dim that they did not light up the street itself. There were but few pedestrians, and my thin clothing was unable to protect me from the chill which made me shiver once or twice. "Autumn is truly here," I said softly. . . .
>
> I stood on a street corner, suddenly remembering that it was the same place where the people had hysterically celebrated the victory for more than a day. A huge crowd had gathered and people were laughing, screaming, jumping, and clowning with one another. Little children were chasing after jeeps, and adults raised their fists in happiness. I too shared their joy. But today, in the darkness, I could find no trace of that laughter. Where had all those people and their laughter gone?

Darkness, chill, and despair are the dominant motifs of *Cold Nights* that also express its sense of betrayal and collapse brought about by the war. The novel opens in the winter of 1944 as the novel's protagonist, Wang Wenxuan, walks home through the eerily empty streets during an air raid. Living under constant threat from Japanese attack and rumors of an imminent Japanese advance on the city, economic deprivation, and the gloom of wartime city life, Wenxuan also faces private torments in the ongoing conflict between his wife, Shusheng, and his widowed mother, who antagonistically share their small apartment. Shusheng, a secretary, is the new Chinese woman who enjoys her life outside the home that Wenxuan's meager salary and increasing illness does not allow him to share. Wenxuan's mother in contrast is resolutely traditional and castigates her daughter-in-law's lifestyle as selfish indulgence. Wenxuan finds himself pulled apart by his love and loyalty to both women. Too meek and indecisive to side with one over the other, Wenxuan eventually is only able to unite both women in their pity for his worsening health that develops into tuberculosis, costing him his job and further worsening his sense of lost control over his family. As the Japanese threat to the city grows, Shusheng is offered a job transfer to Lanchow, a distant, safer city, by the bank manager. Aware of the manager's romantic interest in her, Shusheng resists his offer, but with Wenxuan's encouragement, she eventually departs. Wenxuan's bodily deterioration and the collapse of his marriage are complete when he receives a letter from Shusheng petitioning him to release her from their marriage. "I am not selfish," she writes, "I only want to live, and to live joyfully. I want freedom." Wenxuan dies hearing the sounds of celebration at the news of the Japanese surrender. Throughout the novel the repeated refrain has been that life will be better after victory. *Cold Nights* argues that such a hope is delusional, that the war is more a symptom than a cause, and the conflicts that have split and destroyed Wenxuan's family are endemic in Chinese life. Wenxuan's futilely trying to balance the two polarities between his mother's insistence on traditional imperatives of filial duty and his wife's desire for liberation and self-realization represents China itself caught between its past and present, with Wenxuan, well-intentioned but ineffectual in resolving the conflict, drawn to both but unwilling to choose one over the other. Ultimately, the war has exposed Wenxuan's inadequacies as a son, husband, and father that only his death can relieve. Under the wasting impact of his disease, Wenxuan regresses to become the ideal helpless son that must be nursed by his devoted mother, incapable of providing for his own son or effectively resolving the conflict between his love for his wife and her need for some hopeful future. Ba Jin has turned a realistic domestic drama into a wide-ranging cultural tragedy.

In the novel's epilogue, Shusheng returns to discover that Wenxuan has died and her mother-in-law and son have disappeared. The novel closes with Shusheng suspended between action and paralysis:

> The dead was no more, and the living gone. Even if she waited until the next day, and probably found her husband's gravesite, could she find her son? Could she change her present situation? What should she do? Search for her mother-in-law and her son? Or go back to Lanchow and accept the hand of another?
>
> She had two weeks of vacation, and she must decide within that time: twelve or thirteen days. . . . But why stand in front of the stall and be battered by a chilly wind?
>
> "I still have time to decide," she told herself and walked away slowly and steadily. And suddenly while walking in the darkness she was overcome by a curious feeling. She glanced from time to time at both sides of the street as if afraid that the quivering acetylene lights at the stalls might be extinguished by the chilly wind. The night was so cold . . . so cold.

Cold Nights brings together a national and domestic tragedy, suggesting that both are inextricably linked. In his final novel, Ba Jin has found the means to probe the inner sources of the Chinese cultural and political dilemma, suggesting that reform is far more complicated than a change in government or policy reform. At the core of China's predicament is the Chinese family and its patriarchal past and uncertain future.

Ironically, the truth offered by Ba Jin in his harrowing account of a family's disintegration in *Cold Nights* was unwelcome when the Communists came to power in 1949. Ba Jin published little beyond what was demanded and approved by the new regime. Politically persecuted through the 1950s and 1960s, Ba Jin was officially labeled "a great poisonous weed" and "the

DRACULA 120

(1897)

by Bram Stoker

Dracula *deserves our attention not only because of what it reveals about the times in which it was written but also because it encourages us to reexamine the views of our own day. Certainly the key to the importance of* Dracula *rests in its popularity, a popularity that continues undiminished a century after its initial publication.* Dracula *continues to fascinate us because it both reveals the contradictions of Stoker's own day and points us to the internal tensions of our own.*

—Carol A. Senf, *Dracula: Between Tradition and Modernism*

When *Dracula* appeared in 1897, one of the most prescient responses came from Bram Stoker's mother, Charlotte, who wrote her son: "My dear, it is splendid, a thousand miles beyond anything you have written before, and I feel certain will place you high in the writers of the day. . . . No book since Mrs. Shelley's *Frankenstein* or indeed any other at all has come near yours in originality, or terror—Poe is nowhere. I have read much but I have never met a book like it at all. In its terrible excitement it should make a widespread reputation and much money for you." *Dracula* transformed Stoker from hack to mythmaker, securing his reputation as his mother predicted, though fortunes would be made by the book's many adapters rather than by its creator. With *Dracula,* Stoker produced the prototypical vampire tale and a defining work of modern fictional horror that has achieved an unprecedented degree of cultural saturation. "No other single work," critic Carol A. Senf declares, "with the exception of the Bible, has so influenced Anglo-American culture." Stoker biographer Barbara Belford claims that Count Dracula is "The most filmed character in history after Sherlock Holmes." As much a myth as a novel, *Dracula* has managed such a persistent hold on our collective imagination due to Stoker's ability to embed in his updated gothic tale a mesmerizing combination of threat and seduction whose appeal and power in its seemingly continual subsequent film and fictional reincarnations show no evidence of abating.

Stoker, a Dublin civil servant who became the popular Victorian actor Henry Irving's manager, claimed that the idea for his novel came to him in a nightmare after a dinner of dressed crab. He was probably aware of at least two previous vampire tales: the novel *The Vampyre* (1819) by Lord Byron's friend Dr. John Polidori (composed during the same 1816 storytelling contest that produced Mary Shelley's *Frankenstein*) and the short story "Carmilla" (1871) by Stoker's fellow Dubliner, Joseph Sheridan Le Fanu. Other possible sources include Sir Richard Francis Burton's *Vikram and the Vampire* (1870) and the tales of Hungarian Arminius Vambery, whose legends of vampirism in eastern Europe Stoker heard in April 1890. In August Stoker began work on *Dracula* while on vacation at Whitby, on the Yorkshire coast. It was apparently there that Stoker first learned of Vlad, the 15th-century ruler of Wallachia, now part of Romania. Vlad's father had the title of Dracul, the Order of the Dragon, conferred by the Holy Roman Emperor, and Vlad, called the Impaler for his preferred method of torture, was therefore also known as the son of Dracul, or Dracula. Although he was reputed to have sometimes drunk the blood of his victims, the historical Dracula was never associated with vampirism. Stoker would make this connection in his novel, also moving Dracula's castle from Wallachia to an adjacent Romanian province with the suggestive name of Transylvania, or "the land beyond the forest."

Although Stoker has been called "a hasty writer with the habits of a hack," *Dracula* shows evidence of considerable research and forethought. At Whitby, where the count first lands in England, Stoker made sketches of the town and its graveyard, consulted coast guard logs and weather manuals, and interviewed local people about shipwrecks. In London he gathered vampire lore at the British Museum and asked his surgeon brother about the symptoms and treatment of the injury that kills Renfield. Although he never visited Transylvania, Stoker's descriptions conform to the actual landscape to a remarkable degree. The actual, therefore, anchors the supernatural. Believability and suspense are additionally gained from his complex narrative method of the direct testimonials of alternating viewpoints, in the manner of Wilkie Collins's *The Woman in White*. Participants record their experiences as near as possible to when things happen to them, establishing an immediacy and escalating tension and suspense. Eyewitness accounts are supplemented by documentary sources such as newspaper clippings. All serve to make the extraordinary believable, while the cutting among limited viewpoints enhances suspense.

The novel opens with the journal of Jonathan Harker, a young English solicitor who has gone to Transylvania to help Count Dracula complete the purchase of a London house. Dracula, when he is finally met after a series of dire warnings that Harker chooses to ignore, turns out to be "a tall old man, clean shaven save for a long white moustache, and clad in black from head to foot," with reddish eyes, sharp white teeth, and a pale complexion except for his full, red lips. During his stay of nearly two months at Dracula's castle, Harker gradually realizes that he is being held prisoner, and he eventually discovers the basic characteristics of the vampire. Never seen during daylight and never eating or drinking, Dracula casts no reflection in a mirror. When Harker cuts himself while shaving, Dracula lunges for his throat—only to stop short when he sees a rosary around his victim's neck. Harker is also beset by three phantomlike women vying to kiss him who are driven off by the Count with the admonition that Harker belongs to him. Harker finally discovers the Count in his coffin in a crypt beneath the castle during the day, and realizes that Dracula is preparing to have himself shipped to England. His journal breaks off with his decision to try to climb down the sheer castle wall and the precipice below.

Meanwhile, in England, Mina Murray, Harker's fiancée, learns that her friend Lucy Westenra has received three marriage proposals in one day: from Dr. John Seward, the head of a lunatic asylum; from Quincey Morris, a Texan; and from Arthur Holmwood, the future Lord Godalming. She accept Holmwood's proposal, and the rejected suitors manfully deal with their disappointment by reaffirming the trio's friendship. While awaiting Harker's return, Mina joins Lucy and her mother on vacation in Whitby. When a Russian schooner runs aground in Whitby harbor, the only living creature aboard is a wolflike dog, which leaps ashore and disappears. Almost immediately afterward, Lucy begins having nightmares and resumes her habit of sleepwalking. Mina finds her one night in the churchyard, where a tall man with red eyes is bending over her. Later, Mina notices two tiny holes in Lucy's neck, and Lucy grows progressively weaker and paler. At this point, Mina receives a letter from a hospital in Budapest informing her that Jonathan has been there for six weeks suffering from "brain fever." She goes to join him, and they are married after he has recovered from his delirium.

As Lucy appears to be dangerously ill, Holmwood writes to his friend and former rival, Dr. Seward, asking him to examine his fiancée. Seward calls in his old professor, Abraham Van Helsing of Amsterdam, to consult. A succession of transfusions from Holmwood, Seward, Helsing, and Morris fails to halt Lucy's decline, and she dies shortly after a wolf crashes through the window of her room, killing her mother in fright. Lucy is buried in the family tomb in London. The Harkers return to England with Jonathan believing that his experiences at Castle Dracula were a product of his delirium; but he is shocked to see the much younger-looking Count Dracula on a London street. They receive word from Van Helsing of Lucy's death, and Mina shares with him Jonathan's journal that confirms the doctor's vampiric suspicions. Soon after Lucy's burial, the newspapers report that several small children have disappeared from the vicinity of the cemetery, only to be found the next morning in a weakened condition, their throats marked by small wounds. Each child tells of being lured away by an attractive "bloofer lady." Van Helsing becomes convinced that Lucy, now a vampire, is responsible, and he leads Seward, Holmwood, and Morris back to Lucy's tomb, where they see her returning with another child in tow, whom they rescue. The next night they return to the tomb and drive a stake through Lucy's heart, cut off her head, and stuff her mouth with garlic.

The four men and the Harkers now join forces to track down the Count's various boxes of earth he uses for repose during the day, to render them uninhabitable. They make their headquarters at Dr. Seward's hospital, which is next door to Carfax, the estate Jonathan Harker had gone to Transylvania to help Dracula purchase. Dracula has been given access to the hospital by Dr. Seward's patient Renfield, who is given to devouring small creatures for their "life," and has fallen under the Count's power. Dracula has been visiting Mina and drinking her blood at night. The climax comes when Renfield—who has tried to resist the Count—is found in his cell with a broken back and a fractured skull. Before he dies he tells Van Helsing about Dracula's nocturnal visits. The men burst into the Harkers' bedroom, where they find Jonathan in a stupor and Mina sucking blood from the Count's chest. Dracula flees before the communion host Van Helsing brandishes, and when Van Helsing touches the wafer to Mina's forehead, it sears her flesh, leaving a vivid red mark.

They realize that if the Count is not destroyed, Mina will soon suffer Lucy's fate. They succeed in finding and destroying all but one of Dracula's boxes of earth. Guided by Mina, who is in telepathic communication with the Count, they pursue Dracula to his castle, Van Helsing and Mina by land and the others by boat. Van Helsing stakes the three vampire women who previously attacked Harker, and he and Mina ward off an assault of wolves by drawing a circle in the snow with a crucifix. Soon a band of Gypsies appears with a wagon bearing Dracula's coffin. They are pursued by Harker, Seward, Holmwood, and Morris. Morris is fatally wounded, but he and Harker manage to destroy Dracula before the sun sets.

Despite Stoker's clear limitations as a novelist, particularly in his characterizations, which alternate between grandiloquence and woodenness, *Dracula* succeeds on the level of the thriller, achieving an irresistible forward pressure of threat and suspense. But the novel's persistence derives from the force of its title character and the powerful universal fears and fantasies that Dracula unleashes. It is interesting to note that Dracula appears in only 62 of the 390 pages of the novel's original edition, suggesting that it is less his presence than his implication that is responsible for his hold on the imagination. *Dracula* achieves its power from both its realism and its fantasy. The supernatural is grounded in the trivial details of ordinary life, and out of the conjunction a number of powerful symbols emerge. In the coded method of the novel, bloodsucking becomes a metaphor for sexuality. The Count is irresistible to women and transforms the passive, virtuous Victorian female into an aggressive sexual predator who is in turn seductive and vile. In the only episode of vampirism explicitly described in the novel—in which Mina sucks the blood from Dracula's chest—the virtuous Mina is defiled as a succubus in the making. If she is eventually reclaimed to virtue, her defilement, like Lucy's, is part of the novel's vicarious thrills. In Victorian society, in which female sexuality and aggressiveness were repressed and punished, *Dracula* brings deep-seated gender conflicts to dramatic life. In our own time, Count Dracula is the closest to a modern Satan an irreligious age can conjure, and in an aesthetic tradition that undervalues the clear melodramatic confrontation between good and evil, *Dracula* makes its point in the unmistakably vivid colors of red and black.

121

THE WOMAN IN THE DUNES

(1962)

by Kobo Abé

Abé's labyrinthine underworld is a faithfully detailed mirror image, only turned upside down, of the world we take for granted. The world of Raymond Chandler's novels, by way of contrast, may sometimes become considerably absurd, but it never lapses into the truly Kafkaesque nightmare, and even when good guys and bad guys in Chandler's stories look very much alike, there is always a bottom line of decency that clearly separates them. In Abé's stories, however, the all-too-human and the all-too-inhuman are not simply opposite sides of the same coin; after a while we realize that we have no idea which side of the coin we are seeing or, even worse, on which side our sympathies should lie.

—David Pollack, "The Ideology of Science: Kobo Abé's *Woman in the Dunes*"

It is an irony not missed by Japanese critics that Kobo Abé's *The Woman in the Dunes*, the best-known novel of the best-known postwar Japanese novelist, is probably the least Japanese, owing far more to the works of Franz Kafka, Albert Camus, and Samuel Beckett than to the Japanese literary tradition. As Hisaaki Yamaouchi has pointed out, Abé "is probably the first Japanese writer whose works, having no distinctly Japanese qualities, are of interest to the Western audience because of their universal relevance." Written with a clinical precision that mitigates its abstractions and anchors its nightmarish vision, *The Woman in the Dunes*, with elements derived from Greek myths, symbolism, surrealism, existentialism, and the theater of the absurd, remains one of the enduring modernist allegories on man's fate and the fundamental questions of existence and the meaning of freedom. Different from so many other modern Japanese novelists who located their drama in the conflicts between Western modernism and Japanese traditions, Abé has little sympathy for either a faith in future progress or a consoling nostalgia for the past. Instead his works, described by the critic Thomas Fitzsimmons as "bizarre situations loaded with metaphysical overtones," explode false distinctions and reassuring simplifications in pursuit of timeless relevance and philosophical inquiry.

"Place has no role for me," Abé has asserted. "I am rootless." This sense of alienation and displacement from his Japanese identity and heritage help to explain both the unusual qualities of his works and their universality. His preoccupation with displacement and alienation and his literary interests can be traced directly to his background. Born in Tokyo in 1924, Abé grew up in Manchuria during the Japanese occupation, in Mukden (Shen-yang), where his father, a medical doctor, worked at the Medical University of Manchuria. Attending Japanese schools in Mukden, Abé was estranged both from the native population of Chinese, Mongols, and Russians and from his distant homeland. From his father, Abé inherited his interest in science and his analytical skills; from his mother, who taught Japanese classical literature and was a published novelist, his love of literature. Abé returned to Tokyo in 1942, at the age of 18, to enter Tokyo University Medical School. When unsatisfactory grades threatened his exemption from military service, he forged a medical certificate stating that he was suffering from tuberculosis to be classified unfit for military duty. In 1944, he returned to Mukden to help his father with his medical practice. A year later, a typhus epidemic struck Manchuria and took his father's life. Having opposed Japanese militarism based on the atrocities he witnessed Japanese troops perpetrate during the occupation, Abé greeted the news of Japan's defeat by saying that he was "overjoyed," convinced that Japanese nationalism had been immoral and ruinous. Repatriated back to Tokyo aboard an American landing craft, Abé resumed his medical studies, gaining his degree in 1948, the same year that he began to publish poetry and fiction. His success encouraged him to abandon a medical career for writing. Sympathetic to the concepts of socialism and internationalism, Abé joined the Communist Party and became an enthusiastic participant in Japan's postwar avant-garde literary movement.

In contrast to earlier writers such as Tanizaki and Kawabata who were drawn to rural life for their settings and themes, Abé's focus was almost exclusively urban, reflecting the reality of contemporary postwar Japanese life. "The city," he explained, "is the place where people first had to deal with the stranger who is not an enemy. I think they still have not succeeded completely." To capture the experience of modern urban life and the isolation and alienation it created, Abé turned to techniques derived from European surrealism and the realistic fantasy and transformations of Franz Kafka, whom he greatly admired. Kafka's influence is clear in Abé's prizewinning 1950 story, "Akai Mayu" (translated as "Red Cocoon," 1972), which treats the hallucinatory experiences of a homeless man. His story collection, *Kabe* (*The Wall*, 1951), established his leading theme in the search for some kind of sustaining belief in a hostile world. He produced his first play, *Seifuku* (produced 1955, translated as *Uniform*, 1979), by accident, when a story that he was writing stalled and "it occurred to me that it might be easier to work out something if all I had to do was to write dialogue, and I didn't have to trouble myself with description and the rest." Abé would eventually regard his plays "as necessary and as important as my novels" and became one of Japan's leading experimental dramatists, best known for *Tomaodachi Enemoto Takeaki* (*Friends*, 1967) and *Bo ni Natta Otoko* (*The Man Who Turned into a Stick*, 1969). His first full-length novel to be translated into English was *Dai yon kanpyki* (1959; translated as *Inter Ice Age Four*, 1970), a novel that combines elements from science fiction and surrealism in an absurdist story about the Japanese government harvesting fetuses to preserve the human race under threat of an ecological disaster. His other important novels include *Tanin no Kao* (*The Face of Another*, 1966), *Moetsukita Chizu* (*The Ruined Map*, 1967), *Hako Otako* (*The Box Man*, 1973), and his last novel, *Kangaru Noto* (*The Kangaroo Notebook*, 1991). Abé died of heart failure in 1993.

Abé's most enduring work is *Suna no Onna* (*The Woman in the Dunes*, 1962), a distillation of his preoccupations and techniques as a writer. Written in the spare, analytical style with which Abé is famous, *The Woman in the Dunes* is an imaginative combination of narrative elements, including the detective story and allegory. The novel opens with "just the facts." In the language of a newspaper account or official report a teacher and amateur entomologist, eventually identified as Niki Jumpei, has disappeared after setting off on a seaside holiday to gather specimens for his collection. Since seven years have passed with no solution to the mystery of his disappearance or no body found, he is presumed dead. The novel then picks up the story from Jumpei's departure, having established the novel's central mystery surrounding his fate as well as its dramatic irony in which the reader realizes that all Jumpei's subsequent actions to return from his journey will not be successful. Having taken a train to the seaside town, Jumpei walks near the ocean to an isolated village all but buried by the drifting sand dunes. He is intent on discovering a species of insect living in the dunes that has yet to be classified. In a nod to Kafka's most famous work, *The Metamorphosis*, in which Gregor Samsa wakes up transformed into a giant insect, Abé employs a similar Samsa-like figure, whose name translates as "obedient and average," whose identity becomes attached to an insect that he can name and thereby achieve an identity and distinction he does not possess otherwise. Isolated and alienated from his society, Jumpei finds himself cast into a situation that exemplifies his feelings. Preoccupied by his search, Jumpei misses the last bus out of the village back to the station, and a villager offers him a place to stay in a shack deep within a declivity in the dunes, reachable only by a rope ladder. He is welcomed by an unnamed woman in her 30s, who provides him dinner and a bed. Her husband and daughter were both victims of the ever-encroaching and shifting sands. "I know a little about sand myself," Jumpei, the amateur naturalist pedantically observes. "Let me tell you. Sand moves around like this all year long. Its flow is its life. It absolutely never stops—anywhere. Whether in water or air, it moves about free and unrestricted. So, usually, ordinary living things are unable to endure life in it, and this goes for bacteria too. How shall I put it . . . sand represents purity, cleanliness. Maybe it serves a preservative function, but there is certainly no question of its rotting anything. And, what's more, dear lady, to begin with, sand is a respectable mineral. It couldn't possibly rot away!" Jumpei confronts the reality of his observation and is shocked to learn that all of the woman's efforts are occupied by shoveling the sand from around her shack, and that the entire village depends on the sand for its existence. As she explains, "The village keeps going because we never let up clearing away the sand like this. If we stopped, in ten days the village would be completely buried."

The next day, Jumpei awakes to find that the rope ladder has been removed, and he is trapped, expected to take up the ceaseless labor of digging out from beneath the moving sand. "This entire nightmare could not be happening," he asserts. "Was it permissible to snare, exactly like a mouse or an insect, a man, who had his certificate of medical insurance, someone who had paid his taxes, who was employed, and whose family records were in order? He could not believe it. Perhaps there was some mistake; it was bound to be a mistake. There was nothing to do but assume that it was a mistake." Jumpei, in search of an insect he could name, is now treated like an insect, with all the rather trivial and absurd characteristics of humanity—certificate of medical insurance, paid taxes, employment, and family records in order—overturned in his predicament that combines elements of the myth of Sisyphus and Kafka's *The Trial.* The analogy at work in the novel is Abé's suggestion of the correspondence between human activity and the seemingly overwhelming labor of evading extinction under the onslaught of the obliterating sand, a metaphor for experience itself. Locked into an existential struggle, Jumpei resorts to a number of ways of evading his fate. His attempt to dig his way out by collapsing sections of the dune to use to climb out results in his being half-buried and rescued by the woman; he feigns an injury to show his uselessness as a laborer; he bullies and bargains with the woman to help him; he threatens the villagers with prosecution. Nothing changes his condition. Instead, gradually, Jumpei begins to adjust to his situation. He and the woman have sex, and Jumpei, though never stopping planning his escape, more and more tolerates and even depends on the ordinary routine of his life shoveling the sand. He finally manages to fashion a rope, and, while the woman is sleeping, climbs onto the roof of the shack and uses the rope to reach the top of the dune. The freedom that Jumpei has long struggled for proves to be an illusion, however. Eventually finding his way out of the village to the ocean, he becomes stuck in quicksand and is rescued by the villagers who return him to the woman's care.

Constructing a trap for a crow he plans to use to get a message out, Jumpei discovers how to collect water and thereby evade the villagers' power over him. He makes one final bargain for his release with a villager who agrees to help if he can watch Jumpei and the woman have sex. Failing to persuade the woman, Jumpei tries to force her, but she fights him off, and he begins to realize that the old man has no intention of helping him escape. As the novel concludes, months have passed, and Jumpei accepts the struggle against the sand as a way of life. When the woman, who is now pregnant, needs the villagers' help, they neglect to take away the rope ladder used to lift her from the pit. Using the ladder to climb up for a view of the sea, Jumpei contemplates his next move:

> There was no particular need to hurry about escaping. On the two-way ticket held in his hand now, the destination and time of departure were blanks for him to fill in as he wished. In addition, he realized that he was bursting with a desire to talk to someone about the water trap. And if he wanted to talk about it, there wouldn't be better listeners than the villagers. He would end by telling someone—if not today, then tomorrow.
>
> He might as well put off his escape until sometime after that.

The novel ends with two official documents: a notification of his status as a missing person from the Court of Domestic Relations, finally naming Niki Jumpei, and the court's judgment officially declaring him as missing, and suggesting that his case is now closed.

Bookended by examples of inadequate attempts to solve the novel's mystery of the fate of Jumpei, his actual story enacts a powerful existential fable that allegorizes human activities as little more than a frantic struggle for survival against an implacable and all-powerful foe: the obliterating and ever-shifting sand. The everyman Jumpei, like Camus's Sisyphus, is instructed both in the pointlessness of human labor and its purpose. In the inverted logic of Abé's fable, in the words of the critic David Pollack, "step by step, we have been led to feel that the man trapped in this wretched topsy-turvy world is no longer alienated, anonymous, friendless, and without love. A much more content and fulfilled person than he was before he was trapped, he must acknowledge the truth that we are indeed our own jailers." Abé has provided a powerful object lesson in human identity, the meaning of freedom, and the nature of the human condition, stripped down to its essentials.

122

GONE WITH THE WIND

(1936)

by Margaret Mitchell

If the novel Gone with the Wind *has a theme, the theme is that of survival.*
—Margaret Mitchell, *Wilson Quarterly*, September 11, 1936

Except for the Bible, no book has sold more hardcover copies than *Gone with the Wind*, Margaret Mitchell's sweeping, iconic epic of the American South, the Civil War, and the Reconstruction. A publishing and cultural phenomenon, the novel sold more than 1 million copies in its first year of publication in 1936. It has seldom subsequently sold fewer than 40,000 hardback copies per year since then and considerably more paperback copies. Translated into 27 languages in 37 countries, its popularity has spread worldwide. With the 1939 release of the film version—one of the most successful films in movie history—*Gone with the Wind*'s hold on popular culture has reached an unprecedented level of saturation. It is estimated that more than 90 percent of the American population have seen the film, few of whom have seen it only once. When the film was broadcast on television for the first time in 1976, it drew 110 million viewers, up to that time the largest audience in television history. Mitchell's conception of the South before, during, and immediately after the Civil War has set the archetype, and Scarlett O'Hara, Rhett Butler, and Tara have entered the collective consciousness.

Yet despite its enormous popularity and impact, *Gone with the Wind* has received comparatively little scholarly attention, and its creator has been largely consigned to the critical limbo of the popular romance writer rather than considered as a literary artist. It may be that *Gone with the Wind* is more a popular culture achievement, not a literary one, that the creator of the most popular romantic novel in history should be viewed mainly as the chief progenitor of the modern romance genre. However, Mitchell deserves additional credit for creating an enduring woman-centered fiction that deals in important ways with issues about the ambiguous roles of women in modern society.

Margaret Mitchell was the daughter of a prominent Atlanta, Georgia, couple who was born during the devastating aftermath of the Civil War. Devoted to her native city, Mitchell was exposed to local history from both her parents. As she recalled to a reviewer when *Gone with the Wind* was published, "The genesis of my book . . . lies years back when I was six years old." Mitchell credited her mother with fixing in her imagination the image of the South uprooted by history during tours of ruined plantations, or in her mother's phrase, "Sherman's Sentinels." Mitchell remembered that "She talked about the world those people had lived in, such a secure world, and how it had exploded beneath them. And she told me that my own world was going to explode under me, some day, and God help me if I didn't have some weapon to meet the new world." Mitchell's defense became her writing and storytelling, and her theme how individuals cope in order to survive. Leaving her own secure world first as a debutante and later as a society lady, Mitchell had until 1926 been a reporter and feature writer for the *Atlanta Journal*. When she fell and sprained an ankle that had previously been damaged in two earlier accidents and it failed to heal properly, Mitchell convalesced at home, reading extensively in 19th-century Atlanta history. According to family legend, when few books remained in the library that Mitchell had not read, her husband remarked, "It looks to me, Peggy, as though you'll have to write a book yourself if you're going to have anything to read." This began Mitchell's 10-year labor to produce *Gone with the Wind*. She began with the design to clarify the southern experience of the Confederate defeat, particularly from the perspective of and impact on southern women. She started her story with her heroine's climactic realization on the eventual book's final pages: "She had never understood either of the men she had loved and so she had lost them both." To reach this moment of insight, Mitchell centered her 1,367-page epic on the experience of her main female character, first named Pansy, later to be christened Scarlett O'Hara, when her publisher objected to her first choice because of its homosexual connotations.

Scarlett, one of the most recognizable American heroines, is a complex mixture of modern and traditional values and feminine and masculine traits. On the one hand, she can be seen as a self-centered southern belle, oblivious to people who do not contribute to her sense of entitlement. On the other, she is an aggressive manipulator who rejects passive victimage with a survivalist mentality that fuels her drive for mastery. At the center of Mitchell's novel, therefore, is a morally mixed central protagonist, fascinating and admirable in her passion and resilience, deplorable in her heartlessness and self-centeredness. Ultimately, Scarlett is doomed to exist between the conflicting poles of autonomy and dependence that Mitchell diagnosed as the central dilemma of southern women. In this regard, *Gone with the Wind* offers a fascinating dramatization of gender roles and expectations, relevant not just to the period in the South before and after the Civil War, but increasingly valid to the book's first readers, enduring the struggles of the Great Depression while absorbing the values of the new emancipated women of the post–World War I era. As Anne Jones observes in an insightful essay on the novel, "The Bad Little Girl of the Good Old Days: Gender, Sex, and the Southern Social Order," the novel "questions not only the means but the value of sheer survival, and defines survival quite clearly as psychological and ethical as well as physical. The axes on which Mitchell imagined survival to balance are self-reliance and dependence. Carried to extreme, self-reliance becomes isolation and even solipsism; dependence, at worst, becomes the loss of selfhood and identity. Because the culture [Mitchell] lived in and the culture she imagined both placed these specific values upon one or the other sex, the novel becomes a study in gender roles, in what it means to be a man or a woman in the South." The ambiguity of Scarlett is set from the novel's memorable opening line: "Scarlett O'Hara was not beautiful, but men seldom realized it when caught by her charm as the Tarleton twins were." Scarlett is a complex blend of her mother's feminine side and her father's masculine character, and the novel's events show how both work themselves out in Scarlett's defiance of convention and drive for independence and control. Yet her dominance by traditional values of dependence on the old southern order and its definition of women finally dooms her. Attracted to the equally iconoclastic, masculine, aggressive Rhett, she is pulled back from him by her devotion to the dutiful, chivalric Ashley Wilkes and to the old values of security and protection represented by Tara, the O'Hara plantation. Scarlett is, therefore, both a new woman for her readers' era, as well as one who is incapable of articulating a meaningful role for herself beyond the traditional gender expectation of her past. Rhett, despite his outsider's stance, is no less dominated by traditional gender assumptions. In his own climactic revelation about his relationship with Scarlett and his daughter, Bonnie Blue, Rhett observes:

> I wanted to take care of you, to pet you, to give you everything you wanted. I wanted to marry you and protect you and give you free rein in anything that would make you happy—just as I did Bonnie. . . . I wanted you to stop fighting and let me fight for you. I wanted you to play, like a child—for you were a child, a brave, frightened, bull-headed child. I think you are still a child. . . . I liked to think that Bonnie was you, a little girl again, before the war and poverty had done things to you. She was so like you . . . and I could pet and spoil her—just as I wanted to pet you.

Rhett is no more able to accept the unconventional Scarlett than she is able to rest contentedly in her independence. The men as well as the women in *Gone with the Wind* must ironically be protected in their illusions as the superior guardians of women. The failure of both genders to sustain these reassuring values in the face of the changes wrought by the war and its disruptive aftermath precipitates the novel's tragedy, as Mitchell plays out a number of variations on conventional gender expectations.

The romance genre, reflected both in fiction and later on television through soap operas, borrows much from Margaret Mitchell, particularly her survival plot, endlessly testing characters by circumstances and tangled relationships. Yet few popular romances match the complexity of Mitchell's central female character, preferring instead idealization to Mitchell's richer, three-dimensional portraiture. Most romance novels also cannot resist the pleasing resolution that *Gone with the Wind* insistently avoids. Scarlett, in perhaps one of the most daring and unsettling conclusions in fiction, is left on her own, unsupported by her love for Rhett, with only the consolation that Tara remains and that "Tomorrow is another day." The conflict that Mitchell has exhaustively dramatized between opposing gender assumptions is left unresolved as well, suggesting a basic tension in women and men that continues to await a satisfying synthesis.

Despite her readers' continual pleas for a sequel to resolve the suspense over Scarlett's fate, Mitchell refused to comply and struggled to cope with "the hell on earth" that her popularity brought until she was killed in an accident by an out-of-control taxicab in 1949. *Gone with the Wind* remains one of the defining popular literary expressions of the 20th century, if not for its artistic qualities, then for its ability to captivate a massive audience. Other great female fictional characters—Becky Sharp by Thackeray, Emma Bovary by Flaubert, Anna Karenina by Tolstoy—were the inventions of male novelists. With Scarlett O'Hara, a woman writer offered her own unique point of view to create a riveting central female character and a view of the past and America's central historical tragedy through the lens of a female perspective that continues to express contemporary issues and concerns.

123

THE THREE MUSKETEERS

(1844)

by Alexandre Dumas

The Three Musketeers *is a stirring tale of adventure but it is also a historical saga, a macabre chiller, a thriller, a romance, and a kind of detective novel. It has, in other words, all the ingredients of classic story-telling. Each page moves the action excitingly forward in a variety of moods which run from the drama of the chase through humour to the superreality of an allegorical quest. For what Dumas describes is a Homeric clash of Titans and his characters are gods: it is in this sense that he was, as Anthony Burgess has said, "one of the great myth-makers." Yet ultimately he defies analysis for his attraction lies in the sheer force of his personality and the power of his imagination. Highbrow, lowbrow, young and old surrender to his spell.*

—David Coward, Introduction to *The Three Musketeers*,
World Classics Edition

It is certainly true that there are 19th-century novels of much more artistic and scholarly importance than *The Three Musketeers*, but few would dispute the classic status, popularity, and influence of Alexandre Dumas's rousing tale of intrigue, adventure, and romance set in the France of Louis XIII and Cardinal Richelieu. Influenced by the works of the first great historical novelist, Sir Walter Scott, Dumas brought drama and passion to the genre and in the process introduced countless readers to the pleasures of literature, whetting appetites for swift narration and vivid characters that can eventually be satisfied by greater novelists.

Alexandre Dumas, *père* (1802–70), was almost as dashing a figure as his fictional musketeers. A confirmed womanizer and bon vivant, as well as a prolific and versatile writer, he took part in the Revolution of 1830, stood unsuccessfully for parliament during the Revolution of 1848, and earned—and cheerfully spent—several fortunes. He began his career as a dramatist and rose to fame after embracing the Romantic movement then taking shape among French writers. His first play in the new mode, *Henry III and His Court*, presented in 1829, was a triumph. "Instead of the flat verse and arid passion of classical theatre," writes David Coward, "Dumas gave audiences fiery prose, action, and conflict." By 1836 Dumas was concentrating more on fiction and was impressed by the increasing popularity of the serialized novel, the *roman feuilleton*. In 1838 he began a collaboration with Auguste Maquet (1813–88), a history teacher and writer, revising and rewriting Macquet's works. In 1841, during a visit to Marseilles, Dumas came upon the first volume of *The Memoirs of M. D'Artagnan* (1700) by army captain and romance writer Courtilz de Sandras (1644–1712). A real historical figure, the eponymous character was a career soldier named Charles de Batz-Castelmore, a captain-lieutenant in the king's guards and a D'Artagnan on his mother's side. Borrowing elements of de Sandras's pseudo-memoir and working from Maquet's manuscript outline, Dumas added his own imaginative virtuosity to the material and fashioned what would become his most popular novel and the one he considered his best. *The Three Musketeers* was serialized in *Le Siècle* between March 14, 1843, and July 14, 1844, and was an instant success.

Dumas included a preface to *The Three Musketeers* that playfully credits the source of the story to "The Memoirs of M. Le Comte De La Fere," the name he gives to the musketeer, Athos. At the start of the opening chapter he sets the tone for his tale when he tells the reader that the first scene takes place in the "small town of Meung, the birthplace of the author of the *Romance of the Rose*." It is the spring of 1625, a time, Dumas informs us, of foreign war and civil uneasiness: "There were the nobles, who made war on each other; there was the king who made war on the cardinal . . . then, besides these wars, concealed or overt, secret or public, there were bandits, mendicants, Huguenots, wolves, and lacqueys, who made war on the whole world."

Into this stew of civil and political struggle arrives D'Artagnan, the archetypal adventure hero. He is a proud, passionate, and hotheaded young Gascon, rather callow at first, but increasingly clever and resourceful as the novel progresses. Dumas describes him at his first appearance as "Don Quixote at eighteen." D'Artagnan is on his way to Paris to join the Musketeers of the Guard, who serve the king. He rides into Meung, where he encounters a nobleman, who has a scar on his face and is accompanied by a beautiful young woman. The reader will later learn that she is Milady de Winter, an agent of Cardinal Richelieu and the novel's villainous femme fatale. When D'Artagnan perceives that the nobleman is laughing at his old yellow horse, he challenges him to a duel, only to be beaten senseless by the man's companions.

In Paris D'Artagnan is told by Monsieur de Treville, the captain of the musketeers, that he must serve an apprenticeship as a cadet before becoming a musketeer. De Treville also warns him to beware of the scarred nobleman. D'Artagnan suddenly spots the man from Meung in the street below and rushes off in a fury to accost him. On the way he encounters three musketeers and offends each of them in turn, with the result that three separate duels are arranged. D'Artagnan's first appointment is with Athos, who is accompanied by Porthos and Aramis. Their duel is soon forgotten when the four fight the cardinal's guards, who have arrived to arrest the musketeers for dueling. The musketeers are impressed by D'Artagnan's swordsmanship, bravery, and uprightness, and the four become fast friends. In the days that follow, D'Artagnan learns a little about his new friends. Athos has an aristocratic, melancholy demeanor and seems to carry a secret sorrow. The bragging Porthos is a ladies' man, who hopes to marry a rich widow, while the elegant Aramis insists he is a musketeer only "for a time," and will soon become a priest.

The king rewards D'Artagnan and the musketeers in gold for their escapade with the cardinal's guards, but the money is soon spent and D'Artagnan is unable to pay his rent. His landlord, Bonancieux, will waive payment if D'Artagnan finds and rescues his wife, Constance. A seamstress and devoted lady-in-waiting to Anne of Austria, Constance has been abducted by the scarred nobleman and his minions at the behest of Richelieu, who hopes to learn from Constance details of the rumored romance between the queen and the Duke of Buckingham. Constance escapes her captors and returns home, where a second abduction attempt is foiled by D'Artagnan, now in love with the lovely young woman.

Soon afterward we meet one of history's most renowned political geniuses and the novel's protagonist: Armand-Jean Duplessis, better known as Cardinal Richelieu. "Not," Dumas tells us, "as he is represented—broken down like an old man . . . but such as he really was at this period; that is, a skillful and gallant cavalier . . . upheld by that moral force which made him one of the most unparalleled of mankind." Richelieu despises the queen because she does not love him, preferring instead his political enemy, Buckingham. He also seeks to undermine her influence over the king because she is a member of the powerful Hapsburg family, rulers of two enemies of France, Austria and Spain. Thirdly, the cardinal plans to drive English troops from the Isle of Rhe, where Buckingham has sent them to aid the recalcitrant heretic Huguenots, entrenched in their stronghold, the port city of La Rochelle. "In humiliating England in the eyes of Europe," Dumas tells the reader, "he should humiliate Buckingham in the eyes of the queen."

Richelieu learns from the scarred nobleman, now identified as the Count de Rochefort, that the queen has given Buckingham 12 diamond studs, a gift from the king. He orders Milady to ingratiate herself with the duke and steal two of the studs. He intends to show the two studs to the king at a fete as proof of the queen's infidelity. When Constance learns that the queen is expected to wear the 12 studs at the fete, she begs D'Artagnan to retrieve them. Eager to please his beloved, D'Artagnan sets off at once for England, accompanied by Athos, Porthos, and Aramis. The four are waylaid by the cardinal's agents and only D'Artagnan completes the journey. Buckingham has the missing studs replaced, and D'Artagnan returns to France with the jewels in time to foil the cardinal's plot.

The novel might have ended there, with the successful conclusion of a rousing adventure and the attainment of D'Artagnan's goals (to become a musketeer and to win Constance's love). But Dumas, working within a historical context and possessing a genius for plotting, understood the importance of having his protagonist continue to strive to achieve his aims. The sinister and crafty Richelieu is the instigator of events; his machinations are, observes critic Bill Delaney, "like the mainspring in a clock that keeps the entire mechanism running." The cardinal must either succeed or fail in his endeavors, according to the confines of historical fact; the characters that surround the cardinal must either serve his ends or thwart him, according to Dumas's fictional construct.

When Constance is again seized and imprisoned by Rochefort and his men, D'Artagnan and the three musketeers must find and rescue her. In the meantime, D'Artagnan, in a chance encounter, meets Milady, whom he has recognized as Rochefort's companion from Meung. Intrigued by her and attracted to her beauty, he goes to her room one night pretending to be one of her lovers. After their assignation, Milady gives him a magnificent sapphire ring, which he shows to Athos. The taciturn musketeer, who is revealed as the Comte de la Fere, identifies the ring as one he had given to his wife, a beautiful young woman whom he had discovered was a criminal after seeing that her shoulder was branded with the fleur-de-lis. He begins to suspect that Milady de Winter is his wife, whom he had presumed dead. His suspicion is confirmed after D'Artagnan learns that Milady is the cardinal's spy and confronts her as himself. Enraged, she strikes out at him, and her dress falls from her shoulder, revealing the fleur-de-lis and thus her true identity. She attacks him with a knife, and as he flees, screams that she will get her revenge.

The four friends then leave to fight in the siege of La Rochelle. There, an attempt is made on D'Artagnan's life, and he learns that the architect of the plot was Milady. One evening at an inn the musketeers overhear Richelieu instruct Milady to go to England, where she is to tell Buckingham that he will expose his affair with the queen if he does not withdraw his troops. If he refuses, she is to poison him. In exchange, the cardinal gives her a safe-conduct letter signed by him and agrees to have her enemies, Constance and D'Artagnan, killed. After Richelieu leaves, Athos reveals himself to a terrified Milady as her husband. He orders her to leave France and forces her to give him the safe-conduct letter, which he, in turn, gives to D'Artagnan.

So far, Milady has been a somewhat shadowy, albeit seductive and suggestively venal, presence in the novel. Now readers are treated to the delicious fullness of her villainy. Forewarned of her intention, Milady's English brother-in-law, Lord de Winter, has her arrested and imprisoned when she arrives from France. Her beauty and pretended religious devotion, as well as a lengthy, fabricated story of her seduction by Buckingham, convinces her Puritan jailer, John Felton, of her innocence. He helps her to escape and then, to avenge her, stabs the duke to death. Milady escapes to the French convent where Constance is confined and poisons the young woman before D'Artagnan, Athos, Porthos, and Aramis can reach her. Milady flees just before their arrival at the convent; they track her down, hold a trial, and condemn her to death. She is executed by the public executioner of Lille, who had branded her for her crimes years earlier.

After returning to La Rochelle, D'Artagnan is met by Rochefort, who arrests him and brings him before Richelieu. D'Artagnan is charged with treason but he turns the tables on the cardinal by detailing Milady's many crimes and showing him the safe-conduct letter, signed by Richelieu. Impressed by D'Artagnan's cleverness, the cardinal offers the young man a commission in the musketeers. D'Artagnan offers the commission to Athos, Porthos, and Aramis, each of whom refuses it. La Rochelle surrenders, and the four friends disband. Athos returns to his estate, Porthos marries his rich widow, and Aramis becomes an abbé. D'Artagnan fights several duels with Rochefort, and the two eventually become fast friends.

Dumas's novels, including *The Count of Monte Cristo* (1844–45) and two sequels to *The Three Musketeers—Twenty Years After* (1845) and *The Vicomte de Bragelonne* (1848–50)—made him France's best-selling author as well as the most famous living Frenchman. Over a period of 50 years he wrote 50 plays, published 90 novels, 12 travel books, and numerous histories, biographies, and memoirs. But Dumas's most enduring work remains *The Three Musketeers.* The novel enjoyed steady popularity throughout the 19th century and into the 20th, when it became the perfect vehicle for the movies. As of this writing there have been seven screen versions of *The Three Musketeers,* the first in 1921, as well as radio, television, and children's book adaptations. It is not great literature or an authentic historical document, to be sure, but in the chronicle of D'Artagnan, Athos, Porthos, and Aramis Dumas gave to the world a classic example of storytelling at its best, a novel to be experienced and savored for the sheer love of reading.

THE HOUND OF THE BASKERVILLES

124

(1902)

by Arthur Conan Doyle

Robinson and I are exploring the moor together over our Sherlock Holmes book. I think it will work splendidly—indeed I have already done nearly half of it. Holmes is at his very best, and it is a highly dramatic idea—which I owe to Robinson. We did fourteen miles over the moor to-day and are now pleasantly weary. It is a great place, very sad and wild, dotted with dwellings of prehistoric man, strange monoliths and huts and graves.

—Arthur Conan Doyle to his mother from Dartmoor, April 1901

If space can be found in this listing of the greatest novels for *Uncle Tom's Cabin* for its impact, *The Three Musketeers* for its adventure, and *The Woman in White* for its thrills and suspense, then surely room must be made for arguably the most famous character in all of fiction, Sherlock Holmes, in his finest extended performance, *The Hound of the Baskervilles.* From the great detective's introduction in Doyle's 1887 novel *A Study in Scarlet* to his final adventures, recorded in *The Case-Book of Sherlock Holmes* (1927), over a 40-year period and through four short novels and 53 stories, Doyle's grand "thinking machine," the archetypal private detective, has staked out a place in the world of myth and our collective consciousness. Who does not know Holmes—deerstalker cap, meerschaum pipe, 221B Baker Street, and the line "Elementary, my dear Watson!" (that never was uttered in a Doyle story)? Even those who have never read a Holmes story need no help in conjuring the legend. More than seventy-five years after his final case, as recorded by his creator, Holmes still appears in more fictional works than any other literary character, as if in continuing response to our need for him. He has in fact ceased to be a fictional character at all. As Hesketh Pearson observed, "It is impossible not to believe in his existence. Wholly lacking the mystery and suggestiveness of a great portrait, he is as vivid as a snapshot. . . . More than any other character in fiction he stimulates the sense of association. For those of us who did not live in it, the London of the eighties and nineties of last century is simply the London of Holmes, and we cannot pass down Baker Street without thinking of him and trying to locate his lodgings." Letters addressed to the detective at his Baker Street address for years received a polite response from the bank that inhabits where 221B should be that the detective was unavailable, engaged on a case. Long may he remain so.

Of Doyle's four Holmes novels, *The Hound of the Baskervilles* is the finest, "a real creeper," as the author described the story to his mother. It began, however, not as a Holmes story at all. On a golfing holiday in March 1901, Doyle first heard from a companion, Fletcher Robinson, the local West Country legend of a great spectral hound and the curse of a country family. An April visit to Dartmoor with Robinson sealed Doyle's decision to write a "little book" evoking both the legend and the otherworldly moorland setting. As he began to conceive the story, Doyle needed a strong protagonist to oppose the tale's evil forces, and, as he later recalled, "Why should I invent such a character when I had him already in the form of Holmes?" Sherlock Holmes, however, had last been seen in 1893 in a death grip with his nemesis, Professor Moriarty, plunging over Switzerland's Reichenbach Falls in "The Final Problem." Doyle had tired of his creation and the labor of inventing new cases for him, which prevented the writer from producing the historical romances he wished to publish. For nearly a decade, Doyle had resisted the clamor and the considerable financial inducements to bring Holmes back. It finally took the appeal of Dartmoor and its legend to do so.

After such a long sabbatical from Holmes, Doyle seems in *The Hound of the Baskervilles* refreshed, energized, and willing to push his suspense formula and his detective into new and richer areas. There is no specific reference to a date for the novel's action and, therefore, no necessity to account for Holmes's miraculous survival, since the case can be regarded as one of Holmes's pre-Reichenbach adventures that Watson has finally gotten around to recording. The novel opens familiarly, with Holmes and Watson seated at the breakfast table at 221B with a potential client's walking stick left behind providing the opportunity for an expected bravura performance by Holmes in deduction. The stick's owner, Dr. James Mortimer, soon appears to test the accuracy of Holmes's surmises and to describe the curse of the Baskervilles in which the debauched Sir Hugo Baskerville was long ago killed by a diabolical hound. The same fate seems to have taken the life of the present heir, Sir Charles Baskerville. Mortimer's description of the scene of Sir Charles's death ends with one of the most famous lines in all of Doyle's fiction:

> "Sir Charles lay on his face, his arms out, his fingers dug into the ground, and his features convulsed with some strong emotion to such an extent that I could hardly have sworn to his identity. There was certainly no physical injury of any kind. But one false statement was made by Barrymore at the inquest. He said that there was no traces upon the ground

> round the body. He did not observe any. But I did—some little distance off, but fresh and clear."
>
> "Footprints?"
>
> "Footprints."
>
> "A man's or a woman's?"
>
> Dr. Mortimer looked strangely at us for an instant, and his voice sank almost to a whisper as he answered:
>
> "Mr. Holmes, they were the footprints of a gigantic hound!"

Could there be, therefore, a supernatural explanation for the death of Sir Charles and the working out of a long-active curse that now threatens the new heir, Sir Henry Baskerville? It is the challenge of the supernatural to which the supreme rationalist Holmes must now respond. After a series of near misses apprehending a bearded man who is apparently stalking Sir Henry, and who arrogantly gives his name as "Mr. Sherlock Holmes" to his cabman, tweaking his pursuers, Holmes is prompted to declare, "I tell you, Watson, this time we have got a foeman who is worthy of our steel. . . . It's an ugly business, Watson, an ugly, dangerous business, and the more I see of it the less I like it."

Watson is dispatched to Dartmoor as Sir Henry's protection, and Holmes is kept offstage for nearly six of the novel's 15 chapters. In a sense, it is the absence of Holmes, not his presence, which insures the power and suspense of *The Hound of the Baskervilles.* Without Holmes's invariably right explanations, Watson (and the reader) is plunged into the thick of the confusion unaided. Watson, unlike his buffoonish portrayer, Nigel Bruce, in the Basil Rathbone films, however, has learned from his friend and manages to make headway in uncovering a network of relationships and motives among the circle surrounding the Baskerville estate, including the old family servants, Barrymore and his wife, the litigious neighbor Mr. Frankland, and the naturalist Stapleton and his sister. Helping to animate Watson's investigation is one of Doyle's most evocative settings, Baskerville Hall, a gothic echo of long, dark corridors and sinister family portraits, and, most important, Dartmoor itself, a symbolic setting suggesting primitive regression and human vulnerability. As the butterfly-hunting Stapleton, who has mastered its contours, declares, "It is a wonderful place, the moor, . . . You never tire of the moor. You cannot think the wonderful secrets which it contains. It is so vast, and so barren, and so mysterious." Doyle exploits his setting with its deep symbolic resonance as if he has joined his novel of detection to Emily Brontë's *Wuthering Heights.* In this trackless, disorienting wasteland with its stone huts of long-departed primitive peoples, a spectral hound seems far from implausible, and the uncanny haunts the landscape. In effect it becomes the true nemesis for Holmes—the power of nature and fear and madness that it can produce in the human mind.

Holmes's reentry into the novel comes at the moment when Watson declares that he has "done all that man can do to reach the heart of the mystery." Pursuing the figure of a man whom Watson is convinced may hold the key to the mystery, he awaits his arrival, gun in hand, in one of the primitive stone huts. Hearing his footsteps, Watson is greeted with "It is a lovely evening, my dear Watson, . . . I really think that you will be more comfortable outside than in." Once he comes back onstage, Holmes makes short work of the mystery of the murderer of Sir Charles, and the novel shifts from surprise to suspense: How can the villain be taken? One central mystery, however—of the nature of the spectral hound—is not solved until the novel's exciting climax. As order is once again restored, the novel concludes with the return to the familiar world of 221B.

Despite the resumption of old routines, the novel has tested and exposed Holmes in unprecedented ways. For one of the first times, Holmes confesses his pride and arrogance. Under the impression that his client, Sir Henry Baskerville, has been killed, Holmes declares, "I am more to blame than you, Watson. In order to have my case well rounded and complete, I have thrown away the life of my client. It is the greatest blow which has befallen me in my career." Later, when Holmes hears the hound on the moor, Watson records: "'Where is it?' Holmes whispered, and I knew from the thrill of his voice that he, the man of iron, was shaken to the soul." These are the first examples of the new Holmes who will emerge in the post-Reichenbach stories: less the unfeeling "thinking machine," and more fallible, more vulnerable, and emotionally engaged. These qualities added to the familiar make *The Hound of the Baskervilles* one of most satisfying of the Holmes stories, with its combination of the gothic and the detective story conspiring to create one of the great detective's most worthy and revealing challenges.

Holmes's reappearance was greeted enthusiastically. An old friend was back, and Doyle would subsequently sign a lucrative contract to supply new cases for his detective. When the book first appeared in 1902, one lady observed, "The scenes at the railway bookstands were worse than anything I ever saw at a bargain-sale." Jacqueline A. Jaffe in her critical study of Doyle's works has intriguingly suggested that a possible reason for the enthusiasm for Holmes's return in England was the death of Queen Victoria in January 1901, symbolically signaling the end of an era and a way of life and prompting a cultural soul-searching about the future. An operating principle of order was removed, and into the chaos came the familiar figure of Sherlock Holmes in *The Hound of the Baskervilles* and his subsequent resurrection, a reassuring presence able to solve the baffling randomness and confusion of modern experience, revealing its significance and meaning. Of the conclusion of *The Hound of the Baskervilles*, Jaffe observes, "Holmes is not only saving the last male member of an illustrious family, and thus

TREASURE ISLAND 125

(1883)

by Robert Louis Stevenson

As a teller of a tale Stevenson is the equal of Dumas or Dickens. . . . He had but one main theme, that essential theme of romance, the struggle between the good and the bad, of hero against villain. . . . But compare with his novels all the romantic novels written since . . . and you will see how high he stands. Next to Dumas, he is the best of all the romantic novelists [and] of British nineteenth century writers, he will live longer than any except Dickens.

—John Galsworthy, cited in David Cordingly, introduction to *Treasure Island*, the Modern Library edition, 2001

Stevenson's seminal tale of pirates and the quest for treasure is acknowledged to be the first true adventure story for boys and a classic of its genre. But when *Treasure Island* debuted in the magazine *Young Folks* in weekly installments from 1881 to 1882, it was not received with enthusiasm by the readers for which it was intended. "Captain George North," Stevenson's pseudonym for the story, had failed to supply boys with their basic requirement for adventure fiction: a fantastical plot featuring a glamorous boy hero who triumphs over danger, cunningly outwits the villain, and is acclaimed as a genius by the adults who have turned to him for help. Stevenson's Jim Hawkins, the narrator of *Treasure Island*, and one of the novel's two main protagonists, did not fit the profile. A heroic, thoughtless, and foolish boy by turns, Jim was a fully formed character, too real to appeal to young readers. The story's primary villain, the hypocritically smooth Long John Silver, was similarly too subtle a character, not the pirate king for boys' tastes. It was only after *Treasure Island* was brought out in book form under Stevenson's own name in 1883 that his story caught the imagination of the public. Critiqued by such luminaries as the English prime minister William Gladstone and authors Andrew Lang and Henry James, Stevenson's tale received attention as an important work of fiction and was compared favorably with such illustrious works as Homer's *Odyssey*, *Robinson Crusoe*, *The Last of the Mohicans*, and Walter Scott's historical novels. In his influential 1884 essay, "The Art of Fiction," Henry James advocated for the adventure genre as a serious art form in general and *Treasure Island* in particular. Not just a story for boys, *Treasure Island* took its place in the literary canon as a singular and beloved novel for all ages.

Robert Louis Stevenson (1850–94) was born in Edinburgh, the only child of Thomas Stevenson, a well-to-do harbor and lighthouse engineer, and Margaret Balfour Stevenson, the daughter of a Scots minister. Troubled by lung disease, possibly tuberculosis, for most of his life, Stevenson was frequently bedridden as a child. During these childhood bouts of illness, he made up stories to pass the time and was influenced by such writers as Defoe, Poe, and Hawthorne, as well as by toy theatre plays. Stevenson's father also amused his son with impromptu tales of ships, old sailors, and voyages in the days before steam replaced sailing vessels. Stevenson was expected to pursue the same profession as his father but instead read law at Edinburgh University and further alienated his strict Calvinist parents with his agnosticism and his bohemian existence. In 1871, Stevenson made the decision to become a full-time writer and although he was admitted to the Scottish bar in 1875, he never practiced as a barrister. He was unable to earn a living from his writing, and his father, who initially disapproved of Stevenson's chosen vocation, supported him throughout his 20s. Even the success of *Treasure Island* did not result in an adequate income, and Stevenson did not become financially independent until after his father's death in 1887. Stevenson's first short story was "A Lodging for the Night" (1877), which is set in 15th-century Paris and centers on the poet François Villon. Other early writings included essays and travel sketches, the latter of which grew out of Stevenson's attempt to find a beneficial climate for his health. An 1876 canoe trip around the canals in Belgium and northern France resulted in his first full-length book, *An Inland Voyage* (1878), followed by *Edinburgh: Picturesque Sketches* (1878) and *Travels With a Donkey in the Cévennes* (1879), a chronicle of Stevenson's journey through southern France with his donkey, Modestine. His first play in collaboration with W. E. Henley, *Deacon Brodie*, was published in 1880 and *The New Arabian Nights*, a tribute to the classic series of adventures Stevenson had loved in his youth, appeared in 1882.

While visiting Paris in 1876, Stevenson met and fell in love with Fanny Osbourne, a married American woman with two children. Three years later, Osbourne obtained a divorce and in 1880, she and Stevenson were married in San Francisco. *The Silvarado Squatters* (1883) is an account of the couple's honeymoon at a mining camp on Mount Saint Helena in northern California. After returning to Europe, the Stevensons lived variously in Switzerland, France, and Scotland. In the summer of 1881, while the family was staying at Braemar cottage in Scotland, Stevenson drew a map of an island for the amusement of his 12-year-old stepson, Lloyd Osbourne. Stevenson gave such names to places on the island as Skeleton Island and Spy-Glass Hill, and marked one spot with three red crosses. According to Osbourne, Stevenson wrote "Treasure Island" at the "top right-hand corner" of the map. Osbourne later recounted the story of the novel's inception: "And he seemed to know so much about it too—the pirates, the buried treasure, the man who had been marooned on the island. 'Oh, for a story about it,' I exclaimed, in a heaven of enchantment, and somehow conscious of his own enthusiasm in the idea." Completing one chapter a day, Stevenson wrote the first 15 chapters of an adventure story initially titled *The Sea Cook or Treasure Island* between August and September 1881. He finished the novel in Davos, Switzerland, later in the year. The encouragement of his family, including his father, as well as such visitors to Braemar as Edmund Gosse and Sidney Colvin, made Stevenson give serious thought to the possibility of publishing his tale as a novel. Another visitor, the scholar Alexander Japp, took the first chapters of the tale to James Henderson, the editor of *Young Folks* magazine, who was searching for new writers. Henderson published Stevenson's tale in serial form from October 1881 to January 1882. *Treasure Island* did not boost the magazine's circulation, and some readers even wrote in to complain about the story. Stevenson finally gained the approval of the magazine's readers with the serialization of his next adventure story, *The Black Arrow* (1883).

Stevenson's Jim Hawkins had nothing in common with the superboy protagonists of such *Young Folks* fare as *Don Zalva the Brave*, but if the magazine's readers had cared to look beyond the restraints of pulp adventure fiction for a hero who bridges the gap between the sensational and the ordinary, they might have encountered Homer's wily and indomitable Odysseus, the ancestor of all adventures heroes. Homer's *Odyssey* conforms to the original definition of adventure, from the Old French meaning "a thing about to happen to anyone," but it is Odysseus's response to his destiny and his circumstances that makes him an adventure hero. Odysseus is both heroic and fallible, and his quest—to return home to his country and his family after war—requires a long journey replete with danger, recklessness, daring, and not a little human folly. The will to experience adventure rather than chance alone that puts a protagonist in its way marks the evolution of the genre. Medieval French romances were narratives that featured heroes who experienced a series of adventures during the quest to become reunited with a lady love. The modern adventure story descends from the novel, *Robinson Crusoe* (1719), in which Defoe's eponymous hero defies the wishes of his conventional father and puts to sea, where he endures decades of hardship after he is marooned on a desert island. Defoe's tale spawned the Robinsonade, an adventure subgenre that is loosely defined as a "desert island story"; later 19th-century examples include Johann Wyss's *The Swiss Family Robinson* (1819), R. M. Ballantyne's *The Coral Island* (1858); Jules Verne's *The Mysterious Island* (1874), and H. G. Wells's *The Island of Dr. Moreau* (1896). Swift's *Gulliver's Travels* (1726) is a Robinsonade, as well as a satire of pretentious Enlightenment sensibilities written in the form of an adventure story. Nostalgia for a heroic and more adventurous past, a sense of national virtue together with concepts of heroism and villainy shaped by imperialism, and the romance and promise of adventure suggested by colonized, frequently uncharted, lands were elements in the development of adventure fiction, beginning with the historical novels of Sir Walter Scott and James Fenimore Cooper. During the 19th century, as mass literacy grew, adventure novels became a popular, thriving subgenre of fiction, best exemplified by the romances of Alexandre Dumas, père. The first popular 19th-century adventure stories for boys were those of Captain Frederick Marryat, who began with *The Naval Officer or Scenes and Adventures in the Life of Frank Mildmay* (1829) and continued to produce adventure tales, including Robinsonades, for children and adults until 1848. Adventure stories tinged with melodrama were a feature of English chapbooks and penny dreadfuls, as well as the American dime novel, all of which thrived in the 19th and early 20th centuries. Stevenson's influences for *Treasure Island* include *Robinson Crusoe* and the novels of Ballantyne, Cooper, and W. H. G. Kingston, one of whose characters was a pirate. The character and appearance of the peg-legged Long John Silver were suggested by Stevenson's friend, W. E. Henley, a man of exuberance and energy despite the loss of a foot.

Set in the mid-18th century, *Treasure Island* is narrated by Jim Hawkins, who has been asked by "Dr. Livesey and the rest of these gentlemen" to "write down the whole particulars about Treasure Island, from the beginning to the end, keeping nothing back but the bearings of the island, and that because there is still treasure not yet lifted." Jim's story begins at the Admiral Benbow, an inn near Bristol run by Jim's ailing father, who is under the care of the honorable Dr. Livesey. A mysterious, ragged old sea captain, Billy Bones, arrives at the inn and asks Jim to warn him if he sees a "seafaring man with one-leg." After receiving a piece of paper from the beggar, Blind Pew, on which is a black spot, the pirate symbol of guilt and portent of death, Bones dies. Jim and his mother unlock Billy's sea chest, find a logbook and map, and, avoiding Billy's pursuers, who ransack the inn looking for these items, take the map to Dr. Livesey and Squire Trelawney. The men recognize the drawing as a map of the island where the infamous Captain Flint, the "bloodthirtiest buccaneer that ever lived," buried his treasure, and Trelawney plans an expedition to retrieve it. The captain, Smollett, is a trustworthy man, but Trelawney unwittingly hires many of Flint's former crew, including Long John Silver, taken on as cook aboard the expedition's ship, the *Hispaniola*. Jim is unaware of the charming and mannerly Silver's piratical nature until one night during the voyage, when he hides in an apple barrel and overhears Silver plan a mutiny with the crew. After Jim tells Smollett about the plot, the captain allows the crew leisure time on the island. On a whim, Jim sneaks ashore with the pirates, and, frightened by them, runs off alone. He witnesses Silver's murder of a pirate who refuses to join the mutiny, then flees deeper into the island, where he meets a half-crazed sailor, Ben Gunn, a marooned former member of Flint's crew. The two go to the pirates' stockade, where Silver attempts to negotiate with the captain; when this fails, the pirates attack, and Smollett is wounded. Jim rows out to the *Hispaniola* in Ben's boat, cuts the ship adrift, and manages to struggle aboard. There, he takes control of the ship but is confronted by a drunken wounded sailor, Israel Hands. Israel wounds Jim with a knife and lunges at him, only to be thrown overboard by a sudden twist of the ship. Jim returns to the stockade, where Silver takes him hostage. Silver, whose rebellious men have presented him with the black spot, tries to win Jim over as an ally and leads Jim and the men to the treasure site. There, they discover the treasure gone, excavated by Ben Gunn months earlier, and turn on Silver. Livesey and Ben, who have been hiding in the bushes, fire on the pirates. The men scatter, leaving Jim, Silver, Livesey, and Ben to find the treasure in Ben's cave. Much of the treasure is carried aboard the *Hispaniola*, and Silver is placed in custody; however, he escapes with a portion of the treasure and is never heard from again. The remaining men share the loot; Captain Smollett retires from the sea, and Ben becomes an innkeeper. Although silver bars have remained behind, Jim vows that "oxen and wain-ropes would not bring me back again to that accursed island; the worst dreams that ever I have are when I hear the surf booming about its coasts, or start upright in my bed, with the sharp voice of Captain Flint still ringing in my ears: 'Pieces of eight, pieces of eight!'"

Treasure Island is at heart a coming-of-age story, in which young Jim, who behaves imprudently but also heroically, grows to recognize the shades of gray within the monolithic concepts of good and evil. His understanding of the ambiguity of character is shaped by the unlikeliest of mentors, Long John Silver, part adroit leader and part ruthless pirate, who displays a soft side where Jim is concerned. He is also an entrepreneur, with the share of treasure he obtained before the story begins invested in the bank, real estate, and small business. "It's saving does it," he tells his men in a lecture on economics, as Jim listens from the apple barrel, "and you can lay to that." Stevenson, concerned with his own financial difficulties throughout his adult life, weaves the subject of money throughout *Treasure Island;* every character desires money according to his needs and is motivated to embark upon a potentially dangerous expedition in order to get it. It is the quest for money that anchors the story, but it is Stevenson's subtle characterizations and masterful plotting that make *Treasure Island* not only the most influential and exciting of pirate tales but also one of the purest adventure novels of all time.

NOVELS BY YEAR OF PUBLICATION

11th Century	*The Tale of Genji*
1605, 1615	*Don Quixote*
1678	*The Princess of Cleves*
1719	*Robinson Crusoe*
1722	*Moll Flandors*
1731	*Manon Lescaut*
1747–48	*Clarissa*
1749	*Tom Jones*
1759	*Candide*
1760–67	*Tristram Shandy*
1774	*The Sorrows of Young Werther*
1782	*Les Liaisons dangereuses*
1791	*Dream of the Red Chamber*
1813	*Pride and Prejudice*
1814	*Waverley*
1816	*Emma*
1818	*Frankenstein*
1818	*Persuasion*
1826	*The Last of the Mohicans*
1827, 1840	*The Betrothed*
1830	*The Red and the Black*
1835	*Le Père Goriot*
1836–37	*The Pickwick Papers*
1839	*The Charterhouse of Parma*
1840	*A Hero of Our Time*
1842	*Dead Souls*
1844	*The Three Musketeers*

1847	*Jane Eyre*
1847	*Wuthering Heights*
1847–48	*Vanity Fair*
1849–50	*David Copperfield*
1850	*The Scarlet Letter*
1851	*Moby-Dick*
1852	*Uncle Tom's Cabin*
1852–53	*Bleak House*
1857	*Madame Bovary*
1859	*Oblomov*
1860	*The Woman in White*
1861	*Great Expectations*
1862	*Fathers and Sons*
1862	*Les Misérables*
1866	*Crime and Punishment*
1866–67	*The Last Chronicle of Barset*
1869	*War and Peace*
1871–72	*Middlemarch*
1876	*Daniel Deronda*
1877	*Anna Karenina*
1880	*The Brothers Karamazov*
1881	*The Portrait of a Lady*
1883	*Treasure Island*
1884	*Adventures of Huckleberry Finn*
1885	*Germinal*
1890	*Hunger*
1891	*Tess of the D'Urbervilles*
1895	*The Red Badge of Courage*
1897	*Dracula*
1899	*The Awakening*
1899	*Don Casmurro*
1901	*Buddenbrooks*
1902	*The Hound of the Baskervilles*
1903	*The Ambassadors*
1904	*Nostromo*
1913	*Sons and Lovers*
1913–27	*In Search of Lost Time*
1915	*The Good Soldier*
1916	*A Portrait of the Artist as a Young Man*
1916, 1922	*Petersburg*

1918	*My Ántonia*
1920	*The Age of Innocence*
1920	*Women in Love*
1921–23	*The Good Soldier Švejk*
1922	*Ulysses*
1924	*The Magic Mountain*
1924	*A Passage to India*
1925	*An American Tragedy*
1925	*The Great Gatsby*
1925	*Mrs Dalloway*
1925	*The Trial*
1926	*The Counterfeiters*
1927	*To the Lighthouse*
1929	*Berlin Alexanderplatz*
1929	*A Farewell to Arms*
1929	*Some Prefer Nettles*
1929	*The Sound and the Fury*
1930	*As I Lay Dying*
1930–38	*U.S.A.*
1930–43	*The Man without Qualities*
1932	*The Sleepwalkers*
1934	*Call It Sleep*
1936	*Absalom, Absalom!*
1936	*Gone with the Wind*
1937, 1948	*Snow Country*
1937	*Their Eyes Were Watching God*
1939	*Finnegans Wake*
1939	*The Grapes of Wrath*
1940	*Native Son*
1942	*The Stranger*
1945	*Brideshead Revisited*
1947	*Cold Nights*
1947	*Under the Volcano*
1949	*Nineteen Eighty-Four*
1951	*The Catcher in the Rye*
1951–53	*Molloy, Malone Dies, The Unnamable*
1952	*Invisible Man*
1955	*Lolita*
1957	*Doctor Zhivago*
1957	*On the Road*

1958	*The Leopard*
1958	*Things Fall Apart*
1959	*The Tin Drum*
1962	*The Death of Artemio Cruz*
1962	*Pale Fire*
1962	*The Golden Notebook*
1962	*The Woman in the Dunes*
1964	*Herzog*
1966–67	*The Master and Margarita*
1967	*One Hundred Years of Solitude*
1973	*Gravity's Rainbow*
1979	*A Bend in the River*
1981	*Midnight's Children*
1984	*The Unbearable Lightness of Being*
1984–89	*Cities of Salt*
1985	*The Handmaid's Tale*
1987	*Beloved*
1997	*American Pastoral*

A SECOND HUNDRED (HONORABLE MENTIONS)

S. Y. Agnon	*The Bridal Canopy* (1931)
Isabel Allende	*The House of the Spirits* (1982)
Jorge Amado	*Dona Flor and Her Two Husbands* (1966)
Kingsley Amis	*Lucky Jim* (1954)
Mulk Raj Anand	*Untouchable* (1935)
Ivo Andrić	*The Bridge on the Drina* (1945)
Miguel Angel Asturias	*Mr. President* (1946)
Djuna Barnes	*Nightwood* (1936)
Heinrich Böll	*The Lost Honor of Katharina Blum* (1974)
Elizabeth Bowen	*The Death of the Heart* (1938)
Paul Bowles	*The Sheltering Sky* (1949)
Hermann Broch	*The Death of Virgil* (1945)
Charlotte Brontë	*Villette* (1853)
Fanny Burney	*Evelina* (1778)
Italo Calvino	*Invisible Cities* (1972)
Camilo José Cela	*The Family of Pascual Duarte* (1942)
Louis-Ferdinand Céline	*Journey to the End of Night* (1932)
François-René Chateaubriand	*René* (1802)
J. M. Coetzee	*Disgrace* (1999)
Wilkie Collins	*The Moonstone* (1868)
Joseph Conrad	*Lord Jim* (1900)
	The Secret Agent (1907)
Benjamin Constant	*Adolphe* (1816)
Julio Cortázar	*Hopscotch* (1963)

Robertson Davies	*The Deptford Trilogy* (1970–75)
Don DeLillo	*Underworld* (1997)
Charles Dickens	*Little Dorrit* (1855–57)
Feodor Dostoevksy	*The Idiot* (1869)
Roddy Doyle	*The Barrytown Trilogy* (1987–91)
Theodore Dreiser	*Sister Carrie* (1900)
Lawrence Durrell	*The Alexandria Quartet* (1957–60)
Louise Erdrich	*Love Medicine* (1984)
William Faulkner	*Light in August* (1932)
F. Scott Fitzgerald	*Tender Is the Night* (1934)
Gustave Flaubert	*A Sentimental Education* (1869)
Theodor Fontane	*Effi Briest* (1894)
Carlos Fuentes	*Terra Nostra* (1975)
William Gaddis	*The Recognitions* (1955)
Elizabeth Gaskell	*Wives and Daughters* (1864–66)
Jean Genet	*Our Lady of the Flowers* (1942)
George Gissing	*New Grub Street* (1891)
Oliver Goldsmith	*The Vicar of Wakefield* (1766)
Witold Gombrowicz	*Ferdydurke* (1937)
Nadine Gordimer	*The Conservationist* (1974)
Graham Greene	*The Heart of the Matter* (1948)
Thomas Hardy	*Jude the Obscure* (1895)
	The Mayor of Casterbridge (1886)
Joseph Heller	*Catch-22* (1961)
Ernest Hemingway	*The Sun Also Rises* (1926)
Hermann Hesse	*Steppenwolf* (1927)
Keri Hulme	*The Bone People* (1983)
Joris Karl Huysmans	*Against the Grain* (1884)
Ibuse Masuji	*Black Rain* (1965)
Henry James	*The Golden Bowl* (1904)
	The Wings of the Dove (1902)
Nikos Kazantzakis	*The Last Temptation of Christ* (1955)
Rudyard Kipling	*Kim* (1901)
Lao She	*Camel Xiangzi* (also known as *Rickshaw Boy*) (1936)

D. H. Lawrence	*The Rainbow* (1915)
Harper Lee	*To Kill a Mockingbird* (1960)
Naguib Mahfouz	*The Cairo Trilogy* (1956–57)
Norman Mailer	*The Naked and the Dead* (1948)
André Malraux	*Man's Fate* (1933)
Thomas Mann	*Doctor Faustus* (1947)
Gabriel García Márquez	*Love in the Time of Cholera* (1985)
George Meredith	*The Ordeal of Richard Feverel* (1859)
Henry Miller	*Tropic of Cancer* (1934)
Vladimir Nabokov	*Ada* (1969)
Natsume Sōseki	*Kokoro* (1914)
Ngugi wa Thiong'o	*A Grain of Wheat* (1967)
Frank Norris	*McTeague* (1899)
Flann O'Brien	*At Swim-Two-Birds* (1939)
Alan Paton	*Cry, the Beloved Country* (1948)
Benito Pérez Galdós	*Fortunata and Jacinto* (1886–87)
Ann Radcliffe	*The Mysteries of Udolpho* (1794)
Jean Rhys	*Wide Sargasso Sea* (1966)
Samuel Richardson	*Pamela* (1740)
Alain Robbe-Grillet	*Jealousy* (1957)
Joseph Roth	*The Radetzky March* (1932)
Philip Roth	*Portnoy's Complaint* (1969)
Fernando de Rojas	*La Celestina* (1499)
Jean-Jacques Rousseau	*Julie; or, The New Eloise* (1761)
Marquis de Sade	*Justine* (1791)
Jean-Paul Sartre	*Nausea* (1938)
Walter Scott	*The Heart of Midlothian* (1818)
Mikhail Sholokhov	*Quiet Flows the Don* (1928–40)
Isaac Bashevis Singer	*The Slave* (1962)
Zadie Smith	*White Teeth* (2000)
Aleksandr Solzhenitsyn	*One Day in the Life of Ivan Denisovich* (1962)
Wole Soyinka	*The Interpreters* (1965)
Robert Louis Stevenson	*The Strange Case of Dr. Jekyll and Mr. Hyde* (1886)

Italo Svevo	*The Confessions of Zeno* (1923)
Sigrid Undset	*Kristin Lavransdatter* (1920–22)
John Updike	*Rabbit, Run* (1960)
David Foster Wallace	*Infinite Jest* (1996)
Robert Penn Warren	*All the King's Men* (1946)
Eudora Welty	*Delta Wedding* (1946)
Nathanael West	*Miss Lonelyhearts* (1933)
Edith Wharton	*The House of Mirth* (1905)
Patrick White	*Voss* (1957)

INDEX

C

R

Y